M. Diane O'H...

ROMANS

Also by James Montgomery Boice

Witness and Revelation in the Gospel of John
Philippians: An Expositional Commentary
The Sermon on the Mount
How to Live the Christian Life (originally, *How to Live It Up*)
Ordinary Men Called by God (originally, *How God Can Use Nobodies*)
The Last and Future World
The Gospel of John: An Expositional Commentary (5 volumes in one)
"Galatians" in the *Expositor's Bible Commentary*
Can You Run Away from God?
Does Inerrancy Matter?
The Foundation of Biblical Authority, editor
The Epistles of John
Genesis: An Expositional Commentary (3 volumes)
The Parables of Jesus
The Christ of Christmas
The Minor Prophets: An Expositional Commentary (2 volumes)
Standing on the Rock
The Christ of the Empty Tomb
Foundations of the Christian Faith (4 volumes in one)
Christ's Call to Discipleship
Transforming Our World: A Call to Action, editor
Ephesians: An Expositional Commentary
Daniel: An Expositional Commentary
Joshua: We Will Serve the Lord
Nehemiah: Learning to Lead

ROMANS

Volume 1
Justification by Faith
Romans 1–4

JAMES MONTGOMERY BOICE

BAKER BOOK HOUSE
Grand Rapids, Michigan 49516

Copyright © 1991 by Baker Books
a division of Baker Book House Company
P.O. Box 6287, Grand Rapids, MI 49516-6287

Seventh printing, May 2004

Printed in the United States of America

Library of Congress Cataloging-in-Publication Data

Boice, James Montgomery, 1938-
   Romans/James Montgomery Boice.
         p.   cm.
   Includes bibliographical references and indexes.
   Contents: v. 1. Justification by faith, Romans 1:1–4:25
   ISBN: 0-8010-1002-0 (v. 1)
   1. Bible. N.T. Romans—Commentaries. I. Title.
BS2665.3.B58 1991
227'.1077—dc20   91-7204
                                                                    CIP

For current information about academic books, resources for Christian leaders, and all
new releases available from Baker Book House, visit our web site:
                        http://www.bakerbooks.com

To **HIM**
who was delivered over to death
for our sins
and was raised to life
for our justification

Contents

Preface

I t is a formidable task to begin a study of Paul's great letter to the Romans, and exciting, too. I felt those emotions as I began these studies nearly four years ago, and I still feel them. Perhaps you feel them also, perhaps even as you hold this book in your hand and read this preface.

There are very good reasons for these feelings. For one thing, Romans has probably been the object of more intense study by more highly intelligent and motivated individuals than any document in human history. A document like the United States Constitution has also been intensely studied, of course. But interest in even so important a document as that is confined largely to one nation, while Romans has been of profound interest to people wherever Christianity has spread. Romans has been studied by many millions of persons and for nearly two millennia, that is, from the time of the apostle Paul, its author and the first great missionary of the Christian church, to the present.

The list of the most monumental and helpful commentators on Romans is a virtual history of Christianity. To study this book is to walk in the footsteps, not only of the apostle Paul, but of such theological and pastoral giants as Martin Luther, John Calvin, Robert Haldane, Charles Hodge, D. Martyn Lloyd-Jones, and many others.

But, in my opinion, it is not just this impressive array of prior witnesses that we find daunting. The real reason for our anxiety is the suspicion that a study of Romans will change us profoundly and unalterably. For that is what it was meant to do, after all! And what it has already done! In the opening chapter, I quote F. Godet as saying that there has never been and probably never will be an important spiritual movement in the history of the church that cannot be connected as cause and effect with a deeper knowledge of the truths of this book. That is true. But it is not just church history that has been influenced by Romans. Individuals have been so affected by this great epistle that they have been moved to risk everything for Jesus Christ. If *they* have been, what is to keep this from becoming our own experience?

We all fear change, of course. It makes us anxious. But change is precisely what we need. If we are spiritually moribund, we need to be brought from a state of spiritual death into a state of spiritual life through the gospel. If we are lethargic in our discipleship, we need to be awakened to the glories of a renewed life in Christ. If we are indifferent to the spiritual state of others, we need to be alerted to their peril apart from Christ and be moved to take the gospel to them.

I confess that I have been instructed, moved, and even deeply stirred, by my own studies. Above all, I have been convicted of how shallow I have been in my understanding of the gospel; indeed, how shallow most of our evangelical Christianity, particularly in America, has been. I used to say that American Christianity at best has mastered Romans 1 through 4, and has not even begun to understand Romans 5 through 8, not to mention the remainder of the letter. But today I am not sure we have even mastered the first four chapters. How often do we hear the depravity of the race discussed, as Paul discusses it in Romans 1? How often do we hear that from God's perspective, man is utterly depraved, as Paul says in Romans 3? How often do we hear messages on propitiation, redemption, justification, or faith, the central doctrines of the great latter half of Romans 3? Or the proof of these truths from the Old Testament, which is the burden of Romans 4?

Instead, we cling to man-centered, need-oriented teaching. And our churches show it! They are successful in worldly terms—big buildings, big budgets, big everything—but they suffer from a poverty of soul.

All this means, in my judgment at least, that it is time to get back to the basic, life-transforming doctrines of Christianity—which is to say that it is time to rediscover Romans. I invite you to discover it again with me, through this volume and those to follow. The congregation of Tenth Presbyterian Church in Philadelphia, where I have served as pastor for more than twenty years, has already been doing this, since these are the messages I preached to the morning congregation for nearly two years between September 1986 and June 1988. Listeners of The Bible Study Hour will know that these studies were also aired over the radio from 1987 to 1989. As usual in the preface to my books, I wish to thank the officers and members of Tenth Presbyterian Church for permitting me to invest so much of my time in study and in the preparation of these sermons.

Who knows what God will do for us as we again discover and attempt to live out the great truths of the gospel! May he give us a Great Awakening. We certainly need it. May he even give us a new Reformation.

Philadelphia, Pennsylvania

An Introduction to Romans

Paul, a servant of Christ Jesus, called to be an apostle and set apart for the gospel of God—the gospel he promised beforehand through his prophets in the Holy Scriptures regarding his Son, who as to his human nature was a descendant of David, and who through the Spirit of holiness was declared with power to be the Son of God by his resurrection from the dead: Jesus Christ our Lord. Through him and for his name's sake, we received grace and apostleship to call people from among all the Gentiles to the obedience that comes from faith. And you also are among those who are called to belong to Jesus Christ.

To all in Rome who are loved by God and called to be saints:

Grace and peace to you from God our Father and from the Lord Jesus Christ

(Romans 1:1–7).

With those powerful opening words, written nearly two thousand years ago in the bustling commercial city of Corinth, Greece, a Jewish Christian began a letter to believers whom he had never seen in the far-off city of Rome. What a letter it was! In any other circumstances and by any other hand, the letter might have been a mere incidental piece of correspondence. But the author of this letter was the apostle Paul, and by his hand and under the guidance of the Holy Spirit this bit of ancient writing became for Christians the most influential document ever penned.

Here follow two examples. In the fourth century a distinguished philosopher and teacher named Augustine was under conviction concerning the truthfulness of Christianity. He was a brilliant and attractive man; but he

11

had also lived an immoral life, as many of the pagan intellectuals of his day did, and his past practice of immorality held him in a vise-like grip. He tells about it in the eighth book of his *Confessions,* relating how, although he was convinced of the truthfulness of Christianity, he nevertheless kept putting off a true repudiation of sin and a commitment to Jesus Christ.

One day, while in the garden of a friend's estate near Milan, Italy, Augustine heard a child singing the words *tole lege, tole lege* ("take and read"). He had never heard a song with words like that before, so he received it as a message from God. Obeying the message, he rushed to where a copy of the Bible was lying, opened it at random, and began to read the words that first met his astonished gaze. They were from Romans, the thirteenth chapter: "Let us behave decently, as in the daytime, not in orgies and drunkenness, not in sexual immorality and debauchery, not in dissension and jealousy. Rather, clothe yourselves with the Lord Jesus Christ, and do not think about how to gratify the desires of the sinful nature" (Rom. 13:13–14). This was exactly what was needed by Saint Augustine, as he was later called. The words were the means of his conversion. Afterward he wrote, "Instantly, as the sentence ended—by a light, as it were, of security infused into my heart—all the gloom of doubt was vanished away."[1] Augustine became the greatest figure in the early Christian church between the apostle Paul and Martin Luther.

The second example of the Romans epistle's influence is the Protestant Reformer, Martin Luther. He was no profligate, as Augustine was. Quite the contrary. Luther was a pious, earnest monk—an apparent Christian. But Luther had no peace of soul. He wanted to please God, to be accepted by him. But the harder he worked, the more elusive the salvation of his soul seemed to be. Instead of growing closer to God, he found himself moving away from him. Instead of coming to love God, which Luther knew he should do, he found himself hating God for requiring an apparently impossible standard of righteousness of human beings. In desperation Luther turned to a study of Paul's letter to the Romans and there, as early as the seventeenth verse of chapter 1, he found the solution: "For in the gospel a righteousness from God is revealed, a righteousness that is by faith from first to last, just as it is written: 'The righteous will live by faith.'" As God opened the meaning of this verse to him, Luther realized that the righteousness he needed was not his own righteousness but a righteousness of God, freely given to all who would receive it. Furthermore, this was to be received, not through any works of his own but by faith only *(sola fide).* Faith meant taking God at his word, believing him. Luther did this, and as he did he felt himself to be reborn and to have entered Paradise.

Here is how he put it: "I had no love for that holy and just God who punishes sinners. I was filled with secret anger against him. I hated him,

---

1. Saint Augustine, *Confessions,* trans. J. G. Pilkington, in *Basic Writings of Saint Augustine,* ed. Whitney J. Oates (New York: Random House, 1948), vol. 1, p. 126.

because, not content with frightening by the law and the miseries of life us wretched sinners, already ruined by original sin, he still further increased our tortures by the gospel. . . . But when, by the Spirit of God, I understood the words—when I learned how the justification of the sinner proceeds from the free mercy of our Lord through faith . . . then I felt born again like a new man. . . . In very truth, this language of Saint Paul was to me the true gate of Paradise."[2]

Luther called Romans "the chief part of the New Testament and the very purest gospel"; he believed that "every Christian should know it word for word, by heart, [and] occupy himself with it every day, as the daily bread of his soul."[3]

Samuel Taylor Coleridge, the English poet, called Romans "the profoundest book in existence."

The great Swiss commentator F. Godet wrote that in all probability "every great spiritual revival in the church will be connected as effect and cause with a deeper understanding of this book."[4]

Foundational Christianity

But is that really true? We live in a skeptical age, and it is not unreasonable to think that a sizable percentage of people hearing or reading a statement like that in our day will challenge it. We know that Romans 13:13–14 was used by God to change the life of Saint Augustine and that Augustine altered history by his impact upon the church of the Middle Ages. We know that God used Martin Luther to launch the Reformation. But that was long ago. Augustine lived in the fourth and fifth centuries. Luther labored in the fifteen hundreds. Times have changed since then. Is there any reason to expect a corresponding impact from a study of this ancient letter today?

There is every reason to expect it, and the chief reason is that *Christianity has been the most powerful, transforming force in human history—and the book of Romans is the most basic, most comprehensive statement of true Christianity.*

Not everyone has agreed with this assessment, of course. There have been times when one teacher or another has been enamored with the so-called simple teachings of Jesus and has rejected the writings of Paul as too doctrinaire, too technical, or too harsh. All we really need is to tell people that God loves them, these instructors have said. Others have maintained that it is not what we believe that matters so much as what we do. From that perspective it is the social teachings of Christianity that are its heart; doc-

2. J. H. Merle D'Aubigné, *The Life and Times of Martin Luther,* trans. H. White (Chicago: Moody Press, 1958), pp. 55, 56.

3. Martin Luther, *Commentary on the Epistle to the Romans,* trans. J. Theodore Mueller (Grand Rapids: Zondervan, 1954), p. xi.

4. F. Godet, *Commentary on St. Paul's Epistle to the Romans,* trans. A. Cusin (Edinburgh: T. & T. Clark, n.d.), vol. 1, p. 1.

trines divide, whereas ethics ennoble our lives and unite us. These views all have a seed of wisdom, but they overlook the major issue. The fundamental human problem is not to understand what proper behavior is; generally we know that quite well. The problem is that we do not do what we know we should do. Indeed, we even seem incapable of doing it. This is what Augustine discovered when he tried to reform his life apart from the power of Christ. Again, the problem is not that we need to know that God loves us, though we often doubt that he does. Our hang-up is that we do not love God, as Luther, the pious monk, discovered. We are at war with God. In effect, we hate him; at the very least we do not want him to rule over our lives and resent any meaningful attempts he makes to do so.

Romans shows how God deals with this problem. And because it tells how God deals with this basic dilemma of human life, it necessarily also unveils the true solution to nearly everything else. When we repent of our sin and thus truly come to love God, we discover the secret to an upright and satisfying life, and we become a power for good rather than a disruptive, downward force or merely an indifferent presence in society.

Overview of the Epistle

In the following chapters of this and subsequent volumes, I intend to examine this great ancient document in detail. But because this is an introductory study, it is well at the outset to fix an overview of the entire letter in our minds. Romans has the following parts:

1. *A preliminary personal word and introduction (1:1–15).* Romans is a doctrinal treatise placed between the opening and closing sections of a typical ancient letter. But, unlike most ancient writers, Paul uses the opening section to introduce the theme that will occupy him at length later on. It is "the gospel of God." Gospel means "good news." So Paul is announcing news that is not only good but superlatively good, since it comes from the One who is the Great Good of all.

2. *A brief statement of the theme (1:16–17).* In his introduction Paul shows that the gospel centers in the person of God's Son, the Lord Jesus Christ. But what is this Good News specifically? Paul's short statement shows that it concerns the revelation of God's righteousness to us apart from human works. These were the verses that transformed the life of Martin Luther, for they showed that the answer to life comes not by striving to do good works to please God, but by resting in the finished work of God for us in Jesus Christ.

3. *An analysis of the depravity of human beings and an explanation of the work of Christ as the provision for that need (1:18–4:25).* This is the first major section of the letter, and it contains the most penetrating and perceptive analysis of human nature in its relationship to God ever written. The first thing Paul

shows is that, although people have knowledge of the existence of God through nature, all act as if the true God does not exist. Or, if they acknowledge him verbally, they nevertheless distort their understanding so that they actually worship the creation rather than the Creator. This willful ignorance has not been overlooked by God, since he has punished it by abandoning people to the natural outworking of their sins. This spiritual outworking of sin drags the race downward and enslaves us in invisible chains.

All are involved in this tragedy. The pagan is involved, for the moral disintegration of his life shows him to be held in sin's power. The "moral" individual is also involved, for although he approves of higher behavioral standards, he inevitably fails to live up to those standards. His guilt is even greater than the pagan's. Last of all, Paul unveils the need of the pious, or "religious," individual. The problem with the merely religious person is that the practice of religion alone cannot change the heart.

But here is where the gospel enters in. Although all have been enmeshed in sin's tentacles—so that Paul can remind us, quoting from the Old Testament, that "'There is no one righteous, not even one; there is no one who understands, no one who seeks God. All have turned away, they have together become worthless; there is no one who does good, not even one'" (Rom. 3:10–12)—God has taken the initiative to save us. Through the work of Christ he has provided the righteousness we lack, and he has done this not only for Jews, who might have expected it, but for Gentiles, too. This is why the late Welsh preacher, D. Martyn Lloyd-Jones of London, England, calls Romans 3:21–31, in which this doctrine is stated, "one of the greatest and noblest statements in the whole realm of scripture."[5]

In Romans 4, which is also part of this section, Paul shows that the gospel he has explained in chapter 3 has *always* been God's way of saving lost sinners. It is true that God accomplished salvation through the work of Jesus Christ, who from the perspective of Paul had lived in the not-far-distant past. But the timing is unimportant, says the apostle. Those who lived before Christ were saved by looking forward to his coming, by faith, just as we who have come afterward are also saved by faith as we look back. Paul proves this by Old Testament statements concerning the patriarch Abraham and King David.

4. *A review of the great scope of salvation (5:1–8:39)*. A number of commentators have supposed that in this second major section of his letter, Paul moves from the doctrine of justification by faith to the doctrine of sanctification. But Lloyd-Jones is surely right when he suggests that Paul is actually "showing . . . the certainty, fullness and finality" of what God has done.[6] Sanctification is indeed included in this section. But the author is actually covering the full scope of what God's work in Christ means for the believer.

5. D. M. Lloyd-Jones, *Romans: An Exposition of Chapter 1, The Gospel of God* (Grand Rapids: Zondervan, 1985), p. 25.

6. Ibid.

It gives him a new status before God and new privileges (5:1–11). It joins him to the living Lord Jesus Christ from whom flows a new life of righteousness (5:12–6:23). It releases him from the anguish of trying to attain to moral rectitude by law (7:1–25). It provides victory over sin by the power of the Holy Spirit (8:1–17). It ends in glorification, for the reason that nothing in heaven or earth can ever separate us from the inexpressible love and power of God in Jesus Christ (8:18–39).

5. *A Christian view of history (9:1–11:36).* Those who see a change of subject between chapters 4 and 5 inevitably see an even wider chasm between chapters 8 and 9. Indeed, it is a worse misunderstanding than this! Even many of the best commentators speak of Romans 9–11 as a parenthesis in which, so they suppose, Paul departs from his theme entirely in order to deal with God's different and separate plan for the Jewish people. A correct view, I believe, is that chapters 9 through 11 are a continuation of everything said thus far, particularly Paul's treatment of the believer's eternal security in Christ with which chapter 8 ends. Paul has argued that Jews and Gentiles are alike trapped by sin. He has shown that salvation is by Christ and that this salvation is eternal, being beyond any possibility of repudiation by God. But, some might ask, what of God's ancient chosen people? Most Jews seem to have rejected Christ. If that is so, then one of two things must follow. Either (1) certain people can be saved without Christ (the Jews), which Paul has already said to be impossible; or (2) salvation is not secure, since God has already apparently broken his covenant with the Jews and so should not be trusted.

Paul's answer is that God has not broken faith with Israel. On the contrary, he is doing today as he has always done. God is utterly consistent. There had never been a time in history in which every Jew was saved, just *because* that individual was a Jew. And no one is saved today merely by being what he or she is naturally: a churchgoer, a moral person, a philanthropist, an American (or any other nationality), or even a child of Christian parents. Salvation is by grace through faith, which means that it flows from God's choice and activity. It is God's salvation, after all, not man's. And God will work it out—he *is* working it out—until the fullness of his purpose regarding the salvation of a people for himself is complete.

This is the meaning of history. Its explanation is not found in the rise and fall of empires or in individual accomplishments. It is seen in God's choice of a people for himself and in his work of perfecting and eventually glorifying them. This thought is so wonderful to Paul that he ends this section of his letter with the tremendous doxology of Romans 11:33–36:

> Oh, the depth of the riches of the wisdom
>   and knowledge of God!
> How unsearchable his judgments,
>   and his paths beyond tracing out!

> "Who has known the mind of the Lord?
>   Or who has been his counselor?"
> "Who has ever given to God,
>   that God should repay him?"
> For from him and through him and to him are all things.
>   To him be the glory forever! Amen.

6. *The outworking of Christianity in individual and national life (12:1–15:13).* Paul was no armchair theologian, no ivory-tower divine. His letters always contain and usually end with practical and personal considerations. It is the same here. Having explained the gospel of God's unmerited salvation in Christ and having answered all reasonable objections to it, Paul concludes by showing how the work of God inevitably spills over into the details of individual and national life. His point is not only that Christianity will make a difference in life— though it will—but that it is the only thing that will ever actually make any true alteration in the world.

7. *A conclusion embracing Paul's future plans and final greetings (15:14– 16:27).* Having begun in letter format, the apostle now ends the epistle in the same way. In this section he tells of his hopes for the church at Rome, unveils more of his plans to visit them after having first made a trip to Jerusalem with an offering for the Jewish saints, and sends greetings to Rome from the church at Corinth. Greetings from his fellow workers and a benediction end the letter.

Paul's Regular Teaching

In the nineteenth chapter of Acts, Luke the historian says that during Paul's missionary journeys, the apostle spent two years in Ephesus teaching "the word of the Lord" to all who lived in Asia (v. 10). A marginal note in one ancient manuscript suggests that he did this for five hours each day. Counting six days to each week and fifty-two weeks to each year, that makes 3,120 hours of apostolic instruction, considerably more than most Bachelor or Master of Theology degree programs. What do you suppose Paul taught the residents of Asia during these two long years of instruction? I suggest that he taught them essentially what he has given us in outline form in Romans: the ruin of the human race in sin and the provision of a perfect and eternal remedy for that ruin through the work of Jesus Christ.

Another way of saying the same thing is to say that this is what the apostle Paul would teach if he were to work among us for the same length of time today.

Is Romans relevant today? It is—as long as people of every race, culture and nationality are estranged from God because of sin.

Is Christianity relevant? It is—as long as it can redeem us for God, pro-duce holiness in those who are trapped by sin, explain the meaning of life, and change history. Robert Haldane, the great nineteenth-century Scottish expositor of this letter, said as he drew near his initial summation of the epistle's teaching, "Paul, writing without any of the aids of human wisdom, draws his precepts from the fountain of heavenly truth, and inculcates on the disciples of Jesus a code of duties, which, if habitually practiced by mankind, would change the world from what it is—a scene of strife, jealousy and division—and make it what it was before the entrance of sin, a paradise fit for the Lord to visit and for man to dwell in."[7]

7. Robert Haldane, *An Exposition of the Epistle to the Romans* (MacDill AFB: MacDonald Publishing, 1958), p. 14.

PART ONE

Opening Statements

1

A Man in Christ

Romans 1:1

Paul, a servant of Christ Jesus, called to be an apostle and set apart for the gospel of God. . . .

Lord Lyttleton and Gilbert West were two nineteenth-century English barristers. They were unbelievers who one day took it upon themselves to disprove Christianity. As they discussed their project they decided that there were two main bulwarks of the Christian religion: the resurrection of Jesus Christ and the conversion and apostleship of Paul. West undertook to write against the resurrection of Jesus, while Lyttleton's task was to disprove the factuality of Paul's conversion.

Each was somewhat rusty in his knowledge of the facts, as unbelievers often are. So one lawyer said to the other, "If we are to be honest in this matter, we should at least investigate the evidence." They agreed to do this. While they were preparing their books they had a number of conferences, and in one of them West told Lyttleton that there was something on his mind that he felt he should share. He said that as he had been studying the evidence for Jesus' resurrection he had come to feel that there was something to it, since it was very well attested. Lyttleton replied that he was glad that West had spoken as he had, because on his part he had come to feel that there was some truth in the stories of Paul's Damascus Road conversion. Later, after they had finished their books and the two met again, Lyttleton said to his friend, "Gilbert, as I have been studying the evidence and weighing it by the recognized laws of legal evidence, I have become satisfied that Saul of Tarsus was converted as the New Testament says he was and that Christianity is true; I have written my book from that perspective." West replied that in a similar way he had become convinced of the truth of Jesus' resurrection, had come to believe in Jesus, and had written his book in defense of Christianity. Today their books are found in many good libraries.[1]

Few Christians are surprised by this story, but it has at least one unusual element. Since it is clear that the resurrection of Jesus Christ is foundational to Christianity, it is easy to understand why a nonbeliever like West would want to write a book refuting the resurrection. But the conversion and apostleship of Saint Paul might initially seem to be a much less important matter.

Yet here, as in many other places, first glances are misleading. Paul was not "the founder of Christianity," as some have called him. Jesus alone deserves that title. Yet Paul is so important as the first and greatest of the church's missionaries and as the articulator and systematizer of its theology that discrediting his claim to have been called and taught by Christ would seriously undermine Christianity itself. If Paul was not converted as a result of seeing the risen Lord while on the road to Damascus, as he claimed, and if he did not receive his gospel by a direct revelation from Jesus Christ, then Paul was a charlatan, his writings are not true, and Christianity is bereft of its single most important teacher after Christ.

"Paul"—The Man from Tarsus

Here is the man who meets us at the very beginning of our study, in fact at the very first word. In the Greek text, as well as in nearly all the English versions, the first word of this most important New Testament book is "Paul." It is a miracle that the word is even there. Paul is indeed the writer of this book. But we should remember that it was written to a largely Gentile church and that in his early days Paul was a fanatical Jew who would have little or no concern for any Gentile community, least of all a community that claimed as its Lord a man who had been crucified for blasphemy against the God of Israel only a few years before.

1. Lord Lyttleton, "Observations on the Conversion and Apostleship of Saint Paul" and Gilbert West, "Observations on the Resurrection of Jesus Christ" in *Lord Lyttleton on the Conversion of St. Paul and Gilbert West on the Resurrection of Jesus Christ* (New York: American Tract Society, 1929).

Who was Paul? In an appeal to the Roman commander of the Jerusalem garrison, recorded in Acts, Paul identified himself as a citizen of Tarsus in Cilicia, which he modestly called "no ordinary city" (Acts 21:39). Tarsus was a Greek city, the seat of a well-known university. Therefore, since Paul was apparently from a well-to-do family, we must assume that he received an outstanding Greek or pagan education in Tarsus. He shows some evidence of this by occasionally quoting from the pagan poets.[2]

Important as Paul's Greek education may have been, however, there is no doubt that his education in Judaism was the chief factor in his academic and intellectual development. Paul trained under the renowned Rabbi Gamaliel in Jerusalem where, as he claimed, he acquired a thorough knowledge of Jewish law and traditions (Acts 22:3). The son of a Pharisee (Acts 23:6), he became a Pharisee himself and was so zealous for the Pharisaic ideals of righteousness that he undertook a radical persecution of the early church, which he believed opposed those ideals (Acts 22:4–5; Phil. 3:6). Paul thus had the benefits of the best possible secular and religious educations, which led Charles Hodge to insist in his Romans commentary that "Paul, the most extensively useful of all the apostles, was . . . a thoroughly educated man."[3]

That is worth highlighting. From time to time Christians become skeptical of secular education or even of natural gifts or talents, supposing that these must be opposed to anything done by God's Spirit, but it is unfortunate when Christians think this way. It is possible to clarify the matter by asking three questions. First, what man did God most use in the period of history covered by the Old Testament? The answer obviously is "Moses." Second, what kind of education did Moses have? The answer is "a secular education." He had the best secular education of his day, being instructed "in all the wisdom of the Egyptians," as Stephen observed (Acts 7:22). Third question: What man, aside from Jesus Christ, did God most use in the period of history covered by the New Testament? The answer, again quite obvious, is "Paul," a man who also had the best possible education of his time, first in Tarsus from pagan teachers, whoever they may have been, and then in Jerusalem from Gamaliel, a Jewish teacher and nonbeliever. The conclusion is that there is nothing wrong with either education, whether Christian or secular, or with natural gifts. On the contrary, one's talents are

2. In Acts 17:28 Paul seems to be quoting from two Greek poets: Epimenides, who said, "In him we live and move and have our being" and Aratus, who wrote, "We are his offspring" (*Phaenomena*). He cites Epimenides again in Titus 1:12 ("Cretans are always liars, evil brutes, lazy gluttons"), though the words may actually derive from "Minos" by the earlier Greek poet Callimachus. In 1 Corinthians 15:33 Paul quotes Menander: "Bad company corrupts good character."

3. Charles Hodge, *A Commentary on Romans* (Edinburgh and Carlisle, Pa.: The Banner of Truth Trust, 1972), p. 4. (Original edition 1835.)

God-given, and education is a very great privilege that can enhance them. If we have both, we can thank God for giving them to us.

Still, education in itself is neutral. It can be used for good or for evil. What matters is whether it is given over to God to be used by him as he wills. In his early years Paul used his education and zeal to oppose Christianity. It was only after he had his dramatic encounter with Christ that he was able to use these important tools rightly.

A Servant of Christ Jesus

This leads to the next set of words in Romans: "a servant of Christ Jesus." I have pointed out that Paul was a thoroughly educated man. But important as that is, it is necessary to add that he was also a thoroughly converted man. Paul had met Jesus Christ, and from that moment he was never his own man. He was a servant of the Lord.

In the earlier years of this century the late J. Gresham Machen, at that time Professor of New Testament Literature and Exegesis at Princeton Theological Seminary, wrote a classic study of the apostle Paul titled *The Origin of Paul's Religion*. It was a reply to nineteenth-century attacks on Christianity by men who, like the early Lord Lyttleton, recognized the importance of Paul for the formation of Christian thought and the establishing of Christianity but who, because they rejected a supernatural Jesus, found themselves pressed to account for the nature of the apostle's beliefs. In this book Machen destroyed the liberal views with characteristic thoroughness. On the positive side, he showed that the traditions concerning Paul's contact with the other apostles are sound and that the teachings of Paul were identical with theirs as well as with the teachings of the Lord. He also showed that Paul was convinced of the factualness of the resurrection. On the negative side, Machen showed that Paul could not have derived his beliefs from his Judaistic background or from paganism. "The religion of Paul was rooted in an event, and . . . the event was the redemptive work of Christ in his death and resurrection."[4]

From a scholarly point of view, Machen might have allowed the book to rest there. But the real value of *The Origin of Paul's Religion*, in my judgment, is that this distinguished scholar then carried the argument one step further, showing not only that Paul was convinced of the truth of Christianity, including the great doctrine of the resurrection, but that he had been conquered and captivated by the living Lord Jesus Christ. Paul was in love with Jesus Christ, and it was his love for Christ that alone explains the nature and rigor of his life's work.

4. J. Gresham Machen, *The Origin of Paul's Religion*, the James Sprunt lectures delivered at Union Theological Seminary in Virginia (Grand Rapids: Wm. B. Eerdmans, 1947), p. 316. (Copyright 1925.)

Machen wrote, "Paulinism is to be accounted for [by] the love of Paul for his Savior. . . . The religion of Paul was not founded upon a complex of ideas derived from Judaism or from paganism. It was founded upon the historical Jesus. But the historical Jesus upon whom it was founded was not the Jesus of modern reconstruction, but the Jesus of the whole New Testament and of Christian faith; not a teacher who survived only in the memory of his disciples, but the Savior who after his redeeming work was done still lived and could still be loved."[5]

The conclusion of Machen's book, which I have quoted above, is the point of this first important phrase in Romans: "A servant of Christ Jesus." Paul was a super achiever, after all, so he could have introduced himself by a long list of accomplishments. He could have cited his ancestral tree, his degrees, his success in founding churches—even his writings, since Romans does not seem to have been the first of his letters. But Paul does not do this. Why? It is not because he was embarrassed about these things; he mentions them elsewhere in their proper place. It is certainly not because he did not value them. Paul overlooks these achievements because what he is most concerned about simply overshadows them. Above all else, Paul saw himself as a servant of the Lord.

Paul's letters are always filled with Jesus, no matter what he is writing about. Some letters, like Romans, are theological in nature. Others, like 1 and 2 Corinthians and Galatians, deal with problems in the churches. Some are personal; some are incidental in nature. Whatever his topic or specific purpose, Paul is always thinking about and relating his message to Jesus.

In the first seven verses of Romans, the first half of Paul's opening remarks, Jesus is mentioned by name, pronoun, title, or a descriptive phrase eight times: "Christ Jesus" (v. 1), "his Son," "a descendant of David" (v. 3), "the Son of God," "Jesus Christ our Lord" (v. 4), "him" (v. 5), "Jesus Christ" (v. 6), and "the Lord Jesus Christ" (v. 7).

This provides a very good way of testing our Christianity. Many of us, at least those who take time to read a study of Romans or certain other Bible commentaries, are convinced of the truthfulness of Christianity. Perhaps we can even articulate the doctrines of the faith, as Paul does. We can systematize theology. Ah, but do we love Jesus? Are our thoughts constantly occupied with him? Is he at the forefront? Is he the center? Is he the beginning and the end? When we talk to one another, do we speak often of him? Are we content to let the honors of the world pass by, so long as we can be known as Christ's servants? This gets very close to what is chiefly wrong with our contemporary Christianity. Our religion is one of personalities, plans, and programs, of buildings, books, and bargains. Because it is not the faith of those who love Jesus, it is shallow and selfish, constantly shifting in the ebbs and flows of cultural standards. As we grow in grace we will think less

5. Ibid., p. 317.

of these things and more of him who "loved me and gave himself for me" (Gal. 2:20).

Paul's description of himself as Christ's servant accomplishes a number of other things that are also worth noting:

1. *Paul's description of himself as a servant of Christ puts him in the same category as those to whom he is writing.* In other words, it identifies Paul first and foremost as a Christian. One of the great theological terms of Christianity, which Paul will use in his important explanation of the gospel in chapter 3, is "redemption." In his day it meant to buy in the marketplace, particularly to buy a slave. Slavery to Christ is a special kind of slavery, of course. It is a slavery in which we actually become free. Nevertheless, to become a servant or slave of Christ Jesus is a proper description of what it means to be a Christian. That is why Paul could write to the Corinthians, "Do you not know that your body is a temple of the Holy Spirit, who is in you, whom you have received from God? You are not your own; you were bought at a price. Therefore honor God with your body" (1 Cor. 6:19–20). When Paul identifies himself as "a servant of Christ Jesus," he is saying, among other things, "I am like you. Like you, I, too, have been purchased by Christ and am his follower."

2. *Paul's description of himself as a servant of Christ Jesus emphasizes that his chief function as a disciple of Christ is service.* This is worth noting, because it is a missing element in many of our fellowships.

Not long ago I was talking with a distinguished Christian whom God has used to found a thriving independent church in Texas. The church is now about twenty-five years old, and, according to my friend, the first fifteen years of its existence were spent in trying to convince everyone that it was the only true church in its city (or at least the only good one), and that the cause of Christ would be best served if those belonging to the other churches would simply leave their fellowships and join it. In those fifteen years the church membership grew from perhaps sixty to a hundred and fifty persons. About that time it dawned on the leaders that the way they had marked out was not self-evidently blessed by God, so they decided to take another tack. Instead of urging people to join them and thus contribute to their ministry, the leaders decided to become a church of servants. This meant giving themselves to whatever good work was being done, wherever it was done, and not being fretful if others got credit or even left the home church to further it. With this attitude the church began to grow, and in the last ten years it has swelled to more than two thousand members.

We should learn from this—and from the apostle Paul, who assumed and modeled a servant role. To be more basic, we should learn from Jesus, who said on one occasion, ". . . whoever wants to become great among you must be your servant, and whoever wants to be first must be your slave—just as the Son of Man did not come to be served, but to serve, and to give his life as a ransom for many" (Matt. 20:26–28).

3. *Paul's description of himself as a servant of Christ reminds his readers that he is nevertheless Christ's servant—a servant of Christ first and a servant of man second—and that he is writing to them in this capacity.* This anticipates the next of Paul's phrases.

Called to Be an Apostle

What is an apostle? "Apostle" is one of the least appreciated and even most misunderstood words in the Christian vocabulary. For some it means little more than "disciple." This is unfortunate, because a misunderstanding of this word involves a misunderstanding of much about Christianity.

The best passage for understanding the meaning of the term *apostle* is Acts 1:15–26, in which the eleven apostles elected a twelfth to complete their ranks after the treachery and death of Judas. As Peter explained, it was necessary for the replacement to have known the risen Lord and to have been chosen by him for this office. The disciples nominated two who met the first qualification: Joseph Barsabbas (also known as Justus) and Matthias. Then they drew lots to see whom Jesus himself would select. The choice fell on Matthias. This episode teaches that an apostle was to be a witness to the resurrection of Jesus Christ and that he was also necessarily chosen and equipped by Jesus for this function.

Yet there is more to it even than this. We know that at the very end of the Gospels and at the beginning of Acts, the Lord gives Christians a command we call the Great Commission. It means that we are all to be witnesses to Christ. If this is so, why is the apostolic office a special one? The answer comes from observing the way these chosen representatives of the Lord regarded their office. It is not only that they saw themselves as witnesses. The apostles also knew that they were to witness in an extraordinary, supernatural sense. Because they were apostles, God spoke authoritatively through them, so that what they said as apostles carried the force of divine teaching or Scripture. We see this clearly in Galatians, in which Paul defends his apostleship. At the beginning he stresses the divine origin of his calling, writing, "Paul, an apostle—sent not from men nor by man, but by Jesus Christ and God the Father who raised him from the dead" (Gal. 1:1). After that he links the nature and authority of the gospel to this office: "I want you to know, brothers, that the gospel I preached is not something that man made up. I did not receive it from any man, not was I taught it; rather, I received it by revelation from Jesus Christ" (vv. 11–12).

By calling himself an apostle in Romans, Paul reminds his readers that he is writing as no mere ordinary man but rather as one who has been given a message that should be received by them as the very words of God.

This also has a bearing on ourselves, for it tells us how we are to receive this book and benefit from it. We can study it as a merely human book, of course. That cannot be bad, since Romans is a good piece of writing, one well worth studying, even on limited terms. But if we would profit by it greatly, we must receive it as what it truly is—a message from God to our hearts and minds—and we must obey its teachings, just as we would be obliged to obey God if he should speak to us directly.

Set Apart for the Gospel of God

The third phrase Paul uses to introduce himself to the believers in Rome is "set apart for the gospel of God." This takes us back to the opening overview of Paul's life. In the days before his meeting with Christ on the road to Damascus, Paul was a Pharisee, and the meaning of that word is "separation" or "a separated one." This is the word Paul now uses of his commitment to the gospel. Before he met Christ, Paul was set apart to the Pharisaic traditions. Indeed, he regarded himself as one sublimely set apart. Pharisees crossed the street rather than pass close to some unworthy sinner or vile publican. They held to dietary restraints and sacramental cleansings. The list of things a Pharisee would *not* do was tremendous. But, when Paul met Christ, a life-shattering change occurred in him. Before, he was separated *from* all manner of things, and as a result he was self-righteous, narrow, cruel, and obsessive. Afterward, he was separated *unto* something, unto the gospel. That separation was positive—expansive and joyful, yet humbling. Paul never got over that divinely produced transformation.

Nor should you. Do you know what it is to be released from a negative legalism into the liberation of a positive Christianity? I am sure that in his new calling there were many things that Paul did not do. Certainly he did not make provision for fulfilling fleshly sins. He did not lie or cheat or steal or commit adultery. But Paul never thought of the rejection of these sins as privation, because he had his heart set on something more, and that was so grand a commitment that he always counted his calling to be the greatest of all privileges.

2

God's Grand Old Gospel

Romans 1:1–2

Paul, a servant of Christ Jesus, called to be an apostle and set apart for the gospel of God—the gospel he promised beforehand through his prophets in the Holy Scriptures.

The most important word in the introduction to Paul's letter to the Romans is "gospel." There it occurs six times (vv. 1, 2, 9, 15, 16, 17), and it is important because it is the theme of the epistle. Romans was written to make this great gospel of God more widely known.

We read the word for the first time in verse 1, just nine words into the Greek text. Paul identifies it as "the gospel of God," to which he has been called and set apart. In verse 2 he elaborates a bit, beginning to explain exactly what this gospel is. It is a gospel "promised beforehand through [God's] prophets in the Holy Scriptures regarding his Son." That is, it concerns the Lord Jesus Christ. In verse 9 Paul uses a phrase that firms up that definition, calling it "the gospel of his Son" and adding that he desires to preach it with his whole heart. In verses 15 through 17 he speaks again of his eagerness to preach the gospel: "That is why I am so eager to preach the gospel also to you who are at Rome. I am not ashamed of the gospel, because it is the power of God for the salvation of everyone who believes: first for the Jew, then for the Gentile. For in the gospel a righteousness from God is revealed, a righteousness that is by faith from first to last. . . ."

The Great Good News

Most of us know that the word *gospel (euangelion,* Greek) means "good news." But I am sure that D. Martyn Lloyd-Jones is correct when he suggests in his commentary that most of us stop at the definition and do not actually appreciate how good the good news truly is.[1]

To appreciate the goodness of the gospel we should begin with the fact that aside from Christianity the religions of the world are not at all good news. On the contrary, they are very bad news, a burden. We see this merely by looking into the hard, grim faces of the leaders of the world's other religions—the priests, monks, mullahs, gurus, and holy men who are found in every land and among all races. These are not happy people! And the religions they teach are not happy religions for those who follow them. The reason is not hard to discover. Apart from Christianity all the religions of the world are self-help or "works" religions. That is, they tell you how to find God (or peace, happiness, whatever) by human efforts. If it were possible to do this, religion in general might be good news. But the task is *not* possible. God is too holy, too removed from us because of his holiness and our sin, for us to reach him. Sin has so great a hold on us that it keeps us from the happiness we long for. A religion based on what you or I can do is comfortless because its requirements become burdens that can never be lifted.

This is what Paul himself had found. He had followed a religion of strictly defined good works and high moral standards. But it had not given him peace or even a true sense of achievement. He says later in this epistle that although he had learned what he should do, he found that he could not do it and so was a very "wretched man" (Rom. 7:24).

In our day many people have recognized this and have therefore sought happiness in the religion of "no religion." They have become practical atheists, regarding religion as a tool of some people to control others and therefore something that an enlightened society should throw away. At first this "no religion" seems like good news. But the goodness evaporates as soon as we stop to think about it. If there is no God and if we are therefore free to do as we please without any thought of accountability to a divine authority or punishment by him, we seem to be liberated to joyous independence. But if there is no accountability, because there is nobody to be accountable to, what we do with this great "freedom" becomes meaningless. Moreover, if what we

1. D. M. Lloyd-Jones, *Romans: An Exposition of Chapter 1, The Gospel of God* (Grand Rapids: Zondervan, 1985), p. 55: "If we say that we know the gospel means good news, the really important question, therefore, is whether the gospel has come to us as good news. Is that our real understanding of the thing itself, and not merely the word in which it is described?"

do is meaningless, *we* must be meaningless, too. We are accidental bubbles upon the great cosmic deep, destined only to burst and be forgotten.

"No religion" leads nowhere. It may seem to offer the great good news of human progress, but it actually leaves us with despair over the futility of human existence.

This is where Christianity comes in and proclaims what is really good news. The gospel is good for two reasons. First, it tells us that God is actually there—that he is not merely the figment of human imagination but really exists, that he has made us for fellowship with himself and does hold us accountable for what we do. This gives meaning to life. Second, it tells us that God loves us and has reached out to save us through the work of Jesus Christ. We could not reach God, because our sins separated us from him. But God removed our sins through Christ and so bridged the gap over these very troubled waters. Before, we were groaning after God but could not find him. Now we sing praises to the One who has found us.

Let me make this last point explicitly. Have you ever considered how characteristic it is of Christianity that such large portions of our worship consist of singing praises to God? There is singing in other religions, of course; but it is usually mere chanting, which is itself a religious exercise designed to make the worshiper more "holy" or bring him closer to the deity. Christians do not sing as a good work or as a spiritual discipline. We do not sing to find God. We sing because he has found us and we are happy about it. The very first hymn in many hymnbooks says:

> All people that on earth do dwell,
> Sing to the Lord with cheerful voice;
> Him serve with fear, his praise forthtell,
> Come ye before him and rejoice.

D. Martyn Lloyd-Jones asks, "Has the gospel come to us like that? Can we say honestly at this moment that this is the greatest and best good news that we have ever heard?"[2] If we cannot say that, it may be because we are not really born again, regardless of our profession. Or it may be that we do not actually appreciate the gospel, because we are not walking very close to God.

A "Promised" Gospel

The second thing Paul says about this gospel, this good news, is that it was "promised beforehand" through God's prophets. This is an important point because, new as the Christian gospel seemed when it first burst upon our sin-darkened world, the gospel of the salvation of men by God through the work of Jesus Christ was nevertheless no novelty. On the contrary, it was

---

2. Lloyd-Jones, *Romans: An Exposition of Chapter 1,* p. 58.

the goal to which all prior revelations of God during the Old Testament period led. We find this affirmed in every surviving example of the apostolic preaching.

1. *The preaching of Paul.* The apostle Paul seems never to have tired of showing this connection when he spoke about the gospel. In the thirteenth chapter of Acts, which gives us the first recorded example of Paul's preaching, we find Paul reviewing Israel's history to show (just as he does in Romans 1) that God sent Jesus as a descendant of King David, according to his promise, and that everything that happened to Jesus during the days of his earthly ministry fulfilled the Holy Scriptures. He was condemned and crucified as the prophets had said he would be. Afterward, he was raised from the dead according to these same prophecies. In the latter half of this sermon Paul quotes Psalm 2:7 to prove Christ's deity: "'You are my Son; today I have become your Father'" (Acts 13:33), and Isaiah 55:3 and Psalm 16:10 to confirm that the resurrection was prophesied: "'I will give you the holy and sure blessings promised to David.' So it is stated elsewhere: 'You will not let your Holy One see decay'" (vv. 34–35).

At the end of his sermon in Acts 13, Paul warns of the dangers of unbelief, citing Habakkuk 1:5 ("I am going to do something in your days that you would never believe," v. 41), and announcing that even his proclamation of the gospel to a mixed audience of Jews and Gentiles had been prophesied in Isaiah 49:6 ("I have made you a light for the Gentiles, that you may bring salvation to the ends of the earth," v. 47).

We find this same reference to Old Testament teachings elsewhere. When we are told of Paul's first preaching at Thessalonica, we read, "As his custom was, Paul went into the synagogue, and on three Sabbath days he reasoned with them from the Scriptures, explaining and proving that the Christ had to suffer and rise from the dead" (Acts 17:2–3). Paul also uses this approach in Romans 4, proving the gospel he has explained in Romans 3 on the basis of Old Testament texts about Abraham and King David.

2. *The preaching of Philip.* When we go back a few chapters in Acts and thus to a slightly earlier period in the history of the church, we come to the ministry of the deacon Philip. God used Philip to preach the gospel to an Ethiopian official, and the way he did it was by announcing the fulfillment of Isaiah 53:7–8, which the Ethiopian was reading aloud but did not understand:

> "He was led like a sheep to the slaughter,
>   and as a lamb before the shearer is silent,
>   so he did not open his mouth.
> In his humiliation he was deprived of justice.
>   Who can speak of his descendants?
>   For his life was taken from the earth."
>   Acts 8:32–33

The story relates that "Philip began with that very passage of Scripture and told him the good news about Jesus" (v. 35).

3. *The preaching of Peter.* In the early chapters of Acts we have two examples of Peter's early preaching. The first was at Pentecost, when Peter gave a sermon that was roughly half quotations from the Old Testament; these were explained in the other half of the message. In this sermon Peter quoted Joel 2:28–32 (his chief text, prophesying Pentecost itself), Psalm 16:8–11 (which Paul later quoted in part in his sermon recorded in Acts 13), and Psalm 110:1 (the Old Testament verse most cited in the New). In Peter's sermon (Acts 2:14–36) there are eleven verses of Old Testament quotation and twelve verses of introduction, explanation, and application.

It is recorded in Acts 4:8–12 that Peter also preached on Psalm 118:22, showing that the Old Testament prophesied Jesus' rejection by Israel and his ultimate glorification by God. "He is," said Peter, "the stone you builders rejected, which has become the capstone" (v. 11). This was a favorite text for Peter. He used it again in his first letter, in conjunction with Isaiah 8:14 and 28:16.

4. *The preaching of Jesus Christ.* Where did the apostles get this important Old Testament approach to the gospel, particularly since none of their contemporaries seem to have read the Old Testament books in this fashion? There is only one answer. They got it from the Lord Jesus Christ, their master, who saw his life as a fulfillment of Scripture and also taught his disciples to view it in that way. We remember that after the resurrection, when Jesus was walking to Emmaus with two of his followers, he chided them on their slowness to believe what the Old Testament writers had spoken: "How foolish you are, and how slow of heart to believe all that the prophets have spoken! Did not the Christ have to suffer these things and then enter his glory?" The text continues: "And beginning with Moses and all the Prophets, he explained to them what was said in all the Scriptures concerning himself" (Luke 24:25–27).

Let me emphasize this point. The gospel is good news, of course. But not only that; it is the good news God has been announcing from the very beginning of his dealings with the human race, up to and including the end of the Old Testament—from Genesis 3:15 (the first announcement of the gospel) to Malachi 4:5 (which speaks of the coming of Elijah as Christ's forerunner).

This is the key to understanding the entire Old Testament. It is the key to understanding the New Testament. It is the key to understanding all history—God's saving men and women through the work of his Son, the Lord Jesus Christ, as he announced "beforehand through his prophets in the Holy Scriptures."

"The Holy Scriptures"

Moreover, it is in the Holy Scriptures that this announcement has been made. This phrase is of tremendous importance because it identifies the place at which the announcement of God's great good news may be found and highlights its very essence.

First, the announcement of God's good news is in *writing*, the writings of the prophets. This means that we are not to look elsewhere for it, as if God had chosen to reveal this news by mystical visions, through inward intimations, or in some other nonbiblical or nonobjective way. We have documents to study and words to ponder and understand. Second, the books of the Bible are special, *holy* writings, which means they are not mere human compositions but are the very words of God. They are God's revelation to mankind. As Peter, himself one of the human instruments for God's giving of the New Testament, wrote: ". . . no prophecy of Scripture came about by the prophet's own interpretation. For prophecy never had its origin in the will of man, but men spoke from God as they were carried along by the Holy Spirit" (2 Peter 1:20–21). We should be drawn to the Word in faithful study and meditation—if we really believe the Bible to be God's Holy Scriptures.

I think of how John Wesley expressed his yearning for the Word in that well-known introduction to his sermons:

> I am a creature of a day, passing through life as an arrow through the air. I am a spirit come from God and returning to God, just hovering over the great gulf, till, a few moments hence, I am no more seen; I drop into an unchangeable eternity. I want to know one thing—the way to heaven, how to land safe on that happy shore. God himself has condescended to teach me the way. For this very end he came from heaven. He ha[s] written it down in a book. O give me that book! At any price, give me the book of God! I have it. Here is knowledge enough for me. Let me be *homo unius libri* ("a man of one book"). Here then I am, far from the busy ways of men. I sit down alone. Only God is here. In his presence I open, I read his book—for this end, to find the way to heaven.[3]

I note, as John Murray does in his study of Romans, that the great Karl Barth, usually so perceptive in his exegetical comments, passes over the words *Holy Scripture* without notice in his commentary.[4] Barth valued the gospel, but he did not fully appreciate the nature of the documents in which this gospel is disclosed. It is a flaw in his theology.

---

3. John Wesley, *The Works of John Wesley*, vol. 5, *First Series of Sermons, 1 through 39* (Grand Rapids: Zondervan, n.d.), p. 3. (From the edition of 1872.)

4. Karl Barth, *The Epistle to the Romans*, trans. Edwyn C. Hoskyns (London: Oxford University Press, 1963), p. 28. (Original edition 1933.) See John Murray, *The Epistle to the Romans: The English Text with Introduction, Exposition and Notes*, 2 vols. in 1 (Grand Rapids: Wm. B. Eerdmans, 1977), vol. 1, p. 5. (Original edition 1959, 1965.)

Do not let it be a flaw with you. Recognize, as Paul did, that God has spoken to us in the Bible, and therefore determine to study it carefully and obediently. You should do with it what Francis Bacon said we should do with even the greatest of human books: "taste," "chew," "swallow," and "digest" it, and read it "wholly, and with diligence and attention."[5]

God's Gospel

The final point about the gospel made by Paul in these two verses of Romans is the one with which Paul actually starts, namely, that it is *God's* gospel. It is something God announced and accomplished and what *he* sent his apostles to proclaim. It is something God blesses and through which *he* saves men and women. The grammatical way of stating this is that the genitive ("of God") is a subjective, rather than an objective genitive. It means that God creates and announces the gospel rather than that he is the object of its proclamation.

Note how prominent this point is in these early verses of Romans. God the Father has "promised [the gospel] beforehand through his prophets in the Holy Scriptures" (v. 2). He has sent his Son, the Lord Jesus Christ, to accomplish the work thus promised, with the result that the gospel, then as now, is "regarding" him (v. 3). Finally, it is "through him and for his name's sake" that Paul and the other apostles, exercising a calling received by them from God, were in the process of proclaiming the gospel to men and women everywhere (v. 5).

If God is concerned about his gospel to this extent, will he not bless it fully wherever these great truths are proclaimed?

Let me tell you one story of such a blessing. In the year 1816 a Scotsman by the name of Robert Haldane went to Switzerland. Haldane was a godly layman who, with his brother James Alexander, had been much used of the Lord in Scotland. In Geneva, on this particular occasion, he was sitting on a park bench in a garden in the open air and heard a group of young men talking. As he listened he realized two things. First, these were theological students. Second, they were ignorant of true Christianity. As a result of this encounter and after a few encouraging conversations, Haldane invited the students to his room and began to teach them the Book of Romans, going through it verse by verse, as we will be doing in these studies. God honored this work, and the Holy Spirit blessed it by the conversions of these young men. They were converted one by one, and in turn they were instrumental in a religious revival that not only affected Switzerland but spread to France and the Netherlands.

One of these students was Merle d'Aubigné, who became famous for his classic *History of the Reformation of the Sixteenth Century*. We know it in an

5. Francis Bacon, "Of Studies," *Essays or Councils Civil and Moral* in *Selected Writings of Francis Bacon*, ed. Hugh C. Dick (New York: Modern Library, 1955), p. 129.

abbreviated form as *The Life and Times of Martin Luther.*[6] Another of these men was Louis Gaussen, the author of *Theopneustia,* a book on the inspiration of the Scriptures.[7] The company of those converted through Haldane's exposition of Romans included: Frédéric Monod, the chief architect and founder of the Free Churches in France; Bonifas, who became a great and distinguished theologian; and César Malan, another important religious leader. All were converted as a result of Haldane's exposition of the truths of the Romans epistle.

Why should it be any different today? If it were *our* gospel, we could expect nothing. But it is not our gospel. It is "the gospel of God," that grand old gospel that was "promised beforehand through his prophets in the Holy Scriptures" and achieved for us by the Lord Jesus Christ through his substitutionary death and resurrection. We should proclaim it fearlessly and with zeal, as did Paul.

6. J. H. Merle D'Aubigné, *The Life and Times of Martin Luther,* trans. H. White (Chicago: Moody Press, 1958).

7. S. R. L. Gaussen, *Theopneustia: The Plenary Inspiration of the Holy Scripture* (Chicago: Moody Press, n.d.). (Original edition 1840.)

3

The Gospel of Jesus Christ

Romans 1:2-4

. . . the gospel he promised beforehand through his prophets in the Holy Scriptures regarding his Son, who as to his human nature was a descendant of David, and who through the Spirit of holiness was declared with power to be the Son of God by his resurrection from the dead: Jesus Christ our Lord.

In the previous study I tried to show that Christianity, the religion being explained by the apostle Paul in Romans, is a unique religion, and I gave a number of reasons for saying that. In this chapter we come to the chief reason: Christianity is unique because it is founded upon a unique person, the Lord Jesus Christ.

Yet it is more than this. Not only is Christianity unique because its founder is unique, it is unique because it is uniquely linked to him, in the sense that you simply cannot have Christianity without the Lord Jesus Christ! J.N.D. Anderson, director of the Institute of Advanced Legal Studies at the University of London, has noted that other religions are quite different:

In Confucianism and Buddhism it is the teaching and principles of Confucius and the Buddha which represent the essence of the religion, rather than the teacher who first enunciated them or the facts of his life and death. Even in Islam, the towering figure of Muhammad finds its paramount importance in the divine revelation which it believes was given to mankind through him. It is the *ipsissima verba* of the Almighty, communicated to the prophet by the Archangel Gabriel and subsequently recorded in the Qur'ân, together with that further teaching provided by the inspired *sunna* or practice of the prophet, which constitute the essence of the faith; and a Muslim would point to the Book and the Traditions, rather than to Muhammad himself, as the media of revelation.[1]

By contrast, Christianity *is* Jesus Christ. John R. W. Stott wrote: "The person and work of Christ are the rock upon which the Christian religion is built. If he is not who he said he was, and if he did not do what he said he had come to do, the foundation is undermined and the whole superstructure will collapse. Take Christ from Christianity, and you disembowel it; there is practically nothing left. Christ is the center of Christianity; all else is circumference."[2]

Who Is Jesus Christ?

Obviously this causes us to ask who Jesus Christ is, and, as soon as we do, we find Paul's answer in the words "his Son"—Jesus of Nazareth is the Son of God.

Today, largely as a result of the religious liberalism of the last century, the term "son of God" is understood in a nearly generic sense, usually meaning only "a human being." Liberal theology holds that we are all sons or daughters of God. But this is a rather new heresy and one that none of the New Testament writers would have understood. When they used the words "Son of God" they were not referring to any supposed divine characteristics of human beings or even of some special relationship that we are all supposed to have to God. They meant deity itself. They meant that he who was being called Son of God was uniquely divine; that is, he was and always had been God.

Take the great confession of the apostle Peter, recorded in Matthew 16. Jesus had asked the disciples who the people were saying he was. They gave answers that had been making the rounds: John the Baptist, Elijah, Jeremiah, one of the prophets.

"But what about you?" Jesus asked. "Who do you say I am?"

Peter answered for the rest: "You are the Christ, the Son of the living God" (Matt. 16:16). This answer set Jesus apart from the category of those human figures the people were suggesting. It identified him as the divine Messiah. Moreover, Jesus accepted the designation, assuring Peter and the others that this insight had come not as the result of simple human observa-

1. J. N. D. Anderson, *Christianity: The Witness of History* (London: Tyndale Press, 1970), p. 38.

2. John R. W. Stott, *Basic Christianity* (Downers Grove, Ill.: InterVarsity Press, 1971), p. 21.

tion but as a special revelation from God the Father. It was God who had given Peter this great discernment.

Jesus explicitly taught who he was: "I and the Father are one" (John 10:30). He had also said, "Before Abraham was born, I am!" (John 8:58).

When Thomas fell down to worship Jesus after his resurrection, confessing him "My Lord and my God" (John 20:28), Jesus accepted the designation. Then he gently chided Thomas, not for his worship but for his earlier unbelief.

This is the sense in which Paul begins to unfold the content of the Christian message. Already he has called it "the gospel of God," meaning that God is the source of this great plan of salvation. Now he adds that the gospel concerns "his [God's] Son." This means that Jesus is the unique Son of God and that the person and work of this divine Jesus are the gospel's substance. This is where we start. We do not countenance any modern nonsense about a "Christless Christianity." We begin with the eternal Son of God, and we confess that everything we believe and are as Christians centers in the person and work of that unique individual.

The God-Man

Jesus is not only unique in his divine nature, however. He is also unique in that he became man at a specific point in human history and now remains the God-man eternally. No one else is like that. No one can ever be.

This brings us to a remarkable section of Paul's introduction in which every word is so precisely chosen and of such significance that, even apart from Paul's claims to be writing as an apostle, we ought to think of Romans as more than a "merely human" composition. To begin with, there is an obvious contrast between the two natures of the historical, earthly Jesus. The first is his human nature. In the Greek text the word is *sarx,* translated "flesh." But the term is not limited to describing only the fleshly parts of our body, as the word is in English. It means "the whole man." The translators of the New International Version are therefore right on target when they translate "as to his human nature." This "nature" is contrasted with Christ's divine nature, which is described as "the Spirit of holiness." That phrase does not refer to the Holy Spirit (though many have interpreted it this way), but to Christ's own spiritual or divine nature, which is holy. In other words, the first important thing about this section is its clear recognition of both the human and divine natures of Jesus.

Note also the contrast between "descendant of David" and "Son of God." This corresponds to the aforementioned distinction, because "descendant of David" speaks of Jesus' human nature (it is as a man that he was born into David's family tree), while "Son of God" is linked to his divinity.

The really interesting point is the contrast between the word *was,* the verb used in the first part of this descriptive sentence, and *declared,* which is the verb in part two. However, I need to point out that "was" is a weak rendering of the word Paul actually used. In Greek the word is *ginomai,* which means "become," "take place," "happen" or, in some cases "be born" or even "come into being." "Was" describes a past state or condition, but it can be a timeless state. "Became" shows that something came into existence that was not in existence previously. And, of course, this is precisely what happened in our Lord's incarnation. Before his birth to Mary at what we call the beginning of the Christian era, Jesus was God and always had been God. (That is why the other verb is "declared." He was declared to be God.) But he *became* man at a particular past point in history by the incarnation.

In verses 3 and 4, a brief message of only twenty-eight Greek words (forty-one in English), Paul has provided us with an entire Christology.

Great David's Greater Son

There is a debate among those who have studied Romans as to whether the church to which Paul was writing was predominantly Jewish or predominantly Gentile or a mixture of the two. I believe that it was a predominantly Gentile church and that the epistle should be understood in that light. But, as previously mentioned, it is nevertheless also true that Paul saw the gospel as growing out of its Jewish roots and makes that point frequently.

An example occurs in the words "descendant of David" in verse 3. We have noted that this phrase appears in the long sentence describing the two natures of the Lord Jesus Christ, but it goes beyond what we might have thought necessary for the apostle to say. In contrasting Christ's human nature with his divine nature, it would have been possible for Paul merely to say, "who as to his human nature was *a man* [or a *true man*]." That is indeed the chief point of the passage. But instead of this, he says, "was a descendant of David," thus bringing in the whole matter of Jesus' Jewish ancestry.

Why does Paul do this? There are several reasons.

1. *By referring to Jesus as a "descendant of David," Paul gives substance to his main contention, namely, that Jesus was a true human being.* It is not that Jesus was merely *a* man in some vague, mystical way, but that he became a specific man whose existence was grounded in a particular human ancestry. Although we do not have any pictures of Jesus, if we had lived in his day and had possessed a camera then, we could have taken one. His eyes and hair had a certain color. He weighed so many pounds. Furthermore, we could have talked to him as well as to his mother and father, brothers and sisters and friends. He would have had stories to tell about his human relatives.

2. *By referring to Jesus as a "descendant of David," Paul gives a specific example of the things "promised beforehand" by God "in the Holy Scriptures."* There were many things prophesied concerning the Christ—where he would be born, how he would be treated by his people, the nature of his death, the fact of his resurrection. But one of the chief promises was that he would be born of David's line and would therefore be eligible to sit on David's throne and

reign forever as the true king of Israel. Isaiah said, "A shoot will come up from the stump of Jesse [David's father]; From his roots a Branch will bear fruit" (Isa. 11:1).

Jeremiah was even more explicit:

> "The days are coming," declares the LORD,
>   "when I will raise up to David a righteous Branch,
> a King who will reign wisely
>   and do what is just and right in the land.
> In his days Judah will be saved
>   and Israel will live in safety.
> This is the name by which he will be called:
>   The LORD Our Righteousness."
>
> Jeremiah 23: 5–6

The way in which these prophecies were fulfilled is quite remarkable, because there seemed to be a problem regarding the family from which a claimant to the throne of David might come. The difficulty was that there were two lines of descendency from King David. One was the line of Solomon, who had reigned on David's throne after the death of his father. Normally, there would be no question but that an elder son of a family descended from King Solomon would reign. But in Jeremiah 22:30, in the chapter just before the one prophesying "a righteous Branch" that would arise in David's line, a harsh curse is pronounced on a king named Jehoiachin, the last of the actual reigning kings descended from King Solomon: "Record this man as if childless, a man who will not prosper in his lifetime: for none of his offspring will prosper, none will sit on the throne of David or rule anymore in Judah." Because of God's curse, no king descended in that line could reign legitimately.

There was another strong line of descent, however. King Solomon had an older brother, Nathan, who would have been king if God had not given the throne to Solomon. Nathan had also produced descendants, but any descendant of this line who claimed inheritance of the promises made to King David would have been challenged immediately by descendants in the line that had actually reigned. How could such a dilemma be solved? There was a lack of reigning kings in one line and a curse on the other.

The way God solved the issue was so simple that it confounds the wisest skeptics. The line of Solomon ran on through the centuries until it eventually produced Joseph, who was betrothed to the Virgin Mary and eventually became her husband, though not until after she had conceived and given birth to the Lord Jesus Christ. Jesus was not descended from Joseph; otherwise he would have inherited the curse on that line. But when Joseph took Mary under his protection and thus became the adoptive father of her divine child, he passed the right of royalty to him. And since Jesus was also descended from Mary—who, as it turns out, was a descendant of David through the line of Nathan—Jesus combined the claims of the two lines in his unique personhood and thereby eliminated the possibility of there ever being any other legitimate claimant to the throne. In other words, if Jesus is not the Messiah who has descended from David according to the Old Testament prophecies, there will never be a Messiah. For Jesus had no human children, and each of his brothers (who are the only other possibilities through whom another Messiah might descend) had the curse on him and would have passed it on to his children.[3]

Paul's reference to Jesus' descent from David in Romans 1:3 is quite brief, of course. But these details of his ancestry, as I have given them, would undoubtedly have formed the substance of much longer expositions by Paul in many teaching situations.

3. *By referring to Jesus as a "descendant of David," Paul prepares the way for the exalted title he is going to give him at the end of this great sentence, namely, "Lord."* One of the problems the apostle faced in his missionary work among the Gentiles is that in the eyes of many people the Jesus he preached was only a common criminal, properly executed, and therefore hardly to be extolled. But Jesus is actually a descendant of the great King David, says Paul. And what is even more important, he is the king announced in prophecy—the king who was also the Son of God. He is, therefore, not merely the King of the Jews, but the King of all men. He is the Lord Jesus Christ, the very essence of Christianity.

The Sovereign Son

This brings me to the last point of these verses, based on something Paul says about Jesus in the second half of his long descriptive sentence regarding the Lord's two natures. He says that Jesus "was declared with power to be the Son of God by his resurrection from the dead." How are we to understand that? Particularly, how are we to understand the phrase "with power"?

The most common way of understanding these words is to relate "with power" to "his resurrection," as if Paul was thinking of the resurrection as a striking revelation of God's power. Using this approach, the words "Spirit of holiness" would be seen as referring to the Holy Spirit, viewed as the agent of the resurrection; and this powerful resurrection, accomplished by the Spirit, would be seen as a proof of Christ's deity. It is true, of course, that the resurrection was accomplished by God's power and is itself proof of Christ's claims. But the Bible does not actually speak of the Holy Spirit's

---

3. There is an excellent treatment of the genealogies, their problems, justification, and significance, in Donald Grey Barnhouse, *Man's Ruin,* vol. 1 of *Exposition of Bible Doctrines, Taking the Epistle of Romans as a Point of Departure* (Grand Rapids: Wm. B. Eerdmans, 1952), pp. 44–48. See also my expanded discussion, in James Montgomery Boice, *Standing on the Rock: The Importance of Biblical Inerrancy* (Wheaton, Ill.: Tyndale House, 1984), pp. 103–106.

raising Jesus from the dead. The Father is the One who is said to have done that. Even more significantly, we have already seen that the words "Spirit of holiness" refer to Christ's divine nature—the words *kata pneuma* ("according to spirit") parallel the words *kata sarka* ("according to flesh")—and not to the third person of the Trinity. That alone seems to exclude the most popular interpretation of "with power."

A second understanding links "with power" to the declaration of Christ's deity. That is, it views Paul as thinking of a powerful or effective declaration, one that accomplishes its ends. Charles Hodge and F. Godet held this interpretation.[4]

It is significant, however, that in the Greek text the words "with power" follow immediately after the words "Son of God" so that the text literally reads: ". . . declared the Son of God with power according to a spirit of holiness by the resurrection from the dead." This gives us a third understanding of what is going on in this sentence. In this view the words "with power" are linked to "Son of God," so that we might more properly understand Paul to be speaking of "the Son of God with power" or "the powerful Son of God," which he is declared to be by the resurrection. D. Martyn Lloyd-Jones takes this view, rightly I think, and explains it like this:

> The Lord Jesus Christ . . . was the Son of God before. He is always the Son of God. He was the Son of God before the incarnation and from all eternity. . . . Where then is the variation? . . . It is in the form that he assumes; and what we have been told in verse 3 is that when he came into this world he did not come as the Son of God with power. No! He came as a helpless babe. . . . He was Son of God—yes; but not Son of God with power. In other words, when he came as a babe, the power of the Son of God was veiled in the flesh. . . . But what the apostle says is, that in the resurrection he is "declared to be the Son of God with *power.*" It is there that we realize how powerful he is.[5]

The point of this should be clear to everyone. It is not merely a case of Paul's declaring that the resurrection was a demonstration of the great power of God or even that the resurrection was a powerful demonstration of the validity of Christ's claims. It is not that at all. Rather, it is actually a strong declaration about the Lord's own person—precisely the purpose of this entire section and the point on which Paul will end. It is a declaration that Jesus is the sovereign Son of God and therefore rightly the "Lord" of all men as well as the Savior.

---

4. Charles Hodge, *A Commentary on Romans* (Edinburgh and Carlisle, Pa.: The Banner of Truth Trust, 1972), pp. 19, 20 (original edition 1835). F. Godet, *Commentary on St. Paul's Epistle to the Romans,* trans. A. Cusin (Edinburgh: T. & T. Clark, n.d.), p. 130.

5. D. M. Lloyd-Jones, *Romans: An Exposition of Chapter 1, The Gospel of God* (Grand Rapids: Zondervan, 1985), pp. 115, 116. Robert Haldane takes the same position, *An Exposition of the Epistle to the Romans* (MacDill AFB: MacDonald Publishing, 1958), p. 26.

The conclusion of this, which in this study comes at the end instead of being scattered through the chapter, is that Jesus Christ, the very essence of Christianity, is your Lord and that you ought rightly to turn from all sin and worship him. You may dispute his claims. But if they are true, if Jesus is who the apostle Paul declares him to be in this epistle and others, there is no other reasonable or right option open to you than total and heart-deep allegiance. Colonel Robert Ingersoll, the famous agnostic of the last century, was no friend of Christianity. But he saw certain things clearly; and he said on one occasion, though in a critical vein, "Christianity cannot live in peace with any other form of faith. If that religion be true, there is but one Savior, one inspired book and but one little narrow . . . path that leads to heaven. Such a religion is necessarily uncompromising."[6]

That statement is true because the Lord Jesus Christ is himself uncompromising. He is uncompromising because of who he is. Is he the eternal Son of God now made man for your salvation? Is he the Lord? If he is, you ought to heed his call—the call of the gospel—and follow him.

6. Quoted by Walter R. Martin, *Essential Christianity: A Handbook of Basic Christian Doctrines* (Grand Rapids: Zondervan, 1962), p. 23.

4

Jesus Christ Our Lord

Romans 1:4b

. . . Jesus Christ our Lord.

One of the excellencies of the New International Version is the way it handles the word order of the opening verses of Romans, reserving the words "Jesus Christ our Lord" until the end of verse 4, where they appear as a natural and effective climax. This is an improvement over the King James Version, which does not follow the Greek at this point and inserts the words earlier.

I emphasize this because the words "Jesus is Lord" constituted the earliest Christian creed and were therefore of the greatest possible importance to the early church. From the earliest days it was recognized that if a person confessed "Jesus is Lord," he or she was to be received for baptism. This is because, on the one hand, "No one can say, 'Jesus is Lord,' except by the Holy Spirit" (1 Cor. 12:3) and because, on the other hand, "If you confess with your mouth, 'Jesus is Lord,' and believe in your heart that God raised him from the dead, you will be saved" (Rom. 10:9). To us, reading these records at a later date, it may seem strange that "Jesus is Lord" *(Kyrios 'Iēsous,* Greek) could be so important to our spiritual predecessors, but the reason is that they simply overflow with meaning.

To say that Jesus is Lord implies two things. First, it implies that Jesus is God. Second, it implies that Jesus is the Savior.

"Lord"

The first of these implications is due to the fact that in the Greek version of the Old Testament (the Septuagint), which was well known to the Jewish community of the first century and from which most of the New Testament writers quoted when citing Scripture, *kyrios* ("Lord") is used to translate the Hebrew name for God: Yahweh, or Jehovah. This is why most of our English Bibles do not use the name *Yahweh* but have *Lord* instead. The disciples of Christ knew that this word was repeatedly used to translate this great name for God. Yet, knowing this, they did not hesitate to transfer the title to Jesus, thereby indicating that in their view Jesus is Jehovah.

We need to be careful at this point, of course, because not all uses of "Lord" in the New Testament imply divinity. "Lord" was a bit like our English word *sir.* On the lowest level it could be used merely as a form of polite address. That is why, according to the Gospels, apparent unbelievers frequently called Jesus "Lord." This does not mean that they had received a sudden revelation of who he was but only that they were treating him with the respect due a distinguished rabbi; they were being polite. On the other hand, "Lord" could mean more. When we speak of *Sir* Winston Churchill we are using "sir" as a title. Similarly, those who called Jesus "Lord" were sometimes confessing that he was their "Master" by this greeting. In the most exalted instances, as in Thomas's stirring post-resurrection confession, "My Lord and my God" (John 20:28), the word was linked to the early disciples' belief in Christ's divinity.

This is the meaning of *kyrios* in the Christological passages of the New Testament. Here are some examples.

1. *1 Corinthians 8:4–6.* ". . . We know that an idol is nothing in the world and that there is no God but one. For even if there are so-called gods, whether in heaven or on earth (as indeed there are many 'gods' and many 'lords'), yet for us there is but one God, the Father, from whom all things came and for whom we live; and there is but one Lord, Jesus Christ, through whom all things came and through whom we live." The background for this passage is the polytheism of the Greek world, which Paul is refuting here. He is arguing that there is but one God, who is one with Jesus. The parallelism between "from whom all things came and for whom we live" (applied to God the Father) and "through whom all things came and through whom we live" (applied to Jesus Christ) makes this identification plain.

2. *Luke 2:11.* A second example is from the Christmas story. In this verse the angel tells the shepherds, "Today in the town of David a Savior has been born to you; he is Christ the Lord." The important thing here is that "Lord"

is in the nominative case, as is "Christ," rather than being in the genitive case. If the word had been a genitive, the announcement would have concerned "the Lord's Christ," which would have been perfectly correct but would have meant no more than that Jesus was a specially chosen man, like one of the Old Testament kings, priests, or prophets. Because the word is in the nominative case, the statement actually goes beyond this to mean "Christ [who is] the Lord."

3. *Psalm 110:1.* On one occasion, recorded in Matthew 22:41–46, Jesus asked his enemies who they thought the Christ was to be. They replied, "The son of David." This was true as far as it went; but they were thinking of an earthly, human Messiah, and Jesus wanted them to see farther. So he referred them to this Old Testament text, asking, "How is it then that David, speaking by the Spirit, calls him 'Lord'? For he says, 'The Lord said to my Lord: "Sit at my right hand until I put your enemies under your feet."'" If then David calls him 'Lord,' how can he be his son?" (vv. 43–45). Jesus' point was that if David called the Messiah "Lord," it could only be because the Messiah was to be more than just one of his descendants. He would have to be a divine Messiah, which is what the title "Lord" indicates.

Peter had this text in mind when he told the Sanhedrin, "God exalted him [Jesus] to his own right hand as Prince and Savior . . ." (Acts 5:31).

Paul was also thinking of this when he wrote, "Since, then, you have been raised with Christ, set your heart on things above, where Christ is seated at the right hand of God" (Col. 3:1).

The author of Hebrews used the text early in his letter (and also at two later points): "After he [the Son] had provided purification for [our] sins, he sat down at the right hand of the Majesty in heaven" (Heb. 1:3; cf. 8:1; 12:2).

4. *Philippians 2:5–11.* The great Christological hymn of Philippians 2 is the clearest textual statement that "Jesus is Lord," that is, one with God.

> Your attitude should be the same as that of Christ Jesus:
> Who, being in very nature God,
> did not consider equality with God something to be grasped,
> but made himself nothing,
> taking the very nature of a servant,
> being made in human likeness.
> And being found in appearance as a man,
> he humbled himself
> and became obedient to death—even death on a cross!
> Therefore God exalted him to the highest place
> and gave him the name that is above every name,
> that at the name of Jesus every knee should bow,
> in heaven and on earth and under the earth,
> and every tongue confess that Jesus Christ is Lord,
> to the glory of God the Father.

What is the "name that is above every name"? It is not the name "Jesus" itself, though the wording seems to suggest this to the English reader. It is the name "Lord"; for that is God's own name, and no name can be higher than that.

The meaning of this title shows why the early Christians would not apply the name "Lord" to any other. If they had done so, they would have been repudiating Christ. One famous case is that of the aged Bishop of Smyrna, Polycarp, who was martyred on February 22, A.D. 156. As he was driven to the arena, two of the city officials, who had respect for him because of his age and reputation, tried to persuade him to comply with the demand to honor Caesar. "What harm is there in saying, 'Caesar is Lord,' and burning incense . . . and saving yourself?" they asked. Polycarp refused. Later, in the arena, he explained his position, saying, "For eighty-six years I have been [Christ's] slave, and he has done me no wrong; how can I blaspheme my king who saved me?" Polycarp refused to call Caesar "Lord," because "Lord" meant "God" and there can only be one God. If Polycarp had called Caesar "Lord," then Jesus could not have been "Lord" for Polycarp, and Polycarp could not have been a Christian.

Those who recorded Polycarp's story shared his convictions, for they concluded by saying: "He [Polycarp] was arrested by Herod, when Philip of Tralles was high priest, and Statius Quadratus was governor, *but our Lord Jesus Christ was reigning forever.* To him be glory, honor, majesty and eternal dominion from generation to generation. Amen."[1]

Lord and Savior

The second implication of the title "Lord" is that Jesus is the Savior. This is linked to his lordship because, as John R. W. Stott writes:

> The title "Lord" is a symbol of Christ's victory over the forces of evil. If Jesus has been exalted over all the principalities and powers of evil, as indeed he has, this is the reason why he has been called Lord. If Jesus has been proclaimed Lord, as he has, it is because these powers are under his feet. He has conquered them on the cross, and therefore our salvation—that is to say, our rescue from sin, Satan, fear and death—is due to that victory.[2]

In recent years it has become customary in some parts of the evangelical world to distinguish between the lordship and the saviorhood of Christ in such a way that one is supposed to be able to have Jesus as Savior without

1. "The Martyrdom of Holy Polycarp, Bishop of Smyrna" in *The Apostolic Fathers: An American Translation,* trans. Edgar J. Goodspeed (New York: Harper & Brothers, 1950), pp. 250, 251, 255.

2. John R. W. Stott, "The Sovereignty of God the Son" in *Our Sovereign God: Addresses Presented to the Philadelphia Conference on Reformed Theology 1974–1976,* ed. James M. Boice (Grand Rapids: Baker Book House, 1977), p. 18.

having him as Lord. This is the view, for example, of Charles C. Ryrie, former Dean of Doctoral Studies and Professor of Systematic Theology at Dallas Theological Seminary. Reacting to statements by Arthur W. Pink, J. I. Packer and John R. W. Stott in a variety of publications, Ryrie argues that any attempt to link "Jesus as Lord" to "Jesus as Savior" is the equivalent of adding "commitment" to "faith" in salvation. And since "the message of faith only and the message of faith plus commitment of life cannot both be the gospel . . . one of them is a false gospel and comes under the curse of perverting the gospel or preaching another gospel (Gal. 1:6–9)."[3]

There are two serious mistakes at this point. One involves the meaning of faith, which Ryrie seems to detach from commitment. Is "faith" minus "commitment" a true biblical faith? Hardly! Biblical faith involves three elements: (1) *knowledge*, upon which it is based; (2) *heart response*, which results from the new birth; and (3) *commitment*, without which "faith" is no different from the assent of the demons, who only "believe that and shudder" (James 2:19). Faith without commitment is no true faith. It is a dead faith that will save no one.

The second mistake is even more serious, because it involves the person and work of Jesus himself. Who is this one who has saved us from our sins? He is, as Paul has it, "Jesus Christ our Lord." No true Christian will add anything to the finished work of Jesus. To do so is really to proclaim a false gospel. We direct people to the Lord Jesus Christ. Nevertheless, he is the *Lord* Jesus Christ. This Lord is the object of faith and its content. There is no other. Consequently, if faith is directed to one who is not Lord, it is directed to one who is a false Christ of the imagination. Such a one is not the Savior, and he will save no one.[4]

Is He *Our* Lord?

At this point it is easy for some of us to sit back and congratulate ourselves on having a sound theology. Of course, we know that Jesus must be Lord to be Savior. Of course, we know that true faith involves commitment. But is Jesus really *our* Lord? Are we truly committed to him? In the study of Christ's lordship by John Stott, from which I quoted earlier, six implications are suggested:

1. *An intellectual implication.* If Jesus is our Lord, one thing he must be Lord of is our thinking. He must be Lord of our minds. On one occasion, when the Lord called disciples, he said, "Take my yoke upon you and learn

---

3. Charles Caldwell Ryrie, "Must Christ Be Lord to Be Savior?" in *Balancing the Christian Life* (Chicago: Moody Press, 1973), p. 170. Ryrie is reacting to statements by J. I. Packer in *Evangelism and the Sovereignty of God* (Downers Grove, Ill.: InterVarsity Press, 1967); John R. W. Stott in "Must Christ Be Lord to Be Savior?" *Eternity* (Sept. 1969); and an out-of-print work by Arthur W. Pink, *Present Day Evangelism.*

4. For a fuller discussion of these arguments see James Montgomery Boice, *Christ's Call to Discipleship* (Chicago: Moody Press, 1986), pp. 19–21.

from me . . ." (Matt. 11:29), meaning that he was to be the disciples' teacher. He is to be our teacher today.

How does Jesus do this, seeing that he is not with us physically as he was in the time of the disciples? The answer is that he teaches us through Scripture. That is why we must be men and women of the Book—if we truly are Christ's followers. Left to ourselves, we will stray into many kinds of false thinking just as the world does. But if we regularly read and study the Bible, asking the Holy Spirit to interpret it for us, and then try to live out what we understand, we will increasingly come to think as Christ thinks and discover that we have an entirely new outlook on the world. We will see people from God's perspective, and we will not be taken in by the world's false ideas.

2. *An ethical implication.* In the study I referred to earlier, Stott points out that Jesus is not just Lord of our minds. He is Lord of our wills and of our moral standards also.

> It is not only what we believe that is to come under the lordship of Jesus but also how we behave. Discipleship implies obedience, and obedience implies that there are absolute moral commands that we are required to obey. To refer to Jesus politely as "our Lord" is not enough. He still says to us, "Why do you call me Lord and do not the things that I say?" In today's miasma of relativity we need to maintain unashamedly the absolute moral standards of the Lord. Further, we need to go on and teach that the yoke of Jesus is easy and his burden is light, and that under the yoke of Jesus we have not bondage but freedom and rest.[5]

3. *A vocational implication.* If Jesus is Lord, then he is not only Lord of our minds, wills, and morals, but he is also Lord of our time; this means that he is Lord of our professions, jobs, careers, and ambitions. We cannot plan our lives as if our relationship to Jesus is somehow detached from those plans and irrelevant to them.

Paul is an example at this point. Before he met Christ on the road to Damascus and bowed before him, Paul was pursuing a vocation of his own choice. He was a Pharisee and intent on rising high in the intellectual and ruling structures of Judaism. He knew where he was going. When he met Jesus all this was redirected. The first words Jesus uttered after he had stopped Paul cold by asking, "Saul, Saul, why do you persecute me?" (Acts 9:4) and by identifying himself as Jesus, were: "Now get up and go into the city, and you will be told what you must do" (v. 6). Paul obeyed Jesus and was indeed told what he was to do. He was to be Christ's apostle to the Gentiles. Later, when Paul gave a defense of his activities before King Agrippa, he quoted the Lord as saying to him, "I have appeared to you to appoint you as a servant and as a witness of what you have seen of me and

5. Stott, "The Sovereignty of God the Son," p. 22.

what I will show you. I will rescue you from your own people and from the Gentiles. I am sending you to them to open their eyes and turn them from darkness to light, and from the power of Satan to God . . ." (Acts 26:16–18). Paul concluded, "So then, King Agrippa, I was not disobedient to the vision from heaven" (v. 19).

This is precisely the way we must regard our vocations. We may not be called to be apostles, as Paul was. Only a few are called to what we term "religious work." But whether we work in a church or a factory, in a hospital, a law firm, or our own small business, whether we are homemakers or builders of homes—whatever our calling, we must regard it as a form of Christian service and know that we are obeying our Lord Jesus Christ as we pursue it.

4. *An ecclesiastical implication.* Jesus is also head of the church. This truth can deliver us from two banes. One is disorder. It occurs when those who are members of the church pursue their own course—including what they wish their church to be—without regard to the guidelines for church life laid down in the Bible or without proper consideration for those who are their brothers and sisters in the Lord. The second is clericalism. It occurs when laypeople abandon their God-given roles in the church or when pastors tyrannize the church without acknowledging that they are servants of the people as well as servants of Christ and that they must serve the church as Jesus served it.

5. *A political implication.* Today, when we talk about the lordship of Christ, we face a battle on two fronts. One is an intra-mural contest, which goes on within the Christian fellowship. It is the battle I was speaking about earlier when I repudiated certain attempts to separate the saving work of Christ from his lordship.

But there is another battle also, and it is extra-mural. That is, it is outside the church's fellowship. It comes from those who, in a certain sense, may be quite tolerant of religion, but who insist that religion must be kept in its place—"on the reservation"—and that, above all, it must not intrude into our national life. We are fighting this battle every day. And we are saying—I *hope* we are saying—that Jesus is not only our own personal Lord and not only Lord of the church that he founded; he is also Lord of all life, the life of nations included. He is not merely *our* King; he is the King of kings. He is not merely *our* Lord; he is the Lord of lords. Therefore, we who are Christians stand as his representatives in history to call this world to account. We are here to remind the world that this same Jesus Christ whom we serve has spoken from heaven to reveal what true righteousness is, both for individuals and nations, and that those who disregard him do so at their own peril and must one day give an account.

Yet this must be done correctly. First, it must be done humbly. For none of us is perfect—we, too, must appear before Jesus—and those we speak to are ultimately answerable to him and not to us. Second, we must know that our mission is to be by example and word and not by force. Otherwise we will become triumphalists. We must remember that the Lord did not come to set up an army or even a political organization, but rather a witnessing fellowship. Whenever the church has departed from the Lord's pattern in this area, it has always done so to its harm.

6. *A global implication.* If Jesus is our Lord, the final implication flows from the Great Commission by which, on the basis of his own authority, the Lord sent disciples into the entire world to make and disciple Christians everywhere (Matt. 28:18–20). The lordship of Jesus is the most powerful of missionary incentives. It is as Lord of our lives that he tells us to go; because we know him as Lord, this is exactly what we do. Because we love him, we want everyone to become his disciples.

I close with the questions I asked at the beginning of this list. Is Jesus your Lord? Are you truly committed to him? If you are, your life can never be what it would be otherwise. If he is your Lord, no other can ever take his place.

5

The Obedience of Faith

Romans 1:5

Through him and for his name's sake, we received grace and apostleship to call people from among all the Gentiles to the obedience that comes from faith.

It is a puzzle to me that whenever I write about the lordship of Jesus Christ, as I did in the previous chapter, stressing that one must follow Jesus and submit to him to be a Christian, some people always object that an emphasis like this destroys the gospel. If Jesus must be Lord, then salvation cannot be by "simple" faith, they argue. If we insist that one must follow Christ, we must be mingling works with faith as a means of salvation, which is "another gospel."

No matter that I show what true biblical faith is! No matter that I explain how obedience and faith both necessarily follow from regeneration!

I suppose that Paul had this problem, too, if for no other reason than that the human mind seems to work much the same way in all people. I believe Paul had these difficulties because of the way he develops his thoughts in the opening verses of Romans. In the Greek text the first seven verses of the book are one long sentence, not an unusual form for one writing in good Greek style. Nevertheless, there has been a natural and significant climax at the end of verse 4 in the words "Jesus Christ our Lord." This is the point to which the earlier verses have been leading, and it would have been quite proper, as well as good Greek, if Paul had ended his sentence there. Why does he not do this? Why does he add the thoughts in verse 5 before the wrap-up to the introduction in verses 6 and 7? The answer is along the lines I am describing. The apostle has spoken of Jesus Christ as "Lord." Now, knowing how people think when confronted with that idea, he feels the need to amplify his statement.

Must Jesus be Lord if one is to be saved by him? If he must, this will have an effect on the way we understand the gospel and obey Christ's command to evangelize the world.

Disobedience and Obedience

The key words of verse 5 are those the New International Version translates as "to the obedience that comes from faith" (literally, "unto obedience of faith"). There are two ways this phrase can be interpreted. First, it can be interpreted as referring to the obedience which faith produces or in which it results. I think this is not the true meaning. But it is worth noting that, even if this is the correct interpretation, the point I have been making is still plain, since Paul would be saying that true biblical faith must produce obedience. If the "faith" one has does not lead to obedience, it is not the faith the Bible is talking about when it calls us to faith in Jesus Christ. It may be intellectual assent of a very high order. But it is not a living faith. It does not join us to Jesus Christ, and it will save no one.

Yet the case is even stronger than this, because a proper interpretation of the phrase is not "unto the obedience to which faith leads" (the first interpretation) but rather "unto obedience, the very nature of which is faith" (the second interpretation). Or, to turn it around, we could say, "faith, which *is* obedience."

This is such an important point that I want to establish it a bit more fully before going on to show why it is important. The way I want to do this is to show that it is the view of the most important commentators. Let me cite a few, starting with the most recent and moving backwards.

1. *D. Martyn Lloyd-Jones:* "The Apostle says . . . 'the obedience of faith' in order to bring out this point—that he is talking about an obedience which consists in faith, or, if you like, an obedience of which faith is the central principle."[1]

2. *John Murray:* "It is . . . intelligible and suitable to take 'faith' as in apposition to 'obedience' and understand it as the obedience which consists in faith. Faith is regarded as an act of obedience, or commitment to the gospel of Christ."[2]

---

1. D. M. Lloyd-Jones, *Romans: An Exposition of Chapter 1, The Gospel of God* (Grand Rapids: Zondervan, 1985), pp. 137, 138.
2. John Murray, *The Epistle to the Romans*, 2 volumes in one (Grand Rapids: Wm. B. Eerdmans, 1968), p. 13.

3. *Charles Hodge:* "The obedience of faith is that obedience which consists in faith, or of which faith is the controlling principle."[3]

4. *Robert Haldane:* "The gospel reforms those who believe it; but it would be presenting an imperfect view of the subject to say that it was given to reform the world. It was given that men might believe and be saved. The obedience, then, here referred to, signifies submission to the doctrine of the gospel."[4]

5. *F. Godet:* "The only possible meaning is: the obedience *which consists of* faith itself."[5]

6. *Martin Luther* (contrasting Paul's demand with human arguments): "Paul here speaks of 'obedience to the faith' and not of obedience to such wisdom as first must be proved by arguments of reason and experience. It is not at all his intention to prove what he says, but he demands of his readers implicit trust in him as one having divine authority."[6]

7. *John Calvin:* "By stating the purpose of his call Paul again reminds the Romans of his office, as though he were saying, 'It is my duty to discharge the responsibility entrusted to me, which is to preach the word. It is your responsibility to hear the word and wholly obey it, unless you want to make void the calling which the Lord has bestowed on me.' We deduce from this that those who irreverently and contemptuously reject the preaching of the gospel, the design of which is to bring us into obedience to God, are stubbornly resisting the power of God and perverting the whole of his order."[7]

I have taken several pages to make this point because, as I said at the beginning, it is an extremely important matter. It is important because it affects how we understand the gospel and how we seek to obey Christ's command to evangelize. How is it that most of today's evangelism is conducted? It is true, is it not, that for the most part the gospel is offered to people as something that (in our opinion) is good for them and will make them happy but that they are at perfect liberty to refuse! "The Holy Spirit is a gentleman," we are sometimes told. "He would never coerce anybody." With a framework like this, sin becomes little more than bad choices and faith only means beginning to see the issues clearly.

3. Charles Hodge, *A Commentary on Romans* (Edinburgh and Carlisle, Pa.: The Banner of Truth Trust, 1972), p. 21. (Original edition 1835.)

4. Robert Haldane, *An Exposition of the Epistle to the Romans* (MacDill AFB: MacDonald Publishing, 1958), pp. 30, 31.

5. F. Godet, *Commentary on St. Paul's Epistle to the Romans*, trans. A. Cusin (Edinburgh: T. & T. Clark, n.d.), vol. 1, p. 135.

6. Martin Luther, *Commentary on the Epistle to the Romans*, trans. J. Theodore Mueller (Grand Rapids: Zondervan, 1954), p. 21.

7. John Calvin, *The Epistles of Paul the Apostle to the Romans and to the Thessalonians*, trans. Ross MacKenzie (Grand Rapids: Wm. B. Eerdmans, 1973), pp. 17, 18.

What is missing in this contemporary approach is the recognition that sin primarily is disobedience and that God commands us to repent and repudiate it. As D. Martyn Lloyd-Jones says, "Sin is not just that which I do that is wrong and which makes me feel miserable afterwards . . . not just that which spoils my life and makes me feel miserable and unhappy . . . not just that thing which gets me down and which I would like to overcome." It is that, but it is also much more. Primarily, sin is rebellion against God. "Sin is refusal to listen to the voice of God. Sin is a turning of your back upon God and doing what you think."[8] So, when the gospel is preached, it must be preached not merely as an invitation to experience life to the full or even to accept God's invitation. It must be preached as a command. (This is why Paul is so concerned to stress his role as an apostle, as one called and commissioned to be God's ambassador.) We are commanded to turn from our sinful disobedience to God and instead obey him by believing in and following the Lord Jesus Christ as our Savior.

This is the way Paul himself preached the gospel, though we frequently overlook it because of our own weak methods. Do you remember how Paul concluded his great sermon to the Athenians? "In the past God overlooked such ignorance, but now he *commands* all people everywhere to repent. For he has set a day when he will judge the world with justice by the man he has appointed . . ." (Acts 17:30–31, italics mine). In God's name, Paul commanded the Greeks to repent of their sin and turn to Jesus.

It is the same in Romans. In Romans 6:17 Paul summarizes the response of the Roman Christians to the gospel by saying, "Thanks be to God that, though you used to be slaves to sin, you wholeheartedly *obeyed* the form of teaching to which you were entrusted" (italics mine, here and in the subsequent citations). In Romans 10 he argues that the Jews "did not *submit* to God's righteousness" (v. 3); in verse 16 he says, "But they have not all *obeyed* the gospel . . ." (KJV).[9] At the end of the letter the idea appears again in a great benediction: "Now to him who is able to establish you by my gospel and the proclamation of Jesus Christ, according to the revelation of the mystery hidden for long ages past, but now revealed and made known through the prophetic writings by the *command* of the eternal God, so that all nations might believe and *obey* him—to the only wise God be glory forever through Jesus Christ! Amen" (Rom. 16:25–27).

In my opinion, the weakness of much of our contemporary Christianity can be traced to a deficiency at precisely this point. By failing to present the gospel as a command to be obeyed we minimize sin, trivialize discipleship, rob God of his glory, and delude some into thinking that all is well with their souls when actually they are without Christ and are perishing.

8. Lloyd-Jones, *Romans: An Exposition of Chapter 1*, p. 138.
9. The New International Version unjustifiably changes the word *hypēkousan* to "accept" in this verse ("not all the Israelites accepted the good news"), but it is the same word correctly rendered "obey" or "obedience" elsewhere, including Romans 1:5.

Pelagius and Jonathan Edwards

But there may be an objection at this point. It comes from those who know theology and are aware that, according to Paul's later teaching in Romans, everyone is so deeply ensnared by sin that even though the gospel may be preached to us, apart from the grace of God we are not able to repent and obey God's commands. This was the point that bothered Pelagius and led to his deviant theology and the resulting clash with Saint Augustine. Pelagius felt that if we are commanded to do something, we must be able to do it. "Ought" implies "can." But instead of throwing out the command (which is what most people seem to want to do today), Pelagius threw out the inability, arguing that we can turn from sin, believe on Christ, and pursue obedience in our own strength, entirely unaided by the Holy Spirit.

The problem here is that Pelagius was overlooking the nature of our inability, which he would have understood better had he paid more attention to the command for obedience. The inability of man in his fallen state is not a physical inability, as if God were demanding that a paralyzed person get up and walk to him. A person so impaired really would have an excuse for failing to do that, but that is not the right analogy. The inability we have is not a physical inability but a moral one. That is, we do not obey God, not because we cannot obey him physically, but because we *will* not obey God. It is this that makes the command to obey so important and our disobedience so reprehensible.

Let me give you one illustration. Jonathan Edwards, who is probably the greatest theologian America has produced, wrote his most impressive treatise on the "Freedom of the Will," and at one point toward the end of the treatise he had this answer for those who think the biblical doctrines unreasonable:

Let common sense determine whether there be not a great difference between these two cases: the one, that of a man who has offended his prince, and is cast into prison; and after he has lain there a while, the king comes to him, calls him to come forth; and tells him, that if he will do so, and will fall down before him and humbly beg his pardon, he shall be forgiven, and set at liberty, and also be greatly enriched, and advanced to honor: the prisoner heartily repents of the folly and wickedness of his offense against his prince, is thoroughly disposed to abase himself, and accept the king's offer; but is confined by strong walls, with gates of brass, and bars of iron. The other case is, that of a man who is of a very unreasonable spirit, of a haughty, ungrateful, willful disposition; and moreover, has been brought up in traitorous principles; and has his heart possessed with an extreme and inveterate enmity to his lawful sovereign; and for his rebellion is cast into prison, and lies long there, loaded with heavy chains, and in miserable circumstances. At length the compassionate prince comes to the prison, orders his chains to be knocked off, and his prison doors to be set wide open; calls to him and tells him, if he will come forth to him, and fall down before him, acknowledge that he has treated him unworthily, and ask his forgiveness; he shall be forgiven, set at liberty, and set in a place of great dignity and profit in his court. But he is so stout, and full of haughty malignity, that he cannot be willing to accept the offer; his rooted strong pride and malice have perfect power over him, and as it were bind him, by binding his heart: the opposition of his heart has the mastery over him, having an influence on his mind far superior to the king's grace and condescension, and to all his kind offers and promises. Now, is it agreeable to common sense, to assert and stand to it, that there is no difference between these two cases, as to any worthiness of blame in the prisoners?[10]

When we first come upon an illustration like that, our reaction is to say that it is not an accurate description of our case, that we are not like the stubborn prisoner. But that is precisely what the Bible teaches we are like. Consequently, it is important for the gospel to be presented to the unsaved as a command and to have it stressed that God will hold us accountable if we persist in sin and refuse to bow before our rightful Lord.

Apostle of God's Grace

Yet, as I draw toward the end of this chapter, I must add that although the demand that we repent of sin and turn to the Lord Jesus Christ is a command, it is nevertheless a command that comes to us in the context of the gospel. And, remember, the gospel is not bad news; it is good news. Above all, it is the good news of God's grace.

I suppose that is why the word *grace* appears in verse 5—for the first time in the letter. It will occur again; it occurs just two verses later, in verse 7. In fact, it will be found a total of twenty-two times in the course of the epistle. "Grace" is one of the great words of Romans and a wonderful concept. In my opinion, the word occurs here because even though Paul is stressing the Lordship of Christ and the necessity of obeying God in response to the demands of the gospel, at the same time he is also keenly aware that those who respond to the gospel do so only because God is already graciously at work in them and because the gospel is itself the means by which the unmerited favor of God toward us is made operative.

What is this "grace"? Grace is often defined as God's favor toward the undeserving, but it is more than that. If we have understood Jonathan Edwards's illustration of the stubborn, rebellious prisoner, we know that it is actually God's favor toward those who deserve the precise opposite. What we deserve is hell. We do not even deserve a chance to hear the gospel, let alone experience the regenerating work of God within, by which we are

10. Jonathan Edwards, "A Careful and Strict Inquiry into the Prevailing Notions of the Freedom of the Will," *The Works of Jonathan Edwards*, vol. 1, revised and corrected by Edward Hickman (Edinburgh and Carlisle, Pa.: The Banner of Truth Trust, 1976), p. 66.

enabled to turn from sin and obey Jesus. We deserve God's wrath. We deserve his fierce condemnation. But instead of wrath, we find grace. Instead of condemnation, we find the One who in our place bore God's judgment and now lives to rule over us.

I do not know what went through the mind of Paul as he wrote these words. I know only what I read in the text. But I suspect that Paul was thinking of his own experience of God's grace as he mentions the matter of his apostleship again in verse 5, saying that it was through Christ that he "received grace and apostleship to call people from among all the Gentiles."

There is a passage in 1 Corinthians that gives a clue to what is going on. Paul had been writing of Christ's resurrection appearances and had added that after appearing to James and all the other apostles, Jesus had appeared to him as to one "abnormally born." Then he added, in words that were not demanded by the context but which undoubtedly flowed from Paul's acute sense of God's rich grace toward him, "For I am the least of the apostles and do not even deserve to be called an apostle, because I persecuted the church of God. But by the grace of God I am what I am, and his grace to me was not without effect . . ." (1 Cor. 15:9–10).

Like all who have been truly converted, Paul could never forget what he had been apart from God's grace.

He had been self-righteous.

He had been cruel.

He had been fighting against the goads of God in his conscience.

He had been trying to destroy God's work by his persecution of the infant church.

But God had stopped him and had brought him to a right mind. Up to that point he had been disobeying God. But when Jesus revealed himself to him on the road to Damascus, the rebellious will of the future apostle to the Gentiles was broken and Paul became Jesus' obedient servant and disciple. How could that be? How could one so rebellious be brought to his knees before Jesus? There is only one answer. It was the grace of God. Only the grace of God can produce such changes. Only a gracious God would want to.

Why is it that we so easily fall into either of two wrong emphases when we present the gospel? Either we present the gospel as something so easy and simplistic that it fails to deal with sin and does not really produce conversions. Or else we present a harsh gospel, forgetting that it is only the love of God and not the condemnation of the law that wins anybody.

And there is one more point to be made. It is only the gracious love of God that motivates us to be his ambassadors. We are not apostles, as Paul was, but we have a corresponding function. We are God's witnesses in this world, and, like Paul, we are to take the gospel to the nations. What will motivate us to do that and will actually keep us at it when the going gets hard? There is only one thing: remembrance of the grace of God, which we have first received. Paul said this in 2 Corinthians: "For Christ's love compels us, because we are convinced that one died for all, and therefore all died. And he died for all, that those who live should no longer live for themselves but for him who died for them and was raised again. . . . All this is from God, who reconciled us to himself through Christ and gave us the ministry of reconciliation" (2 Cor. 5:14–15, 18).

6

Those Roman Christians

Romans 1:6–7

And you also are among those who are called to belong to Jesus Christ. To all in Rome who are loved by God and called to be saints: Grace and peace to you from God our Father and from the Lord Jesus Christ.

Perhaps you have at some time picked up a letter, begun to read it, been confused by what was being said, and then flipped to the end—perhaps through several pages of nearly undecipherable handwriting—looking for the signature while you asked yourself, "Who in the world is writing this?" I have done that many times, and I have thought that it would be a lot easier if we began our letters like most ancient writers did.

Writers of old started their letters with three elements: (1) the name of the writer, (2) the name of those to whom he or she was writing, and (3) a greeting. A typical ancient letter might begin like this one from the commander of the Roman garrison at Jerusalem, recorded in Acts 23: "Claudius Lysias, To His Excellency, Governor Felix: Greetings" (v. 26). "Claudius Lysias," the first element in the introduction, is the name of the garrison commander. The second element is "His Excellency, Governor Felix," the name of the person to whom he is writing. Finally, there is the salutation, which in this case is merely "Greetings." The whole is a bit like the start of one of today's inner-office memos. After these formal elements, the commander gets down to the body of the letter, which explains why he is writing it.

Paul's letter to the Romans is styled like this, yet Paul is so filled with his basic theme—the gospel of God centered in Jesus Christ—that he inevitably adds a lot more to the introduction. He begins simply enough: "Paul, a servant of Christ Jesus. . . ." But as he begins to explain a bit further just who he is ("called to be an apostle and set apart for the gospel of God"), the word *gospel* sets him off explaining what that gospel of God is about. It is a gospel "promised beforehand . . . in the Holy Scriptures," concerning God's Son, the Lord Jesus Christ, "who as to his human nature was a descendant of David, and who through the Spirit of holiness was declared with power to be the Son of God by his resurrection from the dead." If we did not know him better, we might think that Paul is already well into his letter at this point. But Paul now brings the description of the gospel back to himself and his apostleship, the point with which he began: "Through him and for his name's sake, we received grace and apostleship to call people from among all the Gentiles to the obedience that comes from faith." Then, having returned to his starting point, he proceeds to the next two elements of the classical introduction: "And you also are among those who are called to belong to Jesus Christ. To all in Rome who are loved by God and called to be saints: Grace and peace to you from God our Father and the Lord Jesus Christ."

This introduction is like a sine wave in mathematics. It begins low, swells to a great peak, and then falls back to an emotional low point again: Paul's reference to the Roman Christians and his greeting to them.

Where Did They Come From?

Yet this wrap-up is not uninteresting. In the first place, it is noteworthy because of the church at Rome itself. Even at this early date—Paul is writing about A.D. 58 or 59, less than thirty years after the death and resurrection of Jesus Christ—the faith of this church was being spoken of "all over the world" (Rom. 1:8). Later, as we know, the church at Rome became increasingly strong, influential, and powerful—eventually corrupt. Even today the church of Rome is a powerful force in Christendom.

Where did this church come from? How did it get started? One thing we can say is that Paul himself did not found it. God had called him to be the apostle to the Gentiles. Rome was a Gentile city. Yet, as he himself says in verse 13, although Paul had wanted to come to Rome many times, he was prevented from doing so, presumably by pressing missionary concerns. Paul got to Rome later, and Luke tells us about it in Acts. But this was many years after the church in Rome had been founded.

Catholic tradition holds that the Roman church was founded by the apostle Peter and that he was the first pope. I do not think it is necessary to argue, as some Protestants have, that Peter was never in Rome. On the contrary, I think an early church document, "The First Letter of Clement to the Corinthians," implies, though it does not prove, that he was there.[1] But that is not the same thing as saying that Peter founded the Roman church, and the evidence on that point is quite the other way. We know from the long list of names in the last chapter of Romans that Paul knew a great deal about the Roman church, even though he had not been there, yet nowhere in that chapter or elsewhere does he mention Peter, which is nearly inconceivable if Peter was in Rome or if he had founded the Roman church. Indeed, Paul says that it had always been his ambition "to preach the gospel where Christ was not known, so that I would not be building on someone else's foundation" (Rom. 15:20). It is hard to see how Paul could have written this in a doctrinal letter to the Roman church if it had already been founded by Peter and received its early teaching from him.

So how did the church become established? The truth is, we do not know. But there is a suggestion in the second chapter of Acts of what may have happened. That chapter tells about Pentecost, and it gives a list of the many nations that were represented in Jerusalem that day, including "visitors from Rome (both Jews and converts to Judaism)" (vv. 10–11). Since the text specifically speaks of "*visitors* from Rome," we are probably right in supposing that most of these visitors returned to their capital city after the Jewish feast days and established the first churches in Italy there. If this is the case, the Roman church existed from the very earliest days of the Christian mission.

Moreover, this is a pattern that would have continued. There was a great deal of travel in the ancient world, much more than we might suppose. Rome was the center of these comings and goings. Undoubtedly, people who had been brought to Christ as a result of Paul's Gentile mission went to and from Rome, and many undoubtedly settled there. This would explain how Paul came to know as many of the Roman Christians as the last chapter shows he did, and it would explain why Paul was not hesitant to write to this church to seek its prayer support for his trip to Jerusalem as well as its financial backing for his projected missionary excursion to Spain (Rom. 15:24, 30–31).

---

1. In the fourth and fifth chapters Clement lists people who have suffered because of jealousy, first giving examples from ancient times and then giving examples from what were for him more modern times. These are presented in pairs: Cain and Abel, Jacob and Joseph, and so forth. The last pair are Peter and Paul, the nature of whose deaths seems to have been well known to Clement. Since Clement lived in Rome and since Paul, one of the pair, is known to have been martyred at Rome, it is reasonable to suppose that Peter was martyred there also, particularly since this is also the ancient tradition of the church. See "The First Letter of Clement to the Corinthians" in Edgar J. Goodspeed, *The Apostolic Fathers: An American Translation* (New York: Harper & Brothers, 1950), pp. 51, 52.

It would also explain why, although the church was undoubtedly composed of both Jews and Gentiles, Paul writes to these believers largely as Gentiles. We see this as early as verse 6, where the phrase "and you also" most naturally picks up from the description of Paul's commission in verse 5: "to call people from among all the Gentiles."

So the first interesting information is that a body of genuine followers of Jesus Christ, whether large or small (we do not know), existed in the capital city of the Roman empire—of all places! We usually think of Rome as the imperial city of the Caesars, glorious in its palaces, marble monuments, and treasures. It was that. But it was also a terrible city, full of horrible sins and gross licentiousness. Vice was everywhere. Yet in this city of gross sin there was a fellowship of people who rejected Rome's sin and instead lived an entirely different kind of life. It was a life marked by holiness, a mutual sharing of burdens, love, and compassion for those who were abused or downtrodden. It was nothing less than a new humanity planted by God atop the deteriorating carcass of the old.

That is what Christianity always is. It is not an outgrowth, not even a quantum leap upward from the world's decaying civilization. It is something utterly new. It is what you are, if you are a Christian—"a new creation" in Christ (2 Cor. 5:17). It is what your church is, if it is composed of true believers.

How Did They Become Different?

Another interesting thing about the second and third parts of the letter's introduction is what they tell us about the spiritual origins of these people. Here is a group of people who were in the midst of a corrupt pagan society, yet were entirely different from the mainstream. How did they get to be different? How did they become Christians? In these verses Paul tells us four important things about the early church at Rome.

1. *The Christians at Rome, like all Christians, were called to belong to Jesus Christ.* This is a general description of Christians, which is different from the similar phrase "called to be saints" that occurs in the next verse. What does it mean? Some people have read verse 6 as if it were describing Christians as people "called by Jesus Christ," because the Greek can be translated that way. But here the New International Version is undoubtedly correct when it inserts the words "to belong to." The sense is not that Jesus has called Christians—that is a work usually attributed to God the Father—but rather that, as a result of God's calling, Christians are attached to Jesus and have their true life in that relationship. Before, as Paul writes in Ephesians 2:1–3, they were "dead in [their] transgressions and sins" and were "by nature objects of wrath." Now, as a result of God's calling, they have been "made alive with Christ" and given "good works" to do (vv. 4, 9).

This is the essential definition of a Christian (a "Christ one"). A Christian is one who belongs to Jesus Christ. This is what makes him or her different and why such a one inevitably seeks the company of others who also belong to Jesus. Nothing is more important than this in a believer's life.

Does this describe you? Do you belong to Jesus Christ? If you do, you will live like it. If you do not, you are no true Christian, regardless of your outward profession.

2. *The Christians at Rome, like all Christians, were loved by God the Father.* This is no bland statement, as if Paul were only declaring that it is God's nature to love and that these citizens of Rome, like all persons, were therefore loved by him. That is not the way the Bible speaks of God's love. This love is an electing, saving love. So the statement "loved by God" actually describes how those who are Christians come to belong to the Lord Jesus Christ in the first place.

How indeed? Some think that people become believers by their own unaided choice, as if all we have to do is decide to trust Jesus. But how could we possibly do that if, as we have seen Paul say, each of us is "dead in . . . transgressions and sins"? How can a dead man decide anything? Some have supposed that we become Christians because God in his omniscience sees some small bit of good in us, even if that "good" is only a tiny seed of faith. But how could God see good in us if, as Paul will later remind us: "All have turned away, they have together become worthless; there is no one who does good, not even one" (Rom. 3:12; cf. Ps. 14:3)? Why, then, *does* God love us? The answer is "because he loves us." There is just nothing to be said beyond that.

Do you remember how God put it in reference to Israel in the days of Moses? "The Lord did not set his affection on you and choose you because you were more numerous than other peoples, for you were the fewest of all peoples. But it was because the Lord loved you . . ." (Deut. 7:7–8). The only explanation of why the Lord loved them was that he loved them. It is love and love only.

This is a tremendous thing, if we are Christians. It is something so great we can hardly begin to take it in. D. Martyn Lloyd-Jones says:

> We are Christians for one reason only and that is that God has set his love upon us. That is the thing that brings us out of the world and out of the dominion of Satan. . . . And therefore it is not surprising that the apostle here should remind these Christians of this wonderful thing. The world hated them; it persecuted them. They might be arrested at any moment, at the whim of any cruel tyrant who happened to be the emperor, and they might be condemned to death and thrown to the lions in the arena. They were oftentimes hated of all men, so Paul is anxious that they should realize this, that they are the beloved of God; that they are in Christ and that God loves them in the same way as he loves Christ. . . . Do not rush on to chapters six, seven and eight, saying, 'I want to know about the doctrine of sancti-

fication.' My dear friend, if you only realized, as you should, that you are loved by God as he loved his own Son, you would learn the most important thing with respect to your sanctification without going any further.[2]

The most important thing is that God has loved us. Therefore, we should love and serve him.

3. *The Christians at Rome, like all Christians, were called to be believers by God.* Here is the same idea that occurs earlier in the phrase "called to belong to Jesus Christ"; but although the meaning of the verb is the same, the emphasis here is different. In the earlier phrase the emphasis was on what it means to be a Christian. A Christian is one who belongs to Jesus Christ; this is his identity. Here the emphasis is on the call itself, and it is a follow-up to the truth that Christians have been loved by God. First, loved. Then, called. The calling is what theologians term "effectual calling."

There are two kinds of calling in any presentation of the gospel. The first is a general calling, which means that all who hear are called to turn from their sin to Jesus Christ. This calling corresponds to the demand for obedience that I was talking about in the previous chapter. Not all who hear will respond to this call. Not all will obey. Nevertheless, when we call in Christ's words, "Come to me, all you who are weary and burdened. . . . Take my yoke upon you and learn from me" (Matt. 11:28–29a), it is a genuine calling. From God's side no barrier is erected. Nothing stands in the way. At the same time, as we also saw, human beings do not obey God if left to themselves. No one responds to God's offer. None want to. So, that some might be saved, God adds to the general call (conveyed to the lost by his servants), a specific call by which God's chosen ones inwardly hear and respond, becoming Christians. The situation is similar to Jesus' call to dead Lazarus. Left to ourselves, we are all spiritual corpses. We cannot do anything. But when God calls savingly, some of these spiritual corpses come to spiritual life and do God's bidding. Anyone who has been saved by God has heard this call in some way and has responded to it.

It may have been—it often is—through preaching. The Word is declared, and somewhere in the church, sitting in a pew with only God looking on, the person involved hears God himself speak. He or she says, "That preacher is describing me. That is my need. It is what I must do." And the person believes! For another it is the quiet witness of a friend who says, "Don't you want to become a Christian? Why don't we pray, and why don't you receive Jesus?" It can be through the quiet reading of the Bible. It can be through a Christian movie, book, or tract. What is common to all these experiences is that God has called and the person has heard him and believed on Jesus Christ.

2. D. M. Lloyd-Jones, *Romans: An Exposition of Chapter 1, The Gospel of God* (Grand Rapids: Zondervan, 1985), pp. 159, 160.

My good friend R. C. Sproul tells of his conversion during his first year in college. He and a college buddy were exposed to the gospel one night and both "accepted" Jesus. For R. C., life was never the same. He was and remains an entirely different person. But his friend came down from his room the next morning and said, "Wasn't that crazy, what we did last night? I guess I just got carried away. You won't tell anybody about it, will you?"[3] The friend had heard only the call of the preacher. But God had called R. C., and this call, being from God himself, had produced a new man through the new birth or regeneration.

4. *The Christians at Rome, like all Christians, are called saints.* Here "saint" does not mean what it has come to mean in large sectors of the Christian church: one who has attained a certain level of holiness and is therefore worthy of some special veneration or even hearing human prayers. In the Bible, being a saint or being sanctified always means being separated to God and his work, precisely what Paul said of himself in verse 1 in the words "set apart for the gospel of God." Having been loved by God and called by him, the Christians at Rome, like all Christians, were then also set apart to him, to live for him and work for him in this world.

This is why the faith of the Roman Christians was "being reported all over the world," as Paul says it was in verse 8. Because they had been called by God and were separated to him, these believers were different from the culture around them. And people noticed it!

Do people today notice the difference in those who profess to be Christians? There is no simple answer to this question, because the answer is often relative and because it is *Yes* in one situation and *No* in another. But notice the connective relationship between the terms in these two verses. Robert Haldane speaks of the believers being *loved* by God, *called* by God and being *saints,* saying rightly, "They were saints because they were called, and they were called because they were beloved of God."[4] That is, their being saints was not the cause but the result of their election. Being elect, they were saints; that is, they were separated to God. So, if it is ever the case that one who professes to have been called by God is not actually separated unto him—I do not mean "not perfect" but "not headed in God's direction"—that person is not saved. He or she is no Christian. The one who has been loved and called by God does obey God and does follow after him.

Grace for the Rugged Upward Way

Yet this involves struggle. It requires the grace and peace of God each step of the rugged upward way.

3. R. C. Sproul tells these stories in a fictional way in his novel *Johnny Come Home* (Ventura, Calif.: Regal Books/GL Publications, 1984), chs. 4–6.
4. Robert Haldane, *An Exposition of the Epistle to the Romans* (MacDill AFB: MacDonald Publishing, 1958), p. 33.

When Paul closes his introduction with the wish that the believers at Rome might experience "grace and peace . . . from God our Father and from the Lord Jesus Christ," he is not merely passing on a traditional (would we say "hackneyed"?) Christian greeting. He is wishing them what they, and we also, need every day we remain on this planet. We have been saved by grace. We must live by grace also. Just as we live moment by moment by drawing breaths of God's good air, so we must live spiritually moment by moment by drawing on his favor. Jesus said, "Apart from me you can do nothing" (John 15:5b). A man who is going through a shattering crisis in his business told me just a short time ago, "The only way I get through it is by spending solid blocks of time with God each morning." And he is doing it! What is more, the crisis is deepening his sense of God's presence and strengthening him, rather than doing the opposite.

And peace? We always need peace, for these are not peaceful times. Only fools think them peaceful. These are troublesome times. But those who are in Christ and are drawing on him for their strength live peacefully in the midst of them.

I close with Paul's own prayer for those great Roman Christians: "Grace and peace to you from God our Father and from the Lord Jesus Christ." What great gifts these are! How needed! What a wonderful and inexhaustible source of supply!

7

A Reputation Worth Having

Romans 1:8

First, I thank my God through Jesus Christ for all of you, because your faith is being reported all over the world.

In the well-known Shakespearean speech "All the world's a stage, and all the men and women merely players," the melancholy Lord Jaques speaks of a soldier as one "seeking the bubble reputation even in the cannon's mouth" (*As You Like It*, Act II, Scene 7). In this speech "reputation" is depicted as worthless, unimportant. How different in *Othello*! Othello, who is also a soldier but who acted foolishly and tragically, says, "I have lost my reputation! I have lost the immortal part, sir, of myself, and what remains is bestial!" (Act II, Scene 3).

How are we to think of reputation? Is it a fragile bubble, or is it immortal? Is it worth having, or is it better for us not even to be concerned with such matters? The answer is that it depends on what we have a reputation for.

In the first chapter of Romans, in a section that is the second, informal introduction to his letter (vv. 8–15), the apostle Paul speaks about a reputation that the Christians at Rome had acquired, and the important point is that he thanks God for it. Their reputation was for faith, and what Paul tells us is that their faith was being spoken about all over the world. This does not mean that every individual in every remote hamlet of the globe had heard of the faith of the Roman Christians, of course, but it does mean that their faith was becoming widely known—no doubt because other Christians were talking about it. "Do you know that there is a group of believers in Rome?" they were asking. "Have you heard how strong their faith is, how faithfully they are trying to serve Jesus Christ in that wicked city?" Since Paul begins his comment by thanking God for this reputation, it is apparent that however worthless some worldly reputations of some worldly persons may be, this reputation at least was worth having.

Why is a reputation for faith worth having? The text suggests four reasons.

A Genuine Faith

The first reason that the reputation of the Christians at Rome was worth having is that the faith on which it was based was genuine. It was a true faith. This is an important place to begin, because there is much so-called faith that is nonbiblical faith and is therefore a flawed and invalid basis for any reputation.

In some people's minds, faith is thought of chiefly as a *subjective religious feeling*, entirely divorced from God's written revelation. I once talked with a young man who thought of faith in this way. When I had asked him if he was a Christian, he said he was. But as we talked I soon discovered that he did not believe in the deity of Jesus Christ, his bodily resurrection, his sacrificial death for our sin, and many other cardinal Christian doctrines. When I asked the young man how he could reject doctrines central to Christian belief and still call himself a Christian, he replied that he did not know how to answer that question but that nevertheless, deep in his heart, he believed he was a Christian. Clearly this was no true faith. It was only a certain variable outlook on life based on his feelings.

Another substitute for true faith is *credulity*. This is the attitude of people who will accept something as true only because they strongly wish it to be true. Sometimes a faith like this is fixed upon a miraculous cure for some terminal disease, like congenital heart failure, AIDS, or cancer. But credulity does not make a cure happen. Wishful thinking is not genuine faith.

A third false faith is *optimism*. Norman Vincent Peale has popularized this substitute faith through his best-selling book *The Power of Positive Thinking*. He suggests that we collect strong New Testament texts about faith, memorize them, let them sink down into our subconscious, and then recall them and recite them whenever we find faith in ourselves wavering. "Everything is possible for him who believes" (Mark 9:23). "If you have faith as small as a mustard seed, you can say to this mountain, 'Move from here to there' and it will move. Nothing will be impossible for you" (Matt. 17:20). Peale says,

"According to your faith in yourself, according to your faith in your job, according to your faith in God, this far will you get and no further."[1]

In this statement, however, faith in yourself, faith in your job, and faith in God are all apparently the same thing, and what this means is that the object of one's faith is irrelevant. John Stott challenges this distortion accurately: "He [Peale] recommends as part of his 'worry-breaking formula' that the first thing every morning before we get up we should say out loud 'I believe' three times, but he does not tell us in what we are so confidently and repeatedly to affirm our belief. The last words of his book are simply 'so believe and live successfully.' But believe *what?* Believe *whom?* To Dr. Peale faith is really another word for self-confidence, for a largely ungrounded optimism."[2] There is some value in a positive outlook on life, of course, just as there is some value in a positive self-image. But this is not the same thing as biblical faith, and it is not the faith for which the apostle Paul thanked God on behalf of the Roman Christians.

Why do I say that the faith of the believers at Rome was a genuine faith in contrast to these other, mistaken views of faith? There are two reasons. First, their faith was in Jesus Christ and in the gospel, which centers in him. Surely this is unmistakable from the context. In the first seven verses of this letter Paul has spoken at length of the gospel, defining it as the gospel "he [God] promised beforehand through his prophets in the Holy Scriptures regarding his Son [Jesus Christ]" and concluding that it had been Paul's task "to call people from among all the Gentiles to the obedience that comes from faith" (vv. 2, 3, 5). Then Paul praises God for the faith of the Roman Christians, and it is evident that it is precisely that kind of faith he has in mind. Their reputation for faith was worth having because theirs was a true faith in Jesus Christ as God's Son and our Savior. As far as salvation is concerned, all other "faiths" are worthless. They will save no one.

Second, this is a faith that God himself brought into being and not something that welled up unaided in the heart of mere human beings. This is why Paul begins by thanking God for these Christians and not by praising them for their commitment. If faith were a human achievement, then Paul should have praised the Roman Christians. He should have said, "First, I thank you for believing in Jesus Christ" or "I praise you for your faith." But Paul does not do this. Faith is worked in us by God as a result of the new birth. Therefore, Paul praises God, not man, for the Roman Christians.

Robert Haldane wrote that in thanking God for the faith of those to whom he is writing "Paul . . . thus acknowledges God as the author of the

1. Norman Vincent Peale, *The Power of Positive Thinking* (New York: Prentice-Hall, 1952), p. 99.

2. John R. W. Stott, *Your Mind Matters* (Downers Grove, Ill.: InterVarsity Press, 1972), pp. 35, 36.

Gospel, not only on account of his causing it to be preached to them, but because he had actually given them grace to believe."[3]

Calvin said of this verse, "Faith is a gift of God."[4]

This is the point to ask whether your faith is like that. Not faith in some nebulous subjective experience or something that you are able to work up by yourself, but a faith worked in you by God, as a result of which you have believed on his Son, the Lord Jesus Christ, as your Savior. If your faith is like that, then yours is a reputation worth having, because it will bring praise to God himself, who is the author of that faith.

A Contagious Faith

The second reason why the reputation for faith that the Christians at Rome had was worth having is that it was a contagious faith. I mean by this that it was a faith not merely heard of and talked about throughout the known world, but that it was also a faith picked up by and communicated to others. Because of this faith, the Roman church grew and the gospel of the Roman congregation spread.

I think this is suggested by verse 17, even though I know the phrase I am referring to can be interpreted in two ways. In Greek the verse contains a repetition of the word *faith* in a phrase that literally reads "from faith to faith" (*ek pisteōs eis pistin*). This can be understood, as the New International Version apparently does understand it, as meaning "by faith from first to last." But it can also mean—and a more literal translation suggests it *does* mean—"from the faith of one who has believed in Christ to another who comes to believe as a result of the first Christian's testimony."

As I say, the phrase "from faith to faith" does not necessarily mean this, since both translations are possible. But I think it does, and whether or not this is the correct meaning, there is no doubt that this is the way the gospel spread in the first Christian centuries, undoubtedly (at least in part) from the strategically located and growing church in the capital city of the Roman empire.

And the church had no modern media at its disposal to "get the message out"! There were no Christian magazines, no inspirational books, no television preachers. How do you suppose these early believers succeeded, as we know they did, without the tools of modern communication? D. Martyn Lloyd-Jones has the answer:

> A revival never needs to be advertised; it always advertises itself. . . . Read the history of the church. When revival breaks out in a little group, it does not

3. Robert Haldane, *An Exposition of the Epistle to the Romans* (MacDill AFB: MacDonald Publishing, 1958), p. 38.

4. John Calvin, *The Epistles of Paul the Apostle to the Romans and to the Thessalonians*, trans. Ross MacKenzie (Grand Rapids: Wm. B. Eerdmans, 1973), p. 20.

matter how small, the news spreads and curiosity is awakened and people come and say, 'What is this? Can we partake in this? How can we get hold of this?' Man does not need to advertise it; it becomes known; it spreads throughout the whole world. It had happened here. This is revival! This is Pentecost! This is the work of the Holy Spirit, and the news had spread like wildfire in that ancient world with its poor means of communication, and its absence and lack of advertising media. Isn't it time we began to think in New Testament terms?[5]

If we think in New Testament terms, we will be concerned with both the quality of our faith and with its contagious nature. We will be concerned that people talk about Christianity and inquire after Christ as the result of our lives and those of our fellow believers.

Faith That Encourages Others

There is a third reason why the reputation for faith that the church at Rome had was worth having: it was an encouragement to other believers elsewhere, including even the apostle Paul himself. In verse 12 Paul speaks of this as an anticipated outcome of his proposed trip to Rome: "that you and I may be mutually encouraged by each other's faith." That expectation was still future. But Paul could look forward to it and speak so confidently of its happening because reports of the Roman Christians' faith had undoubtedly already been a source of encouragement to him.

Did Paul need encouragement? We can be sure he did. Paul was an apostle, of course, a man of great faith. But he is the first to tell us that he was often adversely afflicted by the trials and burdens of his work. In 1 Corinthians he admits that when he came to Corinth it was "in weakness and fear, and with much trembling" (1 Cor. 2:3). In his second letter to Corinth he writes, "We are hard pressed on every side, but not crushed; perplexed, but not in despair; persecuted, but not abandoned; struck down, but not destroyed" (2 Cor. 4:8–9). Yet he concludes, "All this is for your benefit, so that the grace that is reaching more and more people may cause thanksgiving to overflow to the glory of God" (v. 15). Later in the same book, after a lengthy passage listing the many persecutions, hardships, and dangers he endured as Christ's ambassador, he concludes, "Besides everything else, I face daily the pressure of my concern for all the churches" (2 Cor. 11:28).

Everyone needs encouragement, particularly those who are engaged in spiritual warfare against Satan. But what is to encourage them? God, of course. But God also works through human instruments, and one great means of God's encouraging Christian workers is the report of genuine, growing faith on the part of others elsewhere.

This is an encouragement to me. Is it not an encouragement to you?

5. D. M. Lloyd-Jones, *Romans: An Exposition of Chapter 1, The Gospel of God* (Grand Rapids: Zondervan, 1985), pp. 179, 180.

Doesn't your heart respond thankfully when you hear of thriving churches in formerly Communist nations such as Romania, even when believers there have been harassed and sometimes beaten by the civil authorities? Doesn't your spirit rise when you hear of the courageous stand against apartheid by many believers in South Africa?

Isn't your load made lighter when you are told of those in high levels of our own government, in the legislative, executive, and judicial branches, who regularly meet for prayer and Bible study, asking God to lead them as they seek to direct the affairs of the United States of America?

Aren't you also encouraged by the reports of those who are working for Christ in the tough neighborhoods of our cities?

Don't you rejoice when you hear of even one person who has become a Christian?

Let me interject this additional thought. The thing that distinguishes Paul's words to the believers in Rome from what he says elsewhere—to believers in Corinth, Galatia, Ephesus, Philippi or some other city he had visited—is that he had not founded the church in Rome. Although he was planning to visit Rome and be encouraged by a mutual sharing of faith with the Roman Christians, up to this point he had not done so, and I would suppose that for that reason alone he was especially encouraged.

Let me speak personally. I am encouraged when some message or word of mine is used by God to bring another person to faith in Christ, as often happens. I am encouraged when something I do for Christ prospers. But notice: I am especially encouraged, doubly heartened, when the blessing of God occurs elsewhere as the result of someone else's work. Why? Because it means that I am not alone in the work. It means that there are other soldiers in this spiritual warfare and that victory is in the strong hands of our one true commander. I am sure this was true for the apostle Paul and that it was one reason why he thought so buoyantly of the Roman Christians. In hard times it must have cheered him just to know of these Christians and to be aware that their faith was being spoken of "all over the world."

Faith: The Central Item

The last reason why the reputation of the Christians at Rome was worth having is that faith, and not some other attainment or virtue, is *the* essential item in life. Faith in Jesus Christ is what matters. Knowledge is good; Christianity considers knowledge quite important. Good works are necessary; without them we have no valid reason for believing that an individual is saved. The fruit of the Spirit—love, joy, peace, patience, kindness, goodness, faithfulness, gentleness, and self-control (Gal. 5:22–23)—is what we want to see. But faith alone—faith in Christ as Lord and Savior—is essential. For "without faith it is impossible to please God" (Heb. 11:6a). Without faith no one can be justified.

I wonder if we have the spirit of the apostle at this point. Is this the way we actually evaluate other Christian works and testimony?

Here is what I think we do. I think we evaluate other works first on the basis of size. When we hear of a church that has ten thousand members, we are ten times more impressed than if we learn of a church that has only a thousand members. What of a church with a congregation of ten? Let me be clear. I am not against large churches. I am glad for them. I have often said that large churches can do things smaller churches cannot do—launch specialized Christian ministries, for example, or have prospering subgroups that focus on the specific concerns of only some members. Moreover, large churches are often the result of a strong expository ministry, as are some of the largest churches in Southern California, or of strong faith and piety on the part of their members, like the exceedingly large Korean churches. But we must not think, just because the blessing of numbers is good, that a small church is therefore not as favored by God or is not bearing as faithful or strong a testimony. What about the house churches in China, for example? Or the struggling church in North Africa? We may thank God for numerical growth, but what we should be especially thankful for is strong faith.

Is that what we modern Christians are known for? Strong faith? Is our faith, like the faith of the Roman church of Paul's day, spoken of throughout the world?

Another thing we do is evaluate Christian work on the basis of programs. The more the better! Or, the more original the better, particularly if the people involved can write a book about it! Again, I am not against programs. Right programs are for the sake of people and rightly minister to them. But is this the proper way to evaluate churches? Do programs prove God's blessing? You know the answer to that. I do not think the fledgling, first-century church at Rome had many programs, certainly not the kind of things we mean by programs. But it was a famous church—and rightly so. For it was known for what was essential, which is faith.

Is that what we are known for? Do people say of us, "How strong is their faith in God and in Jesus Christ"?

I think we are also impressed—perhaps we are most to be pitied here—by big budgets and big buildings. Again, I am not against either budgets or buildings. Without adequate financing many worthwhile Christian works cannot be done, and without adequate meeting spaces much important activity is hindered. Even in countries like Romania, a chief concern of the thriving Christian congregations has been the repeated attempts of the Communist government to destroy the church structures. Still, a proper concern for budgets and buildings is quite different from evaluating a work on the basis of how large the budget is or how spacious and modern the church structure has become. The Roman church of Paul's day probably just met in people's houses. Yet it was a church whose faith was known throughout the world.

Are we known for that? Or is the best thing that other Christians can say about us is that we have a seven-figure budget or impressive church structures?

Faith really is the essential thing, not numbers or programs, not budgets or buildings. It is by faith that we "demolish arguments and every pretension that sets itself up against the knowledge of God, and we take captive every thought to make it obedient to Christ" (2 Cor. 10:5). The apostle John said, "This is the victory that has overcome the world, even our faith" (1 John 5:4).

I will tell you the kind of reputation I pray we might have at Tenth Presbyterian Church in Philadelphia. I pray that Tenth Presbyterian might be known as a church where people believe what God has told us in the Bible and then actually try to live by what they find there. I want Tenth to be a church known for strong faith in Jesus Christ, where people speak often, lovingly, and fearlessly of him. I want our church to be known for faith where God has placed us, not in some theoretical time or setting, but in the city of Philadelphia, demonstrating that Jesus is the answer to the city's problems and the problems of those who live here. I want Tenth to be rock hard in faith, in adversity as well as in prosperity, when praised as well as when persecuted.

Is that too much to ask? I think not. I think that is a reasonable goal and a reputation worth having.

8

Prayed for Constantly

Romans 1:9-12

God, whom I serve with my whole heart in preaching the gospel of his Son, is my witness how constantly I remember you in my prayers at all times; and I pray that now at last by God's will the way may be opened for me to come to you.

I long to see you so that I may impart to you some spiritual gift to make you strong—that is, that you and I may be mutually encouraged by each other's faith.

About the time I was beginning to prepare for these studies in Romans, I was asked to speak at an anniversary service in a nearby church, and I was given the title: "Passing On the Reformation from Generation to Generation." It was a topic I had never addressed before, and I was not sure how to tackle it. As I thought about the matter, God led me to two sentences, one from the end of the second chapter of the Gospel of Luke and the other from the second chapter of Acts. The first is about Jesus. It says, "And Jesus grew in wisdom and stature, and in favor with God and men" (Luke 2:52). The second is about the early Christian church. It says, "They broke bread in their homes and ate together with glad and sincere hearts, praising God and enjoying the favor of all the people . . ." (Acts 2:46b–47).

What struck me about those two sentences is the word *favor,* for it is an insight into how Christianity must be passed on. Our word for it is "modeling." Jesus so modeled faith that those who looked to him saw he was genuine and therefore favored him and followed him. It was the same with the early church. The early Christians so modeled their profession that those who looked on were attracted to them. We are not surprised to read, immediately after the sentence in Acts 2, that "the Lord added to their number daily those who were being saved" (v. 47b).

That is the way God trains ministers. They see ministry modeled by some other minister before them, and they copy that example.

That is the way God makes evangelists. They learn from others who are already in the work.

That is the way God develops churches. One church models an effective ministry, and other churches learn from it and do the same things themselves.

I begin this way because our subject here is prayer, and the most significant thing to note about it is that our text is a prayer model. Yet this is not a treatise on prayer. It is not a "how-to" for an effective prayer ministry. Rather, it is a glimpse into the apostle Paul's own prayer life—into his pattern of prayer for Christians in the growing church at Rome—and is therefore a model for us as we think about our own prayer patterns, or lack of them.

Work and Pray

There are a number of things I want you to see about this passage, and the first is this: *A strong prayer life is not the least bit inconsistent with vigorous and fervent service for the Lord.*

It should be unnecessary to say this, of course, but we often divorce the two in our thinking. Some are called to pray, we reason. Some are called to work. When we think of what we call "prayer warriors," we often picture old ladies who are strong in faith but unable to "do" much, or we think of people who are hospitalized or bedridden and who can therefore "only" pray. I do not want to be misunderstood at this point, of course. So let me acknowledge that some people are given a special ministry of prayer, perhaps because of precisely these circumstances. Moreover, if you are bedridden or otherwise unable to be outwardly active in Christ's service, I encourage you to spend much prayer time for others. Many who are incapacitated pray for me. I think of a woman named Cherrio Gridley who was crippled through an industrial accident years ago. She listens to The Bible Study Hour and prays regularly for me and my family, the church, and our ministry. Prayer warriors are needed. But this does not mean that those who are active in Christian work (or any kind of work) do not also need to be strong in praying for God's direction and blessing.

Here is where the example of Paul is so helpful. We know of his life from the account of it in Acts, and we have additional insights from what Paul says about himself in his letters. We know that he was a pioneer missionary, taking the gospel of Jesus Christ to places it had not previously been known. In doing this he covered much of the Roman world.

His labors stretched from Syria to Rome.

He crossed deserts and traversed mountain passes.

He traveled by foot and by sea.

He was frequently beaten, once stoned, often imprisoned.

He was shipwrecked.

Everywhere Paul established churches, and after he had established them he constantly kept in touch with the believers, helping them work through their problems. In one place he speaks of the "daily pressure" of his concern for them.

No harried pastor has ever been more pressed for time than Paul.

No busy executive ever carried a greater burden of responsibility.

Yet Paul was a model of a strong and consistent prayer ministry. In our text he says that he remembered the church at Rome—only one of the many churches of a growing Christian movement, and one he had not even visited—"constantly" and "at all times." Do you think Paul was exaggerating? I do not think he was exaggerating at all. I think he really did pray all the time, just as Martin Luther, John Calvin, Jonathan Edwards, and other effective Christian workers did. Luther once said that he had so much to do in a day that he could not get through it without spending at least three or four hours on his knees before God each morning.

Prayer is not inconsistent with fervent service. On the contrary, as Robert Haldane said, "Prayer and labor ought to go together. To pray without laboring is to mock God; to labor without prayer is to rob God of his glory. Until these are conjoined, the gospel will not be extensively successful."[1]

Prayer and God-Directed Service

So we see from Paul's example, as well as from the lives of others, that prayer is not the least bit inconsistent with vigorous Christian activity. On the contrary, and this is the second point: *Prayer directs Christian service properly.*

Again the apostle Paul is our model. We can think of examples of people who are engaged in Christian work but who do not seem to be going about it in the right way. Either they use the world's methods, which produce only the world's results. Or else their goals seem to be secular rather than truly Christian. As we read what Paul says about his prayer life in this chapter, we see that this was not the case with him. He prayed about his work, and as a

1. Robert Haldane, *An Exposition of the Epistle to the Romans* (MacDill AFB: MacDonald Publishing, 1958), p. 40.

result God directed it to be done in a spiritual way and for spiritual ends. He says several things about it.

1. *Paul's service was sincere, or wholehearted.* The older versions of verse 9 say, "whom I serve with my spirit," a literal rendering of the Greek. But the New International Version is surely correct when it paraphrases the text to read, "whom I serve with my whole heart." The point is not that Paul served God by means of or by using his spirit, though one of our modern versions paraphrases the text in this way: "to whom I offer the humble service of my spirit" (NEB). It is rather that Paul served God from the depth of his being—wholeheartedly. What a valid point that is! Not all who profess to serve Christ serve him wholeheartedly. Many are lazy in their service. Many are trying to please other people rather than the Lord. Paul knew of people like this himself. He called them "detestable, disobedient and unfit for doing anything good" (Titus 1:16b). But he was not like them.

What kept Paul from falling into these traps? Clearly it was his relationship to God, sustained by consistent and fervent prayer. As he sought God in prayer, God enabled him to serve the Lord Jesus Christ wholeheartedly.

2. *Paul's service was gospel-centered.* This is the second thing Paul says about his service. It was carried out by his "preaching the gospel of his [God's] Son" (v. 9). We know about the gospel, of course. We know that it is our task to make the gospel known. But it is surprising how many other things squeeze in as a substitute for this one essential thing, and as a result our service is not gospel-centered. We do not mean to let this happen. Other agendas are usually seen as ways to get the gospel out or to make it known, at least at first. But they take on a character and schedule of their own, and they become ends in themselves. What can keep us from this deviation? The answer is prayer. Prayer focuses our attention on God and his gospel, which was clearly Paul's case, as is evident in the opening verses of this letter.

It is this more than anything else that I have found prayer to do for me personally. It has redirected my focus so that I have begun to see things in God's perspective. When that has happened, some of the things in my life that have been most distressing have faded in importance.

3. *Paul's service was for others.* This is the point most evident in Paul's prayer for the Roman Christians, for he is saying that he had been praying to be with them in order that he might be a blessing in their lives. There is a sequence of three important ideas here, and it begins with prayer. First, Paul prayed that he might be permitted to see the Roman Christians. Second, he prayed that he might see them in order to impart a spiritual blessing to them. Third, he prayed that he might see them and impart a spiritual blessing to them so that they might be strengthened in their Christianity. How did Paul propose to do that? The answer is clear. It was by preaching the gospel to them with his whole heart, just as he had preached it to other people.

We need to see the importance of prayer here also, and the best way to see it is to realize that Christians frequently lose the desire to serve others. They lose it in different ways. Criticism will lessen our zeal for service. It is much harder to serve those who criticize us than to serve those who praise and think well of us. Fatigue will lessen it. We grow too tired to serve and thus inevitably think more of ourselves than other persons. Sin also destroys our desire to serve others. This is because sin breaks contact with God, who is the source of right motivation and desire, and because it focuses attention on ourselves. Sin is really self-centeredness rather than other-centeredness. These and other factors turn us from what we are to be as Christ's representatives.

What will keep us on target? The one thing that will keep us from falling to these temptations is prayer. Prayer will overcome an undue oppression from criticism. Prayer will redirect our energies, so we will not be so tired. Prayer will strengthen us for doing what needs to be done in spite of our tiredness. Prayer will keep us from temptation.

> Have we trials and temptations?
> Is there trouble anywhere?
> We should never be discouraged:
> Take it to the Lord in prayer!
> Can we find a friend so faithful,
> Who will all our sorrows share?
> Jesus knows our every weakness:
> Take it to the Lord in prayer!
>
> Are we weak and heavy laden,
> Cumbered with a load of care?
> Precious Savior, still our refuge:
> Take it to the Lord in prayer!
> Do thy friends despise, forsake thee?
> Take it to the Lord in prayer!
> In his arms he'll take and shield thee.
> Thou wilt find a solace there.
>
> Joseph Scriven, 1855

Powerful and Effective Prayer

The third point of this passage is that prayer makes the service of the praying one effective.

A perceptive student may observe at this point that Paul had been praying to visit Rome, and yet, however noble that request may have been, obviously he had not received a favorable answer. Paul was far from Rome. He had not been able to visit the believers in Rome even though he "longed" to see them (v. 11) and had "planned many times to come" (v. 13). At this point he was not even on his way to Rome. Well and good! Our prayers are often the same. But if this is the case, how can we honestly talk about prayer being powerful or about prayer making the service of the praying one effective? There are a number of things to notice.

First, to come to Rome to serve the believers there personally was not the only thing Paul had been praying about. Indeed, what he says is that (1) he remembered them in his prayers at all times; and (2) he prayed that now at last the way might be opened for him to come to them. When he remembered them in his prayers at all times, what do you suppose Paul prayed for as regarding the Roman church? Certainly it was not only that he might have a safe journey to them. Most of his prayers probably had little to do with that. Rather, Paul would have prayed for their maturity in faith, for their safety against Satan's wiles and onslaughts, for their ability to bear an effective witness in the great capital of the empire, with its many perversions and vices. Were these prayers answered? We know they were, because Paul tells us that the faith of the Roman church was being reported all over the world.

If you are praying for someone, do not think your prayers are ineffective just because God is not using *you* to fulfill the request. God has infinite means at his disposal. He may be answering your prayers by others' service.

Second, when Paul prayed that the way might be opened for him to come to Rome, he prayed, as he tells us, that the door might be opened "by God's will" (v. 10). That is, Paul was praying first that the will of God might be done and only secondly that he might come to Rome. He wanted to come to Rome only if that was in God's plan for his life. Do we need proof of this? The proof is in the way Paul graciously submitted to what hindered his plans. We must remember that Paul was a very forceful man and that when he made plans he undoubtedly did everything in his power to stick to them. Moreover, the proposed trip to Rome was no passing fancy on Paul's part. Already we catch a glimpse of how seriously he took it. But in case we miss the point, we find him bringing it up again in chapter 15, saying in several places that his heart had been set on traveling to Rome and then, after being helped on his way by the Roman church, passing on to Spain to preach the Word of God there. Undoubtedly Paul wanted to preach the gospel from one end of the Roman world to the other, from Jerusalem to Tarshish. Nevertheless, when he was hindered in his plans, we do not catch any trace of agitation or frustration on his part. On the contrary, he graciously submitted to God's will for his life and recognized that there was value even in delays. If nothing else, delays gave him additional time to preach the gospel to those in Greece and Asia.

Third—we can hardly miss this—Paul did get to Rome eventually. It was not when he would have chosen, and it certainly was not in the manner he would have chosen. But he *did* get there, and God *did* use him to reach many in the capital. In Philippians he tells us that while he was in prison the gospel spread throughout the Praetorian guard. And we know from other sources that eventually the message of the cross reached even the highest levels of the government. Were Paul's prayers answered? Of course, they were. "The effectual fervent prayer of a righteous man availeth much" (James 5:16b, KJV).

Does Prayer Change Things—Or People?

There is one last thing I want you to see in this section. Not only is prayer not inconsistent with a life of active service for Jesus Christ, and not only (on the contrary) does it direct that service and make it effective—*Prayer also changes the one praying so that he or she increasingly becomes the kind of person through whom God can accomplish his purpose.*

This was true of Paul. By temperament he was not a particularly gracious individual—at least, that is how it seems to me. In his early days he was cruel. He killed those who disagreed with him. Even after he became a Christian I am sure he had his bad moments. He quarreled with Barnabas over John Mark, for instance. Yet how gracious he is in this letter! Paul writes of his desire to visit Rome "so that I may impart to you some spiritual gift to make you strong" (v. 11). But no sooner has he said this than Paul, not desiring to set himself up above the believers at Rome as if he were somehow superior to them, immediately adds as an important qualification, "that is, that you and I may be mutually encouraged by each other's faith" (v. 12). That is an insight into the life of a man who had been changed by prayer and who was being used by God greatly.

Sometimes people ask, "Does prayer change things, or does prayer change people?" It is a good question, and the answer probably is "both." Prayer does change things, since God responds to prayer and frequently alters circumstances because of it. James points to this result when he says, "You do not have, because you do not ask God" (James 4:2b).

On the other hand, I am convinced that far more frequently God uses prayer to change *us.* Because by it he brings us into his presence, opens our eyes to spiritual realities, and makes his perspectives ours.

In Ray C. Stedman's book *Talking to My Father,* the well-known pastor of the Peninsula Bible Church of Palo Alto, California, tells the story of a missionary couple who were returning to the United States by ship after a lifetime of service in Africa. It was during the presidency of Teddy Roosevelt, and Roosevelt, as it happened, was sailing on the same ship. He had been game hunting in Africa, and when he came aboard there was a tremendous fanfare. Bands played. Dignitaries appeared. Crowds of people stationed themselves to see and greet the president. When the ship arrived in America it was more of the same thing. Roosevelt was applauded, and many of the important people of the government came out to welcome him.

Nobody paid any attention to the missionary couple, and it greatly depressed the old man. The two were broken in health. They had no pension; no one had much in those days. They had nowhere to go. They were afraid. "It's not fair," he said to his wife. "We have served God all these years, and when we come home there is not even a single person here to welcome us. We have no money. We have nowhere to go. If God is running the world, why does he permit such injustice?"

His wife said, "You had better go into the bedroom and talk to God about it."

The missionary did, and when he came out a while later a great change had come over him. His wife said, "You feel better now, don't you, dear?"

"Yes," he said. "I began to pray and tell God how unjust the whole thing was. I told him how bitter I was that the president should receive a grand welcome and that we should receive nothing. There was not even a single person to welcome us home. But when I finished, it seemed as if the Lord just placed his hand on my shoulder and said in a quiet voice, 'But you're not home yet.'"[2]

That is quite true, of course. That is the true perspective on what we are doing. But we will see it and live it only as we commune with God in prayer and learn to trust him and look forward to our homecoming.

---

2. Ray C. Stedman, *Talking to My Father: What Jesus Teaches About Prayer* (Portland: Multnomah Press, 1975), pp. 25, 26.

9

Unanswered Prayer

Romans 1:13

I do not want you to be unaware, brothers, that I planned many times to come to you (but have been prevented from doing so until now) in order that I might have a harvest among you, just as I have had among the other Gentiles.

There are very few churchgoers who have not heard the story of the little boy who was praying for a bicycle for Christmas. His was a poor family, so when Christmas morning came there was no bicycle. A friend of the family, who was not too sensitive about such things, said to the lad, "Well, I see God didn't answer your prayer for a bicycle."

The boy replied, "Yes, he did; he said No."

Most of us are aware that No is an answer every bit as much as Yes. But I have always felt that the story of the little boy's prayer does not quite get to the heart of the prayer problem. To receive a bicycle might be nice, but it is clearly not essential. Nor is it spiritual. Most of us understand that when we pray for things like bicycles—a better job, more money, success in a business deal, or the resolution of certain personal problems—there is no real reason why we should expect a Yes answer. God may give what we ask for, but again he may not. We accept that. But what about prayers that really are spiritual? What about prayers that are (or at least seem to be) unselfish?

85

What happens when these prayers are not answered? This is where the real problem with prayer lies and why the people who have trouble with it are not the novices in prayer, as we might suspect—novices do not expect much from prayer anyway—but rather the church's mature believers. It is the saints who feel the burden of unanswered prayer. It is the godly who wrestle with it strenuously.

So what happens? Unfortunately, some persons become somewhat fatalistic about prayer. J. Oswald Sanders pointed to this problem when he wrote, "It is easy to become a fatalist in reference to prayer. It is easier to regard unanswered prayer as the will of God than to . . . reason out the causes of the defeat."[1]

Prayer of an Apostle

In the case of Paul's prayer, recounted in Romans 1, we have a superb example of precisely this problem. Why is it such a good example?

First, it is a prayer by an apostle. The fact that Paul was an apostle does not mean that he was without sin, of course. Nor does it mean that all Paul's prayers were spiritual. Paul did not pray by inspiration, the way he wrote his epistles. In fact, I believe that there is an example of his praying out of the will of God in his prayers to visit Jerusalem with the gifts of the Gentile churches, which Luke tells us about in Acts. God warned Paul not to go to Jerusalem, and even after he went the Lord appeared to him to say, "Leave Jerusalem immediately . . ." (Acts 22:18). Yet Paul did not leave and was eventually imprisoned.

Paul was not without sin as an apostle. Yet he was an apostle, and that says something. It is significant that such a one did not have his prayers answered positively, or at least at once.

Second, Paul's prayer was a proper prayer. I wrote in the previous study that Romans 1:8–12 is not a treatise on prayer in the sense of providing a theological explanation of prayer. It is a prayer model, an example. Still, it is a proper prayer. It is *to the Father* on the basis of *the atoning work of Jesus Christ* and, although Paul does not say so explicitly, it was undoubtedly also *in the Holy Spirit*. Paul puts all three persons of the Godhead together in reference to prayer in one sentence in Ephesians 2:18: "For through him [that is, Jesus Christ] we both [that is, Jews and Gentiles] have access to the Father by one Spirit."

There is one more important thing to see about this prayer, the third item: It was a prayer for right things. Paul might have prayed for something that would only have enhanced his prestige or personal comfort; that is, he might have prayed selfishly. But that was not the case here at all. Paul was praying to come to Rome in order that (1) he might "impart some spiritual

1. J. Oswald Sanders, *Effective Prayer* (Chicago: Moody Press, 1969), p. 19. (Original edition 1961.)

gift" to the end that (2) the believers in Rome might be made "strong" (v. 11). In other words, he wanted to assist in the spiritual growth and fruitfulness of the Roman believers.

This was an entirely worthy and quite spiritual motive. Yet, as I have said, Paul was prevented from coming. His prayer was not answered positively.

Paul does not give an explanation of why his proposed visit to Rome was hindered, at least not here. He only says, "I do not want you to be unaware, brothers, that I planned many times to come to you (but have been prevented from doing so until now) in order that I might have a harvest among you, just as I have had among the other Gentiles." I do not doubt that Paul could have suggested a reason why his prayers were unanswered, perhaps a number of reasons. But he does not, and the fact that he does not opens the door for us to reflect on why prayers like his—including the best of our own prayers—go unanswered.

Not As Necessary As We Think

I want to suggest a number of reasons why perfectly proper prayers may go unanswered and what we may learn from this. The first is: Unanswered prayer may be God's way of teaching that we are not as necessary to the work we are praying for as we think we are. That is so important it is worth saying again. *Unanswered prayer may be God's way of teaching that we are not as necessary to the work we are praying for as we think we are.*

This is clear in Paul's case, is it not? Paul had been praying that he might be permitted to travel to Rome to serve and strengthen the Roman Christians. But noble as this desire may have been, it is also clear that the believers in Rome were doing quite well without him. Indeed, they were doing well without any apostle or noteworthy teacher. Paul testifies to this when he records that their strong faith was being reported on all over the world (v. 8). I do not want to be misunderstood at this point, of course. I have no doubt that if Paul had been allowed to go to Rome, he would have been a blessing to the Christians. Moreover, they apparently did need his teaching, since God directed him to write them the letter we are studying. We, too, need pastors, teachers, and other church leaders. The point is not that Paul could not have been then or eventually a blessing to these Christians, but only that he was not essential to it. God was perfectly able to bless and prosper this church without Paul's personal ministrations.

I do not say that this is something Paul himself necessarily learned by God's refusal to send him to Rome, though it may have been. But it is certainly something we frequently need to learn. I say this because, as I suspect, most of our good prayers—not our selfish or ignorant or carnal prayers, but our good prayers—have ourselves at the center and assume that, if God is to answer them, he must do so through us as his agents.

One thing unanswered prayer may do for us is teach us to pray for blessing on God's work through other people. Years ago, at a management training session for the Servicemaster company, I was taught that good management is "getting the right things done through other people." That is not a bad definition for some prayers. It is at least something we need to practice more frequently.

The great pioneer missionary to China, Hudson Taylor, learned this function of prayer early in his ministry. He had taken literally the verse "owe no man any thing" (Rom. 13:8 KJV) and believed that Christians should never incur debt, even in Christian work. So, when a financial need occurred, he prayed for God to meet it, a lesson he had learned from George Mueller, the founder of the faith orphanages in England. Not long after Taylor had been in China he was moved to pray for two missionaries for each of China's eleven provinces plus Mongolia, twenty-four in all. He had no means of supporting them, so he had to pray for sufficient funds as well. There was not even a society to send them out. But Taylor prayed for this, and God answered—first with the original twenty-four missionaries, then with the thousands who later went to China under the auspices of the China Inland Mission. The growth of the China Inland Mission in those days is a great story.

Was Taylor necessary for this work? Yes, in a way. His prayers were necessary. But he was not the means of conveying the blessing of God to these many provinces of China personally.

Other Things to Do

The second reason why perfectly proper prayers of ours may be unanswered is that *God may have other work for us to do.* This seems to have been the chief (perhaps the only) reason why God did not send the great apostle to Rome earlier. In the fifteenth chapter of Romans, Paul speaks of his ministry among the remote cities of the Gentiles as a fulfillment of Isaiah 52:15—"Those who were not told about him [that is, Jesus] will see, and those who have not heard will understand." Then he adds, somewhat unexpectedly, "This is why I have often been hindered from coming to you" (v. 22). It was his ministry among the people of Asia and Greece that had kept him from the Roman Christians, and that is why he did not chafe under the hindrances God sent. He recognized that delay in reaching Rome was for the sake of the Christian mission elsewhere. We need to learn this, too, and be content through learning it. Let me give some examples.

Here is a man who is in an unrewarding job and who would very much prefer another line of work. He tells the Lord that he is not being fulfilled in his present employment, that he is not using the gifts he believes God has given him, that he is not getting ahead, that he is accomplishing little. Each of those points may be true. The work may be unusually frustrating.

But God does not give him a new job. Why? We cannot say why for certain, but it may be that God still has work for this man in the job he has, even though he cannot see it or believe it is happening. There may be another worker to help. There may be a moral issue to be faced. There may be a person who needs to hear the gospel and be led to Jesus Christ.

Here is a woman who is not married but who wants to be. She tells God that she would be much happier married, that she is not really interested in pursuing a career (though many other women are), that she does not want to grow old alone. Those are perfectly valid desires. Still, God does not answer her prayers positively. Why? It may be that God simply has work for her to do as a single person. He may need her as a single Christian executive, nurse, teacher, businesswoman, secretary, or whatever.

If you are praying for something and God is not answering your request with a Yes, ask what you can accomplish in the meantime and give yourself to that. It does not mean that God may not give you what you are asking for eventually, but in the meantime you will be doing good work.

Spiritual Warfare

The third reason why our prayers may go unanswered for a time is the hardest to understand: *There may be spiritual warfare of which you and I are unaware.* There are examples of this in Scripture. Paul spoke of "a thorn in my flesh, a messenger of Satan, to torment me" (2 Cor. 12:7), saying that he prayed three times for it to be removed but that God had replied, "My grace is sufficient for you, for my power is made perfect in weakness" (v. 9). A second example is Daniel, who prayed for something but did not receive an answer to his prayer for three weeks. When at last he did receive an answer, the angel who brought it explained that when Daniel had begun to pray he had started out with God's answer but that he had been resisted by a spiritual being called "the prince of the Persian kingdom." He was able to come through eventually only because the archangel Michael helped him (Dan. 10:1–14).

Spiritual battles are mysteries to us, because we cannot see the warfare. But there *are* spiritual battles, and we need to know about them. They are an important reason why some of our prayers go unanswered.

Does Prayer Change People?

In the previous study I asked the question, "Does prayer change things or change people?" I answered, "Both." Prayer changes things (or circumstances) because it is a God-ordained way of changing them. I based my view on James 4:2, which says, "You do not have, because you do not ask God." If prayer does not change things, then many of the promises that concern it are at best misrepresentations. Jacques Ellul is quite right, though very bold, when he says, "It is prayer, and prayer alone, which can make history. . . . To pray is to carry oneself toward the future. It is both to expect it as possible, and to will it as history."[2]

But prayer also (perhaps chiefly) changes people, as I pointed out.

I want to return to that point now, because, in addition to all I have said so far, one important reason for God not answering prayer is deficiency in us. And so, prayer needs to change us *before* it changes circumstances. What are our deficiencies? What needs changing in us?

1. *Unconfessed sin.* There are more verses in the Bible saying that God will *not* answer prayers than there are verses that say he will, and one of the chief categories of verses that deal with unanswered prayer concerns sin. Isaiah wrote, "Surely the arm of the LORD is not too short to save, nor his ear too dull to hear. But your iniquities have separated you from your God; your sins have hidden his face from you, so that he will not hear" (Isa. 59:1–2). If God is not answering your prayers—particularly if he is not answering any of them—one thing you should do is ask whether you are cherishing some sin. If so, you need to confess it for full forgiveness and cleansing.

2. *Wrong motives.* James spoke of this when he said, "When you ask, you do not receive, because you ask with wrong motives, that you may spend what you get on your pleasures" (James 4:3). Can a person pray for even spiritual things wrongly? Yes, of course. A woman may pray for the conversion of her husband, but with wrong motives—not for his good, that he may be saved from hell and enjoy fellowship with God in this life—but because it would be much more pleasant for her to have a Christian husband or because other Christians would think better of her.

A pastor may pray with wrong motives—for revival, for instance. How? By praying not chiefly so that people may be saved, but that his church might begin to grow and other pastors might look up to him as an effective teacher and evangelist. In *The Power of Prayer and the Prayer of Power,* R. A. Torrey tells of one minister who was praying for revival so he would not lose his church, and of another who was praying to be baptized with the Holy Spirit because he thought he would be paid more if he was.[3]

If we are praying with wrong motives, we need to be changed by God through prayer so we might pray properly.

3. *Laziness.* It is said of Elijah that he prayed "earnestly" that it would not rain and that it did not rain for three and a half years (James 5:17). Prayer was a serious business with him. One reason our prayers are not answered is that we are not really serious about them.

2. Jacques Ellul, *Prayer and Modern Man,* trans. C. Edward Hopkin (New York: Seabury Press, 1970), p. 132.
3. R. A. Torrey, *The Power of Prayer and the Prayer of Power* (Grand Rapids: Zondervan, 1955), pp. 194, 197.

4. *We are too busy.* Sometimes we are too busy to pray "earnestly." But, as someone has said, "If we are too busy to pray, we are too busy." Each of us has exactly the same amount of time in a day as every other person. If we say we are too busy to pray, what we are really saying is that we consider the things we are doing to be more important than praying. This is a theological misunderstanding.

5. *Idols in the heart.* Some of the elders of Israel once came to Ezekiel to pray with him. But the Lord said to Ezekiel, "These men have set up idols in their hearts and put wicked stumbling blocks before their faces. Should I let them inquire of me at all?" (Ezek. 14:3). Is an idol keeping you from having your prayers answered? Is that idol a person? A boyfriend? A girlfriend? A wife? A husband? Your children? Is it your job? Is it your lifestyle? Your social position? Your worldly reputation? Is it your image of yourself? Are you determined above all else to be "successful"? To place anything ahead of God is idolatry. It is a categorical prayer hindrance.

6. *Stinginess in our giving.* Proverbs 21:13 says, "If a man shuts his ears to the cry of the poor, he too will cry out and not be answered." In other words, if you do not give to the needy, God will not give to you when you ask him for something. Or again, Jesus says, "Give, and it will be given to you. A good measure, pressed down, shaken together and running over, will be poured into your lap. For with the measure you use, it will be measured to you" (Luke 6:38). This is quite clear. Torrey writes, "Here God distinctly tells us that he measures out his benefactions to us in exactly the same measure that we measure out our benefactions to others. And some of us use such [tiny] pint cup measures in our giving that God can only give us a pint cup blessing."[4]

The spiritual life of many Christians can be written in just this one word: stinginess. They began with generous hearts, recognizing that God had been generous to them in salvation. But then they became critical of what God was doing in their lives, or critical of other believers or of the way things were being done in their church—and their generosity dried up. They kept their money for themselves. And God stopped giving! Their abundance leveled off. They plateaued because they could not be trusted with more assets.

7. *Unbelief.* The greatest cause of failure in our prayer, and the area in which we most need to be changed, is unbelief. James told those of his day to "believe and not doubt, because he who doubts is like a wave of the sea, blown and tossed by the wind. That man should not think he will receive anything from the Lord . . ." (James 1:6–7). If we do not believe God's Word unquestioningly, why should we get what we pray for? Is it a surprise that our prayers are unanswered?

4. Ibid., p. 210.

Pray and Do Not Give Up

I close with a hypothetical situation. Here you are, someone who has been praying earnestly for something for a long time and has not had an answer. As we have seen, there are numerous reasons why a positive answer may have been delayed, all the way from spiritual warfare in the heavenlies to our sin or unbelief. What are you to do? Should you keep on battering the brass doors of heaven with ineffectual petitions? Or should you accept God's rejection? Should you quit praying?

The answer is in Jesus' parable of the importunate widow, which, Luke tells us, teaches that we "should always pray and not give up" (Luke 18:1). Prayer may change us. It may change history. But whatever the case, we must keep praying.

Paul kept praying, and he got to Rome eventually.

George Mueller kept praying, too. When Mueller was a young man he had three friends who were not Christians. He began to pray for them. He prayed every day for more than sixty years. It seemed as if his prayers would never be answered. But they were. Two of those men were converted shortly before Mueller's death, one at what was probably the last service Mueller held. The other was converted within a year of Mueller's funeral. Unanswered prayer? How do we ever know it will remain unanswered? Since we do not, we ought always to pray and not give up.

10

The Whole Gospel
for the Whole World

Romans 1:14–15

I am obligated both to Greeks and non-Greeks, both to the wise and the foolish.
That is why I am so eager to preach the gospel also to you who are at Rome.

T he title of this chapter has two parts:
(1) the whole gospel, and (2) the whole world, but I am going to spend
most of it on the second part. The reason is that "the whole world," rather
than "the whole gospel," is the new idea at this point in the exposition. As
far as the gospel goes, we have already learned a great deal about it in the
opening verses of Paul's letter, and we will learn more as our study proceeds. Indeed, the letter of Paul to the Romans is the best treatment of "the
whole gospel" in all Scripture. The point I want to emphasize in this study is
that this full-orbed gospel is for everybody.

Our text expresses it from the perspective of Paul's personal experience:
"I am obligated both to Greeks and non-Greeks, both to the wise and the
foolish. That is why I am so eager to preach the gospel also to you who are
at Rome."

Actually, the gospel has always been for everybody. Thom Hopler in his excellent book on cross-cultural evangelism, *A World of Difference: Following Christ Beyond Your Cultural Walls*, shows this from the Bible as a whole. As early as Genesis 3, we see that the gospel is for both male and female, the first announcement of the gospel being made both to Adam and to Eve (Gen. 3:15). In Daniel we find that it is for the dreaded Babylonians as well as for the persecuted Jews. In the ministry of Jesus Christ the gospel was taught to "publicans and sinners" as well as to those who had the privileges of education and high birth, like Nicodemus. It was disclosed to the Samaritan woman of John 4. Later, at the time of the expanding apostolic ministry, God reminded Peter that the gospel was for Roman military officers, like Cornelius, as well as for those who, like the Jews, were ceremonially "clean." On that occasion Peter made the point by declaring, "I now realize how true it is that God does not show favoritism but accepts men from every nation who fear him" (Acts 10:34–35). Jesus showed the geographical scope of the gospel's proclamation in Acts' version of the Great Commission: "You will receive power when the Holy Spirit comes on you; and you will be my witnesses in Jerusalem, and in all Judea and Samaria, and to the ends of the earth" (Acts 1:8).[1]

How easily we forget this! Christians forget, or at least willfully ignore, that the gospel is for people other than themselves. Unbelievers argue, as an excuse, that the gospel is for other types of people.

To Wise People Everywhere

In Romans 1:14 the first persons to whom Paul says he is obligated as an ambassador of the gospel are Greeks, whom he contrasts with "non-Greeks" or, as some of our more literal versions say, "barbarians."

There is a second contrast in this sentence, "the wise" and the "foolish" (or "unwise"), which indicates how the first category is to be understood. If Paul had contrasted Greeks with Romans—which he could have done, since he was writing to Romans, we would have to understand the distinction between Greeks and non-Greeks in terms of nationality. If he had let the comparison end with "Greeks" and "non-Greeks," not mentioning "wise" and "unwise," the distinction would have been primarily an ethnic one. However, Paul adds the words *wise* and *foolish*, and by doing this he shows that what he is chiefly thinking of is culture or education. Because of their language, long-established Greeks had access to the great historical, epic, dramatic and, above all, philosophical writings of the past. Even the powerful Romans got the bulk of their education through this channel. Apart

---

1. Thom Hopler, *A World of Difference: Following Christ Beyond Your Cultural Walls* (Downers Grove, Ill.: InterVarsity Press, 1981). Hopler surveys the biblical material in the middle chapters of this book.

from the Greek language, others—people of all kinds—could never be considered learned or wise by Greek standards.

So Paul's first claim is that the gospel God sent him to proclaim is for the learned of this world. It is for the wise, whether they are Greeks or Romans or Americans or even the elite among university professors.

The gospel is for you if you are among the educated of our world. You need this ancient Christian gospel. Whatever your educational attainments, however wise you may be, you are still a sinful man or woman and are cut off from the God who made you and to whom you must one day give account for your many sins. You are mortal. One day you will die. You will enter eternity with or without the Lord Jesus Christ—just as surely as any other man or woman.

I know the evasions you might make, because I have been to the same schools and have taken the same courses. I have heard the arguments. You can say, "I was taught in my sociology courses that religions are all relative. They are to be understood by the cultural forces that give them birth. You are a Christian only because you have been born in the West and are the product of an historical stream descending from the Reformation. If you had been born elsewhere, you might as well have been a Buddhist or a Muslim." That is quite true, of course; at least the last part of it is true. But the issue is not where you or I have been privileged (or not privileged) to be born, but whether there is a God and whether or not he is as Christianity presents him. If there is a God, he obviously has some character. He is not everything and nothing all at the same time. Is he the Bible's God? Did God send his Son Jesus Christ to bring us salvation? You cannot escape those questions by mere sociological comparisons.

The Greeks tried to do that even in Paul's day. When he traveled to Athens, the intellectual capital of the world, and spoke of Jesus Christ there, the Greek intellectuals were politely amused by this religious novelty. They thought Paul a proclaimer of "foreign gods." None of this daunted Paul, however. He proclaimed the true God anyway. "Now what you worship as something unknown I am going to proclaim to you," he said (Acts 17:23). He finished his address by speaking of the final judgment and commanding his listeners to repent of their sins.

So also must you.

Perhaps you have another method by which you are trying to evade the gospel's implications. You consider the details of Christianity to be magical or absurd and therefore easy to reject, just as some of the Athenians did. "Who can believe in miracles today?" you protest. "No intelligent person can believe in divine-human beings, people walking on water, resurrections, and such things. We have to reject those old superstitions."

But intelligent people *do* believe these things. They do today, and they always have. What is more, they are convinced that it is those who reject the supernatural who are really the unintelligent.

Let me echo one other "educated" objection. There are people who have taken religion courses in college or graduate school and who now know enough to turn a rather superficial knowledge of biblical studies against the Bible itself. They can speak of "Pauline" verses and "Petrine" theology. They can speak of first and second Isaiah. They think, just because they have a slight acquaintance with such things, that they can sit in judgment on the Bible rather than having it the other way around. "After all, Paul was just a male chauvinist," they say. Or, "If Moses lived when the Bible says he lived, he couldn't even have known how to write—least of all have given us the Pentateuch."

These critical theories have been answered well by conservative, believing scholars, some quite conclusively. Besides, if you honestly want to learn about Christianity, why go to an unbelieving professor to learn about it? Is that not in itself an evasion? Would you not learn more about true piety from that believing pastor who once wanted to help you come to Christ? Or from your believing mother or grandmother who has been praying for you all these many years? Has your skepticism really made your life more comprehensible?

Let me make this first important point again: the gospel is for you—however well educated or intellectually endowed you may be. Your intellect and education are great gifts. But it is God who has given them to you. And if you do not thank him for these gifts and use them in ways that honor him, you are more deserving of judgment than those who are unintelligent. You need a Savior.

The apostle Paul had one of the best educations of his day, having been taught in the wisdom of the Greeks as well as in the religious traditions of Israel. He was a Roman citizen, too! But Paul learned that the gospel of the crucified Son of God alone was true wisdom. It was to people in an important Greek city that he wrote:

> Where is the wise man? Where is the scholar? Where is the philosopher of this age? Has not God made foolish the wisdom of the world? For since in the wisdom of God the world through its wisdom did not know him, God was pleased through the foolishness of what was preached to save those who believe. Jews demand miraculous signs and Greeks look for wisdom, but we preach Christ crucified: a stumbling block to Jews and foolishness to Gentiles, but to those whom God has called, both Jews and Greeks, Christ the power of God and the wisdom of God. For the foolishness of God is wiser than man's wisdom, and the weakness of God is stronger than man's strength.
>
> 1 Corinthians 1:20–25

To "Ordinary" People Everywhere

The Greeks called "barbarians" all who were not Greek, the next category of people to whom Paul says he was obliged to preach the gospel.

"Barbarian" did not have quite the negative overtones to the Greeks as it has for us. The word actually had to do with speech patterns, for when the Greeks heard "foreigners" speak, what they said sounded like babbling, or stammering: *bar, bar bar.* (The Greek word *barbaros* also is linked to the Sanskrit *barbera*, which referred to inarticulate speech.) So barbarians were people who did not speak Greek. But although the word did not have quite the negative overtones it has for us—some of the "barbarians" were quite cultured people—it nevertheless had some. Greek was the language of the educated. Since the histories, epics, and plays were in Greek, to be a barbarian was to be cut off from this cultural storehouse.

Perhaps you are a person who feels yourself similarly disadvantaged. I suppose there are more people today who feel themselves to be cut off from the mainstream of society than there are people who feel a part of it.

You may feel cut off because of a lack of educational opportunities. So many people have been to college. You have not. You have not read the books they have read and talk about. You are not at ease with the buzz words of the intellectual establishment—terms like, well, "buzz word" itself or "interface" or "existential." You do not speak as educated people do. Perhaps you have regional patterns to your speech or make mistakes in grammar.

You may feel cut off because of your race. No matter that others of your race have made it; they are exceptions, you think. You have not, and those who belong to other races, or who belong to your race and have made it to the top, never seem to let you forget your place.

You may feel cut off because of your low income, which shows in the clothes you wear, the neighborhood you live in, the car you drive, and many other distinctions.

For those and other reasons you feel left out. So you look at what the world calls "Christian people" and say, "Those are not *my* people. I don't belong in their company. Christianity is *their* religion. It is not mine."

Here I must ask forgiveness for what has become a terrible sin of the twentieth-century church. Somehow many people feel cut off from the fellowship of believers. As the gospel has succeeded in reaching people and transforming them, bringing them to new levels of opportunity and achievement, it has often taken on these new cultural overtones—just as you have seen. Christians too often forget that Jesus Christ did not go first to the wise, wealthy, or influential citizens of his day, but to the everyday people, whoever and wherever they were. The important people did not like him for it! They called him a friend of drunkards and sinners. Nevertheless, that is where he went. His friends were carpenters, fishermen, tax collectors, and others who worked hard for a living. After his death and resurrection, when the gospel began to spread beyond the geographical borders of Israel, it was among the working people—often among slaves—that it advanced most readily.

I apologize on behalf of any Christian who has given the impression that Christianity is only for the educated, influential, or wealthy. At the same time I urge you not to miss believing on Jesus Christ because of that sadly wrong impression.

In Paul's day there were not many who had the advantages of what we would call a university education, but Paul wrote to the others to say that God had chosen them to expose the foolishness of merely human wisdom:

> Brothers, think of what you were when you were called. Not many of you were wise by human standards; not many were influential; not many were of noble birth. But God chose the foolish things of the world to shame the wise; God chose the weak things of the world to shame the strong. He chose the lowly things of this world and the despised things—and the things that are not—to nullify the things that are, so that no one may boast before him. . . . Therefore, as it is written: "Let him who boasts boast in the Lord."
>
> 1 Corinthians 1:26–29, 31

To Religious People Everywhere

In our text, Romans 1:14–15, Paul limits his "categories" of those who need the gospel to Greeks and non-Greeks, the wise and the foolish. I do not know why he stopped at that point. But it is significant that in the very next verse Paul adds another important category, when he distinguishes between the Jew and the Gentile (v. 16). In the first instance he was proba-bly·thinking of the Romans, who were largely Gentiles. But when he gives the full statement of his thesis in verse 16, he adds this additional category to indicate that the gospel is indeed for the entire world.

Isn't it surprising that Paul feels a need to mention Jews specifically? The gospel is about a Jew, Jesus of Nazareth. It was taught, at least in the early days, exclusively from the Jewish Scriptures. The Old Testament is a Jewish book. The apostles and the early preachers of the gospel were all Jews. Why, then, should Jews specifically be mentioned?

The answer is that Jews as a whole, even more than Gentiles, resisted the gospel. Why? Because it did not fit their strong religious traditions. It is true that the gospel had been promised to Jews in the very Scriptures they defended. But they had imposed their own expectations on those Scriptures and handled them so as to build their own feelings of self-righteousness rather than as a way to recognize sin and their need for the Savior whom God had promised to send. As a result, when God sent Jesus they resented his "independent" spirit and fought him when his moral per-fection exposed their own deep sin.

It is the same today, in the sense that the gospel of salvation by Jesus Christ is resisted most by those who are "religious." Of all persons, religious people often have the least sense of personal need. Above all others, they especially think themselves to have achieved God's standards and deserve commendation by him. They resent being taught that they, too, are sinners, that they, too, need a Savior, that they, too, must come to God through simple faith—just as others. Yet they desperately need Jesus.

Are you one of those people? Do you feel secure in your religion—apart from Jesus? If so, you need to learn that no religion, even Christianity, can save you. Only God can save you. He has made provision for that through the work of Jesus Christ, his own Son, who died for you. That is the gospel. That is what you need. It is needed by everybody.

To Everybody Everywhere

At the close of his statement of obligation to the Greeks and non-Greeks, the wise and unwise, Paul explains his views by declaring, "That is why I am so eager to preach the gospel also to you who are at Rome." When he mentions "you who are at Rome" Paul is not adding a new category, for the Romans fit within the earlier Greek or non-Greek, wise or foolish groupings. The church at Rome included every conceivable type of man or woman and was therefore itself all-embracing. So I think that when Paul says that the gospel is for those at Rome "also" he is actually saying, "The gospel is for you, whoever you may be and wherever you may find yourself."

I present it to you in that way.

You may be a very young person with your whole life stretching before you. You have great plans, and you may have very little place for God in those plans. If so, I tell you that the gospel is for you and that you need it, just as others do. Charles Haddon Spurgeon once said in a talk to children, "You may be young; but you are old enough to sin, and you are old enough to die." As long as that is true, you need a Savior.

You may be an older person, perhaps very along in years. You are thinking that life is almost over for you and that decisions of this scope are for young people. You may be thinking that it is too late to make changes. But you especially need the gospel. Soon you will stand before God, your Maker, and you will have to give an account for your many long years of sinning. You have heard the gospel. Will you have to tell God that you rejected it, that you spurned the offer of grace through his crucified Son, the Lord Jesus? It is not too late. Today can be the day of your salvation. If you turn to him now, you will find that the last years of your life will be the most important and precious of all.

Perhaps you are from a non-Western, non-English-speaking country. You may be reading these words in part because you are a guest in the United States or because you want to learn about America. You may think that what you are reading is something uniquely American, that it is not for you, not for one from your country or from your background. I tell you that it is for you. It is the gospel of the one God and of the one Savior. It is a gospel that has already permeated the entire world. It has come to you now. It is time for you to trust Jesus.

Perhaps you are an American, and you think that you already are a Christian—just because you have been born in a so-called Christian country. Being an American will not save you. Having a Christian tradition or even Christian parents will not save you. Belonging to a church will not save you. You need the gospel. You need to believe in Jesus Christ as your Savior.

The gospel is for those who live in Philadelphia. It is for those in New York. It is for those in Paris or Bombay or Beijing or Mombassa or Bogotá. Whoever you are, you need the gospel. The whole world needs the gospel, and the gospel it needs is the whole gospel of God's grace to sinners through the atoning death of Jesus Christ.

If you are not a Christian, you need to hear this and come to the Lord Jesus Christ as your Savior.

If you are a Christian, you need to make this great good news known to other people, as Paul did.

PART TWO

The Heart of
Biblical Religion

11

The Theme of the Epistle

Romans 1:16–17

I am not ashamed of the gospel, because it is the power of God for the salvation of everyone who believes: first for the Jew, then for the Gentile. For in the gospel a righteousness from God is revealed, a righteousness that is by faith from first to last, just as it is written: "The righteous will live by faith."

In the sixteenth and seventeenth verses of Romans 1, we come to sentences that are the most important in the letter and perhaps in all literature. They are the theme of this epistle and the essence of Christianity. They are the heart of biblical religion.

The reason this is so is that they tell how a man or woman may become right with God. We are not right with God in ourselves. This is what the doctrine of original sin is all about. We are in rebellion against God; and if we are in rebellion against God, we cannot be right with him. On the contrary, we are to be judged by him. What is more, we are polluted by our sin. We are as filthy in God's sight as the most disease infected, loathsome individual could be in ours, and in that state we must be banished from his presence forever when we die.

What is to be done? On our side, nothing can be done. Yet in these sentences Paul tells us that God has done something. In fact, he has done precisely what needs to be done. He has provided a righteousness that is exactly what we need. It is a divine righteousness, a perfect righteousness. And it is received, not by doing righteous things (which we can never do in sufficient quantity anyway), but by simple faith. It is received merely by believing what God tells us.

No One Righteous

In the next chapter, continuing our study of this very important section of the letter to the Roman church, I will show why Paul was not ashamed of this gospel. Here, however, I want to concentrate on the chief idea in these two verses, namely, that in the gospel a righteousness from God is revealed and that this righteousness is received (and has always been received) by faith. The place to begin is with the fact that in ourselves we do not possess this righteousness.

There can be little objection to the statement that we do not possess true righteousness, because this is the point with which Paul begins his formal argument. That is, immediately after having stated his thesis in verses 16 and 17, Paul launches into a section extending from 1:18 to 3:20, in which he shows that far from being righteous before God, men and women are actually very corrupt and are all therefore naturally objects of God's just wrath and condemnation.

I make the point in this way. Notice that in verse 17 (our text here), Paul says that "a righteousness from God is revealed." Then notice that in 3:21, he says virtually the same thing once again: "But now a righteousness from God, apart from law, has been made known to which the Law and the Prophets testify." The words "is made known" mean "is revealed," and the reference to "the Law and the Prophets" corresponds to Paul's citation of a specific statement of the prophet Habakkuk in the earlier verse: "just as it is written: 'the righteous will live by faith.'" So the full exposition of what Paul introduces in 1:17 begins only at 3:21.

So what occupies the intervening verses? They are a statement of the need for this righteousness, introduced by a parallel but deliberate contrast with these two statements. At the start of this section, instead of speaking of any revelation of righteousness, Paul declares: "The *wrath* of God is being revealed from heaven against all the godlessness and wickedness of men who suppress the truth by their wickedness" (v. 18, italics mine).

What Paul says in Romans 1:18 through 3:20 embraces all persons. But he develops his thoughts progressively, moving from a description of those who are openly hostile to God and wicked to those who consider themselves to be either moral, and therefore acceptable to God on the basis of their own good works, or else religious, and therefore acceptable on the basis of their religious practices.

One thing is true of everyone. Left to ourselves, we use either our heathen lifestyle, our claims to moral superiority, or our religion to resist the true God. Paul says that certain facts about God have been revealed to all people in nature. But instead of allowing that revelation to point us to God and then attempting to seek him out as a result of it, we actually suppress the revelation God has given in order to continue in our own wicked ways. This is the real grounds of God's just wrath against us—not that we have failed to do something that we could not do or refused to believe something that we did not even know about, but that we have rejected the knowledge we have in order to pursue wickedness. When he gets to the end of this section Paul is therefore quite right in concluding, quoting from many Old Testament texts:

> As it is written:
> "There is no one righteous, not even one;
>   there is no one who understands,
>   no one who seeks God.
> All have turned away,
>   they have together become worthless;
> there is no one who does good,
>   not even one."
> "Their throats are open graves;
>   their tongues practice deceit."
> "The poison of vipers is on their lips."
>   "Their mouths are full of cursing and bitterness."
> "Their feet are swift to shed blood;
>   ruin and misery mark their ways,
> and the way of peace they do not know."
>   "There is no fear of God before their eyes."
>
> Romans 3:10–18

We may not like this description of ourselves (who would?), but it is God's accurate assessment of our depraved lives and civilization.

A Righteousness from God

In all literature there is no portrait of the human race so realistic, grim, or hopeless as this summation of Paul's. Yet it makes the wonder of the gospel all the more glorious, for it is against this background that "a righteousness from God" is made known.

We need to see several important things about it.

1. *This righteousness from God is the righteousness of the Lord Jesus Christ.* In 1:17 and 3:21, Paul says that righteousness "comes through faith in Jesus Christ." But it is surely right to add, in view of what Paul said in the opening section of this letter (and says elsewhere), that this is the very righteousness of Christ, which God gives to us. Righteousness is revealed in the gospel—Paul says so—but the gospel concerns Jesus Christ (1:2–3). So it is

Christ who has this righteousness, and it is from him that we both learn about it and receive it.

Jesus possesses righteousness in two senses, both important. First, Jesus is intrinsically righteous. That is, being God, he is utterly holy and without sin. That is why he could say during the days of his flesh, "I always do what pleases him [that is, God]" (John 8:29b) or, as he said to his enemies on another occasion, "Can any of you prove me guilty of sin?" (John 8:46a). His words left them speechless.

Jesus is also righteous in that he achieved a perfect righteousness by his obedience to the law of God while on earth. When John the Baptist resisted Jesus' call for baptism, saying, "I need to be baptized by you, and do you come to me?" Jesus replied, "Let it be so now; it is proper for us to do this to fulfill all righteousness" (Matt. 3:14–15). By saying that it was proper for him to be baptized in order "to fulfill all righteousness," Jesus showed that he intended to fulfill the demands of the law while he lived among us. And he did. D. Martyn Lloyd-Jones has written:

> He rendered a perfect obedience to the law; he kept it in every jot and tittle. He failed in no respect. He fulfilled God's law completely, perfectly, and absolutely. Not only that! He has dealt with the penalty meted out by the law upon all sin and upon all sins. He took your guilt and mine upon himself, and he bore its punishment. The penalty of the law was meted out upon him, and so he has honored the law completely, positively and negatively, actively and passively. There is nothing further the law can demand; he has satisfied it all.[1]

When Paul says that righteousness from God is revealed in the gospel, he means that the gospel shows how we can acquire the righteousness we need. But this does not exclude the truth that the existence and nature of this righteousness are also revealed to us in Christ's person. In Christ we can see that righteousness truly exists and can be offered to us by God.

2. *God offers this righteousness of Jesus Christ freely, apart from any need to work for it on our part.* This is the heart of the Good News, of course. For unless God were willing to give this righteousness to us and actually does give it, the mere existence of a perfect righteousness would not be good news at all. On the contrary, it would be very bad news, for it would increase our sense of condemnation.

It was the discovery of this truth that transformed Martin Luther and through him launched the Reformation. Luther was aware that Jesus exhibited a perfect righteousness and that this was a standard of character rightly demanded from all human beings by God. But Luther did not have this righteousness. In fact, the more he tried to achieve this righteousness, the

1. D. M. Lloyd-Jones, *Romans: An Exposition of Chapter 1, The Gospel of God* (Grand Rapids: Zondervan, 1985), p. 302.

more elusive it became. It was Luther's very piety that created the problem. He wanted to be righteous. He wanted to please God. But the more he worked at pleasing God, the more he knew that pleasing God involved more than merely doing certain things and refusing to do others. He knew that pleasing God involved even the very attitudes in which he did or did not do these things. Basically he needed to love God, and he knew he did not love God. He actually hated God for making the standard of righteousness so impossible.

As I pointed out in the introductory chapter of this book, Luther wrote, "I had no love for that holy and just God who punishes sinners. I was filled with secret anger against him."[2]

But then Luther discovered that he had misunderstood God's intention in revealing the nature and existence of this righteousness. It was not revealed so that men and women like Luther might strive toward it and inevitably fail desperately, as Luther did. It was revealed as God's free gift in Christ, so that those who came to know Christ might stop their fruitless striving and instead rest in him. They could rest in his atoning death on their behalf, since he took the punishment of their sins upon himself and paid for them fully so that their sins might never rise up to haunt them again. They could rest in righteousness, knowing that God had given it to them and that they could thereafter stand before God, not in their own self-righteousness, which is no righteousness at all, but in the very righteousness of Christ.

The term for the application of the righteousness of Christ to the sinner is "imputation." It is like putting the infinite moral capital of the Lord Jesus Christ in our empty bank account. It is having the riches of heaven at our disposal. When Luther saw this, it was as if the doors of heaven had been opened and he was able to pass through "the true gate of Paradise."[3]

3. *Faith is the channel by which sinners receive Christ's righteousness.* Paul lived many centuries before the Reformation, but he seems to have anticipated the sixteenth-century battles over the role of faith in salvation by the way he emphasizes faith both in this initial statement of his thesis and in his fuller development of the role of faith in receiving the gospel in 3:21–31. In Romans 1:17, he speaks of "a righteousness that is *by faith* from first to last, just as it is written: 'The righteous will live *by faith*,'" quoting Habakkuk 2:4 (italics mine). In 3:21–31 he refers to "faith" eight times.

What is faith? Initially Luther thought of faith as a work and therefore grimly regarded it as something else to be attained. But faith is not a work. It is believing God. It is opening a hand to receive the righteousness of Christ that God offers.

2. The quote is from J. H. Merle D'Aubigné, *The Life and Times of Martin Luther*, trans. H. White (Chicago: Moody Press, 1958), p. 55. I refer to it in full in this volume on pages 12, 13.

3. Ibid., p. 56

Faith consists of three elements. First, it consists of *knowledge*. It is no mere attitude of mind; it involves content. We must have faith in "something." In the case of salvation that content (and the object of our knowledge) is the revelation of what God has done for us in Jesus Christ.

Second, faith consists of a *heart response* to the gospel. This is because faith is not assent to some principle that is true but nevertheless has little relationship to us. It involves the love of God for us in saving us through the death of Jesus Christ, his Son. Unless this touches our hearts and moves them, we do not really understand the gospel.

Finally, faith consists of *commitment*, commitment to Christ. At this point, Jesus becomes not merely a Savior in some abstract sense or even someone else's Savior, but *my* Savior. Like Thomas, I now gladly confess him to be "*My* Lord and *my* God" (John 20:28, italics mine).

In an excellent little book entitled *All of Grace,* the great Baptist preacher Charles Haddon Spurgeon wrote, "Faith is not a blind thing; for faith begins with knowledge. It is not a speculative thing; for faith believes facts of which it is sure. It is not an unpractical, dreamy thing; for faith trusts, and stakes its destiny upon the truth of revelation. . . . Faith . . . is *the eye* which looks. . . . Faith is *the hand* which grasps. . . Faith is *the mouth* which feeds upon Christ."[4]

One person who read Romans 10:8 ("'The word is near you; it is in your mouth and in your heart'") exclaimed, "Give me a knife and a fork and a chance." He had the idea. He was prepared to receive the gospel personally.

Another who had the idea was Count Zinzendorf. His great hymn about justification through the righteousness of Christ received by faith comes to us through the translation of John Wesley:

> Jesus, thy blood and righteousness
> My beauty are, my glorious dress;
> 'Midst flaming worlds, in these arrayed,
> With joy shall I lift up my head.
>
> Bold shall I stand in thy great day,
> For who aught to my charge shall lay?
> Fully absolved through these I am,
> From sin and fear, from guilt and shame.
>
> O let the dead now hear thy voice;
> Now bid thy banished ones rejoice;
> Their beauty this, their glorious dress,
> Jesus, thy blood and righteousness.

4. Charles Haddon Spurgeon, *All of Grace* (Chicago: Moody Press, n.d.), pp. 46, 47, 50, 51.

It was by faith in the completed work of Christ and God's gift of Christ's righteousness to believing men and women that Zinzendorf expected to stand before God in the day of judgment and be accepted by him.

"Nothing in My Hands"

This was Paul's expectation and experience, too. He tells of his experience of God's grace in Philippians.

Paul had been an exceedingly moral man: ".... If anyone else thinks he has reasons to put confidence in the flesh, I have more: circumcised on the eighth day, of the people of Israel, of the tribe of Benjamin, a Hebrew of Hebrews; in regard to the law, a Pharisee; as for zeal, persecuting the church; as for legalistic righteousness, faultless" (Phil. 3:4–6). But Paul learned to count his attainments as nothing in order to have Christ "and be found in him, not having a righteousness of my own that comes from the law, but that which is through faith in Christ—the righteousness that comes from God and is by faith" (v. 9). This is a vivid, personal statement of what he also declares at the beginning of Romans.

In Philippians, Paul uses a helpful metaphor, saying that before he met Christ his thoughts about religion involved something like a lifelong balance sheet showing assets and liabilities. He had thought that being saved meant having more in the column of assets than in the column of liabilities. And since he had considerable assets, he felt that he was very well off indeed.

Some assets he had inherited. Among them were the facts that he had been born into a Jewish family and had been circumcised according to Jewish law on the eighth day of life. He was neither a proselyte who had been circumcised later in life, nor an Ishmaelite who was circumcised when he was thirteen years of age. He was a pure-blooded Jew, having been born of two Jewish parents ("a Hebrew of Hebrews"). As an Israelite he was a member of God's covenant people. He was of the tribe of Benjamin. Moreover, Paul had assets he had earned for himself. He was a Pharisee, the strictest and most faithful of the Jewish religious orders. He was a zealous Pharisee, proved by his persecution of the church. And, as far as the law was concerned, Paul reckoned himself to be blameless, for he had kept the law in all its particulars so far as he had understood it.

These were great assets from a human point of view. But the day came when God revealed his own righteousness to Paul in the person of Jesus Christ. When Paul saw Jesus he understood for the first time what real righteousness was. Moreover, he saw that what he had been calling righteousness, his *own* righteousness, was not righteousness at all but only filthy rags. It was no asset. It was actually a liability, because it had been keeping him from Jesus, where alone true righteousness could be found.

Mentally Paul moved his long list of cherished assets to the column of liabilities—for that is what they really were—and under assets he wrote "Jesus Christ alone."

Augustus M. Toplady had it right in the hymn "Rock of Ages":

> Nothing in my hand I bring,
> Simply to thy cross I cling;
> Naked, come to thee for dress;
> Helpless, look to thee for grace;
> Foul, I to the fountain fly;
> Wash me, Saviour, or I die.
>
> Rock of Ages, cleft for me,
> Let me hide myself in thee.

When those who have been made alive by God turn from their own attempts at righteousness, which can only condemn them, and instead embrace the Lord Jesus Christ by saving faith, God declares their sins to have been punished in Christ and imputes his own perfect righteousness to their account.

12

Not Ashamed

Romans 1:16-17

I am not ashamed of the gospel, because it is the power of God for the salvation of everyone who believes: first for the Jew, then for the Gentile. For in the gospel a righteousness from God is revealed, a righteousness that is by faith from first to last, just as it is written: "The righteous will live by faith."

At first glance it is an extraordinary thing that Paul should say that he is "not ashamed" of the gospel. For when we read that statement we ask, "But why should anybody be ashamed of the gospel? Why should the apostle even think that something so grand might be shameful?" Questions like that are not very deep or honest, since we have all been ashamed of the gospel at one time or another.

The reason is that the world is opposed to God's gospel and ridicules it, and we are all far more attuned to the world than we imagine. The gospel was despised in Paul's day. Robert Haldane has written accurately:

By the pagans it was branded as atheism, and by the Jews it was abhorred as subverting the law and tending to licentiousness, while both Jews and Gentiles united in denouncing the Christians as disturbers of the public peace, who, in their pride and presumption, separated themselves from the rest of mankind. Besides, a crucified Savior was to the one a stumbling-

111

block, and to the other foolishness. This doctrine was everywhere spoken against, and the Christian fortitude of the apostle in acting on the avowal he here makes was as truly manifested in the calmness with which, for the name of the Lord Jesus, he confronted personal danger and even death itself. His courage was not more conspicuous when he was ready "not to be bound only, but also to die at Jerusalem," than when he was enabled to enter Athens or Rome without being moved by the prospect of all that scorn and derision which in these great cities awaited him.[1]

Is the situation different in our day? It is true that today's culture exhibits a certain veneer of religious tolerance, so that well-bred people are careful not to scorn Christians openly. But the world is still the world, and hostility to God is always present. If you have never been ashamed of the gospel, the probable reason, as D. Martyn Lloyd-Jones suggests, is not that you are "an exceptionally good Christian," but rather that "your understanding of the Christian message has never been clear."[2]

Was Paul tempted to shame, as we are? Probably. We know that Timothy was, since Paul wrote him to tell him not to be (2 Tim. 1:8). However, in our text Paul writes that basically he was "*not* ashamed of the gospel," and the reason is that "it is the power of God for the salvation of everyone who believes: first for the Jew, then for the Gentile. For in the gospel a righteousness from God is revealed, a righteousness that is by faith from first to last, just as it is written: 'The righteous will live by faith.'"

In this study, following the treatment of D. Martyn Lloyd-Jones, I want to suggest eight reasons why we should not be ashamed of this gospel.[3]

The Gospel Is "Good News"

The first reason why we should not be ashamed of the gospel is the meaning of the word *gospel* itself. It means "good news," and no rational person should be ashamed of a desirable proclamation.

We can understand why one might hesitate to convey bad news, of course. We can imagine a policeman who must tell a father that his son has been arrested for breaking into a neighbor's house and stealing her possessions. We can understand how he might be distressed at having to communicate this sad message. Or again, we can imagine how a doctor might be dismayed at having to tell a patient that tests have come out badly and that he or she does not have long to live, or how a person involved in some great moral lapse might be ashamed to confess it. But the gospel is not like this. It

1. Robert Haldane, *An Exposition of the Epistle to the Romans* (MacDill AFB: MacDonald Publishing, 1958), p. 45.

2. D. M. Lloyd-Jones, *Romans: An Exposition of Chapter 1, The Gospel of God* (Grand Rapids: Zondervan, 1985), p. 260.

3. Lloyd-Jones devotes four chapters to developing these points (*Romans: An Exposition of Chapter 1*, chs. 20–23, pp. 256–309).

is the opposite. Instead of being bad news, it is good news about what God has done for us in Jesus Christ. It is the best news imaginable.

The Way of Salvation

The second reason why we should not be ashamed of the gospel is that it is about "salvation." And not just any salvation. It is about the saving of ourselves.

The background for this side of the Good News is that, left to ourselves, we are in desperate trouble. We are in trouble now because we are at odds with God, other people, and ourselves. We are also in trouble in regard to the future; for we are on a path of increasing frustration and despair, and at the end we must face God's just wrath and condemnation. We are like swimmers drowning in a vast ocean of cold water or explorers sinking in a deep bog of quicksand. We are like astronauts lost in the black hostile void of outer space. We are like prisoners awaiting execution.

But there is good news! God has intervened to rescue us through the work of his divine Son, Jesus Christ. First, he has reconciled us to himself; Christ has died for us, bearing our sins in his own body on the cross. Second, he has reconciled us to others; we are now set free to love them as Jesus loved us. Third, he has reconciled us to ourselves; in Jesus Christ (and by the power of the Holy Spirit) we are now able to become what God has always meant for us to be.

We can say this in yet other ways. Salvation delivers us from the guilt, power, and pollution of sin. We are brought back into communication with God, from whom our sins had separated us. And we are given a marvelous destiny, which Paul elsewhere describes as "the hope of the glory of God" (Rom. 5:2). In 1 Corinthians 1:30 Paul expresses these truths somewhat comprehensively when he writes that "Christ Jesus . . . has become for us wisdom from God—that is, our righteousness, holiness and redemption." Paul was not ashamed of the gospel, because it was about a real deliverance—from sin and its power—and about reconciliation to God.

God's Way of Salvation

The third reason why Paul was not ashamed of the gospel is that it is God's way of salvation and not man's way. How could Paul be proud of something that has its roots in the abilities of sinful men and women or is bounded by mere human ideas? The world does not lack such ideas. There are countless schemes for salvation, countless self-help programs. But these are all foolish and inadequate. What is needed is a way of salvation that comes not from man, but from God! That is what we have in Christianity! Christianity is God's reaching out to save perishing men and women, not sinners reaching out to seize God.

Paul speaks about this in two major ways, contrasting God's way of salvation with our own attempts to keep the law, on the one hand, and, on the other hand, with our attempts to know God by mere human wisdom.

As to the law, he says, "For what the law was powerless to do in that it was weakened by the sinful nature, God did by sending his own Son in the likeness of sinful man to be a sin offering. And so he condemned sin in sinful man, in order that the righteous requirements of the law might be fully met in us, who do not live according to the sinful nature but according to the Spirit" (Rom. 8:3–4). This means that, although we could not please God by keeping the law's demands, God enables us to please him, first, by condemning sin in us through the work of Jesus Christ and, then, by enabling us to live upright lives through the power of the Holy Spirit.

As to wisdom, Paul writes, "For since in the wisdom of God the world through its wisdom did not know him, God was pleased through the foolishness of what was preached to save those who believe" (1 Cor. 1:21).

The Power of God

This leads to the fourth reason why Paul was not ashamed of the gospel, the matter he chiefly emphasizes in our text: The gospel is powerful. That is, it is not only good news, not only a matter of salvation, not only a way of salvation from God; it is also powerful enough to accomplish God's purpose, which is to save us from sin's pollution.

It is important to understand what is involved here, for it is easy to misconstrue Paul's teaching. When Paul says that "the gospel . . . is the power of God for salvation," he is not saying that the gospel is *about* God's power, as if it were merely pointing us to a power beyond our own. Nor is Paul saying that the gospel is the *source* of a power we can get and use to save ourselves. Paul's statement is not that the gospel is about God's power or even a channel through which that power operates, but rather that the gospel is *itself* that power. That is, *the gospel is powerful;* it is the means by which God accomplishes salvation in those who are being saved.

Since Paul puts it this way, we are right to agree with John Calvin when he emphasizes that the gospel mentioned here is not merely the work done by God in Jesus Christ or the revelation to us of that work, but the actual "preaching" of the gospel "by word of mouth."[4] He means that it is in the actual preaching of the gospel that the power of God is demonstrated in the saving of men and women.

In the previous section I quoted what the King James Version calls "the foolishness of preaching" (1 Cor. 1:21), and since that is Paul's own phrase, we can see it as proof that Paul was himself aware of how foolish the proclamation of the Christian message is if considered only from a human point

4. John Calvin, *The Epistles of Paul the Apostle to the Romans and to the Thessalonians,* trans. Ross MacKenzie (Grand Rapids: Wm. B. Eerdmans, 1973), p. 27.

of view. Some years ago I had the task of talking about "The Foolishness of Preaching" as one message of seven in a weekend conference on reformed theology. My address came after a break for lunch in the middle of what was a very long Saturday, and I began by saying that if there was anything more foolish than the foolishness of preaching, it was preaching about the foolishness of preaching after lunch on a day during which the listeners had already heard a number of other very distinguished preachers. It was a way of capturing what every preacher feels at one time or another as he rises to proclaim a message that to the natural mind is utter folly and that is as incapable of doing good in the hearers as preaching a message of moral reformation to the corpses in a cemetery—*unless* God works.

But that is just the point! God does work through the preaching of this gospel—not preaching for its own sake, but the faithful proclamation of God's work of salvation for sinful men and women in Jesus Christ.

Let me say this another way since it is so important. We read in the first chapter of Acts that when the Lord Jesus Christ dispatched his disciples to the world with his gospel, he told them: ". . . you will receive power when the Holy Spirit comes on you; and you will be my witnesses in Jerusalem, and in all Judea and Samaria, and to the ends of the earth" (v. 8). Earlier they had been asking about the kingdom of God, no doubt thinking of an earthly, political kingdom, which they highly valued and hoped for. But Jesus' reply pointed them to something far greater. His was a spiritual kingdom—not spiritual in the sense of being less than real, but a kingdom to be established in power by the very Spirit of God—and they were to be witnesses for him. Moreover, as they witnessed, the Holy Spirit, which was to come upon them, would bless their proclamation and lead many to faith.

And so it happened. Three thousand believed at Pentecost. Thousands more believed on other occasions.

So also today. The world does not understand this divine working, but it is nevertheless true that the most important thing happening in the world at any given time is the preaching of the gospel. For there the Spirit of God is at work. There men and women are delivered from the bondage of sin and set free spiritually. Lives are transformed—and it is all by God's power. As D. Martyn Lloyd-Jones says, "The thing to grasp is that the apostle is saying that he is not ashamed of the gospel, because it is of God's mighty working. It is God himself doing this thing—not simply telling us about it: doing it, and doing it in this way, through the gospel."[5]

A Gospel for Everyone

The fifth reason why Paul was not ashamed of this gospel is that it is a gospel for everyone—"everyone who believes." It is "first for the Jew" and then also "for the Gentile."

5. Lloyd-Jones, *Romans: An Exposition of Chapter 1*, p. 291.

Paul's phrase "first for the Jew, then for the Gentile" has led readers to think that he was saying something like "to the Jew above the Gentile" or "to the Jew simply because he is a Jew and therefore of greater importance than other people." But, of course, this is not what Paul intends. In this text Paul means exactly the same thing Jesus meant when he told the woman of Samaria that "salvation is from the Jews" (John 4:22). Both were speaking chronologically. Both meant that in the systematic disclosure of the gospel the Jews had occupied a first and important place. This was because, as Paul says later in Romans, theirs was "the adoption as sons; theirs the divine glory, the covenants, the receiving of the law, the temple worship and the promises. Theirs are the patriarchs, and from them is traced the human ancestry of Jesus Christ . . ." (Rom. 9:3–5). No one can fully understand the gospel if he or she neglects this historical preparation for it.

But this does not mean that Paul is setting the Jew above the Gentile in this text or, as some would desire by contrast, that he is setting the Gentile above the Jew. On the contrary, Paul's point is that the gospel is for Gentile and Jew alike. It is for everybody.

Why? Because it is the power of God, and God is no respecter of persons. If the gospel were of human power only, it would be limited by human interests and abilities. It would be for some and not others. It would be for the strong but not for the weak, or the weak but not for the strong. It would be for the intelligent but not the foolish, or the foolish but not the wise. It would be for the noble or the well-bred or the sensitive or the poor or the rich or whatever, to the exclusion of those who do not fit the categories. But this is not the way it is. The gospel is for everyone. John wrote, "For God so loved the world that he gave his one and only Son, that *whoever* believes in him shall not perish but have eternal life" (John 3:16, italics mine). At Pentecost Peter declared, "*Everyone* who calls on the name of the Lord will be saved" (Acts 2:21; cf. Joel 2:32). Indeed, the Bible ends on this note: "The Spirit and the bride say, 'Come!' And let him who hears say, 'Come!' *Whoever* is thirsty, let him come; and *whoever* wishes, let him take of the free gift of the water of life" (Rev. 22:17). (I have added italics to these passages to emphasize this important point.)

How can one be ashamed of a gospel which offers hope to the vilest, most desperate of men, as well as to the most respectable person? How can we be ashamed of anything so gloriously universal.

Salvation Revealed to Sinners

The sixth reason why Paul was not ashamed of the gospel is that God has revealed this way of salvation to us. The gospel would be wonderful even if God had not revealed it. But, of course, if he had not revealed it, we would not know of it and would be living with the same dreary outlook on life as the unsaved. But the gospel *is* revealed. Now we not only know about the Good News but are also enabled to proclaim God's revelation.

And there is this, too: When Paul says that the gospel of God "is revealed," he is saying that it is only by revelation that we can know it. It is not something we could ever have figured out for ourselves. How could we have invented such a thing? When human beings invent religion they either invent something that makes them self-righteous, imagining that they can save themselves by their own good works or wisdom—or they invent something that excuses their behavior so they can commit the evil they desire. In other words, they become either legalists or antinomians. The gospel produces neither. It does not produce legalists, because salvation is by the accomplishment of Christ, not the accomplishments of human beings.

Christians must always sing: "Nothing in my hand I bring, / Simply to thy cross I cling." But at the same time, simply because they have been saved by the Lord Jesus Christ and have his Spirit within them, Christians inevitably strive for and actually achieve a level of practical righteousness of which the world cannot even dream.

A Righteousness from God

The seventh reason why Paul was not ashamed of the gospel is the one we considered most fully in the previous chapter, namely, that it concerns a righteousness from God, which is what we need. In ourselves we are not the least bit righteous. On the contrary, we are corrupted by sin and are in rebellion against God. To be saved from wrath we need a righteousness that is of God's own nature, a righteousness that comes from God and fully satisfies God's demands. This is what we have! It is why Paul can begin his exposition of the Good News in chapter 3 by declaring, "But now a righteousness from God, apart from law, has been made known, to which the Law and the Prophets testify" (v. 21). (As previously mentioned, this verse is a repetition of the thesis presented first in Romans 1:17.)

By Faith from First to Last

The eighth and final reason why the apostle Paul was not ashamed of the gospel is that the means by which this glorious gift becomes ours is faith, which means that salvation is accessible to "everyone who believes."

What does Paul mean when he writes, *ek pisteōs eis pistin* (literally, "from faith to faith")? Does he mean, as the New International Version seems to imply, "by faith entirely" (that is, "by faith from first to last")? Does he mean "from the faith of the Old Testament to the faith of the New Testament" or, which may be almost the same thing, "from the faith of the Jew to the faith of the Gentile"? Does he mean "from weak faith to stronger faith," the view apparently of John Calvin?[6] In my opinion, the quotation from Habakkuk throws light on how the words *ek pisteōs* are to be taken. They mean "by

6. Calvin, *The Epistles of Paul the Apostle*, p. 28.

faith"; that is, they concern "a righteousness that is by faith." If this is so, if this is how the first "faith" should be taken, then, the meaning of the phrase is that the righteousness that is by faith (the first "faith") is revealed to the perceiving faith of the believer (the second "faith").[7] This means that the gospel is revealed to you and is for you—if you will have it.

7. This is the view of F. Godet, *Commentary on St. Paul's Epistle to the Romans*, trans. A. Cusin (Edinburgh: T. & T. Clark, n.d.), vol. 1, pp. 160, 161; Haldane, *op. cit.*, p. 49; and Lloyd-Jones, *op. cit.*, pp. 307, 308. Haldane defines it as "the righteousness . . which is received by faith, is revealed to faith, or in order to be believed."

13

Martin Luther's Text

Romans 1:17

For in the gospel a righteousness from God is revealed, a righteousness that is by faith from first to last, just as it is written: "The righteous will live by faith."

In the year 1920 an English preacher by the name of Frank W. Boreham published a book of sermons on great Bible texts, in each case linking his text to the spiritual history of a great Christian man or woman. He called his book *Texts That Made History*.[1] There was David Livingstone's text: Matthew 28:20 ("Surely I will be with you always, to the very end of the age"). There was John Wesley's text: Zechariah 3:2 ("Is not this man a burning stick snatched from the fire?"). There were twenty-three sermons in this book, and Boreham published four more similar books in his lifetime.

Of all the texts that are associated with the lives of great Christians, none is so clearly one man's text or so obviously a driving, molding force in that man's life as Roman 1:17. And, of course, the man whose text it was is Martin Luther.

1. F. W. Boreham, *A Bunch of Everlastings or Texts That Made History* (Philadelphia: The Judson Press, 1952). (Original edition 1920.)

119

I propose that we study Romans 1:17 from the standpoint of Luther's life. Already we have seen that Romans 1:16–17 are the theme verses of this important Bible book. We have studied them from two perspectives. The first study focused on the chief idea: that there is a righteousness from God, which God freely offers human beings and which alone is the basis of their justification before him. It is received by faith. The second study worked through these verses in detail, showing eight reasons why Paul could say (and all true believers today can continue to say) that they are not ashamed of God's gospel. In this study we want to see the outworking of that gospel in the life of just one man, Martin Luther.

In the Convent at Erfurt

Martin Luther began his academic life by studying law, which was his father's desire for him. But although he excelled in his studies and gave every promise of becoming successful in his profession, Luther was troubled in soul and greatly agitated at the thought that one day he would have to meet God and give an account before him. In his boyhood days he had looked at the frowning face of Jesus in the stained-glass window of the parish church at Mansfeld and had trembled. When friends died, as during his college days two of his closest friends did, Luther trembled more. One day he would die—he knew not when—and he knew that Jesus would judge him.

On August 17, 1505, Luther suddenly left the university and entered the monastery of the Augustinian hermits at Erfurt. He was twenty-one years old, and he entered the convent, as he later said, not to study theology but to save his soul.

In those days in the monastic orders there were ways by which the seeking soul was directed to find God, and Luther, with the determination and force that characterized his entire life, gave himself rigorously to the Augustinian plan. He fasted and prayed. He devoted himself to menial tasks. Above all he adhered to the sacrament of penance, confessing even the most trivial sins, for hours on end, until his superiors wearied of his exercise and ordered him to cease confession until he had committed some sin worth confessing. Luther's piety gained him a reputation of being the most exemplary of monks. Later he wrote to the Duke of Saxony:

> I was indeed a pious monk and followed the rules of my order more strictly than I can express. If ever a monk could obtain heaven by his monkish works, I should certainly have been entitled to it. Of this all the friars who have known me can testify. If it had continued much longer, I should have carried my mortification even to death, by means of my watchings, prayers, reading and other labors.[2]

2. J. H. Merle D'Aubigné, *The Life and Times of Martin Luther*, trans. H. White (Chicago: Moody Press, 1958), p. 31.

Still, Luther found no peace through these exercises.

The monkish wisdom of the day instructed him to satisfy God's demand for righteousness by doing good works. "But what works?" thought Luther. "What works can come from a heart like mine? How can I stand before the holiness of my Judge with works polluted in their very source?"[3]

In Luther's agony of soul, God sent him a wise spiritual father by the name of John Staupitz, the vicar-general of the congregation. Staupitz tried to uncover Luther's difficulties. "Why are you so sad, brother Martin?" Staupitz asked one day.

"I do not know what will become of me," replied Luther with a deep sigh.

"More than a thousand times have I sworn to our holy God to live piously, and I have never kept my vows," said Staupitz. "Now I swear no longer, for I know that I cannot keep my solemn promises. If God will not be merciful towards me for the love of Christ and grant me a happy departure when I must quit this world, I shall never with the aid of all my vows and all my good works stand before him. I must perish."

The thought of divine justice terrified Luther, and he opened up his fears to the vicar-general.

Staupitz knew where he himself had found peace and pointed it out to the young man: "Why do you torment yourself with all these speculations and these high thoughts? . . . Look at the wounds of Jesus Christ, to the blood that he has shed for you; it is there that the grace of God will appear to you. Instead of torturing yourself on account of your sins, throw yourself into the Redeemer's arms. Trust in him—in the righteousness of his life—in the atonement of his death. Do not shrink back. God is not angry with you; it is you who are angry with God. Listen to the Son of God."[4]

But how could Luther do that? Where could he hear the Son of God speak to him as Staupitz said he would? "In the Bible," said the vicar-general. It was thus that Luther, who had only first seen a Bible in his college days shortly before entering the cloister, began to study Scripture.

He studied Romans, and as he pondered over the words of our text the truth began to dawn on him. The righteousness we need in order to stand before the holy God is not a righteousness we can attain. In fact, it is not human righteousness at all. It is divine righteousness, and it becomes ours as a result of God's free giving. Our part is merely to receive it by faith and to live by faith in God's promise. Guided by this new light, Luther began to compare Scripture with Scripture, and as he did he found that the passages of the Bible that formerly alarmed him now brought comfort.

In his sermon on Luther's text, Boreham describes a famous painting that represents Luther at this stage of his pilgrimage. The setting is early morning in the convent library at Erfurt, and the artist shows Luther as a

3. Ibid., p. 32.
4. Ibid., pp. 37, 38.

young monk in his early twenties, poring over a copy of the Bible from which a bit of broken chain is hanging. The dawn is stealing through the lattice, illuminating both the open Bible and the face of its eager reader. On the page the young monk is so carefully studying are the words: "The just shall live by faith."[5]

The Road to Rome

In 1510, five years after he had become a monk and two years after he had begun to teach the Bible at the new University of Wittenberg, Luther was sent by his order to Rome.[6]

On the way, while being entertained at the Benedictine monastery at Bologna, Luther fell dangerously ill and relapsed into the gloomy dejection over spiritual matters that was so natural to him. "To die thus, far from Germany, in a foreign land—what a sad fate!" D'Aubigné wrote, ". . . the distress of mind that he had felt at Erfurt returned with renewed force. The sense of his sinfulness troubled him; the prospect of God's judgment filled him once more with dread. But at the very moment that these terrors had reached their highest pitch, the words of St. Paul, 'The just shall live by faith,' recurred forcibly to his memory and enlightened his soul like a ray from heaven."[7] Luther was learning to live by faith, which was what the text was teaching. Comforted and eventually restored to health, he resumed his journey across the hot Italian plains to Rome.

"Thou Holy Rome, Thrice Holy"

Luther had been sent to Rome on church business. But, in spite of this, he approached the ancient imperial city as a pilgrim. When he first caught sight of Rome on his way south he raised his hands in ecstasy, exclaiming, "I greet thee, thou holy Rome, thrice holy from the blood of the martyrs." When he arrived, he began his rounds of the relics, shrines, and churches. He listened to the superstitious tales that were told him. At one chapel, when told of the benefits of saying Mass there, he thought that he could almost wish his parents were dead, because he could then have assured them against purgatory by his actions.[8]

Yet Rome was not the center of light and piety Luther had imagined. At this time, the Mass—at which the body and blood of Jesus were thought to be offered up by the priests as a sacrifice for sins—was the center of Luther's devotion, and he often said Mass at Rome. Luther performed the

5. Boreham, *A Bunch of Everlastings*, p. 19.
6. Some historians place this journey in 1511 or 1512.
7. D'Aubigné, *The Life and Times of Martin Luther*, p. 50.
8. Thomas M. Lindsay, *A History of the Reformation*, vol. 1, *The Reformation in Germany from Its Beginnings to the Religious Peace of Augsburg* (Edinburgh: T. & T. Clark, 1963), p. 207. (Original edition 1906.)

ceremony with the solemnity and dignity it seemed to him to require. But not the Roman priests! They laughed at the simplicity of the rustic German monk. Once, while he was repeating one Mass, the priests at an adjoining altar rushed through seven of them, calling out in Latin to Luther, "Quick, quick, send our Lady back her Son." On another occasion, Luther had only reached the gospel portion of the Mass when the priest administering beside him terminated his. "*Passa, passa,*" he cried to Luther. "Have done with it at once."

Luther was invited to meetings of distinguished ecclesiastics. There the priests often ridiculed and mocked Christian rites. Laughing and with apparent pride, they told how, when they were standing at the altar repeating the words that were to transform the bread and wine into the body and blood of the Lord, they said instead (no doubt with solemn intonation), "*Panis es, et panis manebis; vinum es, et vinum manebis*" ("Bread you are, and bread you will remain; wine you are, and wine you will remain"). Luther could hardly believe his ears. Later he wrote, "No one can imagine what sins and infamous actions are committed in Rome; they must be seen and heard to be believed. Thus, they are in the habit of saying, 'If there is a Hell, Rome is built over it; it is an abyss whence issues every kind of sin.'" He concluded, "The nearer we approach Rome, the greater number of bad Christians we meet with."[9]

Then there occurred the famous incident told many years later by Luther's son, Dr. Paul Luther, and preserved in a manuscript in the library of Rudolfstadt. In the Church of St. John Lateran in Rome there is a set of medieval stone stairs said to have originally been the stairs leading up to Pilate's house in Jerusalem, once trod upon by the Lord. For this reason they were called the *Scala Sancta* or "Holy Stairs." It was the custom for pilgrims, like Luther, to ascend these steps on their knees, praying as they went. At certain intervals there were stains said to have been caused by the bleeding wounds of Christ. The worshiper would bend over and kiss these steps, praying a long time before ascending painfully to the next ones. Remission of years of punishment in purgatory was promised to all who would perform this pious exercise.

Luther began as the others had. But, as he ascended the staircase, the words of our text came forcefully to his mind: "The just shall live by faith."

They seemed to echo over and over again, growing louder with each repetition: "The just shall live by faith," "The just shall live by faith." But Luther was not living by faith. He was living by fear. The old superstitious doctrines and the new biblical theology wrestled within him.

"By fear," said Luther.

"*By faith!*" said St. Paul.

"By fear," said the scholastic fathers of medieval Catholicism.

"*By faith!*" said the Scriptures.

9. D'Aubigné, *The Life and Times of Martin Luther*, pp. 52, 53.

"By fear," said those who agonized beside him on the staircase.

"*By faith!*" said God the Father.

At last Luther rose in amazement from the steps up which he had been dragging himself and shuddered at his superstition and folly. Now he realized that God had saved him by the righteousness of Christ, received by faith; he was to exercise that faith, receive that righteousness, and live by trusting God. He had not been doing it. Slowly he turned on Pilate's staircase and returned to the bottom. He went back to Wittenberg, and in time, as Paul Luther said, "He took 'The just shall live by faith' as the foundation of all his doctrine."[10]

This was the real beginning of the Reformation, for the reformation of Luther necessarily preceded the reformation of Christendom. The later began on October 31, 1517, with the posting of his "Ninety-Five Theses" on the door of the Castle Church at Wittenberg.

J. H. Merle D'Aubigné, the great nineteenth-century historian of the Reformation, wrote:

> This powerful text had a mysterious influence on the life of Luther. It was a creative sentence both for the reformer and for the Reformation. It was in these words God then said, "Let there be light! and there was light." . . . When Luther rose from his knees on Pilate's Staircase, in agitation and amazement at those words which Paul had addressed fifteen centuries before to the inhabitants of that same metropolis—Truth, till then a melancholy captive, fettered in the church, rose also to fall no more.[11]

"Here I Stand"

When Luther rose from his knees on the steps of the *Scala Sancta*, the high point of his long career—his refusal to recant his faith before the imperial diet at Worms—was still eleven years away. But Luther was already prepared for this challenge. He would be ready to defend his position, because he now saw that a man or woman is not enabled to stand before God by his or her own accomplishments, however devout, still less by the pronouncements of ecclesiastical councils or popes, however vigorously enforced, but by the grace and power of Almighty God alone. And if a person can stand before God by grace, he can certainly stand before men.

Luther was summoned before the diet by the newly elected emperor, Charles V. But it was really the Roman See that had summoned him, and the champions of Rome were present to secure his condemnation. Upon his arrival at the town hall assembly room at four o'clock on the afternoon of April 17, Luther was asked to acknowledge as his writings a large stack of books that had been gathered and placed in the room. He was also asked

10. Boreham, *A Bunch of Everlastings*, p. 20.
11. D'Aubigné, *The Life and Times of Martin Luther*, p. 55.

whether he would retract their contents, which called for reform of abuses rampant in the church, asserted the right of the individual Christian to be emancipated from priestly bondage, and reaffirmed the fundamental doctrine of justification by faith.

Luther asked that the titles might be read out. Then he responded, "Most gracious emperor! Gracious princes and lords! His imperial majesty has asked me two questions. As to the first, I acknowledge as mine the books that have just been named. I cannot deny them. As to the second, seeing that it is a question which concerns faith and the salvation of souls, and in which the Word of God, the greatest and most precious treasure either in heaven or earth, is interested, I should act imprudently were I to reply without reflection. . . . For this reason I entreat your imperial majesty, with all humility, to allow me time, that I may answer without offending against the Word of God."

It was a proper request in so grave a matter. Besides, by taking reasonable time to reflect on his answer, Luther would give stronger proof of the firmness of his stand when he made it. There was debate concerning this request, but at last Luther was given twenty-four hours to consider his response.

When he appeared the next day, the demand was the same: "Will you defend your books as a whole, or are you ready to disavow some of them?"

Luther replied by making distinctions between his writings, trying to draw the council into debate and thus have an opportunity to present the true gospel. Some of his books treated the Christian faith in language acceptable to all men. To repudiate these would be a denial of Jesus Christ. A second category attacked the errors and tyranny of the papacy. To deny these would lend additional strength to this tyranny, and thus be a sin against the German people. A third class of books concerned individuals and their teachings. Here Luther confessed that he may have spoken harshly or unwisely. But if so, it was necessary for his adversaries to bear witness of the evil done. Luther said he would be the first to throw his books into the fire if it could be proved that he had erred in these or any others of his writings.

"But you have not answered the question put to you," said the moderator. "Will you, or will you not, retract?"

Upon this, Luther replied without hesitation: "Since your most serene majesty and your high mightiness require from me a clear, simple, and precise answer, I will give you one, and it is this: I cannot submit my faith either to the pope or to the councils, because it is clear to me as the day that they have frequently erred and contradicted each other. Unless therefore I am convinced by the testimony of Scripture, or by the clearest reasoning— unless I am persuaded by means of the passages I have quoted—and unless they thus render my conscience bound by the Word of God, I cannot and I will not retract, for it is unsafe for a Christian to speak against his conscience."

Then looking around at those who held his life in their hands, Luther said: "Here I stand. I can do no other. May God help me. Amen." Thus did the German monk utter the words that still thrill our hearts after four and a half centuries.[12]

The Master of All Doctrines

Later in life Luther was to write many things about the doctrine of justification by faith, which he had learned from Romans 1:17. He would call it "the chief article from which all our other doctrines have flowed." He called it "the master and prince, the lord, the ruler and the judge over all kinds of doctrines." He said, "If the article of justification is lost, all Christian doctrine is lost at the same time." He argued, "It alone begets, nourishes, builds, preserves, and defends the church of God, and without it the church of God cannot exist for one hour."[13]

What a heritage! What a rebuke against the weak state of present-day Christianity!

If justification by faith is the doctrine by which the church stands or falls, our contemporary declines are no doubt due to our failure to understand, appreciate, and live by this doctrine. The church of our day does not stand tall before the world. It bows to it. Christians are not fearless before ridicule. We flee from it. Is the reason not that we have never truly learned to stand before God in his righteousness? Is it not because we have never learned the truth: "If God is for us, who can be against us?" (Rom. 8:31b)? The church will never be strong unless it is united around faithful men and women who firmly hold this conviction.

12. Luther's words are quoted from D'Aubigné, *The Life and Times of Martin Luther*, pp. 423–434.

13. Martin Luther, *What Luther Says: An Anthology*, compiled by Ewald M. Plass, vol. 2, *Glory—Prayer* (St. Louis: Concordia Publishing House, 1959), pp. 702–704.

PART THREE

The Race in Ruin

14

The Angry God

Romans 1:18

The wrath of God is being revealed from heaven against all the godlessness and wickedness of men who suppress the truth by their wickedness.

Today's preaching is deficient at many points. But there is no point at which it is more evidently inadequate and even explicitly contrary to the teachings of the New Testament than in its neglect of "the wrath of God." God's wrath is a dominant Bible teaching and the point in Romans at which Paul begins his formal exposition of the gospel. Yet, to judge from most contemporary forms of Christianity, the wrath of God is either an unimportant doctrine, which is an embarrassment, or an entirely wrong notion, which any enlightened Christian should abandon.

Weakness of Contemporary Preaching

Where do most people begin when making a presentation of Christian truth, assuming that they even speak of it to others? Where does most of today's Christian "preaching" begin?

Many begin with what is often termed "a felt need," a lack or a longing that the listener will acknowledge. The need may involve feelings of inadequacy; a recognition of problems in the individual's personal relationships or work or aspirations; moods; fears; or simply bad habits. The basic issue may be loneliness, or it may be uncontrollable desires. According to this theory, preaching should begin with felt needs, because this alone establishes a point of contact with a listener and wins a hearing. But does it? Oh, it may establish a contact between the teacher and the listener. But this is not the same thing as establishing contact between the listener and God, which is what preaching is about. Nor is it even necessarily a contact between the listener and the truth, since felt needs are often anything but our real needs; rather, they can actually be a means of suppressing them.

Here is the way Paul speaks of a felt need in another letter: "For the time will come when men will not put up with sound doctrine. Instead, to suit their own desires, they will gather around them a great number of teachers to say what their itching ears want to hear" (2 Tim. 4:3). "What their itching ears want to hear" is a classic example of a felt need. In this passage the apostle warns Timothy not to cater to it. Obviously he himself did not structure the presentation of his gospel around such "needs."

Another way we present the gospel today is by promises. We offer them like a carrot, a reward to be given if only the listener accepts Jesus. Through this approach, becoming a Christian is basically presented as a means of getting something. Sometimes this is propounded in a frightfully unbiblical way, so that what emerges is a "prosperity gospel" in which God is supposed to be obliged to grant wealth, health, and success to the believer.

We also commonly offer the gospel by the route of personal experience, stressing what Jesus has done for us and commending it to the other person for that reason.

The point I am making is that Paul does not do this in Romans, and in this matter he rebukes us profitably. D. Martyn Lloyd-Jones puts it like this:

> Why is he [Paul] ready to preach the gospel in Rome or anywhere else? He does not say it is because he knows that many of them [the Romans] are living defeated lives and that he has got something to tell them that will give them victory. He does not say to them, "I want to come and preach the gospel to you in Rome because I have had a marvelous experience and I want to tell you about it, in order that you may have the same experience—because you can if you want it; it is there for you."
>
> This is not what Paul does. . . . There is no mention here of any experience. He is not talking in terms of their happiness or some particular state of mind, or something that might appeal to them, as certain possibilities do—but this staggering, amazing thing, the wrath of God! And he puts it first; it is the thing he says at once.[1]

---

1. D. M. Lloyd-Jones, *Romans: An Exposition of Chapter 1, The Gospel of God* (Grand Rapids: Zondervan, 1985), p. 325.

The reason, of course, is that Paul was God-centered, rather than man-centered, and he was concerned with that central focus. Most of us are weak, fuzzy, or wrong at this point. Paul knew that what matters in the final analysis is not whether we feel good or have our felt needs met or receive a meaningful experience. What matters is whether we come into a right relationship with God. And to have that happen we need to begin with the truth that we are not in a right relationship to him. On the contrary, we are under God's wrath and are in danger of everlasting condemnation at his hands.

Wrath: A Biblical Idea

There is a problem at this point, of course, and the problem is that most people think in human categories rather than in the terms of Scripture. When we do that, "wrath" inevitably suggests something like capricious human anger or malice. God's wrath is not the same thing as human anger, of course. But because we fail to appreciate this fact, we are uneasy with the very idea of God's wrath and think that it is somehow unworthy of God's character. So we steer away from the issue.

The biblical writers had no such reticence. They spoke of God's wrath frequently, obviously viewing it as one of God's great "perfections"—alongside his other attributes. Says J. I. Packer, "One of the most striking things about the Bible is the vigor with which both Testaments emphasize the reality and terror of God's wrath."[2] Arthur W. Pink wrote, "A study of the concordance will show that there are more references in Scripture to the anger, fury, and wrath of God than there are to His love and tenderness."[3]

In the Old Testament more than twenty words are used to refer to God's wrath. (Other, very different words relate to human anger.) There are nearly six hundred important passages on the subject. These passages are not isolated or unrelated, as if they had been added to the Old Testament at some later date by a particularly gloomy redactor. They are basic and are integrated with the most important themes and events of Scripture.

The earliest mentions of the wrath of God are in connection with the giving of the law at Sinai. The first occurs just two chapters after the account of the giving of the Ten Commandments: "[The Lord said,] 'Do not take advantage of a widow or an orphan. If you do and they cry out to me, I will certainly hear their cry. My anger [wrath] will be aroused, and I will kill you with the sword; your wives will become widows and your children fatherless'" (Exod. 22:22–24).

Ten chapters later in Exodus, in a very important passage about the sin of Israel in making and worshiping the golden calf (a passage to which we

2. J. I. Packer, *Knowing God* (Downers Grove, Ill.: InterVarsity Press, 1973), pp. 134, 135.
3. Arthur W. Pink, *The Attributes of God* (Grand Rapids: Baker Book House, 1975), p. 82.

will return), God and Moses discuss wrath. God says, "Now leave me alone so that my anger [wrath] may burn against them and that I may destroy them. . . ." But Moses pleads, "Why should your anger burn against your people, whom you brought out of Egypt with great power and a mighty hand? Why should the Egyptians say, 'It was with evil intent that he brought them out, to kill them in the mountains and to wipe them off the face of the earth'? Turn from your fierce anger; relent and do not bring disaster on your people" (Exod. 32:10–12).

In this early and formative passage, Moses does not plead with God on the grounds of some supposed innocence of the people—they were not innocent, and Moses knew it—nor with the fantasy that wrath is somehow unworthy of God's character. Rather Moses appeals only on the grounds that God's judgment would be misunderstood and that his name would be dishonored by the heathen.

There are two main words for wrath in the New Testament. One is *thymos*, from a root that means "to rush along fiercely," "to be in a heat of violence," or "to breathe violently." We can capture this idea by the phrase "a panting rage." The other word is *orgē* which means "to grow ripe for something." It portrays wrath as something that builds up over a long period of time, like water collecting behind a great dam. In his study of *The Apostolic Preaching of the Cross*, Leon Morris notes that apart from the Book of Revelation, which describes the final outpouring of God's wrath in all its unleashed fury, *thumos* is used only once of God's anger. The word used in every other passage is *orgē*. Morris observes, "The biblical writers habitually use for the divine wrath a word which denotes not so much a sudden flaring up of passion which is soon over, as a strong and settled opposition to all that is evil arising out of God's very nature."[4]

John Murray describes wrath in precisely this way when he writes in his classic definition: "Wrath is the holy revulsion of God's being against that which is the contradiction of his holiness."[5]

We find this understanding of the wrath of God in Romans. In this letter Paul refers to wrath ten times.[6] But in each instance the word he uses is *orgē*, and his point is not that God is suddenly flailing out in petulant anger against something that has offended him momentarily, but rather that God's firm, fearsome hatred of all wickedness is building up and will one day result in the eternal condemnation of all who are not justified by Christ's righteousness. Romans 1:17 says, on the basis of Habakkuk 2:4, that "the righteous will live by faith." But those who do *not* live by faith will not live; they will perish. Thus, in Romans 2:5 we find Paul writing, "Because of

4. Leon Morris, *The Apostolic Preaching of the Cross* (Grand Rapids: Wm. B. Eerdmans, 1955), pp. 162, 163.

5. John Murray, *The Epistle to the Romans* (Grand Rapids: Wm. B. Eerdmans, 1968), p. 35.

6. In 1:18; 2:5, 8; 3:5; 4:15; 5:9; 9:22; 12:19, and 13:4, 5.

your stubbornness and your unrepentant heart, you are storing up wrath against yourself for the day of God's wrath, when his righteous judgment will be revealed."

Wrath Revealed

But it is not only a matter of God's wrath being "stored up" for a final great outpouring at the last day. There is also a present manifesting of this wrath, which is what Paul seems to be speaking of in our text when he says, using the present rather than the future tense of the verb, "The wrath of God *is being revealed* from heaven against all the godlessness and wickedness of men who suppress the truth by their wickedness." How is this so? In what way is the wrath of God currently being made manifest?

Commentators on Romans suggest a number of observations at this point, listing ways in which God's wrath against sin seems to be disclosed. Charles Hodge speaks of three such manifestations: "the actual punishment of sin," "the inherent tendency of moral evil to produce misery," and "the voice of conscience."[7]

D. Martyn Lloyd-Jones lists "conscience," "disease and illness," "the state of creation," "the universality of death," "history," and (the matter he thinks Paul mainly had in view) "the cross" and "resurrection of Christ."[8]

Robert Haldane has a comprehensive statement:

The wrath of God . . . was revealed when the sentence of death was first pronounced, the earth cursed and man driven out of the earthly paradise, and afterward by such examples of punishment as those of the deluge and the destruction of the cities of the plain by fire from heaven, but especially by the reign of death throughout the world. It was proclaimed by the curse of the law on every transgression and was intimated in the institution of sacrifice and in all the services of the Mosaic dispensation. In the eighth chapter of this epistle the apostle calls the attention of believers to the fact that the whole creation has become subject to vanity and groaneth and travaileth together in pain. This same creation which declares that there is a God, and publishes his glory, also proves that he is the enemy of sin and the avenger of the crimes of men. . . . But above all, the wrath of God was revealed from heaven when the Son of God came down to manifest the divine character, and when that wrath was displayed in his sufferings and death in a manner more awful than by all the tokens God had before given of his displeasure against sin.[9]

7. Charles Hodge, *A Commentary on Romans* (Edinburgh and Carlisle, Pa.: The Banner of Truth Trust, 1972), p. 35. (Original edition 1935.)

8. Lloyd-Jones, *Romans: An Exposition of Chapter 1*, pp. 342–350.

9. Robert Haldane, *An Exposition of the Epistle to the Romans* (MacDill AFB: MacDonald Publishing, 1958), pp. 55, 56.

Each of these explanations of the present revelation of the wrath of God is quite accurate. But in my opinion Paul has something much more specific in view here, the matter that Charles Hodge alone mentions specifically: "the inherent tendency of moral evil to produce misery." This is what Paul goes on to develop in Romans 1. In verses 21 through 32 Paul speaks of a downward inclination of the race by which the world, having rejected God and therefore being judicially abandoned by God, is given up to evil. It is set on a course that leads to perversions and ends in a debasement in which people call good evil and evil good. Human depravity and the misery involved are the revelation of God's anger.

A number of years ago, Ralph L. Keiper was speaking to a loose-living California hippie about the claims of God on his life. The man was denying the existence of God and the truths of Christianity, but he was neither dull nor unperceptive. So Keiper directed him to Romans 1, which he described as an analysis of the hippie's condition. The man read it carefully and then replied, "I think I see what you're driving at. You are saying that I am the verifying data of the revelation."

That is exactly it! The present revelation of God's wrath, though limited in its scope, should be proof to us that we are indeed children of wrath and that we need to turn from our present evil path to the Savior.

Turning Aside God's Wrath

Here I return to that great Old Testament story mentioned earlier. Moses had been on the mountain for forty days, receiving the law. As the days stretched into weeks, the people waiting below grew restless and prevailed upon Moses' brother Aaron to make a substitute god for them. It was a golden calf. Knowing what was going on in the valley, God interrupted his giving of the law to tell Moses what the people were doing and to send him back down to them.

It was an ironic situation. God had just given the Ten Commandments. They had begun: "I am the LORD your God, who brought you out of Egypt, out of the land of slavery. You shall have no other gods before me. You shall not make for yourself an idol in the form of anything in heaven above or on the earth beneath or in the waters below. You shall not bow down to them or worship them; for I, the LORD your God, am a jealous God, punishing the children for the sin of the fathers to the third and fourth generation of those who hate me, but showing love to thousands who love me and keep my commandments" (Exod. 20:2–6). While God was giving these words, the people whom he had saved from slavery were doing precisely what he was prohibiting. Not only that, they were lying, coveting, dishonoring their parents, committing adultery, and no doubt also breaking all the other commandments.

God declared his intention to judge the people immediately and totally, and Moses interceded for them in the words referred to earlier (Exod. 32:11–12).

At last Moses started down the mountain to deal with the people. Even on a human level, quite apart from any thought of God's grace, sin must be judged. So Moses dealt with the sin as best he knew how. First he rebuked Aaron publicly. Then he called for any who still remained on the side of the Lord to separate themselves from the others and stand beside him. The tribe of Levi responded. At Moses' command they were sent into the camp to execute the leaders of the rebellion. Three thousand men were killed, approximately one-half of one percent of the six hundred thousand who had left Egypt at the Exodus (Exod. 32:28; cf. 12:37—with women and children counted, the number may have been more than two million). Moses also destroyed the golden calf. He ground it up, mixed it with water, and made the people drink it.

From a human standpoint, Moses had dealt with the sin. The leaders were punished. Aaron was rebuked. The allegiance of the people was at least temporarily reclaimed. But Moses stood in a special relationship to God, as Israel's representative, as well as to the people as their leader. And God still waited in wrath on the mountain. What was Moses to do?

For theologians sitting in an ivory-tower armchair, the idea of the wrath of God may seem to be no more than an interesting speculation. But Moses was no armchair theologian. He had been talking with God. He had heard his voice. He had receive his law. Not all the law had been given by this time, but Moses had received enough of it to know something of the horror of sin and of the uncompromising nature of God's righteousness. Had God not said, "You shall have no other gods before me"? Had he not promised to punish sin to the third and fourth generation of those who disobey him? Who was Moses to think that the judgment *he* had imposed would satisfy a God of such holiness?

Night passed, and the morning came when Moses was to ascend the mountain again. He had been thinking, and during the night a way that might possibly divert the wrath of God had come to him. He remembered the sacrifices of the Hebrew patriarchs and the newly instituted rites of the Passover. God had shown by such sacrifices that he was prepared to accept an innocent substitute in place of the just death of the sinner. God's wrath could sometimes fall on the substitute. Moses thought, *"Perhaps God would accept. . . ."*

When morning came, Moses ascended the mountain with great determination. Reaching the top, he began to speak to God. It must have been in great anguish, for the Hebrew text is uneven and Moses' second sentence breaks off without ending (indicated by a dash in the middle of Exod. 32:32). This is the strangled sob welling up from the heart of a man who is asking to be damned if his own judgment could mean the salvation of those he had come to love. The text reads: "So Moses went back to the LORD and said, 'Oh, what a great sin these people have committed! They have made themselves gods of gold. But now, please forgive their sin—but if not, then blot me out of the book you have written" (Exod. 32:31–32). Moses was offering to take the place of the people and accept judgment on their behalf.

On the preceding day, before Moses had come down from the mountain, God had said something that could have been a great temptation. If Moses would agree, God would destroy the people and start again to make a new Jewish nation from Moses (Exod. 32:10). Even then Moses had rejected the offer. But, after having been with his people and being reminded of his love for them, his answer, again negative, rises to even greater heights. God had said, "I will destroy the people and save you."

Now Moses replies, "Rather destroy me and save them."

Moses lived in the early years of God's revelation and at this point probably had a very limited understanding of God's plan. He did not know, as we know, that what he prayed for could not be. He had offered to go to hell for his people. But Moses could not save even himself, let alone Israel. He, too, was a sinner. He, too, needed a savior. He could not die for others.

But there is One who could. Thus, "But when the time had fully come, God sent his Son, born of a woman, born under law, to redeem those under law, that we might receive the full rights of sons" (Gal. 4:4–5). That person is Jesus, the Son of God. His death was for those who deserve God's wrath. And his death was fully adequate, because Jesus did not need to die for his own sins—he was sinless—and because, being God, his act was of infinite magnitude.

That is the message Paul will expound in this epistle. It is the Good News, the gospel. But the place to begin is not with your own good works, since you have none, but by knowing that you are an object of God's wrath and will perish in sin at last, unless you throw yourself upon the mercy of the One who died for sinners, even Jesus Christ.[10]

---

10. Material in this chapter sometimes closely parallels the chapter on "The Wrath of God" in James Montgomery Boice, *Foundations of the Christian Faith: A Comprehensive and Readable Theology* (Downers Grove, Ill.: InterVarsity Press, 1986), pp. 246–255.

15

Natural Revelation

Romans 1:18–20

The wrath of God is being revealed from heaven against all the godlessness and wickedness of men who suppress the truth by their wickedness, since what may be known about God is plain to them, because God has made it plain to them. For since the creation of the world God's invisible qualities—his eternal power and divine nature—have been clearly seen, being understood from what has been made, so that men are without excuse.

No one likes to talk about the wrath of God, particularly if it is thought of in relation to ourselves. But if we have to think about it, as our study of Romans 1:18–20 obviously forces us to do, we find ourselves reacting generally in one of two ways. Either (1) we argue that wrath is somehow unworthy of God, a blotch on his character, and therefore a mistaken notion that should be abandoned at once by all right-thinking people; or (2) we reply by denying that we merit God's wrath, that we do not deserve it.

The second reaction is the more serious of the two. So it is the one Paul tackles in the development of his argument for the need we all have of the Christian gospel.

Romans 1:18–20 contains three important concepts, which together explain why the wrath of God against men and women is justified. The first is *wrath* itself. It is being revealed from heaven against the ungodly, Paul says. The second is the *suppression* of the truth about God by human beings, a point picked up and developed more fully in verses 21–23. The third idea is God's prior *revelation* of himself to those very people who suppress the truth about him. These concepts need to be studied in inverse order, however. For when they are considered in that order—revelation, suppression, and wrath—they teach that God has given a revelation of himself in nature sufficient to lead any right-thinking man or woman to seek him out and worship him, but that, instead of doing this, people suppress this revelation. They deny it so they do not have to follow where it leads them. It is because of this willful and immoral suppression of the truth about God by human beings that the wrath of God comes upon them.

Revelation of God in Nature

There has been so much debate about what theologians call "natural revelation" that it is important to begin a discussion of this subject with some important definitions and distinctions.[1] First, a definition: natural revelation means what it sounds like, namely, the revelation of God in nature. It is sometimes called "general revelation," because it is available to everybody. Natural revelation is distinguished from "special revelation," which goes beyond it and is the kind of revelation we find in the life and ministry of Jesus Christ, the Bible, and the revelation of the Bible's meaning to the minds of those who read it by the Holy Spirit.

When Paul talks about a knowledge of God made plain to human beings, as he does in this text, it is the general or natural revelation, not a specific scriptural revelation, that he has in mind.

The second concept that needs to be defined here is "knowledge of God." This is necessary because we can use the words *know* or *knowledge* in different ways.

1. *Awareness.* To begin on the lowest level, when we say that we know something we can be saying only that we are aware of its existence. In this sense we can say that we know where somebody lives or that we know certain things are happening somewhere in the world. This is true knowledge, but it is not extensive knowledge. It is knowledge that affects us very little. It does not involve us personally.

2. *Knowing about.* Knowing about something goes a step further, because knowledge in this sense may be detailed, extensive, and important. This is the

---

1. One recent but classic battle over natural revelation occurred between two noted Swiss theologians: Karl Barth, who denied the validity of natural revelation, and Emil Brunner, who affirmed it.

kind of knowledge a physicist would have of physics or a doctor of medical facts. To come more to the point, a theologian can have knowledge about God, a theology by which he might be called a very learned man—and still not be saved.

3. *Experience.* The word *know* can also be used to refer to knowledge acquired by experience. To go back to the two previous categories, we could have this kind of knowledge of where a person lives if, for example, we had actually lived in his or her home ourselves. Again, a doctor could have knowledge like this if he were actually to experience the diseases he treats or undergo the operations he performs. Knowledge of a disease by having it is obviously quite different from merely having read of its causes and symptoms and how to treat the ailment.

4. *Personal.* The last kind of knowledge is the highest and most important level. It is what we would call personal knowledge, the kind of knowing we can only have of God, of ourselves, or of another human being. When the Bible speaks of knowing God in a saving way, this is what it has in mind. It involves the knowledge of ourselves in our sin and of God in his holiness and grace. It involves the knowledge of what he has done for us in Christ for our salvation and an actual coming to know and love God through knowing Jesus Christ. It involves head knowledge, but it also involves heart knowledge. It expresses itself in piety, worship, and devotion. It is what Jesus was speaking of when he prayed, "This is eternal life: that they may know you, the only true God, and Jesus Christ, whom you have sent" (John 17:3).

Some people grow impatient with definitions of this sort and wish that the teachers making them would just get on with explaining the Bible. But distinctions are necessary in this case, since they alone isolate the particular kind of knowledge of God available to men and women in nature for which God holds them accountable.

In the context of our text, this is not knowledge in the last of the four senses mentioned; if it were, all persons would be saved. Nor is it even (except in a very limited sense) knowledge about God or knowledge by experience. It is basically *awareness.* Nature reveals God is such a way that, even without the special revelation of God that we have in the Bible, all men and women are at least aware that God exists and that they should worship him. This awareness of God will not save them. But it is sufficient to condemn them if they fail to follow nature's leading, as they could and should do, and seek out the true God so revealed.

Eternal Power and Divine Nature

The apostle is precise here as he explains what the natural revelation involves. It consists of two elements: first, "God's eternal power" and, second, God's "divine nature" (v. 20). The second means quite simply that there *is* a God. In other words, people have no excuse for being atheists.

The first means that the God, whom they know to exist, is all-powerful. People know this by definition, since a god who is not all-powerful is not really God. We can express these two ideas philosophically by the term "Supreme Being." "Being" (with a capital "B") refers to God's existence. "Supreme" denotes his ultimate power. What Paul is saying is that nature contains ample and entirely convincing evidence of the existence of a Supreme Being. God exists, and we know it. That is his argument. Therefore, when people subsequently refuse to acknowledge and worship God (as we do), the problem is not in God or in a lack of evidence for his existence but in our own irrational and resolute determination not to know him.

I need to add several more important things at this point, and the first concerns the extensiveness of this nevertheless incomplete revelation. I have pointed out that the revelation of God in nature is the *limited* disclosure of God's existence and supreme power. There is no revelation of his mercy, holiness, grace, love, or the many other things necessary for us to learn if we are to know God savingly. Still, we are not to think of this limited revelation as minimal, as if somehow its limited quality alone can excuse us. According to the Bible, this natural revelation of God, though limited, is nevertheless extensive and overwhelming in its force.

In the Old Testament the great counterpart to Romans 1:18–20 is the first half of Psalm 19 (vv. 1–6). It speaks of the revelation of God in the heavens:

> The heavens declare the glory of God;
>   the skies proclaim the work of his hands.
> Day after day they pour forth speech;
>   night after night they display knowledge.
> There is no speech or language
>   where their voice is not heard.
> Their voice goes out into all the earth,
>   their words to the ends of the world.
>
> In the heavens he has pitched a tent for the sun,
>   which is like a bridegroom coming forth from his pavilion,
>   like a champion rejoicing to run his course.
> It rises at one end of the heavens
>   and makes its circuit to the other;
>   nothing is hidden from its heat.

In these verses it is the "glory" or majesty of God that is said to be revealed in nature. But the emphasis here is on the universal nature of the revelation rather than on its content. It is heard in every human "speech" and "language." It is known in "all the earth" and "to the ends of the world."

Another classic Old Testament passage about natural revelation is the interrogation of Job recorded in chapters 38 and 39 of that book. God is the interrogator, and his point is that Job is far too ignorant even to question God or presume to evaluate his ways. In the context of that negative argument—"See how little you know"—God unfolds an overwhelming list of evidences for his wisdom, power, and great glory, which Job (like all people everywhere) should know and before which he should marvel:

> "Where were you when I laid the earth's foundation?
>   Tell me, if you understand.
> Who marked off its dimensions? Surely you know!
>   Who stretched a measuring line across it?
> On what were its footings set,
>   or who laid its cornerstone—
> while the morning stars sang together
>   and all the angels shouted for joy?
>
> "Who shut up the sea behind doors
>   when it burst forth from the womb,
> when I made the clouds its garment
>   and wrapped it in thick darkness,
> when I fixed limits for it
>   and set its doors and bars in place,
> when I said, 'This far you may come and no farther;
>   here is where your proud waves halt'?"
>
>   Job 38:4–11

God's interrogation of Job goes on in that fashion for two chapters. Then, after Job responds by a confession of his own ignorance, God launches into the same type of questioning for one chapter more. These chapters stress that God is all-powerful and all-wise, and the evidence they present for these divine attributes is nature.

Kindness in Nature

There may be one other matter to be mentioned, though I must be careful not to claim too much for it here. When Paul and Barnabas came to Lystra in Lycaonia on their first missionary journey, the people wanted to worship them because they thought they were gods as a result of a miracle they did. Paul rebuked their error and began to teach them better, in one place speaking of God's revelation of himself in nature in these words: "God . . . made heaven and earth and sea and everything in them. In the past, he let all nations go their own way. Yet he has not left himself without testimony: He has shown kindness by giving you rain from heaven and crops in their seasons; he provides you with plenty of food and fills your hearts with joy" (Acts 14:15b–17).

If these words are to be taken at their face value—and why should we not take them that way?—they say that God has also revealed his *kindness* in nature. Theologians call this common grace. Instead of sending us all to hell at this instant, as he has every right to do, God takes care of us in a common, general way so that most of us have food to eat, clothes to wear, and places to live. True, the evidence for common grace is not unambiguous. There are bad things in this world, too: hurricanes, terrible diseases, and so on. But generally the world is a reasonably pleasant place. So it is not only God's glory, power, and wisdom that we see in nature, according to the Bible. We see God's goodness or kindness as well, and this attribute especially increases our guilt when we refuse to seek God so that we may thank and worship him.

Awareness Within

The second idea I need to add here is that God's revelation of himself in nature does not stop with the external evidence for his existence, power, wisdom, and kindness—the attributes I have mentioned—but it has what can be called an internal or subjective element as well. That is, not only has God given evidence for his existence; he has also given us the capacity to comprehend or receive it—though we refuse to do so. The text says, "What may be known about God is *plain to them*, because *God has made it plain to them*," and "God's invisible qualities—his eternal power and divine nature—have been *clearly* seen, being *understood* from what has been made" (vv. 19–20, italics mine).

Charles Hodge writes of these verses, "It is not of a mere external revelation of which the apostle is speaking, but of that evidence of the being and perfections of God which every man has in the constitution of his own nature, and in virtue of which he is competent to apprehend the manifestation of God in his works."[2]

John Calvin says that we are "blind" to God's revelation but "*not so blind* that we can plead ignorance without being convicted of perversity."[3]

Let me use an illustration. Suppose you are driving down the street and come to a sign that says, "Detour—Turn Left." But you ignore this and drive on. It happens that there is a police officer present, who stops you and begins to write out a ticket. What excuse might you have? You might argue that you didn't see the sign. But that would carry very little weight if the sign was well placed and in bright colors. Besides, it makes no difference. As long as you are driving the car, the responsibility for seeing the sign and obeying it is yours. What is more, you are accountable if, having ignored the

---

2. Charles Hodge, *A Commentary on Romans* (Edinburgh and Carlisle, Pa.: The Banner of Truth Trust, 1972), p. 36. (Original edition 1935.)

3. John Calvin, *The Epistles of Paul the Apostle to the Romans and to the Thessalonians*, trans. Ross MacKenzie (Grand Rapids: Wm. B. Eerdmans, 1973), p. 31.

sign, you recklessly race on and either harm yourself and your passengers or destroy property.

Paul's teaching fits this illustration. He is saying, first, that there is a sign. It is God's revelation of himself in nature. Second, you have "vision." Although blind to much, you can nevertheless see the revelation. Therefore, if you choose to ignore it, as we all do apart from the grace of God, the disaster that follows is your own fault. Your feelings of guilt are well founded.

Let me try this again. Paul is not saying that there is enough evidence about God in nature so that the scientist, who carefully probes nature's mysteries, can be aware of him. (Carl Sagan has done this as well as anybody, but he acknowledges no Supreme Being.) Paul is not saying that the sign is there but hidden, that we are only able to find it if we look carefully. He is saying that the sign is *plain*. It is a billboard. In fact, it is a world of billboards. No one, no matter how weak-minded or insignificant, can be excused for missing it.

There is enough evidence of God in a flower to lead a child as well as a scientist to worship him. There is sufficient evidence in a tree, a pebble, a grain of sand, a fingerprint, to make us glorify God and thank him. This is the way to true knowledge. But people will not do this. They reject the revelation, substitute nature itself or parts of nature for God, and thereby find their hearts increasingly darkened.

John Calvin gives this just conclusion: "But although we lack the natural ability to mount up unto the pure and clear knowledge of God, all excuse is cut off because the fault of dullness is within us. And, indeed, we are not allowed thus to pretend ignorance without our conscience itself always convicting us of both baseness and ingratitude."[4]

Suppressing the Truth

When Calvin speaks of baseness and ingratitude, he brings us to the second point of Paul's argument in this section of Romans, the point that justifies and leads to God's wrath. We have already been talking about this. It is human rejection of the revelation God has given.

Paul's description of what people have done in regard to natural revelation is in the phrase "who suppress the truth by their wickedness" (v. 18). In Greek the word translated "suppress" is *katechein*, which means "take," "hold," "hold fast," "hold back," "keep," "restrain," or "repress." In a positive sense the word can be used to mean holding to something that is good, as when Paul speaks of holding on to the word of life (cf. Phil. 2:16). In a negative sense it means wrongly to suppress something or hold it down. This is the way Paul is using it here. Thus, the newer translations of the Bible speak

4. John Calvin, *Institutes of the Christian Religion*, 2 vols., ed. John T. McNeill, trans. Ford Lewis Battles (Philadelphia: Westminster Press, 1960), pp. 68, 69.

in Romans 1:18 of those who "suppress the truth in unrighteousness" (NASB), "keep truth imprisoned in their wickedness" (Jerusalem Bible) or "stifle" truth (NEB). Why do we do this? It is because of our wickedness, because we prefer sin to that to which the revelation of God would take us.

This leads to the matter we are going to study in the next chapter, what R. C. Sproul has called "the psychology of atheism."[5] It leads to an explanation of why natural revelation by itself does not work, in the sense of actually bringing us to God.

But before we turn to that topic, I need to say that if, as Paul maintains, the revelation of God in nature is fully adequate to condemn people who do not allow it to bring them to worship and serve this true God, how much more terrible and awful is the case of the vast numbers of people, particularly in our country, who have not only the natural revelation to lead them to God but also have the Bible and the proclamation of its truths in virtually every town and hamlet of our land and (by means of radio and television) at almost any hour. "Without excuse"? The people of Rome were without excuse, and they had nothing but nature. No Bible! No churches! No preachers! What about us who have everything? If we reject what God tells us, we are a thousand times more guilty.

No excuse! "How shall we escape if we ignore such a great salvation?" (Heb. 2:3).[6]

5. R. C. Sproul, *If There Is a God, Why Are There Atheists? A Surprising Look at the Psychology of Atheism* (Minneapolis: Dimension Books, 1978). (Originally *The Psychology of Atheism*.)

6. Portions of this chapter are borrowed with changes from "Knowing God" and "The Unknown God" in James Montgomery Boice, *Foundations of the Christian Faith: A Comprehensive and Readable Theology* (Downers Grove, Ill.: InterVarsity Press, 1986), pp. 19–34.

16

The Psychology of Atheism

Romans 1:18-20

The wrath of God is being revealed from heaven against all the godlessness and wickedness of men who suppress the truth by their wickedness, since what may be known about God is plain to them, because God has made it plain to them. For since the creation of the world God's invisible qualities—his eternal power and divine nature—have been clearly seen, being understood from what has been made, so that men are without excuse.

In 1974 theologian R. C. Sproul produced a book from which I have drawn the title of this study: *The Psychology of Atheism.* Sproul's book (later reissued as *If There Is a God, Why Are There Atheists?*) is an attempt to understand why people reject God either philosophically, becoming philosophical atheists, or practically, becoming practical atheists. (Practical atheists may say that they believe in God, but they "act as if" God does not exist.) Sproul's answer is that atheism has nothing to do with man's supposed ignorance of God—since all people know God, according to Romans 1—but rather with mankind's dislike of him. People do not "know" God, because they do not *want* to know him.

145

Sproul writes:

The New Testament maintains that unbelief is generated not so much by intellectual causes as by moral and psychological ones. The problem is not that there is insufficient evidence to convince rational beings that there is a God, but that rational beings have a natural antipathy to the being of God. In a word, the nature of God (at least the Christian God) is *repugnant* to man and is not the focus of desire or wish projection. Man's desire is not that Yahweh exists, but that he doesn't.[1]

The Sovereign God

But why are people so determined to reject God? Up to this point we have looked at three great ideas in our study of Romans 1:18–20: (1) the *wrath* of God, which is directed against all the godlessness and wickedness of men; (2) the *suppression* by human beings of the truth about God revealed in nature; and (3) the prior *revelation* of God's eternal power and divine nature through what God has made. But we have seen that the historical sequence of these ideas is the reverse of the above listing. First, God has revealed himself. Second, people have rejected the truth thus revealed. Third, the wrath of God is released upon them because of this rejection.

Still, the question remains: Why do so-called rational beings react in what is clearly such an irrational manner? If the truth about God is as plainly understood as Romans 1:18–20 maintains it is, why should anyone suppress it? The answer, of course, is what I began to talk about in the previous chapter and am now to carry further in terms of Sproul's thesis. *Men and women reject God because they do not like him.* They may like a god of their own imagining, a god like themselves, and therefore say that they like God. But the truth is that they do not like the God who really is.

Paul's words for this universal dislike of God are "godlessness" and "wickedness" (v. 18). "Godlessness" means that people are opposed to God. They are not like God and do not like him. "Wickedness" refers to what people do because of this determined opposition. They reject the truth about God, thereby trying to force God away.

What is it that people do not like about God? The answer is, nearly everything. Let me show this by a look at some of the most important of God's attributes.

The first thing men and women dislike about God is his sovereignty, his most basic attribute. For if God is not sovereign, God is not God. Sovereignty refers to rule; in the case of God, it refers to the Being who is ruler over all. Sovereignty is what David was speaking about in his great prayer recorded in 1 Chronicles 29:10–13.

---

1. R. C. Sproul, *If There Is a God, Why Are There Atheists? A Surprising Look at the Psychology of Atheism* (Minneapolis: Dimension Books, 1978), pp. 56, 57. (Originally *The Psychology of Atheism.*)

Praise be to you, O LORD,
  God of our father Israel,
  from everlasting to everlasting.
Yours, O LORD, is the greatness and the power
  and the glory and the majesty and the splendor,
  for everything in heaven and earth is yours.
Yours, O LORD, is the kingdom;
  you are exalted as head over all.
Wealth and honor come from you;
  you are the ruler of all things.
In your hands are strength and power
  to exalt and give strength to all.
Now, our God, we give you thanks,
  and praise your glorious name.

God shows his sovereignty over the material order by creating it and ruling it according to his own fixed laws. Sometimes he shows his sovereignty by miracles. God shows his sovereignty over the human will and therefore also over human actions by controlling them. Thus, he hardens Pharaoh's heart so that Pharaoh refuses to let the people of Israel leave Egypt; and then God judges him. In a contrary way, God melts the hearts of some individuals and draws them to Jesus.

But why should the sovereignty of God be so objectionable to human beings? If we look at matters superficially, we might think that all people would quite naturally welcome God's sovereignty. "After all," we might argue, "what could be better than knowing that everything in the world is really under control in spite of appearances and that God is going to work all things out eventually?" But it is only when we look at externalities that we can think like that. When we peer below the surface we discover that we are all in rebellion against God because of our desire for autonomy.

This was Adam's problem. It was the root sin. God had told Adam that he was to be as free as any creature in the universe could be. Adam was to rule the world for God. Moreover, he was free to go where he wished and do as he wished. He could eat whatever he wished, with one condition: As a symbol of the fact that he was not autonomous, that he was still God's creature and owed his life, health, fortune, and ultimate allegiance to God, Adam was forbidden to eat of a tree that stood in the midst of the Garden of Eden. He could eat of all the trees north of that tree, all the trees east of that tree, all the trees south of that tree, all the trees west of that tree. But the fruit of that one tree was forbidden to him, upon penalty of death. "When you eat of it you will surely die," was God's warning.

Nothing could have been more irrational than for Adam to eat of that tree. God had never lied to him, so he could believe God. Moreover, Adam owed God utter and unquestioning obedience in this and every other matter. Besides, he had been warned that if he ate he would die. There was nothing to be gained from eating! There was everything to lose! Still, as Adam looked at the tree it was a great offense to him. The tree stood for a limitation on his personal desires. It represented something he was not allowed to do. So Adam said in effect, "That tree is an offense to my autonomy. I do not care if I can eat of all the trees north of here, east of here, south of here, and west of here. As long as I allow that tree to remain untouched, I feel less than human. I feel diminished. Therefore, I am going to eat of it and die, whatever that may mean."

So Adam ate of the tree of the knowledge of good and evil, and death, the punishment for sin, came upon the race.

That is the condition of every human heart. We hate God's sovereignty because we want to be sovereign ourselves. We want to run our own lives. We want to roam free, to know no boundaries. When we discover that there are boundaries, we hate God for the discovery.

We react like the rulers of the nations in Psalm 2: "The kings of the earth take their stand and the rulers gather together against the LORD and against his Anointed One. 'Let us break their chains,' they say, 'and throw off their fetters'" (vv. 2–3).

We say, "We will not have this God to rule over us."

The Holy God

It is not only the sovereignty of God that is repugnant to us in our natural, sinful state, however. We oppose God for his holiness as well. One reason is obvious: We hate holiness because we are not holy. God's holiness exposes our sin, and we do not like exposure. But there is more to it than that. Let me explain.

Holiness is one of the greatest of all God's attributes, the only one that is properly repeated three times over in worship statements ("Holy, holy, holy is the Lord Almighty . . ." [Isa. 6:3; cf. Rev. 4:8]). We think of holiness as utter righteousness, that God does no wrong. But although holiness includes righteousness, holiness is much more than this and is not basically an ethical term at all. The basic idea of holiness is "separation." For example, the Bible is called holy (the Holy Bible), not because it is without sin, though it is inerrant, but because it is set apart and different from all other books. Religious objects are holy because they have been set apart for worship. In reference to God, holiness is the attribute that sets him apart from his creation. It has at least four elements.

1. *Majesty*. Majesty means "dignity," "authority of sovereign power," "stateliness" or "grandeur." It is the characteristic of strong rulers and of God, who is ruler over all. Majesty links holiness to sovereignty.

2. *Will*. A second element in holiness is will, the will of a sovereign personality. This makes holiness personal and active, rather than abstract and passive. Moreover, if we ask what the will of God is primarily set on, the

answer is on proclaiming himself as the "Wholly Other," whose glory must not be diminished by the disobedience or arrogance of men. This element of holiness comes close to what the Bible is speaking of when it refers to God's proper "jealousy" for his own honor. "Will" means that God is not indifferent to how men and women regard him.

3. *Wrath.* Wrath is part of holiness because it is the natural and proper stance of the holy God against all that opposes him. It means that God takes the business of being God so seriously that he will permit no other to usurp his place.

4. *Righteousness.* This is the matter mentioned earlier. It is involved in holiness not because it is the term by which holiness may most fully be understood but because it is what the holy God wills in moral areas.

Here is our problem. Precisely because holiness is not an abstract or passive concept, but is instead the active, dynamic character of God at work to punish rebellion and establish righteousness, the experience of confronting the holy God is profoundly threatening. Holiness intrigues us, as the unknown always does. We are drawn to it. But at the same time we are in danger of being undone, and we fear being undone, by the resulting confrontation. When Isaiah had his encounter with the holy God in the passage referred to above, he reacted in terror, crying, "Woe to me! I am ruined! For I am a man of unclean lips, and I live among a people of unclean lips, and my eyes have seen the King, the LORD Almighty" (Isa. 6:5).

When God revealed himself to Habakkuk, the prophet described the experience by saying, "I heard and my heart pounded, my lips quivered at the sound; decay crept into my bones, and my legs trembled . . ." (Hab. 3:16).

Job said, "Therefore I despise myself and repent in dust and ashes" (Job 42:6).

Peter exclaimed when he caught only a brief glimpse of Jesus' holiness, "Go away from me, Lord; I am a sinful man!" (Luke 5:8).

The point I am making is this: If confrontation with the holy God is an unpleasant and threatening experience for the best of people—for the saints and prophets of biblical history, for example—how much more threatening must the holiness of God be for outright and unregenerate sinners. For them the experience must be totally overwhelming. No wonder they resist God, make light of him, or deny his existence. A. W. Tozer has written, "The moral shock suffered by us through our mighty break with the high will of heaven has left us all with a permanent trauma affecting every part of our nature."[2] Tozer is right. Therefore, the holiness of God as well as God's sovereignty drive us from him.

2. A. W. Tozer, *The Knowledge of the Holy* (New York: Harper & Row, 1961), p. 110.

The Omniscient God

In his study of atheism, Sproul has a particularly good chapter on God's "omniscience." This term means that God knows everything, including ourselves and everything about us. We do not like this, as Sproul indicates. He proves his point by looking at four modern treatments of the fear of being known, even by other human beings.

The first is by Jean-Paul Sartre, the French existentialist. Sartre has analyzed the fear of being beneath the gaze of someone else in a number of places, but the best known is in his play *No Exit*. In this play four characters are confined in a room with nothing to do but talk to and stare at each other. It is a symbol of hell. In the last lines of the play this becomes quite clear as Garcin, one of the characters, stands at the mantelpiece, stroking a bronze bust. He says:

> Yes, now's the moment: I'm looking at this thing on the mantelpiece, and I understand that I'm in hell. I tell you, everything's been thought out beforehand. They knew I'd stand at the fireplace stroking this thing of bronze, with all those eyes intent on me. Devouring me. (*He swings around abruptly.*) What? Only two of you? I thought there were more; many more. (*Laughs.*) So this is hell. I'd never have believed it. You remember all we were told about the torture chambers, the fire and brimstone, the "burning marl." Old wives' tales! There's no need for red-hot pokers. Hell is—other people![3]

The final stage directive says that the characters slump down onto their respective sofas, the laughter dies away, and they "gaze" at each other.

The second modern treatment of the fear of being known by others is from Julius Fast's *Body Language*. This book is a study of nonverbal communication, how we express ourselves by various body positions, nods, winks, arm motions, and so forth. There is a discussion of staring, and the point is made that although it is allowable to stare at objects or animals, even for long periods of time, it is not acceptable to stare at human beings. If we do, we provoke embarrassment or hostility or both. Why? Because we associate staring with prying, and we do not want anybody prying into what we think or are.

The third modern study of the significance of the human fear of exposure is Desmond Morris's *The Naked Ape*. The naked ape is, of course, the human being, the only animal who has no hair or other covering.

The fourth person whose works Sproul studies is the Danish philosopher Søren Kierkegaard. He wrote of a human need for hiddenness or solitude.

What emerges from these studies of modern attitudes toward exposure is a strange ambivalence. On the one hand, we want people to look at us, to notice us. If they ignore us, we feel diminished or hurt. At the same time, if they look too long or too intently, we are embarrassed and upset, because

3. Jean-Paul Sartre, *No Exit and Three Other Plays* (New York: Vintage Books, 1949), p. 47.

we are ashamed of who we are and do not want others to know us very well. If this is the case in our reaction to other human beings, who never really know us deeply even when they pry, and who are in any case sinners like ourselves, how much more traumatic is it to be known by the omniscient God, before whom all hearts are open, all desires known?

Exposure like this is intolerable. So human beings suppress their knowledge of God—because of his omniscience as well as because of his other attributes.

The Immutable God

At the very end of Sproul's book there is a short "conclusion" in which the author tells how, after he had written the bulk of his study, he remembered a sermon by the great New England preacher and theologian Jonathan Edwards, entitled "Men [Are] Naturally God's Enemies."[4] Sproul wondered how Edwards handled the subject he had been dealing with. So he hunted up the sermon and found Edwards saying that human beings hate God as "an infinitely holy, pure and righteous Being." They hate him because his omniscience is a "holy omniscience" and his omnipotence is a "holy omnipotence."[5] So far, Edwards seemed to be making the same points Sproul was making.

Then Edwards said, "They do not like his immutability."

Immutability? thought Sproul. *Why immutability?*

Immutability means that God does not change. But why should human beings dislike that about God? Edwards explained that it is "because by this he never will be otherwise than he is, an infinitely holy God."[6] As he thought about this, Sproul began to understand what the great theologian was saying. Men and women hate God for his immutability because it means that he will never be other than he is in all his other attributes.

If the time could come when God might cease to be sovereign, like a retiring chairman of the board, then his sovereignty would not seem particularly bad to us. We are eternal creatures. We could wait him out. When he retires, we could take over.

Again, the holiness of God would not be so offensive to us if the time might come when God would cease to be holy. What God forbids now he might someday condone. Tomorrow or next week or next month he might begin to think differently and change his mind. We could wait to do our sinning.

Omniscience? The time might come when God's memory would begin to fail and he would forget bad things he knows about us. We could live with that.

---

4. Jonathan Edwards, *The Works of Jonathan Edwards* (Edinburgh and Carlisle, Pa.: The Banner of Truth Trust, 1976), vol. 2, pp. 130–141.

5. Ibid., p. 131.

6. Ibid.

But not if God is immutable! If God is immutable, not only is God sovereign today; God will be sovereign tomorrow and the next day and the day after that. God will always be sovereign. In the same way, not only is God holy today. God will always be holy. And not only is God omniscient today. God will always be omniscient. God will never change in any of these great attributes. He is the sovereign, holy, omniscient, and immutable God. He always will be, and there is nothing you or I or anyone else can do about it.

We may suppress the truth about God out of a wicked rejection of his sovereignty, saying, "We will not have this God to rule over us." But whether we appreciate his rule or not, God's sovereignty is precisely what we need. We need a God who is able to rule over our unruly passions, control our destructive instincts, and save us. We may hate God for his holiness. But hate him or not, we need a holy God. We need an upright standard, and we need one who will not cease from working with us until we attain it. We may hate God for his omniscience. But we need a God who knows us thoroughly, from top to bottom, and who loves us anyway. We need a God who knows what we need. We may hate God for his immutability, since he does not change in any of his other attributes. But we need a God we can count on.

17

Without Excuse

Romans 1:20

For since the creation of the world God's invisible qualities—his eternal power and divine nature—have been clearly seen, being understood from what has been made, so that men are without excuse.

No human being is infinite. Infinitude belongs exclusively to God. Yet, in spite of our finite nature, human beings do seem to have an almost infinite capacity for some things. One of them is for making excuses for reprehensible behavior. Accuse a person of something, and regardless of how obvious the fault may be, the individual immediately begins to make self-serving declarations: "It wasn't my fault," "Nobody told me," "My intentions were good," "You shouldn't be so critical." The two least spoken sentences in the English language are probably "I was wrong" and "I am sorry."

Some people try to brazen things out by denying the need to make excuses. Walt Whitman once wrote, "I do not trouble my spirit to vindicate itself or be understood." The French have a saying that has a similar intent: "Qui s'excuse, s'accuse" ("He who excuses himself, accuses himself").[1] But

1. Quotations are from *Roget's International Thesaurus* (New York: Thomas Y. Crowell, 1953), pp. 637, 638.

153

that is an excuse itself, since it means that the person involved is too great to need to make apologies.

Our text says that in spite of our almost infinite capacity to make excuses, we are all "without excuse" for our failure to seek out, worship, and thank the living God.

"I Didn't Know God Existed"

The first of our excuses is that we do not know that God exists or at least that we do not know for sure. Every era has had its characteristic excuses for failure to seek and worship God, but in our "scientific age," this is certainly a very common rationalization. We remember that when the Soviet cosmonaut Yuri Gagarin returned to earth from his short time in space, he said with typical atheistic arrogance, "I did not see God." The fact that he could not see God was supposed to be proof of God's nonexistence. Unfortunately, what Gagarin said is typical of many millions of people in our time, both in the communist East and the capitalistic West. It is the argument that science either has disproved God or else has been unable to give adequate evidence for affirming his existence.

It should be clear by this point, however, that if the Bible is from God, as Christians claim, then whatever *we* may think about the matter, God at least does not agree with our assessment.

We say, "There is no evidence for God." Or, "There is insufficient evidence for God."

God says that quite the contrary is the case. God says that nature supplies evidence that is not only extensive but is also "clearly seen" and fully "understood." In other words, there is no excuse for atheism.

The alternative put forward today is that the universe is eternal because matter is eternal, and that all we see has come about over a long period of time as the result of chance or random occurrences. This is the view of Carl Sagan, who affirms the eternity of matter. "In the beginning was the cosmos," cries Sagan. But think through the problems. Suppose everything we see did evolve over long periods of time from mere matter. Suppose our complex universe came from something less complex, and that less complex something from something still less complex. Suppose we push everything back until we come to "mere matter," which is supposed to be eternal. Have we solved our problem? Not at all! We are trying to explain the complex forms of matter as we know them today, but where did those forms come from? Some would say that the form or purpose we see was somehow in matter to begin with. But, if that is the case, then the matter we are talking about is no longer "mere matter." It already has purpose, organization, and form, and we need to ask how these very significant elements got there. At some point we must inevitably find ourselves looking for the Purposer, Organizer, or Former.

Moreover, it is not just form that confronts us. There are personalities in the cosmos. We are personalities. We are not mere matter, even complex matter. We have life, and we know ourselves to be entities possessing a sense of self-identity, feelings, and a will. Where could those things come from in an originally impersonal universe? Francis Schaeffer has written, "The assumption of an impersonal beginning can never adequately explain the personal beings we see around us, and when men try to explain man on the basis of an original impersonal, man soon disappears."[2]

Until recently, the most popular fallback from these truths has been the argument that whatever the difficulties may be for supposing an evolution of what we see from mere matter, such is nevertheless possible, given an infinite amount of time and chance occurrence. But there are two problems here.

First, what is chance? People talk as if chance were an entity that could bring about the universe. But chance is merely a mathematical abstraction with no real existence. Suppose you are about to flip a coin and were to ask, "What are the chances of its coming up heads?" The answer is fifty percent (ignoring the possibility that it may stick in the mud on its side). Suppose further that you do flip the coin and that it comes up heads. What made it come up heads? Did chance do it? Of course not. What made it come up heads was the force of your thumb on the coin, the weight of the coin, the resistance of the air, the distance from your hand to the ground, and other variables. If you knew and could plot every one of those variables, you would be able to tell exactly what would happen—whether the coin would land either heads or tails. You do not know the variables. So you say, "Chances are that it will come up heads fifty percent of the time." But the point I am making is that chance didn't do it. Chance is nothing. So to say that the universe was created by chance is to say that the universe was created by nothing, which is a meaningless statement.

What about there being an infinite amount of time? As I have pointed out, even with an infinite amount of time nothing with form or purpose comes into being apart from an original Former or Purposer. But supposing it could. Even this does not explain the universe, for the simple reason that the universe has not been around for an infinite amount of time. Science itself tells us that the universe is in the nature of fifteen to twenty billion years old. It speaks of an original beginning known popularly as the Big Bang. True, fifteen to twenty billion years is a long time, more time than we can adequately comprehend. But such time is not infinite! That is the point. And if it is not infinite, then an appeal to infinity does not explain the existence of our very complex universe.

"I didn't know God existed"? Can anyone really affirm that in face of the evidence for the existence of God in nature? The Bible says we cannot, and

2. Francis A. Schaeffer, *Genesis in Space and Time* (Downers Grove, Ill.: InterVarsity Press, 1972), p. 21.

even a secular analysis of the options supports the Bible's statement. Ignorance is no excuse for failing to seek and worship God, *because we are not ignorant.*

"I Have Too Many Questions"

There are people who might follow what I have said to this point and even agree with most of it but who would nevertheless excuse themselves on the ground that they still have too many questions about Christianity. They recognize that the God we are talking about is not just "any god" but the God who has revealed himself in Scripture. And when they think about that they have a host of questions. They suppose that these are valid excuses for their rejection of the deity. For example:

1. *What about the poor innocent native in Africa who has never heard of Christ?* Every preacher gets asked this question. In fact, it is probably the question most asked by Christians and non-Christians alike. But it is also true that Romans 1:18–20, the text we have been studying, answers it. The implication behind this question is that the "innocent" native is going to be sent to hell for failing to do something he has never had an opportunity to do, namely, believe on Jesus Christ as his Savior, and that a God who would be so unjust as to condemn the "innocent" native cannot be God. And that is true! God must be just, and God would be unjust if he condemned a person for failing to do what he or she obviously did not have the opportunity of doing.

But that is not the case in regard to the so-called innocent in Africa. To be sure, the native is innocent of failing to believe on Jesus if he or she has never heard of Jesus. But it is not for this that the native or anyone else who has not heard of Jesus is condemned. As Romans 1 tells us, the native is condemned for failing to do what he or she actually knows he or she should do, that is, seek out, worship, and give thanks to the God revealed in nature. Everyone falls short there. A person might argue that the native actually does seek God, offering in proof the widespread phenomenon of religion in the world. Man has rightly been called *homo religiosus.* But that is no excuse either, for the universality of religion, as Paul is going to show in the next verses, is actually evidence of man's godlessness. Why? Because the religions that man creates are actually attempts to escape having to face the true God. We invent religion—not because we are seeking God, but because we are running away from him.

To repeat what we have seen in the last two studies: (1) all human beings know God as a result of God's revelation of himself to us through nature, but (2) instead of allowing that revelation to lead us to God, we repress the revelation and instead set up false gods of our own imaginations to take the true God's place. The reason, as we have also seen, is that (3) we do not like the God to which this natural revelation leads us.

2. *Isn't the Bible full of contradictions?* This is an excuse we also often hear, but it is as unsubstantial as the first one. We are told that as the data from science has come in, so many errors have been found in the Bible that no rational person could possibly believe that it is God's true revelation. It follows that at best the Bible is a collection of insightful human writings, so no one can intelligently buy into Christianity on the basis of the biblical "revelation."

The problem with this argument is its premise. It assumes that the accumulation of historical and scientific facts has uncovered an increasing number of textual and other problems, but actually the opposite is the case. As the data has come in over the decades, particularly over the last few decades, the tendency is for the Bible to be vindicated. *Time* magazine recognized this in a cover story in the December 30, 1974, issue. The story was captioned "How True Is the Bible?" In this essay the magazine's editors examined the chief radical critics of the recent past—Albert Schweitzer, Rudolf Bultmann, Martin Dibelius, and others—but concluded:

> The breadth, sophistication and diversity of all this biblical investigation are impressive, but it begs a question: Has it made the Bible more credible or less? Literalists who feel the ground move when a verse is challenged would have to say that credibility has suffered. Doubt has been sown, faith is in jeopardy. But believers who expect something else from the Bible may well conclude that its credibility has been enhanced. After more than two centuries of facing the heaviest scientific guns that could be brought to bear, the Bible has survived—and is perhaps the better for the siege.
>
> Even on the critics' own terms—historical fact—the scriptures seem more acceptable now than they did when the rationalists began the attack.[3]

It is hard to see how anyone can use the alleged "contradictions" in the Bible to justify a failure to seek out and worship the Bible's God, especially after he or she has investigated the evidence thoroughly.

3. *If there is a God and the God who exists is a good God, why does he tolerate evil?* The argument has two forms. One form is philosophical, asking how evil could have entered a world created and ruled by a benevolent God. The other is personal and practical, asking why things happen to me that I do not like or why God does not give me what I ask him for or do what I tell him in my prayers I want him to do.

The philosophical problem is difficult. If we ask how evil could originate in an originally perfect world, there is no one, so far as I know, who has ever answered that puzzle adequately. If God made all things good, including Adam and Eve, so that nothing within them naturally inclined toward evil in any way, then it is difficult (if not impossible) to see how Adam or Eve or any other perfect being could do evil. But I must point out that although

---

3. *Time*, Dec. 30, 1974, p. 41.

Christians may not have an adequate explanation for the origin of evil (at least at this point in the history of theological thought), our difficulty here is at least only half as great as that of the unbeliever. For the unbeliever has the problem not only of explaining the origin of evil; he has the problem of explaining the origin of the good as well. In any case, our failure to understand how evil came about does not disprove its existence any more than it disproves the existence of God.

The second form of this problem is personal and practical. It is the form of the question that probably troubles most people: "Why does God tolerate evil, particularly in my life? Why do bad things happen to me? Why doesn't God answer my prayers as I would like?"

Part of the answer to this problem is that if we got what we deserved, we would be suffering not merely the evils we now know but rather those eternal torments that are to be the lot of the unregenerate in hell. In other words, instead of saying, "Why do bad things happen to me?" we should be saying, "Why do good things happen to me?" All we deserve is evil. If our life has any good in it, that good (however minimal) should point us to the God from whom all good comes. That we do not follow that leading, but instead complain about God's treatment, only increases our guilt. It shows us to be precisely what Paul declares we are in Romans 1:18: godless and wicked.

Let me illustrate how this works. After I had preached the sermon that is printed as chapter 16 of this volume ("The Psychology of Atheism"), I received an unsigned note in which someone objected to my comments about the natural man's hatred of God's sovereignty. He (or she) said, "Preach sermons to your congregation, not to the radio audience. Deal with the hard questions. The difficulty is not that I am not sovereign but that the sovereignty of God does not seem good. When the answers to my prayers seem to make no sense, what then am I to think of God? Deal with that one."

The tone of this note was a bit insulting, as you can see. But the problem is not that it was insulting to me. The problem is that it was insulting to God. Moreover, it was itself a refutation of the point it was making. The questioner was saying that he or she had no difficulty with the concept of God's sovereignty, only with what God does—if God exists. But, of course, what is that if not a challenge to God's sovereignty? It is a way of saying, "God, I am not going to believe in you unless you come down from your lofty throne, stand here before little me and submit to my interrogation. I will not acknowledge you unless you explain yourself to me." Could anything be more arrogant than that? To demand that God justify his ways to us? Or even to think that we could understand him if he did? Job was not challenging God's sovereignty. He was only seeking understanding. But when God interrogated him, asking if he could explain how God created and sustains the universe, poor Job was reduced to near stammering. He said, "I despise myself and repent in dust and ashes" (Job 42:6).

It is interesting that the same week in which I got this note, demanding that God explain himself on our level before we believe on him, I got another letter that was quite different. This person described a particularly horrible week that he had just gone through. But then he said, "Seeing the situation in the light of God's sovereignty made it possible for me to ask forgiveness for my anger and open my eyes to what God wants me to see, namely, that my life will frequently be 'disordered,' but he will never let it get out of control." Do you see the difference?

Is it right to have questions about why God acts as he does? Of course! Who has not had them? It is right to believe and then seek understanding.[4] But to use an inability to understand some things as an excuse for failing to respond to what we do know is that deliberate repression of the truth about which Paul was speaking in our text.

"I Didn't Think It Was Important"

The weakest excuse that anyone can muster is the statement that "I just didn't think it was important." That is obviously faulty—if God exists and we are all destined to meet him and give an account of our actions some day. Nothing can be as important as getting the most basic of our relationships right: the relationship of ourselves to God. And yet, for one reason or another—perhaps just because the press of life's many demands seems more important—we push this greatest of all issues aside.

How do you think that is going to sound when you appear before God at the last day?

"I didn't think it was important"?

"I didn't think *you* were important"?

"I didn't think my repression of the truth about you mattered"?

A little later on in Romans, Paul tells what is going to happen in that last day. Men and women are going to appear before God with their excuses, but when they do, says Paul, "Every mouth [will] be silenced and the whole world [will be] held accountable to God" (Rom. 3:20). Even in this day there are no valid excuses, as Paul declares in Romans 1:20. But in *that* day the excuses will not even be spoken, so obvious will it be that all human beings—from the smallest to the greatest—are guilty of godlessness.

Since today is not yet that final day, there is still time to turn from the arrogance that pits finite minds and sinful wills against God.

Do you remember Methuselah? He lived longer than any other man—969 years. His name means "When he is gone it shall come." "It" was the great flood of God's judgment. That flood destroyed the antediluvian

---

4. This was the philosophy of the great medieval scholar Anselm, who expressed it by the Latin phrase *fides quarens intellectum* ("faith in search of understanding").

world. But the reason I refer to Methuselah and his longevity is that he is a picture of God's great patience with those who sin against him. During the early years of Methuselah's life God sent a preacher named Enoch to turn the race from its sin. Enoch preached that judgment was coming: "See, the Lord is coming with thousands upon thousands of his holy ones to judge everyone, and to convict all the ungodly of all the ungodly acts they have done in the ungodly way, and of all the harsh words ungodly sinners have spoken against him" (Jude 14–15). After Enoch died, Noah continued the preaching. For the entire lifetime of Methuselah, all 969 years, the flood did not come. God was gracious, "patient . . . not wanting anyone to perish, but everyone to come to repentance" (2 Peter 3:9). But, though patient, God was not indifferent to sin, and at last Methuselah died, and wrath did indeed come.

We live in a similar age today. Today is the day of God's grace. But wrath is gathering. We see it about us like the rising waters of the flood. Do not wait to be overtaken by it. Do not make excuses. Admit that you are "without excuse" in God's sight and quickly take refuge in the Savior.

18

Base Ingratitude

Romans 1:21

For although they knew God, they neither glorified him as God nor gave thanks to him, but their thinking became futile and their foolish hearts were darkened.

In many Bibles the twenty-first verse of Romans 1 begins a new paragraph, and rightly so. In the previous verses Paul has explained the fearful state of men and women as exposed to the wrath of Almighty God, and he has explained why this is our condition. We are objects of God's wrath because we have rejected the knowledge of God, which all persons possess as a result of God's extensive disclosure of himself in the works of nature. Now Paul is going to take that description of the human race further by showing the sad results for man of this rejection.

Yet the paragraphs are also tied together. This is because Paul does not immediately speak of the results of our rejection of God, which is his ultimate purpose. Instead he first cites two more things of which sinful men and women are guilty. This means that there are three failures in all, one of which we have already studied and two additional ones added here. First, we have *suppressed the truth about God*, being unwilling to come to God to whom the revelation in nature leads. (This is the sin studied in detail in the last chapter.) Second, we have *refused to glorify (or worship) God*. This is in

161

spite of our genuine knowledge of him. Third, we have *forgotten to be thankful*. To know God is to know ourselves as his creatures and thus to know that all we have and enjoy is from him. Yet, because we willingly block the knowledge of God from our minds, we thus obviously also refuse to glorify God *as* God and are ungrateful.

Ungrateful! John Milton spoke of "base ingratitude" (*Comus*, line 776). William Shakespeare wrote, "Blow, blow thou winter wind; thou art not so unkind as man's ingratitude" (*As You Like It*, Act 2, Scene 7). The Russian writer Fyodor Dostoyevsky said of man, "If he is not stupid, he is monstrously ungrateful! Phenomenally ungrateful. In fact, I believe that the best definition of man is the ungrateful biped."[1]

No Praise, No Glory

There is a connection between these three human failures, however. So to understand the nature of our ingratitude to God, we need first to understand that we have not "gloried him as God," which is how Paul states it.

The word *glory*, from which the words *glorify* and *glorification* derive, is quite interesting. In the Greek language the original words are *dokeo* (the verb) and *doxa* (the noun), from which we get our word *doxology*. Originally the verb meant "to appear" or "to seem," and the noun that came from this then meant an "opinion." A person's opinion of someone or something is how that person or thing appears to the one observing it. From *doxa* we get our English words *orthodox* (which means a "straight or correct opinion"), *heterodox* (which means a "different or wrong opinion") and *paradox* (which means a "contrary or irreconcilable opinion"). At one time *doxa* and *dokeo* were concerned with either a good opinion or a bad opinion about someone. But eventually they came to refer to a good opinion only. At this point the noun came to mean the "praise" or "honor" due to one about whom such good opinions were held, and the verb referred to rendering an individual such honor. Kings possessed "glory" because they merited the praise of their subjects. The word is used in this sense in Psalm 24, which speaks of God as the King of glory: "Who is he, this King of glory? The LORD Almighty—he is the King of glory" (v. 10).

At this point it is easy to see the effect of using the word *glory* or *glorify* of God. Who can "glorify" God? Obviously, only one who has a right opinion about him, that is, one who knows and properly appreciates God's attributes. The one who knows God as sovereign, holy, omniscient, immutable, loving, merciful, and so on—and who praises the Almighty for these things—glorifies him.

And there is this, too: The English language has another entirely different word that means almost the same thing as "glory" and that might

---

1. Fyodor Dostoevsky, "Notes from Underground" in *Existentialism from Dostoevsky to Sartre*, ed. Walter Kaufmann (New York: Meridian Books, 1956), p. 74.

well have been used for it had not the French word *gloire* superseded it in everyday speech. This is the Anglo-Saxon word *worth,* which also refers to a person's intrinsic merit or character. Man's worth is man's character. God's worth is God's glory. Now, using this term, what happens when you acknowledge God's character as he himself reveals it? Well, you acknowledge his "worth-ship," or, as we say, you "worship" him. "Worth-ship" is hard for us to say. So either we shorten it and speak of "worshiping" God, or we abandon the Anglo-Saxon term and switch to the Latin word and speak of "glorifying" God instead.

The point I am making is that each of these three ideas is the same. Linguistically, the *worship* of God, the *praise* of God, and the *giving of glory* to God are identical.

Of course, this is precisely what Paul says the human race has not done. Moreover, its failure to worship or glorify God follows naturally from its willful suppression of the truth about God, which God has revealed to us in nature. We have already seen that we reject the things God has revealed because we do not like the God to which the truth about God leads us. We do not like him for his sovereignty; God's sovereignty negates our autonomy. We do not like him for his holiness; God's holiness opposes and condemns our sin. We do not like him for his omniscience; his omniscience terrifies us because we fear exposure. We do not like God for his immutability, because immutability means that God will never be other than he is in all his other attributes. We cannot stand these truths. So we repress them, denying their existence. It is obvious that if we do this, we are not going to praise God for these same characteristics.

On the contrary, we do what the Jews did when they had been brought out of Egypt but had rebelled against God by making the golden calf. We take the attributes that belong to God only and ascribe them to idols, saying, "These are your gods, O Israel, who brought you up out of Egypt" (Exod. 32:8). We are going to examine how we do that in greater detail as we study the latter half of Romans 1.

Not Thankful

There are times in my study of the major Bible commentators when I am seriously disappointed, and this is one of them. For the third great failure for which Paul cites the human race is ingratitude—"nor gave thanks," he says—and yet this important idea receives very little treatment by these commentators. Haldane, great in nearly all respects as a commentator, gives just nine lines to this matter.[2] Godet has five lines.[3] Even John Calvin says only,

2. Robert Haldane, *An Exposition of the Epistle to the Romans* (MacDill AFB: MacDonald Publishing, 1958), p. 61.
3. F. Godet, *Commentary on St. Paul's Epistle to the Romans,* trans. A. Cusin (Edinburgh: T. & T. Clark, n.d.), vol. 1, pp. 173, 174.

"It is not without reason that Paul adds that *neither gave* they *thanks*, for there is no one who is not indebted to God's infinite kindnesses, and even on this account alone he has abundantly put us in his debt by condescending to reveal himself to us."[4]

In working on this idea I was therefore pleased to discover that in his book on "doubt," entitled *In Two Minds*, the British writer Os Guinness (now living in America) devotes an entire chapter to ingratitude, viewing it rightly, I believe, as a major cause for doubt and thus as a step away from faith toward failure.

Guinness's thesis is that doubt is not unbelief but rather a middle place between faith and unbelief, hence his title. But that middle position is an unstable one. If we are doubting, we will not merely doubt for long. Either we will move from doubt in the direction of a stronger faith, or we will move from doubt in the direction of unbelief. And whether we do one or the other depends on how we deal with what causes us to be unsettled. Guinness sees the causes of our unsettling as: ingratitude, a faulty view of God, weak foundations, lack of commitment, lack of growth, unruly emotions, and fearing to believe. He calls them "seven families of doubt." Ingratitude is the cause of doubt he starts with.

Why is ingratitude so dangerous? Because it is based upon a willful unawareness of the most basic facts about God and upon our lack of a proper relationship to him. In other words, it is because of the very problem about which Paul is teaching.

Romans 1:18–20 teaches that the existence of God is abundantly disclosed in nature. This means, of course, not merely that God exists but also that all we are, see, and have has been brought into being by him. He is the Creator of everything. So if we have life, it is from God. If we have health, it is from God. The food we eat, the clothes we wear, the friends we share—everything good is from God. If we fail to be grateful for this, it is because we are not really acknowledging him or are rejecting a proper relationship to him. Someone may say, "But we sometimes experience bad things, too. We suffer pain and hunger. We get sick. Eventually we die." But even here we show our ingratitude. For we deny the fact that if we got what we deserve, we would all be in hell, sinners that we are. Our very existence, as sinners, should cause us to praise God not only for his sovereignty, holiness, omniscience, and all the other attributes I have mentioned, but for his abundant mercy, too. But we are not conscious of this. So we erect a great mass of ingratitude upon our earlier sins of suppressing the truth and refusing God worship.

Guinness refers to Romans 1:21 as a sober reminder that "rebellion against God does not begin with the clenched fist of atheism but with the self-satisfied heart of the one for whom 'thank you' is redundant."[5]

4. John Calvin, *The Epistles of Paul the Apostle to the Romans and to the Thessalonians*, trans. Ross MacKenzie (Grand Rapids: Wm. B. Eerdmans, 1973), p. 32.

5. Os Guinness, *In Two Minds: The Dilemma of Doubt and How to Solve It* (Downers Grove, Ill.: InterVarsity Press, 1976), p. 72.

Martyn Lloyd-Jones, who spends a little more time on ingratitude than the other commentators, writes:

> Man does not thank God for his mercy, for his goodness, for his dealings with us in providence. We take the sunshine for granted; we are annoyed if we do not get it. We take the rain for granted. How often do we thank God for all these gifts and blessings! . . . God is "the giver of every good and perfect gift"; he is "the Father of mercies." Yet people go through the whole of their lives in this world and they never thank him; they ignore him completely. That is how they show their attitude toward God. In this way they suppress the truth that has been revealed concerning [him].[6]

Remember and Give Thanks

Guinness's chapter on ingratitude makes another important contribution, and that is its emphasis on the biblical theme of "remembering to give thanks." This has "tremendous emphasis," he says. "The man or woman of faith is the one who gives thanks. Unbelief, on the other hand, has a short and ungrateful memory."[7]

When the people of Israel left Egypt to travel to the Promised Land, they were the recipients of many great blessings. They had been delivered from slavery, protected from Pharaoh's pursuing armies, provided with water to drink and manna to eat, and they were given guidance in the form of the great cloud that covered them by day to protect them from the sun's fierce heat and turned into a pillar of fire by night to provide both light and warmth. If ever a people should have been fervently grateful to God, it was this people. Yet they were not grateful. They had asked for freedom. But when they received it and found that it was not precisely to their liking, they wanted to lynch Moses, turn around, and go back to Egypt. When they were given manna, they cried out for a different diet. No matter what God did, there was always something else they wanted.

Moses knew where such ingratitude would lead. He knew they would be made rebellious by ingratitude. So this great leader constantly reminded the Jewish people of their past, of God's blessings to them, and of their need to be thankful. After they had been delivered from Pharaoh's pursuing armies, Moses composed a song that said:

> I will sing to the LORD,
>   for he is highly exalted.
> The horse and its rider
>   he has hurled into the sea.

6. D. M. Lloyd-Jones, *Romans: An Exposition of Chapter 1, The Gospel of God* (Grand Rapids: Zondervan, 1985), p. 382.

7. Guinness, *In Two Minds*, p. 75.

The LORD is my strength and my song;
  he has become my salvation.
He is my God, and I will praise him,
  my father's God, and I will exalt him. . . .

Who among the gods is like you, O LORD?
  Who is like you—
  majestic in holiness,
  awesome in glory,
  working wonders?
Exodus 15:1–2, 11

Moses wanted Israel to remember God's past blessings. Later when God gave the Ten Commandments and other portions of the law, Moses said, "Be careful that you do not forget the LORD, who brought you out of Egypt, out of the land of slavery" (Deut. 6:12).

David, too, was strong on the need to be thankful, and he wrote much about it. After the ark of the covenant had been brought back to Jerusalem, David wrote a psalm beginning: "Give thanks to the LORD, call on his name; make known among the nations what he has done" (1 Chron. 16:8; cf. Ps. 105:1). David also said, "I will give you thanks in the great assembly; among throngs of people I will praise you" (Ps. 35:18). In the same way, Psalms 106, 107, 118, and 136 begin with thanksgiving: "Give thanks to the LORD, for he is good; his love endures forever."

Psalm 100, titled "A Psalm. For giving thanks," says:

Shout for joy to the LORD, all the earth.
  Worship the LORD with gladness;
  come before him with joyful songs.
Know that the LORD is God.
  It is he who made us, and we are his;
  we are his people, the sheep of his pasture.
Enter his gates with thanksgiving
  and his courts with praise;
  give thanks to him and praise his name.
For the LORD is good and his love endures forever;
  his faithfulness continues through all generations.

What was true for those living in the time of the Old Testament is true also for those living in New Testament times. When Jesus healed the ten lepers, only one of them came back, after showing himself to the priests, and thanked Jesus. Jesus asked, "Were not all ten cleansed? Where are the other nine? Was no one found to return and give praise to God except this foreigner?" (Luke 17:17–18). Jesus seemed to be bothered by the others' ingratitude. Similarly, Paul emphasized thanksgiving in his commands to the Philippians about prayer, saying, "Do not be anxious about anything, but in everything, by prayer and petition, *with thanksgiving*, present your requests to God. And the peace of God, which transcends all understanding, will guard your hearts and your minds in Christ Jesus" (Phil. 4:6–7, italics mine). Paul was concerned that in making new requests of God (which is proper) we nevertheless remember to thank him for what we have already received.

The point I am making is that thankfulness is a mark of those who truly know God—even though we sometimes forget to be thankful. Ingratitude, by contrast, is the mark of those who repress the truth about him.

Are We Thankful?

Although this section is a study of the psychology and acts of those who are in rebellion against God—the focus of Romans 1:18–32—all of it clearly has bearing on those who profess to know God. There are two pertinent questions: Are we who know God thankful? *and* Do we express our thanks verbally?

It is interesting to note that in many of the world's languages "giving thanks" is the basic meaning of at least one word for prayer. A very important Greek word for prayer is *eucharisteo*, from which is derived the liturgical word *Eucharist*. The Eucharist is the Lord's Supper, and it refers to that aspect of the communion service that involves thanksgiving to God for Christ's atoning death. *Eucharisteō* means "to give thanks." One of the most important Latin words for prayer is *gratia*, from which we have derived the French and English words *grace*. It has two meanings. On the one hand, it means God's "unmerited favor." That is the most common meaning of the word in English. It is the meaning in the hymn "Amazing Grace." But *gratia* also means "thanksgiving," the meaning we retain when we speak of saying "grace" before a meal. Isn't it interesting that so many of these words for prayer mean thanksgiving? Isn't it significant that the chief element in the opening of the heart of man to God in prayer should be gratitude?

Yet how little this is actually the case! We pray, but our prayers are often only versions of "God bless me and my wife, my son John and his wife, us four and no more. Amen."

Or they are strings of requests: "Give me this, give me that; do it quickly, and that's that."

Our prayers should follow the order of that little prayer acrostic ACTS: Adoration, Confession, Thanksgiving, and (only then) Supplication. We should ask for things only after we have already thanked God for what he has given.

What a difference it would make if we would all actually learn to glorify and worship God and be thankful! I think Reuben A. Torrey wrote wisely when he said:

> Returning thanks for blessings already received increases our faith and enables us to approach God with new boldness and new assurance. Doubtless the reason so many have so little faith when they pray is because they take so

little time to meditate upon and thank God for blessings already received. As one meditates upon the answers to prayers already granted, faith waxes bolder and bolder, and we come to feel in the very depths of our souls that there is nothing too hard for the Lord.[8]

This is what Os Guinness is saying, too! Doubt is the middle position between faith and unbelief. But if we learn to thank God for who he is and for his many blessings, we inevitably move from doubt to faith, rather than from doubt to even greater rebellion.

8. R. A. Torrey, *How To Pray* (New York: Fleming H. Revell, 1900), p. 76.

19

Fools!

Romans 1:21–23

For although they knew God, they neither glorified him as God nor gave thanks to him, but their thinking became futile and their foolish hearts were darkened. Although they claimed to be wise, they became fools and exchanged the glory of the immortal God for images made to look like mortal man and birds and animals and reptiles.

I have often spoken of the rebellion of the first man and woman against God, pointing out that, although the woman was deceived by Satan, having been led to think that her disobedience would result in good both for herself and her husband, the man was not deceived and therefore knew what he was doing. Adam deliberately set his face against God. He said in effect, "As long as that tree is in the middle of the garden of Eden and I am not able to eat of it, I feel demeaned as a human being. I am not autonomous. So I am going to eat of it and die, whatever that may be." Because he understood what he was doing, Adam's sin was greater than Eve's.

Yet there was a measure of "deception" in Adam's case also—deliberate deception. For how else can we explain what Adam did? Adam was no ignoramus. He knew that he was rebelling against God and that he was rejecting the truth about himself and the world, which God had revealed. What did

169

Adam think he was going to put in the place of God and God's truth? In place of God, he wanted to put himself! That much is obvious. In place of the truth, he no doubt wanted to put a "truth" of his own making!

This is what Satan had actually offered Eve earlier. When she replied to the serpent—the great deceiver—about the tree of the knowledge of good and evil, saying that she and her husband were not to eat of it or touch it lest they die, Satan had declared, "You will not surely die. . . . For God knows that when you eat of it your eyes will be opened, and you will be like God, knowing good and evil" (Gen. 3:4–5). Ah, "like God!" That was what Eve and Adam wanted to become. God is the sovereign God, and one aspect of his sovereignty is that he makes the rules. Adam wanted to make his own rules. He wanted to say what was to be true and what was to be false. And yet, in rebelling against God, he became anything but sovereign or wise. He became the opposite, losing what strength and wisdom he had. Instead of becoming more like God, which Satan had promised the woman, Adam became like Satan. Instead of rewriting the truth so that it would better suit his own warped desires, Adam began a process in which he and the human race after him turned from the truth of God to lies.

Substitution and Moral Foolishness

What happened to Adam back in the earliest moments of earth's history is what Paul declares in Romans 1 to be true now of every human being. Our study of Romans 1:18–21 has shown what human beings have done in terms of their relationships to God. They have (1) suppressed the truth about God; (2) refused to glorify, or worship, God; and (3) neglected to be thankful. Because of the first and perhaps also because of the second and third of these transgressions, the wrath of God has already begun to come upon them.

But the problem not only involves people's relationships to God. It also involves what happens to them as a secondary result of their breaking of the ties that should exist between this holy and loving Creator and his rational creatures. When Adam rebelled against God it was not only his relationship to God that was broken. His relationship to Eve was broken also, and this, too, was to affect the history of mankind. Adam acted the fool, and he became one. So also with the race as a whole. Thus, having spoken of that cosmic rebellion by which the human race has set its face against God, Paul goes on to declare, "For although they knew God, they neither glorified him as God nor gave thanks to him, but their thinking became futile and their foolish hearts were darkened. Although they claimed to be wise, they became fools and exchanged the glory of the immortal God for images made to look like mortal man and birds and animals and reptiles" (vv. 21–23). According to these words, the first result of man's rebellion against God, so far as he himself is concerned, is that he became a fool. His heart was darkened.

The words in this paragraph are wonderfully expressive and deserve careful attention. I start with three that are related.

1. *Dialogismois.* This is the word translated "thinking" in the New International Version, "imaginations" in the King James Version, and "argumentations" in J. B. Phillips's paraphrase. It refers to the working of the human mind apart from revelation. We have it in our word *dialogue.* The point is that, having rejected the truth about God that God has revealed to all human beings in nature (and later through Jesus Christ and the Bible), human beings have been left to their own mental devices, which are, however, inadequate for working out or discovering reality. We will not have God. So, having rejected God, we can use our minds only to rearrange error.

2. *Sophoi.* This word is translated "wise" in most Bible versions, but its force comes from its use in words like sophistry, sophisticated, sophomore, philosophy, philosopher, and philosophical. A philosopher is one who loves wisdom. A sophisticate thinks himself to be very worldly-wise. This is what those who have rejected the truth about God imagine themselves to have become. It is what Adam imagined he had become. In ourselves we think that we are all very intelligent and sophisticated individuals.

Let me quote D. Martyn Lloyd-Jones on this point:

> Instead of accepting revelation they became philosophers. And what is a philosopher? A philosopher is a man who claims that he starts by being skeptical about everything, that he is an agnostic. "I am going to have the data," he says, "and then I am going to apply my mind to it. I am going to reason it out and I am going to work it out." And that is exactly what such men have done; they became foolish and wicked in their reasonings, in their thoughts, in their own conjectures and speculations and surmisings. And what is the cause of it all? Paul uses the word "vain" and it means not only foolish, but it means wicked as well. . . . The cause of the whole trouble was wickedness, and it is still wickedness.[1]

Paul's point is that such persons are not being honest with the data they claim to be treating, and the reason they are not honest with the data is that they do not like the direction to which the data points them. Therefore, instead of using their minds to recognize and pursue the truth, they use them to provide philosophical justifications for their actions.

3. *Emōranthēsan.* This is a long Greek word, but it is derived from a very simple root found within it: *mōros,* which means "fool." It is used in the sentence, "Although they claimed to be wise, they became fools" (v. 22).

---

1. D. M. Lloyd-Jones, *Romans: An Exposition of Chapter 1, The Gospel of God* (Grand Rapids: Zondervan, 1985), p. 377.

What kind of fools? Well, in the Greek language, "fool" does not mean merely to be guilty of intellectual folly, though it includes this error, but to be guilty of moral folly or wickedness as well. That is why in the Bible it is so often connected with a denial of the existence of God, as in Psalm 14:1 ("The fool says in his heart, 'There is no God'"). It is why it is such a reprehensible term (cf. Matt. 5:22). If "fool" referred only to a deficiency of intellect, it could hardly be a bad thing, at least in terms of our relationship to God. None of us can ever know God fully; he is infinitely above us. But if the word includes a moral or ethical element, as it does, then it is truly bad, for it refers to our willful rejection of whatever truth about God we are capable of receiving.

This compounds our guilt, for it adds the sin of hypocrisy to the prior sin of rebellion. We have rebelled against God by rejecting the knowledge about himself that he has revealed to us. In addition to that, while willfully scorning the truth, we make exalted but ridiculous claims to great wisdom.

The Downward Sliding Path

Beginning in verse 24, Paul is going to show that turning away from God launched the race upon a downward path, leading inevitably to great moral depravity. We are going to look at that aspect of the slide of the human race in detail when we come to those verses. But even here it is important to see that what is involved is a falling away from a high level of truth, received by revelation, and not an upward climb to it.

It is important to see this, because the world believes exactly the opposite. It tries to teach that the path of the race has been consistently upward from its original "animal" beginnings and that our present world religions or philosophies are a step upward from whatever religious sensibilities went before them. We have been taught that primitive ages of the race were marked by animism and that animism progressed upward to polytheism, which in turn produced monotheism.

But this is not the way it happened. Some years ago a student of comparative religions named Robert Brow published a book entitled *Religion: Origins and Ideas* in which he argued correctly that this popular theory of evolutionary religious development simply does not fit the facts. On the contrary, he argued, the work of anthropologists suggests that the original form of religion was monotheism and that the polytheistic or animistic religions we see today among certain "primitive" peoples are actually a falling away from that much higher standard. Brow wrote, "Research suggests that the tribes are not animistic because they have continued unchanged since the dawn of history. Rather, the evidence indicates degeneration from a true knowledge of God."[2]

2. Robert Brow, *Religion: Origins and Ideas* (Chicago: InterVarsity Press, 1966), p. 11.

In his reconstruction Brow argues that an early knowledge of the true God came first, accompanied by animal sacrifices that were a way of acknowledging that the worshiper had offended God and needed to make atonement for his or her offenses. In time polytheism entered, providing a pantheon of gods and goddesses who were worshiped not because they were imagined to be higher or greater than the original true God but because they were lesser and therefore less to be feared. At this point priests emerged to take over the functions of sacrifice, and the religions degenerated even further. So it has continued. According to Brow, the so-called primitive tribesman is actually closer to the truth of religion than our civilized and sophisticated contemporaries.[3]

If this is true, as the Bible also declares it to be, then our pretension to progress in religion is only another sharp example of our great wickedness and inordinate folly. Claiming to be wise, we have become fools. For what could be more foolish than to have "exchanged the glory of the immortal God" for gods of our own devising?

Trauma, Repression, Substitution

In the midst of these important verses, Paul introduces another word that is extremely significant for understanding the nature of nonbiblical religions and the human psychology that has produced them. This is the word *exchanged*. It occurs in the verses we are studying, where Paul says, ". . . [they] exchanged the glory of the immortal God for images made to look like mortal man and birds and animals and reptiles" (v. 23). Two verses further on it occurs again: "They exchanged the truth of God for a lie, and worshiped and served created things rather than the Creator—who is forever praised. Amen" (v. 25).

This word explains why the human race has been so determined to invent religions to replace worship of the one true God. It explains it by a term we in our day are particularly well equipped to understand.

In psychology there is a recognized sequence of common human experiences known as *trauma*, *repression*, and *substitution*. Here is an example of the way these concepts are used: Suppose that a certain man is having difficulty concentrating on his work and that he cannot sleep at night. Not knowing what is wrong, he goes to a psychiatrist for help. "I can't seem to concen-

---

3. Of course, Frederick Godet saw and described the same thing earlier: "Far from being a first step towards the goal of Monotheism, Polytheism is on the contrary the result of degeneracy, an apostasy from the original Monotheism, a darkening of the understanding and heart, which has terminated in the grossest fetishism. The history of religions, thoroughly studied as it is now-a-days, fully justifies Paul's view. . . . It proves that at the root of all pagan religions and mythologies, there lies an original Monotheism, which is the historical starting-point in religion for all mankind" (*Commentary on St. Paul's Epistle to the Romans*, trans. A. Cusin [Edinburgh: T. & T. Clark, n.d.], vol. 1, p. 176). He cites Pfleiderer's treatise on other religions in *Jahrbuecher fuer protestantische Theologie* (1867).

trate," he says. "I like my job. I am not particularly pressured by it. But I am not doing well, and at night I can't sleep. Something is wrong. I don't know what it is. Can you help me?" The psychiatrist says he will try. So he asks the man to tell something about himself. When was the first time he noticed being unable to concentrate? What was his life like at that time? How was his relationship with his wife? How was his relationship with his children? How have things been at home? Did anything happen at that time that might have upset him?

Suppose that during these exploratory sessions, the psychiatrist notices that every time he mentions the house in which this man lives, the man's brow furrows and his answers to the therapist's questions get shorter. This happens a number of times, and eventually the psychiatrist, who is trained to observe such things, asks, "Did anything bad ever happen to your home? Do you have any bad memories about it?"

The man furrows his brow again and says, "No."

"Are you sure there isn't something bothering you about it?"

The man assures the doctor that there is nothing. Nevertheless, as the doctor probes this area he discovers that about the time the man began to have trouble with his job, his house was burglarized one evening, and both he and his wife were threatened by the burglar. Suppose in addition that the psychiatrist discovers that the robber was never caught, that the man has installed the most sophisticated burglary devices, and that he is constantly calling home. When these facts emerge it is not hard for the psychiatrist to explain what has happened. The robbery and the threat to his wife were so traumatic to this man that ever since he has been worried that another robbery (or something worse) might occur. The man has not admitted these fears to himself. In fact, he has repressed the experience, perhaps because he thinks he is not supposed to show such unmanly emotions as fear. But the trauma is with him, and his inability to concentrate at work is one evidence that the problem has never been dealt with adequately. To do so the psychiatrist will get the man to talk about his experience, face up to his fears and try to work with them.

What the man has experienced are the three stages of trauma, repression, and substitution, which I mentioned earlier. The robbery was so traumatic that the man repressed his memories of it. But the trauma did not go away. The memory of the event was only repressed. So a set of unnatural behavioral patterns emerged to fill the void.

This is precisely what Paul says has happened to the human race. Because of our primitive break with God in Adam and the resulting sinful state in which we live, whenever we experience the revelation of God in nature (or in Jesus Christ, the Bible, Christian preaching, or whatever), we find echoes of the original trauma emerging and inevitably attempt to repress them. But we cannot erase the trauma, and an act of substitution takes place by which we become "religious," creating substitutionary deities to take the true God's place.

This is the explanation of the universality of religion on this planet. The fact that people are religious does not prove that we are all seeking God. It proves the contrary. It proves that we are all running away from God. Although we are unwilling to know God and do not want him, we are nevertheless unable to do without him and try to fill the void with our substitute gods.

R. C. Sproul has dealt with this very well in the book I referred to earlier: *If There Is a God, Why Are There Atheists?* He puts it like this:

> In the case of God's revelation, man encounters something ominously threatening which is traumatic. The memory of conscious knowledge of the trauma is not maintained in its lucid threatening state but is repressed. It is "put down" or "held in captivity" in the unconsciousness. That which is repressed is not destroyed. The memory remains though it may be buried in the subconscious realm. Knowledge of God is unacceptable to man and as a result man does his best to blot it out or at least camouflage it in such a way that its threatening character can be concealed or dulled. That the human psyche is capable of such repression has been thoroughly demonstrated in a multitude of ways. The critical factor, however, . . . is that the knowledge is not obliterated or destroyed. It remains intact though deeply submerged in the unconscious.
>
> In the substitution-exchange process, the repressed knowledge manifests itself outwardly in a disguised or veiled form. The original knowledge is threatening; its disguised form is much less threatening. . . . In theological terms, what results from the repression is the profession of atheism either in militant terms, or its less militant form of agnosticism, or a kind of religion that makes God less of a threat than he really is. Either option, atheism or religion, manifests an exchange of the truth for a lie.[4]

From Darkness to Light

There is one more word that we need to look at before bringing this chapter to a close, and that is the word *darkness*. It occurs in verse 21: "For although they knew God, they neither glorified him as God nor gave thanks to him, but their thinking became futile and their foolish hearts were darkened." Darkness is an image, of course. It is the equivalent of Paul's saying that "their thinking became futile" or "they became fools" or "exchanged the glory of the immortal God for images made to look like mortal man and birds and animals and reptiles."

4. R. C. Sproul, *If There Is a God, Why Are There Atheists? A Surprising Look at the Psychology of Atheism* (Minneapolis: Dimension Books, 1978), pp. 76, 77. (Originally *The Psychology of Atheism*.)

When men and women turn away from God, they do not admit this, of course. Instead, they speak of "bright new ideas," "enlightenment" or "seeing the light." One whole movement in philosophy in Europe a century or so ago was called the Enlightenment. But, since God is the sole source of light, any ideas of enlightenment apart from him that we may think we have are an illusion. And what we need is the revelation and power of God to bring us back from self-inflicted darkness into God's light.

That is what has happened to Christians. We do not have any ability to rediscover the light of God by ourselves. Before God worked in us we were as much in the dark as anybody. Paul writes in Ephesians of what we were like in our unsaved state, much as he writes of the heathen in Romans: "They [the unsaved] are darkened in their understanding and separated from the life of God because of the ignorance that is in them due to the hardening of their hearts" (Eph. 4:18). However, as the result of God's illuminating work, ". . . you were once darkness, but now you are light in the Lord" (Eph. 5:8). To return to our illustration from psychiatry, in the case of Christians God has uncovered for us the cause of our great spiritual trauma. He has dealt with our rejection of his revelation (as well as with all our other sins) in Christ, making that known to us. Then he has brought us back into harmony with himself so that we no longer need fear him or run away from him but rather bask in his light.

We are also to live by his light. For in the passage from Ephesians cited above, Paul goes on to say, "Live as children of light (for the fruit of the light consists in all goodness, righteousness and truth) and find out what pleases the Lord" (Eph. 5:8–10). If we are of the light, we must live by the light. If we know God, we must show it by being like him.

20

God Gave Them Up

Romans 1:24–28

Therefore God gave them over in the sinful desires of their hearts to sexual impurity for the degrading of their bodies with one another. They exchanged the truth of God for a lie, and worshiped and served created things rather than the Creator—who is forever praised. Amen.

Because of this, God gave them over to shameful lusts. Even their women exchanged natural relations for unnatural ones. In the same way the men also abandoned natural relations with women and were inflamed with lust for one another. Men committed indecent acts with other men, and received in themselves the due penalty for their perversion.

Furthermore, since they did not think it worthwhile to retain the knowledge of God, he gave them over to a depraved mind, to do what ought not to be done.

I do not know whether Oscar Wilde was reflecting more on the divine nature or human nature in saying, "When the gods wish to punish us they answer our prayers."[1] But, according to the Book of Romans, he may well have been doing both, and have been correct in both instances.

1. *Roget's International Thesaurus* (New York: Thomas Y. Crowell, 1953), p. 532.

Thus far in our study of Romans we have been concentrating on human rebellion against God, and we have seen—indeed, Paul has explicitly told us—that the wrath of God "is being revealed from heaven" against men and women because of this rebellion. In what way is God showing wrath? It is clear what *we* have done. We have (1) suppressed the truth about God; (2) refused to glorify, or worship, God as God; and (3) declined to be thankful. As a result human beings have become "darkened" in their thinking. We have become fools. Nevertheless, up to this point we have not been told specifically of anything that God has actually done to unleash his wrath upon humanity. Now this changes. For the first time in the letter we are told—three times in succession—that God has abandoned men and women to perversion. The sentence says, "God gave them over." It is found in verses 24, 26, and 28.

But here is the irony. And here is why I quoted Oscar Wilde. Man's punishment is to be abandoned by God. But, of course, this is precisely what man has been fighting for ever since Adam's first rebellion in the Garden of Eden. Man has wanted to get rid of God, to push him out of his life. In contemporary terms he is saying, "God, I just want you to leave me alone. Take a seat on that chair over there. Shut up, and let me get on with my life as I want to live it."

And so God does!

Like the father of the Prodigal Son, he releases the rebellious child, permitting him to depart with all his many possessions and goods for the far country.

Adrift in God's Universe

Well! Isn't that what we want? Yes, it is what we think we want. But the problem is that it doesn't turn out as we anticipate. In fact, it turns out exactly the reverse. We think of God as a miser of happiness, keeping back from us all that would make us happy. We think that by running away from him we will be happy, wild, and free. But it doesn't work that way. Instead of happiness we find misery. Instead of freedom we find the debilitating bondage of sin.

Many who have studied the Bible for a long time know the phrase I have quoted in the King James wording, but this is a case in which the modern translations do better in capturing the meaning for our day. The King James Version of the Bible used the words "God gave them up" at this point. The King James translators knew what they meant, of course. They meant a judicial abandonment of the human race to the consequences of its rebellion. But, unfortunately, for most of us today those words sound like a simple hands-off policy in which men and women really are freed up to pursue and practice whatever they think will please them. That is not quite the idea. "God gave them up" sounds as if God simply let people drift off to nowhere, like releasing a porcelain pitcher in space. The actual idea is seen much better in the New International Version. For it is not that God gives the human race up to nothing, but rather that he gives it over to the consequences of the rebellious, sinful directions it has taken.

It is like releasing the porcelain pitcher on earth rather than in space. When you let go of the pitcher it does not drift off into nowhere. You release it from your hand to the law of gravity, and when you do that it falls downward and breaks—if the fall is far enough and the ground hard.

The reason for this is in the very nature of things, and in the fact that what they are can never be otherwise. We need to see this. If you or I were God, then we could get away with the kind of rebellion or sin without consequences that we seem to want. We could make the universe run the way we want it. But we cannot do that. The universe with all its laws, physical and moral, is a given—because God is a given. Since God can never be other than he is, the universe will always be as it is. And this means that when you and I rebel against God, we must by the very nature of the case do it on God's terms and according to God's laws rather than our own. When we run away from God we think our way will be uphill, because we want it to be so. But the way is actually downhill. We are pulled down by the law of moral gravity—when God lets go.

The Downhill Slope

What happens is illustrated in the case of Jonah, the prophet who tried to run away from God. He rejected God's call for him to go and preach to Nineveh and instead set off for Tarshish at the far end of the Mediterranean. But he didn't get where he was going, and his path was constantly downhill until God turned him around and got him going to Nineveh. In the King James Bible, which makes this point a bit neater than the New International Version, we are told four times over that the prophet's path was downhill. We read that he went "*down* to Joppa" and that when he found a ship bound for Tarshish he went "*down* into it" (Jonah 1:3). Then we are told that he had gone "*down* into the sides of the ship" (v. 5). Still later, after he had been cast overboard, he recounted the experience, saying, "I went *down* to the bottoms of the mountains" (Jonah 2:6). (The italics are mine.)

Down! Down! Down! Down! It is a sad life history, but it is the experience of all who run from God, and Paul says all men and women do run from God, trying to rearrange the universe to fit their own desires.

In Romans, Paul marks this downward lemming-like rush of the human race in three stages.

1. "*Therefore God gave them over in the sinful desires of their hearts to sexual impurity for the degrading of their bodies with one another*" (v. 24). I do not know why, when he set out to trace this downward moral path of human beings, the apostle Paul concentrated on sexual sins, since he could clearly have

chosen other sins as well. Perhaps it is because sexual sins are so visible (sins of the spirit are harder to detect) or because the damage in this area is so evident or because this was the obvious, stinking cesspool of corruption in his day and, therefore, something those to whom he was writing would clearly understand. Whatever the reason—and there may be even more reasons than these—it is an excellent example.

Sex is a wonderful gift, a gift imparted to the human race by God. It is a gift to be enjoyed. *But* it is be enjoyed within the bonds of marriage, not outside of marriage and, above all, not in casual entanglements. If it is, the result is always what Paul declares it will be, namely, "impurity" and the "degrading" of one's body.

It is evident that hardly anything in Romans 1 is more contemporary so far as our own culture is concerned. Today we are witnessing a frantic pursuit of pleasure that has been called rightly, even by the secular media, "the new hedonism." That is, ours is seemingly a culture in which casual sex and every other kind of casual pleasure is an ideal. And it is an ideal that has been actualized by many! With what results? At the start of this path the Prodigal Son would no doubt extol it for its freedoms. He would speak of being free to think new thoughts, have new experiences, and shake off all that old inhibiting sense of guilt that bound him previously. But, given time, the feeling changes, and the one who is running away comes inevitably to feel used, taken advantage of, dirty, and betrayed.

Not long ago CBS television ran an hour-long special on the freewheeling lifestyle in California, interviewing particularly many women who had been caught up in it. Interestingly, their nearly universal opinion was that they had been betrayed by the sexual revolution. As one woman said, "All men want from us is our bodies; we have had enough of that to last a lifetime."

Isn't it the case that these women were expressing precisely what Paul says in verse 25, when he observes that those who act this way "have exchanged the truth of God for a lie"? Let's say it clearly, as the world is beginning to recognize: The "new hedonism" and the "sexual revolution" are a deception!

But there is more. There is a second downhill step on this path. . . .

2. *"Because of this, God gave them over to shameful lusts. Even their women exchanged natural relations for unnatural ones. In the same way the men also abandoned natural relations with women and were inflamed with lust for one another. Men committed indecent acts with other men, and received in themselves the due penalty for their perversion"* (vv. 26–27).

I wrote a moment ago that there is nothing more contemporary in terms of today's culture than Paul's description of a declining society in this great first chapter of Romans. This has been clear already in terms of today's forms of hedonism and the sexual revolution. Unfortunately, the decline becomes even more apparent as Paul, with almost shocking candor, begins to talk about sexual perversions, namely, lesbianism and male homosexuality. For centuries these matters were hardly spoken of in western society. Although some were no doubt practicing these acts, they were considered so reprehensible that a moral person not only was not to speak about them, but he or she was not even to know what such vices involved. But today? Today they are written about with explicit detail in virtually every newspaper and magazine in our land. Grade-school children discuss them. Not only are we not shocked—but we have become complacent, as if this were a natural expression of an upright spirit.

"Natural" is the important word here—Paul uses it in verse 27, and the opposite term, "unnatural," in verse 26—because it explains why this stage is a *further* step along the downward moral path.

Let me elaborate on that statement. Fornication and adultery (which are in view in verse 24) are not "unnatural" sins, for they are not against nature. Of course, they are true sins, for they break the moral law of God. They result in "impurity" and in the "degrading" of our bodies, as Paul says. But they are not unnatural. On the contrary, they are in one sense quite natural. They are accomplished by using one's body in a natural way. Not so with homosexuality! Homosexuality is "unnatural," and it is accomplished by using one's body in an unnatural way, that is, against nature. In the first case, we may well need the Bible to tell us that fornication is wrong. The popular song asks, "How can it be wrong when it seems so right?" But in the case of homosexuality we do not even need this special revelation. A look at one's sexual apparatus should convince anyone that practices of this kind are not normal. They were not meant to be.

Perhaps this is why at this point, and at no other point in his discussion of the results of our rebellion, Paul speaks of a specific judgment of God upon the sin itself: "Men committed indecent acts with other men, and received in themselves the due penalty for their perversion" (v. 27). Up to this point Paul has not been saying that God punishes these or other particular sins with particular penalties, but rather that the abandonment of human beings to the committing of the sin is itself the punishment. That is, God punishes you by letting you do what you want. But not here, at least not *only* that. Here Paul speaks of a particular penalty "received in themselves" by those who sin in this way.

Is Paul speaking of AIDS (acquired immunodeficiency syndrome)? No! He had never heard of AIDS, though he was probably thinking at least in part of other sexual diseases. But the point is irrelevant. What Paul is saying is that sin does and will have consequences, and "unnatural" sins will have particularly "unnatural" consequences.

Indeed, it is not only Paul who would say this. Not long ago *Time* magazine ran a cover story on AIDS, called "The Big Chill: Fear of AIDS," in which even this obviously secular magazine spoke religiously. It spoke of AIDS as "a vague sort of retribution, an Old Testament-style revenge." It quoted novelist Erica Jong, author of *Fear of Flying* and a former high priest-ess of sexual abandon, as saying, "It's hard enough to find attractive single men without having to quiz them on their history of bisexuality and drug use, demand blood test results and thrust condoms into their hands. Wouldn't it be easier to give up sex altogether and join some religious order?" *Time* also quoted a Los Angeles entertainment writer: "AIDS pushes monogamy right back up there on the priority list."[2]

Why is this? Why are even secular magazines and newspapers beginning to sound like prophets? It is because of the given, because of the unchange-able physical and moral character of the universe in which we live. We may not like it; most of us don't. We would change it if we could. But we cannot. It is God's universe. It does not change. Therefore, the only wise thing is to come to terms with it, repent of sin, and come back to God in the way he has provided: through faith in the sacrifice of himself for us by Jesus Christ.

Yet there is something more. . .

3. *"Furthermore, since they did not think it worthwhile to retain the knowledge of God, he gave them over to a depraved mind, to do what ought not to be done"* (v. 28). The first time I began to think about this threefold repetition of the sen-tence "God gave them over" in this section of Romans, it seemed to me that at this point something was apparently wrong with the order. Paul is tracing a downward declining path, resulting from humanity's rebellion against God, yet here the order doesn't seem to be downward. We can understand that when men and women abandoned God, God abandoned them: first, to sexual impurity and, second, to sexual perversions. That is surely downhill. But now we find that God abandons them "to a depraved mind." Isn't that something that should have come first? Doesn't sin originate in the mind? Shouldn't the third of these consequences have been listed first, *before* the other two consequences?

I was puzzled by this sequence until I realized that the "depraved mind" about which Paul is writing is not just any sinful mind—he has earlier talked about the generally foolish minds and generally darkened hearts of human beings—but about the specifically "depraved mind" created by continuing down this awful path for a lifetime. At the end is a mind not merely foolish or in error, but totally depraved. It is a mind so depraved that it begins to think that what is bad is actually good and that what is good is actually bad. May I say it? It is the mind of the devil, which is what Adam chose to pursue when he followed the dangling carrot: "You will be like God, knowing good and evil" (Gen. 3:5). Adam did not become "like God," knowing good and evil; he became "like Satan." And, being like Satan, in time he came to call the good bad and the bad good. How else can one explain man's continual flight from him from whom alone all good gifts come (cf. James 1:17)?

2. *Time*, February 16, 1987, p. 51.

The evidence of this bottom stage of depravity is disclosed in verse 32, the end of Romans 1: "Although they know God's righteous decree that those who do such things deserve death, they not only continue to do these very things but also approve of those who practice them." The new word here is "approve." It is not only that people do what is sinful. A person might do that, be ashamed of his or her action, and then repent of it. But here, at the very end of this awful downhill path of judicial abandonment described in this chapter of Romans, the individuals involved actually come to *approve* of what is evil.

How do you appeal for good to a person who has become like that? Every argument you could possibly use would be reversed. The case is hopeless.

"How Can I Give You Up?"

Hopeless? Yes, but not for God. For if it were, why would Paul even be writing this letter? As a matter of fact, if it were hopeless, *he* would not be writing it, for he was one of the most hopeless cases of all, as he reminds us several times in his epistles.

We are focusing here on the idea that "God gave them up." The way I want to state this is to say that although in a sense God has certainly given the race *over* to the natural outworkings of its rebellious ways—a judgment we see about us on all hands—in another sense God has not "given up" at all. At least he has not given up on those on whom he has set his affection. I think of the way in which he speaks through Hosea to the sinful nation of Israel:

> "How can I give you up, Ephraim?
>   How can I hand you over, Israel?
> How can I treat you like Admah?
>   How can I make you like Zeboiim?
> My heart is changed within me;
>   all my compassion is aroused.
> I will not carry out my fierce anger,
>   nor devastate Ephraim again."
>   Hosea 11:8–9

If God actually did give up on humanity forever, all would be hopeless. The Lord Jesus Christ would not have come. He would not have died for our sin. There would be no gospel. But that is not the case. Jesus did come. There is a gospel. The way back to the eternal, sovereign, holy God is open. This is the Good News. Hallelujah!

And need I say more? If there is the gospel, if this is still the age of God's grace, if God has not given up on us ultimately and forever—though he will eventually do that for some one day—then we are not to give up on other people either. How can we, if we have tasted the elixir of grace ourselves?

We tend to give up, at least if the sin of the one we are abandoning is different from our own. We think of others as too far gone, or as having sinned beyond the point of a genuine repentance. Or, terrible as it is, we think of their sin as proof, evidence, that God has abandoned them forever. Many have done that with homosexuals. They regard AIDS as the kind of divine judgment on this sin that precludes our having any pity on the victims or working to bring them the only salvation they can know. Is AIDS a judgment? I believe it is, just like many other consequences of sin. But it is not the final judgment. And until that final judgment breaks forth on our race, it is still the day of grace in which all who know the Good News and are obeying the voice of Christ in taking it to the lost can be hopeful.

Someone once spoke to John Newton, the man who had been a slave trader and a "slave to slaves" earlier in his life, about a person he regarded as a hopeless case. He despaired of him. Newton replied, "I have never despaired for any man since God saved me." We should not despair either. The consequences of sin are dreadful. But they alone, if nothing else, should compel us forward as agents of God's great grace and reconciliation.

21

Lifting the Lid on Hell

Romans 1:29–31

They have become filled with every kind of wickedness, evil, greed and depravity. They are full of envy, murder, strife, deceit and malice. They are gossips, slanderers, God-haters, insolent, arrogant and boastful; they invent ways of doing evil; they disobey their parents; they are senseless, faithless, heartless, ruthless.

For several chapters we have been studying the most dreadful description of the sinful human race in all literature, the description provided by the apostle Paul in Romans 1:18–32. It began with the rejection of God by all people and has proceeded to God's abandonment of us, as a result of which human beings rapidly fall into a horrible pit of depravity, to their own hurt and the hurt of others.

In the last verses of Romans 1, to which we come now, Paul rounds out his description by a catalogue of vices. It is a long list, containing twenty-one items. But how are we to handle this? How can we face such a devastating unmasking of ourselves? Some will not face it at all, of course. Indeed, even many preachers will not. These verses detail what theologians call "total depravity," and people do not want to hear about that. So many preachers change their message to fit today's cultural expectations. They speak of our

185

goodness, the potential for human betterment, the comfort of the gospel—without speaking of that for which the gospel is the cure.

Jesus said, "Love the Lord your God with all your heart and with all your soul and with all your mind" and "your neighbor as yourself" (Matt. 22:37, 39). But, as one writer says, "Man as sinner hates God, hates man, and hates himself. He would kill God if he could. He does kill his fellow man when he can. [And] he commits spiritual suicide every day of his life."[1]

The interesting thing about this, however, is that although the pulpit has been muted in its proclamation of the truth of man's depravity, the secular writers have not. They write as if they have never met a good man or a virtuous woman. Psychiatrists say that if you scratch the surface and thus penetrate beneath the thin veneer of human culture and respectability, you "lift the lid of hell."[2]

All Kinds of Wickedness

At the beginning of this section Paul wrote that "the wrath of God is being revealed from heaven against all the godlessness and wickedness of men who suppress the truth by their wickedness" (v. 18). In that verse the second use of "wickedness" refers to man's suppression of the truth about God. But at the beginning of the verse, where the term is used for the first time, "wickedness" is distinguished from "godlessness"; godlessness and wickedness are employed to designate two great categories of human evil. The first embraces all sins against God, that is, sins of the first table of the law. The second embraces the sins of man against man, those of the second table of the law. Generally speaking, it is the sins of "godlessness" that we have been looking at to this point; they are fundamental. However, in these last verses Paul lists examples of man's "wickedness."

1. *Wickedness.* It is probably to indicate that he is now moving to this second category of sins that Paul begins his catalogue of vices with this term. For "wickedness" in verse 29 is the same word that is used in verse 18. In Greek it is a composite negative term, made up of the positive word for "righteousness" (*dikaios*), preceded by the negative particle *a,* meaning "not." Literally it means "not righteous," or "unjust." Since what is "right" is determined by the character or law of God, this term denotes everything that is opposed to that divine law or character. It embraces what follows.

2. *Evil.* The Greek word is *ponēria,* which is a general term for badness. One commentator says, "This refers to the general inclination to evil that reigned among the heathen and made them practice and take pleasure in

---

1. John H. Gerstner, "The Atonement and the Purpose of God" in James Montgomery Boice, ed., *Our Savior God: Man, Christ and the Atonement* (Grand Rapids: Baker Book House, 1980), p. 107.

2. Ibid.

vicious and unprofitable actions."[3] But, of course, it is not just the heathen who are evil, unless we rightly call everyone by that name. We, too, are evil.

3. *Greed.* In other places, this word (*pleonexia*) is translated "covetousness." It is what God prohibits in the tenth of the Ten Commandments and what is nevertheless the apparent basis of our western economies. It is the desire always to want a little more. There is a proper kind of ambition, of course. There is a proper desire to improve oneself, particularly for the benefit of others. But that is not what is referred to by this term. It is "the passion for more," the lust to advance oneself even at the expense of others.

4. *Depravity.* This word denotes that deliberate wickedness that delights in doing other people harm. It could be translated "maliciousness."

As I have mentioned, there are twenty-one terms for evil in these verses, and these are just the first four. But these four belong together in Paul's listing, since they are vices with which Paul says the human race is "filled." What holds them together? They seem primarily to describe injustices that humans commit against the property of other people, and thus also against their well-being.

Hatred of One's Fellowman

Having shown in the earlier part of this chapter of Romans that human beings hate God and would kill him if they could, Paul now shows how they also hate and attempt to destroy their fellows. In other words, the first four terms describe sins against the property and well-being of others. In the next five terms Paul details sins against the very persons of other human beings. The sins are: envy, murder, strife, deceit, and malice.

5. *Envy.* Earlier Paul has spoken of "greed," indicating that people never seem to be satisfied with what they have but instead clamor for more, often at the cost of others. Here he goes further. Envy is related to greed, but it goes beyond it, because it shows that the chief factor in our greed is jealousy over the fact that other people have more. Or worse! It is possible that they have less and that we are still greedy for what they have, simply because we envy them. In ancient Greece there was a man whose name was Aristides. He was a great man and was called "Aristides the Just." But he was put on trial for something, as many just men were, and a citizen of Athens came to him not knowing who he was and asked him to vote for his own banishment. Aristides asked, "But what harm has Aristides done you?"

The man said, "None. I am just tired of hearing him called 'Aristides the Just.'" That is envy in its most destructive form.

3. Robert Haldane, *An Exposition of the Epistle to the Romans* (MacDill AFB: MacDonald Publishing, 1958), p. 67.

6. *Murder.* The Greek word for "murder" (*phonou*) sounds like the word for "envy" (*phthonou*), which is why they probably appear together so often in ancient texts. But they belong together naturally, too, since murder often flows from envy. Cain's murder of his brother Abel, the first murder in history, is an example. "And why did he murder him?" John asks. "Because his own actions were evil and his brother's were righteous" (1 John 3:12). Another early example is Lamech, who killed a young man who had injured him (perhaps only verbally) and then boasted about the deed (Gen. 4:23). We must remember here also that, according to Jesus, murder is not only the outward act of taking a life. It is also the hatred in the heart that leads to it (cf. Matt. 5:21–22).

7. *Strife.* The root meaning of this word is "debate." But it came to mean the bad side of debate, which is contention, quarreling, or wrangling.

8. *Deceit.* Paul is going to return to this word in his summation of human depravity in chapter 3, saying in verse 13 that the "tongues" of the wicked practice this vice. It denotes outright treachery by which words are used to ensnare the unwary for the deceiver's personal gain. Much of the business of the western world is carried on by this means.

9. *Malice.* This word is derived from two Greek words: *kakos*, which means "bad," "evil," "worthless," or "pernicious" (we have it in our word *cacophony*, which is a bad or discordant sound) and *ethos*, which means "habit," "custom" or "usage." So the word has the idea of customary or habitual evil. The malicious person is one who is normally set against other people and is out to harm them.

The Central Sins

It is hard to group these vices to give logic to Paul's treatment, and it may even be wrong to try to see meaningful groupings in his arrangement. Nevertheless, if the first four terms catalogue sins against the property or well-being of others, and the next five list sins against other persons, it may be that the next six terms are, as one commentator suggests, "those of which pride is the center."[4] They are certainly among the most harmful of these vices.

10. *Gossips.* Some words in every language sound like what they describe, and this is the case here. We have words like hiss, buzz, thump, and bang, for example. This Greek word is *psithuristas*, which sounds like a whisper and is, in fact, sometimes translated "whisperings." It refers to the slanderous gossip that is often spread in secret and that is so harmful to another's reputation. It is a deadly vice. It is interesting that the Hebrew word that

4. F. Godet, *Commentary on St. Paul's Epistle to the Romans*, trans. A. Cusin (Edinburgh: T. & T. Clark, n.d.), vol. 1, p. 184.

denotes the murmuring of a snake charmer is translated in the Septuagint by the verb form of this very word: to whisper.

11. *Slanderers.* Slander carries gossip one step further, since gossip is unleashed in secret but slander is done openly. The Greek word literally means "to speak against" someone, or "defame" him.

12. *God-haters.* At first glance, this word seems to be out of place in this listing, because here we are dealing with man's sins against man and "God-hater" seems more properly to belong in the earlier verses, in which man's opposition to God was examined. For this reason some have taken the word in a passive sense, meaning "hated by God," that is, as a term for hardened sinners. But surely it cannot mean that in a list of human vices. Actually, it does belong here, since it comes between the sin of slander and the sin of pride. It is as if Paul notes that in his "slander" man does not merely slander other human beings but is slandering God, too, not failing to speak even against the Almighty. That is the essence of insolence and arrogance, the next items the apostle mentions.

Not many people would admit that they hate God, choosing rather to think of themselves as rather tolerant of him. But nowhere do they show their hatred more than in their condescending attitudes. Scratch beneath the surface, allow something to come into their lives that they consider unwarranted or unfair, and their hatred of God immediately boils over. "How could God let this happen to me?" they demand. If they could, they would strangle him!

13. *Insolent.* This is the great Greek word *hubris,* which means "pride." But it is a special kind of pride. It is pride that sets a human being up against God. The Greeks regarded this as the greatest of flaws, one the gods would not tolerate. No translation can convey all this in one English word, but the New International Version does a fair job when it renders it "insolent."

14. *Arrogant.* Today people almost think of arrogance as a virtue, considering it a properly belligerent attitude toward hostile society. But it is rightly included in this list of vices. Arrogance rises from a feeling of personal superiority that regards others with haughtiness. Robert Haldane characterizes the word as describing those who are "puffed up with a high opinion of themselves" and who regard others "with contempt, as if they were unworthy of any intercourse with them."[5]

15. *Boastful.* Boasting is based on pride. It is to seek admiration by claiming to be or have what one actually is not or does not possess.

5. Haldane, *An Exposition of the Epistle to the Romans,* p. 69.

Creators of Evil

Up to this point all the vices mentioned are but one word in Greek. But now Paul seems to need two words each to describe the next evils: "inventors of evil things" (*epheupetas kakōn*) and "disobedient to parents" (*goneusin apeitheis*).

16. *They invent ways of doing evil.* Real creativity belongs to God alone, since at best we can only think his thoughts after him. But here, in an ironical way, Paul suggests that the one area in which our creativity excels is inventing new ways to do evil. The old ways are not enough for us. They are too slow, too ineffective, too unproductive, too dull. So we expend our efforts to make more. This was a term used by the author of 2 Maccabees to describe Antiochus Epiphanes and by Tacitus to describe Sejanus. It is this kind of invention that the psalm is speaking of when it says that people "provoked him [God] to anger with their inventions" (Ps. 106:29 KJV).

17. *They disobey their parents.* Few things more characterize our day than children's utter disregard of their parents' wishes. But this must have been common enough in antiquity, too, since so much is said against it in the Bible. The fifth of the Ten Commandments, the first of the second table, says: "Honor your father and your mother" (Exod. 20:12a). Paul refers to it in Ephesians, noting that it is the first commandment with a promise attached: "that it may go well with you and that you may enjoy long life on the earth" (Eph. 6:2).

Senseless, Faithless, Heartless, Ruthless

The Greek word for disobedience (the seventeenth vice listed) is a compound word beginning with the prefix *a,* meaning "not," just like the term "not righteous" was used for "wickedness" in verse 29. That sound apparently stuck in Paul's mind and led to a series of four similar terms, which conclude this devastating catalogue: *asynetous, asynthetous, astorgous,* and *aneleēmonas.* The New International Version captures a bit of this flavor by rendering the four terms as: senseless, faithless, heartless, ruthless.

18. *Senseless.* To most of us "senseless" probably means unconscious, but that is not the thought here. "Without understanding" is a fuller translation, but even so we need to make clear the kind of lack of understanding we mean. Haldane has it right in saying that "the persons so described were not destitute of understanding as to the things of this world." As to these they might be "most intelligent and enlightened." Rather it was "in a moral sense, or as respects the things of God, [that] they were unintelligent and stupid. . . . All men are by nature undiscerning as to the things of God, and to this there never was an exception."[6]

6. Ibid., p. 70.

19. *Faithless.* This word is not built on the Greek word for faith (*pistis*), which has to do with belief or trust in God. Rather, the root is *tithēmi* ("put" or "place"), and the term Paul uses actually has to do with breaking an appointment or covenant. "Breaking faith" is the idea. It means that what people solemnly commit themselves to cannot be trusted.

20. *Heartless.* This word literally means "without natural affection." It can be seen in the mother who intentionally aborts or abandons her child or the father who abandons his family.

21. *Ruthless.* The Greek word means "without mercy." Godet writes, "It calls up before the mind the entire population of the great cities flocking to the circus to behold the fights of gladiators, frantically applauding the effusion of human blood, and gloating over the dying agonies of the vanquished combatant. Such is an example of the unspeakable hardness of heart to which the whole society of the Gentile world descended."[7] Ah, but it was not only in the ancient world that people lacked mercy. Ours is a particularly ruthless age. We tend to think that others are unmerciful, particularly when they deal harshly with us. But the truth is that cruelty is at the heart of even the most gentle human being.

One commentator observes that as we scan these lists, "we cannot but be impressed with the apostle's insight into the depravity of human nature as apostatized from God, the severity of his assessment of these moral conditions, and the breadth of his knowledge respecting the concrete ways in which human depravity came to expression."[8]

The Road to Hell

I began this section by saying that it is hard to imagine anything more horrible than this great catalogue of human vices, not merely because they are horrible in themselves, but also because they are with us everywhere. To study a list like this does not mean that every individual is equally guilty of each vice or that there have not been periods of history when they have been either more or less prominent. But, at best, these are all just below the surface of our respectability, and they quickly become apparent whenever you cross our sinful human nature or scratch this surface.

Yet, horrible as this is, it is only a foretaste of what hell itself will be like. For hell is only what is described in these verses, going on and on for eternity. Lloyd-Jones writes, "Hell is a condition in which life is lived away from God and all the restraints of God's holiness."[9] That is precisely what is described in this passage. The basic point is that the human race has cho-

7. Godet, *Commentary on St. Paul's Epistle to the Romans*, p. 185.

8. John Murray, *The Epistle to the Romans* (Grand Rapids: Wm. B. Eerdmans Publishing Company, 1968), p. 50.

9. D. M. Lloyd-Jones, *Romans: An Exposition of Chapter 1, The Gospel of God* (Grand Rapids: Zondervan, 1985), p. 392.

sen to go its way without God and that as a result of this choice God has abandoned the race to the result of its own sinful choices. We have made earth a hell! And we will carry that hell with us into hell, making hell even more hellish than it is already! We and hell itself will go on becoming more and more hell-like for eternity.

Oh, the horror of our choice!

Oh, the glory of the gospel!

A few weeks before I preached this study, after my earlier sermon on "The Psychology of Atheism," I was roundly chastised in a local paper for preaching such a harsh message, as if I had no word of love in my teaching. It may have been that the love of God was not as apparent in that message as it might have been, and if so, I need to correct that fault. But I do know that it is only an awareness of the horror of our sin that ever leads us to appreciate the gospel when we hear it. What if we think we are basically all right before God? What if we think ourselves good? Then we think we do not need the gospel. We think we can do without God, which is exactly what these verses are describing.

When our blinders are stripped off and the depravity of the race—to which we contribute—is unfolded before us, the glory of the gospel bursts forth, and Romans 1:16 and 17 becomes for us what Martin Luther found it to be for him, namely, "the door to Paradise." The gospel is then seen to be "the power of God for the salvation of everyone who believes"—no matter how sinful, no matter how corrupt.

We do not deserve this gospel. How could we? We could not even invent it. But because God is not like us—because he is not "wicked," "evil," "greedy," "depraved," "envious," "senseless," "faithless," "heartless," "ruthless," or anything else that is bad—he not only could invent it, he did!

22

How Low Can You Go?

Romans 1:32

Although they know God's righteous decree that those who do such things deserve death, they not only continue to do these very things but also approve those who practice them.

Over the years I have collected questions about the Christian life that I wish someone had answered for me when I was much younger. One is "Why can't a person sin just a little bit?" I think this is an important question, because it is where most of us find ourselves much of the time. Most of us would not admit to wanting to sin in big ways, and we probably don't. We know that sin is destructive. We do not want to make an utter shipwreck of our lives. But we wonder from time to time why we can't sin "just a little bit." God forbids all sin, of course. But surely all sins are not equally terrible. What would be so bad about our just dipping into sin now and then—to sort of satisfy our appetite for it, have our fling, and then get back out and go on with our "upright" Christian lives?

Having studied most of the first chapter of Romans carefully, we should know the answer to that question. The problem with just dipping into sin is that sin never stops at that point. The problem with sinning "just a little bit"

193

is that each bit is followed by just a little bit more, until God has been banished from life's horizons entirely and we have ruined everything.

The Downhill Path

The way this happens is spelled out in the second half of Romans 1 by a threefold repetition of the phrase "God gave them over," which we have already studied. (It occurs in verses 24, 26, and 28.) Just before this, Paul has shown how we reject God. We reject God by suppressing the knowledge about him that we have received from nature and by allowing the God-like vacuum in our lives to be filled with substitutes. We do it by saying, in effect (though we often do not admit it even to ourselves), "God, we do not want you. We want you to get out of our lives and leave us alone. We want to do our own thing without your interference."

So that is just what God does! God does not abandon us in the absolute sense, since this is still God's world and we still have to live in it and conform to the laws of this world, whether we want to or not. But God does abandon us to our own devices in the sense that he withdraws his restraints. He allows us to go our own way, abandoning us judicially to sin's consequences.

That path is definitely downhill!

It cannot be any other way, of course. If God is the source of all good, as the Bible declares him to be, then to abandon God is to abandon the good and to launch oneself on a path leading in progressive measure to all that is evil. If we will not have God, who is truth, we will find falsehood. If we will not seek God, who is holy, we will pursue perversions. If we will not have God, who is the source of all reality, we will have unreality. We will pursue fantasies and dreams and be disillusioned.

A review seems appropriate at this point. In declaring that God gives us over to our own devices, Paul describes a downhill slide that looks like this:

1. *God gave them over to sexual impurity* (v. 24). The reference is to fornication and adultery, which, Paul says, have two outcomes. First, they result in the degrading of our bodies. People who have had a variety of sexual partners often testify to this. Second, they result in exchanging what is good and true for what is bad and a deception. Paul calls it "a lie." Again, many who have sought personal fulfillment through sexual experimentation testify that promises of the "liberated" life were deceptions. The promised satisfaction and fulfillment did not materialize.

2. *God gave them over to shameful lusts* (v. 26). This refers to perversions, chiefly male homosexuality and lesbianism, and it is a step downward from mere sexual experimentation. This is because, in addition to being merely sinful, these perversions are "unnatural." That is, they are against nature. Bodies were not meant to function in these ways. Those who sin in these

ways do so, therefore, not only against God's revelation in the Old and New Testaments, but also against the very order of creation.

3. *God gave them over to a depraved mind* (v. 28). When we looked at this verse before, I asked why this is a step further down the ladder of abandonment by God than items one and two. After all, sins of the mind precede sins of the flesh; a person has to think sin before practicing it. So why should this be the third item, rather than the first?

The answer, as we saw earlier, is that this is not the kind of mental depravity Paul is thinking of. It is true that thoughts about evil generally precede evil actions. But here Paul is speaking about the kind of thought perversion that results in the person involved regarding what is good as what (to him or her) appears evil, and what is evil as what (to him or her) appears good. This brings us to the verse with which this great chapter of Romans ends, our text for this study. Verse 32 says of those who have sunk to this point, "Although they know God's righteous decree that those who do such things deserve death, they not only continue to do these very things but also approve of those who practice them." The key word here is "approve." It means that these people sanction both the evil and the evildoers.

Moral Insanity

This is insanity, of course—moral insanity. But it is important to see that this is exactly the point to which rejection of God and suppression of the truth about God lead us.

It is helpful at this point to think of the story of King Nebuchadnezzar of Babylon, as told in the early chapters of Daniel. The theme of Daniel is the identity of the Most High God, and it is established early in the book when we are told that after Nebuchadnezzar had conquered Jerusalem, he carried articles from the temple of God in Jerusalem "to the temple of his god in Babylonia and put [them] in the treasure house of his god" (Dan. 1:2). This was a way of saying that, in Nebuchadnezzar's opinion, his god was stronger than the Jewish God. And so it seemed! Nebuchadnezzar had conquered Jerusalem. He did not understand that God had used him merely as an instrument of judgment upon his disobedient people, as he had repeatedly said he would do.

But Nebuchadnezzar was not really interested in proving that his *god* was stronger than the Jews' God; he was not all that religious. Nebuchadnezzar's god was only a projection of himself, an *alter ego*, and the real struggle of the book is therefore actually between Nebuchadnezzar himself and Jehovah. In other words, it is exactly the struggle that Paul depicts in Romans as being between sinful humanity and God. Nebuchadnezzar did not want to acknowledge God, precisely what Paul says *we* do not want to do. He wanted to run his own life, achieve what he wanted to achieve and then claim the glory for himself for those achievements.

The climax of his rebellion, recorded in Daniel 4, came when Nebuchadnezzar looked over Babylon from the roof of his palace and claimed the glory of God for himself, saying, "Is not this the great Babylon I have built as the royal residence, by my mighty power and for the glory of my majesty?" (Dan. 4:30). This is the cry of the secular humanist. It describes life as of man, by man, and for man's glory.

The point for which I introduce this illustration comes now, in the nature of the judgment pronounced upon this powerful but arrogant emperor. Sometimes, when we think of God's dispensing of judgments, we think of him as acting somewhat arbitrarily, as if he were merely going down a list of punishments to see what punishment he has left for some special sinner. "Let's see now," he might muse. "Nebuchadnezzar? What will it be? Not leprosy, not kidney stones, not paralysis, not goiter. Ah, here it is: *insanity*. That's what I'll use with Nebuchadnezzar." We may think that is what happened, when we read about the voice "from heaven" that declared: "This is what is decreed for you, King Nebuchadnezzar: Your royal authority has been taken from you. You will be driven away from people and will live with the wild animals; you will eat grass like cattle. Seven times will pass by for you until you acknowledge that the Most High is sovereign over the kingdoms of men and gives them to anyone he wishes" (Dan. 4:31–32).[1]

But this is not the way it happened. God is not arbitrary. He does not operate by sorting through a list of options. Everything God does is significant. So when God caused Nebuchadnezzar to be lowered from the pinnacle of human pride and glory to the baseness of insanity, it was God's way of saying that this is what happens to all who suppress the truth about God and take the glory of God for themselves. The path is not uphill. It is downhill, and it ends in that moral insanity by which we declare what is good to be evil, and what is evil to be good.

Bestial Behavior

But it is not only insanity that we see in the case of Nebuchadnezzar. We see a dramatization of bestial behavior, too, in the words decreeing that Nebuchadnezzar would "live with the wild animals [and] eat grass like cattle." Indeed, what came to pass was even worse. We are told that "he was driven away from people and ate grass like cattle. His body was drenched with the dew of heaven until his hair grew like the feathers of an eagle and his nails like the claws of a bird" (Dan. 4:33). It is a horrible picture. But it is merely a dramatic Old Testament way of describing what Paul is saying in Romans: If we will not have God, we will not become like God ("like God, knowing

1. This must be a description of insanity and the customary treatment of the insane in those days, because later in the story Nebuchadnezzar himself speaks of his "sanity" being restored (Dan. 4:34).

good and evil," Gen. 3:5); on the contrary, we will become like and live like animals.

At this point I always think of Psalm 8, verses 4 through 7, which say:

> When I consider your heavens,
>   the work of your fingers,
> the moon and the stars.
>   which you have set in place,
> what is man that you are mindful of him,
>   the son of man that you care for him?
> You made him a little lower than the heavenly beings
>   and crowned him with glory and honor.
> You made him ruler over the works of your hands;
>   you put everything under his feet:
> all flocks and herds,
>   and the beasts of the field.

These verses fix man at a very interesting place in the created order: lower than the angels, or heavenly beings, but higher than the animals—somewhere between.[2] This is what Thomas Aquinas saw when he described man as a mediating being. He is like the angels in that he has a soul. But he is like the beasts in that he has a body. The angels have souls but not bodies, while the animals have bodies but not souls.

But here is the point. Although man is a mediating being, created to be somewhere between the angels and the animals, in Psalm 8 he is nevertheless described as being somewhat lower than the angels rather than as being somewhat higher than the beasts. In other words, although between the angels and the beasts, man is nevertheless destined to look, not downward to the beasts, but upward to the angels and beyond the heavenly beings to God, becoming increasingly like him. If he will not look up and thus become increasingly like God, he will inevitably look down and become like the animals. Like Nebuchadnezzar, he will become beastlike.

Over the last ten or so years I have noticed something very interesting about our culture. I have noticed a number of articles (and sometimes books) that have tended to justify or at least explain bestial human behavior on the ground that we are, after all, "just animals." We have perversions, but—well, the animals have perversions, too.

Some time ago an article appeared in a scientific journal about a certain kind of duck. Two scientists had been observing a family of these ducks, and they reported something that they called "gang rape" in this duck family. I am sure they did not want to excuse this crime among humans by the

---

2. It is true that portions of verses 4–6 occur in Hebrews 2 in reference to Jesus Christ. But in Psalm 8 they are used of men and women in general, and they are used of Jesus in Hebrews only because of his having become a man. That is, he became "a little lower than the angels" in order to be like us. In this way he became our "brother" (cf. Heb. 2:11).

inevitable comparison they were making. But I think their point was that gang rape among humans is at least understandable, given our animal ancestry. These scientists had an evolutionary, naturalistic background, and I think they were saying, "After all, gang rape is not that surprising when you consider that even the ducks do it."

A story of a similar nature appeared in the September 6, 1982, issue of *Newsweek* magazine. It was accompanied by a picture of a baboon presumably killing an infant baboon, and over this there was a headline which read: "Biologists Say Infanticide Is as Normal as the Sex Drive—And That Most Animals, Including Man, Practice It." The title says everything. It identifies man as an animal, and it justifies his behavior on the basis of this identification. The logic goes like this: (1) man is an animal; (2) animals kill their offspring; (3) therefore, it is all right (or at least understandable) that human beings kill their offspring. But, of course, the argument is fallacious. Most animals do not kill their offspring. They protect their young and care for them. And even if, in a few rare instances, some animals do kill their young, this is still nothing to compare to the crimes regarding the young of which human beings are capable. In this country alone, for example, we kill over one and a half million babies each year by abortion—in most instances, simply for the convenience of the mother.

Worse Than the Animals

I want to take this a step further, however, and to do that I share the following story. Dr. John Gerstner, Professor Emeritus of Pittsburgh Theological Seminary, was teaching about the depravity of man, and to make his point he compared men and women to rats. After he had finished his address there was a question-and-answer period, and someone who had been offended by the comparison asked Gerstner to apologize. Gerstner did. "I do apologize," he said. "I apologize profusely. The comparison was terribly unfair . . . to the rats." He then went on to show that what a rat does, it does by the gifts of God that make it ratlike. It does not sin. But we, when we behave like rats, behave worse than we should and even worse than rats. We are worse than "beasts" in our behavior.

Do ducks commit rape? I have never observed that particular family of ducks, and I do not know if they do or do not. Perhaps so. But I do know that if rape occurs in the animal world, it is uncommon. Not so with us. In the human race it is frightfully common. Or again, I do not know if baboons actually kill their young. They may. But they do not systematically murder them for their own convenience, as we do.

Is There a Bottom Rung?

Everything I have been describing to this point has concerned the downhill passage of the human race when it turns away from God, based on

Romans 1:32, the last verse of this first great section of Paul's letter. This verse describes the nadir of man's fall. I have called it the lowest point, the worst point on the downward sliding scale.

But is it really the lowest point? Is it the bottom? Or *is* there a bottom? Is there a point beyond which sin will not go?

I have asked this last question from time to time in terms of our declining western culture—not so much in an absolute sense but in terms of the moral sensibilities of our nation. I have asked, "Is there a point at which we will pull back from our increasingly rapid decline and say, 'This is where we stop; this is terrible; this is a point beyond which we will not go'?" Is there such a point in our culture?

If there is, it is certainly not adultery. We have plenty of that.

It is not prostitution. In fact, prostitution is actually legal in some places.

It is not pornography, though Christians have been opposing pornography effectively in some areas.

Where is the point beyond which our culture does not want to go?

I have noticed that in recent years there has been an attempt to define this point at the place where perversions impinge upon children. The argument would go, "It is not possible to forbid anything to adults as long as they want to do something or consent with each other to do it. But we must not allow these things to affect children. Pornography? Yes, but not child pornography. Prostitution? Yes, but not child prostitution." That sounds good, of course. It gives us the feeling that we are both tolerant—God forbid that we should be intolerant—and moral. But it is sheer hypocrisy. I remember noticing, the first time I was beginning to think along these lines, that at the very time articles were appearing to protest against child pornography and child prostitution, a movie appeared starring Brooke Shields, who was only twelve years old at the time but who played the part of a child prostitute in a brothel in New Orleans at the turn of the century. It was called *Pretty Baby*. Certain elements of the media suggested that the young actress "matured" through her experience.

Do you see what I am saying? When we are sliding downhill we delude ourselves into thinking that we are only going to dip into sin a little bit or at least that there are points beyond which we will never go, lines we will never cross. But this is sheer fantasy. When we start down that downhill path, there are no points beyond which we will not go and no lines we will not choose to cross—if we live long enough. And even if we die, hell (as I commented in the previous study) is merely our continuing along this dismal, destructive, downhill path forever.[3]

3. For a fuller study of the fall of Nebuchadnezzar and what it teaches concerning the downward slide of the human race, see James Montgomery Boice, *Daniel: An Expositional Commentary* (Grand Rapids: Zondervan, 1989), chs. 1–6.

God's Image Restored

I do not want to leave this section with us at the edge of this awful bottomless pit, however. It is true that our rejection of God has left us looking to the beasts and becoming increasingly like them—indeed, even worse than the beasts—and that left to ourselves there can be no end to this grim descent into depravity. But the gospel, for the sake of which Romans was written, tells us that God has not left us to ourselves. In Christ, he has acted to restore what we are intent on destroying.

I see this in five steps:

1. We were made in God's image.
2. We rejected God in Adam and therefore lost that image; we became, not like God, knowing good and evil, but like Satan.
3. Having lost the image of God and having ceased to become increasingly like him, we became like beasts and, as I have been pointing out here, even worse than beasts.
4. Christ became like us, taking a human form upon himself.
5. He died for us and opened up the possibility of our renewal after his image.

Paul writes about this in 2 Corinthians 3, first speaking of a veil that has come between ourselves and God, and then adding: "But whenever anyone turns to the Lord, the veil is taken away. . . . And we, who with unveiled faces all reflect the Lord's glory, are being transformed into his likeness with ever-increasing glory, which comes from the Lord, who is the Spirit" (vv. 16, 18).

When we come to Christ, the question is not "How low can you go?" We are done with that. The question is "How high can you rise?" And to that question the answer also is: no limit. We are to become increasingly like the Lord Jesus Christ throughout eternity.

23

The First Excuse: Morality

Romans 2:1–3

You, therefore, have no excuse, you who pass judgment on someone else, for at whatever point you judge the other, you are condemning yourself, because you who pass judgment do the same things. Now we know that God's judgment against those who do such things is based on truth. So when you, a mere man, pass judgment on them and yet do the same things, do you think you will escape God's judgment?

At first glance the opening words of Romans 2 seem redundant—an echo of what we have already seen in the letter. In Romans 1:20, after Paul has explained how men and women suppress the truth about God, which God has revealed in nature, Paul concludes by saying, "So . . . men are without excuse." Now he says the same thing—"You, therefore, have no excuse"—as he continues to build the case that all persons, whoever they are or whatever they have or have not done, are under God's judgment.

Paul is not being redundant, of course, as we will see. But even if he were, the point of the repetition is well taken. Paul's repetition dramatizes the fact that human beings never seem able fully to admit their wrongdoing and never tire of making excuses for their bad behavior. Dale Carnegie, in his perennial best seller, *How to Win Friends and Influence People*, bases his approach to people-management on the premise that others rarely admit to having done anything wrong and that it is therefore pointless to criticize them. My favorite example from the book is a saying of Al Capone, the Chicago gangland leader who for years was the Federal Bureau of Investigation's "Public Enemy Number One." Capone was as sinister as they come, a hardened killer. But he said of himself, "I have spent the best years of my life giving people the lighter pleasures, helping them to have a good time, and all I get is abuse, the existence of a hunted man."[1]

Carnegie's point, and mine as well, is that people habitually attempt to excuse their wrong behavior. If as hardened a man as Al Capone thought well of himself, how much more do the normal, "morally upright" people of our society think well of themselves!

Jew or Gentile

This is why Romans 2 was written. In Romans 1, Paul has shown that the human race has turned away from God in order to pursue its own way and that the horrible things we do and see about us are the result. All have become part of this rebellion. Later on (in Romans 3:10–11), he is going to conclude:

> As it is written:
> "There is no one righteous, not even one;
>   there is no one who understands,
>   no one who seeks God.
> All have turned away,
>   they have together become worthless;
>   there is no one who does good,
>   not even one."

No one wants to admit that, however. So, instead of acknowledging that what Paul said about the human race is true, most of us make excuses, arguing that although Paul's description may be true of other people, particularly very debased individuals or the heathen, it is certainly not true of us. "We know better than that," we say. "And we act better, too." In the second chapter of Romans Paul is going to disabuse us of these erroneous ideas.

But who is it who thinks like this? To whom particularly is Paul speaking when he says in verse 1: "You, therefore, have no excuse, you who pass judgment on someone else"?

There has been a great deal of discussion of this among commentators. Some maintain that in Romans 2:1–16 Paul is addressing the "virtuous heathen," that is, the particularly moral or upright persons of his society. Others maintain that he is thinking of Jews. Later on, of course, Paul does

---

1. Dale Carnegie, *How to Win Friends and Influence People* (New York: Cardinal edition, Pocket Books, 1963), p. 20.

mention Jews specifically—"Now you, if you call yourself a Jew . . ." (v. 17)—but the question is whether he is also thinking of Jews at the start of the chapter. If he is not, he is dealing with three classes of people: (1) pagans in chapter 1; (2) moral or virtuous people in 2:1–16; and (3) religious people or Jews in 2:17–29. If he *is* thinking of Jews, he is dealing with two classes of people: (1) Gentiles in chapter 1; and (2) Jews in chapter 2.

The reformers, John Calvin among them, took the former view. Calvin wrote, "This rebuke is directed at the hypocrites who draw attention by their displays of outward sanctity, and even imagine that they have been accepted by God, as though they had afforded him full satisfaction." He distinguishes between "sanctimonious persons" and those guilty of "the grosser vices."[2]

Today most commentators believe that Paul was thinking of Jews throughout the chapter, even though he does not mention Jews specifically until later. John Murray is an example. He finds four reasons for this position:

1. "The propensity to judge the Gentiles for their religious and moral perversity was peculiarly characteristic of the Jew."

2. "The person being addressed is the participant of 'the riches of his [God's] goodness and forbearance and longsuffering,'" and this applies to Jews more than to Gentiles.

3. "The argument of the apostle is . . . that special privilege or advantage does not exempt from the judgment of God." This fits Jews particularly.

4. "The express address to the Jew in verse 17 would be rather abrupt if now for the first time the Jew is directly in view, whereas if the Jew is the person in view in the preceding verses then the more express identification in verse 17 is natural."[3]

Support of this position is fairly strong today, as I have indicated. Yet I am not fully convinced. Murray argues that Jews were particularly prone to judge Gentiles. But I would argue that, although that was true, it is nevertheless also a basic human characteristic, practiced by Gentiles on one another as well as by Jews on Gentiles. Again, Murray thinks that "the riches of his goodness and forbearance and longsuffering" describes Jews more than Gentiles. But I think a broader reference is required by the thrust of chapter 1. It is because of God's longsuffering that the people described in chapter 1 are still living and not in hell. Likewise, I would argue that the "special privilege" Murray refers to in his third argument does not actually come in until later, when the Jews *are* being considered. As to the fourth argument, that the reference to Jews in verse 17 is too abrupt, I feel that it is

2. John Calvin, *The Epistles of Paul the Apostle to the Romans and to the Thessalonians*, trans. Ross MacKenzie (Grand Rapids: Wm. B. Eerdmans, 1973), p. 40.

3. John Murray, *The Epistle to the Romans* (Grand Rapids: Wm. B. Eerdmans, 1968), pp. 55, 56. This view was also held by Charles Hodge, Frederic Godet, and Robert Haldane.

no more abrupt than the way verse 1 introduces those "who pass judgment on someone else."

I think Paul first introduces those, both Jew and Gentile, who consider themselves above others, and then, midway through the chapter, those, in this case Jews particularly, who rely on their religious advantages.

Let me say, however, that in a sense it does not matter much. If Paul is thinking of Jews in verses 1–16, he is at least thinking of them in regard to their morally superior attitude, from which we are not exempt, though we be Gentiles. And if he is thinking of Gentiles, he is at least embracing Jews at the point at which they might indulge in similarly wrong thinking.

What's Wrong with Morality?

Paul has described the race as being under the wrath of God, and he has shown the depths to which our rebellion against God has led us. He has not minced words. He has described the race as being "filled with every kind of wickedness, evil, greed and depravity. . . . full of envy, murder, strife, deceit and malice. . . . gossips, slanderers, God-haters, insolent, arrogant and boastful; they invent ways of doing evil; they disobey their parents; they are senseless, faithless, heartless, ruthless" (Rom. 1:29–31). This is a dreadful denunciation, and at this point someone, perhaps everyone, reacts by saying that although that description of vice may fit other individuals, it certainly does not fit him. "I am not like this," he might say.

It would be perfectly proper if Paul had answered such an objector by pointing out that the important question is not whether he or she has done the specific blameworthy things mentioned, but whether the person measures up to the perfect standard of God. God, being perfect, cannot be satisfied with anything less than perfection. That important point, which Paul is also quite capable of making, means that we fall short of this divine standard and are therefore deserving of judgment, however good we may be.

But that is not the way Paul answers. Paul does not let the objecting person off the hook by acknowledging, somewhat reluctantly, that he (or she) may indeed be innocent of the vices mentioned, but that he nevertheless falls short of God's righteous, higher standard. On the contrary, Paul argues that the objector is guilty of these very things—perhaps even more guilty than the pagans to whom he feels superior. The very fact that this supposedly moral person is objecting shows that he has some kind of moral conscience. He "passes judgment on someone else" in declaring the other's actions bad, as distinct from his own actions, which are good. But this does not mean that he is innocent of what he sees and condemns in others. On the contrary, he is guilty of these very actions: ". . . at whatever point you judge the other, you are condemning yourself, because you who pass judgment do the same things" (v. 1).

Paul is not appealing to God's standard as that by which self-styled moral individuals will be judged, though he had every right to do so. Rather, he is appealing to their own standard, whatever it is.

Condemned by Any Standard

This is worth thinking through carefully. What are the standards by which you or I might judge sin in others?

1. *The Ten Commandments.* The most widely acknowledged standard of morality, at least in the western world, is the Decalogue, containing what most of us call the Ten Commandments, as recorded in Exodus 20 (cf. Deut. 5:6–21). Much civil law is based on it. For example, when we pass laws recognizing the responsibility of children to obey their parents up to a certain age, we are affirming the fifth of the Ten Commandments, which says, "Honor your father and your mother" (v. 12). When we pass laws against killing, even by such things as excessive speed on the highways, we are affirming the sixth commandment, which says, "You shall not murder" (v. 13). We have laws protecting marriages and against adultery, laws against stealing other people's property, laws against perjury, and so on. These laws grow out of a common recognition of the moral principles embodied in the Ten Commandments.

"Well, that is what we are talking about," says someone. "Paul's condemnation of sin in Romans 1 might have been proper in that far-off heathen context. But it does not apply to us. We have the Ten Commandments and do not do that for which the pagans are condemned."

Don't we? Don't you?

You appeal to the fifth commandment, which requires you to honor your father and your mother. But have you never dishonored your parents? Have you never spoken to them in a dishonoring way? Acted in a dishonoring way? Have you always been properly thankful, respectful, and obedient to them?

You appeal to the sixth commandment, which forbids murder, and you feel good about this because you have never actually murdered anybody. But have you forgotten that God looks on the heart and judges by thoughts and wishes as well as by actions? Have you never been angry enough with somebody to want to murder that person? Jesus said on one occasion that even speaking a defamatory word is sufficient to incur God's wrath for breaking this commandment (Matt. 5:21–22).

You appeal to the seventh commandment, but are you guiltless here? This commandment forbids adultery; but many have done this, and others have desired it or contemplated it. Jesus said that we are guilty of this even if we only lust after another person (Matt. 5:28).

Have you never stolen? Never shaded the figures on your income tax in order to pay less than you actually owed? Never kept the change when you were given more than you should have received? Never borrowed something and then failed to return it, even though you remembered it later?

Have you never lied? Never misrepresented the truth?

And what about the commands I did not even mention the first time around? What about the tenth of the commandments, which says that we must not "covet"? To covet means to want something that someone else has just because he or she has it and you do not. There is no one in our society who is innocent of this, because our entire advertising and marketing industry is based on it.

There are also the four commandments that make up the first table of the law, those that deal with God and our responsibility to worship him. Who has never placed another god before God? Who has never made an idol of something? Who has not misused God's name? Who has remembered even a single Sabbath day, not to mention every Sabbath day, by keeping it holy?

If you say, "My standard is the morality of the Ten Commandments," you are condemned by this standard.

2. *The Sermon on the Mount.* There may be people who have followed my argument to this point but are still not convinced how useless it is to make excuses. They might admit the force of judgments based on the Ten Commandments. "But," they might say, "that was another age and a particularly difficult set of standards. We live in the Christian era now, and I go by the teachings of the gentle Jesus. My standard is the Sermon on the Mount."

If anybody thinks this way, that person's thinking proves how little he or she really understands Christ's sermon. For the Sermon on the Mount does not weaken the Old Testament standards; it rescues them. I have already made that clear in using Matthew 5 to interpret murder and adultery properly. The Sermon on the Mount shows that God is not satisfied with mere external adherence to his laws but requires an inner conformity as well. Our hearts and minds also must be purified.

However, I suppose that what most persons have in mind if they appeal to the Sermon on the Mount, are the Beatitudes, with which it begins. Jesus said:

> "Blessed are the poor in spirit,
>   for theirs is the kingdom of heaven.
> Blessed are those who mourn,
>   for they will be comforted.
> Blessed are the meek,
>   for they will inherit the earth.
> Blessed are those who hunger and thirst for righteousness,
>   for they will be filled.
> Blessed are the merciful,

> for they will be shown mercy.
> Blessed are the pure in heart,
>   for they will see God.
> Blessed are the peacemakers,
>   for they will be called sons of God.
> Blessed are those who are persecuted because of righteousness,
>   for theirs is the kingdom of heaven."
>
> Matthew 5:3–10

Most "moral" people see themselves in this description. They think themselves meek, merciful, pure, peacemakers. They imagine that they actually thirst for righteousness and are even sometimes persecuted because of it. But who really embodies these characteristics? Is it anyone you know? Hardly! The only person who has ever really embodied them is the one who spoke them: Jesus of Nazareth. He was gentle in spirit; he mourned for sin; he was meek, merciful, and pure; he alone embodied righteousness—and he suffered for it.

You see my point. If Jesus has shown what it means to keep the standards of the Sermon on the Mount, then none of us has done it. And so, if we appeal to the Sermon on the Mount as the measure by which we judge others and put ourselves above them, we condemn ourselves, as Paul indicates.

3. *The Golden Rule.* "But wait a minute," someone interrupts. "You have referred to the Beatitudes as an important part of Jesus' teaching, and that is right. But it is not all he taught, even in this sermon. What about the 'heart' of the sermon: the Golden Rule. What is wrong with the part that goes: 'In everything, do to others what you would have them do to you, for this sums up the Law and the Prophets' (Matt. 7:12)?"

Is that the part by which you judge others and by which you want to be judged? Have you always treated others exactly as you have wanted them to treat you? Have you never been impatient with them? Never gotten angry with them unjustly? Never accused them falsely? Never taken advantage of another's weakness? The Golden Rule accuses you, as it must if it is truly the summation of the law, as Jesus teaches.

4. *Fair Play.* Let me try once more. What about the "Englishman's virtue," as some have called it. What about the simple, rock-bottom standard of fair play? The point is obvious. There is no one who is ever fair to other people always and in all ways.

Calling Sinners to Repentance

A number of years ago Thomas A. Harris wrote a book of pop psychology called *I'm O.K., You're O.K.,* and about that time the Philadelphia Conference on Reformed Theology was holding its annual meetings on the depravity of man. One of the speakers was John H. Gerstner, Professor Emeritus of

Pittsburgh Theological Seminary. He used the book as a jumping-off place for the following story.

Gerstner and his wife had been in Kashmir, and they were returning from a shopping expedition in a little boat that had just pulled up beside a larger junk near the shore. There was a bump, and some water splashed on them. The owner of the boat got very agitated and gestured for them to get out. Gerstner told how he remembered saying to his wife, "See how excitable this fellow is. We get a little water splashed on us, and you would think it was a catastrophe of the first order." The man got more and more agitated. "It's okay, Kusra," Gerstner said. "It's okay."

Finally, the owner of the boat got so excited that he broke out of the dialect he had been using, which the Gerstners had been unable to understand, and shouted, "It no okay!"

At this they got the message and climbed onto the shore. The owner then threw his grandchild up to them and climbed out himself. When they turned around, the boat was gone. The hull had been punctured. and the undertow had swallowed their craft. It was eventually tossed up about six boats further on; if the Gerstners had delayed a moment longer, they would have been swallowed up with it.[4]

That is the message of these early chapters of Romans: "I am not O.K. You are not O.K. No one is O.K." And the sooner we admit that we are *not* okay and turn to the One who knows that we are not, but who offers us a way of salvation anyway, the better off we will be. Jesus does not excuse us; he forgives us. He calls us sinners. Yet he says, "I have not come to call the righteous, but sinners to repentance" (Luke 5:32). The most important thing in life is to know that Jesus is able to save you from sin. The second most important thing is to know that you require it.

---

4. Gerstner tells the story in "Man the Sinner" in James Montgomery Boice, ed. *Our Savior God: Studies on Man, Christ and the Atonement* (Grand Rapids: Baker Book House, 1980), pp. 56, 57.

24

The Long-Suffering God

Romans 2:4

Or do you show contempt for the riches of his kindness, tolerance and patience, not realizing that God's kindness leads you toward repentance?

In my library in Philadelphia I have a large number of books that deal with the attributes of God. They are among my favorite volumes. I think, for example, of A. W. Tozer's books on knowing God: *The Pursuit of God* and *The Knowledge of the Holy.*[1] Or Arthur Pink's studies of God's character: *The Attributes of God* and *Gleanings in the Godhead.*[2] Some are heavy theological works, like Emil Brunner's *The Christian Doctrine of God,*[3] Herman Bavinck's *The Doctrine of God*[4] and Carl F.

---

1. A. W. Tozer, *The Pursuit of God* (Harrisburg, Pa.: Christian Publications, 1948) and *The Knowledge of the Holy* (New York: Harper & Row, 1961).

2. Arthur W. Pink, *The Attributes of God* (Grand Rapids: Baker Book House, 1975) and *Gleanings in the Godhead* (Chicago: Moody Press, 1975). The second volume includes the first plus additional material.

3. Emil Brunner, *The Christian Doctrine of God, Dogmatics: Vol. 1* (Philadelphia: The Westminster Press, 1950).

4. Herman Bavinck, *The Doctrine of God* (Edinburgh and Carlisle, Pa.: The Banner of Truth Trust, 1977).

H. Henry's multivolumed *God, Revelation and Authority*.[5] There is also the well-deserved popular favorite: *Knowing God,* by J. I. Packer.[6]

I find as I look over these books that there is little in them concerning two of the three attributes we are to study in this chapter: tolerance (forbearance) and patience (longsuffering). Why is this? Pink calls attention to it, saying, "It is not easy to suggest a reason . . . for surely the longsuffering of God is as much one of the divine perfections as is his wisdom, power or holiness, and as much to be admired and revered by us."[7]

The reason many of us ignore these attributes may be precisely what Paul suggests it may be, when he asks in our text, "Do you show contempt for the riches of his [God's] kindness, tolerance and patience, not realizing that God's kindness leads you toward repentance?" The reason why we do not think often of God's tolerance and patience is our insensitivity to sin and our reluctance to turn from it.

The Goodness of God

I have said that two of the three attributes mentioned in our text are frequently neglected: tolerance and patience. But the first of the three attributes is "goodness" (KJV), or "kindness" (NIV), and goodness is not usually ignored. I suppose this is because goodness is so desirable a part of God's nature. Our word *God* points in that direction. It comes to us from Anglo-Saxon speech, where "God" originally meant "The Good." This was an important insight, for it meant that in the minds of the Anglo-Saxons, God was not only "the Greatest" of all beings, though they recognized that as well, but that he was also "the Best." All the goodness there is originates in God. That is why the apostle James could write, "Every good and perfect gift is from above, coming down from the Father of the heavenly lights, who does not change like shifting shadows" (James 1:17). In the language of philosophy the simplest of all definitions of God is *summum bonum,* the chief good.

Yet, when Paul speaks of the goodness of God in Romans 2, he is not thinking of this as having to do primarily with what God is in himself, but as having to do with God's actions toward us. This may be why the New International Version renders the Greek term *chrēstotēs* (later, *chrēstos*) as "kindness" rather than "goodness," as it is in the King James Bible.

1. *Creation.* The first place at which the goodness of God is seen is in creation. We remember that on each of the successive days of creation, after God had made the heavens and the earth, the sea and the land, and all the creatures that live in the sea, inhabit the land, and fly in the air, God said,

---

5. Carl F. H. Henry, *God, Revelation and Authority,* 4 vols. (Waco, Tex.: Word Books, 1976–1979).

6. J. I. Packer, *Knowing God* (Downers Grove, Ill.: InterVarsity Press, 1973).

7. Pink, *The Attributes of God,* p. 61.

"It is good." And it really was good—and continues to be, in spite of the increasing spoilage of creation that has come to it because of human sin.

The world about us is good, and this is a great proof of God's goodness. Every time we breathe God's good air, we demonstrate how indebted we are to this goodness. Every time we use the resources of the world to make homes and clothes and to grow food, we show that God is kind toward us. And what of our bodies? How suited are our hands to perform useful work! How valuable are our arms and legs! How amazing our eyes! How marvelous our minds! Paul Brand's study of the wonders of the human body—cells, bones, skin, and motion—*Fearfully and Wonderfully Made*,[8] highlights some of this goodness.

2. *Providence.* God's goodness is also revealed in providence, that is, by his continual ordering of the world and world events for good. Providence is seen in what theologians call "common grace." Jesus spoke of this when he observed that God "causes his sun to rise on the evil and the good, and sends rain on the righteous and the unrighteous" (Matt. 5:45).

3. *The Gospel Call.* But the kindness of God toward us is seen not only in the physical creation and providence. It is also seen in many spiritual matters. Above all, it is seen in the widespread proclamation of the gospel. To be sure, the gospel has not yet penetrated everywhere. There are still many millions of people who have not heard that Jesus loves them and has died for them. But *you* have! You at least know God's goodness in the gospel.

Charles Haddon Spurgeon, the great Baptist preacher of the nineteenth century, wrote on Romans 2:4:

> Myriads of our fellow men have never had an opportunity of knowing Christ. The missionary's foot has never trodden the cities wherein they dwell, and so they die in the dark. Multitudes are going downward, downward; but they do not know the upward road. Their minds have never been enlightened by the teachings of God's word, and hence they sin with less grievousness of fault. You are placed in the very focus of Christian light, and yet you follow evil! Will you not think of this? Time was when a man would have to work for years to earn enough money to buy a Bible. There were times when he could not have earned one even with that toil. Now the word of God lies upon your table, and you have a copy of it in almost every room of your house. Is not this a boon from God? This is the land of the open Bible, and the land of the preached word of God. In this you prove the richness of God's goodness. Do you despise this wealth of mercy? . . . Is this a small thing?[9]

8. Paul Brand and Philip Yancey, *Fearfully and Wonderfully Made* (Grand Rapids: Zondervan, 1980).

9. Charles Haddon Spurgeon, "Earnest Expostulation" in *Metropolitan Tabernacle Pulpit,* vol. 29 (Edinburgh and Carlisle, Pa.: The Banner of Truth Trust, 1971), p. 196. (Originally published in 1884.)

The kindness of God is not a small thing. We dare not despise it, as Paul tells us.

The Tolerance of God

The second attribute of God in our text is tolerance, and this, as I wrote earlier, *is* frequently neglected. The Greek word is *anochēs*, variously translated "tolerance," "forbearance," "holding back," "delay," "pause," or "clemency."

The new idea introduced by this term is that of human offense to God's goodness, offense that should evoke an immediate outpouring of fierce judgment but which God actually endures. We see this quality at the beginning of the Bible. God had warned Adam that on the day he ate of the forbidden tree he would die (Gen. 1:17). But when God came to Adam and Eve in the garden to confront our first parents with the fact of their disobedience, he did not actually execute the sentence. Someone has pointed out that Adam and Eve did die in their spirits, which they proved by running away from God when he came calling. That is true. But they did not die physically, at least not at once. And they never did die eternally, because God came with an offer of salvation through a future deliverer who would defeat Satan, which they then believed and trusted. This first great outcropping of sin and God's dealings with it show God's tolerance.

So it is with us all. We sin, but God does not immediately implement the judgment we deserve. He bears with us, enduring the affront to his great majesty and holiness. And he offers us salvation!

The irony is that we do not appreciate this and instead actually turn God's temporary tolerance of some sin into an accusation against him. Do you remember the question raised by those who had witnessed a few instances of evil in the days of Jesus Christ? Apparently some Galileans had been visiting Jerusalem and had been worshiping at the temple. While they were in the midst of their pious acts, soldiers from Pilate fell upon them and killed some of them. Again, about this same time a tower fell over and killed eighteen persons who were standing beside it. Jesus was asked how it was possible that something like this could happen in a world ruled by a just yet merciful God. Was it because these people were worse sinners than others? Or was it because God was either too weak to avert the tragedies or just didn't care?

Jesus replied, "Do you think that these Galileans were worse sinners than all the other Galileans because they suffered this way? I tell you, no! But unless you repent, you too will all perish. Or those eighteen who died when the tower of Siloam fell on them—do you think they were more guilty than all the others living in Jerusalem? I tell you, no! But unless you repent, you too will all perish" (Luke 13:2–5).

Jesus' point was that our way of asking that question is entirely wrong. The question is not why God somehow "lets down" and allows others to perish, but rather why he has spared us, we being the sinners we are. If we could understand how sinful we are, we could understand that the soldiers should have killed us, or the tower should have fallen on us. We should be dead and in hell this very instant. That we are not in hell is an evidence of God's tolerance. He has not yet confined us to the punishment we deserve.

God's tolerance should lead us to repentance, before it is too late.

The Patience of God

The last of these three attributes is the greatest from the point of view of our text, for it is linked to the call for repentance in that God spares us for a very long time that we might do so. The Greek word *makrothymia* is interesting, because the first half of it, *makro* (macro), emphasizes how great God's longsuffering, or patience, is.

Here is a good place to put these three terms together and compare them. I quote first from Robert Haldane. He thinks these words apply to the Jews explicitly, which I do not. But his definitions and contrasts are significant nevertheless: "Goodness imports the benefits which God hath bestowed on the Jews. Forbearance denotes God's bearing with them, without immediately executing vengeance—his delaying to punish them. . . . Long-suffering signifies the extent of that forbearance during many ages."[10] Here is another quotation, from Charles Hodge: "The first means kindness in general, as expressed in giving favors; the second, patience; the third, forbearance, slowness in the infliction of punishment."[11]

I would define each of these three terms as aspects of God's goodness: the first as goodness to man without any specific relationship to sin; the second as goodness in relation to sin's magnitude; the third as goodness in relation to sin's endurance or continuation. Spurgeon was thinking along these lines when he wrote, "Forbearance has to do with the magnitude of sin; longsuffering with the multiplicity of it."[12]

"Patience" means that God bears with sin a long time. Here are some examples:

First, God was patient with those who sinned in the early ages of the race before the great flood. This was a particularly evil time. Some of the evil is described in Genesis 4, which begins with Cain's murder of his brother Abel and ends with Lamech's boast about having killed a man just for wounding him. This evil is summarized in Genesis 6:5, where we are told, "The LORD saw how great man's wickedness on the earth had become, and that every inclination of the thoughts of his heart was only evil all the time." What a devastating statement—"only evil all the time"! This was a dreadful age. Yet,

10. Robert Haldane, *An Exposition of the Epistle to the Romans* (MacDill AFB: MacDonald Publishing, 1958), p. 77.
11. Charles Hodge, *A Commentary on Romans* (Edinburgh and Carlisle, Pa.: The Banner of Truth Trust, 1972), p. 48. (Original edition 1935.)
12. Spurgeon, "Earnest Expostulation," p. 197.

in spite of this great evil, God was patient with the antediluvian generation. He spared it for 120 years while Noah was in the process of constructing and outfitting the ark. It was only at the end of that period, after ample warnings from Noah and the other pre-flood preachers, like Enoch, that the flood came.

A second example is Israel, with whom God was exceptionally patient. He was patient with the Jews for forty years in the wilderness, as Paul reminds us in a sermon to Gentiles and Jews at Antioch ("He endured their conduct for about forty years in the desert," Acts 13:18). Later, when the Israelites entered the Promised Land and were soon found following the debased customs and worship of the nations around them, God did not immediately chastise his people but instead sent a long line of deliverers. Even when their sin was so great that a judgment by invasion and deportment was inevitable, God still sent generations of prophets to warn both Israel and Judah and turn them from sin.

What of ourselves? Arthur W. Pink writes:

> How wondrous is God's patience with the world today. On every side people are sinning with a high hand. The divine law is trampled under foot and God himself openly despised. It is truly amazing that he does not instantly strike dead those who so brazenly defy him. Why does he not suddenly cut off the haughty infidel and blatant blasphemer, as he did Ananias and Sapphira? Why does he not cause the earth to open its mouth and devour the persecutors of his people, so that, like Dathan and Abiram, they shall go down alive into the Pit? And what of apostate Christendom, where every possible form of sin is now tolerated and practiced under cover of the holy name of Christ? Why does not the righteous wrath of heaven make an end of such abominations? Only one answer is possible: because God bears with "*much* longsuffering the vessels of wrath fitted to destruction."[13]

Repent or Perish

Yet, much as I appreciate Arthur Pink and value his description of God's longsuffering toward those of our own time, I do not think his statement that "only one answer is possible" is correct. Pink asks, "Why does God not immediately destroy all wrong doers?" He answers, "Because God is longsuffering toward the vessels of wrath fitted for destruction." That means: simply because God *is* long-suffering. Sinners will perish eventually anyway, but God is nevertheless willing to endure them for a very long time.

Well, that is part of the answer. God does endure for a long time those who eventually will perish. But if our text—which speaks so eloquently of the goodness, tolerance, and patience of God—means anything, it certainly

13. Pink, *The Attributes of God*, p. 64.

means that God also has quite another purpose in his patience. Paul says that it is to lead us to repentance.

There are two ways we can go, of course. Paul is clear about them. One way is repentance, the way Scripture urges. The other is defiance, or spite toward God's goodness.

Which will it be for you? You can defy God. You can set yourself against his goodness, tolerance, and patience—as well as against his other attributes like sovereignty, holiness, omniscience, and immutability, which you also despise. But why should you do that? I have previously pointed out that it is quite understandable how a sinner who does not wish to leave his or her sin must hate God's holiness. It is obvious that a rebellious subject will resent God's sovereignty. But why should you "show contempt for the riches of his kindness, tolerance and patience"? These are winsome qualities. A kind, tolerant, and patient God is a good God. Why should you fail to realize that God's exercise of these attributes toward you is for a good end?

I want to give you three reasons why you should allow these attributes to lead you to repentance and should no longer despise the goodness of God.

First, if God is a good God, then whatever you may think to the contrary in your fallen state, to find this good God will mean finding all good for yourself. You do not normally think this way. You think that your own will is the good. You think that if you have to turn from what you think you want—and desperately do want—you will be miserable. Can you not see that it is your own sinful way, and the ways of millions of other people just like you, that is the cause of your miseries. God is not the cause. God is good. God is the source of all good. If you want to find good for yourself as well as others, the way to find it is to turn from whatever is holding you back and find God. God has provided the way for you to turn to him through the death of his Son, the Lord Jesus Christ. He died for your sin to open the door to God's presence.

Not long ago I was talking to a young girl who had gotten into trouble because of her rebellion against nearly everyone who was in authority over her, had ended up in an institution for troubled teenagers, and had had a very rough time. But in the counseling and small-group sessions she learned something important. As we talked she said, "I learned that the people I thought were my enemies were actually my friends, because they told me the truth, and I learned that my trouble was not caused by other people. I caused it. If I am going to get anywhere, I have to change."

This teenager had become a lot smarter than many people who fight against God by blaming him for their misery. If you are to be wise and not foolish, you must allow the goodness of God to lead you to repentance.

Second, if God is tolerant of you, it is because he has a will to save you. If he wanted to condemn you outright, he could have done it long ago. If he is tolerant, you will find that if you come to him he will not cast you out. One commentator wrote, "If God is good even to the unkind and the unthankful, surely the door of entrance to the divine favor is open to the penitent."[14]

Third, if God is patient with you in spite of your many follies, it is because he is giving you an opportunity to be saved. The apostle Peter wrote, "The Lord is not slow in keeping his promise, as some understand slowness. He is patient with you, not wanting anyone to perish, but everyone to come to repentance" (2 Peter 3:9). If God were not good, you might have room to doubt this. You might think of God as a cat playing with a mouse. You might think of him as being patient with you only for his own amusement. But this is not the case at all. If God is good in his patience, his reason for being so must be to do good. His patience must be to give you opportunity to turn to him. Do not make the mistake of thinking that because God is tolerant he will not judge sin. God will judge it. He is just, as well as patient. But now he is patient, and if he has allowed you to live twenty, forty, or even eighty or ninety years, it is so that you might come to him now—before you die and the opportunity for salvation is gone forever.

Paul says that God's goodness "leads" you to repentance. If he is leading, he will not turn you away if you follow him. If he bids you repent, he will not spurn your repentance.

14. William S. Plumer, *Commentary on Romans* (Grand Rapids: Kregel Publications, 1979), p. 86. (Original edition 1870.)

25

Wrath Stored Up

Romans 2:5

But because of your stubbornness and your unrepentant heart, you are storing up wrath against yourself for the day of God's wrath, when his righteous judgment will be revealed.

In Romans 2:5 we come for a second time to the idea of the wrath of God, and for the second time we need to defend wrath as a proper element in God's character. It is strange this should be so.

Several years ago newspapers reported the discovery of a "house of horrors" in north Philadelphia. A man named Gary Heidnik had been luring prostitutes and other rootless women to his home, imprisoning and torturing them, and finally killing some. When his crimes were uncovered, two women were found chained to the walls of the basement, and body parts of others were discovered in Heidnik's refrigerator. Heidnik was criminally insane, of course. But the interesting thing about this case is that much of the outrage it engendered was directed, not so much at this man, who was obviously insane, but at the police, who had been alerted to the strange goings-on in the house earlier by neighbors but had done nothing. The police maintained that until they were finally told about Heidnik by a woman who had been in his home but had escaped, they did not have "probable cause" to interfere.

The position of the police may have been technically and legally correct, of course. But the point I am making is that people naturally feel that evil demands both intervention and outrage, and they are deeply upset if this does not happen. If nothing is done or if the situation is allowed to continue unchallenged for a long time, the outrage is intensified!

Why are we unwilling to grant the rightness of a similar outrage to God. The only possible reason is that we consider our sins and those of most other people to be excusable—forgetting that in the sight of the holy God they are not much different from those of Gary Heidnik. They are measured not by our own relative and wavering standards of good and evil, but by God's absolute and utterly upright criteria.

Wrath Revealed

The first time we came in Romans to the idea of the wrath of God, we were at the beginning of the first great section of the letter. There Paul wrote, "The wrath of God is being revealed from heaven against all the godlessness and wickedness of men who suppress the truth by their wickedness" (Rom. 1:18). This is a thematic verse and therefore very important, for it is saying that the wrath of God is not something merely saved up until some long-delayed but final day of judgment, but rather is something that God has been revealing to us even now. Romans 2:5 is going to say that there is also a day of wrath to come, but the first thing Paul says about God's wrath is that it is already being revealed from heaven.

This means that the wrath of God is a very real thing. Moreover, we can know the certainty of a future day of wrath by noting the past and present revelation of that wrath.

How has the wrath of God been revealed? Robert Haldane says:

It was revealed when the sentence of death was first pronounced, the earth cursed, and man driven out of the earthly paradise, and afterward by such examples of punishment as those of the deluge, and the destruction of the cities of the plain by fire from heaven. . . .But, above all, the wrath of God was revealed from heaven when the Son of God came down to manifest the divine character, and when that wrath was displayed in his sufferings and death, in a manner more awful than by all the tokens God had before given of his displeasure against sin. Besides this, the future and eternal punishment of the wicked is now declared in terms more solemn and explicit than formerly. Under the new dispensation, there are two revelations given from heaven, one of wrath, the other of grace.[1]

1. Robert Haldane, *An Exposition of the Epistle to the Romans* (MacDill AFB: MacDonald Publishing, 1958), pp. 55, 56.

I do not anywhere know a statement regarding the nature of the revelation of God's wrath that is more complete or accurate than this statement by Haldane. Yet, in Romans 1, Paul's point is that the wrath of God is revealed to us chiefly in the debilitating downward drag of sin upon our lives. We think when we sin that we can sin "just a little bit." But we cannot! Sin captures us and pulls us down inexorably, until—if we are allowed to continue in sin long enough—we end up calling what is good, evil and what is evil, good. And we perish utterly!

This means that the moral turmoil and chaos of the world, including our own personal world, is evidence that the wrath of God is no fiction. This is something to be gravely concerned about.

Wrath Deserved

In Romans 2:5, Paul has other things to say about wrath, and his first point is that the wrath of God toward the sin of men and women is deserved. That should be perfectly evident by now, of course—at least if we have understood the argument of Romans 1. God's wrath is deserved, because our ignorance of God is a willful ignorance and our refusal to seek him out and worship him is a willful refusal. We have already seen that God has revealed his existence and power in nature and that this alone should be sufficient to lead every man, woman, and child on the face of the earth to give thanks to God. But we do not do it, and the fact that we do not do it is proof that we do not want to.

But the case is even stronger than this, which is what Paul is chiefly teaching in chapter 2. Romans 1 declared God's wrath on the basis of the evidence for the existence of God in nature, which we refuse to acknowledge. Chapter 2 goes beyond this, with verse 5, our text here, speaking of the wrath of God as coming to us because of our stubborn refusal to repent.

The word *repent* takes us back to verse 4. For in that verse Paul has spoken of two paths open to human beings as a result of God's kindness, tolerance, and patience. One path is the path of contempt for God's blessings. The other path, the one Paul recommends, is repentance. Paul argues that the kindness, tolerance, and patience of God are to lead us to repentance. But will this happen? Is it happening now? The answer appears in verse 5, where Paul speaks of our "stubborn" and "unrepentant" hearts. Apparently, the kindness, tolerance, and patience of God do not have the effect by themselves of leading men and women to repentance. On the contrary, those who have already suppressed the truth about God revealed in nature now add to their evil a hardening of their hearts against the kindnesses that have been bestowed upon them for their good.

So the wrath of God against the race is deserved on two counts: (1) we have rejected the natural revelation; and (2) we have shown contempt for God's patience and kind acts.

Wrath Proportionate to Sin

In my judgment, the most important teaching in this verse is that the wrath of God is proportionate to human sin, in the sense that those who sin much will be punished much and that those who sin less will be punished less. This has been a problem for some Christian people who have thought of hell's punishments as being poured out on unbelievers only because of their adamant refusal to accept Jesus Christ. Since that sin—a great sin, to be sure—seems to be the same for everybody, the punishments of hell should be equal, such persons feel.

But this is not correct. For one thing, even the basic premise is in error, for not everyone has a chance to hear of Jesus Christ, and therefore not all will be punished for refusing to believe on him. We saw this in our study of Romans 1, when we dealt with whether it is just for God to condemn those who, like the natives in a far-off island jungle, have never had a chance to hear the gospel. We saw there that God does not condemn people for failing to do what they did not even know they should do, but rather for failing to follow the revelation they do have. The native is condemned, not for failing to believe on Jesus, about whom he has never heard, but for failing to seek God out on the basis of the revelation of God found in nature.

If this is true, however, as it is, then it also follows that some people are more guilty than others and must be punished accordingly. The native is perhaps least guilty, in spite of what we may regard as his particularly debased worship and immoral practices. The person who has heard of Jesus but has refused to come to God through faith in Jesus Christ is more guilty. He has rejected not one but two sources of revelation: the revelation in nature and the special revelation of the gospel of God's grace in Jesus Christ disclosed in Scripture.

What of those, like ourselves, who have heard the gospel repeatedly and have even seen its power demonstrated in the lives of other persons? If we refuse that repeated and amplified revelation, we are the guiltiest of all.

There is an interesting image suggested by Paul's language at this point, for Paul speaks of the stubborn and unrepentant person "storing up wrath" for the day of God's judgment. It is the image of a greedy individual, a miser, who has been storing up wealth which, contrary to his expectations, is destined to destroy him. I think of this man as storing up a great horde of gold coins, placing them in an attic above his bed where he thinks no one will find them and where they will be safe. He keeps this up for years, amassing a great weight of gold. But one day, while he is sleeping and oblivious to his danger, this great weight of gold breaks through the ceiling of his bedroom, comes crashing down onto his bed, and kills him. He thought of his wealth as salvation, but it was death.

That is the way it is for those who pile sin upon sin and show contempt for God's kindness. They think of their sins as building up a life of future happiness and freedom. But each sin is actually a storing up of wrath.

Haldane says, "A man is rich according to his treasures." Therefore, "the wicked will be punished according to the number and aggravation of their sins."[2]

This is true even of the good we receive and enjoy without giving proper thanks to God.

Each little indulgence of sin is a coin of wrath stored up.

Each neglect of others is a saved-up ingot of anger.

Each angry word, each selfish thought, each mean retort, each harmful act, is a piling up of wrath's treasures.

Each pleasure enjoyed without genuine thanks to God builds wrath.

Each year of grace, each day enjoyed without the experience of God's swift and immediate judgment, each moment of indifference to the mercy of God, is wrath's accumulation.

If life has been good to you, you only increase your guilt and build a treasure of future punishment by ignoring God's kindness.

Certain Wrath

There is another thought about wrath in verse 5, and it is that the wrath of God against sin is certain. People who spurn God's patience inevitably think that in the end they will somehow get free and escape what they deserve. That is what the people being addressed in this chapter were thinking. They looked at the debased moral practices of the heathen and concluded that they themselves would escape God's wrath because of their imagined superiority to the heathen in such things. But it is not so, Paul says. In fact, it is quite the contrary. Their very awareness of high moral standards, coupled with their refusal to repent of sin and come to God, intensifies their guilt and assures their final condemnation.

Certainty of judgment is seen in the phrase "the day of God's wrath." Why is the time of the outpouring of the wrath of God called a "day"? In my opinion it is not because it is to unfold in what we would call a twenty-four-hour day, like the day of the invasion of the Normandy beaches in World War II, which one writer called *The Longest Day*. I think the Bible speaks of various and manifold judgments that may actually be spread out over a considerable period of time. The use of the word *day* in the phrase "day of wrath" is similar to its use in the phrase "the day of Jesus Christ." In that phrase the word encompasses the events of a thirty-three-year ministry.

Why, then, is the day of God's wrath called a "day"? It is because it is as fixed in God's calendar as any day you can mention—December 7, 1941, to give just one example. That day is determined! So when the day rolls around, the wrath of God *will* be poured out, whatever you or anyone else may hope to the contrary.

A great German preacher by the name of Walter Luethi wrote:

2. Ibid., pp. 79, 80.

If the time should ever come (for these things are conceivable nowadays) when we should succeed in demonstrating that black is white and white black, that good is evil and evil good, if we should ever be successful in invalidating the fundamental moral principles of the universe, so that sin were no longer hated and everyone took a fancy to evil, then there would still be a stronghold where evil would be hated, and that is heaven. And there would still be one who has sworn to fight the evil in the world to the last drop of his blood, and that is God, whose "wrath is revealed from heaven against all ungodliness and wickedness of men."[3]

Wrath That Is Just

Romans 2:5 makes another point about wrath that we also need to see. God's wrath is a just wrath, not arbitrary or petulant but rather according to "righteous judgment." When Paul mentions judgment he brings in thoughts of God's law and reminds us that the judgment of God will be according to law. Indeed, as he is going to show, those who have done good—it there are any—will receive good from God, while those who have done evil will receive evil.

One great problem with sin is that it leads to self-justification, so that anything that happens to us that we do not like is immediately perceived as being unjust, a reason to fault God for his ordering of the universe. The cry of the rebellious heart is always: "The only thing I want from God is justice."

God forbid that you should receive justice from God!

The justice of God will condemn you. And the terror of the very thought of justice is that God is indeed a just God. The God of all the earth does do right, as Abraham well knew (cf. Gen. 18:25). Sin is punished now in large measure, and it will be punished fully and equitably in the life to come. Do not ask God for justice. Seek mercy. Seek it where salvation from the wrath of God may alone be found.

Wrath Poured Out

Where is that salvation to be found? If God's wrath is deserved by us, proportionate to our sin, as certain as the calendar, just, and even partially disclosed in the natural unfolding of the effects of sin in our lives, how can it possibly be avoided—since we *are* sinners?

The only place is in Christ, who bore the full measure of the wrath of God in our place. Do we doubt that God's wrath is real and threatening? If we do, we need only look at Jesus in the hours preceding his crucifixion. He was not like Socrates who calmly quaffed the hemlock that was to end his life. Jesus' soul was "troubled" (John 12:27), and he agonized in the Garden

---

3. Walter Luethi, *The Letter to the Romans: An Exposition*, trans. Kurt Schoenenberger (Edinburgh and London: Oliver and Boyd, 1961), pp. 20, 21.

of Gethsemane, asking that the "cup" God had prepared for him might be taken away (Matt. 26:36–44). Jesus was not afraid of death. He had as much courage in that respect as Socrates. The reason Jesus trembled before death is that his death was not to be like the death of mere mortals. Jesus was not going to die for himself. He was going to die for others. He was going to take upon himself the full measure of the wrath of God that they deserved. He was to drink the cup of wrath to the very dregs—in order that the justice of God might be satisfied and sinners might be spared.

And so it was!

The time came when Jesus was led away to be crucified. He was hung on the cross, midway between earth and heaven, a bridge between sinful man and a holy God. There he, who knew no sin, was made sin for us. There God's wrath was poured out.

For centuries the wrath that men and women had been storing up had been accumulating—like coins in the attic or water behind a great dam. Oh, here and there a little of the flood of God's judgment had sloshed out over the top as God reached the end of his patience in some small area, and a Sodom and Gomorrah were destroyed or a Jerusalem was overthrown. But, for the most part, the wrath of God merely accumulated, growing higher and broader and deeper and increasingly more turbulent. Then Jesus died! When he died the dam was opened, and the great weight of the accumulated wrath of God was poured out upon him. He took God's wrath for us. He bore its impounded fury in our place. No wonder his righteous soul shrank back from the atonement. He had never committed a single sin. He was spotless and without blame. Yet because he was blameless and because he was God, he was able to stand in the breech for us and secure our salvation.

God demonstrated clearly that he had! In Jerusalem there was a temple the central feature of which was a room called the Most Holy Place. God was understood to dwell symbolically in that place. Before it hung a thick curtain, symbolizing the barrier that sin has raised between God in his holiness and ourselves in our sin. For anyone to penetrate beyond that barrier meant instant death, as occasionally happened, for the wrath of God must flame out against any sin that would intrude upon holiness. That curtain was torn in two when Jesus died. For centuries it had hung there, proclaiming that God was holy, that man was sinful, and that the way to God was therefore strictly barred. But now that Jesus had died for sin, taking the place of any who would trust him and receive the benefit of his sacrifice, the wrath of God was expended, the way was open, and there was nothing left but God's great love and kindness.

This is the gospel. It is what is open to you if you will approach God, not on the basis of your own good deeds or works, which can only condemn you, but on the basis of Christ's having borne the wrath of God in your place.

That wrath is thundering down the chasm of history toward the day of final judgment, and one day it must break upon you unless you stand before God in Jesus Christ. Martin Luther began his spiritual pilgrimage by fearing God's wrath and then came to find peace in Christ. But he never forgot the reality of the final judgment, and he always warned his hearers to flee from it to Christ. He said in one place, "The Last Day is called the day of wrath and of mercy, the day of trouble and of peace, the day of destruction and of glory."[4] Luther was right. It must be one or the other. If it is to be a day of mercy and peace for you, rather than a day of wrath and trouble, it must be because you are trusting in Christ.

4. Martin Luther, *Luther's Works*, vol. 25, *Lectures on Romans*, ed. Hilton C. Oswald (St. Louis: Concordia, 1972), p. 176.

26

Good for the Good, Bad for the Bad

Romans 2:6–11

God "will give to each person according to what he has done." To those who by per-
sistence in doing good seek glory, honor and immortality, he will give eternal life. But
for those who are self-seeking and who reject the truth and follow evil, there will be
wrath and anger. There will be trouble and distress for every human being who does
evil: first for the Jew, then for the Gentile; but glory, honor and peace for everyone who
does good: first for the Jew, then for the Gentile. For God does not show favoritism.

I am sure you have been in situations
in which a person, perhaps yourself, has been caught doing something
wrong and has immediately begun to make excuses. "I didn't mean to do
it," the accused one might say. Or, "But so-and-so did it first." Or, "You just
don't understand my circumstances."

It may be the case in any given instance that the person involved really
was "innocent," because of his or her motive or because of circumstances.
This is one reason why our judicial system takes so much trouble to determine motives and circumstances in criminal cases. Generally, however, the
excuses people make are exactly that, excuses, and they need to be seen for
what they really are. This is particularly true in our relationships to God.
God accuses us of repressing the truth about himself and of violating his

225

moral law even while we pass judgment on others for doing the same things, but as soon as we hear these truths we begin to make excuses. We claim that we did not know what was required of us, that we did not do what we are accused of doing, or that our motives were actually good. Whenever we find ourselves doing this, we need to rediscover the principles of God's just judgment, which Romans 2 explains.

One important principle is that God's judgment is *according to truth* (v. 2). On the basis of this principle alone we find ourselves to be guilty. For God, who is the God of truth, declares that we ourselves do what we find deserving of blame in others.

Another principle is that God's judgment is *according to our deeds* (v. 6). We cannot plead extenuating circumstances with God, because it is what we do that counts. This principle is unfolded in verses 6 through 11 and is developed further in verses 12 through 15.

Two Different Paths

These verses speak of two very different paths. One is the path of good deeds, the end of which is glory, honor, peace, and eternal life. The other is the path of evil, the end of which is trouble, distress, wrath, and anger. The verses teach that a person is on either one path or the other.

Up to this point, particularly as a result of our earlier study of verse 5, a person might conclude that the judgment of God will be a finely graded thing—extending all the way from perfect happiness and bliss on the one hand to utter misery and torment on the other, and that most of us will fall somewhere in between. This is because of the principle of proportionality in judgment, which we developed from the idea of "storing up wrath" in verse 5. As we look at people, we see that some are better than others, and some are worse. Therefore, we reason, in the life to come some should be treated well, some should be treated badly, *and the differences should be relative.* A person reasoning along these lines might conclude that our future existence in heaven or hell (or whatever) should be somewhat the same as our present existence, which means a mixture of good and bad for most people.

Our text refutes this error. According to these verses, the two paths are mutually exclusive.

The Path of the Just

The first path is that of the person who does good. In our text Paul speaks of such people in two places. Putting together these verses, we have the following: "To those who by persistence in doing good seek glory, honor and immortality, he [God] will give eternal life. . . . There will be . . . glory, honor and peace for everyone who does good: first for the Jew, then for the Gentile" (vv. 7, 9–10).

There are two things that such a person is described here as doing: (1) he or she *does good* and (2) *persists in doing good*. There are three things that are highlighted as his or her essential motivation: (1) *glory*, (2) *honor*, and (3) *immortality*. Elsewhere in Paul's writings, these terms are used of the Christian's ultimate expectations. "Glory" refers to the transformation of the believer into the image of God's Son, by which the glory of God will be reflected in that person (cf. Rom. 5:2; 8:18, 30; 9:23; 1 Cor. 2:7; 15:43; 2 Cor. 3:12–18; 4:17). "Honor" refers to God's approval of believers, as contrasted with the dishonor and even scorn accorded to them by the world (cf. Heb. 2:7; 1 Peter 1:7). "Immortality" refers to the resurrection hope of God's people (cf. 1 Cor. 15:42, 50, 52–54). One commentator writes, "The three terms have indisputably in the usage of Paul redemptive associations, and this consideration of itself makes it impossible to think that the eschatological aspiration referred to is anything less than that provided by redemptive revelation. The three words define aspiration in terms of the highest reaches of Christian hope."[1]

Likewise, there are four things that God is said to dispense to such people as rewards for their aspirations: (1) *eternal life*, (2) *glory*, (3) *honor*, and (4) *peace*. "Eternal life" refers to salvation—life in heaven with God rather than damnation. "Glory" and "honor" are two of the goals the people described are striving for. The last term, "peace," seems to parallel "immortality" and therefore points, not to peace *with* God, which we can enjoy now as the result of Christ's death for us and our resulting justification, or even to that supernatural peace *of* God, which "transcends all understanding" (Phil. 4:7), but to the peace of heaven. It is deliverance from sin and its conflicts.

But here comes the big question. Has anyone ever chosen this path by his or her own will and then walked along it by his or her own strength? Does anyone of himself or herself actually do good and persist in it apart from the gospel?

I have spoken of the aspirations of the one who walks this path being "Christian" aspirations. Therefore, it is a path walked by Christians. But the question I am asking is whether any of us actually choose this path and then persist in it *of ourselves*, that is, unaided by the work of the Holy Spirit in turning us from sin to faith in Christ and by joining us to him. I hope that by this time we know the answer to that question. It is no! No one chooses to do good (as God defines it) or seeks glory, honor, or immortality by the path of rigorous morality. In fact, as we will see when we get to Paul's summation of the human condition in Romans 3:10–12:

> As it is written:
> "There is no one righteous, not even one;
>   there is no one who understands,
>   no one who seeks God.

1. John Murray, *The Epistle to the Romans* (Grand Rapids: Wm. B. Eerdmans, 1968), p. 64.

> All have turned away,
>   they have together become worthless;
> there is no one who does good,
>   not even one."

This first path would be a wonderful option if anyone could actually walk along it. But none can! And none do! Therefore, when God judges men and women by an accurate and comprehensive examination of their deeds, as he says he will do, all will be condemned. "For God does not show favoritism" (Rom. 2:11).

The Way of Sinners

The second path is the one all persons naturally take, apart from the intervention of God. It is the way of destruction. Again, Paul speaks of it in two verses of our text. Putting these together we have: "For those who are self-seeking and who reject the truth and follow evil, there will be wrath and anger. There will be trouble and distress for every human being who does evil: first for the Jew, then for the Gentile" (vv. 8–9).

In these verses there are four things that the wicked are said to be or do, which reveal their sinfulness. First, they are "self-seeking." This is the opposite of the first and second "greatest" commandments, which say, "Love the Lord your God with all your heart and with all your soul and with all your mind. . . . [and] your neighbor as yourself" (Matt. 22:37, 39). It is the sin of Satan who said, "I will make myself like the Most High" (Isa. 14:14b). Second, they "reject the truth." In the context of these early chapters of Romans, this refers to the rejection of the truth of God revealed in nature and, of course, all other rejections of truth that flow from it. Third, such a person "does evil." Romans 1:29–31 was an exposition of what this means, and there are other like passages later on (cf. Rom. 3:13–18). Fourth, they "follow evil." This could mean simply that they *do* evil, but this would be redundant in light of verse 9. Here it probably refers to the continuing downward path of evil described in 1:18–32.

What is the result of these choices? Again, there are four items: "wrath and anger" and "trouble and distress." The first two and the last two closely parallel each other, and there is a relationship between the first pair and the second. "Wrath and anger" both concern God's fierce and absolute opposition to all evil. "Trouble and distress" refer to the effect of God's resulting judgment upon evildoers. The words are frequently used of the sufferings of the wicked in the life to come (cf. Isa. 8:22; Zeph. 1:15, 17).

This is what awaits the ungodly and why even those who think that they are better than other people also need the gospel.

The Two Paths in Scripture

Many people find this section of Romans to be extremely difficult, for it seems to be saying that salvation is by good works. If you do good and persist in it, you will be saved. If you do evil, you will be lost. This is not what Romans 2:6–11 is saying, of course. No one is saved other than by the work of Jesus Christ and by faith in him. Nevertheless, it is significant that the inspired apostle does speak of two paths, and he does not encourage us to suppose that a person can reach the goal of eternal life without actually being on the path of righteousness.

Should we be surprised at this? Hardly!

This is the message of Psalm 1, which speaks of the righteous man "who does not walk in the counsel of the wicked or stand in the way of sinners or sit in the seat of mockers," but rather delights "in the law of the LORD," and speaks also of the wicked man who is "like chaff that the wind blows away" (vv. 1, 2, 4). This has present implications. But, like Paul's parallel thoughts in Romans, it has eternal implications as well. "Therefore the wicked will not stand in the judgment, nor sinners in the assembly of the righteous" (v. 5), and "the wicked will perish" (v. 6).

Matthew 19:16–21 records that the Lord Jesus Christ replied in similar terms to the rich young man who asked him, "Teacher, what good thing must I do to get eternal life?"

We might have expected Jesus to reply that the man should have faith in him. But instead Jesus said to obey the commandments: "'Do not murder, do not commit adultery, do not steal, do not give false testimony, honor your father and mother,' and 'love your neighbor as yourself.'"

The young man thought he had already done this. "All these I have kept," he said.

Again, instead of telling him to have faith in himself or even pointing out that he had not actually kept these commandments as God intended he should, Jesus merely brought to mind the young man's debilitating love of possessions: "If you want to be perfect, go, sell your possessions and give to the poor, and you will have treasure in heaven. Then come, follow me" (v. 21).

The introduction to the parable of the good Samaritan is along the same lines. An expert on the law tried to test Jesus by asking the same question posed by the rich young ruler: "Teacher, what must I do to inherit eternal life?" (Luke 10:25).

Jesus pointed him to the law: "'Love the Lord your God with all your heart and with all your soul and with all your strength and with all your mind'; and 'Love your neighbor as yourself'" (v. 27). The parable that followed was given to show who one's neighbor is and what it means to love him.

The most striking of Jesus' words setting out the two paths are those that come at the end of his last great sermon before the crucifixion, the sermon preached on the Mount of Olives:

[Jesus said,] "When the Son of Man comes in his glory, and all the angels with him, he will sit on his throne in heavenly glory. All the nations will be gathered before him, and he will separate the people one from another as a shepherd separates the sheep from the goats. He will put the sheep on his right hand and the goats on his left.

"Then the King will say to those on his right, 'Come, you who are blessed by my Father; take your inheritance, the kingdom prepared for you since the creation of the world. For I was hungry and you gave me something to eat, I was thirsty and you gave me something to drink, I was a stranger and you took me in, I needed clothes and you clothed me, I was sick and you looked after me, I was in prison and you came to visit me.'

"Then the righteous will answer him, 'Lord, when did we see you hungry and feed you, or thirsty and give you something to drink? When did we see you a stranger and invite you in, or needing clothes and clothe you? When did we see you sick or in prison and go to visit you?'

"The King will reply, 'I tell you the truth, whatever you did for one of the least of these brothers of mine, you did for me.'

"Then he will say to those on his left, 'Depart from me, you who are cursed, into the eternal fire prepared for the devil and his angels. For I was hungry and you gave me nothing to eat, I was thirsty and you gave me nothing to drink, I was a stranger and you did not invite me in, I needed clothes and you did not clothe me, I was sick and in prison and you did not look after me.'

"They will also answer, 'Lord, when did we see you hungry or thirsty or a stranger or needing clothes or sick or in prison, and did not help you?'

"He will reply, 'I tell you the truth, whatever you did not do for one of the least of these, you did not do for me.'

"Then they will go away to eternal punishment, but the righteous to eternal life."

Matthew 25:31–46

I do not want anyone to think that I am substituting good works for faith as a means of salvation. I am not. If good works are even added to faith—not to mention being substituted for faith—as a grounds of salvation, this becomes a false gospel and deserves the anathema Paul pronounces on such error (Gal. 1:8–9). Salvation is achieved by Christ for all who are to be saved, and it becomes theirs by simple faith in him and his work. But we must not mock God either! It is an equal error, as Paul also shows, to think that one can be saved by faith and then continue down the same path he or she has been treading, doing no good works at all. A person doing that is not saved, regardless or his or her profession.

Here is the wonder of the Christian gospel. On the one hand, it is utterly by grace received through faith—and even that faith is of grace (cf. Eph. 2:8). No one who is saved can possibly boast of anything. We are saved on the sole grounds of Jesus' death in our place. But, at the same time and on the other hand, those who are saved by grace through faith are placed on a path of righteousness where they do indeed perform such good works as the world about them cannot even begin to dream.

That is why Jesus could say, "For I tell you that unless your righteousness surpasses that of the Pharisees and the teachers of the law, you will certainly not enter the kingdom of heaven" (Matt. 5:20). "Righteousness" in this verse means "good deeds." So the teaching is that the people of God will—if they truly are the people of God—do good works surpassing even the best of the righteous (but unsaved) people of Christ's day.

Getting on the Right Path

What can you do if you are on the wrong path? How do you get out of the company of the wicked—who are rejecting the truth, pursuing evil, and thereby treasuring up wrath against the day of God's judgment—and into the company of those who are doing good deeds and who seek glory, honor, and immortality? Let me ask that twofold question again more clearly: What do you do if you are on a wrong path in order to get off the wrong path and onto a right one? Here are some specific answers:

1. *Recognize that you are on the wrong path.* Nobody is ever going to get off a wrong path and onto a right one as long as he or she entertains some hope that the present road will eventually lead to where he or she wants to go. So long as you think the way of your own self-seeking and of the rejection of the biblical truth about God is going to get you to happiness or fulfillment or salvation in the life to come (or whatever), you are never going to take even the first small step toward being saved. You must begin by recognizing that you are on the wrong path and that the end of that path is destruction.

2. *Admit that the path itself will not change.* Strangely, some travelers will admit that they are on a wrong road, but rather than go back to the right one they keep hoping that the road itself will change or that they will find a fork they can take that will get them to their proper destination. That will not happen in the physical world—nor in the spiritual! The path of self-seeking will always take you further from God and happiness. It is the downward path of Romans 1. It ends in the wrath of Romans 2.

3. *Turn around and face the opposite direction.* This is a way of speaking about what the Bible calls repentance or conversion. "Repentance" means to have a change of mind, to think differently and act differently as a result. "Conversion" literally means to turn around. You need to reject the way you are going and choose a different path entirely.

4. *Commit yourself to the Lord Jesus Christ, trusting in his death on your behalf.* This is the fullest meaning of faith, which does not stop merely with an intellectual assent to certain truths about God or Jesus but involves a commitment to Jesus as one's personal Lord and Savior. You must be able to say,

as Thomas did when Jesus appeared to him a week after his resurrection, "My Lord and my God!" (John 20:28).

5. *Get on with following Jesus and obeying his commands.* When you are wandering down the path of your own self-seeking and finally begin to realize what you are doing, you sense that you are hopelessly far from the true path—and in a sense you are. As long as you continue as you are going you will always be far from it. God seems infinitely removed. The return to God seems hopeless. But when you stop and turn around, beginning to seek God rather than your own will and pleasure, you will find (much to your surprise) that Jesus is not far away at all. In fact, you find him right there beside you. It was because he was with you and was calling you that you even turned around. That is why in the Bible repentance and faith always go together, so closely together that it is often impossible to say which comes first and which second. To believe on Jesus is to turn from sin—and *vice versa.*

And there is something else, too.

In the same instant you turn from sin and believe on Jesus, you find that you are already on the right road. You do not have to seek it, because the first step on that road *is* believing on Jesus. It is being where he is. He starts with you at that precise point. Therefore, as you step forward you find the darkness dispel, the light break through, and a glimpse of glory, honor, immortality, and eternal life rise up before you as your goal.

27

Not Hearers Only, But Doers

Romans 2:12-15

All who sin apart from the law will also perish apart from the law, and all who sin under the law will be judged by the law. For it is not those who hear the law who are righteous in God's sight, but it is those who obey the law who will be declared righteous. (Indeed, when Gentiles, who do not have the law, do by nature things required by the law, they are a law for themselves, even though they do not have the law, since they show that the requirements of the law are written on their hearts, their consciences also bearing witness, and their thoughts now accusing, now even defending them.)

I mentioned previously that every preacher who spends time trying to answer questions people have about Christianity has heard the question about the heathen over and over again. "What about the poor heathen in a far-off jungle who has never heard about Jesus Christ? Will God condemn him for failing to believe on a person about whom he has not even heard?"

I have answered that question in various ways over the years. One of the answers I have sometimes given, particularly to those who are not yet Christians, is that if someday we get to heaven and discover that a number or even all of these untaught natives have arrived in heaven despite our failure to tell them about Jesus, all we will be able to do is praise God for his great mercy and unfathomable ways. We will be happy! But if, on the contrary, we get to heaven and discover that not one of the untaught heathen is there, all of them having been condemned for failing to do what they knew they should do (on the basis of the *natural* revelation), we will still praise God for his mercy (to those to whom it was extended) and acknowledge his justice in the heathens' case, since the Judge of all the earth always *does* do right (cf. Gen. 18:25).

However, when I come to Romans 2:12, as we do now, I am reproved for this answer. For the text does not suggest that the heathen may somehow get to heaven in spite of their ignorance of the gospel, but rather that they will be condemned like the others. Not for failing to believe on Jesus, of whom they have not heard, of course! But for failing to do what they knew they should do, even apart from God's *special* revelation.

Verse 12 of our text supports this view, using the powerful word *perish.* "All who sin apart from the law will perish apart from the law, and all who sin under the law will be judged by the law."

Principles of Judgment

It can hardly be otherwise, of course, given the nature of man and the principles of God's judgment spelled out in this important second chapter of Romans. It is true that after reading verses 7 and 10 we might have some excuse for thinking that God may save some persons apart from the gospel, since those verses describe the hypothetical case of those who do good by God's standards. "To those who by persistence in doing good seek glory, honor and immortality, he will give eternal life. [There will be] glory, honor and peace for everyone who does good: first for the Jew, then for the Gentile." This might suggest that there are some untaught persons who, in spite of their ignorance of the gospel, nevertheless do good, strive for immortality, and therefore will be saved. But the fact that this is an entirely hypothetical case is proved by verse 12. If anyone actually could persist in doing good, there would be the reward of eternal life with God. But no one does! Therefore, "all who sin apart from the law will also perish."

I mentioned the principles of God's judgment as a reason why no one will be saved without Christ. Based on Romans 2, it is worth reviewing them at this point.

1. *God's judgment is according to truth* (v. 2). Human judgment tries to live up to this standard. Witnesses in our courts are required to "tell the truth, the whole truth, and nothing but the truth." But obviously human judgment is at best according to partial truth, and it is often misled entirely when witnesses inadvertently misrepresent the facts or lie about them. God's judgment is infinitely superior to human judgment at this point. It is according to full knowledge and perfect truth, because all secrets are known and all hearts are open to God. And no one will be able to lie in God's court.

2. *God's judgment is proportionate to human sins* (v. 5). This is why Paul speaks of sinners as "storing up wrath" against the day of God's wrath. Those who sin much will be punished much. Those who sin less will be judged accordingly.

3. *God's judgment is according to righteousness* (v. 5). Paul points to "his righteous judgment." There will be nothing wrong about it. It will be according to the highest possible standard and a faultless moral code.

4. *God's judgment is impartial* (v. 11). In human courts we often find the accused hoping to receive preferential treatment for one reason or another, and judges sometimes comply. Not so with God. At the final judgment all will be judged according to the same impartial standards and procedures, for, as Paul writes, "God does not show favoritism."

5. *God's judgment is according to people's deeds* (vv. 6–10, 12–15). Considering the number of verses dealing with this principle, this must have been the most important point of all according to Paul's way of thinking. Indeed, it is found throughout Romans 2, even in verses that seem to be making another point. Take verse 1, as an example. Paul is writing of persons who try to excuse their wrongdoing by saying that they have a firmer sense of what is right and wrong than other people. Paul's reply is that these persons are nevertheless guilty, because they "do the same things." That is, they are judged on the basis of their actual deeds. That phrase—"do the same things"—is also implied in verse 2 and repeated in verse 3. Finally, in verse 6, Paul says, "God 'will give to each person according to what he has done.'"[1] It is not what we know or even what we say we do that matters. It is how we actually perform.

Sinners *Under* the Law

How hard it is for our perverted sense of being righteous in God's sight to die! As we read these verses we can discern at once what Paul was dealing with and how he is replying. I said earlier, when we began to study Romans 2, that in my judgment Paul is dealing chiefly with the virtuous pagan in the first half of the chapter (vv. 1–16) and with the Jew in the second half (vv. 17–29). But, although this is generally true, he nevertheless is also probably thinking of the Jew in this section. Paul can undoubtedly visualize the Jew's response. He has spoken of those who are "under," or exposed, to the law as perishing. But the Jew would not want to accept this. According to Jewish teaching, salvation was by the law. The pious Jew spent long hours meditating on the law and could always be found in the synagogue attending to its

---

1. Paul seems to be quoting from Psalm 62:12, Proverbs 24:12, or both, which gives added weight to this principle. Since he has quoted these words, verses 7–15 should probably be seen as an exposition of them.

reading and exposition. I suppose Paul could almost hear the Jew gearing up to rattle off his accomplishments.

"I am not like all other men—robbers, evildoers, adulterers—or even like this tax collector."—"I fast twice a week."—"I give a tenth of all I get" (cf. Luke 18:12).

"All these I have kept since I was a boy" (cf. Luke 18:21).

As a matter of fact, Paul had thought like this himself before he met Christ: ". . . circumcised on the eighth day, of the people of Israel, of the tribe of Benjamin, a Hebrew of Hebrews; in regard to the law, a Pharisee; as for zeal, persecuting the church; as for legalistic righteousness, faultless" (Phil. 3:5–6).

Later, Paul is going to deal with the religious person's false hopes more directly, but here he focuses on such people's actual performance. "I know you know the law," Paul is acknowledging. "But do you keep it?" He reminds them that "it is not those who hear the law who are righteous in God's sight, but it is those who obey the law who will be declared righteous" (v. 13).

Not hearers only, but doers! That is the point of this passage, and it is the point at which each of us falls down. At the time of the release of the Tower Report on the investigation of arms sales to Iran, the newspapers carried a headline in which President Ronald Reagan was quoted as admitting, "Everyone fell short." That is it exactly—except that in the matter of our standing before God, the outcome is of far greater importance. Since we are condemned by the law, all of us having failed to live up to its standards, we must seek salvation in another way entirely.

Sinners *Apart From* the Law

There is another problem here: the problem of Gentiles (whom Paul had chiefly in mind) who would excuse themselves on the grounds that, unlike the Jews, they had not been given the law. They would agree with the justice of God in the Jews' condemnation. God had told the Jews how to live, and they had not done it. Indeed, they were even hypocritical about it, which is what Paul seems to bring out in the latter half of the chapter (vv. 17–24). The Jews had sinned *under* the law. But the Gentiles did not have the law of God. How, then, could they be condemned by it? In fact, how could they even be accused of sinning? Yet Paul wrote, "All who sin apart from the law will also perish apart from law" (v. 12a). How can there be sin *apart from* a divine law code or revelation?

Paul's answer is in verses 14 and 15. It has two parts. First, the Gentiles, even though they do not possess the law of God given to the Jewish people, nevertheless have a law "written on their hearts." Second, they also possess "consciences" that tell them they ought to obey this law and condemn them when they do not.

This is a very important point, for it introduces for the first time in Paul's letter what the older theologians called "the moral law" or "the law of nature." Earlier we dealt with "natural revelation," which means the revelation that God has given of himself in creation. (See chapter 15 of this volume.) It involves his "eternal power and divine nature" (Rom. 1:20); that is, confirms that there is a Supreme Being. But that is not what is involved here. In the earlier case, the natural revelation was seen to be sufficient to condemn all men and women, because on its basis they are obliged to seek out, thank, and worship the true God, which they do not do. But this goes beyond the natural revelation in that it involves a moral code or order that, Paul says, is possessed by all people. They may not have the revealed law of God. But they have something like it. They have "a law for themselves," which condemns them.

No person has talked about this moral law more effectively in recent years than the late Cambridge professor C. S. Lewis. It is the initial argument in his classic defense of the faith, *Mere Christianity*. Lewis begins with the observation that when people argue with one another, an angry person almost always appeals to some basic standard of behavior that the other person is assumed to recognize: "They say things like this: 'How'd you like it if anyone did the same to you?'—'That's my seat, I was there first'—'Leave him alone, he isn't doing you any harm'—'Why should you shove in first?'—'Give me a bit of your orange, I gave you a bit of mine'—'Come on, you promised.' People say things like that every day, educated people as well as uneducated, and children as well as grown-ups."[2]

What interested Lewis about these remarks is that the people making them are not merely saying that the other person's behavior just does not happen to suit them, but rather that the behavior of the other person is wrong:

> The man who makes [these remarks] . . . is appealing to some kind of standard of behavior which he expects the other man to know about. And the other man very seldom replies, "To hell with your standard." Nearly always he tries to make out that what he has been doing does not really go against the standard, or that if it does there is some special excuse. He pretends there is some special reason in this particular case why the person who took the seat first should not keep it, or that things were quite different when he was given the bit of orange, or that something has turned up which lets him off keeping his promise. It looks, in fact, very much as if both parties had in mind some kind of Law or Rule of fair play or decent behavior or morality or whatever you like to call it, about which they really agreed. And they have. If they had not, they might, of course, fight like animals, but they could not *quarrel* in the human sense of the word. Quarrelling means trying to show that the other man is in the wrong. And there would be no sense in trying to do that unless you and he had some sort of agreement as to what Right and

2. C. S. Lewis, *Mere Christianity* (New York: The Macmillan Company, 1958), p. 3.

Wrong are, just as there would be no sense in saying that a footballer had committed a foul unless there was some agreement about the rules of football.[3]

Lewis had a marvelously fresh gift for stating deep things simply. But it cannot escape us that this is precisely what Paul is saying in Romans 2:14–15, in reference to the Gentiles, though in more theological terms. It is true that Gentiles did not have the Jews' law. But they had a law within, a law that did not merely say that some kinds of behavior seem to work better than others or produce better responses from other people, but, rather, went far beyond that either to accuse or excuse them of wrongdoing.

Witnesses for the Prosecution

There are three important witnesses against the natural man in these verses. We must see what they are.

1. *The law of nature.* Lewis points out that today the law (or laws) of nature usually refers to physical phenomena like gravity, the bonding of elements, combustion, or nuclear energy. But, when the ancient theologians used this term, it meant, as it does here, "the law of *human* nature." The law of human nature is like natural physical law in that it comes from without and is meant to govern the way things operate or function. But there is this difference: In the physical realm an object has no choice as to whether or not it will observe the physical law. Those laws always operate. But in the human or moral realm people do have a choice, and the law is universally violated.

I know that many people object to belief in a universal moral law, pointing to the fact that some (the insane, for example) do not seem to be aware of it or to the fact that moral standards vary among different races or cultures. But those objections are not valid. It is true that there are people who do not seem to be aware of moral standards, and the insane are among them. But the very fact that we call such persons "insane" shows that *we* nevertheless recognize and want to adhere to the standards, regardless of what the problem may be in that individual's case. If an insane man commits a crime, we usually excuse him; but we do not excuse others. The problem is the person, not the standard. Again, although there are obvious differences in the way various races and cultures look at morals, there is nevertheless far more agreement than we might think at first. Regardless of the culture, there is (with few exceptions) a general regard for life, honor, bravery, selflessness, and such things. And the law codes and moral treatises of the ancients are remarkably like our own.

Regardless of what people say or even how they act, the real proof of the moral law is in people's objection when they perceive themselves to be mis-

3. Ibid., pp. 3, 4.

treated. If they speak of "unfair treatment," as all people do at one time or another, "have they not let the cat out of the bag and shown that, whatever they say, they really know the Law of Nature just like anyone else?" as Lewis argues.[4]

2. *Conscience.* The second accuser in these verses is the conscience, which Paul introduces as "also bearing witness" (v. 15). Some have confused the law of nature and the conscience, but they are two very different concepts. The first is an objective standard of which all are aware; it involves knowledge, knowledge of the right. The conscience is the part of our being that tells us we ought to do the right thing personally. Robert Haldane says, "Knowledge shows what is right; the conscience approves of it and condemns the contrary."[5]

3. *The Memory.* The third of the prosecuting witnesses in man is something we have not touched on yet, but which is introduced in the very last phrase we are studying: "their thoughts now accusing, now even defending them" (v. 15). It is the memory. Why is the memory so important? Obviously because it is something within ourselves that can (and will) condemn us, even without an external, judging word from God.

What a picture we have here! Three accusers, combining their witness to prove that even the person without the law will perish!

Donald Grey Barnhouse was known for his vivid and often very original illustrations, and at this point in his treatment of Romans he refers to the famous Revolutionary War painting "The Spirit of '76." It shows a drummer, a standard-bearer, and a fifer marching briskly down the road. Barnhouse says that our conduct (measured by the moral law), our conscience, and our memory are like those figures:

> Your conduct beats the drum that declares by your resounding good works that you know there is a divine law. Your conscience waves the flag that reminds you that often you have trampled your principles in the dust as you rushed past on your way to complete the desires of your own will. And the fife of your memory shrieks its refrain to remind you that you have sinned. The excuses and accusations of your thought run like shrill arpeggios in the counterpoint of your guilt. And the trio, conduct, conscience and mind, are all in step, in a perfect unison of condemnation because you have followed the road of your own will, refusing the road that forks at the cross of Jesus Christ that will lead you, if you follow it, even into eternal life.[6]

4. Ibid., p. 5.

5. Robert Haldane, *An Exposition of the Epistle to the Romans* (MacDill AFB: MacDonald Publishing, 1958), p. 91.

6. Donald Grey Barnhouse, *Epistle to the Romans*, part 8 (Philadelphia: The Bible Study Hour, 1950), p. 390.

Shall Not Perish

That is the point to which we should be led, of course. We should be led away from attempts to justify ourselves by our works, as the Jews did, or excuse ourselves as people who do not know what we should do, as the Gentiles did. Instead we should turn to Christ, where alone salvation may be found.

At the beginning of this study I spent some time talking about Romans 2:12, which says, "All who sin apart from the law will also perish apart from the law." I made the point that we must never think any person will ever be saved in any way other than by faith in Jesus Christ. Apart from him they will "perish." But whenever we see that word *perish*, with all its proper force and terror, we must also think of probably the best-known verse in the Bible, John 3:16, in which Jesus uses that word but says that it need not be our end: "For God so loved the world that he gave his one and only Son, that whoever believes in him shall not perish but have eternal life."

John 3:16 speaks of two destinies: eternal life and perishing, the very ends Paul speaks about in Romans 2 (vv. 7, 12). From birth we are all headed toward the second end, destined to perish miserably, without God and without hope (cf. Eph. 2:12). But Jesus died to make another and entirely different destiny possible. It is the way of atonement, with Jesus dying in our place, taking our punishment for sin upon himself. This is a wonderful end. It is, as Lewis says, "a thing of unspeakable comfort."[7] Still, it does not begin with comfort. It begins with the knowledge of sin, so that we might turn from sin to faith in Jesus.

7. Lewis, *Mere Christianity*, p. 25.

28

All Hearts Open, All Desires Known

Romans 2:16

This will take place on the day when God will judge men's secrets through Jesus Christ, as my gospel declares.

I am not very attracted to liturgical prayers because, although liturgical language is often quite beautiful (like that of Shakespeare's plays), the mere repetition of prayers tends, in my opinion, toward a love of language for its own sake and not meaning. There are exceptions, of course, and sometimes a particular phrase sticks in mind as expressing a great truth admirably.

I think of one such expression as we come to Romans 2:16: "This will take place on the day when God will judge men's secrets through Jesus Christ, as my gospel declares." The main idea is the uncovering of human secrets by God at the final judgment, and the liturgical expression of that truth, which I love, is from the opening collect of the Anglican Order for the Administration of Holy Communion. It begins, "Almighty God, unto whom all hearts are open, all desires known, and from whom no secrets are hid. . . ." I think that is a powerful expression—and helpful if it is used rightly. It reminds us that in a world ordered by an omniscient God there are, in the final analysis, *no secrets*. We may have secrets here, hiding from others what we are or do. But there will be no secrets on the day when all secrets will be brought to light before God.

The All-Knowing God

God knows all things even now, of course. God spoke of the Jewish people to Isaiah, saying, "For I know their works and their thoughts" (Isa. 66:18 KJV). King David wrote of himself:

> O LORD, you have searched me
>   and you know me.
> You know when I sit and when I rise;
>   you perceive my thoughts from afar.
> You discern my going out and my lying down;
>   you are familiar with all my ways.
> Before a word is on my tongue
>   you know it completely, O LORD.
>
> Psalm 139:1–4

The author of Hebrews declared, "Nothing in all creation is hidden from God's sight. Everything is uncovered and laid bare before the eyes of him to whom we must give account" (Heb. 4:13).

This is one reason why unregenerate people repress their knowledge of God, as Romans 1:18–20 declares they do. We looked at this when we were studying those verses. If God knows all things, as he must if he is God, he knows us not as we wish to project ourselves before others but as we really are, and none of us can stand the thought of such perfect and penetrating knowledge.

I pointed out in that earlier study that this is one of the characteristics of human nature perceived by the existentialist philosopher and playwright Jean-Paul Sartre. In his analysis of man, Sartre rooted man's uniqueness in his being a subject, who observes, rather than an object, which is observed. A subject observes and acts. An object is observed and acted upon. The former pleases us. The latter is disturbing. In one of his works, Sartre imagines himself as a man who is standing in a hallway, looking through a keyhole at another person. As long as he is the observer and the other person is the object observed, Sartre is content. He is in control. But suddenly he hears footsteps in the hall, turns around, and realizes that someone has been looking at him as he has looked through the keyhole. Now he is no longer content. He is no longer in control, and he is overcome with feelings of shame, fear, guilt, and embarrassment. According to Sartre, to be fully human, man must be the ultimate subject rather than an object.[1]

---

1. Jean-Paul Sartre, *Being and Nothingness*, trans. Hazel E. Barnes (New York: Washington Square Press, 1953), p. 319.

But what about God? How can one escape being an object before him, since God sees us always? Sartre's solution was to banish God from his own private universe, to become an atheist.

In a series of essays called *The Words*, Sartre tells how he came to this point. He was a child at the time. He had been raised a Catholic, and as one of his assignments in the Catholic school he attended he had written a paper on the Passion of Christ. When the awards were presented for these papers, Sartre was given only a silver medal rather than the gold. He resented it and blamed God. Sartre wrote, "This disappointment drove me into impiety. . . . For several years more, I maintained public relations with the Almighty. But privately, I ceased to associate with him."[2]

Then he tells how, during these years, there was a time when he felt that God existed: "I had been playing with matches and burned a small rug. I was in the process of covering up my crime when suddenly God saw me. I felt his gaze inside my head and on my hands. I whirled about in the bathroom, horribly visible, a live target. Indignation saved me. I flew into a rage against so crude an indiscretion, I blasphemed, I muttered like my grandfather: 'God damn it, God damn it, God damn it.' He never looked at me again."[3]

That story alone explains the life and philosophy of Sartre. Yet it is sad and tragic. Sad, because it is mistaken. Sartre says, "He [God] never looked at me again." But in reality God never ceased to look at Sartre. God looks on all things and sees them perfectly. Actually, it was Sartre who had ceased to look at God. Tragic, because by turning his back on God, Sartre turned from the one being in the universe who could have helped him.

I said earlier that Sartre's solution to the problem of being beneath the gaze of God and of being overcome by natural feelings of shame, fear, guilt, and embarrassment was to banish God from his universe—to become an atheist. But it does not require a philosophical genius to realize that this is only whistling in the dark. If there is a God, as even Sartre indirectly attests, then he cannot be so banished, certainly not by human beings. Moreover, if God is omniscient, as he must be if he is God, then not only has he seen all the evil deeds we have done and known the evil thoughts we have had. He also remembers them. And one day he will produce them for exposure and judgment.

It is what Paul speaks about when he writes of "the day when God will judge man's secrets through Jesus Christ."

Naked Before God and Man

I now take you from that day of judgment to one of the very first days of human history. It is the day when Adam and Eve stood before God in the

2. Jean-Paul Sartre, *The Words*, trans. Bernard Frechtman (Greenwich, Conn.: Fawcett Publications, 1966). p. 64.
3. Ibid.

Garden of Eden shortly after having sinned by eating of the fruit of the tree of the knowledge of good and evil. The story is in Genesis 3, but the theme is set in the previous chapter, before the fall, where it is said: "The man and his wife were both naked, and they felt no shame" (Gen. 2:25).

I have said many times in considering this story that I have no doubt that this was a literal physical nakedness. Otherwise the matter of their making fig-leaf clothes for themselves, which we are told about later, has no meaning. But it was a psychological nakedness, too. Adam and Eve were not ashamed in their nakedness before they sinned. It was only after they had sinned that they were conscious of it.

Why were they unashamed before the fall? The answer is obvious. Nakedness has to do with exposure, not only with external, physical exposure but, more importantly, with internal exposure. They were not ashamed in their nakedness before the fall because they had nothing to be ashamed about.

1. *They were unashamed before God.* Adam and Eve had done nothing that would have been any cause for shame. They were without sin at the time, and their relationship to God was one of utter openness. They delighted to see God when he came to them in the garden. They conversed with him freely. We cannot do this, of course, and the reason we cannot do it is sin. Sin causes us to hide from God, as Adam and Eve later did when God came to them. Sin causes us to flee from him.

Some flee into atheism, as Sartre did.

Some flee into materialism.

Even Christians run away from God when they persist in sin.

Donald Grey Barnhouse had been preaching on a college campus and had been invited to speak in one of the women's dorms following a meeting that had been held elsewhere that evening. When he finished, one of the young women remained behind, obviously offended by his teaching. Her face was scowling. "I used to believe that stuff, but I don't believe it anymore," she said.

Barnhouse asked, "What class are you in?"

"I'm a freshman."

"What kind of a family do you come from?" The girl said that she came from a Christian family.

"Do you have a Bible?"

"Yes."

"Do you read it?"

"I used to read it," the student said, "but I don't read it anymore. I told you I no longer believe that stuff."

"Can you remember when you stopped reading it?" Barnhouse asked. The girl said that she had stopped reading it around Thanksgiving. "Tell me," said Barnhouse, "what happened in your life around November the tenth?" The girl began to cry, and it soon came out that at that time she had started to live in sin with a young man, and it was because of this that she could no longer tolerate the gaze of God when she read her Bible.

Wesley said it well: "The Bible will keep you from sin, or sin will keep you from the Bible." This is because the God who confronts us in Scripture is the holy God before whom all hearts are open.

2. *They were unashamed before each other.* Before the fall, it was not only God before whom Adam and Eve were unashamed. They were also unashamed before each other, and for the same reason. They had nothing to be ashamed about. They had not lied to one another. They had not falsely accused one another, as they later did, trying to shift the blame for their sin to others. They had not harmed one another. As a result they could be completely themselves. Today no one can be completely open in a relationship. In some good relationships we come close. But still, there is a residue of ourselves that we keep hidden even from a spouse or very close friend. Why? Because we are ashamed of ourselves, and we fear that if we reveal the fault, the other will cease to love us or respect us.

3. *They were unashamed in their own eyes.* Both Adam and Eve were without shame as they looked on themselves. In those first days, Adam could look at himself and know he had nothing to hide. And Eve could look at herself and know she had nothing to hide.

What about us? Today, most of us will hardly stop our mad race through life long enough even to take a brief glance at who we are. Generations ago, people lived more slowly; they could reflect on who they were and where they were going. Modern life has intensified the pace. Most of us cannot even come into a room and sit down for two minutes without feeling the need to snap on the television set or radio to fill our heads with stimulation—anything to keep from thinking. "All the news, all the time!" That is what we want. And the reason we want it is that we do not want to consider that we are naked before God and that nothing is hidden from him before whom we must give account.

Hiding from Thee

What we are and do comes out in the continuation of the Genesis story. Adam and Eve sinned, in spite of the warning God had given them concerning the tree of the knowledge of good and evil. So when God came to them in the garden they hid themselves—or at least they tried to.

Actually, they had already tried to hide, first from themselves and then from each other. They did it by trying to make clothing from fig leaves. Sometimes when people are trying to be funny they speak of prostitution as the oldest human profession, but they are wrong in this. The oldest profession is not prostitution but the clothing industry. Later, sin showed itself in sexual sins as well as in other ways. But the very first effect of sin was the opening of the eyes of Adam and Eve to perceive that they were naked, in response to which "they sewed fig leaves together and made coverings for themselves" (Gen. 3:7). In other words, as sinners they found their psychological exposure intolerable and tried to cover up. At first they used leaves. Later, when God appeared to question them, they used evasions and excuses and tried to put the blame on God.

I have sometimes spoken of these leaves as good works and of the attempt to be covered by them as "fig-leaf righteousness." It was a way of saying, "We are all right. We are not sinners. We are good people." Well, as long as it was just the two of them, they got by, since they were both sinners. But the fig leaves were inadequate when they finally stood before God, just as our good works will be useless at the judgment.

I do not know what happened to those fig leaves when God finally appeared to Adam and Eve and called them to stand before him. Perhaps they fell off. But whether or not they did, they might as well have, for nothing could have hidden from God what they were or had done. So it will be in *our* judgment. We commit our sins in secret. We present a false face to the public. We declare that God does not exist. We brand ourselves atheists. We think we are safe. But we do not need reporters hiding in the bushes to observe what we are doing and report it in the *National Enquirer.* We do not need a talk-show host to reveal our cover-up transactions. God knows. God remembers. And one day he "will judge men's secrets through Jesus Christ."

What a dreadful last scene to human history!

The Psalmist said, "If you, O LORD, kept a record of sins [and he does], O LORD, who could stand?" (Ps. 130:3).

Naked—Yet Clothed by God

I come to the climax of the story of Adam and Eve's sin, and it is chiefly for this that I tell it. God told Adam and Eve that the punishment for their eating of the tree of the knowledge of good and evil would be death. But when he confronted them in their sin and exposed it, the death he had promised fell not on them but on a substitute. And here is a truly thrilling point: *It was with the skin of the substitute that they were clothed.*

The Bible tells it tersely, saying, "The LORD God made garments of skin for Adam and his wife and clothed them" (Gen. 3:21). The text does not indicate what animals God killed in order to get the skins with which he clothed Adam and Eve, but in view of the development of this idea later in the Bible, I tend to think that they were lambs and that the skins were lambskins. Certainly, the incident is meant to point to Jesus Christ as the only sufficient atonement for sin, and Jesus is pictured as "the Lamb of God, who takes away the sin of the world" (John 1:29). Whatever they were, God must have killed animals in order to have the skins with which he clothed our first parents.

Think what this must have meant to Adam and Eve. Their first thought, when they saw the animals lying dead in front of them, must have been, "So this is what death is!" They must have regarded the scene with horror. God had told them, "You must not eat from the tree of the knowledge of good and evil, for when you eat of it you will surely die" (Gen. 2:17). But if they had not witnessed death before this, which we are to suppose they had not, they probably did not take this threat seriously. Now suddenly death was before them, and they must have sensed for the very first time how serious it is to disobey God. In that instant it must have dawned on them that if death is the result of sin, then sin is far worse than anything they could possibly have imagined. Moreover, *they* were sinners, and their sin was damnable.

But there is something else that must have gripped them in that instant, and that was a deep and growing wonder at God's mercy. God had told them that their sin would be punished by death. And it was! But wonder of wonders, it was not themselves who died but the animals. They had broken God's law. God had every right to take their lives in forfeit of his broken commandment. But instead, he showed that there could be a substitution. An innocent could die for them.

And there was another marvel, too. They were exposed as sinners. All the secrets they had were revealed. But although their sins were exposed—their nakedness was a symbol of it—they did not have to remain naked. Rather, God clothed them with the skins of the slain animals. So they were both exposed and covered at the same time.

This is what must be done for us. We cannot escape from our guilt. The guilt is there and is well documented. We can try to deny it, but everything in our lives, culture, and psychological makeup will refute the denial. We show our guilt by doors and blinds and shower curtains and the clothing industry—as well as by our calculated attempts to hide from one another. These patterns testify to the truthfulness of the Word of God. But the gospel tells us that God deals with this guilt. He does not just deny, forgive, or forget it. He deals with it in Jesus Christ. Christ died for sin; the penalty of sin has been paid. Now God clothes those who have believed in Christ with Christ's righteousness:

> Jesus, thy blood and righteousness
> My beauty are, my glorious dress;
> 'Midst flaming worlds, in these arrayed,
> With joy shall I lift up my head.

Whoever you are, the day is coming when you will stand before the judgment bar of God, and God will judge even the deepest secrets of your heart. How will you manage in that day? You can appear before God in only one of two ways. Either you will stand before him in the righteousness of Christ, your sin atoned for by his death, or you will stand in the horror of your own spiritual and moral nakedness. The Bible speaks of people who will be like that. It describes their terror. "Then the kings of the earth, the princes, the generals, the rich, the mighty, and every slave and every free man hid in caves and among the rocks of the mountains. They called to the mountains and the rocks, 'Fall on us and hide us from the face of him who sits on the throne and from the wrath of the Lamb! For the great day of their wrath has come, and who can stand?'" (Rev. 6:15–17).

Do not wait until the day when God will expose and judge all secrets. Flee to Christ for his righteousness today.[4]

4. A portion of this chapter has already appeared in slightly different form in James Montgomery Boice, *Genesis*, vol 1, *Genesis 1:1–11:32* (Grand Rapids: Zondervan, 1982), pp. 118–122, 189–193.

29

The Second Excuse: Religion

Romans 2:17-24

Now you, if you call yourself a Jew; if you rely on the law and brag about your relationship to God; if you know his will and approve of what is superior because you are instructed by the law; if you are convinced that you are a guide for the blind, a light for those who are in the dark, an instructor of the foolish, a teacher of infants, because you have in the law the embodiment of knowledge and truth—you, then, who teach others, do you not teach yourself? You who preach against stealing, do you steal? You who say that people should not commit adultery, do you commit adultery? You who abhor idols, do you rob temples? You who brag about the law, do you dishonor God by breaking the law? As it is written, "God's name is blasphemed among the Gentiles because of you."

It should be evident from study of the earlier portions of Romans that nearly everything that has been said thus far applies to all men and women. That is, it applies to ourselves—apart from the supernatural work of God in us through the Holy Spirit. Regardless of our achievements, our vaunted moral standards or our outward position in life, we are all in exactly the same situation as the hedonistic pagan described in Romans 1. We have suppressed the knowledge of God disclosed to us in nature and have therefore launched ourselves along the path of moral and spiritual decline that the chapter describes. The propensity to condemn others for what we ourselves do, which is unfolded in Romans 2, also describes us.

But we are great at making distinctions, particularly when these are to our advantage, and it is to another of these self-serving "excuses" that we now come. We have already seen one such distinction, used by the moralist, who admits that there are indeed pagans like those portrayed in Romans 1 but who denies that he or she is like them—because the person knows better and has "standards." (See my chapter 13.) The new distinction, the one that enters in here, is made by individuals who consider themselves to be religious.

In Paul's day such a person was the Jew, which is how Paul begins the section: "Now you, if you call yourself a Jew. . . ." Today the person who fits this category could be an ardent Fundamentalist, any churchgoing Protestant (regardless of denomination), a devout Catholic, or some other variety of "religious" individual.

Let's imagine what this religious person might be thinking. He or she has been listening to Paul describe the pagan morality of the day and has been quick to join Paul in condemning it. "I am glad that you have spoken as you have," this person might tell Paul, "because things really are in a terrible state today. The divorce rate is up. Our political leaders lie to us. Nobody wants to work. The schools are breaking down. Crime, venereal disease, prostitution, gambling and other vices are increasing. Moreover, if God is a God of justice and truth, as we suppose he must be, he will certainly judge all these wicked people severely. So preach to them. The drug dealers, the crime lords, the politicians—all, no doubt, will profit from your gospel.

"But leave me out of it! I am a very religious person, and my religious commitments exempt me from your blanket condemnations. I have been a churchgoing person all my life. I have been baptized and confirmed. I go to communion. I give to the church's support."

Paul replies that these are genuinely good things and not to be ignored. "But you still need the gospel," he says.

"Why?"

"Because God is not interested in outward things alone—things like church membership, the sacraments, stewardship—but rather in what is within."

God says, "Man looks at the outward appearance, but the LORD looks at the heart" (1 Sam. 16:7b).

A Catalogue of Advantages

I have put this argument in simple contemporary language, but when we turn to Romans 2:17–20 we find the Jew (the "religious person" of Paul's day) to be making eight important claims. Four are about the Jews' special spiritual advantages. Four are about their religious privileges.[1] The claims having to do with the Jews' spiritual advantages are:

1. God has given us his law.
2. He has entered into a special relationship with us.
3. Because we have been given his law, we know his will, and
4. We approve only the most excellent of human moral standards.

The claims having to do with their privileges are:

1. To be a guide for the blind,
2. To be a light for those who are in the dark,
3. To be an instructor for the foolish, and
4. To be a teacher of infants.

To evaluate these claims properly, we must begin by seeing that *so far as they go,* each is absolutely true. Many of our contemporaries would regard such claims as mere spiritual arrogance or prejudice, believing that no religion has any special claim to truth. But no Christian can think like this, nor can any true Jew. The Jew in Paul's day boasted of having received a unique and special revelation from God: first from the hands of Moses on Mount Sinai and then by a long succession of writings from selected generals, kings, chroniclers, and prophets. And he was correct in this boast! In fact, Christians as well as Jews receive the writings of the Old Testament as the very words of God, not as mere human inventions. The apostle Peter wrote, "For prophecy never had its origin in the will of man, but men spoke from God as they were carried along by the Holy Spirit" (2 Peter 1:21).

In the same way, it is also absolutely true that God had entered into a special relationship with the Jews. He had begun with Abraham, and from

1. These have been handled differently by different commentators, though their underlying points are the same. Charles Hodge speaks of three Jewish advantages: (1) their covenant relationship to God, (2) their superior advantages as to divine knowledge, and (3) their circumcision. The first two are covered in the present paragraph (cf. *A Commentary on Romans* [Edinburgh and Carlisle, Pa.: The Banner of Truth Trust, 1972], p. 59). Robert Haldane lists six advantages: (1) their bearing the name of a Jew, (2) having received the law, (3) having the true God as their God, (4) knowing his will, (5) discerning what is evil, and (6) their ability to teach and guide other men (cf. *An Exposition of the Epistle to the Romans* [MacDill AFB: MacDonald Publishing, 1958], p. 94). Frederick Godet sees the advantages as falling into these categories: (1) the gifts of God, (2) the superior capabilities which these gifts confer on the Jews, and (3) the part which the Jew thereby thought himself called to play toward other nations (cf. *Commentary on St. Paul's Epistle to the Romans*, trans. by A. Cusin [Edinburgh: T. & T. Clark, n.d.], vol. 1, p. 213).

Abraham's days onward Jews had enjoyed the advantages of a covenant relationship.

Jesus taught this in his conversation with the Samaritan woman whom he met at Jacob's well near Sychar (John 4:1–26). When he touched upon her sin, she tried to get him into a theological discussion—just like many people today do when so confronted. They try to escape dealing with the evil in their lives. This woman asked a question about the proper place for worship—undoubtedly often discussed in the towns of Samaria in her day. Was it Jerusalem, as the Jews obviously claimed? Or was it upon Mount Gerazim, as the Samaritans believed? (vv. 19–20).

Jesus answered the woman in two ways. First, he opened her eyes to a new era of worship, which he was bringing in, a time in which worship would be neither in Jerusalem exclusively nor in Samaria. Rather, he said, ". . . a time is coming and has now come when the true worshipers will worship the Father in spirit and truth . . . they are the kind of worshipers the Father seeks. God is spirit, and his worshipers must worship in spirit and in truth" (vv. 23–24).

Second, Jesus dealt with the specific question she raised. This has forever settled the matters both of the authority of the Old Testament and of the priority of Jews in spiritual matters. Jesus said, "You Samaritans worship what you do not know; we worship what we do know, for salvation is from the Jews" (v. 22). It follows from this that until the inauguration of the church age at Pentecost, although salvation was available for Gentiles, the way was by the gate of Judaism only.

Again, the Jew addressed by Paul in our text was right in claiming that because he possessed a true revelation from God in what we call the Old Testament, he really did know God's will. Or at least he had the proper foundation for knowing it. In Romans 2:18 "will" is not referring to the secret or hidden counsels of God—for an obvious reason: the hidden counsels of God are indeed hidden. Rather, it refers to the revelation in Scripture of what, as Haldane put it, "is agreeable to him, what he requires them to do, what he commands, what he prohibits, what he approves, and what he rewards."[2] We have an example of what this means in the three specific commandments that Paul cites in verses 21 and 22.

Finally, the Jew was right in his claim that because he was instructed by the law he had a valid basis for approving what was excellent or superior in human moral standards. In other words, he could evaluate any lesser standards because he possessed an absolute rule or yardstick by which to measure them.

Out of these four basic spiritual advantages grew an equally impressive set of privileges, couched here in somewhat metaphorical language. The Jew saw himself as being "a guide for the blind, a light for those who are in the dark, an instructor of the foolish, a teacher of infants"—all because he

2. Haldane, *An Exposition of the Epistle to the Romans*, p. 95.

had "the embodiment of knowledge and truth" in the Scriptures (vv. 19–20). And so he did! So he was! The knowledge of the true God and the way of this true God were indeed a light in the dark labyrinth of pagan superstition and culture.

The Eighth Commandment

Alas, knowledge of God and of the way of this true God was not enough! This is because, as we have already seen, God judges according to truth and not according to appearances, according to what men and women actually do and not according to their mere professions.

At this point Paul brings forth three examples of that "superior" way of the Jew, which came as a result of his possessing the revealed law of God: the eighth of the Ten Commandments, the seventh of the Ten Commandments, and a statement embracing the first two of the Ten Commandments. The eighth commandment said, "You shall not steal" (Exod. 20:15). This was part of the Jewish instruction properly passed to others. But, Paul asks, did the Jew himself steal? The seventh commandment said, "You shall not commit adultery" (Exod. 20:14). But did the Jew commit adultery? The first and second commandments declared: "You shall have no other gods before me. You shall not make for yourself an idol in the form of anything in heaven above or on the earth beneath or in the waters below. You shall not bow down to them or worship them; for I, the LORD your God, am a jealous God, punishing the children for the sin of the fathers to the third and fourth generation of those who hate me, but showing love to a thousand generations of those who love me and keep my commandments" (Exod. 20:3–6). But did the Jew break these two commandments?

So far I have written about Romans 2:17–24 as if it is dealing with Jews almost exclusively. But here we must break away from that more limited view and get back to what I said at the beginning, namely, that these verses speak to all kinds of "religious" people: Fundamentalists, churchgoing Presbyterians, Baptists, Catholics, whatever. It is a charge, as one commentator puts it, "against the orthodox."

So I ask, "We who preach against stealing, do we steal?"

The idea that one should not steal is a generally accepted standard of human behavior, but it is just as generally broken. We should not think that we have kept this commandment just because we have not forced our way into another person's home and walked off with his possessions. We steal from God when we fail to worship him as we ought or when we set our own concerns ahead of his. We steal from an employer when we do not give the best work of which we are capable or when we overextend our coffee breaks or leave work early. We steal if we waste company products or use company time for personal matters. We steal if we sell something for more than it is worth. We steal from our employees if the work environment for which we are responsible harms their health, or if we do not pay them enough to guarantee a healthy, adequate standard of living. We steal when we borrow something and do not return it. We steal from ourselves when we waste our talents, time, or money.

The Seventh Commandment

After citing the eighth of the Ten Commandments, Paul moves backward to the seventh and asks: "You who say that people should not commit adultery, do you commit adultery?"

What are we to answer to this question, particularly if we live in the United States of America where adultery, fornication, and a variety of forms of sexual experimentation are not only excused, but even encouraged and applauded? What are we to answer in view of the revelation of sexual sins in the lives of prominent national figures, both secular and religious? What are we to say in view of Jesus' teaching that the seventh commandment has to do with the thoughts of our minds and the intents of our hearts and not only with external actions. According to Jesus' teaching, lust is the equivalent of adultery, just as hate is the equivalent of murder (Matt. 5:27–28; cf. vv. 21–22). The biblical standard is purity before marriage and fidelity afterward.

There is hardly an area of our cultural life so in opposition to God's standards. The media use the lure of sex to push materialism and glamorize the pursuit of pleasure. Television fills our living rooms with sex-filled advertisements, and its programs are increasingly explicit in portraying immoral sexual relationships and practices. Movies are worse. Even the most respectable areas of our cities frequently feature X-rated films.

At one time people would defend high sexual standards, even though they often did something quite different on the side. But today we do not even hold to the morality. "If it feels good, do it!" That is the cry of our age and the practice of the great majority.

The First and Second Commandments

The third of Paul's examples of preaching one thing but doing another is a reference to the first and second commandments: "You who abhor idols, do you rob temples?"

It is not as easy to understand this question as it is to understand the first two. There are several problems. First, the second half of the sentence does not match the first in the same way the parts of the first two questions match. When Paul says, "You who preach against stealing, do you steal?" he is charging the religious person with doing exactly what that person says others should not do. In other words, the religious person says, "Do not steal," yet he does steal. So also with the second example. The religious person says, "Do not commit adultery," but he commits adultery himself. In the case of this third example, the parts do not match. The prohibition is: "Do not worship idols." But Paul's accusation is not idolatry, which we might expect, but rather sacrilege or robbery of the heathen temples.

The second problem is equally if not more puzzling. So far as we know, the Jews did not "rob temples." Does this mean, then, merely that they robbed God of the honor properly due to him? Does it refer to the trafficking in offerings conducted in the courtyard of the temple in Jerusalem, which Jesus condemned? Does it refer to Jews possessing (perhaps as art objects) items that had been taken from heathen temples by Gentile armies and later sold? Does it refer to actual temple spoilage? It is hard to say what this means, although there are arguments in favor of each of these views.

What we can say is that, regardless of the particular way the ancient Jew may have broken the first and second of the Ten Commandments (which we may or may not understand), we certainly understand how *we* have broken them—even the most religious among us.

The first commandment is a demand for our exclusive and zealous worship of the true God: "You shall have no other gods before me" (Exod. 20:3). To worship any god but the biblical God is to break this commandment. But we need not worship a clearly defined "god" to break this commandment—Zeus, Minerva, Buddha, Allah, or one of the countless modern idols. We break it whenever we give some person or some object or some worldly aspiration the first place in our lives, a place that belongs to God alone. Often today the substitute god is ourselves or our image of ourselves. It can be such things as success, fame, material affluence, or power over others. To keep this commandment would be, as John R. W. Stott says, "to see all things from his [God's] point of view and do nothing without reference to him; to make his will our guide and his glory our goal; to put him first in thought, word and deed; in business and leisure; in friendships and career; in the use of our money, time and talents; at work and at home."[3]

Now consider the second commandment, which says: "You shall not make for yourself an idol in the form of anything in heaven above or on the earth beneath or in the waters below. You shall not bow down to them or worship them; for I, the LORD your God, am a jealous God, punishing the children for the sin of the fathers to the third and fourth generation of those who hate me, but showing love to a thousand generations of those who love me and keep my commandments" (Exod. 20:4–6). If the first commandment deals with the *object* of our worship, forbidding the worship of any false God, this commandment deals with the *manner* of our worship, forbidding us to worship even the true God unworthily.

This means that we should take the utmost care to discover what God is truly like and thus increasingly worship him as the only great, transcendent, spiritual, and inscrutable God he is. But we do not do this. Instead, as Paul

3. John R. W. Stott, *Basic Christianity* (Grand Rapids: Wm B. Eerdmans, 1958), p. 65.

argued at the beginning of his discussion, we suppress the knowledge of God and find that our foolish hearts are darkened (Rom. 1:18, 21).[4]

When Paul comes to the end of this paragraph, which describes the true state of the orthodox, or "religious," person, he quotes the Old Testament to show that "God's name is blasphemed among the Gentiles because of you" (v. 24; cf. Isa. 52:5; Ezek. 36:22). This is always the case when ostensibly devout persons violate the very standards they proclaim. It is a terrible thing!

But there is something even more terrible, and that is for these same persons to continue nevertheless along this wrong path, supposing that they are on the best of standings with God—just because they are religious—when actually they are, like the utter pagans around them, on a swift journey to destruction. William Barclay begins his discussion of these verses with the words: "To a Jew a passage like this must have come as a shattering experience."[5] He is right, of course. But it is not only for the Jew that a passage like this is or should be shattering. It should be shattering to us all, particularly if we find ourselves thinking that our case is somehow different from that of other persons—because of our religious leanings.

If you have been trusting in your baptism,

If you have been trusting in your confirmation,

If you have been trusting in your church membership, or your knowledge of the Bible or doctrine, or in your generous stewardship,

If you have been trusting in your Christian upbringing,

If you have been trusting in *anything* other than Jesus Christ and his death upon the cross in your place, throw whatever it is completely out of your mind. Abandon it. Stamp upon it. Grind it down. Dust off the place where it lay.

Then turn to Jesus Christ alone, and trust him only.

4. A fuller discussion of these four commandments, from which some of the above material has been taken, may be found in James Montgomery Boice, *Foundations of the Christian Faith* (Downers Grove, Ill.: InterVarsity Press, 1986), pp. 227–231, 239–243.

5. William Barclay, *The Letter to the Romans* (Edinburgh: The Saint Andrew Press, 1969), p. 42.

30

Circumcision

Romans 2:25–29

Circumcision has value if you observe the law, but if you break the law, you have become as though you had not been circumcised. If those who are not circumcised keep the law's requirements, will they not be regarded as though they were circumcised? The one who is not circumcised physically and yet obeys the law will condemn you who, even though you have the written code and circumcision, are a lawbreaker.

A man is not a Jew if he is only one outwardly, nor is circumcision merely outward and physical. No, a man is a Jew if he is one inwardly, and circumcision is circumcision of the heart, by the Spirit, not by the written code. Such a man's praise is not from men, but from God.

When my wife and I lived in Basel, Switzerland, we became acquainted with the annual Swiss celebration known as Faschnacht, which is the equivalent of the Mardi Gras—"Fat Tuesday." This term refers to the time of indulgence immediately preceding Lent (which always begins on a Wednesday) in which people do things they expect to have to give up for the solemn days leading up to Good Friday. Basel is a Protestant city, so its citizens hold Faschnacht during the first week of Lent—in bold defiance of Catholic custom. But otherwise their week of riotous abandon is precisely the same as found elsewhere. The Swiss have

257

many jokes about it. One of the standard jokes concerns the number of ille-
gitimate babies that will be born in Basel about nine months later.

In Switzerland the Salvation Army is evangelical, and each year it uses
Faschnacht to witness to the claims of Christ. I remember from the time I was
there that in the days immediately before the celebration of Faschnacht billboards appeared bearing the name of the Salvation Army, an address or phone
number where one could get spiritual council, and a sentence in German that
went: *Gott sieht hinter deine Maske.* It means "God sees behind your mask."

I have reflected on that many times, remembering that it is a statement
of a great biblical principle, found explicitly for the first time in 1 Samuel
16:7. That text says, "Man looks at the outward appearance, but the Lord
looks at the heart."

Last Retreat of the Orthodox

This is what Paul is getting at in the last paragraphs of Romans 2, as he
deals for the final time with the objections of those who consider themselves to be so thoroughly religious that they do not need the gospel. The
issue is the Jewish sacrament of circumcision and the accompanying claim
that all who have been circumcised will be saved.

Robert Haldane writes that "Paul here pursues the Jew into his last
retreat."[1] The Jew, who was the chief example in Paul's day of the thoroughly religious person, had begun his defense against Paul's gospel by the
argument that he (or she) possessed the law. As we have seen in the previous study, Paul argued that possession of the law, although undoubtedly a
great privilege, is of no value if the one possessing the commands of God
fails to keep them. The law says, "You shall not steal" (Exod. 20:15). But
knowing that is no help if you do steal, for then the law condemns rather
than exonerates the individual. It is the same with other commandments:
"You shall not commit adultery" (Exod. 20:14) and "You shall have no other
gods before me" (Exod. 20:3). The Jew, along with everybody else, had broken those laws. So it was not sufficient to say, "I have the law, and therefore
I do not need the gospel." On the contrary, the law is given to reveal our
need of God's grace.

Still, the Jew had one last card to play, one final argument. He had been
circumcised, and circumcision had brought him into visible outward fellowship with that body of covenant people to whom God had made salvation
promises. It was like saying that circumcision (our counterpart is baptism)
had made him a member of that body, and because of that membership his
salvation was certain.

The Jew really did believe this—just as many people today believe they
are saved merely by being members of a church! In the various commen-

1. Robert Haldane, *An Exposition of the Epistle to the Romans* (MacDill AFB: MacDonald,
1958), p. 100.

taries I possess, the most thorough documentation of this point is by Charles Hodge, who drew it from a variety of scholars. I quote his summary here:

> Rabbi Menachem in his *Commentary on the Books of Moses* (fol. 43, col. 1) says, "Our Rabbins have said that no circumcised man will see hell." In the *Jalkut Rubeni* (num. 1) it is taught, "Circumcision saves from hell." In the *Medrasch Tillim* (fol. 7, col. 2) it is said, "God swore to Abraham that no one who was circumcised should be sent to hell." In the book of *Akedath Jizehak* (fol. 54, col. 2) it is taught that "Abraham sits before the gate of hell, and does not allow that any circumcised Israelite should enter there."[2]

The argument is that salvation is for Jews and that what makes one a Jew is circumcision.

Today, of course, even Jews are not quite certain about what it is that makes a true Jew. The most common answer is that a Jew is a person who has descended from Abraham. Yet what about Ishmael and those who descended from him, the Arabs? Ishmael was Abraham's son, but Ishmael's descendants are not Jews, though they are of Semitic stock. To account for this, the official Jewish definition is that a Jew is a person who has a Jewish mother. By this reasoning, Isaac alone would be Jewish and Ishmael would be excluded. But what about a child born of a good Jewish mother (or even of two good Jewish parents) who converts to Christianity? Is such a person Jewish? According to the official theory, a child of a Jewish mother who converts to Christianity would be Jewish. Yet in many Jewish circles conversion to Christianity is considered grounds not only for denying that the person is Jewish but also for excluding such a one from his or her own biological family.

What is a Jew?

Paul's answer to this important question is radical. But notice: Paul does not say (since he is dealing with salvation matters) that one does not have to be a Jew to be saved, but rather that one has to be a *true* Jew which, as he points out, is not a matter of external criteria—such as possession of the law, descent from Abraham, or circumcision—but of conduct, which flows from spiritual changes within. "A man is not a Jew if he is only one outwardly, nor is circumcision merely outward and physical. No, a man is a Jew if he is one inwardly, and circumcision is circumcision of the heart, by the Spirit, not by the written code . . ." (vv. 28–29).

It is what we found earlier in Romans 2. God's concern is not chiefly with our knowing the truth but with our doing it (vv. 1–3). It is not a matter of our having the law but of obeying its precepts (vv. 21–23).

Let me quote William Barclay:

2. Charles Hodge, *A Commentary on Romans* (Edinburgh and Carlisle, Pa.: The Banner of Truth Trust, 1972), p. 63. (Original edition 1935.) Hodge draws his material from Eisenmenger's *Entdecktes Judenthum*, part 2, p. 285.

Jewishness, [Paul] insists, is not a matter of race at all; Jewishness has nothing to do with circumcision. Jewishness is a matter of conduct. If that is so, there is many a so-called Jew who is a pure descendent of Abraham and who bears the mark of circumcision in his body, who is no Jew at all; and equally there is many a Gentile who never heard of Abraham and who would never dream of being circumcised, who is a Jew in the real sense of the term. . . . With one stroke Paul was abolishing the very basis of Jewish thought. He was shutting out from real Jewishness many and many a Jew, and he was introducing a new conception which made Jewishness a thing available to every nation, a thing as wide as the earth itself.[3]

What Is a Sacrament?

Most of us are not personally affected by contemporary debate over the definition of a true Jew, of course. But the matter of godly conduct accomplished in us by the work of the Holy Spirit (v. 29) is our concern. And, as far as the sacraments go (our sacraments are baptism and the Lord's Supper, rather than circumcision), the issue is whether these reflect the necessary inward change and reality.

What is a sacrament?

Peter Lombard, who lived in the twelfth century, called a sacrament "a sign of a sacred thing."[4] John Calvin, in a more comprehensive statement, wrote that a sacrament is "an outward sign by which the Lord seals on our consciences the promises of his good will toward us in order to sustain the weakness of our faith; and we in turn attest our piety toward him in the presence of the Lord and of his angels before the eyes of men."[5] The important thing in each definition is that a sacrament is a "sign" of a spiritual reality rather than the reality itself.

Let me define a sacrament from a Christian point of view. There are four elements:

1. *A sacrament is a divine ordinance instituted by Christ himself.* This links the sacraments to other things that Christ also commanded us to do: for instance, to pray. But it separates it from things that we may do but are not commanded to do: to kneel when we pray or to sing hymns when we worship, to give just two examples. In this, the New Testament sacraments of baptism and the Lord's Supper, which were commanded by Christ, are like

3. William Barclay, *The Letter to the Romans* (Edinburgh: The Saint Andrew Press, 1969), p. 42.

4. Peter Lombard, *The Four Books of Sentences*, book 4, I, 2, in Eugene R. Fairweather, ed., *A Scholastic Miscellany: Anselm to Ockham*, The Library of Christian Classics, vol. 10 (Philadelphia: The Westminster Press, 1956), p. 338.

5. John Calvin, *Institutes of the Christian Religion*, ed. John T. McNeill, trans. Ford Lewis Battles (Philadelphia: The Westminster Press, 1960), vol. 2, p. 1172.

the Old Testament sacrament of circumcision, which God himself imposed on Abraham and his descendants.

2. *A sacrament uses material elements as visible signs of God's blessing.* In baptism the sign is water. In the Lord's Supper the signs are bread, which signifies the Lord's body, and wine, which signifies his shed blood. The Old Testament sign was a cutting away of the flesh.

This is an important matter, for it sets the sacraments off from other proper but nonsacramental activities that do not use material elements as signs. Moreover, the element distinguishes the sacrament from that to which it points. For example, if you are driving along the New Jersey Turnpike and see a sign that reads "New York 30 miles," you realize that the sign is pointing to New York. The sign is not itself New York. Again, if you see a sign saying "Drink Coca-Cola," you know that the sign is not Coca-Cola. It is only pointing you in that direction. It is in this way that the sacraments point to spiritual realities. Baptism signifies our identification with Jesus Christ by faith. The Lord's Supper signifies our vital participation and union with him. The sign is secondary, outward, and visible. The reality is primary, inward, and invisible.

3. *A sacrament is a means of grace.* This does not mean that spiritual life is automatically communicated to the one who participates in the sacraments in some magical way, so that he or she is automatically saved. This is the point Paul is denying in his discussion of circumcision in our text. But this negative truth is not the same thing as saying that the sacraments have no value. Indeed, immediately after denying in Romans 2 that one is saved by circumcision, Paul goes on to speak of the "value" of circumcision in the next chapter, as we shall see.

What is the value of baptism and the Lord's Supper? John Murray answers:

> Baptism is a means of grace and conveys blessing, because it is the certification to us of God's grace and in the acceptance of that certification we rely upon God's faithfulness, bear witness to his grace, and thereby strengthen faith. . . . In the Lord's Supper that significance is increased and cultivated, namely, communion with Christ and participation of the virtue accruing from his body and blood. The Lord's Supper represents that which is continuously being wrought. We partake of Christ's body and blood through the means of the ordinance. We thus see that the accent falls on the faithfulness of God, and the efficacy resides in the response we yield to that faithfulness.[6]

4. *A sacrament is a seal, certification, or confirmation of the grace it signifies.* Earlier I pointed out that a sign points to something other than itself, like

---

6. John Murray, *Collected Writings,* vol. 2, *Select Lectures in Systematic Theology* (Edinburgh: The Banner of Truth Trust, 1977), pp. 367, 368.

the sign directing a traveler to New York or encouraging him to drink Coca-Cola. But a sign frequently does something else as well: It indicates ownership. A sign saying "Joe's Restaurant," means that the restaurant belongs to Joe. A sign reading "United States Courthouse" means that the building on which it is found is the property of the federal government. In a similar way, some signs authenticate documents. A seal on a passport or on an academic transcript validates that document.

Theologians refers to sacraments as "signs and seals" of some reality: signs because they point to them, seals because they authenticate the one submitting to the sacrament.

This is what made baptism such an important sign for Martin Luther. There were times in the midst of the fearful events and enervating pressures of the Reformation when Luther, who went up and down emotionally, as forceful leaders often do, became confused about everything. In his most bleak periods he questioned the value of the Reformation; he questioned his own faith; he even questioned the value of the work of the Lord Jesus Christ on his behalf. But we are told that when that happened he would frequently write on the table in front of him in chalk the Latin words *baptizatus sum!* ("I have been baptized!"). That sign would point him to spiritual reality, and he would be reassured that he really was Christ's and had been identified with him in his death and resurrection.[7]

Being a Jew is important. In fact, in a sense every saved person must be a member of that covenant people. But only if you are a true Jew (cf. Gal. 6:16)! That is, one must be a Jew inwardly and spiritually, not necessarily by physical descent from Abraham. In the same way, circumcision is of value, but only if it points (like baptism and the Lord's Supper) to the reality of a changed heart.

Summary of Romans 2

We have now come to the end of Romans 2, and it is time to summarize Paul's teaching in that chapter. The apostle has been dealing with persons who would agree with his condemnation of the heathen (as expressed in chapter 1), but who would excuse themselves on the grounds either (1) of being very moral, that is, people who know higher standards of conduct than those possessed by the heathen; or (2) of being thoroughly religious and therefore of being saved by the possession of the revealed law of God and by participation in the sacraments.

Do you know of any people like that today? Of course, you do. You may even be one of them. Here is what the apostle Paul says to such people:

7. I have treated these points more fully in James Montgomery Boice, *Foundations of the Christian Faith* (Leicester, England, and Downers Grove, Ill.: InterVarsity Press, 1986), pp. 595–597.

1. *Knowledge alone, even knowledge of the highest spiritual and moral principles, does not win God's approval.* On the contrary, superior knowledge actually leads to even greater condemnation—if it is not accompanied by adherence to the higher standard. Both the moral pagan and the orthodox Jew were found wanting, not because they did not have a moral code or divine revelation, but because, having that code or revelation, they nevertheless failed to live up to it. The pagan did "the same things" he condemned in others (vv. 1–3). The Jew likewise "broke the law" (vv. 21–23).

2. *Membership in a religious society, whether the covenant nation of Israel or the visible church of Christendom, does not guarantee that we have obtained God's favor.* It is not that belonging to the visible company of God's people is unimportant. It is. But salvation is not won by any external associations if (as we have seen) God looks not on outward appearances but on the heart. Jews have been saved; they are being saved. But it is not because they are Jews! Church members are likewise being saved. But it is not because they are church members! If any of us could perfectly keep the law of God, we would be saved by keeping it. But none of us can. We have all broken it. Therefore, we can be saved only as the result of Christ's death on the cross and the application of that work to us by the Holy Spirit. This alone brings us into the true company of God's elect people and develops a life consistent with that new identity.

3. *The sacraments, either of the Old Testament or the New Testament periods, save no one.* They point to what saves, but they are not the reality themselves. Hodge observes, "According to the apostle, the true idea of a sacrament is not that it is a mystic rite, possessed of inherent efficacy or conveying grace as a mere *opus operatum*; but that it is a seal and sign, designed to confirm our faith in the validity of the covenant to which it is attached; and from its significant character to present and illustrate some great spiritual truth."[8]

4. *God judges according to truth and performance, and by that standard every human being is condemned.* We may not like the concluding part of that sentence, but we can hardly disagree with the rightness and value of the first part. Would it be right for God to judge in any other than the highest and most righteous fashion? Could he judge in any way other than by truth? Could he admit falsehood or deception before the bar of his justice? Could he allow pretense or wishful thinking or mere intentions, rather than actual deeds, to slip by? Could he overlook sin, just because a person is a Jew? Or a church member? Or just because he or she might know better? Obviously, none of these perversions of justice can occur with God, though they are all too common in human systems. If this is true, then of themselves no human beings will be justified.

8. Hodge, *A Commentary on Romans*, p. 67.

5. *If we are to be saved, it must be by the labor of Jesus Christ applied to us by the Father through the ministry of the Holy Spirit.* When David sinned and then confessed his sin in Psalm 51, even though he confessed his sin genuinely and thoroughly he did not suppose that it was the mere fact of his confession that would save him. On the contrary, he looked entirely to God. He prayed: (1) "Cleanse me with hyssop . . ." (v. 7). Hyssop was used to sprinkle the blood of the animals used in the Jewish sacrificial system. So this was a plea for cleansing by the blood of the atonement. And he added: (2) "Create in me a pure heart" (v. 10). As the next verse makes clear, David understood this to be something that could only be accomplished by the Holy Spirit, which is precisely the point to which Paul comes at the conclusion of the chapter.

I end with one last observation. In the final sentence of Romans 2, Paul has a pun, which is untranslatable in English but which takes us back to the identification of a true Jew, with which we began. The word *Jew* comes from the name of Judah, the fourth son of Jacob (or Israel, Gen. 32:28), and the pun is found in the fact that Judah means "praise." When Leah gave birth to Judah she said, "This time I will praise the Lord," and the text adds, "So she named him Judah [or 'praise']" (Gen. 29:35). Similarly, when Jacob/Israel was dying, he said, using the same pun, "Judah, your brothers will praise you" (Gen. 49:8a).

This is the pun Paul uses at the end of the chapter: "Such a man's praise is not from men, but from God." He means, "True Jewishness (Judah) is from God and is spiritual. It does not come from men by outward things like circumcision."

31

Do Jews Have an Edge?

Romans 3:1

What advantage, then, is there in being a Jew, or what value is there in circumcision?

Every profession has its favorite stories, and the legal profession is no exception. A lawyer friend tells a story of a novice attorney defending a man accused of biting another man's ear off during a barroom brawl. A witness to the fight was on the stand, and the lawyer was cross-examining him. "Did you actually see the defendant bite this man's ear off?" the young attorney asked.

"No, sir," the witness replied.

That was the answer the attorney wanted and needed, but he made a mistake not uncommon to young lawyers. Instead of ending his cross examination when he was ahead and on a winning track, he continued to ask questions.

"What exactly did you see?" he queried.

"I saw him spit it out," said the witness.

The point is that going too far or failing to quit when you're ahead is a mistake in legal squabbling.

The Problem with Paul's Argument

It is a like charge—that he has gone too far—that the apostle Paul seems to hear an opponent raise as he comes to the end of Romans 2 and begins chapter 3. We know what Paul has been trying to prove: that all persons, Jews as well as Gentiles, are guilty of sin before God and therefore need a Savior. No one can save himself. But Paul has argued this case so forcefully that he has virtually equated the Jew, who was thought to have great religious advantages, with the Gentile, who had none. He has said, "There will be trouble and distress for every human being who does evil: first for the Jew, then for the Gentile; but glory, honor and peace for everyone who does good: first for the Jew, then for the Gentile. For God does not show favoritism" (Rom. 2:9–11). Then, when he reaches the end of the chapter, he defines Jewishness in a way that has virtually nothing whatever to do with a person's religious or ethnic heritage: "A man is a Jew if he is one inwardly; and circumcision is circumcision of the heart, by the Spirit, not by the written code . . ." (v. 29).

"But doesn't that prove too much?" an opponent would be arguing. If God treats Jews and Gentiles alike, not showing favoritism, and if the only thing that makes one truly Jewish is an inward transformation by the Holy Spirit, then what advantage is there in being a Jew?

Or, to put it in other terms, what is the Old Testament all about? Why did God bother to choose Abraham and establish his descendants, the Jews, as a special covenant people if there is no advantage to being Jewish? And why did God institute circumcision? If Paul is right, these things are pointless. Or, since we know that what God does is not pointless and must have a proper purpose to it, isn't it the case that Paul must be wrong in his conclusions—whether or not we can detect the weak point in his arguments?

This is a very important matter—for Jews as well as for non-Jews. We have been talking about the Jewish people's spiritual advantages or lack of them. But, although the Jew's apparent advantages are different from the Gentile's, his situation and the Gentile's are parallel. For we who call ourselves Christians must ask, "What advantage, then, is there is being a godly, churchgoing person? What value is there in baptism, church membership, communion, or any other religious exercise if we are all under condemnation anyway?"

I have titled this study "Do Jews Have an Edge?" But I might as well have asked, "Do any religious people have an edge?" If we do not, then why should we bother with religion at all? Let's enjoy ourselves and sin right along with the heathen. If we *do* have an edge, then isn't it the case that it is possible to please God by our religious practices and be saved by them after all?

The Jews' Advantages

Paul's answer is that circumcision and being Jewish are true advantages, although they are not the kind of advantages we are thinking of if we wrongly suppose that one can be saved by them.

To do justice to Paul's thinking, we need to look ahead to the list of Jewish advantages appearing not here in Romans 3 but in chapter 9. The passage at hand encourages us to do this, because after Paul asks, "What advantage, then, is there in being a Jew, or what value is there in circumcision?" he answers, "Much in every way! *First of all,* they have been entrusted with the very words of God" (vv. 1–2, italics mine). The very fact that Paul says "first" leads us to look for what is also second and third and so on.

Paul lists only one advantage in Romans 3: "the very words of God." This had led some commentators to note that the Greek word *proton* (translated "first of all") can also mean "chiefly" or "as a matter of first importance."[1] But, as John Murray points out, "It makes little difference whether we regard the word he uses as 'first' or 'chiefly,'" since both inevitably suggest other advantages.[2]

As mentioned, we do find a list of these advantages in Romans 9. Speaking of the Jews, Paul says, "Theirs is the adoption as sons; theirs the divine glory, the covenants, the receiving of the law, the temple worship and the promises. Theirs are the patriarchs, and from them is traced the human ancestry of Christ, who is God over all, forever praised! Amen" (vv. 4–5). These ideas are worth looking at individually.

1. *The adoption as sons.* This first term embraces what follows, for it speaks of a sovereign act of God, who—for his own good reasons and according to his own good pleasure—drew the Jewish people into a special family relationship with himself. There is a real difference between Jews, who were adopted into God's family, and Christians (both Jews and Gentiles), who enter the family of God by a new birth, being born again. But the advantages are similar. Among them, obviously, is the privilege of approaching God directly as one's Father.

2. *The divine glory.* In the context of Jewish history, this phrase refers to God's revelation of himself in glory on Mount Sinai at the time of the giving of the law, in the Most Holy Place of the Jewish temple, and in a few other places. No other nation had this privilege.

3. *The covenants.* This word is plural, so it probably refers to the full scope of those special bondings of God to Israel generally known as the Abrahamic covenant, the Mosaic covenant, and the Davidic covenant. In

1. "The original denotes *primarily*, which is not a priority of order, but a priority in dignity and advantage" (Robert Haldane, *An Exposition of the Epistle to the Romans* [MacDill AFB: MacDonald Publishing, 1958], p. 107).

2. John Murray, *The Epistle to the Romans* (Grand Rapids: Wm. B. Eerdmans, 1968), p. 92.

each case, God promised to be certain things to his people and to do certain things for them, not because of any good in them or in anticipation of any special performance on their part, but solely for his own good pleasure.

4. *The receiving of the law.* This is the item Paul refers to as "first of all" or "chiefly" in Romans 3. We will see why this is the most important advantage later and in our next study.

5. *The temple worship.* This was an obvious advantage because, in the early days, God actually manifested himself in the tabernacle or temple. However, since the emphasis here is on "worship," the advantage actually referred to is the way in which this worship pointed the pathway to God by atoning sacrifices for sin, which prefigured the only perfect sacrifice of Jesus Christ. Indeed, each item in the temple design and furnishings pointed forward to Jesus and was fulfilled by him.

6. *The promises.* The Old Testament (like the New Testament) is filled with promises to God's people. These are of very wide scope, covering all we could possibly need. They are sure and reliable, since it is God who has made and spoken them.

7. *The patriarchs.* This word means "fathers" and can refer to any one of the giants of Israel's past. Chiefly it refers to the first three fathers: Abraham, Isaac, and Jacob (or Israel). God calls himself by their name, saying to Moses, "I am the God of your father, the God of Abraham, the God of Isaac and the God of Jacob" (Exod. 3:6; cf. Matt. 22:32). It was an advantage to have had such ancestry, because God had worked through these men greatly. Also, they were models of faith and godliness to their descendants.

8. *The human ancestry of Jesus Christ.* Being related to Christ did not secure salvation for Jewish people, but it was still better to be close to him and his ministry in this way than to be far from him. If nothing else, there was at least a cultural affinity out of which it was easier to understand the meaning of his teaching.

The Very Words of God

I suppose that if Paul had been asked to interrupt himself after the first two verses of Romans 3, he might have listed those eight items. And if he had been pressed even further, he might have developed a whole book or preached a whole sermon or sermons on each one. Each is a great advantage, and seeing the whole picture requires us to think a bit about each of them.

Still, we must not miss the fact that when Paul is answering the specific question "What advantage, then, is there in being a Jew?" in Romans 3, it is not the whole list but rather the matter of possessing the very words of God alone that he stresses. In fact, although he has also asked, "What value is there in circumcision?" he does not speak of the sacraments or any other external sign as an advantage in this context. Just Scripture! That is the chief item and, in Romans 3, the only one.

This is of immense importance to us, because it is the only blessing in this long list of Jewish advantages in which Gentiles share. We cannot say as Gentiles, "Ours is the adoption as sons," for we have not been adopted as a people. We cannot say, "Ours is the divine glory" (we have never seen God's glory), or "Ours are the covenants" (though there is a covenant of grace for Christian people). We cannot claim the advantages of the temple worship or the promises made to Israel or the patriarchs or an ancestral relationship to Jesus Christ.

But we *can* say, "Ours are the Scriptures"—if we have been fortunate enough, as virtually all of us have been, to have been given the very words of God in our language.

Can any of us experience anything in life of greater personal advantage to our souls than possession of the Holy Scriptures? Of course not! Without them we are utterly confused, adrift on a sea of human speculation where all the great questions of life are concerned. Is there a God? We do not know; at least, in our sinful state we are unable to admit the full personal significance of there being a God. Who are we? We do not know the answer to that important question. Apart from Scripture, we cannot know that we have been created in the image of the one true God and are called to glorify him and to enjoy him forever. How do we come to God? How is our sin to be dealt with? What way of life is best? Does what we do here matter? It is only from the revelation of God in the Bible that we can have sure answers to any of these life-and-death questions.

What Advantage to the "Christian"?

At this point I am sure you can see where this study is going, since I am obviously trying to take what Paul has said to the thoroughly religious person of his day, the Jew, and apply it to the thoroughly religious person of our time. Paul is answering an argument. His answer is a digression from what he has been setting out to prove in Romans 1:18–3:20. Nevertheless, the issue the apostle is dealing with here is of vital importance to everyone. No one is saved by such things as baptism, sacraments, or church attendance. No one is even saved by such an important thing as having—yes, even studying—the Bible. But that does not mean that religious practices are of no use to us or that one is acting wisely if he or she abuses, neglects, or disregards them.

So I ask this question: "What advantage, then, is there in being a godly, churchgoing 'Christian' person?" I suggest three answers.

1. *Even if God never saves you by drawing you from the darkness of your sin to saving faith in Jesus Christ, you will at least sin less because of these advantages and therefore be punished less severely.*

Some will think this a strange place to begin, but we need to begin with the hardest situation in order that we might understand, on the one hand, that there are genuine spiritual advantages (for those who will have them) and, on the other hand, that these in themselves do not save anyone. We must remember that our situation is desperate. We can do nothing for ourselves. Even knowing the truth does not save us, because in our unregenerate state we are unresponsive and even hostile to it. No one can be saved who is not born again, and the work of spiritual regeneration is God's doing.

Still, we have seen that there are degrees of punishment for sin. In Romans 2:5, Paul has spoken of individuals "storing up wrath" by frequent and persistent sin. The Lord Jesus Christ made the point when he described a servant who knows his master's will and disobeys it being beaten with many blows, while another servant who does not know his master's will and therefore unintentionally disobeys it being beaten with "few blows" (Luke 12:47–48). Even the author of the letter to the Hebrews seems to make the point when he speaks of "every violation [of the law] and disobedience" receiving "its just punishment" (Heb. 2:2). So I say, if nothing else, knowing the law of God and living in the company of people who are trying to obey God's commands and encourage each other to live godly lives is of value—even if you are not saved. For it will at least mean that you will be committing fewer sins for which you will one day be punished.

2. *Going to church and listening to the preaching of the Word of God, if you are in a good, Bible-believing church, will at least cause you to know the way of salvation, even if you do not respond to it.*

A person might argue that knowing how to be saved and yet not responding to that revelation, in fact rejecting it, is not an advantage but a disadvantage in that it undoubtedly increases one's guilt. It is a case of the servant knowing his master's will but not doing it. This is true, of course. Moreover, it is compounded if together with your knowledge you also acquire the habit of thinking of yourself as a rather fine Christian specimen. You are worse off if you think that God must somehow think better of you just because you know much.

But it does not need to work that way. In fact, it is meant to work quite the other way. Instead of becoming proud because of your knowledge, you should be humbled by it. The first thing you learn from the Bible, if you are really profiting from it, is that you are a sinner hopelessly lost by virtue of your own sinful nature and your deliberately wicked choices; indeed, that you are under God's just wrath and doomed to perish utterly and horribly unless God is gracious to you and reaches out to save you through the work of Christ. This is what Romans is all about thus far. Who can read the first three chapters of Romans intelligently and remain proud? Who can read these chapters and fail to see the need of throwing oneself utterly upon God's mercy? As I said, knowledge of the way of salvation, including your need of it as a sinner, in itself will not save you. But it is hard to see how you can be saved without it. This is because without such knowledge you will not even begin to seek God. Most likely, you will consider yourself already saved or at least not needing salvation.

3. *The third great advantage of regular church attendance and, above all, faithful adherence to the preaching and study of the Word of God is that, although you cannot claim this as a right from God, it is through the reading and preaching of the Bible that God is most likely to save you.*

How is one born again, after all? Peter writes that we are "born again, not of perishable seed, but of imperishable, through the living and enduring word of God. For,

> All men are like grass,
>> and all their glory is like the flowers of the field;
> the grass withers and the flowers fall,
>> but the word of the Lord stands forever.
>> 1 Peter 1:23–25

To hear the Word of God is the most assured path to salvation.

In the same way James wrote, "He [God] chose to give us birth through the word of truth, that we might be a kind of firstfruits of all he created" (James 1:18).

Benefiting from One's "Edge"

Years ago, when I was preaching through John, I came to the ninth chapter, where we are told the story of a man who was born blind but who was healed by Jesus from spiritual as well as physical blindness. I remember reflecting on how desperate this man's plight was and how this is intended to be a picture of our own desperate condition apart from Jesus Christ.

What was his state? For one thing, he was blind. He could not see. Others could see, but he could not. And this meant that he could not see Jesus. If Jesus had said, as Peter and John later said to a crippled man at the temple gate called Beautiful, "Look at us [me]," the man could not have looked, for he was blind. This is the state of the lost today. Jesus is preached, but they cannot see him. That is, they cannot understand who he actually is or what he has accomplished. They cannot understand the gospel. The Bible says, "The man without the Spirit does not accept the things that come from the Spirit of God, for they are foolishness to him, and he cannot understand them, because they are spiritually discerned" (1 Cor. 2:14).

Again, the man whose story is told in John 9 had been blind from birth, which meant that he probably did not even greatly value sight, having never known what it was. He knew he was missing something, of course, just like many people today are vaguely aware of a missing dimension in their lives. But he did not really know what this was or even think of having his condition cured. In the story we notice that he did not ask the Lord to heal him.

Again, he was a beggar. It is a beggar's task to beg, but he did not beg for sight. He was in the habit of asking the passers-by for money, because he had none. This means that, even if sight could have been procured for some great sum, the man's case would still have been hopeless, as grim as before. For how could he buy his sight, having nothing? In his poverty the blind man reminds us of how bankrupt we are before God.

No, there is very little to be said for this man at the moment Jesus found him. He was blind, unaware, and bankrupt. But, when I was preparing my studies of this story, I came across a saying of one of the older preachers, who observed that, although little could be said for this man, there was this one thing: he was at least in a place where Jesus was likely to go. He was by the gate leading into the temple grounds, where Jesus frequently passed by, and it was there that Jesus looked at him (he could not look at Jesus), loved him, healed him, and drew him to himself.[3]

I apply this to you if you are reading these words but are not born again:

Your condition is not good. You are lost and under God's wrath. You are blind to God's truth. You are spiritually bankrupt. But there is this one thing. Although you cannot save yourself, as long as you can hear this or any other gospel message, you are at least where Jesus is likely to go. He loves to bless the preaching and teaching of his Word. Therefore, though your condition may be desperate, it is no worse than that of any other lost sinner before he or she was saved. The mere hearing of the Word is your advantage. Do not despise it, then. Do not say, "So, then, what advantage is there in religion?" There is a great advantage in it. "Much in every way!" (Rom. 3:2). Cling to it. Wring every possible "edge" from it. Who knows but that God will use the very Word you hear to save your soul?

3. See James Montgomery Boice, *The Gospel of John: An Expositional Commentary*, 5 vols. in 1 (Grand Rapids: Zondervan, 1985), pp. 586, 599.

32

"Give Me That Book!"

Romans 3:1-2

What advantage, then, is there in being a Jew, or what value is there in circumcision? Much in every way! First of all, they have been entrusted with the very words of God.

In the third chapter of Romans, in what seems almost to be an incidental reference, the apostle uses a term for the Bible that ascribes to it the highest possible authority. In the New International Version the term is rendered in English as "the very words" of God. The King James Version has the word *oracles*. In Greek this important word is *logia*. It was the possession of these *logia*, or oracles, that constituted the chief advantage of a person's having been born a Jew, according to Paul's teaching.

God's Word or Man's Word

The fact that Paul calls this the first or chief advantage of the Jew is in itself reason to study this further—more than we were able to do in the last study. But I return to this now because of its bearing on one of the most important matters dividing today's church. The issue is the nature of the Bible. What is the Bible? Is it a divine book or a human book? Is it supernat-

273

ural or natural? Is it something that is binding upon our minds and morals, or is it simply a collection of noble thoughts, which we may use or neglect according to our own perception of the issues?

Let me clarify this division by saying that there are really only three basic positions that a person can hold in regard to the Bible. Either: (1) the Bible is the Word of God, which is what this important term of Paul affirms; or (2) the Bible is a collection of the ideas and words of mere men; or (3) the Bible is a combination of the two.

The first is the classic, evangelical doctrine. That is, it is the view that has been held throughout church history. Thus, even when there were debates about the nature of Jesus Christ, the Trinity, justification by faith, and other theological issues, it was always the Bible to which those disagreeing on these matters appealed. Even heretics regarded the Bible as the Word of God. They disagreed with what the church taught, thinking the church to be wrong in its interpretation. They themselves had to be corrected in the course of things. But everyone understood that the Bible is God's Word and is therefore entirely without error and authoritative in all it teaches. It is only in recent years that this position has been questioned.

Irenaeus, who lived and wrote in Lyons, France, in the early years of the second century, said that we should be "most properly assured that the Scriptures are indeed perfect, since they were spoken by the Word of God and his Spirit."[1] Martin Luther said, "Scripture, although also written of men, is not of men nor from men, but from God."[2]

John Calvin wrote:

> This is the principle that distinguishes our religion from all others, that we know that God has spoken to us and are fully convinced that the prophets did not speak of themselves, but, as organs of the Holy Spirit, uttered only that which they had been commissioned from heaven to declare. All those who wish to profit from the Scriptures must first accept this as a settled principle, that the Law and the prophets are not teachings handled on at the pleasure of men or produced by men's minds as their source, but are dictated by the Holy Spirit.[3]

When we speak of the Bible as the Word of God, we do not deny that the message of the Bible is also expressed in human language, the point Luther

---

1. Irenaeus, *Against Heresies*, II, xxvii, in *The Ante-Nicene Fathers*, vol. 1, ed. Alexander Roberts and James Donaldson (Grand Rapids: Wm. B. Eerdmans, n.d.), p. 399. (Original edition 1885.)

2. Martin Luther, "That Doctrines of Men Are to Be Rejected," in *What Luther Says: An Anthology*, compiled by Ewald M. Plass, vol. 1 (Saint Louis: Concordia Publishing House, 1959), p. 63.

3. John Calvin, *Calvin's Commentaries*, vol. 10, *The Second Epistle of Paul the Apostle to the Corinthians and the Epistles to Timothy, Titus and Philemon*, trans. T. A. Smail (Grand Rapids: Wm. B. Eerdmans, 1964), p. 330.

was making in the words I quoted. We must stress this, because some have fallen into thinking that the words of the Bible were made known to the human writers in a mechanical way so that they were mere scribes, thereby bypassing their own vocabularies and thought processes. But, of course, this is not the evangelical view. Each of the writers I have quoted understood that.

When we speak of the classic church view—that the Bible is the very Word of God—we mean that by the process known as inspiration, which we freely admit we do not fully understand, God so guided the human authors that the result, in the whole and in the parts, is what God desired to be expressed. The Bible is expressed in human words; but it is also the Word of God from beginning to end, and it is entirely truthful because God is truthful.

The second view, that the Bible is the words of mere men, is the view of liberalism and neoorthodoxy, though many of the neoorthodox theologians were willing to listen to the Bible carefully. Karl Barth is a chief example. Neoorthodoxy held that God is so transcendent, so far above us, so separated from where we are, that he does not actually speak in human words but rather reveals himself in ways that we cannot even talk about. So what we have in the Bible is men testifying in their own words to what they believed God said in this nonverbal fashion.

Of course, classic liberalism is a step below this. Liberalism sees the Bible only as a collection of human writings—inspiring at times, perhaps even embodying the highest thoughts, ethics, and aspirations of the human race, but nevertheless only a human book and therefore without any absolute authority. To the liberal, the Bible can, in principle, be rejected utterly.

The third position is the one the evangelical church is particularly wrestling with today. It is the view that the Bible is the Word of God and the words of men combined—not in the sense that God has spoken infallibly through the human authors, the classic view, but in this sense: When you read the Bible you find things there that have certainly come to us from God and are therefore truthful. But we also have to admit (so the argument goes) that when we read the Bible we also find things that are not truthful, things we know to be in error. Because we know that God does not speak that which is untruthful, these things must come from mere human beings, from human beings alone. Therefore the Bible is a mixture of human words and divine words, and it is the task of scholarship to separate the two, extracting the kernels of divine truth from the human chaff.

Of course, what happens in this framework is that the scholar becomes God so far as the revelation is concerned. That is, the scholar becomes the authority who tells us what is true and what is not true, what is of God and what is not of God, what we are to believe and what we are not to believe. And the danger is that, because we are sinners (which includes the scholars who, perhaps at this point, are even greater sinners than the rest of us), we try to weed out the things we do not want to hear and so refashion the divine revelation to suit our own desires or notions. Thus the powerful, reforming voice of God in the church is forgotten.[4]

"The Oracles of God"

Romans 3:2 has bearing on this controversy, as I said. And the reason is that it uses a word for the Scriptures that identifies them in the whole and in their parts as God's very words. The term (*logia*) occurs in three other passages (Acts 7:38, Heb. 5:12, and 1 Peter 4:11), and in each case the word indicates that the Old Testament Scriptures, to which these New Testament verses refer, were regarded by the New Testament authors as "oracular."

No one has written more effectively on the full authority of the Bible, nor has anyone more carefully analyzed these and other key terms, than Benjamin Breckinridge Warfield, Professor of Didactic and Polemic Theology at Princeton Theological Seminary from 1887 to 1921. During those years the full storm of German liberalism was breaking over the American churches, and Warfield set out to counter it academically, thereby producing a remarkable collection of carefully reasoned studies of the Bible's words for itself and its teaching. These have been brought together in a volume entitled *The Inspiration and Authority of the Bible*, which is in my opinion still the most important single work on the nature and authority of the Bible in the English (and probably any) language.

In the chapter of this work dealing with the term *logia*, Warfield explores four separate bodies of literature. First, he looks at the word in the classical Greek authors, that is, as it was used by such writers as Aristophanes, Euripides, Herodotus, Thucydides, and others. His conclusion is that: "In *logion* [the singular form of *logia*] we have a term expressive, in common usage at least, of the simple notion of divine revelation, an oracle, and that independently of any accompanying implication of length or brevity, poetical or prose form, directness or indirectness of delivery. This is the meaning of *logion* in the mass of profane Greek literature."[5]

Next Warfield examined the Septuagint, the Greek translation of the Old Testament made between 250 and 150 B.C., and found that in this translation *logia* was regularly used as a rendering of *'merah*, which means "utterances," particularly the utterances of God.

Third, Warfield examined the works of the Philo, the Hebrew-Christian philosopher of Alexandria. Philo used *logia* to express whatever in the highest sense was a word from God, that is, an oracle from heaven. Moreover, he identified those words with what is recorded in the Scriptures of the Old and New Testaments. Says Warfield, "To Philo all that is in Scripture is orac-

---

4. The material in this section is borrowed with some changes from James Montgomery Boice, *Standing on the Rock* (Wheaton, Ill.: Tyndale House, 1984), pp. 46, 47.

5. Benjamin Breckinridge Warfield, "The Oracles of God" in *The Inspiration and Authority of the Bible*, ed. Samuel G. Craig (London: Marshall, Morgan & Scott, 1969), pp. 365, 366.

ular, every passage is a *logion*, of whatever character or length; and the whole, as constituted of these oracles, is *ta logia*, or perhaps even *to logion*—the mass of logia or one continuous logion."[6]

The last body of material examined by Warfield was the writings of the early Christian fathers: Clement of Rome, Irenaeus, Clement of Alexandria, and Ignatius. Here again he found usage consistent with what had gone before.

Warfield then gives this summary of the use of *logia* and *logion*:

> No lower sense can be attached to it in these instances than which it bears uniformly in its classical and Hellenistic usage: it means, not "words" barely, simple "utterances," but distinctively "oracular utterances," divinely authoritative communications, before which men stand in awe and to which they bow in humility: and this high meaning is not merely implicit, but is explicit in the term. It would seem clear again that there are no implications of brevity in the term: it means not short, pithy, pregnant sayings, but high, authoritative, sacred utterances. . . . It characterizes the utterances to which it is applied as emanations from God.[7]

In reference to Romans 3:2, which he discusses at the end of his study, Warfield says, "The very point of this use of the word is that it *identifies* the Sacred Books with the Oracles."[8] He elaborates:

> That is to say, we have unobtrusive and convincing evidence here that the Old Testament Scriptures, as such, were esteemed by the writers of the New Testament as an oracular book, which in itself not merely contains, but is the "utterance," the very Word of God; and is to be appealed to as such and as such deferred to, because nothing other than the crystallized speech of God. . . . Let him that thinks them something other and less than this, reckon, then, with the apostles and prophets of the New Covenant—to whose trustworthiness as witnesses to doctrinal truth he owes all he knows about the New Covenant itself, and therefore all he hopes for through this New Covenant.[9]

Strength and Weakness

I do not want anyone to think, just because I have taken so much space to record Warfield's careful work in this area, that the issues are of mere academic interest. The case is exactly the opposite. The point at issue is that if the Scriptures of the Old and New Testaments are the Word of God, as Paul affirms by the use of the word *logia* in Romans 3:2, then they inevitably bear within themselves the truth, authority, and power of God. And where

6. Ibid., p. 384.
7. Ibid., p. 403.
8. Ibid., p. 404.
9. Ibid., pp. 406, 407.

they are known, studied, and believed, there God is and will be powerfully at work. In other words, God will be doing what he said he would do through his word in Isaiah 55: "My word . . . will not return to me empty,/but will accomplish what I desire/and achieve the purpose for which I sent it" (v. 11).

I do not hesitate to say that the weaknesses of the liberal church and the strengths of the evangelical church (for all its failures) can be traced precisely to this point: their understanding of and, consequently, their use of (or failure to use) Scripture.

Several years ago I had the task of finding a person to write a foreword to a small booklet on "Freedom and Authority," written by J. I. Packer, which the International Council on Biblical Inerrancy produced as part of its ten-year program to "elucidate, vindicate and apply the doctrine of biblical inerrancy as an essential element for the authority of Scripture and a necessity for the health of the church." At once I thought of Charles W. Colson because of his years in government and his work with Prison Fellowship. I thought he could put the case for a link between freedom and authority well.

Colson agreed to write the foreword, but what I got back was not what I expected. It was better. Colson told how, when he had first heard of the International Council on Biblical Inerrancy, he thought that its cause did not concern him. He was dealing with "practical" issues, not "ivory-tower theology." But he said that he changed his mind when he saw the effects of a high and low view of Scripture on the front lines of spiritual warfare in the prisons. Colson wrote:

> Experiences in the past two years have profoundly altered my thinking. The authority and truth of Scripture is not an obscure issue reserved for the private debate and entertainment of theologians; it is relevant, indeed critical for every serious Christian—layman, pastor, and theologian alike.
>
> My convictions have come, not from studies in Ivory Tower academia, but from life in what may be termed the front-line trenches, behind prison walls where Christians grapple in hand-to-hand combat with the prince of darkness. In our prison fellowships, where the Bible is proclaimed as God's holy and inerrant revelation, believers grow and discipleship deepens. Christians live their faith with power. Where the Bible is not so proclaimed (or where Christianity is presumed to rest on subjective experience alone or contentless fellowship) faith withers and dies. Christianity without biblical fidelity is merely another passing fad in an age of passing fads. In my opinion, the issue is that clear-cut.[10]

Why is it that "believers grow and discipleship deepens" when the Bible is proclaimed as God's inerrant revelation? It is because of what God does through it. Let me list a few of the things God does.

10. Charles W. Colson, "Foreword" in J. I. Packer, *Freedom and Authority* (Oakland, Calif.: International Council on Biblical Inerrancy, 1981), p. 3.

1. *Unsaved men and women are born again by the work of the Holy Spirit operating through the Bible.* That is why Peter tells Christians, "For you have been born again, not of perishable seed, but of imperishable, through the living and enduring word of God" (1 Peter 1:23), and why James declares, "He chose to give us birth through the word of truth, that we might be a kind of firstfruits of all he created" (James 1:18). Nothing else will save a lost sinner—not philosophy, not history, not science. Jesus says, "Flesh gives birth to flesh, but the Spirit gives birth to spirit" (John 3:6). If we are to experience divine life, we must experience it in the only way it can come—through the Bible as the Holy Spirit works through it.

2. *Christians are convicted of sin and enabled to turn from it by the power of the Holy Spirit speaking through the Bible.* Paul speaks of this in 2 Timothy 3:16: "All Scripture is God-breathed and is useful for teaching, rebuking, correcting and training in righteousness." Scripture teaches us in a general way, of course. But it also rebukes our sin, corrects us, and then leads us in righteousness.

3. *Christians are sanctified, or made holy, through the Bible.* Jesus spoke of this when he prayed to his Father in that great intercessory prayer for the church recorded in John 17: "Sanctify them by the truth; your word is truth" (v. 17). To be sanctified means to be "set apart" for God and his purposes; it is what every Christian should be. Jesus says that we attain this commitment or orientation by our study of and obedience to God's Word.

4. *Christians learn the will of God through the Bible, and it is through the Bible that they are given wisdom to apply the details of Scripture to their daily lives.* The Bible does not give us magical instructions for making the many thousands of decisions we need to make in life. But it does give sound principles to guide us in our choices. As we read and study the Bible, God speaks to us by means of these principles and leads us in the ways of truth and righteousness.

This World's Most Precious Possession

The end of this study is in the form of questions, and they are these: When you hold a copy of the Word of God in your hands, do you recognize what the Bible truly is? Do you see it as God's Book? Do you thank God for it? Do you prize it above all earthly possessions? Do you make it your chief goal in life to know it and live by it?

Let me tell you what John Wesley, that great evangelist of the eighteenth century, wrote about the Bible:

I am a creature of a day, passing through life as an arrow through the air. I am a spirit come from God and returning to God, just hovering over the great gulf 'till, a few moments hence, I am no more seen; I drop into an unchangeable eternity! I want to know one thing—the way to heaven, how to land safe on that happy shore. God himself has condescended to teach me the way. For this very end he came from heaven. He hath written it down in a book. O give me that book! At any price, give me the book of God! I have it: Here is knowledge enough for me. Let me be *homo unius libri* [a man of one book]. Here then I am, far from the busy ways of men. I sit down alone. Only God is here. In his presence I open, I read his book—for this end, to find the way to heaven. Is there a doubt concerning the meaning of what I read? Does anything appear dark or intricate? I lift up my heart to the Father of Lights: "Lord, is it not thy word, 'If any man lacks wisdom, let him ask of God'? Thou hast said, 'If any be willing to do thy will, he shall know.' I am willing to do, let me know thy will."[11]

That should be the cry of your heart if you know the Bible to be what it truly is: "the very words of God."

Only the Spirit of God working through that book, the Bible, will bring you to spiritual life and save your soul. Only that book and the Spirit of God working through it will sanctify you, making you like Jesus. Only that working will avert that great downward spiral of sin, both personal and cultural, which is described in Romans.

11. John Wesley, *The Works*, vol. 5 (Grand Rapids: Zondervan, n.d.), p. 3. (From the authorized edition of 1872.)

33

Two More Questions

Romans 3:3–8

What if some did not have faith? Will their lack of faith nullify God's faithfulness? Not at all! Let God be true, and every man a liar. As it is written:

> *"So that you may be proved right when you speak*
> *and prevail when you judge."*

But if our unrighteousness brings out God's righteousness more clearly, what shall we say? That God is unjust in bringing his wrath on us? (I am using a human argument.) Certainly not! If that were so, how could God judge the world? Someone might argue, "If my falsehood enhances God's truthfulness and so increases his glory, why am I still condemned as a sinner?" Why not say—as we are being slanderously reported as saying and as some claim that we say—"Let us do evil that good may result"? Their condemnation is deserved.

It is not often that you or I get to witness an exceptional mind at work, particularly in a debate or other confrontational situation. The presidential debates, which have become a staple of our election process every four years, should provide it. But they do not. Usually they are only presentations of well-rehearsed positions, with little true interaction, and they are slanted to the media and what we have come to call "image building" and "nonverbal communication." Law courts, where legal questions are argued and decided, could provide an example, but the discussions are usually humdrum and technical. Besides, few of us actually have opportunities to witness trials. The closest examples of settings in which most of us can see keen minds at work are those rare television programs like Ted Koppel's "Nightline" or William Buckley's "Firing Line."

The apostle Paul was a keen-thinking individual, perhaps one of the sharpest men who ever lived. But we do not have copious places at which to observe his mind in action. In Acts, which records the progress of his missionary journeys, we are told repeatedly that Paul went into the Jewish synagogues and "reasoned" with the Jews (cf. Acts 9:22; 17:2–3, 17; 18:4, 28; 19:8). But there is almost no record of the form these debates took or of how Paul dealt with the questions his opponents would have been asking.

As I say, there are not many places where we can see Paul's sharp mind in action. But here in the third chapter of Romans we at least get a glimpse into the kind of back-and-forth reasoning that must have taken place again and again in the setting of Paul's missionary expositions.

The first two chapters of Romans contain the bedrock teaching of the apostle as to the nature and universality of human sin. All that he has said in those chapters is to be summarized in chapter 3. But Paul seems to have been hearing in his mind the questions that sharp Jewish opponents had thrown up at him over the years, and he is therefore reluctant to move on to his summary without dealing with at least the most important of them. We have already looked at one of these questions: "What advantage, then, is there in being a Jew, or what value is there in circumcision?" (Rom. 3:1). In following Paul's logic at this point, we have seen that there are genuine advantages to the possession of spiritual things, even though they in themselves do not guarantee salvation. In particular, it is a great advantage to possess the Word of God.

In verses 3 through 8 of this chapter Paul deals with two more questions. In the text there are actually seven question marks as the apostle phrases these questions, no doubt reflecting ways in which they had been voiced to him. But there are really only two basic questions, and it is these that Paul answers before moving on to the great summary of verses 9 through 20.

The First Question: God's Faithfulness

The question Paul raises in verse 3—"What if some did not have faith? Will their lack of faith nullify God's faithfulness?"—grows out of what was being discussed previously.

In the first verses of the chapter Paul has defended the value of circumcision (the chief Jewish sacrament) and the possession of the Old Testament (the Jews' Bible), while at the same time maintaining his chief point:

namely, that Jews are not saved by these things any more than Gentiles are saved by human morality or good works, and that Jews and Gentiles all therefore equally stand under the just condemnation of God apart from faith in Jesus Christ. "But," says Paul's opponent, "if Jews are not saved by these things and are therefore perishing in unbelief (since we all know that the majority of Jews do not believe in Jesus), isn't God then proved to be unfaithful to his people—since he has made an eternal covenant with them?" If Paul is right, God would have to be unfaithful. But since God *is* faithful, as both Paul and his opponents would acknowledge, isn't it true that Paul's arguments about the Jews being lost without Jesus Christ are erroneous?

This is an important question. And one way we know it is important is that Paul returns to it in the second major section of Romans (chapters 9–11), where he carefully answers two questions: Has God failed with the Jews? and Is God unjust in his treatment of them?

In these later chapters Paul deals with the issue by making the following six points:

1. *God is sovereign in human affairs and does all things justly, even if this means passing over the mass of Jewish people for a time (Rom. 9:1–21).* Paul makes this point by reviewing God's sovereign choice of Abraham, Isaac, and Jacob in order to form the Jewish people and establish the Messiah's line—while passing over Ishmael and Esau. If salvation is by election and therefore by grace, there can be no injustice in God's choosing to pass over anybody.

2. *God prophesied that Israel as a whole would reject Christ and that he would offer the gospel to the Gentiles (Rom. 9:22–33).* This was meant to keep Israel conscious of the very nature of the gospel, namely, that it is by grace—since Jews could never claim salvation as a right. Because of these prophecies (and warnings), the unbelief of the Jews, so very evident in Paul's day, should have come as a surprise to no one.

3. *The offer of the gospel to the Gentiles was nevertheless for Israel's own good, since it was intended to provoke them to jealousy and therefore faith (Rom. 10:1–21).* It was a "last resort" by God to reach out to those who had already rejected him.

4. *In spite of the universal offer of the gospel to Gentiles as well as Jews and Israel's jealousy of that fact, a remnant of Jews is nevertheless being saved (Rom. 11:1).* Paul cites himself as an example. "I ask then: Did God reject his people? By no means! I am an Israelite myself, a descendant of Abraham, from the tribe of Benjamin."

5. *This situation is no different from what it has always been, because even in earlier days all Jews were not saved, but rather it was only a remnant that believed and was faithful (Rom. 11:2–24).* The apostle's example here is Elijah, who in the days of Ahab considered himself to be the only faithful Israelite left, but to

whom God disclosed that there were seven thousand who had not worshiped Baal. The number was larger than Elijah imagined, but it was nevertheless just seven thousand. The many other thousands of Jews living at that time were not saved.

6. *Notwithstanding Israel's present and persistent unbelief, there will yet be a day of national blessing in which God's promises to Israel will be completely fulfilled (Rom. 11:25–36).* This truth is so marvelous that Paul closes this important section of the letter with a doxology.

Not all these points are made in Paul's much briefer treatment in Romans 3. But I have given them here because they provide the framework in which the words Paul does give must be taken. When Paul asks the question, "Will their lack of faith nullify God's faithfulness?" and when he answers, "Not at all!" it is clear that he is embracing at least two of the points he makes later: (1) that God is sovereign and that all he does is just; and (2) that God will not break his promises and that, as a result, his pledges to Israel will certainly be fulfilled in the end. Again, when Paul says, "What if some did not have faith?" he indicates: (1) that in spite of great national unbelief, "some" Jews, now as then, have believed in the Messiah; and that (2) then as now the way of salvation is through the channel of faith in God's promises.

In our sin all of us naturally presume on God, trying to manipulate him in the sense that we try to oblige him to save us regardless of what we either believe or do. The Jew did it by claiming that God must save him because of God's promises to the nation. We Christians do it by believing that God will save us because our parents were saved, because we have been baptized or confirmed or some such thing. But we cannot do that. God is faithful. He will save those he has promised to save. But not apart from faith! And not mechanically! If you are to be saved, it must be by faith in Jesus Christ, God's Son, whom God has appointed Savior.

Later Paul will say, ". . . if you confess with your mouth, 'Jesus is Lord,' and believe in your heart that God raised him from the dead, you will be saved. For it is with your heart that you believe and are justified, and it is with your mouth that you confess and are saved. As the Scripture says, 'Everyone who trusts in him will never be put to shame'" (Rom. 10:9–11).

The Second Question: Our Sin

I indicated in an indirect way when dealing with verses 3 and 4 that the question there was at least reasonable and important, for it deals with the matter of God's faithfulness and rightly asks how God can be faithful to his promises if each and every member of the covenant people of Israel is not saved. That question is so important that Paul later takes three whole chapters to answer it, as we have seen. It is not this way with the second question.

Did I say, "question"? It is a quibble. It is playing around. It is toying with theological matters and, as a result, deserves the scorn Paul gives it.

Yet Paul must have heard it a lot, just as we do. We gather this from the fact that he seems compelled to present it in three forms.

1. *God's role as judge.* The first form of the question has to do with God's role as judge of all the earth and could be rephrased as asking, "If our unrighteousness (or sin) is the necessary background against which God displays his wisdom, love, and mercy in salvation, how can God judge us for what therefore obviously has a good end?" We might think at this point that Paul would reply with some carefully reasoned distinction or with some truth that has formerly been hidden from us. He might reply that a good end does not justify a bad means, much the way Godet does at this point in his commentary. Godet refers to this logical error as utilitarianism:

> It [the argument that good ends justify evil means] has always been sought to justify the greatest crimes in history by representing the advantages they have resulted to the cause of humanity. There is not a Robespierre who has not been transformed into a saint in the name of utilitarianism. But to make such a canonization valid, one would require to begin by proving that the useful result sprang from the evil committed as its principle. Such is the teaching of Pantheism. Living Theism, on the contrary, teaches that this transformation of the bad deed into a means of progress, is the miracle of God's wisdom and power continually laying hold of human sin to derive from it a result contrary to its nature. On the first view, all human responsibility is at an end, and the judgment becomes a nullity. On the second, man remains fully responsible to God for the bad deed as an expression of the evil will of its author, and despite the good which God is pleased to extract from it. Such is scriptural optimism, which alone reconciles man's moral responsibility with the doctrine of providential progress.[1]

This is an argument Paul might have used to answer the quibble of his opponent. But, as I say, he does not. Instead, he replies merely by a categorical statement regarding the certainty of God's judgment. "Certainly not! If that were so, how could God judge the world?" (v. 6). The argument is: If there is a world, there must be a God who made it, to whom all who live and act in this world are responsible. Therefore the judgment of God is a given, and any argument that would suggest it is not is fallacious.[2]

1. F. Godet, *Commentary on St. Paul's Epistle to the Romans*, trans. A. Cusin (Edinburgh: T. & T. Clark, n.d.), vol. 1, p. 233.

2. John Murray says, "Paul appeals to the fact of universal judgment and he does not proceed to prove it. He accepts it as an ultimate datum of revelation, and he confronts the objection of verse 5 with this fact. About the certainty of God's judgment there can be no dispute. Once the judgment is accepted as a certainty, then all such objection as is implied in verses 5, 7, 8 falls to the ground. . . . The answer to objections is proclamation" (John Murray, *The Epistle to the Romans* [Grand Rapids: Wm. B. Eerdmans, 1968], p. 99).

2. *My condemnation.* The second form of the objection is like the first, but it centers more on one's own contemplated judgment than on God's role as judge. The first says, "How can God judge sin if sin actually leads to what in the end is beneficial?" Paul's answer is that God is going to judge sin regardless. The second form of the objection says, "If my sin enhances God's truthfulness and so increases his glory, how can he condemn me?" Paul does not even answer this, but instead passes on to the third form of the question, after which he concludes: "Their condemnation is deserved" (v. 8b).

3. *Doing evil that good may result.* The last form of the question is the most extreme, but it seems to have been the way in which Paul most heard it—both because of the way Paul refers to it here and the fact that he deals with it in other places (cf. Rom. 6:1–23). Here Paul admits that this charge had been widely disseminated against him: "Why not say—as we are being slanderously reported as saying and as some claim that we say—'Let us do evil that good may result'?" (v. 8a). That is, the more one sins, the more God is glorified. I believe this is the most extreme form of the question because, in addition merely to dismissing the judgment of God or excusing sin, this argument actually encourages the indulgence of the sinful nature and appetite by allegedly Christian people.

You have heard this argument, too. It goes by the theological name of Antinomianism: "If we are saved by grace through faith, entirely apart from any works of the law, then what does it matter whether we live righteous lives or not? Indeed, isn't it good that we sin, because then God is given even greater glory as our Savior?"

Faith, Justification, and Good Works

As soon as I put the argument in that form, we recognize—even if we have not done so before—that although Paul is answering questions put to him long centuries ago, the issue is not a past issue but a current and very critical one. Indeed, it concerns the very nature of the gospel. Is it true that the gospel of salvation by grace leads to sin? Or at least that it excuses it? Is it enough to sin and then claim glibly, "I am forgiven," without genuine repentance expressed in a repudiation of the evil and a decision to live differently, not to mention a desire to make restitution? If it is—if this is where Christianity leads—then I for one want nothing to do with it. It is a mockery. It is an offense to God's justice. But if, on the other hand, we insist on Christians doing righteous deeds—declaring, as Paul does, that we must not sin that grace may abound—how do we preserve the true gospel of grace apart from human merit?

Here is where Roman Catholic theology and Protestant theology part company most radically. Catholics have a proper concern for works; no one can ever say that it is all right to sin and yet be saved, according to true Catholic teaching. But Catholic theology brings works into salvation in the sense that God justifies us in part by producing good works in us, so that we are saved by faith plus those good works. The Catholic formula for justification is:

$$\text{Faith} + \text{Good Works} = \text{Justification}$$

Protestants reply that we are justified by faith in Jesus Christ alone. No works enter into justification; not even faith is a work. But Protestants add (or *should* add—there is a great deal of deficient Protestant theology at this point) that good works must follow faith if we are justified. The Protestant formula would be:

$$\text{Faith} = \text{Justification} + \text{Good Works}$$

What of the deficient Protestant theology I mentioned parenthetically? What would be the formula of Antinomianism? That formula is:

$$\text{Faith} = \text{Justification} - \text{Good Works}$$

In other words, "Let us go on sinning so that grace may increase" (cf. Rom. 6:1).

It does not take an accomplished theologian to see that this is not true Christianity. Think, for example, how Jesus insisted on a radical change of behavior for all who would follow him. He said, "If anyone would come after me, he must deny himself and take up his cross daily and follow me" (Luke 9:23). He admonished those whose "faith" was only verbal, "Why do you call me, 'Lord, Lord,' and do not do what I say? I will show you what he is like who comes to me and hears my words and puts them into practice. He is like a man building a house, who dug down deep and laid the foundation on rock. When a flood came, the torrent struck that house but could not shake it, because it was well built. But the one who hears my words and does not put them into practice is like a man who built a house on the ground without a foundation. The moment the torrent struck that house, it collapsed and its destruction was complete" (Luke 6:46–49). Furthermore, he told the Jews of his day, ". . . unless your righteousness surpasses that of the Pharisees and the teachers of the law, you will certainly not enter the kingdom of heaven" (Matt. 5:20).

The reason all this can be said is that God never justifies a person without regenerating him or her; that is, the person being saved is given a new nature, which must and will hate sin and strive for righteousness. Paul does not spell this out in Romans 3, being content merely to scorn the position that thinks it possible to be on good terms with God and yet continue to sin. But he gets to it later—in chapter 6. There he shows that all who are saved are joined to Christ. Because Christ lives in them, they increasingly want what Christ wants. And if they find that they are not increasingly coming to hate sin and love righteousness, they are not really Christ's. They are not true Christians.

By definition, Christianity must be the most beneficial (I would say, the *only* ultimately beneficial) force in the world. Why? Because it is the work of God, and only God is or can be ultimately beneficent.

Do you doubt this? If so, you have not understood the first two chapters of Romans. Those chapters have told us of the nature and extent of human sin. They have demonstrated that men and women, left to themselves, are on a path leading away from God, the only source of true good, and that the progression along that path is always and inevitably downhill. No original or ultimate good comes from any mere man or woman, only evil. Therefore, if good is to be seen anywhere, it must be from God himself and be seen in those in whom he has planted his very nature.

What a calling, if you are a Christian! What a destiny!

"Do evil that good may result"? If you find yourself thinking that way, you are no true Christian. You are no Christian if evil in yourself and in others does not distress you. You are no Christian if you can take the transgressions of God's law lightly. If you are a Christian, you will hate sin, repudiate it, fight against it, and strive for righteousness.

34

No One Righteous, Not Even One

Romans 3:9–11

What shall we conclude then? Are we any better? Not at all! We have already made the charge that Jews and Gentiles alike are all under sin. As it is written:

"There is no one righteous, not even one;
there is no one who understands,
no one who seeks God."

In the third chapter of Romans, beginning with verse 9, the apostle summarizes the condition of every human being apart from the grace of God in Jesus Christ. It is not a pretty picture. According to Paul, Jews are not better than Gentiles, and neither are Gentiles better than Jews. Instead, all are alike under sin, and all are thus subject to the wrath and final judgment of Almighty God. Quoting from Psalm 14:1–3, Psalm 53:1–3, and Ecclesiastes 7:20, Paul declares: "As it is written: 'There is no one righteous, not even one; there is no one who understands, no one who seeks God.'"

This is a serious charge, indeed a devastating picture of the race, because it portrays human beings as unable to do even a single thing either to please, understand, or seek after God. It is an expression of what theologians rightly call man's "total depravity."

The doctrine of total depravity is hard for the human race to accept, of course, for one of the results of our being sinners is that we tend to treat sin lightly. Most people are willing to admit that they are not perfect. It takes an extraordinary supply of arrogance for any mere human being to pretend that he or she has no flaws. Generally we do not do that. But this is far different from admitting that we are utterly depraved so far as our having any natural ability to please God is concerned. We are willing to admit that we are not perfect, but not that we are not righteous. We are willing to admit that there are things not known to us, but not that we are devoid of all spiritual understanding. We are willing to admit that we wander off the true path at times, but not that we are not even on the right path. Instead of admitting that we are running away from God, we pretend that we are seeking him.

It is vitally important that we come to terms with this bad tendency to run from the truth about ourselves. Without an accurate knowledge of our sin, we will never come to know the meaning of God's grace. Without an awareness of our pride, we will never appreciate God's greatness, nor will we come to God for the healing we so desperately need. The situation is a bit like being sick and needing a doctor. As long as we are convinced we are well (or at least almost well), we will not seek medical care. But if we know we are spiritually sick, we will turn to the Great Physician, Jesus Christ, who alone is able to heal us.

How Bad Is It?

In making the previous point—that we need to recognize how desperate the situation is so we will turn to God for help—I have used the analogy of being sick and needing a physician. But now I want to say, as I have already suggested, that according to Romans 3:9–11 the situation is even worse than that. As long as someone is merely sick, the situation is not hopeless. He or she may get better and survive. But, according to these verses and others, apart from the grace of God a person is not only spiritually sick but dead. The sinner is moribund.

The uniqueness of the Bible's teaching can be seen by noting that in the long history of the human race there have been only three basic views of human nature: (1) that man is well; (2) that man is sick; and (3) that man is dead. There are variations in these views, of course. Optimists will say that man is well, but they may disagree on exactly how well he is; perhaps he might not be as well as he possibly could be. Or again, although more pessimistic observers will agree that man is sick—that there is something wrong with him—they will differ over how serious the illness is. Man may be acutely sick, critically sick, mortally sick, and so on. In spite of these variations, there are nevertheless only three basic views.

The first view—that man is essentially well—is the view of Liberalism and, for that matter, of most persons today. If people admit that anything at all is wrong with man, generally it is only that he is not as fully healthy as he could perhaps be. This view holds that, morally and spiritually speaking, all people need is a little exercise, spiritual vitamins, perhaps a psychological checkup once a year, and so on. Many would say that the human race is even getting better and better. This is the view of all optimists.

The second view—that man is sick—is the view of the pessimist, which is to say: anyone who has reflected seriously on the true facts of human nature. Those who believe that man is sick have looked at the general optimism of the last hundred years and have found it wanting. In those earlier days, flushed with the heady success of the industrial revolution, encouraged by technological and medical advances, and goaded by the beguiling doctrine of universal and inevitable evolution, people began to believe that the human race was ascending like a rocket and that within a reasonable time all human problems would be solved. Wars would cease. Starvation would be eliminated. Disease would be conquered. Indeed, people would learn to live and work together in a spirit of universal brotherhood and cooperation. But those who look at this blithe optimism today are rightly critical: If human nature is only "slightly flawed," as the optimists believe, how come the world has not been perfected by now? Why are there still wars? Why hasn't starvation or disease been eliminated? Why can't people get along with one another? The pessimist looks at this and concludes wisely that the situation is not good. In fact, it is terrible. Pessimists believe that man is very sick indeed.

But not dead!

The pessimist believes that man is sick—very sick, even mortally ill—but adds, "As long as there's life there's hope." Sure, man may be ready to blow himself off the face of the earth and even destroy the planet while he is doing it. But the situation is still not hopeless, says the pessimist. We must work hard, tackle our ills and defeat them. There is no need to call the mortician yet.

The third view, the one the Bible presents, is that we humans are not well, nor even sick. We are dead so far as our being able to do anything to please, understand, or find God is concerned. That is, we are as God declared we would be when he warned Adam and Eve against eating of the tree of the knowledge of good and evil. God said, ". . . you must not eat from the tree of the knowledge of good and evil, for when you eat of it you will surely die" (Gen. 2:17). Our first parents did eat of it, and they did die. Thus it is true of us, as Paul said in writing to the Ephesians, that we are "dead in [our] transgressions and sins" (Eph. 2:1). Of ourselves we are as unable to respond to God as any corpse would be if someone, believing it alive, told it to do *anything.*

The Moral Nature: None Righteous

In the first part of his summary of the hopeless condition of man, the apostle speaks of man's moral nature and concludes that the human race is unrighteous. This does not mean merely that man is a bit less righteous than he needs to be to please God and somehow get to heaven. We cannot have understood the first chapter of Romans and think in those terms. Actually, when Paul says that "there is no one righteous," he means that *from God's point of view* human beings have no righteousness at all.

I emphasize "from God's point of view," not to suggest that any view other than God's is ever ultimately valid but merely to make clear that it is from this viewpoint that we need to assess the situation. This is because, if we assess the human condition from man's perspective, we will always conclude that at least some people are good—simply because they are better than what we think we observe in others.

Our problem at this point is that we think of the good we do (or *can* do), our righteousness, as being the same thing as God's righteousness, when it is actually quite different. We assume that by simply accumulating human goodness we can please God.

Let me give an illustration. Suppose that during the Vietnam War a platoon of American soldiers was captured and interred by the North Vietnamese. Imagine further that at some point in their captivity a Red Cross package arrived at the camp and that it contained, among other things, a game of Monopoly. The donor simply thought the soldiers would like to while away the long hours of their imprisonment playing it. The soldiers were glad to get the Monopoly game, but not for the reason the folks back home sent it to them. They were glad to have it because it gave them "money" with which to do camp business. Before this, if someone wanted to get something from another soldier—a cigarette, for example—he had to beg, borrow, or steal it. Now he could buy it with the Monopoly money. So the soldiers distributed the gold, yellow, blue, green, and white money and went into business.

It seems always the case among a group of Americans that one person is a naturally gifted capitalist, and this platoon was no exception. Because one man was a genius at buying low and selling high, in time he accumulated almost all the money in the camp.

Suppose further that eventually there was a prisoner-of-war exchange, and a group of North Vietnamese were exchanged for this platoon of Americans. A helicopter comes, picks them up, flies them to Da Nang, and from there it is only a matter of hours before they are back in the States on the California coast. Almost immediately the successful capitalist/soldier enters the First National Bank of San Francisco and steps up to the counter. The teller is pleased to open an account for him. "We are glad to help our veterans," she says. "How much do you want to deposit?"

"About half a million," the ex-prisoner answers, as he pushes $500,382 in Monopoly money over the counter and through the teller's window. Of course, the teller reaches down, not for a deposit slip but for the alarm button that will call someone to take this poor deranged man away.

That is the difference between human righteousness, on the one hand, and the righteousness God requires of us, on the other. Human righteousness is like Monopoly money. It has its uses in the game we call life. But it is not real currency, and it does not work in God's domain. God requires divine righteousness, just as in America only United States dollars are legal tender. We are going to find a little bit further along in Romans that Paul will write of Israel's failure to find God, using this very distinction: "Since they did not know the righteousness that comes from God and sought to establish their own, they did not submit to God's righteousness" (Rom. 10:3). That is, Israel wanted God to accept their own currency rather than come to Christ for the genuine currency he alone can provide.

So the first thing Paul says about the human race in his summary of its lost condition is that it has no righteousness. Verse 12 adds, "'All have turned away, they have together become worthless; there is no one who does good, not even one.'"

The Sinful Mind: None Understands

The second pronouncement Paul makes about human beings in their sinful condition is that no one understands spiritual things. Again, we need to view this as a lack of spiritual perception and not merely a lack of human knowledge. If we think on the human level, comparing the "understanding" of one person with that of another, we will observe rightly that some people obviously understand a great deal about our world. And since we are impressed by that, we will be misled. We need to see that in spiritual matters the important thing is that no one truly understands God or seeks to know him.

The best commentary upon this phrase is found in the first two chapters of 1 Corinthians. The people in the church at Corinth were mostly Greeks. They prized the wisdom of the Greek philosophers, as virtually all Greeks did. Paul writes that when he was with them he did not attempt to impress them with such wisdom, but rather that he determined to know nothing while among them "except Jesus Christ and him crucified" (1 Cor. 2:2). Why? He explains his decision in two ways.

First, human wisdom has shown itself bankrupt so far as coming to know God is concerned. Paul says that "the message of the cross is foolishness to those who are perishing, but to us who are being saved it is the power of God. For it is written: 'I will destroy the wisdom of the wise; the intelligence of the intelligent I will frustrate.' Where is the wise man? Where is the scholar? Where is the philosopher of this age? Has not God made foolish the wisdom of the world? For since in the wisdom of God the world through its wisdom did not know him, God was pleased through the foolishness of what was preached to save those who believe" (1 Cor. 1:18–21). In making this indictment, Paul was only echoing what the best of the Greeks had themselves concluded. The philosophers already knew they had been unable to discover God through human reasoning or scholarship.

The second way Paul explains his decision to know nothing while among the Greeks but Christ crucified is the statement that spiritual matters can only be known by God's Spirit: "The man without the Spirit does not accept the things that come from the Spirit of God, for they are foolishness to him, and he cannot understand them, because they are spiritually discerned" (1 Cor. 2:14).

This does not mean that a person cannot have a rational understanding of Christianity or what the Bible teaches apart from the illumination of his or her mind by the Holy Spirit. In one sense, a scholar can understand and explain theological principles as well as any other area of human knowledge. An unbelieving philosopher can lecture accurately on the Christian idea of God. An unbelieving historian can analyze to near perfection the nature of the Reformation and describe the meaning of justification by faith. When I was at Harvard University there were non-Christian professors who could present the doctrines of Christianity so brilliantly that Christians would marvel at their lectures and be edified by them. and even unbelieving students would rise to their feet and applaud. But these professors did not believe what they were teaching. If they had been asked their opinion of what they were so accurately presenting, they would have said that it was all utter nonsense. It is in this sense that they, not being "spiritual," were unable to understand Christianity.

If we return to Romans 1, we are reminded of the cause of this ignorance. It is not that the doctrine of God (or any other doctrine of the Christian faith) is difficult to comprehend. It is rather that we do not want to move in the direction these doctrines lead us. So we suppress the truth about God, refusing to glorify or give thanks to him, and as a result our thinking becomes "futile" and our foolish hearts are "darkened" (v. 21).

The Captive Will: None Seeks God

Having spoken of our moral and intellectual failures, Paul moves at last to the area of the corrupt human will and concludes rightly that no one "seeks God."

Here again we must not think in merely human terms. If we do, we will conclude, contrary to Paul's teaching, that "seeking after God" has actually been the history of our race. I have already dealt with the academic expression of this view in our analysis of Romans 1:21–23, referring to Robert Brow's *Religion: Origins and Ideas*.[1] Brow maintains that study of primitive peoples suggests, not that the human race has moved from primitive conceptions of God to higher conceptions of him—thus seeking after "God" constantly—but rather that the human race has been consistently running

---

1. Robert Brow, *Religion: Origins and Ideas* (Chicago: InterVarsity Press, 1966).

away from ideas of a high and holy God. He argues that primitive peoples generally have a truer picture of God than we do, though they do not worship him. They believe in a great and true God who stands behind their pantheon of animistic deities or lesser gods, but they do not worship this God, because they do not fear him as much as they do the immediate and hostile powers.

F. Godet saw this and wrote, "At the root of all pagan religions and mythologies, there lies an original Monotheism, which is the historical starting-point in religion for all mankind."[2]

But here I want to focus on the way this negative principle works in our lives and society. Consider a man who believes himself to be the perfect refutation of Paul's statement that there is *no one* who seeks God. "But I *do* seek him," this man argues. "In fact, I have been seeking him all my life. I was born into a Baptist family; but I could not find God in my Baptist home or church. So, when I grew old enough to select a church on my own, I joined a Presbyterian church. Unfortunately, that was a bad church. No one could find God there. So I joined an Episcopalian church. Over the years I have attended almost every kind of church there is. I have been to Lutheran churches, Pentecostal churches, Methodist churches, Bible churches, independent churches. I have been seeking God all my life, but I haven't found him."

The answer to this man's argument is that he has not been *seeking* God. He has been running away from him. When God got close to him in his Baptist home and church, he left that church and joined a Presbyterian congregation. And when things got hot for him there—God can work in Presbyterian churches—he joined an Episcopal church. When God got too close to him there, he left it for a succession of other denominations. If he gets to the end of this circle, he will probably look around carefully to see if anyone is looking and then jump back in at the beginning.

This man is not seeking God. He is merely using religious trappings to disguise his intention of running away from the Almighty and everything true commitment and faith would entail.

Pursued by God

I come back to where I was at the beginning of this study and say that according to the Bible no one unaided by the Spirit of God (1) has any righteousness by which to lay a claim upon God; (2) has any true understanding of God; or (3) seeks God. But what we do not have and cannot do and have not done, God has done for those who are being saved.

What exactly has God done? First, God has sought us. We had run from him, but like "The Hound of Heaven" God pursued us relentlessly. Some of

2. F. Godet, *Commentary on St. Paul's Epistle to the Romans*, trans. A. Cusin (Edinburgh: T. & T. Clark, n.d.), vol. 1, p. 176.

us ran from God for a long time and can recall the days of our waywardness well. If God had not pursued us, we would have been lost eternally. We would never have come to God by ourselves. Now we know that no one is ever saved who has not first been pursued by God and been found by him. Second, God has given us understanding. He has done this by making us alive in Jesus Christ by the power of the Holy Spirit, as a result of which our eyes have been opened to see things spiritually. This does not mean that we perfectly comprehend all things about God and his ways, but we now truly "understand" in the sense that we believe these things and respond accordingly. Last of all, God has given us a righteousness that we did not have in ourselves and, in fact, could never have had—*his* righteousness, which is the righteousness of Jesus Christ and is the ground of our salvation.

35

The Bondage of the Will

Romans 3:11

". . . there is no one who understands, no one who seeks God."

Early in my study of Paul's letter to the Romans, I had an opportunity to teach this book to two separate groups of people for a week at a time. I covered a large number of Bible doctrines, touching on everything from election to glorification. But in both of those settings the point the listeners kept coming back to in question periods was the matter of the human will and its freedom or bondage.

I had said that if we are as desperately lost in sin as Romans 1:18–3:20 says we are, then, unaided by the Spirit of God, no one can come to God, choose God, or even believe on Jesus Christ and be saved—unless God first makes that person alive in Christ and draws him or her. But this is what troubled many. It did not seem consistent with what they knew of their ability to choose what they wanted to choose or reject what they wanted to reject. What is more, it seemed inconsistent with the many free offers of the gospel found throughout Scripture. What does the Bible mean when it says that we are "dead in [our] transgressions and sins" (Eph. 2:1)? Does that mean that we are really unable to respond to God in any way, even when the gospel is proclaimed to us? Or do we still have at least that ability? If we

297

can respond, what did Jesus mean when he said, "No one can come to me unless the Father who sent me draws him" (John 6:44a), or "No one can come to me unless the Father has enabled him" (John 6:65)? On the other hand, if we cannot respond, what is the meaning of those passages in which the gospel is offered to fallen men and women? For example, the Lord said through the prophet Isaiah, "Come, all you who are thirsty, come to the waters; and you who have no money, come, buy and eat!" (Isa. 55:1). What about such invitations? Furthermore, how can a person be held responsible for failing to believe in Jesus if he or she is unable to do so?

These questions come to us from Romans 3:10–11 because of the words with which Paul sums up man's spiritual condition. He has said that we are all unrighteous: "'There is no one righteous, not even one.'" Now he adds: "'There is no one who understands, no one who seeks God.'" The way we interpret this verse has a lot to do with how we regard man's rock-bottom inability (or ability) where spiritual things are concerned.

The Debate in Church History

We might suspect, even if we knew nothing of the past, that a question as important as this must have been discussed often in church history, and this is indeed the case. In fact, the very best way of approaching the subject is through the debates that took place between the theological giants of past days.

The first important debate was between Pelagius and Saint Augustine toward the end of the fourth and the beginning of the fifth century. Pelagius argued for free will. He did not want to deny the universality of sin, at least at the beginning. He knew that "all have sinned and fall short of the glory of God" (Rom. 3:23a), and in this he wanted to remain orthodox. But Pelagius could not see how we can be responsible for something if we do not have free will in that matter. If there is an obligation to do something, there must be an ability to do it, he argued. Pelagius believed that the will, rather than being bound by sin, is actually neutral—so that at any moment or in any given situation it is free to choose either good or evil.

This worked itself out in several ways. For one thing, it led to a view of sin as only those deliberate and unrelated acts in which the will actually chooses to do evil. Thus any necessary connection between sins or any hereditary principle of sin within the race was forgotten. Pelagius argued further that:

1. The sin of Adam affected no one but himself, and

2. Those born since Adam have been born into the same condition Adam was in before his fall, that is, into a position of neutrality so far as sin is concerned, and

3. Today human beings are able to live free from sin if they want to.

This is probably the root view of most people today, including many Christians. But it is faulty, because it limits the nature and scope of sin and because it leads to a denial of the necessity for the unmerited grace of God in salvation. Moreover, even when the gospel is preached to a fallen sinner (according to this view), what ultimately determines whether he or she will be saved is not the supernatural working of God through the Holy Spirit, but rather the person's will, which either receives or rejects the Savior—and this gives human beings glory that ought to go to God.

In his early life Augustine had thought along the same lines. But when he became a Christian and as he studied the Bible, Augustine came to see that Pelagianism does not do justice to either the biblical doctrine of sin or the grace of God in salvation.

Augustine saw that the Bible always speaks of sin as more than mere isolated and individual acts. It speaks of an inherited depravity as a result of which it is simply not possible for the individual to stop sinning. Augustine had a phrase for this fundamental human inability: *non posse non peccare*. It means "not able not to sin." That is, unaided by God, a person is just not able to stop sinning and choose God. Augustine said that man, having used his free will badly in the fall, lost both himself and his will. He said that the will is free of righteousness, but it is enslaved to sin. It is free to turn from God, but not to come to him.

As far as grace is concerned, Augustine saw that apart from grace no one can be saved. Moreover, it is a matter of grace from beginning to end, not just of "prevenient" grace or partial grace to which the sinner adds his or her efforts. Otherwise, salvation would not be entirely of God, God's honor would be diminished, and human beings would be able to boast in heaven. Any view that leads to such consequences must be wrong, for God has declared: "It is by grace you have been saved, through faith—and this not from yourselves, it is the gift of God—not by works, so that no one can boast" (Eph. 2:8–9).

In defending his views, Augustine won the day, and the church supported him. But Christianity gradually drifted back in the direction of Pelagianism during the Middle Ages.

At the time of the Reformation the battle erupted again, first between Martin Luther and a Dutch humanist, Erasmus of Rotterdam, and then between Jacob Arminius and the followers of John Calvin.

The most interesting debate was between Luther and Erasmus. The latter had been sympathetic to the Reformation in its early stages because, like most wise people of the time, he saw that the church badly needed to be reformed. But Erasmus did not have Luther's spiritual undergirdings, and at last he was prevailed upon to challenge the reformer. Erasmus chose to write on the freedom of the will. He said that the will must be free—for reasons very much like those given by Pelagius. Still, the subject did not mean a great deal to Erasmus, and he counseled moderation, no doubt hoping that Luther would do likewise.

It was no small matter to Luther, however, and he did not approach the subject with detached moderation. Luther approached the matter zealously, viewing it as an issue upon which the very truth of God depended. In one place, in the midst of demolishing the Dutch humanist's views, Luther wrote: "I give you hearty praise and commendation on this . . . account—that you alone, in contrast with all others, have attacked the real thing, that is, the central issue."[1]

In this work, *The Bondage of the Will*, which Luther considered his greatest theological writing, the reformer did not deny the psychological fact that men and women do make choices. This is so obvious that no one can really deny it. What Luther affirmed was that *in the specific area of an individual's choice of God or failure to choose God*, the will is impotent. In this area Luther was as determined to deny the will's freedom as Erasmus was determined to affirm it. We are wholly given over to sin, said Luther. Therefore, our only proper role is humbly to acknowledge our sin, confess our blindness, and admit that we can no more choose God by our enslaved wills than we can please him by our sullied moral acts. All we can do is call on God for mercy, knowing even as we seek to do so that we cannot even call for mercy unless God is first active to convict us of sin and lead us to embrace the Lord Jesus Christ for salvation.

In trying to convey Luther's thought, I used to say that although we have free will in many areas, we do not have free will in all areas. That is, we can choose what we want in some things—little things like what we will select from a menu, what color tie we will put on, what job we will take. But we do not have free will in the important areas. If I have an intelligence quotient of 120, I cannot make it 140 just by the exercise of my free will. Unless I am an Olympic-class athlete, I cannot choose to run a mile in four minutes or the hundred-yard dash in nine seconds. I used to say that in exactly the same way, none of us can choose God by the mere exercise of our will.

Edwards's "Freedom of the Will"

I do not present the matter that way anymore, however, and the reason I do not is that in the meantime I have read Jonathan Edwards's treatise on the freedom of the will and now think differently. Not on the basic issue or in my conclusions—but in the way I define the will.

Let me explain.

It can hardly escape anyone who looks at Edwards's treatise that at least on the surface Edwards seemed to be saying the exact opposite of what Saint Augustine and Martin Luther had said. Luther titled his study *The Bondage of the Will*, in opposition to Erasmus's *Freedom of the Will*, whereas Jonathan Edwards's treatise is titled "A Careful and Strict Inquiry into the

1. Martin Luther, *The Bondage of the Will*, trans. J. I. Packer and O. R. Johnston (Westwood, N.J.: Fleming H. Revell, 1957), p. 319.

Prevailing Notions of the Freedom of the Will."[2] The title does not specifically state that Edwards was asserting the will's "freedom," only that he was going to investigate the prevailing ideas about it, but, it is not by chance that Edwards used words opposite to Luther's. In the end, Edwards came out on the same side as Luther and of all the great biblical theologians before him. But along the way he made a unique contribution to the subject for which the idea of the "freedom" of the will was appropriate.

In this important work the first thing Edwards did was to define the will. Strangely, no one had done this previously. Everyone had operated on the assumption that we all know what the will is. We call the will that mechanism in us that makes choices. Edwards saw that this was not accurate and instead defined the will as "that by which *the mind* chooses anything." That may not seem to be much of a difference, but it is a major one. It means, according to Edwards, that what we choose is not determined by the will itself (as if it were an entity to itself) but by the mind, which means that our choices are determined by what we think is the most desirable course of action.

Edwards's second important contribution was in the treatment of what he termed "motives." He asked, "Why is it that the mind chooses one thing rather than another?" His answer: The mind chooses as it does because of motives. That is, the mind is not neutral. It thinks some things are better than other things, and because it thinks that way it always chooses the "better" things. If a person thought one course of action was better than another and yet chose the less desirable alternative, the person would be acting irrationally or, to use other language, he would be insane.

Does this mean that the will is bound, then? Quite the contrary. It means that the will is free. It is always free. That is, it is free to choose (and always will choose) what the mind thinks is best.

But what does the mind think is best? Here we get to the heart of the problem as it involves choosing God. When confronted with God, the mind of a sinner never thinks that the way of God is a good course. The will is free to choose God; nothing is stopping it. But the mind does not regard submission to God and serving God as being desirable. Therefore, it turns from God, even when the gospel is most winsomely presented. It turns from God because of what we saw in Romans 1. The mind does not want God to be sovereign. It does not consider the righteousness of God to be the way to personal fulfillment or happiness. It does not want its true sinful nature exposed. The mind is wrong in its judgments, of course. The way it chooses is actually the way of alienation and misery, the end of which is death. But human beings think sin to be the best way. Therefore, unless God changes the way we *think*—which he does in some by the miracle of the new birth—our minds always tell us to turn from God. And so we do turn from him.

2. Jonathan Edwards, "A Careful and Strict Inquiry into the Prevailing Notions of the Freedom of the Will," *The Works of Jonathan Edwards*, vol. 1, revised by Edward Hickman with a memoir by Sereno E. Dwight (Edinburgh: Banner of Truth Trust, 1976), pp. 3–93.

Moral Inability

The third great contribution Edwards made to understanding why the will never chooses God, although it is free, concerns responsibility, the matter that had troubled Pelagius so profoundly. Here Edwards wisely distinguished between what he called "natural" inability and what he termed "moral" inability. Let me give a simple illustration.

In the natural world there are animals that eat nothing but meat. They are called carnivores from *caro, carnis,* which means "meat." There are other animals that eat nothing but grass or plants. They are called herbivores from *herba,* which means vegetation. Imagine that we have captured a lion, a carnivore, and that we place a bundle of hay or a trough of oats before him. He will not eat the hay or oats. Why not? Is it because he is physically, or naturally, unable to eat them? No. Physically he could munch on the oats and swallow them. But he does not and will not, because it is not in his nature to eat this kind of food. Moreover, if we could ask why he will not eat the herbivore's meal and the lion could answer, he would say, "I cannot eat this food, because I hate it. I will only eat meat."

Now think of the verse that says, "Taste and see that the LORD is good" (Ps. 34:8a) or of Jesus' saying, "I am the living bread that came down from heaven. If a man eats of this bread, he will live forever . . ." (John 6:51). Why will a sinful man or woman not "taste and see that the Lord is good" or feed upon Jesus as "the living bread"? To use the lion's words, it is because that person "hates" such food. The sinner will not come to Christ—because he does not want to. It is not because he cannot come physically.

Someone who does not hold to this teaching (there are many today) might say, "But surely the Bible says that anyone who will come to Christ may come to him. Didn't Jesus invite us to come? Didn't he say, 'Whoever comes to me I will never drive away'" (John 6:37b)? The answer is yes, that is exactly what Jesus said. But it is beside the point. Certainly anyone who wants to come to Christ may come to him. That is why Jonathan Edwards insisted that the will is not bound. The fact that we may come is what makes our refusal to seek God so unreasonable and increases our guilt. But who is it who wills to come? The answer is: No one, except those in whom the Holy Spirit has already performed the entirely irresistible work of the new birth so that, as a result of this miracle, the spiritually blind eyes of the natural man are opened to see God's truth, and the totally depraved mind of the sinner, which in itself has no spiritual understanding, is renewed to embrace the Lord Jesus Christ as Savior.

Old and Practical Doctrine

This is not new teaching, of course, although it seems new to many who hear it in our own quite superficial age. It is merely the purest and most basic form of the doctrine of man embraced by most Protestants and even (privately) by many Catholics. The Thirty-Nine Articles of the Church of England say: "The condition of man after the fall of Adam is such, that he cannot turn and prepare himself by his own natural strength and good works to faith, and calling upon God; wherefore we have no power to do good works, pleasant and acceptable to God, without the grace of God by Christ preventing us [that is, being present beforehand to motivate us], that we may have a good will, and working with us when we have that will" (Article 10).

In the same way the Westminster Larger Catechism states, "The sinfulness of that state whereinto man fell, consisteth in the guilt of Adam's first sin, the want of that righteousness wherein he was created, and the corruption of his nature, whereby he is utterly indisposed, disabled, and made opposite to all that is spiritually good, and wholly inclined to all evil, and that continually" (Answer to Question 25).

I suppose that at this point there are people who are willing to agree, somewhat reluctantly, that the inability of the will to choose God or believe on Christ is the prevailing doctrine of the church and perhaps even the teaching of the Bible. But they are still not certain of this teaching's value and may even consider it harmful. They ask, "If we teach that men and women cannot choose God (even if this is true), don't we destroy the main impetus to evangelism and undercut the missionary enterprise? Isn't it better just to keep quiet about it?"

It should be a sufficient answer to this worry to say that the very person who gave us the Great Commission said, "No one can come to me unless the Father who sent me draws him."

But let me answer instead by saying that, contrary to this doctrine being a hindrance to evangelism, it is actually the greatest possible motivation for spreading the gospel. If it is true that the sinner, left alone, never *naturally* seeks out God, how is that individual ever going to find God unless other people, sent by God, carry the gospel to him (or her). "Ah, but even then the person cannot respond," says the objector. True enough. Not by himself. But it is through the preaching and teaching of the gospel that God chooses to call people to faith, and anyone who obeys God and takes the gospel to the lost can be encouraged to know that God will work through this means. Moreover, the evangelist will pray for the sinner, since nothing but the work of God—certainly not the eloquence or charm of man—can save him.

"But surely you must not tell the sinner that he cannot respond unless God first does a work of regeneration in him?" argues a skeptic. On the contrary, that is exactly what the sinner needs to know. For it is only in such understanding that sinful human beings learn how desperate their situation is and how absolutely essential is God's grace. If we are hanging on to some confidence in our own spiritual ability, no matter how small, we will never seriously worry about our condition. There will be no sense of urgency.

"Life is long. There will be time to believe later," we say, as if we can bring ourselves to believe when we want to, perhaps on our deathbed after we have done what we wish with our lives. At least we are ready to take a chance on it. But if we are truly dead in sin, as Paul says we are, and if that involves our will as well as all other parts of our psychological and spiritual makeup, we will find ourselves in near despair. We will see our state as hopeless apart from the supernatural and totally unmerited workings of the grace of God.

And that is what God wants! He will not have us boasting of even the smallest human contribution to salvation. It is only as we renounce all such vain possibilities that he will show us the way of salvation through Christ and lead us to him.[3]

---

3. Much of this chapter has been taken with alterations from James Montgomery Boice, *Foundations of the Christian Faith* (Downers Grove, Ill.: InterVarsity Press, 1986), pp. 208–216.

36

No One Who Does Good

Romans 3:12

*"All have turned away, they have together become worthless;
there is no one who does good, not even one."*

I do not know why God should bother
to speak to us about something more than once, like a parent trying to correct a naughty child: "Johnny, get out of the mud. Johnny, stop climbing in
the tree; you'll fall. Johnny, don't speak like that to your sister." But God
does speak to us again and again; and it is good he does, because we need
it. Indeed, most of us have trouble hearing him even then.

To my knowledge, nothing in the Bible is repeated as frequently or as
forcefully as the words summing up mankind's sinful nature, which we find
in Romans 3:10–12, particularly verse 12. Psalm 14:2 and Psalm 53:2, where
a question is posed by the psalmist, form the basis for the apostle's answer
in verses 10 and 11. Verse 12 is a verbatim quotation (from the Septuagint).
Psalm 14:3 says, "All have turned aside, they have together become corrupt;
there is no one who does good, not even one." Psalm 53:3 almost exactly
repeats that charge: "Everyone has turned away, they have together become
corrupt; there is no one who does good, not even one." Now, in Romans
3:12, the words are written out for us one more time: "All have turned away,

they have together become worthless; there is no one who does good, not even one."

You would think that we might begin to get the message at this point. If God says something once, we should listen to what he says very carefully. If he says the same thing twice, we should give him our most intense and rapt attention. What if he repeats himself a third time? Then surely we should stop all else, focus our minds, seize upon each individual word, memorize what is said, and ponder the meaning of the saying intensely, attempting to apply the truth of God's revelation to our entire lives.

A More Manageable View

Yet we do not do this, and the reason we do not is that the revelation of God is too intense, too penetrating, too devastating for us to deal with it. What we do, even as Christians, is blandly to admit what God is saying while nevertheless recasting it in less disturbing terms.

I remember as a child being taught a Sunday-school lesson about sin. The teacher used a blackboard, and she began the lesson by drawing a yard-stick in a vertical position on the left side of the blackboard. The yardstick was labeled "the divine measure," and a verse was written beside it: Matthew 5:48 ("Be perfect, therefore, as your heavenly Father is perfect"). A line was drawn across the top of the blackboard at the point to which the top of the yardstick reached. This was the standard. The teacher then asked, "Has any-one ever lived up to this standard?"

After a few suggestive hints, one of the students answered, "Yes, the Lord Jesus Christ lived up to it."

"That's right," said the teacher. So she drew a line parallel to the yard-stick, reaching from the bottom of the blackboard to the line at the top that represented perfection. She labeled this line "Jesus Christ."

"Has anybody else lived up to this standard?" she continued. We agreed that nobody else had, although, as she pointed out, some people have done better than others. To show that some persons are better than others but that no one had reached perfection she drew a number of vertical lines, all of which fell short of the "perfection" standard. There was a line labeled "98 percent" for very good people, lines labeled "90 percent" and "80 per-cent" for fairly normal people, and a line labeled "40 percent" for pretty bad people. Then Romans 3:23 was added, the teacher pointing out that although some people are better than others, with God "there is no differ-ence, for all have sinned and fall short of [his] glory."

As I look back on that lesson I do not doubt that it taught some very valuable things, primarily that although some people look quite good to us by our standards, all people nevertheless fail to please God and need a Savior. As a tool for teaching this, the lesson was effective.

But the illustration on which the lesson was based has one great weak-ness. By putting the lines representing "98 percent" people, "90 percent" people, "80 percent" people, and "40 percent" people parallel to the line representing Jesus Christ, the diagram inevitably suggests that human goodness is essentially the same as divine goodness and that all people really need is that little bit of additional goodness which—added to their own efforts and attainments—will make up the required "100 percent." That error needs to be repudiated.

Is that what Psalm 14:3, Psalm 53:3, and Romans 3:12 teach us? Not at all! If we are to express the teaching of these verses by our diagram, we must either eliminate the lines representing human beings from the diagram entirely or else represent them not as lines stretching upward in the direction of divine perfection, but downward in varying degrees of opposition to God and his righteousness. God does not merely say that people fail to live up to his standard, although that is also true and is one way of expressing sin's nature. He says rather that we have all "turned away." We have "together become worthless; there is no one who does good, not even one."

All, Like Sheep . . .

I suggested earlier that when God says something more than once we should pay the most rapt attention to it, memorizing and pondering each word. I would like to do something like that now, taking one phrase of Romans 3:12 at a time. The first is: "All have turned away."

This phrase is expressed in just two words in Greek: *pantes*, properly translated "all," and *exeklinan*, a past form of a verb meaning "to deviate," "wander" or "depart" from the right way. That "right way" is outlined in the opening chapter of Romans; it is to recognize God's eternal power and divine nature and then to glorify, thank, worship, and serve him (vv. 21, 25). But it is precisely from this right way that we have deviated. Instead of seeking God and worshiping him in thankful service, we have suppressed the truth about him and gone our own way, inventing false gods to take the true God's place and finding our intellect and morals to be increasingly debased as a result.

This indictment includes every human being. At the beginning of the verse the inclusiveness is expressed positively by the strong word *all*. At the end it is expressed negatively by the words *not even one*. One commentator writes, "As respects well-doing there is not one; as respects evil-doing there is no exception."[1]

But Paul's words do not only draw our attention to Romans 1, where the departure of men and women from the right way is spelled out. They also make us think of that well-known verse in Isaiah, where sinners are compared to sheep who cannot find their way: "We all, like sheep, have gone astray, each of us has turned to his own way . . ."(Isa. 53:6). Ah, that is the

1. John Murray, *The Epistle to the Romans* (Grand Rapids: Wm. B. Eerdmans, 1968), p. 104.

problem! Not only have we not gone God's way, we have not even gone in ways marked out by other people. We have each gone *our own* way. Consequently, each of us is basically set against all others, and we pursue our own well-being and desires to the neglect or hurt of other people.

I like some words that the great Swiss theologian Karl Barth offers at this point in his famous commentary on Romans, for they suggest that Paul's condemnation of the race is not merely a matter of biblical revelation but is the judgment of history as well. "The whole course of history pronounces this indictment against itself," Barth begins. So "how can a man be called 'historically minded' if he persistently overlooks it?" He continues:

> If all the great outstanding figures in history, whose judgments are worthy of serious consideration, if all the prophets, psalmists, philosophers, fathers of the church, reformers, poets, artists, were asked their opinion, would one of them assert that men were good or even capable of good? Is the doctrine of original sin merely one doctrine among many? Is it not rather, according to its fundamental meaning . . . , *the* doctrine which emerges from all honest study of history? Is it not the doctrine which, in the last resort, underlies the whole teaching of history? Is it possible for us to adopt a "different point of view" from that of the Bible, Augustine and the Reformers? What then does history teach about the things which men do or do not do?
>
> Does it teach that some men at least are like God? No, but that—*There is none righteous, no not one.*
>
> Does it teach that men possess a deep perception of the nature of things? or that they have experienced the essence of life? No, but that—*There is none that understandeth.*
>
> Does it provide a moving picture of quiet piety or of fiery search after God? Do the great witnesses to the truth furnish a splendid picture, for example, of "prayer"? No—*There is none that seeketh after God.*
>
> Can it describe this or that individual and his actions as natural, healthy, genuine, original, right-minded, ideal, full of character, affectionate, attractive, intelligent, forceful, ingenuous, of sterling worth? No—*They have all turned aside, they are together become unprofitable; there is none that doeth good, no, not so much as one.*[2]

Commentator Robert Haldane says, "The Prophet here teaches us what is the nature of sin [and] . . . what are its consequences. For as the man who loses his way cannot have any rest in his mind, nor any security, it is the same with the sinner. And as a wanderer cannot restore himself to the right way without the help of a guide, in the same manner the sinner cannot restore himself, if the Holy Spirit comes not to his aid."[3]

2. Karl Barth, *The Epistle to the Romans*, trans. from the sixth edition by Edwyn C. Hoskyns (London: Oxford University Press, 1933), pp. 85, 86.

3. Robert Haldane, *An Exposition of the Epistle to the Romans* (MacDill AFB: MacDonald Publishing, 1958), p. 119.

Corrupt and Useless

The second phrase in Romans 3:12 is also composed of just two Greek words, and the impact is similar. The first word is *hama*. It means "together." It is the equivalent of "all" in phrase one. The second word is *ēchreōthēsan*, the past tense of a verb meaning "useless" or "corrupt." I say "useless" *or* "corrupt" because the word in Greek (the language in which Paul is writing) and the word in Hebrew (the language in which the word occurs in Psalms 14 and 53) have these two closely related meanings respectively. Together they say what Jesus meant when he described his followers as "the salt of the earth," adding, "But if the salt loses its saltiness, how can it be made salty again? It is no longer good for anything, except to be thrown out and trampled by men" (Matt. 5:13).

What do you do if something is corrupt or useless? You throw it away and start again. I remember a scene from the movie on the life of the great renaissance painter Michelangelo, called *The Agony and the Ecstasy*, which made this point. Michelangelo was unhappy with his first attempt at painting the Sistine Chapel, and he was mulling the problem over in a local bar. The bartender served a flagon of wine drawn from a new barrel, but the wine was sour.

"This wine is sour, bartender," shouted Michelangelo.

The bartender came to the table, tasted the wine, and then spit it out. Very decisively he went over to the wine barrel, struck the bung from it with a wooden hammer and allowed the many gallons of wine to pour out into the street. "If the wine is sour, throw it out," he retorted.

Michelangelo mulled this over and then applied the principle to his first inadequate designs. He went back to the Sistine Chapel, destroyed his original frescoes—and began again.

"Useless!" "Corrupt!" We do not like to hear those words applied to ourselves, but they are God's verdict all the same. We must accept them. However, when we do, we can know that God does not merely pour us out like wine to be trodden on by passers-by. Rather, like Michelangelo, he begins again and produces a brand-new work of art. He begins anew in order to make us entirely new creations, like Jesus Christ.

No One Who Does Good

The last of Paul's phrases is the most straightforward. Indeed, it is so precise and outspoken that we can hardly miss what he is saying: "There is no one who does good, not even one." No one at all does good—*no one!*

This verse always takes my mind back to the Old Testament, to Genesis, where there appears a similar statement of man's utter inability to please God by any human effort: "The LORD saw how great man's wickedness on the earth had become, and that every inclination of the thoughts of his heart was only evil all the time" (Gen. 6:5). That verse says not only that men and women do not do good, as God counts goodness; they do precisely the opposite. They do evil and that continually. I have pointed out, in a detailed exposition of this text in *Genesis: An Expositional Commentary*, that Genesis 6:5 teaches that sin is *internal* (rising from the "thoughts" and inclinations of the "heart"), *pervasive* (affecting our "every inclination" so that our deeds are "only evil") and *continuous* (that is, operating "all the time").[4]

I suppose there are people who might recognize the truth of these statements, at least in the sense that they accurately express the opinions of Paul and of Moses (who wrote Genesis). But they might dismiss them as merely the harsh and gloomy thoughts of these men. Paul had been a Pharisee—and Pharisees thought poorly of everyone, didn't they? And Moses? Well, he was the great lawgiver, so he might be inclined to pessimism. What about Jesus? What did he think? Wouldn't the gentle, loving, and compassionate Jesus have a more uplifting outlook?

I think here of a section of an address given at one of the Philadelphia Conferences on Reformed Theology by Professor Roger R. Nicole of Gordon Conwell Theological Seminary. It was called "The Doctrines of Grace in Jesus' Teaching," and the pertinent section stressed Christ's view of human evil. Nicole wrote:

> Our Lord Jesus Christ, with all the concern, compassion and love which he showed to mankind, made some very vivid portrayals of man's condition. He did not mince words about the gravity of human sin. He talked of man as salt that has lost its savor (Matt. 5:13). He talked of man as a corrupt tree which is bound to produce corrupt fruit (Matt. 7:7). He talked of man as being evil: "You, being evil, know how to give good things to your children" (Luke 11:13). On one occasion he lifted up his eyes toward heaven and talked about an "evil and adulterous generation" (Matt. 12:39), or again, "this wicked generation" (v. 45). In a great passage dealing with what constitutes true impurity and true purity he made the startling statement that out of the heart proceed murders, adulteries, evil thoughts and things of that kind (Mark 7:21–23). He spoke about Moses having to give special permissive commandments to men because of the hardness of their hearts (Matt. 19:8). When the rich young ruler approached him, saying, "Good Master," Jesus said, "There is none good but God" (Mark 10:18). . . .
>
> Jesus compared men, even the leaders of his country, to wicked servants in a vineyard (Matt. 21:33–41). He exploded in condemnation of the scribes and Pharisees, who were considered to be among the best men, men who were in the upper ranges of virtue and in the upper classes of society (Matt. 23:2–39).
>
> The Lord Jesus made a fundamental statement about man's depravity in John 3:6: "That which is born of the flesh is flesh." He saw in man an unwillingness to respond to grace—"You will not come to God" (John 5:40), "You have not the love of God" (v. 42), "You receive me not" (v. 43), "You believe

4. James Montgomery Boice, *Genesis: An Expositional Commentary*, vol. 1, *Genesis 1:1–11:32* (Grand Rapids: Zondervan, 1982), pp. 250–254.

not" (v. 47). Such sayings occur repeatedly in the Gospel of John. "The world's works are evil" (John 7:7); "None of you keeps the law" (v. 19). "You shall die in your sins," he says (John 8:21). "You are from beneath" (v. 23); "Your father is the devil, who is a murderer and a liar" (vv. 38, 44); "You are not of God" (v. 47); "You are not of my sheep" (John 10:26); "He that hates me hates my Father" (John 15:23–25). This is the way in which our Lord spoke to the leaders of the Jews. He brought to the fore their utter inability to please God.

Following another line of approach he showed also the blindness of man, that is, his utter inability to know God and understand him. Here again we have a whole series of passages showing that no man knows the Father but him to whom the Son has revealed him (Matt. 11:27). He compared men to the blind leading the blind (Matt. 15:14). He mentioned that Jerusalem itself did not know or understand the purpose of God and, as a result, disregarded the things that concern salvation (Luke 19:42). The Gospel of John records him as saying that he that believed not was condemned already because he had not believed on the Son of God (John 3:18). "This is the condemnation, that . . . men loved the darkness rather than light, because their deeds were evil" (v. 19). He said that only the one who has been reached by grace can walk not in darkness but have the light of life (John 8:12). The Lord Jesus emphasized that it is essential for man to be saved by a mighty act of God if he is to be rescued from his condition of misery (John 3:3, 5, 7–16). Even in the Lord's Prayer the Lord teaches us to say, "Forgive us our debts" (Matt. 6:12). And this is a prayer that we need to repeat again and again. He said, "The sick are the people who need a physician" (Matt. 9:12). We are those sick people who need a physician to help us and redeem us. He said that we are people who are burdened and heavy-laden (Matt. 11:28). . . .

The people who were most readily received by the Lord were those who had this sense of need and who therefore did not come to him with a sense of the sufficiency of their performance. The people he received were those who came broken-hearted and bruised with the sense of their inadequacy.[5]

After such a review of Jesus' teaching, Paul's words in Romans seem almost mild by comparison.

Grace That Is Greater Than Sin

But they are not mild, of course! They are devastating, as I indicated at the beginning of this study. Why? Why does God speak to us in these terms? The answer is obvious. It is so we might see our true condition, stop trying to excuse ourselves or whittle down the scope of God's judgment, and instead open ourselves up to God's grace. For that is what we need: grace!

5. Roger R. Nicole, "The Doctrines of Grace in Jesus' Teaching" in *Our Sovereign God: Addresses Presented to the Philadelphia Conference on Reformed Theology 1974–1976,* James M. Boice, editor (Grand Rapids: Baker Book House, 1977), pp. 38–41.

> Grace, grace, God's grace,
> Grace that will pardon and cleanse within;
> Grace, grace, God's grace,
> Grace that is greater than all our sin.

We have this grace in Jesus Christ. He alone can save us from our depravity.

37

The Race in Ruin

Romans 3:13-18

"Their throats are open graves;
their tongues practice deceit."
"The poison of vipers is on their lips."
"Their mouths are full of cursing and bitterness."
"Their feet are swift to shed blood;
ruin and misery mark their ways,
and the way of peace they do not know."
"There is no fear of God before their eyes."

We have already had one very grim description of the human race in the verses that end Romans 1. There humanity was described as being "filled with every kind of wickedness, evil, greed and depravity. They are full of envy, murder, strife, deceit and malice. They are gossips, slanderers, God-haters, insolent, arrogant and boastful; they invent ways of doing evil; they disobey their parents; they are senseless, faithless, heartless, ruthless" (vv. 29–31). After a list of such vices we might think that a further catalogue would be unnecessary. Yet, as Paul gets to the end of this first main section of Romans, in which the need of people for the gospel of grace is so clearly and comprehensively pointed out, he seems to sense a need to do it all over again.

313

So he writes:

> "Their throats are open graves;
>   their tongues practice deceit."
> "The poison of vipers is on their lips."
>   "Their mouths are full of cursing and bitterness."
> "Their feet are swift to shed blood;
>   ruin and misery mark their ways,
> and the way of peace they do not know."
>   "There is no fear of God before their eyes."
>
> Romans 3:13–18

The difference between this and the passage in Romans 1 is that each of these sentences is a quotation from the Old Testament, whereas the earlier passage was made up merely of the apostle's own descriptive terminology. In other words, the verses in Romans 1 are a description of the world as Paul saw it, though he is also writing as an apostle and by the inspiration of the Holy Spirit. The verses in Romans 3 are more specifically and obviously God's own description of the race's depravity.

Wicked Words from Wicked Men

Verses 13 and 14 are made up of three quotations from the Old Testament: Psalm 5:9, Psalm 140:3, and Psalm 10:7, though there are other passages that are similar. What is striking about them is that they all refer to the organs of speech: throat, tongue, lips, and mouth. And they describe how the words spoken by these organs are used to harm others. In the previous verses we have been shown how people harm themselves by turning away from God. Here we learn how they also harm others by the organs of speech that God gave them.

What do you think of first when you read these verses? If you are like me, you notice the words *cursing* and *bitterness* and think, first of all, of harsh speech, which is meant to wound another person. Perhaps when you were a child and other children said hurtful things to you, you were taught this little saying by a parent or a family friend: "Sticks and stones may break my bones, but words will never hurt me."

Unfortunately, I am sure you also learned—if you thought about it—that this little saying is not really true. It is a way of bolstering our egos to help us get through some difficult times, but it is not true that words do not hurt us. Words do hurt; they hurt deeply. In fact, they often hurt permanently. When I think back on my childhood I can remember times when I suffered some physical injury. I broke my collarbone, damaged two teeth, tore the cartilage in my left leg, and suffered scores of bumps, bangs, and bruises. But, although I can sometimes recall the incidents, I cannot remember even one bit of the pain. Yet I remember the pain of words. I remember harsh things other people said, and I still hurt when I recall them. Sticks and stones *do* hurt our bones—temporarily. But words wound forever.

Yet, I think that what Paul is saying here goes deeper. Indeed, it is clear that it does, because the words that describe the outcome of the harmful words of the ungodly all have to do, not with psychological injury, but with death.

Martin Luther has written the most penetrating study of this passage of any commentator I have studied, and he, with characteristic insight and brilliance, relates these evil words not just to hurtful things someone may say to us, but to false teachings or heresy, which are able to kill the soul. Luther suggests that those who teach falsely do three things:

1. *They devour the dead.* This means that they devour those who are spiritually dead already. Here he writes vividly: "Their teaching . . . swallows up the dead, who have gone from faith to unbelief, and swallows them up in such a way that there is no hope of returning from the death of this unbelief, unless they can be recalled by the most wonderful power of God before they descend to hell, as the Lord showed in the case of Lazarus who had been dead for four days. He says, moreover, that the grave is 'open' because they devour and seduce many people." Luther quotes Psalm 14:4 ("Have they no knowledge, all the evildoers who eat up my people as they eat bread?"), then continues: "That is, just as there is squeamishness about eating bread, even though it is eaten more frequently than other foods, so also they do not cease to devour their dead, and their disciples are never satisfied." Luther concludes, "Heresy, or faithless teaching, is nothing else than a kind of disease or plague which infects and kills many people, just as is the case with the physical plague."[1]

And, of course, this is precisely the business the world's purveyors of words are engaged in, even those who are highly regarded by our society. I was once talking with Josh D. McDowell, the popular Christian apologist who speaks widely on college campuses for Campus Crusade for Christ and is author of the best-selling books *Evidence That Demands a Verdict* and *More Evidence That Demands a Verdict.* McDowell was in the process of launching a nationwide campaign called "Why Wait?" whose purpose was to encourage today's teens to reject sexual experience before marriage. We were discussing this campaign and some of the pressures on today's young people. He mentioned television, pointing out that the average young person today will have seen more than ninety thousand explicit sexual encounters on television before he or she reaches the age of nineteen. Whenever anyone on television says, "I love you" to another person, the two always end up in bed. This is all "love" is allowed to mean. Moreover, the young person will probably not see even one example of anyone contracting a sexual disease

---

1. Martin Luther, *Luther's Works*, vol. 25, *Lectures on Romans*, ed. Hilton C. Oswald (St. Louis: Concordia, 1972), p. 228.

as the result of such open sex practices. Nor will the TV screen show the pain or psychological damage that promiscuous sex brings. As we were talking about these things, McDowell said, "On television immorality has become morality. Sin is the norm."

But immorality kills! That is the thrust of the first three chapters of Romans and the point of Paul's specific quotations from the Old Testament. Can you see this? If you can, you need to start thinking differently about the contemporary media—television, newspapers, magazines, and movies. Their messages are not harmless entertainment, as we sometimes think. They are a death machine. They are killing our young people and many older people as well. They are an open grave for the unwary.

2. *They teach deceitfully.* The second thing Luther noticed about those who disseminate false teaching is that they teach deceitfully, which is what Paul says. "Their tongues practice deceit" (v. 13).

Luther notices the difference between the mouth, which has teeth and chews—it is referred to later ("Their mouths are full of cursing and bitterness")—and the tongue, which is soft. He says: "'To teach deceitfully' is to teach a pleasing and wanton doctrine, as if it were holy, salutary, and from God, so that people who have been thus deceived hear this doctrine as if from God and believe that they are hearing him. For the message appears good to them and truthful and godly. . . . The tongue is soft, it has no bones, and it licks softly. Thus their every speech only softens the heart of men to be pleased with themselves in their own wisdom, their own righteousness, their own word or work. As it says in Isaiah 30:10: 'Speak to us smooth things. Prophesy not to us what is right.'"[2]

Isn't this what we hear in the words of the world around us? The world generally does not speak warnings—except as threats to *other* people. On the contrary, we are encouraged to think that everything is all right with us—that we can do anything we wish, satisfy any desire, avoid any responsibility, above all, never express true repentance for anything—and everything will come out right in the end. This is damnable heresy in the literal sense! It is false teaching that will transport many to hell.

3. *They kill those who have been taught such things.* In the third of his three points Luther comes to the end result of false teaching, showing that it leads to death. "This . . . same flattering and pleasing doctrine . . . not only does not make alive those who believe it but [it] actually kills them. And it kills them in such a way that they are beyond recovery."[3] Paul has already said the same thing himself in Romans 2: "But for those who are self-seeking and who reject the truth and follow evil, there will be wrath and anger . . . trouble and distress" (vv. 8–9). He says it even more clearly later: "For the wages of sin is death" (Rom. 6:23a).

2. Ibid., pp. 229, 230.
3. Ibid.

Violent Acts from Violent Men

We are not to think that this grim description is limited to mere words, however, still less to charming (though deceptive) words. In verse 14 the deceitful and poisonous speech of verse 13 boils over into harsh "cursing and bitterness" on those who refuse to be deceived. And in verses 15–17 those who teach falsehood move from words to violent actions. These verses, quoted from Isaiah 59:7–8, describe three acts of violent men, beginning with the end result of these acts. To see the progression, we need to take them in reverse order.

1. *"The way of peace they do not know"* (v. 17). This relates to people as they are in themselves apart from God. They know no personal peace—". . . the wicked are like the tossing sea, which cannot rest, whose waves cast up mire and mud" (Isa. 57:20). But this also describes the effects such persons have upon others. Having no peace themselves, they disrupt the peace of other people. Commentator Haldane says rightly, "Such is a just description of man's ferocity, which fills the world with animosities, quarrels and hatred in the private connections of families and neighborhoods; and with revolution, wars and murders among nations. The most savage animals do not destroy so many of their own species to appease their hunger, as man destroys of his fellows to satiate his ambition, revenge or cupidity."[4]

There are three ways in which men and women lack peace apart from God. First, they are not at peace with God; they are at war with him. Second, they are not at peace with one another; they hate and attack one another. Third, they are not at peace in themselves; they are restless and distressed. The only way we can find peace is by coming to the cross of Christ, where God has himself bridged the gap to man and has made peace. There sinners find peace with God and within themselves. And they are drawn together into fellowship with those who have likewise found peace and who are therefore able to live in peace with one another.

2. *"Ruin and misery mark their ways"* (v. 16). Again, this is something wicked persons experience themselves; their way is misery and ruin. But it is also something they bring on others. In other words, this verse has an active and not just a passive sense. Without a changed nature, human beings naturally labor to destroy and ruin one another, as Paul has already shown earlier.

3. *"Their feet are swift to shed blood"* (v. 15). Working backward, we come to the last of these deceitful actions. Their end is death—and not just physical death, though that would be bad enough in itself—but spiritual death, which is the death of the soul and spirit in hell. Death means separation.

4. Robert Haldane, *An Exposition of the Epistle to the Romans* (MacDill AFB: MacDonald Publishing, 1958), p. 120.

Physical death is the separation of the soul and spirit from the body. Spiritual death is the separation of the soul and spirit from God. It is forever.

No Fear of God

The last phrase of this great summary of the human race in ruin is from Psalm 36:1, and it is an apt conclusion. It tells why all these other violent and wicked acts have happened: *"There is no fear of God before their eyes."*

You know, I am sure, that the word *fear* in this sentence does not mean exactly what we usually mean by the word. We mean "fright" or "terror," but in the Bible the word *fear,* when used of God, denotes a right and reverential frame of mind before him. It has to do with worshiping him, obeying him, and departing from evil. That is why we read in Proverbs 9:10: "The fear of the LORD is the beginning of wisdom, and knowledge of the Holy One is understanding." This means that if we approach God rightly, all other things will fall into their proper places. When Romans 3:18 declares that the human race has not done this, it is saying what Paul has been stating all along. Because men and women will not know God, choosing rather to suppress the truth about him, their minds are darkened and they become fools. They claimed to be wise but "exchanged the glory of the immortal God for images made to look like mortal man and birds and animals and reptiles" (Rom. 1:22).

One commentator says, "To be destitute of the fear of God is to be godless, and no indictment could be more inclusive and decisive than the charge here made."[5]

I find it interesting, however, that Paul here also refers to "eyes." This is the sixth of the specific body references Paul makes in these verses in order to make his accusations vivid. He has referred to throats, tongues, lips, mouths, and feet. Now he mentions eyes.

Since eyes are our organs of vision, to have the fear of God before our eyes means that we have God constantly in our thoughts and in a central position in everything that concerns us. It means that we are ever looking toward him. Here I remind you of what we see in Psalm 8:5, where man is described as being "a little lower than the heavenly beings." Earlier I pointed out, in discussing man's downward path, that it is our destiny as those made in God's image to look up to the heavenly beings and beyond them to God and thus become increasingly like God. To have the "fear of God before [our] eyes" is to do just that. It is the way of all blessing, growth, and knowledge. But if we will not do that, we will inevitably look down and become like the beasts who are below us.

I began this section with a reminder that "fear" in regard to God does not mean "fright" or "terror," but rather a right and reverential frame of

5. John Murray, *The Epistle to the Romans* (Grand Rapids: Wm. B. Eerdmans, 1968), pp. 104, 105.

mind before him. But I need to add that if we will not come to God as he presents himself to us in Jesus Christ (as Savior), it is not inappropriate to be actually afraid of the Almighty. God's wrath hangs over us. His terrible judgment awaits us as the proper recompense for our unatoned sins.

The irony of the state of human beings in our sin, however, is that we do *not* fear the one, holy, and judging God. Instead, we fear lesser entities. The pagan of Paul's day feared the vast pantheon of Babylonian, Greek, Roman, and an assortment of other gods. The pagan in the distant jungle fears the rivers, rocks, and trees. He fears the sky, the thunder, the spirits of the night. The "civilized" pagan—that is, a contemporary man or woman—fears the future, hostile neighbors, disease, technological breakdown, and a host of other dangers.

Above all, everyone fears death.

What irony: To fear these things, all of which pass away eventually, and yet not fear God, to whom all of us must one day give an accounting. God spoke through the prophet Isaiah: ". . . you fear mortal men, the sons of men, who are but grass, [but] you forget the LORD your Maker, who stretched out the heavens and laid the foundations of the earth, [and] you live in constant terror every day because of the wrath of the oppressor . . ." (Isa. 51:12–13). No wonder the psalmist says, "Blessed are all who fear the LORD, who walk in his ways" (Ps. 128:1).

Mercy Alone

As we near the end of our studies of this first and most important section of Romans, it is helpful to note what others have written in summary about these words. One man who has written wisely is John Calvin:

> In his conclusion [Paul] again repeats, in different words, what we stated at the beginning, namely, that all wickedness flows from a disregard of God. When we have forsaken the fear of God, which is the essential part of wisdom, there is no right or purity left. In short, since the fear of God is the bridle by which our wickedness is held back, its removal frees us to indulge in every kind of licentious conduct. . . .
>
> David, in Psalm 14:3, says that there was such perversity in men that God, when looking on them all in succession, could not find even one righteous man. It therefore follows that this infection had spread into the whole human race, since nothing is hidden from the sight of God. . . . In other psalms he complains of the wickedness of his enemies, foreshadowing in himself and his descendants a type of the kingdom of Christ. In his adversaries, therefore, are represented all those who, being estranged from Christ, are not led by his Spirit. Isaiah expressly mentions Israel, and his accusation therefore applies still more to the Gentiles. There is no doubt that human nature is described in these words, in order that we may see what man is when left to himself, since Scripture testifies that all who are not regenerated by the grace of God are in this state. The condition of the saints

would be not better unless this depravity were amended in them. That they may still, however, remember that they are not different from others by nature, they find in what remains of their carnal nature, from which they can never escape, the seeds of those evils which would continually produce their effect in them, if they were not prevented by being mortified. For this they are indebted to the mercy of God and not to their own nature.[6]

How could our salvation be due to anything but mercy if we really are as ruined as Paul describes us? Ruined? Yes! But we may be saved from ruin by the glorious work of our divine Savior, Jesus Christ.

---

6. John Calvin, *The Epistles of Paul the Apostle to the Romans and to the Thessalonians,* trans. Ross MacKenzie (Grand Rapids: Wm. B. Eerdmans, 1973), p. 67.

38

Silence at Last

Romans 3:19

Now we know that whatever the law says, it says to those who are under the law, so that every mouth may be silenced and the whole world held accountable to God.

Now the apostle Paul comes to the end of the first main section of his letter, concluding that every human being is (1) accountable to God for what he or she has done; (2) guilty of having done countless wrong things; and (3) will never be justified by God on the basis of any supposed good works. His exact words in Romans 3:19–20 are: "Now we know that whatever the law says, it says to those who are under the law, so that every mouth may be silenced and the whole world held accountable to God. Therefore no one will be declared righteous in his sight by observing the law; rather, through the law we become conscious of sin."

These two verses are very important, because to understand them is to understand the first great foundational truths of Christianity.

A Diagnostic Question

I want to study these verses in two separate messages, however, and one of my reasons for dividing them is that verse 19 has played an important part in the conversion of many, many people.

From 1927 to 1960 the pastor of Tenth Presbyterian Church in Philadelphia (the church I now pastor), was Donald Grey Barnhouse, a gifted
Bible teacher whom God used wonderfully in preaching and conference
ministries throughout this country and around the world. He dealt with
many people's problems in his ministry, and early on he developed what he
came to call a series of diagnostic questions to help him analyze where
those he was trying to help were coming from spiritually. First, he tried to
determine whether or not the individual involved was a Christian. "Are you
born again?" he would ask. If the person gave a clear-cut testimony to his or
her faith in Christ, Barnhouse would then go on to deal with the specific
problem that had been raised. If not, he would proceed as follows:

"Perhaps I can help clarify your thinking with a question. You know that
there are a great many accidents today. Suppose that you and I should go
out of this building and a swerving automobile should come up on the side-
walk and kill the two of us. In the next moment we would be what men call
'dead.' We brush aside that absurd folly that we are going to meet St. Peter
at the gate of heaven. (That exists only in jokes about two Irishmen.) We
are going to meet God. Now suppose that in that moment of ultimate reckoning God should say to you, 'What *right*—note my emphasis on the word
right—what *right* do you have to come into my heaven?' What would be your
answer?"

Barnhouse found, as he used this approach again and again in counseling situations, that only three possible answers can be given to it. That is, all
the many varieties of answers ultimately boil down to just three. One of
them involves the text I am considering, which is why I tell this story.

"Justified by Good Works"

The first answer people give to the question is a common one. It is that
they have done certain good things and therefore want to be accepted by
God on the basis of these achievements. Some people have a very high
opinion of themselves, of course. They think they have been models of righteous conduct—that they have never done anything bad, only what is good.
In fact, they believe they have done a great deal of good! Others know that
they have not been consistently good, but they still want God to take note of
what good works they have done and accept them into heaven on that basis.
Some have kept the Golden Rule, they say—or tried to keep it. Others have
tried to help their neighbors, and so on.

If a person replied to Barnhouse's question with any of those claims, he
took them to Galatians 2:16b, which says that we ". . . put our faith in Christ
Jesus that we may be justified by faith in Christ and not by observing the
law, because by observing the law no one will be justified." Barnhouse
showed that no one can satisfy God's perfect standards by tainted human
righteousness.

Then he frequently told the following story. Early in his ministry he knew a man who lived near Tenth Presbyterian Church to whom he would often speak about the gospel. This man usually replied to the preacher's message by laughing patronizingly. He wasn't the kind of person who needed the church or any kind of religion, he would say. He belonged to a lodge, the chief function of which was to do good works. He was active in that lodge and lived up to its high moral principles. If he ever met God, he felt he would be all right on the basis of his lodge associations.

Years went by, during which the man resisted all attempts by Barnhouse to explain the gospel to him.

One day word came that the man was quite ill. He had been stricken with a fatal disease and was not expected to live out the day. Barnhouse went to see him. A member of his lodge was present on what is called "the deathwatch," since no member of the lodge was supposed to be allowed to die alone. This lodge member was seated across the room from the bed on which the other was dying. He was reading a newspaper. As Barnhouse entered, the replacement for this man also entered the room, and the shift was changed. The first man got up and left; the second took his place.

Barnhouse realized that the situation was desperate and decided on a bold course of action. He sat down by the bed and spoke along these lines: "You don't mind my staying here for a few minutes and watching you, do you? I have often wondered what it would be like for a person to die without Jesus Christ. I have known you for quite a few years, and you have always said that you do not need Christ and that your lodge obligations are enough. I would like to observe a person end his life with those beliefs and see what it is like."

The man on the bed was struck through the heart. He looked at Barnhouse like a wounded animal. "You . . . wouldn't . . . mock . . . a dying man . . . would you?" he said.

Barnhouse then asked his diagnostic question. "You are going to appear before God in a very short while. Suppose he asks you, 'What right do you have to come into my heaven?' What will you say?"

This time the man looked back in agonized silence, and great tears flowed from his frightened eyes and down his pale, wrinkled cheeks. Then, while he listened attentively, Barnhouse told him how he might approach God through the merits of the Lord Jesus Christ. The man replied that his mother had taught him those truths as a child but that he had abandoned them. He had lived without faith. But now, in his final moments on earth, he came back to God through Jesus Christ, confessed his faith in Christ and then had someone call his family members so he might give his newfound testimony to them. He asked Barnhouse to tell his story at his funeral, which took place a few days later.

You must clearly understand this. No one is going to be justified before the bar of God's justice on the basis of his or her good works, however great they may be. Your record will not save you. It is your record that has gotten you into trouble in the first place. Your record will condemn you. The only way anyone will ever be saved is by faith in Jesus Christ, who paid the penalty of our misdeeds for us and, in place of our misdeeds, offers us the gift of his own great righteousness.

"Not a Thing to Say"

The second answer that can be given to Barnhouse's question involves our text in Romans, but it, too, is connected with a story. One summer Barnhouse was crossing the Atlantic by ship, and about the second or third day out, which was a Sunday, he preached for the passengers. This led to several fruitful conversations, one with a young woman who was a professor of languages at one of the eastern colleges. In the course of their conversation Barnhouse asked his question: "If this ship should suddenly suffer some great catastrophe and sink to the bottom of the sea and we died, and if, when you appeared before God, he should ask you, 'What right do you have to come into my heaven?' what would you say?"

The woman answered, "Why, I wouldn't have a thing to say."

Barnhouse replied, "You are quoting Romans 3:19." She didn't know what he meant, so he opened his Bible and showed the verse to her: "Now we know that whatever the law says, it says to those who are under the law, so that every mouth may be silenced and the whole world held accountable to God." He explained that she had said it in American idiom: "I wouldn't have a thing to say." God had said, "Every mouth [will] be silenced." But it is the same thing. At God's judgment no one will be able to offer any good works as grounds for his or her justification or proffer any valid excuses for bad conduct. All mouths will be made mute, and everyone will know that he or she is guilty and deserves God's just condemnation.

The reason, of course, is that this is *God's* judgment. The person we must appear before is *God.* We do not have the same experiences when we appear before mere men or answer before a mere earthly tribunal.

Here we have trials by our peers. But our peers are like us. They are also sinful. Frequently juries excuse bad behavior.

Not even judges are always entirely upright in their decisions. In some cases they can be bribed. Or they simply make mistakes.

Moreover, human law is inexact and imperfect. It has loopholes. We can plead extenuating circumstances. And even if we lose our case, we can generally appeal to a higher court and to a court beyond that. If we finally exhaust our legal options and perhaps are sent to prison, we can still carry on our efforts at self-vindication. We can write letters. We can write a book. We can argue. We can refuse to be silenced.

Ah, but before God every mouth will be silenced! Then we will all know that we are not righteous and that there is not a word that can be spoken in our defense.

As evidence for this statement I bring forward the experience of the saints. Surely, if anyone could stand before God and be able to speak in his or her own defense, it would be an upright biblical character. But this is not what we find such people doing. Whenever a biblical "hero" has a glimpse of God's glory, the result is not a loosing of the tongue but a feeling of utter worthlessness before God—and of silence.

Job is an example. Job wanted answers to an important question: Why do the righteous suffer? His friends had no satisfactory answers, although Job discussed the options with them at length. But when at last God spoke, revealing himself to Job and asking a series of probing questions that go on and on in the book that bears Job's name (chapters 38–41), Job was overcome with confusion and answered:

> "I am unworthy—how can I reply to you?
> I put my hand over my mouth.
> I spoke once, but I have no answer—
> twice, but I will say no more."
> Job 40:4–5

Job was silenced.

Isaiah had the same experience. When God revealed himself to Isaiah in the great vision recorded in chapter 6 of his prophecy, Isaiah replied, "Woe to me! I am ruined! For I am a man of unclean lips, and I live among a people of unclean lips, and my eyes have seen the King, the LORD Almighty" (v. 5). How interesting that Isaiah's response focused on his lips and the lips of his people! He recognized that anything he might say was unworthy, unclean, sinful. He was silenced. He said no more. It was only after God sent a seraph with a coal from the altar to purge his lips that Isaiah was freed to speak again and obey the command to take God's message to God's people.

When Habakkuk had a revelation of God, he testified:

> I heard and my heart pounded,
> my lips quivered at the sound;
> Decay crept into my bones,
> and my legs trembled.
> Habakkuk 3:16

Habakkuk's lips trembled, but no sound came out.

Even John, the beloved disciple of the Lord, when he saw the risen Christ in that awesome vision recorded in the first chapter of Revelation, had no words for him. Instead, he fell at Christ's feet "as though dead" and did not move until Jesus placed his hand upon him and performed something like a physical resurrection (Rev. 1:17).

In his treatment of our text Barnhouse suggests that if there will be any words spoken before the bar of God by those who have rejected the grace of God in this life and are being sent to outer darkness forever, it will be—not excuses—but a resentful acknowledgment of the truth of God and the justice of their own condemnation.

They will cry, "It was all true, God. I was wrong. I knew I was wrong when I made my excuses. But I hated and still hate the principle of righteousness by the blood of Christ. I must admit that those despised Christians were right who bowed before you and acknowledged their dependence on you. I hated their songs of faith then, and I hate them now. They were right, and I hated them because they were right and because they belonged to you. I wanted my own way. I still want my own way. I want heaven, but I want heaven without you. I want heaven with myself on the throne. That is what I want, and I do not want anything else and never, never will want anything other than heaven with myself on the throne. I want my own way. And now I am going to the place of desire without fulfillment, of lust without satisfaction, or wanting without having, of wishing but never getting, of looking but never seeing, and I hate, I hate, I hate, because I want my own way. I hate you for not letting me have my way. I hate, I hate. . . ."

Their voices will drift off into outer nothingness, and there will be silence at last.[1]

The Only Saving Answer

It is clear from what I have been saying that the only *saving* answer to the question being posed—"What right do you have to come into God's heaven?"—focuses not on the works of the sinner, but on the achievements of Jesus Christ. If we are to be saved, it will not be on the basis of anything we have ever done or can do, but solely on the basis of what he has done for us. Christ died for us. He suffered in our place. He bore the punishment of our sins. All who come to God on that basis and with that answer will be saved. No others will be. Only those who come to God trusting in the Lord Jesus Christ will enter heaven.

Some years ago there was an Arthur Murray dance instructor who had been out late on a Saturday evening. In the wee hours of the morning he staggered back to his hotel room, fell into bed, and went to sleep. The next morning he was suddenly jolted awake by his clock radio. A man was speaking, and he was asking this question: "If in the next few moments some great disaster should happen and you should be killed and if you should find yourself before God and he should ask you, 'What right do you have to come into my heaven?' what would you say?"

The dance instructor was amazed and confounded by this question. He had never heard a question like that before. He realized that he did not have an answer. He had not a single thing to say. His mouth, filled with

1. Barnhouse tells the foregoing stories in Donald Grey Barnhouse, *God's Wrath: Exposition of Bible Doctrines, Taking the Epistle to the Romans as a Point of Departure*, vol. 2, Romans 2:1–3:20 (Grand Rapids: Wm. B. Eerdmans, 1953), in the study "Silence Before God," pp. 263–273.

empty words just hours before, was suddenly stopped. He sat silently on the edge of his bed while Barnhouse—he was the preacher on that radio program—explained the answer to him.

That dance instructor was D. James Kennedy, now pastor of the Coral Ridge Presbyterian Church in Fort Lauderdale, Florida, and author of the popular witnessing and evangelism program known as "Evangelism Explosion." Kennedy believed on Jesus Christ that day in his hotel room, and the question that had been used to save him became the chief tool in his evangelism strategy. Since that day many thousands of people have come to Christ through his program.

What Is *Your* Answer?

I end by asking that same question of you. Someday you will die. You will face God, and he will say to you, "What right do you have to come into my heaven?" What will your response be?

Perhaps you will say, "Well, here is my record. I know that I have done some bad things, but I have done a lot of good things, too. I want you to look at these and see if they are not enough for me to have deserved heaven. Add it up. All I want from you is justice." If you say that, justice is exactly what you will get. You will be judged for your sin and be condemned. Your good works, however fine they may seem in your sight or even in the sight of other people, will not save you. For, as we have seen, God has said:

> "There is no one righteous, not even one;
> there is no one who understands,
> no one who seeks God.
> All have turned away,
> they have together become worthless;
> there is no one who does good,
> not even one."

No one will be declared righteous in God's sight by the law of good works, for it is by the law that "we become conscious of sin" (Rom. 3:20).

Perhaps you will not plead your good works, but instead will stand before God silenced. This is better. At least you will have recognized that your goodness is not adequate before God. You will know you are a sinner. But it is still a most pitiful position to be in: silent before the one great Judge of the universe, with no possibility of making a defense, no possibility of urging extenuating circumstances, no hope of escaping condemnation.

So what will you say? I trust you will be able to answer—I hope this study had helped you to the point of being able to answer, if you have not come to it already—"My right to heaven is the Lord Jesus Christ. He died for me. He took the punishment for my sin. He is my right to heaven, because he has become my righteousness."

39

None Justified by Good Works

Romans 3:20

Therefore no one will be declared righteous in his sight by observing the law; rather, through the law we become conscious of sin.

In the New International Version of Romans, the word *therefore* has already occurred two times: once in Romans 1:24, where Paul speaks of God's having given mankind up to its wickedness ("Therefore God gave them over . . ."), and once in Romans 2:1, where he speaks to the morally sensitive but unbelieving person ("You, therefore, have no excuse . . ."). However, in the Greek manuscripts, the proper and strongest word for "therefore" (*dioti*) occurs for the first time in Romans 3:20, which is our text. *Dioti* literally means "on account of which thing" (*dia ho ti*). So it is appropriate that it is found here, where it marks a conclusion based on all that has been said in the first major section of Paul's letter.

From Romans 1:18, where the argument began, and up to this point, Paul has been proving that the entire race lies under the just condemnation of God for its wickedness. His argument is an all-embracing negative, which precedes the even greater positive statements of Romans 3:21 and what is to follow. How is this great argument summarized? Quite simply. Paul says that no one will be saved by good works: "Therefore no one will be declared righteous in [God's] sight by observing the law; rather, through the law we become conscious of sin."

But why? Why is it that no one will be saved by good works? If not the utterly immoral person, why not at least the virtuous pagan or the religious Jew? Why not you? Why not me? Paul's answer takes us back over the chief points of the preceding chapters.

Wrath: The Rejection of God

The first plank in Paul's argument is one we have already looked at several times in various forms. It is that, far from pursuing God and trying to please him (which is what most of us mistakenly think we are doing), the entire race is actually trying to get away from God and is resisting him as intensely and thoroughly as possible. You remember from our previous studies how Paul says that we "suppress" the truth about God, much of which is revealed even in nature, not to mention the written revelation of God, which is the Bible. But because we do not want to serve a deity who is like the One we know is there—the God who is sovereign over his creation, altogether holy, omniscient, and immutable—we suppress the truth about this true God and try to construct substitute gods to take his place. And, says Paul, "The wrath of God is being revealed from heaven against all [this] godlessness and wickedness" of mankind (Rom. 1:18).

"But what about the good things human beings do?" asks someone. "You can't deny that people are often kind and helpful to one another or go out of their way for others. Don't these things count for anything?"

Let me answer this question by an illustration from a book by Robert M. Horn, a staff member of British InterVarsity (the Universities and Colleges Christian Fellowship). It is entitled *Go Free! The Meaning of Justification*, and the illustration is borrowed in turn from a book by Loraine Boettner (*The Reformed Doctrine of Predestination*), who borrowed it from W. D. Smith (*What Is Calvinism?*).[1] These writers imagine a sailing ship manned by a crew of pirates. The pirates are on good terms with one another. They work hard at their jobs, are honest among themselves (according to a certain "pirate code"), help one another, and even defend one another. Their hard work really is hard work. Their kindness to each other really is kindness. But all these "good" actions are also and at the same time "bad" or wrong behavior, because they are aimed at maintaining themselves in violation of international maritime law. Their good deeds are highly selective; they do not help everyone, only themselves or those like themselves. They actually rob, maim, and murder many other people. And even their kindnesses to each other grow out of their rebellion, expressing and actually reinforcing it.

1. Robert M. Horn, *Go Free! The Meaning of Justification* (Downers Grove, Ill.: InterVarsity Press, 1976), pp. 16, 17. See Loraine Boettner, *The Reformed Doctrine of Predestination* (Grand Rapids: Wm. B. Eerdmans, 1932, 1960), pp. 69, 70.

Here is a more modern example. Some years ago Mario Puzo wrote a book called *The Godfather*, which later became a movie, and a sequel to the movie. The book was a study of the so-called Mafia, the powerful crime families who control much of the illegal gambling, prostitution, drug dealing, and other criminal activity in America and other parts of the world. This book and the films based on it showed the tremendous violence exerted by these crime families to achieve their goals. But what made the violence particularly shocking is that it seemed to exist alongside tender and otherwise noble feelings and actions of these figures. Mafia dons are often quite kindly family men. They love their wives and children. They are loyal to each other. They defend each other. In fact, they are ruthless in righting a wrong done to a member of their own crime family. Ah, but they are still crime-oriented, and the structure and ethical code of the family is created only to enhance their own well-being in violation of the law and at the expense of other people.

That parallels our situation in respect to mankind's universal rebellion against God. We may do good things (at least "good" as they appear to us), but our good is actually bad, because it is designed to maintain our rebellion against the only sovereign God and his laws.

No Excuse: God's Law Broken

The second reason why no one will be declared righteous in God's sight by observing the law is that no one actually does observe it. This is the explanation of the apparent contradiction between Romans 2:13, which says that "it is those who obey the law who will be declared righteous," and Romans 3:20, which says that "no one will be declared righteous in [God's] sight by observing the law." Both are true because, although anyone who perfectly obeys the law would be declared righteous—the righteousness of God requires it—in point of fact no one actually does this; rather, all disobey God's law.

At this point Paul speaks in almost identical terms to both the Jew, who actually possessed the revealed law of God, and to the Gentile, who did not possess it. To the Jew he says, "You who preach against stealing, do you steal? You who say that people should not commit adultery, do you commit adultery? You who abhor idols, do you rob temples? You who brag about the law, do you dishonor God by breaking the law? As it is written: 'God's name is blasphemed among the Gentiles because of you'" (Rom. 2:21b–24). The point of these statements is that the laws these religious people broke are in their Scriptures. In fact, they are from the very heart of the Old Testament, the Ten Commandments given to Moses on Mount Sinai. It is the Ten Commandments that say, "You shall have no other gods before me" (Exod. 20:3), "You shall not commit adultery" (v. 14), and "You shall not steal" (v. 15). These were laws of which the Jews were most proud. But they had broken them, as indeed all human beings have.

It is exactly the same idea in the case of the Gentile. The Gentile of Paul's day, the Greek or Roman of the first century, did not have the Old Testament law for the most part (though some did). But Gentiles had a code of ethics of their own. They knew that they should do good. They knew that they should seek the prosperity of other human beings. They knew that stealing and all other harmful practices were wrong. But they did bad things all the same, just as we do! Paul tells the Gentile, "You, therefore, have no excuse, you who pass judgment on someone else, for at whatever point you judge the other, you are condemning yourself, because you who pass judgment do the same things" (Rom. 2:1).

This means that whenever we are offended at another person's actions, as we frequently are, we condemn ourselves before God. For what we find blameworthy in another, we also do. Is a person rude to you and are you offended? If so, your reaction condemns you, since you are often rude to other people. Are you angry when someone takes unfair advantage of you? You are right to be angry; a violation of fairness is wrong. But you still condemn yourself, because you are also unfair to others. You may not always admit it, but it is true. Whatever standard you raise by which you approve one set of actions and disapprove another set of actions in others—that very standard condemns you, because you cannot and do not live up to it.

So the second reason why no one will be declared righteous by observing the law is that no one actually does observe it. We fail to observe even the tiniest part, and we certainly do not observe the whole!

The Actual Case: Great Wickedness

The third reason why no one will be declared righteous in God's sight by observing the law is that, far from observing the law (or even trying to observe the law), we are all actually violating the law in every conceivable way and on every possible occasion and are therefore actively, consistently, thoroughly, and intentionally wicked.

This is the meaning of the two long lists of descriptive vices found in Romans 1:29–31 and Romans 3:10–18. Apart from these lists, a person might reluctantly admit that at least at times he or she breaks even the lowest possible standard for decent behavior and might say, "I do not pretend to be able to do even a single right thing all the time or in every possible situation." But that is a far cry from admitting that one is thoroughly wicked in God's sight. And as long as a person is unwilling to admit that, there is always the feeling that somehow (regardless of the person's admitted shortcomings) the good that a person does will be acknowledged by God, and justification by good works will at least become possible.

But look at how God sees human beings: "They have become filled with every kind of wickedness, evil, greed and depravity. They are full of envy, murder, strife, deceit and malice. They are gossips, slanderers, God-haters, insolent, arrogant and boastful; they invent ways of doing evil; they disobey their parents; they are senseless, faithless, heartless, ruthless" (Rom. 1:29–31). It is from this viewpoint that Paul declares:

> As it is written:
>> "There is no one righteous, not even one;
>>> there is no one who understands,
>>> no one who seeks God.
>> All have turned away,
>>> they have together become worthless;
>> there is no one who does good,
>>> not even one."
>> "Their throats are open graves;
>>> their tongues practice deceit."
>> "The poison of vipers is on their lips."
>>> "Their mouths are full of cursing and bitterness."
>> "Their feet are swift to shed blood;
>>> ruin and misery mark their ways,
>> and the way of peace they do not know."
>>> "There is no fear of God before their eyes."
>>>> Romans 3:10–18

These verses do not mean that every human being has done every bad thing possible, but they do mean that the human race is like this. We are members of that human race, and, if the truth be told, the potential for every possible human vice is in everyone. We may not get a chance to murder someone. We may not even be tempted to do so. But given due provocation, right circumstances, and the removal of the societal restraints provided to limit murderous acts, we are all capable of murder and will murder, just as others have. So also with God's other commandments.

It is because of this inward potential that Scripture says, "The LORD saw how great man's wickedness on the earth had become, and that every inclination of the thoughts of his heart was only evil all the time" (Gen. 6:5).

Circumcision: No Substitutes

The fourth reason why no one will be declared righteous before God by observing the law is that God is concerned with true or actual observance—that is, with the attitudes and actions of the heart—and not with any outward acts that appear pious but actually mean nothing.

The chief example of this wrongheaded attempt at justification is the faith that certain people have placed in circumcision. This was not a case of simple pagan superstition or of the mere traditions of the elders, because the rite of circumcision was prescribed for Israel by God in the Old Testament. It was a rite given to Abraham, who was to circumcise all the males in his household and pass on this rite to those who were their descendants (Gen. 17:9–14). Circumcision was to be a mark of membership in the

special chosen family of God's people. This was such an important requirement that later in Jewish history we find a scene in which God was dis-
pleased with Moses and was about to kill him, evidently because he had
neglected to circumcise his own son. He was saved only when Zipporah, his
wife, performed the rite for him (Exod. 4:24–26).

Circumcision is neither extra-biblical nor unimportant. It was an important rite, just as baptism, the observance of the Lord's Supper, church membership, and similar religious practices are important today. But the error of
the Jew (and the error of many contemporary Christians) is in thinking that
a person can be declared righteous before God by these things. That is not
possible. Sacraments do have value once one is justified; that is, they are
valuable signs of something that has occurred internally (if it has occurred
internally), and they are meant to remind us of that experience and
strengthen it. But no one can be saved by circumcision or by any other
external religious act.

Paul writes, "Circumcision has value if you observe the law, but if you
break the law, you have become as though you had not been circumcised. . . .
A man is not a Jew if he is only one outwardly, nor is circumcision merely
outward and physical. No, a man is a Jew if he is one inwardly; and circumcision is circumcision of the heart, by the Spirit, not by the written code"
(Rom. 2:25, 28–29a).

"But circumcision is commanded in the law!" says the Jew.

True, but not as a means by which a man or a woman can be justified.

"But aren't we commanded to be baptized?" asks the Christian.

Yes, but as an outward sign of a prior, inward faith. It is not baptism that
saves us, but God who works in us inwardly.

"But aren't we told to observe the Lord's Supper?" the believer wonders.

Yes, if we have been justified by faith in him whose death the communion service signifies. But to eat the bread, which signifies the Lord's
broken body, and drink the wine, which signifies the Lord's shed blood,
without faith in him is to eat and drink condemnation to oneself (1 Cor.
11:29).

God is not taken in by mere externals. There are no substitutes for faith.

The Law's Good Function

I come back to our text, which says that "no one will be declared righteous in his sight by observing the law; rather, through the law we become
conscious of sin." We have been looking at the first part of this sentence,
the negative, and we have gone back over the opening section of Romans to
see why this great negative is true.

Yet this is only one part of the sentence. The first part of the sentence
makes this definite negative statement, declaring that no one will be
declared righteous by observing God's law. It tells us what the law cannot
do. By contrast, the second half of the sentence contains a great positive

statement, telling us that, although the law is unable to justify anybody, all of us being sinners, it is nevertheless able to show where we fall short of God's standards and thus point us to the Lord Jesus Christ, in whom alone God provides salvation.

J. B. Phillips is an Englishman who has written a very lively paraphrase of the New Testament, called *The New Testament in Modern English*. Because he is an Englishman and not an American, Phillips has occasionally used British terms for concepts that would be described in an entirely different way by Americans. Therefore, for Americans at least, Phillips throws new light on key passages. This is true of Romans 3:20. In England what we call a ruler or yardstick is called a straightedge. So when Phillips came to this verse and wanted to show what the law does for us (even though the law is not a means by which we can be justified), he paraphrased the text by writing, "'No man can justify himself before God' by a perfect performance of the Law's demands—indeed it is the straightedge of the Law that shows us how crooked we are."

Apart from God's law we may consider ourselves to be quite upright, model citizens who are fit candidates for heaven. But when we look into the law closely we soon see that we are not fit candidates at all. We are not upright. We are morally crooked. And we discover that if we are to become acceptable to the only upright, holy God, we must be changed by him.

One commentator has compared the law of God to a mirror. What happens when you look into a mirror? You see yourself, don't you? And what happens if your face is dirty and you look into a mirror? The answer is that you see that you should wash your dirty face. Does the mirror clean your face? No. The mirror's function is to drive you to the soap and water that will clean you up.

With that analogy in mind, let me give you a verse written by Robert Herrick, an English poet who lived about the time of William Shakespeare. It uses an image drawn from classical mythology in which the great Greek hero Hercules was sent to perform what was thought to be an impossible task: to clean up the immense, filthy stables of King Augeas. Comparing his heart to those stables, Herrick wrote:

> Lord, I confess that thou alone art able
> To purify this Augean stable.
> Be the seas water and the lands all soap,
> Yet if thy blood not wash me, there's no hope.

That is it exactly. If you are placing your hope in your supposed ability to keep God's law or even just in your ability to do certain good things, your case is most hopeless. Your heart needs cleansing, and no effort of your own can ever cleanse it.

Where will you find cleansing? You will find it only in Christ, to whom the law drives you. William Cowper, an eighteenth-century poet, found cleansing there and wrote:

> There is a fountain filled with blood,
> Drawn from Immanuel's veins;
> And sinners, plunged beneath that flood,
> Lose all their guilty stains.
>
> The dying thief rejoiced to see
> That fountain in his day;
> And there have I, as vile as he,
> Washed all my sins away.

I trust you also have found cleansing where Robert Herrick, William Cowper, and so many others have found it. The apostle Peter declared, "Salvation is found in no one else, for there is no other name under heaven given to men by which we must be saved" (Acts 4:12).

PART FOUR

God's Remedy in Christ

40

But Now . . .

Romans 3:21

But now a righteousness from God, apart from law, has been made known, to which the Law and the Prophets testify.

For two and a half chapters of Romans (and thirty-nine of these studies), we have been looking at the sad story of the ruin of the race because of sin. Now we reach a new and glorious point in Paul's letter. Instead of reviewing the grim story of sin and God's wrath, we turn with relief to the wonderful news of God's great grace to sinners through the Lord Jesus Christ.

Understanding the Bible depends in no small measure on understanding the Bible's main words—words like *justification, redemption, faith, substitution, obedience, grace,* and many others. No one can claim really to understand the Bible unless he or she knows something about the meaning of these terms. But it is also the case that understanding the Bible sometimes depends on what we might be inclined to think of as less important words. I think of the "so" in John 3:16, for instance: "For God *so* loved the world that he gave his one and only Son. . . ." What does "so" mean? To ask that question and answer it, we must go deeper into the meaning of this most popular verse than we might at first have thought possible.

339

We come to two such words at the beginning of Romans 3:21: "But now"!

What tremendous words they are! One expositor calls them "the great turning point" in God's dealings with the human race, and a turning point in the letter.[1] Another calls them "God's great 'nevertheless' in the face of man's failure."[2] If we had not studied the first two and a half chapters of Romans carefully, we would not be in a position to appreciate these words, because the change they speak of would not seem to be a change at all. With no understanding of the past, we can never appreciate the present.

But now we can! We have studied the past. Therefore these two words become for us a cry of great joy and a paean of victory.

The Turning Point

Where should we begin? The obvious place is with the word *now*, which indicates that there has been a change in time or in history. Before, something bad had existed. *Now* that has changed.

The contrast between "then" and "now" is a very great one for Paul, as a careful study of his writings shows. The reason is plain. The change between a past sad state of affairs and a glorious present state is one that Paul had himself experienced. It occurred on the Damascus road. Before that event, Paul had been an enemy of Jesus Christ and of his followers. He had been trying to get rid of them, and he thought he was doing right, as fanatics generally do. But the future apostle was actually in great darkness, ignorant of God and opposed to him. It was on the road to Damascus that Jesus appeared to Paul, revealing himself as the Son of God, the one whom Paul was persecuting. In that moment the scales fell from Paul's eyes, the truth of heaven broke in upon his darkened heart, flooding it with new light, and he turned from his old life of pride, prejudice, and persecution to a new life of serving Christ and his gospel. Like the blind man who had been healed by Jesus, Paul could now say, "One thing I know. I was blind *but now* I see!" (cf. John 9:25).

In his letter to the Philippians, Paul puts this change in theological language but with precisely this emphasis: "If anyone else thinks he has reasons to put confidence in the flesh, I have more: circumcised on the eighth day, of the people of Israel, of the tribe of Benjamin, a Hebrew of the Hebrews; in regard to the law, a Pharisee; as for zeal, persecuting the church; as for legalistic righteousness, faultless. *But* whatever was to my profit I *now* consider loss for the sake of Christ. What is more I consider everything a loss

1. D. M. Lloyd-Jones, *Romans: An Exposition of Chapters 3:20–4:25, Atonement and Justification* (Grand Rapids: Zondervan, 1970), p. 23.

2. Ray C. Stedman, *From Guilt to Glory*, vol. 1, *Hope for the Helpless* (Portland: Multnomah Press, 1978), p. 87.

compared to the surpassing greatness of knowing Christ Jesus my Lord . . ."
(Phil. 3:4–8, italics mine).

Meeting Jesus on the way to Damascus, in the midst of his campaign to arrest and kill Christians, made all the difference between life and death for the apostle.

From Wrath to Righteousness

Yet, in the context of his letter to the Romans, Paul speaks of this great temporal or historical change not so much as something that occurred to him personally but as something that God had done to provide for the salvation of the race. If God had not done this, our present condition and future prospects would be bleak. They would be only what we have already found in Romans 1:18 through 3:20. We would be under wrath, in spiritual and moral decline, and without any possibility of helping or saving ourselves by human righteousness. We would be, as Paul said of the Ephesians in their unregenerate state, "without hope and without God in the world" (Eph. 2:12b). *But now* things are different. There is hope because of what the Lord Jesus Christ has accomplished. The incarnation, life, death, and resurrection of Jesus have changed everything.

What specifically has changed? Paul's use of "now" in this and other texts suggests changes in the following areas:

1. *Wrath and righteousness.* The first change is the one most obvious from our text. When Paul says, "But now a righteousness from God, apart from law, has been made known," it is clear that he is contrasting this with the earlier declaration: "The wrath of God is being revealed from heaven against all the godlessness and wickedness of men . . ." (Rom. 1:18). Before, the wrath of God was being revealed against us. *Now* the righteousness of God is made known.

Several weeks before writing this sermon, I was preaching to a gathering of missionaries in southern France, and one of my messages was on Genesis 3, the story of the fall of our first parents. I said in the course of that message that when God clothed Adam and Eve with the skins of animals, this was a picture (which they no doubt clearly understood) of the way in which God would one day clothe with Christ's righteousness all who would believe on the Lord Jesus Christ. When I finished, an older missionary expressed appreciation for the emphasis on being clothed with Christ's righteousness, saying, "We don't hear that often enough; it is an important teaching."

I agreed that it was certainly an important teaching. But there is a sense in which teaching about the wrath of God is almost as important. If we do not understand that apart from Jesus Christ we are under God's wrath and destined for an eternity of judgment, we can hardly appreciate the greatness of what God has done for us in providing salvation through Christ's atonement.

People in our day generally think that they are on great terms with God or that, if they are not, it is only because God is a bit out of sorts and peevish—though he will probably get over it. That is not the case at all. On the contrary, the case is as Paul presents it in the first chapter of Romans. We have rejected God, suppressing the truth about him in spite of the fact that God has revealed it to us; as a result, God is already in the process of unleashing his wrath. He has given us up to the consequences of our sin. In Romans 1:29–31, Paul describes the end of this abandonment. There is "every kind of wickedness, evil, greed and depravity." He says that people are "full of envy, murder, strife, deceit and malice. They are gossips, slanderers, God-haters, insolent, arrogant and boastful; they invent ways of doing evil; they disobey their parents; they are senseless, faithless, heartless, ruthless." These things are an expression of what happens to the human race when God displays his wrath by abandoning us to our own evil devices.

How are we to escape from such captivity? In ourselves we cannot. "*But now,*" says Paul, in place of wrath "a righteousness from God has been made known." This is the one single way of salvation from the wrath to which our sin has subjected us. But thank God there is this one way.

2. *Condemnation and justification.* The second change is from condemnation to justification. This is evident from the continuation of Romans 3, where Paul writes, "There is no difference, for all have sinned and fall short of the glory of God, and are justified freely by his grace . . ." (vv. 22b–24). Yet it is not only here that we see this truth; nor do these verses necessarily present it in the strongest language. Think rather of Romans 8:1: "Therefore, there is *now* no condemnation for those who are in Christ Jesus," and Romans 5:9, which declares, "Since we have *now* been justified by his blood. . . ."

Most people do not think of themselves as being under condemnation, obviously because the sentence hanging over them has not yet been fully executed. They are alive and well. They expect to remain so. Nevertheless, they are still under condemnation and will perish eventually. Jesus said this clearly: "For God did not send his Son into the world to condemn the world, but to save the world through him. Whoever believes in him is not condemned, but whoever does not believe stands condemned already because he has not believed in the name of God's one and only Son. This is the verdict: Light has come into the world, but men loved darkness instead of light because their deeds were evil" (John 3:17–19). These words are a close parallel to what Paul says about human beings suppressing the truth about God in their wickedness. They are already under wrath.

But now, because of Christ's work, there can be justification rather than condemnation. There is justification "through the redemption that came by Christ Jesus" (Rom. 3:24).

3. *Bondage and freedom.* Sin does not only bring us under God's just wrath and condemnation. It also enslaves us so that we cannot live truly good lives. Yet things can be different. In Romans 7:6 Paul uses those two important words again: "*But now,* by dying to what once bound us, we have been released from the law so that we serve in the new way of the Spirit, and not in the old way of the written code" (italics mine). This is a very important matter, which we will look into in detail later in these studies. But the chief point is that, although apart from Christ we are under law but unable to keep it since we are bound by sin, being united to Christ by the Holy Spirit delivers us from bondage and enables us to live holy lives.

Paul says this earlier when he writes, "But now that you have been set free from sin and have become slaves to God, the benefit you reap leads to holiness, and the result is eternal life" (Rom. 6:22).

4. *Exclusion and participation.* The final contrast is one Gentiles should particularly appreciate. Paul expresses it best in writing to the Ephesians, saying, "But now in Christ Jesus you who once were far away have been brought near through the blood of Christ" (Eph. 2:13).

Paul never forgot that—although Jews need Christ just as much as Gentiles need him, for no one, either Jew or Gentile, can be saved apart from faith in Jesus—the Jews of his day nevertheless had great spiritual advantages that non-Jews did not possess. They had "the adoption as sons . . . the divine glory, the covenants, the receiving of the law, the temple worship and the promises," as Paul observes in Romans 9:4. Gentiles were cut off from these things. Nevertheless, those who had been excluded from this earthly citizenship had *now* come together with believing Jews into a new relationship. "Consequently," Paul says, "you are no longer foreigners and aliens, but fellow citizens with God's people and members of God's household" (Eph. 2:19).

A New But Ancient Gospel

I have been claiming that the words "but now" indicate that something new has come into the world in terms of a believing person's relationship to God. Yet I need to say also that, although this is true in one sense—something new actually happened in history through the work of Christ—there is another sense in which this is not "new" at all, but is rather only an expression of the same plan through which God had been saving people since the beginning of the world. It is new in a historical sense, but as the way of salvation it has always existed in the mind of God. Paul says this explicitly in 2 Timothy 1:9b–10, where he writes, "This grace was given us in Christ Jesus before the beginning of time, but it has now been revealed through the appearing of our Savior. . . ."

Paul makes this same point in Romans 3:21 by saying that this "righteousness from God" is something "to which the Law and the Prophets testify."

This refers to the Old Testament, of course. So we ask: Where and in what ways does the Old Testament testify to the grace that has come into the world through Jesus Christ?

It is not hard to answer that question. We think back to the earliest part of the Old Testament, which records how God came to Adam and Eve after their rebellion in eating of the forbidden tree. God pronounced a judgment on them, cursing the serpent who had brought the temptation and punishing Adam and Eve for yielding to it. But then, in the middle of these stern and frightening words, God said, speaking to the serpent: "And I will put enmity between you and the woman, and between your offspring and hers; he will crush your head, and you will strike his heel" (Gen. 3:15).

This speaks of the coming of Jesus Christ, who would be wounded by Satan. Although Satan would strike his heel, Christ would crush Satan's head, destroying Satan and his works forever. As I have pointed out elsewhere, Adam and Eve believed this prophecy and were saved by looking forward in faith to this mighty one who was to come, just as we are saved by looking back to him by the same faith.[3]

Further on in Genesis, we see God telling Abraham more about this redeemer. From the beginning he had said to Abraham that "all peoples on earth will be blessed through you" (Gen. 12:3b). But as the story unfolds we see God adding more to that initial cryptic revelation, until finally, in that magnificent account of the test by which Abraham was commanded to offer Isaac, his only son, on Mount Moriah, we learn that it was not through Abraham himself that the nations were to be blessed but through his "offspring" (Gen. 22:18). Paul would later point out that this word is singular, indicating not the whole of the descendants of Abraham, the nation of Israel, but that one special descendant who would redeem the race by dying for it (cf. Gal. 3:8, 15–16). The near sacrifice of Isaac was a striking picture of how God would one day give his only Son for us on that identical mountain.

The ceremonial law of Israel points to Jesus Christ, for he is the Lamb of God who takes away the world's sin. He fulfilled the meaning of the sacrifices. More than that, each item of the temple furnishings and each detail of the rites of Israel's worship point to him.

In the psalms we have many great words about Jesus.

Psalm 16:10 prophesies the Lord's resurrection: "You will not abandon me to the grave, nor will you let your Holy One see decay." It was quoted by Peter at Pentecost (Acts 2:27) and by Paul before the Gentiles at Pisidian Antioch (Acts 13:35).

Psalm 22 describes the crucifixion. The Lord quoted the opening lines of this prophecy while hanging on the cross (see Matt. 27:46 and parallels).

3. See James Montgomery Boice, *Genesis: An Expositional Commentary*, vol. 1, *Genesis 1:1–11:32* (Grand Rapids: Zondervan, 1982), pp. 183–188. The chapter is entitled "Living by Faith."

Psalm 23 portrays Jesus as the Good Shepherd, a theme that the Lord expounded, as recorded in John 10.

Psalm 24 describes Jesus' glorious ascension into heaven.

And what of the Old Testament prophets? The many specific references to Jesus in the prophetic books are too numerous to list. But we cannot overlook the great Suffering Servant passages of Isaiah, particularly this one:

> He was despised and rejected by men,
>   a man of sorrows and familiar with suffering.
> Like one from whom men hide their faces
>   he was despised, and we esteemed him not.
> Surely he took up our infirmities
>   and carried our sorrows,
> yet we considered him stricken by God,
>   smitten by him and afflicted.
> But he was pierced for our transgressions,
>   he was crushed for our iniquities;
> the punishment that brought us peace was upon him,
>   and by his wounds we are healed.
> We all, like sheep, have gone astray,
>   each of us has turned to his own way;
> and the LORD has laid on him
>   the iniquity of us all.
>
> Isaiah 53:3–6

These prophecies of the salvation that was to come through Jesus Christ can be multiplied hundreds if not thousands of times throughout the Old Testament.

Saying Those Words

The important thing, however, is not so much whether you understand or even know of these Old Testament prophecies, but whether the change they speak about is a reality for you. You may not know much theology. Terms like "justification," "propitiation," and "redemption" may be only vague generalities for you. But you know what your past life has been. You remember your past sins. You are aware of your failures. Is that truly a former, past state for you? Can you say, "That was true of me once. I really was like the person described in the first two and a half chapters of Romans. But that was before. Now Christ has come. He has saved me, and I have become an entirely new creature because of him"?

D. Martyn Lloyd-Jones suggests that this is one way by which you can test whether or not you are a true Christian, and by which you can reassure and strengthen yourself if you are:

When the devil attacks you and suggests to you that you are not a Christian and that you have never been a Christian because of what is still in your heart or because of what you are still doing or because of something you once did—when he comes and thus accuses you, what do you say to him? Do you agree with him? Or do you say to him: "Yes, that was true, but now . . ."? Do you hold up these words against him? Or when, perhaps, you feel condemned as you read the Scripture, as you read the Law in the Old Testament, as you read the Sermon on the Mount, and as you feel that you are undone, do you remain lying on the ground in hopelessness, or do you lift up your head and say, "But now"? This is the essence of the Christian position; this is how faith answers the accusations of the Law, the accusations of conscience and everything else that would condemn and depress us. These are indeed very wonderful words, and it is most important that we should lay hold of them and realize their tremendous importance and their real significance.[4]

Can you say those words? You can, if you trust in Jesus and his death on your behalf.

Can you say:

"Once I was blind, *but now* I see"?

"Once I was lost, *but now* I am found"?

"Once I was subject to the just wrath of God. *But now* I have been saved by Jesus, having received the gift of God's righteousness through faith in him"?

4. Lloyd-Jones, *Romans: An Exposition of Chapters 3:20–4:25*, p. 27.

41

Righteousness Apart from Law

Romans 3:21-24

But now a righteousness from God, apart from law, has been made known, to which the Law and the Prophets testify. This righteousness from God comes through faith in Jesus Christ to all who believe. There is no difference, for all have sinned and fall short of the glory of God, and are justified freely by his grace through the redemption that came by Christ Jesus.

$\mathbf{I}$n Romans 3:21–31 we are dealing with themes that are the very heart, not only of Paul's letter, but of the entire Bible and therefore of reality itself. In all life and history there is nothing more important than these teachings. But who today thinks this way? Who is willing to acknowledge this in an age when abstract thought—indeed, even thinking itself—is suspect? Who even among the masses of Christian people really appreciates what Paul is saying here? Ours is an age in which people are self-absorbed and focus on immediate gratification. We tend to evaluate any religious teaching according to its apparent relevance to our present "needs" and short-term goals.

No one can have success teaching basic truths about man and the universe unless our closed ways of thinking are changed. But, then, this has always been the case. It was no easier for the apostle Paul to preach the message of salvation to a generation that was busy entertaining itself by sex and circuses than for today's Christians to minister that same word to an age that has anesthetized itself through television.

But we must try! We must try as Paul did! We must teach the Word of God, because it is by the Word alone that God speaks to us about what really matters.

Four Great Doctrines

We have already seen how Paul introduces this section of his letter—with the words "but now." These words indicate that something of great importance has taken place, and that this is the substance of the good news being proclaimed by Paul and the other messengers of the gospel. Here is a simple outline of this teaching:

1. *God has provided a righteousness of his own for men and women, a righteousness we do not possess ourselves.* This is the very heart or theme of the Word of God. Although it is new in its fulfillment, it had nevertheless been fully prophesied in the Old Testament.

2. *This righteousness is by grace.* We do not deserve it. In fact, we are incapable ever of deserving it.

3. *It is the work of the Lord Jesus Christ in dying for his people, redeeming them from their sin, that has made this grace on God's part possible.* This is the reason for the "now" in "but now." It is because of Jesus' death that there is a Christian gospel.

4. *This righteousness that God has graciously provided becomes ours through simple faith.* Believing and trusting God in regard to the work of Jesus is the only way anyone, whether Jew or Gentile, can be saved.

The importance of these teachings will become increasingly clear in our exposition of them. But we can see their importance even at this point by noticing that they are a nearly exact repetition of what Paul has already stated as the thesis of the letter. They were stated in his opening address, for example: "Paul, a servant of Christ Jesus, called to be an apostle and set apart for the gospel of God—the gospel he promised beforehand through his prophets in the Holy Scriptures regarding his Son, who as to his human nature was a descendant of David, and who through the Spirit of holiness was declared with power to be the Son of God by his resurrection from the dead: Jesus Christ our Lord. Through him and for his name's sake, we received grace and apostleship to call people from among all the Gentiles to the obedience that comes from faith" (Rom. 1:1–5). The teachings of Romans 3:21–31 are all there. It is the same gospel.

Again, it is also what we have found in the initial statement of Paul's thesis in Romans 1:16–17: "I am not ashamed of the gospel, because it is the power of God for the salvation of everyone who believes: first for the Jew, then for the Gentile. For in the gospel a righteousness from God is revealed, a righteousness that is by faith from first to last, just as it is written: 'The righteous will live by faith.'"

So I repeat what I said at the beginning of this study: *There is nothing in all life and history that is more important than these teachings.* The issues of eternity hang on these truths, and we must be faithful to them regardless of the resistance or scorn of our contemporaries.

Objective and Subjective Genitives

We begin with the first of these four doctrines, namely, that "God has provided a righteousness of his own for men and women." You will notice, if you read the text carefully, that in Romans 3:21 the New International Version speaks of "a righteousness *from* God," while I have implied (echoing the King James Version) that this is the "righteousness *of* God," that is, suggesting that it is God's own righteousness. Which is correct? Is this a righteousness from God? Or is it the righteousness of God? And is there a difference?

The variations in translations stem from the fact that the Greek text contains a simple genitive construction, which we usually translate in English by using the word "of." But in Greek, as in English, this can be either what grammarians call a subjective genitive or an objective genitive. A subjective genitive is one in which the word following "of" is the subject or source of the idea. An example is "love of God." The phrase usually means that this is God's love. He is the source of the love and the subject of the action. A nonbiblical example is the "novels of Charles Dickens." It means that Dickens is the author of the novels. He wrote them. It does not mean that they are about him. The other type of genitive is what grammarians call an objective genitive. It refers to a situation in which the word following "of" is the object of the first word. An example might be "world of misery." This does not mean that misery is the source of the world or even the source of the world's problems but rather that the world is characterized by misery. It is a miserable world. The word *misery* functions as an adjective in this construction.

How, then, is the phrase "righteousness of God" to be interpreted? If this is a case of an objective genitive, it is a righteousness determined by God's own nature. That is, as we can also say, it is his righteousness or divine righteousness. This is what the editors of the Scofield Bible seem to have thought, for they appended a note to Romans 3:21, which reads: "The righteousness of God is all that God demands and approves, and is ultimately found in Christ himself, who fully met in our stead every requirement of the law." They support this interpretation by a reference to 1 Corinthians 1:30: "Christ . . . has become . . . our righteousness."

I find support for this idea in the text, because Paul's chief point is that the righteousness of God *has been disclosed* in the person and work of Christ.

Before, we did not have any truly adequate way of understanding what this righteousness is like. But now we do, since we can see it in the Savior.

On the other hand, if this is a subjective genitive (rather than an objective genitive), we should then understand Paul to be teaching that God is the source of this righteousness and that it is in Jesus Christ that God *makes it available to us.* The translators of the New International Version seem to have preferred this idea, for they have written: "But now a righteousness *from* God . . . has been made known."

Surely this is a case where we do not have to choose between the two ideas, for both are correct. Righteousness *is* to be seen in the Lord Jesus Christ, but it is also *his* righteousness, rather than our own, that we need. Apart from him we might compare ourselves only with one another and thus have an utterly inadequate idea of what the holy God requires. This is what Paul himself had been doing prior to his encounter with Jesus on the road to Damascus. He had compared himself with other people, even the most moral people of his day, and had concluded that there was much he could boast about: "If anyone else thinks he has reasons to put confidence in the flesh, I have more" (Phil. 3:4). But when he saw Jesus in the Damascus road vision, for the first time he came to understand what true righteousness is and learned to reckon his own good deeds as worthless. "For [his] sake," wrote Paul, "I have lost all things. I consider them rubbish, that I may gain Christ and be found in him, not having a righteousness of my own that comes from the law, but that which is through faith in Christ—the righteousness that comes from God and is by faith" (vv. 8b–9).

At the same time—it is explicitly stated in the last of those three verses from Philippians—the righteousness *of* God, which is revealed in Christ, is also a righteousness that comes to us *from* God. For if God did not give it, there is no way any of us could possibly win it for ourselves. This is another way of saying that salvation is a gift. It is the ground on which the redeemed will ascribe *all* their praise to God for saving them.

Apart from the Law

These ideas need to be held together. And they need to be remembered in everything we say both about our inability to attain righteousness by ourselves and about the way God has provided it for us through the work of Jesus Christ.

The phrase Paul uses in our text to state how the righteousness of God can *not* come to us is "apart from law." This does not mean that the law has no value, of course. The very sentence reminds us of one of its values, for it says that "the Law and the Prophets" testified to the righteousness that would come (and eventually did come) in Jesus Christ. (In our last study we looked at some of the texts that do just that.) Again, at the very end of Romans 3, we find Paul returning to the subject of the law, saying, "Do we, then, nullify the law by this faith? Not at all! Rather, we uphold the law" (v. 31). The law clearly had value in the Old Testament period and continues to have value in the Christian era.

Theologians usually speak of the function of God's law in two areas: (1) to restrain evil, much as secular law is meant to do; and (2) to reveal man's sin and thus point us to the need for Jesus Christ. These are important functions. But the one thing the law cannot do and was never meant to do was save a person by his or her observance of it.

This is why Paul speaks of a righteousness of God "apart from law" and why this announcement is such good news, although hard for unsaved people to understand or accept. The law, as Paul will say later in Romans, is "holy, righteous and good" (Rom. 7:12). If we could be saved by law, the law of God would save us. But we cannot! And it cannot! We cannot keep God's commandments. If the law is to have any benefit for us, it must be by enabling us to see our inability to satisfy the standards of God by our own efforts and thus turn us to Christ. That is why Paul says that "this righteousness from God comes [not by law but] through faith in Jesus Christ to all who believe . . ." (Rom. 3:22).

Another way of putting this is to say that when the law was given to Israel on Mount Sinai, the very books that listed these unyielding commandments of the holy God also contained instructions for the sacrifice of the lamb on the Day of Atonement. God gave the commandments, but he also gave the altar and taught the principle of substitution. It is as if he were saying, "These are my commandments; you must keep them or be lost. But I know you cannot keep them. So, rather than trusting in your ability to do what you never will be able to do, I point you to my Son, who will die for you. It is on the basis of his future work that I am giving you a righteousness you could never achieve yourselves. Trust him."

A Unique Religion

This idea is so important that I want to state it another way, showing the utter uniqueness of Christianity in this fundamental matter. Paul has said that this righteousness from God, which we need, is "apart from law," by which he means primarily "apart from the law of God given to Israel." He means, as John Murray has said in his commentary, that "in justification there is no contribution, preparatory, accessory or subsidiary, that is given by works of law."[1]

But "law" also embraces all human effort to attain righteousness, and this means that the fundamental principle of this verse (as well as of the Bible as a whole) is that God's righteousness is to be received apart from any human doing whatsoever.

1. John Murray, *The Epistle to the Romans* (Grand Rapids: Wm. B. Eerdmans, 1968), p. 109.

This is the point at which Christianity is distinguished categorically from every other human religion. All religions have their distinguishing points, of course. Some call God, the Supreme Being, by a different name. Some emphasize one path to God, some another. Some are mystical, some very ritualistic. But all, except for Christianity, suppose that there is something human beings can do for the Deity to convince him to save them. They teach a human way to achieve eternity, a man-made ladder to the bliss of the life to come. Only Christianity humbles man by insisting that there is nothing at all we can do to work out our salvation.

Of course, once we are saved we have the obligation and privilege of doing much, since Jesus calls us to discipleship. But we are not saved by such doings. All our actions can bring upon us, even the best of our actions, is the judgment from God that we deserve. Therefore, it is vitally important to examine ourselves to see if we are really trusting in Jesus and what he has done, or whether we are trusting in what we suppose we can do. Commentator Donald Barnhouse has written:

> Look into your own heart and see whether you are trusting, even in a small fraction, in something that you are doing for yourself or that you are doing for God, instead of finding in your heart that you have ceased from your works as God did from his and that you are resting on the work that was accomplished on the cross of Calvary. This is the secret of reality: Righteousness apart from law. Righteousness apart from human doing. Christianity is the faith that believes God's Word about the work that is fully done, completely done. . . .
>
> Righteousness without law. Righteousness apart from human character. Righteousness without even a consideration of the nature of the being that is made righteous. Righteousness that comes from God upon an ungodly man. Righteousness that will save a thief on the cross. Righteousness that is prepared for you. Righteousness that you must choose by abandoning any hope of salvation from anything that is in yourself. And underline this—it is the only righteousness that can produce practical righteousness in you.[2]

The *Really* Good News

When a person is first presented with this pure core of Christianity, the reaction is usually revulsion. We want to save ourselves, and anything that suggests that we cannot do so is abhorrent to us. We do not want a religion that demands that we throw ourselves entirely upon the grace and mercy of God. But Christianity is not only the religion we *need* so desperately. It is also the only religion *worth having* in the long run. Let me explain.

2. Donald Grey Barnhouse, *God's Remedy: Exposition of Bible Doctrines Taking the Epistle of Romans as a Point of Departure*, vol. 3, *Romans 3:21–4:25* (Grand Rapids: Wm. B. Eerdmans, 1954), p. 12.

1. *If salvation is by the gift of God, apart from human doing, then we can be saved now.* We do not have to wait until we reach some high level of attainment or pass some undetermined future test. Many people think in these terms, because they know (if they are honest with themselves) that their lives and actions are far from what they should be now and they keep striving. But this means—I am sure you can see it—that salvation can never be a present experience but is something always in the future. It is something such persons hope to attain, though they are afraid they may not. It is only in Christianity that this future element moves into the present. And the reason it can is that salvation is not based on our ability to accumulate acceptable merits with God, but rather on what God has *already* done for us. When Jesus said on the cross, "It is finished," he meant what he said. His finished work is the sole grounds for our being declared righteous by God. And since it is a past accomplishment, salvation can be ours now, solely by the application of Christ's righteousness to us as God's gift.

This is why Paul can say, "Therefore, there is now no condemnation for those who are in Christ Jesus" (Rom. 8:1). It is also why he declared, "I tell you, now is the time of God's favor, now is the day of salvation" (2 Cor. 6:2).

It is why Joseph Hart, one of our great hymnwriters, wrote:

> Come, ye weary, heavy laden,
> Bruised and broken by the Fall;
> If you tarry till you're better,
> You will never come at all:
> Not the righteous, not the righteous,
> Sinners Jesus came to call.
>
> Let not conscience make you linger,
> Nor of fitness fondly dream;
> All the fitness he requireth
> Is to feel your need of him:
> This he gives you; this he gives you;
> 'Tis the Spirit's rising beam.

2. *If salvation is by the gift of God, apart from human doing, then salvation is certain.* If salvation is by human works, then human works (or a lack of them) can undo it. If I can save myself, I can unsave myself. I can ruin everything. But if salvation is of God from beginning to end, it is sure and unwavering simply because God is himself sure and unwavering. Since God knows the end from the beginning, nothing ever surprises him, and he never needs to alter his plans or change his mind. What he has begun he will continue, and we can be confident of that. Paul expressed this confidence in regard to the church at Philippi, saying that "he who began a good work in you will carry it on to completion until the day of Christ Jesus" (Phil. 1:6).

3. *If salvation is by the gift of God, apart from human doing, then human boasting is excluded, and all the glory in salvation goes to God.* I doubt any of us would want to be in a heaven populated by persons who got there, even in part, by their own efforts. The boasting of human beings is bad enough in this world, where all they have to boast of is their own good looks (for which they are not responsible), their money, their friends, or whatever. Imagine how offensive it would be if they were able to brag about having earned heaven: "Old Joe down there—he's in the other place—just didn't have what it takes, I suppose. He should have lived a good life, like me." Even if the only thing that determines a person's salvation is faith (thought of as something of which we *are* capable), it would still be intolerable for some people to boast of having believed, though others had refused to do so.

But it is not going to be like that! Salvation is a gift. It is receiving God's righteousness—apart from law, apart from human doing. It is, as Paul wrote to the Ephesians, "not by works, so that no one can boast" (Eph. 2:9). No one in heaven will be praising man. In heaven the glory will go to God only. *Soli deo gloria!*

Thank God it is that way.

42

Amazing Grace

Romans 3:22–24

There is no difference, for all have sinned and fall short of the glory of God, and are justified freely by his grace through the redemption that came by Christ Jesus.

In the last study I introduced four doctrines found in Romans 3:21–31: (1) God has provided a righteousness of his own for men and women, a righteousness we do not possess ourselves; (2) this righteousness is by grace; (3) it is the work of the Lord Jesus Christ in dying for his people, redeeming them from their sin, that has made this grace on God's part possible; and (4) this righteousness, which God has graciously provided, becomes ours through simple faith. We have already looked at the first of these four doctrines: the righteousness that God has made available to us apart from law. Now we will examine the second doctrine: that this righteousness becomes ours by the grace of God alone, apart from human merit.

That is the meaning of grace, of course. It is God's favor to us *apart from human merit*. Indeed, it is favor when we deserve the precise opposite. D. Martyn Lloyd-Jones has written, "There is no more wonderful word than 'grace.' It means unmerited favor or kindness shown to one who is utterly undeserving. . . . It is not merely a free gift, but a free gift to those who

355

deserve the exact opposite, and it is given to us while we are 'without hope and without God in the world.'"[1]

But how are we to do justice to this great concept today? We have too high an opinion of ourselves even to understand grace, let alone to appreciate it. We speak of it certainly. We sing, "Amazing grace—how sweet the sound—That saved a wretch like me!" But we do not think of ourselves as wretches needing to be saved. Rather, we think of ourselves as quite worthy. One teacher has said, "Amazing grace is no longer amazing to us." In our view, it is not even grace.

There Is No Difference

This is why the idea expressed in Romans 3:23 is inserted at this point. For many years, whenever I came to this verse, I had a feeling that it was somehow in the wrong place. It was not that Romans 3:23 is untrue. Obviously it is, for that is what Romans 1:18–3:20 is all about. What bothered me is that the verse did not seem to belong here. I felt that the words "there is no difference, for all have sinned and fall short of the glory of God" belonged with that earlier section. The verse seemed somehow an intrusion here, because Romans 3:21–31 is not talking about sin but about the way of salvation.

I think differently now, however. And the reason I think differently is that I now understand the connection between this verse and grace. The reason we do not appreciate grace is that we do not really believe Romans 3:23. Or, if we do, we believe it in a far lesser sense than Paul intended.

Let me use a story to explain what I mean. In his classic little book *All of Grace*, Charles Haddon Spurgeon begins with the story of a preacher from the north of England who went to call on a poor woman. He knew that she needed help. So, with money from the church in his hand, he made his way through the poor section of the city to where she lived, climbed the four flights of stairs to her tiny attic apartment, and then knocked at the door. There was no answer. He knocked again. Still no answer. He went away. The next week he saw the woman in church and told her that he knew of her need and had been trying to help her. "I called at your room the other day, but you were not home," he said.

"At what time did you call, sir?" she asked.

"About noon."

"Oh, dear," she answered. "I was home, and I heard you knocking. But I did not answer. I thought it was the man calling for the rent."[2]

This is a good illustration of grace and of our natural inability to appreciate it. But isn't it true that, although most of us laugh at this story, we unfor-

1. D. M. Lloyd-Jones, *Romans: An Exposition of Chapters 3:20–4:25, Atonement and Justification* (Grand Rapids: Zondervan, 1970), p. 57.

2. Charles Haddon Spurgeon, *All of Grace* (Chicago: Moody Press, n.d.), p. 5.

tunately also fail to identify with it? In fact, we may even be laughing at the poor woman rather than at the story, because we consider her to be in a quite different situation from ourselves. She was unable to pay the rent. We know people like that. We feel sorry for them. But we think that is not our condition. We *can* pay. We pay our bills here, and we suppose (even though we may officially deny it) that we will be able to pay something—a down payment even if not the full amount—on our outstanding balance in heaven. So we bar the door, not because we are afraid that God is coming to collect the rent, but because we fear he is coming with grace and we do not want a handout. We do not consider our situation to be desperate.

But, you see, if the first chapters of Romans have meant anything to us, they have shown that spiritually "there is no difference" between us and even the most destitute of persons. As far as God's requirements are concerned, there is no difference between us and the most desperate or disreputable character in history.

I have in my library a fairly old book entitled *Grace and Truth*, written by the Scottish preacher W. P. Mackay. Wisely, in my judgment, the first chapter of the book begins with a study of "there is no difference." I say "wisely," because, as the author shows, until we know that in God's sight there is no difference between us and even the wildest profligate, we cannot be saved. Nor can we appreciate the nature and extent of the grace needed to rescue us from our dilemma.

Mackay illustrates this point with an anecdote. Someone was once speaking to a rich English lady, stressing that every human being is a sinner. She replied with some astonishment, "But ladies are not sinners!"

"Then who are?" the person asked her.

"Just young men in their foolish days," was her reply.

When the person explained the gospel further, insisting that if she was to be saved by Christ, she would have to be saved exactly as her footman needed to be saved—by the unmerited grace of God in Christ's atonement—she retorted, "Well, then, I will not be saved!" That was her decision, of course, but it was tragic.[3]

If you want to be saved by God, you must approach grace on the basis of Romans 1:18–3:20—on the grounds of your utter ruin in sin—and not on the basis of any supposed merit in yourself.

Common Grace

It is astonishing that we should fail to understand grace, of course, because all human beings have experienced it in a general but nonsaving way, even if they are not saved or have not even the slightest familiarity with Christianity. We have experienced what theologians call "common grace," the grace that God has shown to the whole of humanity. Jesus spoke of it

3. W. P. Mackay, *Grace and Truth* (Loizeaux Brothers, n.d.), pp. 3, 4.

when he reminded his listeners that God "causes his sun to rise on the evil and the good, and sends his rain on the righteous and the unrighteous" (Matt. 5:45b).

When Adam and Eve sinned, the race came under judgment. No one deserved anything good. If God had taken Adam and Eve in that moment and cast them into the lake of fire, he would have been entirely just in doing so, and the angels could still have sung with great joy: "Holy, holy, holy is the Lord God Almighty, who was, and is, and is to come" (Rev. 4:8). Or, if God had spared Adam and Eve, allowing them to increase until there was a great mass of humanity in the world and then had brushed all people aside into everlasting torment, God would still have been just. God does not owe us anything. Consequently, the natural blessings we have are due not to our own righteousness or abilities but to common grace.

Let me try to state this clearly once more. If you are not a believer in Jesus Christ, you are still a recipient of God's common grace, whether you acknowledge it or not. If you are alive and not in hell at this moment, it is because of God's common grace. If you are in good health and not wasting away in some ward of hopeless patients in a hospital, it is because of common grace. If you have a home and are not wandering about on city streets, it is because of God's grace. If you have clothes to wear and food to eat, it is because of God's grace. The list could be endless. There is no one living who has not been the recipient of God's common grace in countless ways. So, if you think that it is not by grace but by your merits alone that you possess these blessings, you show your ignorance of spiritual matters and disclose how far you are from God's kingdom.

Unmerited Grace

But it is not common grace that Paul is referring to in our Romans text, important as common grace is. It is the specific, saving grace of God in salvation, which is not "common" (in the sense that all persons experience it regardless of their relationship to God), but rather is a gift received only by some through faith in Jesus Christ, apart from merit.

This is the point we need chiefly to stress, of course, for it takes us back to the story of the preacher's visit to the poor woman and reminds us that the reason we do not appreciate grace is that we think we deserve it. We do not deserve it! If we did, it would not be grace. It would be our due, and we have already seen that the only thing rightly due us in our sinful condition is a full outpouring of God's just wrath and condemnation. So I say again: *Grace is apart from good works.* Grace is apart from merit. We should be getting this by now, because each of the blessings enumerated in this great chapter of Romans is apart from works, law, or merit—which are only various ways of saying the same thing.

The righteousness of God, which is also *from* God, is apart from works.

Grace, which is the source of that righteousness, is apart from works.

Redemption, which makes grace possible, is apart from works.

Justification is apart from works.

Salvation from beginning to end is apart from works. In other words, it is free. This must have been the chief idea in Paul's mind when he wrote these verses, for he emphasizes the matter by repeating it. He says that we are "justified *freely* by his *grace* through the redemption that came by Christ Jesus" (v. 24, italics mine).

One of the most substantial works on grace that I have come across is by Lewis Sperry Chafer, the founder of Dallas Theological Seminary, and it goes by that title: *Grace.* In the very first chapter Chafer has a section captioned "Seven Fundamental Facts About Grace." I am not happy with everything he says in this section, particularly the last two of these points. But I refer to him here because of what he says about grace and demerit:

1. "Grace is not withheld because of demerit" and
2. "Grace cannot be lessened because of demerit."[4]

These are important points, since they emphasize the bright side of what usually appears to us as undesirable teaching.

Most of us resent the thought of "free" grace. We want to earn our own way, and we resent the suggestion that we are unable to scale the high walls of heaven by our own devices. We must be humbled before we will even give ear to the idea.

But if we have been humbled—if God has humbled us—the doctrine of grace becomes a marvelous encouragement and comfort. It tells us that the grace of God will never be withheld because of anything we may have done, however evil it was, nor will it be lessened because of that or any other evil we may do. The self-righteous person imagines that God scoops grace out of a barrel, giving much to the person who has sinned much and needs much, but giving only a little to the person who has sinned little and needs little. That is one way of wrongly mixing grace with merit. But the person who is conscious of his or her sin often imagines something similar, though opposite in direction. Such people think of God's withholding grace because of their great sin, or perhaps even putting grace back into his barrel when they sin badly.

Thank God grace is not bestowed on this principle! As Chafer says:

---

4. Lewis Sperry Chafer, *Grace* (Chicago: The Bible Institute Colportage Association, 1939), pp. 4, 5.

God cannot propose to do less in grace for one who is sinful than he would have done had that one been less sinful. Grace is never exercised by him making up what may be lacking in the life and character of a sinner. In such a case, much sinfulness would call for much grace, and little sinfulness would call for little grace. [Instead] the sin question has been set aside forever, and equal exercise of grace is extended to all who believe. It never falls short of being the measureless saving grace of God. Thus, grace could not be increased, for it is the expression of his infinite love; it could not be diminished, for every limitation that human sin might impose on the action of a righteous God has, through the propitiation of the cross, been dismissed forever.[5]

Grace humbles us, because it teaches that salvation is apart from human merit. At the same time, it encourages us to come to God for the grace we so evidently need. There is no sin too great either to turn God from us or to lessen the abundance of the grace he gives.

Abounding Grace

That word *abundance* leads to the final characteristic of grace to be included in this study. It is taught two chapters further on in a verse that became the life text of John Newton: Romans 5:20. Our version reads, ". . . . But where sin increased, grace increased all the more." But the version Newton knew rendered this, "But where sin abounded, grace did much more abound" (KJV).

John Newton was an English clergyman who lived from 1725 to 1807. He had a wide and effective ministry and has been called the second founder of the Church of England. He is best known to us for his hymns.

Newton was raised in a Christian home in which he was taught many great verses of the Bible. But his mother died when he was only six years old, and he was sent to live with a relative who mocked Christianity. One day, at an early age, Newton left home and joined the British Navy as an apprenticed seaman. He was wild and dissolute in those years, and he became exceedingly immoral. He acquired a reputation of being able to swear for two hours without repeating himself. Eventually he deserted the navy off the coast of Africa. Why Africa? In his memoirs he wrote that he went to Africa for one reason only and that was "that I might sin my fill."

In Africa he fell in with a Portuguese slavetrader in whose home he was cruelly treated. This man often went away on slaving expeditions, and when he was gone the power in the home passed to the trader's African wife, the chief woman of his harem. This woman hated all white men, and she took out her hatred on Newton. He tells us that for months he was forced to grovel in the dirt, eating his food from the ground like a dog and beaten unmercifully if he touched it with his hands. For a time he was actually

5. Ibid., p. 5.

placed in chains. At last, thin and emaciated, Newton made his way through the jungle, reached the sea, and there attracted a British merchant ship making its way up the coast to England.

The captain of the ship took Newton aboard, thinking that he had ivory to sell. But when he learned that the young man knew something about navigation as a result of his time in the British Navy, he made him ship's mate. Even then Newton fell into trouble. One day, when the captain was ashore, Newton broke out the ship's supply of rum and got the crew drunk. He was so drunk himself that when the captain returned and struck him in the head, Newton fell overboard and would have drowned if one of the sailors had not grabbed him and hauled him back on deck in the nick of time.

Near the end of the voyage, as they were approaching Scotland, the ship ran into bad weather and was blown off course. Water poured in, and she began to sink. The young profligate was sent down into the hold to pump water. The storm lasted for days. Newton was terrified, sure that the ship would sink and he would drown. But there in the hold of the ship, as he pumped water, desperately attempting to save his life, the God of grace, whom he had tried to forget but who had never forgotten him, brought to his mind Bible verses he had learned in his home as a child. Newton was convicted of his sin and of God's righteousness. The way of salvation opened up to him. He was born again and transformed. Later, when the storm had passed and he was again in England, Newton began to study theology and eventually became a distinguished evangelist, preaching even before the queen.

Of this storm William Cowper, the British poet who was a close friend of John Newton's, wrote:

> God moves in a mysterious way,
>   His wonders to perform;
> He plants his footsteps in the sea
>   And rides upon the storm.

And Newton? Newton became a poet as well as a preacher, writing some of our best-known hymns. This former blasphemer wrote:

> How sweet the Name of Jesus sounds
>   In a believer's ear!
> It soothes his sorrows, heals his wounds,
>   And drives away his fear.

He is known above all for "Amazing Grace":

> Amazing grace—how sweet the sound—
>   That saved a wretch like me!
> I once was lost, but now am found—
>   Was blind, but now I see.

> 'Twas grace that taught my heart to fear,
>   And grace my fears relieved;
> How precious did that grace appear
>   The hour I first believed.
>
> Through many dangers, toils, and snares,
>   I have already come;
> 'Tis grace has brought me safe thus far,
>   And grace will lead me home.

Newton was a great preacher of grace. And no wonder! He had learned what all who have ever been saved have learned: namely, that grace is from God, apart from human merit. He deserved nothing. But he found grace through the work of Jesus.

43

Bought with a Price

Romans 3:24

. . . justified freely by his grace through the redemption that came by Christ Jesus.

On September 17, 1915, the distinguished Professor of Didactic and Polemic Theology at Princeton Theological Seminary, Benjamin Breckinridge Warfield, stood in Miller Chapel to deliver an address to the newly arrived students. The subject had been announced: "'Redeemer' and 'Redemption,'" and the young men were probably prepared for a difficult and weighty presentation. Instead Warfield talked about how wonderful the two words *Redeemer* and *redemption* are.

"There is no one of the titles of Christ which is more precious to Christian hearts than 'Redeemer,'" the professor began. True, other titles are more often on our lips: "Lord," "Savior," others. But "Redeemer" is more intimate and therefore more precious. Warfield explained:

> It gives expression not merely to our sense that we have received salvation from [Jesus], but also to our appreciation of what it cost him to procure this salvation for us. It is the name specifically of the Christ of the cross. Whenever we pronounce it, the cross is placarded before our eyes and our hearts are filled with loving remembrance not only that Christ has given us salvation but that he paid a mighty price for it.

363

How do we know this is true? In proof of his statement, Warfield appealed, not to great works of theology dealing with the cross—though there are many of them—but to the church's hymnody. Many of the hymns in the hymnbook used that day at Princeton celebrated the Lord as Redeemer, and Warfield listed them:

> Let our whole soul an offering be
>> To our *Redeemer's* name;
> While we pray for pardoning grace,
>> Through our *Redeemer's* name;
> Almighty Son, Incarnate Word,
>> Our Prophet, Priest, *Redeemer*, Lord; . . .
> O for a thousand tongues to sing
>> My dear *Redeemer's* praise; . . .
> All hail, *Redeemer*, hail,
>> For thou hast died for me; . . .
> · All glory, laud and honor
>> To thee *Redeemer*, King.

Those are only six of the hymns he listed. He cited twenty-eight. But then, in case the students had missed his point, he did the same thing all over again with the words *ransom* and *ransomed*, which are near synonyms of "redeem" and "redeemed." He found twenty-five examples.[1]

"Redemption" and "Redeemer" are the words to which we now come in our phrase-by-phrase exposition of Romans 3:21–31—"God's Remedy in Christ." We have outlined the passage by citing four great doctrines found in it: (1) the righteousness of God, (2) grace, (3) redemption, and (4) faith, by which these blessings are conveyed to the individual. This is the third doctrine. It is most precious to us, because it describes what the Lord Jesus Christ did for us by dying.

A Misunderstood Doctrine

In his address Warfield spoke of the "cost" of redemption. But here a problem develops for some people. "Isn't salvation supposed to be free?" they ask. "Haven't you just talked about grace, the unmerited favor of God toward us? Salvation can't be bought or sold. If you talk about God extracting a price for his favor, you make God cheap, begrudging, and mercenary. How can anyone believe that this is accurate?"

1. Benjamin Breckinridge Warfield, "'Redeemer' and 'Redemption'" in *The Person and Work of Christ* (Philadelphia: Presbyterian and Reformed Publishing, 1950), pp. 325–348.

Because of such reasoning some scholars have tried to change the meaning of "Redeemer" and "redemption" from what I have suggested these words mean (and do mean) to something more like "release" or "deliverance," that is, to the process of setting someone free without any idea of paying a price for it. They point to Luke 24:21 in which the Emmaus disciples used the word *redeem* in their conversation with Jesus, saying, "We had hoped that he was the one who was going to redeem Israel." Obviously they were thinking of a political deliverance, not a commercial transaction. Or they point to Ephesians 1:14, ". . . a deposit guaranteeing our inheritance until the redemption of those who are God's possession." They argue that there is no suggestion of a price in that statement. Rather, it is speaking only of our deliverance from the power of sin at the return of Christ.

Three Great Words

How should we respond to this objection? There are a number of ways. We could point out that the Emmaus disciples obviously misunderstood the nature of Christ's redemptive work. We could emphasize that, although redemption includes the idea of deliverance and is a word sometimes used for "deliverance," it is nevertheless a larger and more embracing concept. We might observe that, even though in the Bible a price for redemption is paid, it is never a case of our paying for redemption—we have no means of paying for it—but rather of *God's* paying the price in Christ, so that salvation might be free for us.

These points are all valid. Nevertheless, in my judgment, the best way of getting to the meaning of redemption is by a careful examination of the biblical words used for it. There are three Greek words, plus two important Hebrew words or concepts.

The first Greek word is *agorazō*. It comes from the noun used to describe an open marketplace in Greek-speaking lands, an *agora*. An *agora* is where all sorts of things—wine, grain and oil, pottery, silver and gold ornaments, horses, slaves, clothing and household wares—were bought and sold. The verb *agorazō*, which is based upon the word *agora*, meant "to buy" something in such a marketplace. Clearly a price was involved. Not long ago I discovered that the Greek Orthodox community of Philadelphia was using the word for an annual outdoor bazaar at which those of Greek descent raise money for their church. It is advertised as "A Greek Agora." *Agorazō* suggests that Christ's saving work involves his purchasing us for himself in this world's marketplace.

The second Greek word for "redemption" is related closely to the first. It is *exagorazō*. Clearly it is only the first word with the addition of the prefix *ex*, which means "out of." So *exagorazō* means "to buy *out of* the marketplace," with the idea that the object or person purchased might never have to return there again.

It is hard to illustrate this in terms of contemporary purchases. The closest we can come is redeeming an object from a pawnshop. But if we remember that in the ancient world some of the chief objects of commerce were slaves and that slaves could be purchased out of the marketplace (redeemed) by the payment of a price, this becomes a rich idea for us. According to the Bible, we are all slaves to sin. By ourselves we cannot escape from this slavery. But Jesus has freed us. He has done it by paying the price of our redemption by his blood. That is why Peter writes, "For you know that it was not with perishable things such as silver or gold that you were redeemed from the empty way of life handed down to you from your forefathers, but with the precious blood of Christ, a lamb without blemish or defect" (1 Peter 1:18–19). Here the idea of Christ's death being the cost or price of our redemption is inescapable.

The third pertinent Greek word is actually a group of words based on the root verb *yō*. They carry further the idea of being purchased out of the marketplace, for the chief thought of these words is "to loose" or "to set free." These words have an interesting development. *Yō* itself meant only "to loose or loosen," as in taking off a suit of clothes or unbuckling one's armor. When used of persons, it signified loosening bonds so that, for example, a prisoner might be released. It was usually necessary to pay a ransom price to free a prisoner, however. So in time a second word developed from *yō* to signify this "ransom price." It was *lytroō*. From it another verb developed: *lytroō* which, like *yō*, meant "to loose" or "to set free" but, unlike *yō*, always meant to free by paying the redemption price. From these last two words the proper Greek term for redemption came about: *lytrōsis* (and the cognate word *apolytrōsis*). These words always had to do with freeing a slave by paying for him. In Christian vocabulary they mean that Jesus freed us from sin's slavery by his death. Thus:

> Long my imprisoned spirit lay
> Fast bound in sin and nature's night;
> Thine eye diffused a quick'ning ray,
> I woke, the dungeon flamed with light:
> My chains fell off, my heart was free,
> I rose, went forth and followed thee.

As long as we know that the death of the Lord Jesus Christ accomplished that, we will love him for being our Redeemer.

Old Testament Background

Important as a study of these Greek words for redemption may be, it is nevertheless true that the richest words for understanding the redemptive work of Christ are in the Old Testament. I refer here to two of them.

First, *kōpher*, which, like *lytron*, means "a ransom price." But it is richer than the Greek idea, because it refers to the redemption of a person who, apart from that redemption, would die. Let me explain. Suppose a person in Old Testament times owned an ox that had gored somebody to death. Under certain circumstances (we might describe this as manslaughter rather than homicide), the owner of the ox would be fined. But suppose there had been negligence. Suppose the ox was known to be dangerous and the owner had failed to secure the animal properly. In this case the owner of the ox could be killed. That is, he would have to forfeit his life for the one whose life had been taken. There would be little to be gained by one more death, of course. So Old Testament law provided a way by which, if the owner could come to an agreement with the relatives of the dead man, it would be possible for him to pay a ransom price, an indemnity, instead of dying. This ransom price was called the *kōpher*.

As I say, this term enriches our understanding of what the Lord Jesus Christ did in dying for us. For it is not only that in some way his death freed us from sin's power. Christ did deliver us from sin's power, but he also delivered us from *death*, which is the punishment God had established for transgressions ("The soul who sins . . . will die," Ezek. 18:4b). Therefore, for us to be redeemed means life.

The final words I bring into this study of "redemption" are *gā'al*, which means "to redeem," and the related noun, *gō'ēl*, which means "kinsman-redeemer." This latter term requires explanation.

It was a principle of Jewish law that property should remain within a family as much as possible. Therefore, if a Jewish person lost his or her share of the land through debt or by some other means, a solemn obligation evolved on a near relative (if there was one) to buy the property back again. This person, because of close relationship to the one who had lost the property, was a "kinsman," and if willing and able to purchase the property and restore it to the family, he became a "kinsman-redeemer." In some cases, where there was no male heir to inherit the property, the duty of the kinsman extended to marrying the widow in order to raise up heirs.

A kinsman-redeemer had to fulfill three qualifications:

1. He had to be a close relative (a stranger would not do),
2. He had to be willing to take on this responsibility (nobody could be compelled to do this work), and
3. He had to be able to pay the ransom price (he had to have sufficient means at his disposal).

A Romance of Redemption

Those three conditions apply to and were fulfilled in the case of Jesus Christ. But to make them vivid, let me develop them in the context of an

Old Testament story, the only story in the Bible in which we see a kinsman-redeemer in action. It is the story of Ruth and her "redeemer," Boaz.

In the days of the Judges there was a famine in Israel, and a man from Bethlehem, whose name was Elimelech, left Judah with his wife, Naomi and two sons to live in Moab. Not long after this, Elimelech died, and shortly after that the sons married Moabite women. One was Orpah, and the other was Ruth. About ten years later the sons also died, and Naomi and the two daughters-in-law were left. Apparently the three were quite poor, so when Naomi heard that the famine in Judah had passed and that there was food there, she decided to go back to her homeland and live again in Bethlehem. Orpah took her mother-in-law's advice and went back to her family, but Ruth insisted on staying with Naomi. Her entreaty (Ruth 1:16–17), which Naomi heeded, is one of the most beautiful passages in the Bible. Ruth said:

> "Don't urge me to leave you or to turn back from you. Where you go I will go, and where you stay I will stay. Your people will be my people and your God my God. Where you die I will die, and there I will be buried. May the Lord deal with me, be it ever so severely, if anything but death separates you and me."

Back in Bethlehem, Naomi and Ruth were still quite poor, in spite of the fact that Naomi seems to have owned a piece of land (cf. 4:3), and the only way they could survive was by Ruth's going into the fields at harvest time to "glean" behind the reapers. Gleaning means that she was allowed to follow the workmen and pick up any small bits of grain they discarded. The law of Israel established this right for poor persons.

Ruth went to a field belonging to an affluent man named Boaz who, as it turned out, was a close relative of Naomi, a kinsman of her deceased husband Elimelech. Boaz was kind to Ruth, in spite of the fact that she was a foreigner. He encouraged her to remain in his fields and instructed the workmen to protect her and be generous to her, allowing a good supply of the grain to fall behind.

Can we say that Boaz fell in love with Ruth the Moabitess? Yes, we can, even though these are not the words in which the ancients recounted such events. (Strikingly, the word *love* does not occur in the entire Book of Ruth, though it is a love story.)

Naomi seems to have recognized what was happening as well as realizing that God was arranging circumstances so that Boaz could perform the office of a kinsman-redeemer for herself, in regard to her inheritance, and for Ruth, in regard to raising up an heir. So she advised Ruth how to make her claim known to Boaz. When she did, Boaz was delighted, for it meant that Ruth was interested in him also and had not, as he said, "run after the younger men, whether rich or poor" (Ruth 3:10). Unfortunately, there was a kinsman closer to Naomi and Ruth than himself. Boaz promised to raise the matter with this kinsman and to perform the office of kinsman-redeemer if the other was unable or unwilling.

As it turned out, the other relative was interested in the land but was unable to fulfill the obligation to Ruth. So Boaz willingly bought the land and married Ruth. The story ends by relating that they had a son named Obed, who became the father of Jesse, who was the father of King David.

What a beautiful story! What a beautiful redemption for Ruth! J. Vernon McGee comments:

> From the very beginning there was a marvelous development in the status of Ruth. First, she was found in the land of Moab, a stranger from the covenants of promise, without hope and without God in the world. Next she was brought by providence into the field of Boaz, under the wings of the God of Israel. Then she was sent to the threshing floor of Boaz; and there she was seen asserting her claim for a kinsman-redeemer. Finally, in this last chapter of the Book of Ruth, she is seen as a bride for the heart of Boaz and as a mother in his home. What splendid progress! What scriptural evolution! From a very lowly beginning she was lifted to the very pinnacle of blessing. All this was made possible by a *goel* who loved her.[2]

In redeeming us, Jesus fulfilled a similar set of qualifications: (1) He became our kinsman by the incarnation, being born in this very town of Bethlehem; (2) he was willing to be our Redeemer, because of his great love for us; and (3) he was able to redeem us, because he alone could provide an adequate redemption price by dying. We rightly sing:

> There was no other good enough
> To pay the price of sin;
> He only could unlock the gate
> Of heaven, and let us in.

The redemption of Ruth may not have cost Boaz a great deal, at the most only money, but our redemption cost Jesus Christ his life.

The Death of Great Words

At the beginning of this study I referred to the address of the gifted theologian B. B. Warfield, given to the incoming class of students at Princeton Seminary in 1915. I return to it now because of something else it contains. Warfield had spoken of "Redeemer" and "redemption" as being among the most precious words in the Christian vocabulary. But he confessed, as he came to the end of his address, that this seemed to be changing. The pre-

2. J. Vernon McGee, *In a Barley Field* (Glendale, Calif.: Regal Books, G/L Publications, 1968), p. 93.

cise biblical meanings of these words was being lost, and with them something precious about Christianity. Warfield said:

> What we are doing today as we look out upon our current religious modes of speech, is assisting at the deathbed of a word. It is sad to witness the death of any worthy thing—even of a worthy word. And worthy words do die, like any other worthy thing—if we do not take care of them. . . . I hope you will determine that, God helping you, you will not let them die thus, if any care on your part can preserve them in life and vigor.
>
> But the dying of the words is not the saddest thing which we see here. The saddest thing is the dying out of the hearts of men of the things for which the words stand. . . . The real thing for you to settle in your minds, therefore, is whether Christ is truly a Redeemer to you, and whether you find an actual redemption in him. . . . Do you realize that Christ is your Ransomer and has actually shed his blood for you as your ransom? Do you realize that your salvation has been bought, bought at a tremendous price, at the price of nothing less precious than blood, and that the blood of Christ, the Holy One of God? Or, go a step further: do you realize that this Christ who has thus shed his blood for you is himself your God?[3]

We have fallen a great deal further away from these great concepts since Warfield's time, and we are spiritually impoverished as a result. Yet the issue is the same. The questions are unchanged. Is Jesus truly your Redeemer? Are you trusting in him? Your answer to those questions will determine your entire life and destiny.[4]

---

3. Warfield, "'Redeemer' and 'Redemption,'" pp. 344, 345, 347.

4. There are many worthwhile studies of the words "Redeemer" and "redemption" in addition to the few cited in this chapter. For further study see: James Denney, *The Death of Christ* (Chicago: InterVarsity Press, 1964); Leon Morris, *The Apostolic Preaching of the Cross* (Grand Rapids: Wm. B. Eerdmans, 1956); Arthur W. Pink, *The Satisfaction of Christ* (Swengel, Pa.: Bible Truth Depot, 1955); and John R. W. Stott, *The Cross of Christ* (Downers Grove, Ill.: InterVarsity Press, 1986).

44

Propitiation: The Forgotten Doctrine

Romans 3:25

God presented him as a sacrifice of atonement, through faith in his blood.

There are a number of texts in Romans that have been especially used by God in the conversion of important Christian leaders. We have already studied one: Romans 1:16–17, which was used to bring Martin Luther to faith. It became his life text. Romans 13:11–14 was used to save Saint Augustine. In Romans 3:25 we come to a verse that has opened the door of Paradise to many.

William Cowper and John Bunyan

William Cowper was an eighteenth-century English poet who authored some of our most beloved hymns. He had a miserable childhood. His mother died when he was only six years old, and he was immediately bundled off to a boarding school where, being slight of build and of a sensitive nature, he was mercilessly badgered, bullied, and beaten by the older boys. Cowper struggled through this time and through his later early years as a law student. But terrors overwhelmed him, and on more than one occasion his mind seemed to fail. Twice he tried to commit suicide. At last, in the year 1756, the twenty-five-year-old Cowper was committed to a private asylum under the care of a man whose name was Dr. Cotton.

Two hundred years ago, being confined to an asylum often meant receiving the most terrible treatment. But Cowper's doctor was a devout old gentleman, and he treated the distraught poet in a way that brought him out of his depression and introduced him to salvation through the work of Christ.

Cowper had been much troubled by his sin, often crying out, "My sin! My sin! Oh, for some fountain open for my cleansing!" But he had known of no such fountain. Now, under the care of this gentle Christian doctor, he discovered the only fountain that has ever washed away one's sins.

Here is how Cowper himself told about it:

> The happy period which was to shake off my fetters and afford me a clear opening of the free mercy of God in Christ Jesus was now arrived. I flung myself into a chair near the window, and, seeing a Bible there, ventured once more to apply to it for comfort and instruction. The first verses I saw were in the third chapter of Romans: "Being justified freely by his grace through the redemption that is in Christ Jesus, whom God hath set forth to be a propitiation, through faith in his blood, to manifest his righteousness." Immediately I received strength to believe, and the full beams of the Sun of Righteousness shone on me. I saw the sufficiency of the atonement he had made, my pardon in his blood, and the fullness and completeness of his justification. In a moment I believed and received the gospel.

Cowper said afterwards that he could have died with gratitude and joy, so overwhelmed was his spirit in that moment. He was utterly transformed. Later he wrote of his conversion:

> There is a fountain filled with blood
> Drawn from Immanuel's veins;
> And sinners, plunged beneath that flood,
> Lose all their guilty stains.
>
> The dying thief rejoiced to see
> That fountain in his day;
> And there have I, as vile as he,
> Washed all my sins away.
>
> E'er since by faith I saw the stream
> Thy flowing wounds supply,
> Redeeming love has been my theme,
> And shall be till I die.

It is an interesting sidelight to this story that it was exactly one hundred years before this, in 1656, that the same text brought deliverance to John Bunyan, the author of *Pilgrim's Progress*. Bunyan's account of his conversion reads, "As I was walking up and down in the house, as a man in a most woeful state, the Word of God took hold of my heart." Here he quotes our text. Then he says, "Oh, what a turn it made upon me! I was as one awakened out of some troublesome dream."[1]

The Modern Revolt

Obviously, there is power in a text that has been so greatly used in the conversion of these and other Christian leaders. But how are these ideas received today? How many in our day are likely to be saved by Romans 3:25?

One difficulty is with the word *propitiation* (the word used in the King James Version of Rom. 3:25). Few understand what propitiation means, let alone love and respond to the concept. "Redemption" we can understand, at least in part. It is an image for Christ's work drawn from the world of buying and selling, and since we do so much of both, the idea of redemption is at least not foreign to us. But "propitiation" is drawn from the world of ancient religion. It signifies what the worshiper does when he or she presents a sacrifice to a deity. It is an "atoning sacrifice," an act by which the wrath of the offended deity is appeased or turned aside. Because this ancient world of sacrifices is so far from our experience, the idea of propitiation is hard to understand.

Then, too, there are our "theological" objections. Propitiation (as commonly defined) presupposes the wrath of God—a wrath that needs to be appeased or turned aside. But right here many modern thinkers stop, regarding wrath as highly inappropriate for Christianity. Such persons might say, "We can understand how the idea of propitiation might be appropriate in an ancient, pagan society, where God was not known and was thought to be vacillating, capricious, and often angry. But certainly this is not the God of Christianity. According to the Christian revelation, God is not angry. He is loving. He does not need to be appeased by us. All we need to do is recognize that he loves us and receive his forgiveness."

One theologian states sharply: "[Those who hold to] the 'fire and brimstone' school of theology, who revel in ideas such as that Christ was made a sacrifice to appease an angry God, or that the cross was a legal transaction in which an innocent victim was made to pay the penalty for the crimes of others, a propitiation of a stern God, find no support in Paul. These notions came into Christian theology by way of the legalistic minds of the medieval churchmen; they are not biblical Christianity."[2]

How extraordinary!

1. The story of William Cowper and John Bunyan is told by F. W. Boreham in *A Bunch of Everlastings: Or Texts That Made History* (Philadelphia: The Judson Press, 1920), pp. 120–128.

2. William Neil, *Apostle Extraordinary* (London: Religious Education Press, 1965), pp. 89, 90. He is quoted by John R. W. Stott, *The Cross of Christ* (Downers Grove, Ill.: InterVarsity Press, 1986), pp. 172, 173.

One result of this modern objection to the biblical idea of propitiation has been a retranslation of Bible passages that use it. The chief culprit here is the well-known British theologian C. H. Dodd. According to Dodd, it is not God who is to be propitiated but ourselves. So the important idea is not the turning aside of God's wrath toward us, but rather the covering over of our guilt which, according to Dodd, is best expressed by the word *expiation.* As a result of this argument, "expiation" rather than "propitiation" has been used in the relevant passages of the Revised Standard and the New English versions of the Bible, upon which Dodd has had an influence (Rom. 3:25; Heb. 2:17; 1 John 2:2; 4:10).

But is this interpretation correct? Can words rightly be reassigned new meanings in this fashion? Surely, as Leon Morris says in his discussion of the term, "When we reach the stage where we must say, 'When the [writers] used "propitiation" they did not mean "propitiation,"' it is . . . time to call a halt."[3]

It is certainly that time for anyone who has been studying Romans, for if anything is clear at this point (after having made our way through the first two and a half chapters of the letter), it is that it is precisely the wrath of God that is our problem. We are under wrath because of sin. Therefore, if the wrath of God cannot be turned aside by someone or in some way, we are lost. It is precisely this concept that we should be looking for. John Murray wrote, "Instead of stumbling at this concept we should rather anticipate that the precise category suited to the need and liability created by the wrath of God would be enlisted to describe or define the provision of God's grace."[4]

We can rightly express some appreciation for Dodd, of course, for he has distinguished between the mistaken pagan ideas of a god who *is* capricious and easily angered and the Christian God who is not. The Lord is indeed gracious. Besides, Dodd has made clear that it is not in our power to turn God's wrath aside or in any way alter his attitude toward us. But this is not the whole of the matter, and the correct approach is not to reinterpret the biblical data, but rather to seek a deeper and correct interpretation of it.

Here are two important points to remember:

1. *Although God's wrath is not like the capricious anger of the pagan deities, his wrath is nevertheless a true wrath against sin; and it is this true and proper wrath that must be dealt with.*

We may feel, because of our particular cultural prejudices, that the wrath of God and the love of God are incompatible. But the Bible teaches that God is both wrathful and loving at the same time. What is more, his wrath is not just a small and insignificant element alongside his far more significant

3. Leon Morris, *The Apostolic Preaching of the Cross* (Grand Rapids: Wm. B. Eerdmans, 1956), p. 155.

4. John Murray, *The Epistle to the Romans* (Grand Rapids: Wm. B. Eerdmans, 1968), pp. 116, 117.

and overwhelming love. Actually, God's wrath is a strong character element. God hates sin and must punish it. The wrath of God is revealed in the Bible all the way from the opening chapters of Genesis to the final cataclysmic judgments recorded in the Book of Revelation.

2. *Although propitiation means turning the wrath of God aside, in the biblical framework this is never a case of mere human beings appeasing the divine wrath, but rather of God himself satisfying his wrath through the death of his own Son, Jesus.*

In pagan rituals, sacrifices were made by people trying to placate God. In Christianity, it is never humans who take the initiative or make the sacrifice. It is God himself who, out of his great love for sinners, provides the way by which his wrath against sin may be averted. In Jesus, God placates his own wrath against sin so that his love may go out to save sinners. As John Stott points out, "This was already clear in the Old Testament, in which the sacrifices were recognized not as human works but as divine gifts. They did not make God gracious; they were provided by a gracious God in order that he might act graciously towards his sinful people. 'I have given it to you,' God said of the sacrificial blood, 'to make atonement for yourselves on the altar' (Lev. 17:11)."[5]

The Ark of the Covenant

Having mentioned the Old Testament system of blood sacrifices, I come to one of the most beautiful pictures of the work of Christ to be found in all the Bible. When God gave Moses the law, he told him to build a portable tabernacle to house the Ark of the Covenant and be the focal point of Israel's worship. The tabernacle was an enclosure of skins that could be easily assembled and disassembled whenever the people camped or marched. Within it was an enclosure consisting of an outer chamber called the Holy Place and an inner chamber called the Most Holy Place. The Ark of the Covenant was placed within this inner chamber.

The Ark was a gold-covered wooden box about a yard long, containing the stone tables of the law that Moses had received on Mount Sinai. (The first set of tables had been broken, but a new set had been written. It was these that were placed there.) This box had a cover called the Mercy Seat, and upon the Mercy Seat, at each end and facing one another, were statues of cherubim (angels) whose wings stretched upward and then forward, almost meeting directly over the Ark. In a symbolic way, God was imagined to dwell above the Ark, over or between the outstretched wings of the cherubim.

As it stands, the Ark is a picture of terrible judgment, intended to produce dread in the worshiper through a disclosure of his or her sin. For what does God see as he looks down upon earth from between the outstretched

5. Stott, *The Cross of Christ*, pp. 173, 174.

wings of the cherubim? Clearly, he sees the law of Moses, which each of us has broken. He sees that he must act toward us in judgment. God cannot ignore sin; sin must be punished.

But this is where the Mercy Seat comes in, and why it is called the *Mercy Seat*. Once a year, on the Day of Atonement, the Jewish high priest entered the Holy of Holies to make atonement for the people's sins. He entered to make *propitiation*, the very word that (in Greek) was used to translate "Mercy Seat." Moments before, he had offered a sacrifice for his own sin and the sins of his family in the outer courtyard of the tabernacle. Then he had sacrificed a second animal. Now he took the blood of that second animal and very carefully—lest he somehow violate the laws surrounding the sacrifice or intrude unworthily upon God's holiness and be struck down, as others who had done so had been—he entered the Most Holy Place and sprinkled the blood of the sacrifice on the Mercy Seat.

What is symbolized here? Now, as God looks down from between the outstretched wings of the cherubim, he does not see the law of Moses that we have broken, but instead sees the blood of the innocent victim. He sees that punishment has been meted out. Propitiation has been made. And his love goes out to save all who come to him, not on the basis of their own righteousness or good works, but through faith in that sacrifice.

We know, of course, that the blood of animals did not take away sin. The Bible tells us so (see Heb. 10). But the animal sacrifice pointed forward to the only sufficient sacrifice of Jesus Christ, who by his atoning death became our true propitiation.

"God, Be Mercy-Seated"

There are not many places in the Bible where the concept of "propitiation" occurs, but I turn to one of them in closing. It is a passage in which the idea is embedded in a story recorded in Luke 18:9–14.

Jesus told a parable about two men who went to the temple to pray. One was a Pharisee. The other was a publican, or tax collector. (We have a bad opinion of Pharisees today because of some of the things Jesus said about them, but they were highly regarded by their contemporaries.) The Pharisee stood up to pray—as everyone would have agreed he had the right to do. In fact, if he had not prayed, he would probably have been asked to do so: "Come here, Mr. Pharisee. Stand up where we can all hear you. Now be quiet, everybody. The Pharisee is going to pray."

Pray he did. He prayed about himself: "God, I thank you that I am not like all other men—robbers, evildoers, adulterers—or even like this tax collector. I fast twice a week and give a tenth of all I get" (vv. 11–12). I do not think the Pharisee was lying. I think he really did give a tenth of his income to the temple and really did fast twice a week. I do not believe he was a thief or an adulterer. Moreover, I think others would have concurred in this evaluation. Here was an outstanding citizen, a credit to his community. If anyone could be accepted by God on the basis of his character or good works, it was this Pharisee.

But then there was that other person, the tax collector. He "stood at a distance"—where he belonged. Most people regarded him as a no-good, money-grubbing, cheating, Roman collaborator. Jesus said of him, "He would not even look up to heaven, but beat his breast and said, 'God, have mercy on me, a sinner'" (v. 13). And why not? He *was* a sinner. He had plenty to beat his breast about.

It is hard to imagine a greater contrast than the one between these two men. As to occupation, noble versus base. As to bearing, proud versus shameful. As to self-evaluation, self-confident versus cringing. Yet, when the Lord concluded his parable, he reversed the judgment every one of his listeners had been making and declared: "I tell you that this man [the tax collector], rather than the other [the Pharisee], went home justified before God. For everyone who exalts himself will be humbled, and he who humbles himself will be exalted" (v. 14).

No dime-store novel, no cinematic melodrama ever had a more surprising ending than this parable.

And yet, it is an illustration of the very purest gospel! Can you see the point? Why did the tax collector, rather than the Pharisee, go home "justified"? At first glance we might suppose that we have been overly hasty in our appraisal of the two men. The Pharisee appeared righteous, but perhaps he was not. Perhaps he had done things he was pretending he had not done. Perhaps he was a thief. Perhaps he was an adulterer. As for the tax collector—well, maybe he was better than he seemed. Perhaps, like the fictitious prostitute, he had "a heart of gold." Or perhaps he was actually doing good in the guise of a tax collector. Perhaps he was a Zealot operating "under cover."

We know perfectly well that this is not the way the story should be taken. It is true that the Pharisee was not justified. He *was* a sinner. But so was the tax collector. The only differences between the two men were that (1) the tax collector knew he was a sinner, while the Pharisee did not know it; and (2) the tax collector approached God, not on the basis of his good works (which he did not have), but on the basis of the provision of God for him, symbolized by the Mercy Seat and by the propitiation that took place there. Literally, his prayer was, "God, be 'Mercy-Seated' [propitiated] to me, a sinner."

That prayer is worth exploring. It is one of the shortest prayers in the Bible—only seven words in English (NIV), six in Greek—but it is one of the most profound.

Consider the beginning and ending. The first word is "God." The last word is "sinner." Those alone are profound, because they show what results when a human being actually becomes aware of the true God. When anyone becomes conscious of God, he (or she) does not proceed unchanged in his supposed "righteousness," as the Pharisee did. (It is how we know that the Pharisee did *not* know God.) Rather, he is conscious of sin, and the more so, the closer to God he comes. We know that despite his reputation the tax collector knew God—because he came to God as a sinner.

Then—this is the great part of the prayer—between the beginning of the prayer ("God") and the end of it ("me, a sinner") are the words "have mercy on me," or "be Mercy-Seated to me."

Can you see what was involved? This tax collector did not only know God and know himself as a sinner, the starting point of all true religion. He also knew the heart of the gospel, since he understood propitiation, he knew that between the presence of the Holy God, who looked down in judgment upon the law that he had broken, and himself, there needed to come the blood of the sacrificial victim. And this meant that he was not actually pleading for mercy—though the prayer sounds like it—but was coming to God on the basis of the mercy already provided by God through the sacrifice. He was saying, "Treat me on the basis of the blood sprinkled upon the Mercy Seat."

That is why we must preserve this and the other great words describing the achievement of the Lord Jesus Christ for our salvation. We cannot be saved without propitiation. The wrath of God must be turned aside. God has shown how it is turned aside. He has made propitiation.

Will you pray that prayer, the tax collector's prayer? No one will ever be saved without it.[6]

---

6. The material on the Pharisee and the tax collector closely parallels a chapter on this parable in James Montgomery Boice, *The Parables of Jesus* (Chicago: Moody Press, 1983), pp. 83–91.

45

Just and the Justifier

Romans 3:25–26

God presented him as a sacrifice of atonement, through faith in his blood. He did this to demonstrate his justice, because in his forbearance he had left the sins committed beforehand unpunished—he did it to demonstrate his justice at the present time, so as to be just and the one who justifies those who have faith in Jesus.

The Australian scholar Leon Morris points out, in *The Apostolic Preaching of the Cross*, that the first impression one has in turning to the subject of justification, after dealing with the words for salvation already treated in Romans, is the abundance of the material to be considered.

The word *propitiation*, though of great importance for understanding the nature of the atonement, is found only four times in all the New Testament (and not in all translations). *Redemption*, though frequent in contemporary Christian vocabulary and in the Old Testament, is not used very often in the New Testament. *Reconciliation* occurs in just five passages, all of them Pauline. "By contrast," says Morris, "he who would expound justification is confronted with eighty-one occurrences of the adjective *dikaios*, ninety-two of the noun *dikaiosynē*, two of the noun *dikaiōsis*, thirty-nine of the verb *dikaioō,* ten of the noun *dikaiōma,* and five of the adverb *dikaios.*"[1] Thus, the frequency of the words alone would indicate that "justification" is the central or pivotal idea in the doctrine of salvation.

John Calvin, the father of the Presbyterian and Reformed churches, called justification "the main hinge on which salvation turns."[2]

Thomas Cranmer, the framer of the Church of England, believed that justification is "the strong rock and foundation of Christian religion." He declared that "whosoever denieth [this doctrine] is not to be counted for a true Christian man . . . but for an adversary of Christ."[3]

Thomas Watson, one of the finest of the Puritans, said, "Justification is the very hinge and pillar of Christianity. An error about justification is dangerous, like a defect in a foundation. Justification by Christ is a spring of the water of life. To have the poison of corrupt doctrine cast into this spring is damnable."[4]

The great Reformer Martin Luther, in the words quoted earlier in this volume, wrote, "When the article of justification has fallen, everything has fallen. . . . This is the chief article from which all other doctrines have flowed. . . . It alone begets, nourishes, builds, preserves, and defends the church of God; and without it the church of God cannot exist for one hour." Luther said that justification is "the master and prince, the lord, the ruler, and the judge over all kinds of doctrines."[5]

These statements are not exaggerations. They present simple truth, because justification is indeed God's answer to the most important of all human questions: How can a man or a woman become right with God? We are not right with God in ourselves. We are under God's wrath. Justification is vital, because we must become right with God or perish eternally.

A Salvation Triangle

Here is another question—one that is also important, at least so far as our understanding of the Book of Romans is concerned. If justification is as critical a doctrine as the frequency of the words for justification and the quotations from Calvin, Cranmer, Watson, and Luther seem to indicate, why have we not encountered it before now? Why have we not been studying justification earlier—in Romans 3 at least, if not in the previous chapters?

1. Leon Morris, *The Apostolic Preaching of the Cross* (Grand Rapids: Wm. B. Eerdmans, 1956), p. 224.

2. John Calvin, *Institutes of the Christian Religion,* ed. John T. McNeill, trans. Ford Lewis Battles (Philadelphia: The Westminster Press, 1960), p. 726.

3. Thomas Cranmer, "Sermon on Salvation" in *First Book of Homilies* (London: Society for the Propagation of Christian Knowledge, 1914), pp. 25, 26. (Original edition 1547.)

4. Thomas Watson, *A Body of Divinity* (London: The Banner of Truth Trust, 1970), p. 226. (Original edition 1692.)

5. Martin Luther, *What Luther Says: An Anthology,* compiled by Ewald M. Plass (St. Louis: Concordia, 1959), vol. 2, pp. 702–704, 715.

The answer, of course, is that this is precisely what we have been doing. The Greek word for "justification" (*dikaiosynē*) is built on the word for "right" or "righteousness" (*dikaios*), and it is a lack of precisely this righteousness and our need for a righteousness (or justification) not our own that has concerned us. As far back as Romans 1:17, we saw that "in the gospel a righteousness from God is revealed, a righteousness that is by faith from first to last. . . ." What is this if not justification? Or again, in Romans 3, we saw that "a righteousness from God, apart from law, has been made known, to which the law and the prophets testify" (v. 21). This also is a reference to justification. In between those two verses—between Romans 1:17 and Romans 3:21—is a long section showing that no one is able to be justified by his or her own merits or good works. In fact, this section ends by saying, "Therefore no one will be declared righteous [that is, no one will be justified] in his [God's] sight by observing the law; rather, through the law we become conscious of sin" (Rom. 3:20).

In other words, thus far at least, the entire Book of Romans has been about this doctrine.

Another way of showing this is to indicate how each of the ideas that describes Christ's work in dying for us—redemption and propitiation—which we have already studied, is tied into justification. It is not possible to have any one of these without the others.

I find it helpful to portray this by what I call the salvation triangle. Imagine a triangle with one of its three sides on the bottom. Imagine further that the three points of the triangle represent (1) God the Father (the point at the top of the triangle), (2) the Lord Jesus Christ (the point on the bottom and to the left), and (3) ourselves (the point on the bottom and to the right). Imagine in addition that each of the three sides of the triangle represents one of the three salvation doctrines that we have been studying.

The line at the bottom stands for "redemption." It links the Lord Jesus Christ and mankind, because it describes what Jesus does in relation to his people. He redeems them. He purchases them at the price of his own shed blood. Because this describes what Jesus does for us, and not what we do, turn that bottom line into an arrow pointing from Jesus to us. He is the subject of the action. We are the objects.

The line on the left, connecting the Lord Jesus Christ and God the Father, stands for "propitiation." It is there because propitiation describes what the Lord Jesus Christ did for us in relationship to his Father. As we saw when we studied that word, it is not ourselves that need to be propitiated. It is God. His wrath against sin needs to be turned aside. Moreover, we are unable to make propitiation. The work is beyond us. God himself must make propitiation, and this is what he does in Christ. Jesus, who is God, turns God's wrath aside. This line can also be turned into an arrow too—an arrow pointing from Jesus to the Father. As in the former case, Jesus is the subject of this action, but here the Father is the object.

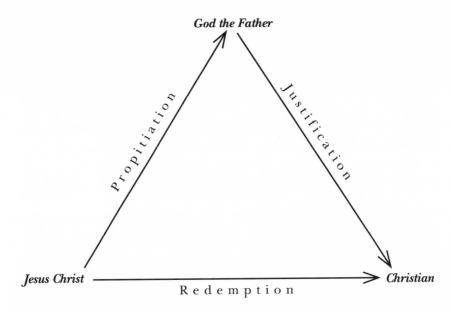

The final line of the salvation triangle connects God the Father with ourselves, and this (as we anticipate) represents "justification." This arrow
points toward us, for God is the subject of the action—he justifies us—and
we are the object—we are justified.

This diagram tells us a great deal about how God saves fallen men and
women. As you picture it in your mind, you will see that two of these actions
(redemption and propitiation) issue from the Lord Jesus Christ. This indicates
that he is the one who has achieved our salvation. It is *his* work. We are the
recipients of two actions (redemption and justification). We contribute nothing to salvation. "Salvation comes from the LORD" (Jonah 2:9b). God the
Father is the recipient of one action (propitiation) and the author of one
action (justification). This makes clear that it is on the basis of Christ's work of
propitiation that we are justified. It is because Jesus paid the price of our salvation by dying in our place that God can justify the ungodly—as we will see.

The point I am making here, however, is that these three works are inex-
tricably bound together. It is not possible to have even a single one without
the others. Consequently, everything we have been studying is in one sense
a part of justification.

An Image from the Law Courts

But what does justification refer to specifically? Redemption, as we saw, is
a term borrowed from the marketplace. It concerns buying and selling and
indicates the price Jesus paid for our deliverance. Because the word was so
often used in ancient times for buying slaves, it has overtones of delivering

us from sin's slavery. Christ freed us from sin's slavery by his death. Propitiation, as we saw in the previous study, is a term borrowed from the world of ancient religion. It describes the sacrifice by which the wrath of God is turned from us. In ancient times pagan worshipers thought they could turn aside God's wrath by themselves, presenting sacrifices commensurate with their transgressions. But, although the idea is the same, in Christianity it is understood that no mere human being can placate or turn aside God's wrath. Only God can do that, and that is precisely what he has done through the only sufficient sacrifice of Jesus Christ.

What about justification? This word comes from the world of the law courts and describes the act of a judge in acquitting an accused person. As Leon Morris says, "Justification . . . is a legal term indicating the process of declaring righteous."[6]

It is important to note those two legalistic words: "acquitting" and "declaring." This is because the single most serious error in trying to understand justification is to suppose that it means "to *make* righteous" in the sense of actually producing righteousness in the one justified. As we will see in our final study of Romans 3, actual righteousness does follow on justification—so closely that we are correct in saying that if it does not, the one involved is not justified. But justification in itself does not refer to this change. The English word might lead us to think so. It is composed of the two Latin words: *justus*, meaning "just" or "righteous," and *facio*, meaning "to make." At first glance this is precisely what the word seems to indicate: "to make righteous." But, as I say, this is not the right idea. Justification only indicates that the person involved has a right standing before the bar of God's justice. It does not indicate how he or she got that way, which is why the other terms—redemption and propitiation—are so necessary.

Let me put it in another way. Justification is the opposite of condemnation. When a defendant is found to stand in a wrong relationship to the law, he or she is condemned or pronounced guilty by the judge. Condemnation of that defendant does not make the person guilty. He or she is only declared to be so. In the same way, in justification the person is declared to be just or in a right relationship to the law, but not made righteous. A person *could* be declared righteous on the basis of his or her own righteousness; such a one would be pronounced innocent in a court of law. But in salvation, since we have no righteousness of our own and are not innocent, we are declared righteous on the grounds of Christ's atonement.

A Well-Developed Doctrine

It helps to realize that the full New Testament doctrine of justification is not merely justification alone but, to state it fully: *justification by grace through faith in Jesus Christ.*

6. Morris, *The Apostolic Preaching of the Cross*, p. 271.

This is exactly what Paul is declaring in the verses that are the basis of this study, Romans 3:24–26: "[Those who believe] are justified freely by [God's] grace through the redemption that came by Christ Jesus. God presented him as a sacrifice of atonement, through faith in his blood. He did this to demonstrate his justice, because in his forbearance he had left the sins committed beforehand unpunished—he did it to demonstrate his justice at the present time, so as to be just and the one who justifies those who have faith in Jesus."

Let's take that definition a step at a time, as John R. W. Stott does in his treatment of it in *The Cross of Christ*.[7]

1. *The source of our justification is the grace of God* (v. 24). Since "there is no one righteous, not even one" (Rom. 3:10), it is patently clear that no one can make or "declare [himself or herself] righteous" (v. 20). How, then, is salvation possible? It is possible only if God does the work for us—which is what "grace" means, since we do not deserve God's working. As we saw earlier, Paul emphasizes this by adding the word *freely* to the word *grace,* which is redundant but nevertheless good writing.

2. *The ground of our justification is the work of Christ* (v. 25). We have seen this in our discussion of the words *propitiation* and *redemption,* both of which are used by Paul here (redemption in v. 24, and propitiation [KJV] in v. 25). It is because these works have been done that God is able to forgive justly.

"Justification," writes Stott, "is not a synonym for amnesty, which strictly is pardon without principle, a forgiveness which overlooks—even forgets (*amnēstia* is 'forgetfulness')—wrongdoing and declines to bring it to justice. No, justification is an act of justice, of gracious justice. . . . When God justifies sinners, he is not declaring bad people to be good, or saying that they are not sinners after all; he is pronouncing them legally righteous, free from any liability to the broken law, because he himself in his Son has born the penalty of their law-breaking. . . . In other words, we are 'justified by his blood.'"[8]

I fear that this pivotal doctrine is slipping away from people today. But it was not always in such low esteem. It was precious to Charles Haddon Spurgeon, to name just one past warrior—and it was the means of his conversion. Here is how he tells it:

When I was under the hand of the Holy Spirit, under conviction of sin, I had a clear and sharp sense of the justice of God. Sin, whatever it might be to other people, became to me an intolerable burden. It was not so much that I feared hell, but that I feared sin. I knew myself to be so horribly guilty that I remember feeling that if God did not punish me for sin he ought to do so. I

7. John R. W. Stott, *The Cross of Christ* (Downers Grove, Ill.: InterVarsity Press, 1986), pp. 189–192.
8. Ibid., p. 190.

felt that the Judge of all the earth ought to condemn such sin as mine. . . . I had upon my mind a deep concern for the honor of God's name, and the integrity of his moral government. I felt that it would not satisfy my conscience if I could be forgiven unjustly. The sin I had committed must be punished. But then there was the question how God could be just, and yet justify me who had been so guilty. . . . I was worried and wearied with this question; neither could I see any answer to it. Certainly, I could never have invented an answer which would have satisfied my conscience.[9]

But then, as the great Baptist preacher recounted, light dawned on his soul. He saw that "Jesus has borne the death penalty on our behalf. . . . Why did he suffer, if not to turn aside the penalty from us? If then, he turned it aside by his death, it is turned aside, and those who believe in him need not fear it. It must be so, that since expiation is made, God is able to forgive without shaking the basis of his throne."[10]

It is not difficult to see that this was precisely the problem Paul was dealing with in his cryptic reference to God's leaving "the sins committed beforehand unpunished" and "to demonstrate his justice at the present time." Paul was thinking in temporal terms, acknowledging that before the incarnation and death of Christ there had been something like a stain on God's name. For centuries he had been refusing to condemn and instead had actually been justifying sinful men and women—men like Abraham, who was willing to compromise his wife's honor to save his own life; Moses, who killed an Egyptian; David, who committed adultery with Bathsheba and then murdered her husband, Uriah, to cover it up; and women like Rahab, the prostitute of Jericho. God had been saving these people. When they died he did not send them to hell. It would seem to anyone looking on that he had merely been passing over their sins—forgiving them, yes, but unjustly.

Was God unjust?

No, says Paul. In the death of Christ, God's name is vindicated. It is now seen that on the basis of his death, God had been just when he justified the ungodly (and *is* just when he continues to justify them).

3. *The means of our justification is faith* (vv. 25–26). Faith is the channel by which justification comes to us or becomes ours. This is the subject of our next study, but here we need to say at least two things.

First, faith is not a good work. It is necessary, absolutely essential. But it is not a good work. In fact, it is not a work at all. Faith is itself God's gift, as Paul makes clear in Ephesians 2:8–9. "For it is by grace you have been saved, through faith—and this not from yourselves, it is the gift of God—not by works, so that no one can boast."

9. Spurgeon's account of his conversion appears in Charles Haddon Spurgeon, *All of Grace* (Chicago: Moody Press, n.d.), pp. 27, 29.

10. Ibid.

Second, although faith is the means of our justification, it is also the only means. Luther expressed it by the words *sola fide* ("by faith alone"), thus adding a word not present in the text of Scripture but nevertheless catching the essence of the idea. Clearly, if faith is not a good work but only receiving what God has done for us and freely offers, then it is by faith alone that we can be justified—all other acts or works being excluded by definition. The only means by which any person can ever be justified is by believing God and receiving what he offers.

4. *The effect of our justification is union with Christ.* This idea is not stated explicitly in our passage, being held for Paul's later unfolding of the full nature of the gospel. But it does come later. It is the grounds of the benefits of salvation unfolded in Romans 5:1–11 and of our victory over sin explained in Romans 5:12–8:17.

John Stott explains it this way:

> To say that we are justified "through Christ" points to his historical death; to say that we are justified "in Christ" points to the personal relationship with him which by faith we now enjoy. This simple fact makes it impossible for us to think of justification as a purely external transaction; it cannot be isolated from our union with Christ and all the benefits which this brings. The first is membership of the Messianic community of Jesus. If we are in Christ and therefore justified, we are also the children of God and the true (spiritual) descendants of Abraham. . . . Secondly, this new community, to create which Christ gave himself on the cross, is to be "eager to do what is good," and its members are to devote themselves to good works. . . .
>
> To be sure, we can say with Paul that the law condemned us. But "there is now no condemnation for those who are in Christ Jesus."[11]

The question is—it is the third of my questions in this study—are *you* in Christ? Are you justified through faith in what he achieved for you at Calvary? There are many important questions in this world: Who am I? What am I here for? Where am I going? Who is God? How can I please God? But the greatest questions are: How can I become *right* with God, justified in his sight? And: Am *I* justified?

If you are not, you need to come to God as the tax collector came to him, confessing your sin and asking that he be merciful to you on the basis of Christ's atonement. Jesus said of the tax collector that "this man . . . went home justified before God" (Luke 18:14a). So may you be. It is that easy.

11. Stott, *The Cross of Christ*, pp. 191, 192.

46

Faith

Romans 3:25-26

God presented him as a sacrifice of atonement, through faith in his blood. He did this to demonstrate his justice, because in his forbearance he had left the sins committed beforehand unpunished—he did it to demonstrate his justice at the present time, so as to be just and the one who justifies [those] who have faith in Jesus.

It is time to talk about faith.

Wonderful as the salvation that has been accomplished by Jesus Christ may be, it is of no use to us unless it becomes ours personally—and the way the work of Christ becomes ours personally is through faith. That is why the Bible says, "And without faith it is impossible to please God . . ." (Heb. 11:6) and why the apostle Paul speaks of faith so often in the section of Romans we are now studying—eight times in verses 21 through 31.[1]

When we began our study of this section, I suggested a four-part outline of the doctrines Paul was presenting here. The outline was not inclusive, but it indicated the general direction of the passage. The points were these: (1) God has provided a righteousness of his own for men and women, a

---

1. "Faith" occurs in verses 22, 25, 26, 27, 28, 30 (twice), and 31. But "believe," which is the same root word in Greek, also occurs in verse 22, and both words appear frequently in Romans 4.

righteousness we do not possess ourselves; (2) this righteousness is made available to us by grace; that is, we do not deserve it and in fact are incapable ever of deserving it; (3) it is the work of the Lord Jesus Christ in dying for his people, redeeming them from their sin, that has made this grace on God's part possible; and (4) the righteousness that God has graciously provided becomes ours through simple faith. In pursuing this outline we looked at the third point carefully—considering the various ways in which the work of Christ is presented to us—and this led to a study of justification, which is another way of talking about God's gift to us of his righteousness.

But we have done that, and we have now come to the fourth and last point of the outline: "The righteousness that God has graciously provided becomes ours through simple faith."

You can hardly miss this point if you read Romans 3:21–31 with care (but I will nonetheless add italics for emphasis). In those verses Paul tells us: "This righteousness of God comes through *faith* in Jesus Christ to all who believe" (v. 22). He says that "God presented him as a sacrifice of atonement, through *faith* in his blood" (v. 24). He teaches that God "justifies those who have *faith* in Jesus" (v. 26), maintaining that "a man is justified by *faith* apart from observing the law" (v. 28). Paul concludes that "there is only one God, who will justify the circumcised by *faith* and the uncircumcised through that same *faith*" (v. 30). This message is clear. Faith is not a good work. It does not earn salvation. It does not put God in debt to us. Nevertheless, faith is essential, for only those who believe on Jesus Christ are saved.

What Is Faith?

What exactly is faith? There have been many attempts to define faith, some of them misleading. Here are several good ones.

First, a definition by John Calvin: "We shall possess a right definition of faith if we call it a firm and certain knowledge of God's benevolence toward us, founded upon the truth of the freely given promise in Christ, both revealed to our minds and sealed upon our hearts through the Holy Spirit."[2] Calvin emphasizes what is stated by Paul in Romans, namely, that true faith is in God's freely offered salvation through the work of Christ. But he adds, as Paul suggests in Ephesians 2:8–10 though not in Romans 3, that this is the work of the Holy Spirit in us.

Here is another definition—by Charles Haddon Spurgeon: "Faith is believing that Christ is what he is said to be. and that he will do what he has promised to do, and then to expect this of him."[3]

2. John Calvin, *Institutes of the Christian Religion*, ed. John T. McNeill, trans. Ford Lewis Battles (Philadelphia: The Westminster Press, 1960), p. 551.

3. Charles Haddon Spurgeon, *All of Grace* (Chicago: Moody Press, n.d.), p. 47.

I like that definition, but I remember something Spurgeon said in the chapter of *All of Grace* in which he provides it. He told of an uneducated preacher who read a chapter of the Bible to his people at the start of his sermon and then said that he was going to "confound" it. He meant "expound" it. But Spurgeon noted that there is always danger of doing that where faith is concerned. We can explain it until no one understands it. "Faith is the simplest of all things," he said.[4] It is perhaps its very simplicity that makes it so hard to comprehend.

How can we explain faith? How can we make the very complex definitions of the textbooks manageable?

The First Element: Knowledge

Most theologians and Bible teachers divide faith into three parts: "knowledge, belief and trust"[5] or "awareness, assent and commitment"[6] or some variation of those ideas. But, in nearly every case, the point with which they begin is "knowledge of the truth" or what I call "content." Faith without content is no true faith at all.

Of the writers on faith, Calvin is perhaps strongest on this point, for he found it necessary to oppose a very serious error about faith that had developed in the teaching of the medieval church. In the years before the Reformation the church had been derelict in teaching the Scriptures to the people. Consequently, most people were ignorant of the true gospel of salvation, and most clergy were ignorant of it also. How, then, were such ignorant communicants to be saved? The church answered that it was by "implicit" faith. That is, it was not necessary for the faithful actually to know anything. All they had to do was trust the church implicitly. The church and its teachings were right, even if its members did not know what those right teachings were, and they would be all right, too, if they just believed or trusted the church.

The situation reminds me of a contemporary story in which a man was being interviewed by a group of church officers before being taken into membership. They asked him what he believed about salvation, and he replied that he believed what the church believed.

"But what does the church believe?" they probed.

"The church believes what I believe," he answered.

The committee was a bit exasperated by this time. But they tried again: "Just what do you and the church believe?"

The man thought this over for a moment and then replied, "We believe the same thing."

4. Ibid., 44.

5. Ibid.

6. D. M. Lloyd-Jones, *Romans: An Exposition of Chapters 3:20–4:25, Atonement and Justification* (Grand Rapids: Zondervan, 1970), p. 45.

The situation was not unlike that of most people in the Middle Ages. So this was what Calvin attacked. He argued that "the object of faith is Christ" and that "faith rests upon knowledge, not upon pious ignorance." Calvin wrote, "We do not obtain salvation either because we are prepared to embrace as true whatever the church has prescribed, or because we turn over to it the task of inquiring and knowing. But we do so when we know that God is our merciful Father, because of reconciliation effected through Christ (2 Cor. 5:18, 19), and that Christ has been given to us as righteousness, sanctification and life. By this knowledge, I say, not by submission of our feeling, do we obtain entry into the Kingdom of Heaven."[7]

This ancient debate has bearing upon the "faith" of many persons today, for although many probably do not exercise "implicit" faith in the church or in any other authority, they seem to have implicit faith in themselves or merely "faith in faith," which turns out to be almost the same thing.

The greatest offender at this point is Norman Vincent Peale, who has popularized a subjective faith in his best-selling book *The Power of Positive Thinking*. He suggests that we collect a few of the Bible's strong statements about faith—statements like "All things are possible to him who believes" (Mark 9:23) and "If you have faith as a grain of mustard seed, you will say to this mountain, 'Move from here to there,' and it will move; nothing will be impossible to you" (Matt. 17:20)—memorize them and then let them sink down into our subconscious minds and transform us. In this way, says Peale, we will become believers in God and in ourselves: "According to your faith in yourself, according to your faith in your job, according to your faith in God, thus far will you get and no further."[8] His last words are: "So believe and live successfully."

But believe *what*? And believe *whom*?

The advice Peale gives may be very useful for a salesman or for a person who is worried about doing well at school or at work. But this is not biblical faith. It is, as John Stott notes, only another word for "self-confidence" or "optimism."[9]

To anyone who thinks that faith in God is roughly the same thing as faith in his or her job success or in oneself, the Christian must reply that this is not so. If it were, the object of faith would be irrelevant. But in the gospel the object of faith is the all important thing. Our faith must be in Christ and his work rather than in ourselves. We are inadequate for what needs to be done. Therefore, we must trust Christ, whom God has sent to be the Savior.

7. Calvin, *Institutes of the Christian Religion*, pp. 542, 544, 545.

8. Norman Vincent Peale, *The Power of Positive Thinking* (New York: Prentice-Hall, 1952), p. 99.

9. John R. W. Stott, *Your Mind Matters* (Downers Grove, Ill.: InterVarsity Press, 1972), p. 36.

Faith and the Word of God

In his *Institutes of the Christian Religion*, Calvin is so concerned about stressing the importance of knowledge as the first element in faith that he rightly presents it in another way, showing the necessary link between faith and the Word of God, or the Bible. Reduced to its basics, Calvin shows that: (1) faith is *defined* by God's Word; (2) faith is *born* of God's Word; and (3) faith is *sustained* by God's Word.

The first of these points is particularly clear in Romans 3. For Paul speaks of faith after having spoken of the righteousness of God (that is, the gospel) "to which the Law and the Prophets testify" (v. 21). It is after this that he says, "This righteousness from God comes through faith in Jesus Christ to all who believe" (v. 22). In other words, the faith in Christ about which he is speaking is faith in that work of Christ previously revealed in and explained by the Old Testament. It has this specific content. It is not nebulous. Moreover—lest we miss this—the next chapter of Romans proves that the way of salvation was disclosed in the cases of Abraham and David who, Paul says, were saved by the same faith with which we are saved. He cites Genesis 15:6 and Psalm 32:1–2 as evidence.

There cannot be any true faith without the Word of God, for it is in the Word alone that we learn what we are to believe. Calvin says, "There is [therefore] a permanent relationship between faith and the Word. . . . Take away the Word and no faith will then remain."[10]

The second way in which faith is linked to the Word of God is that faith is created, born, or awakened in us by that Word. Apart from the Word, we are like Lazarus—as dead in our transgressions as he was dead in his cold Judean tomb. What will awaken us from that sleep of death? Nothing but the voice of Christ calling to us: "John, come forth! . . . Mary, come forth! . . . Charles, come forth!" Only the call of the life-giving God can produce such new life. But where can we hear that call? Not in the words of mere men or women. Not in human books. The only place we can hear it is in the pages of the Bible, where alone God speaks.

That is why Peter speaks of our being "born again, not of perishable seed, but of imperishable, through the living and enduring word of God" (1 Peter 1:23).

The third link between faith and the Bible is that it is through the Bible that faith is strengthened or sustained. Why? Because the Bible directs us to God and his promises, and only God is strong enough to support us in this matter of salvation. Calvin says, "Therefore, if faith turns away even in the slightest degree from this goal toward which it should aim, it does not keep its own nature, but becomes uncertain credulity and vague error of mind."[11] The conclusion is that if you wish to be strong in faith and grow in

---

10. Calvin, *Institutes of the Christian Religion*, pp. 548, 549.
11. Ibid., p. 549.

it, you must spend time studying the Bible and appropriating the promises of God that are found there.

The Second Element: Moving of the Heart

The second element in true biblical faith is what I call the "moving of the heart" or what others have called "belief" (Spurgeon) or "assent" (Lloyd-Jones). The idea here is that, important as the biblical content of faith is and which Calvin stressed so strongly, it is nevertheless possible to know this content and yet be lost—if it has not touched the individual personally. An example is the devil, who undoubtedly knows the Bible and understands theology better than we do, yet who does not believe it in this fuller sense. "Even the demons believe" but "shudder" (James 2:19).

The best example of what this second element in faith means comes from the conversion of John Wesley, the great evangelist. This took place in May 1738. Wesley had been an active preacher and evangelist for years before this. He knew Christian doctrine, but it had not affected him at a genuinely personal level. Although he "believed" in a sense, he did not really love Christ or trust him personally. However, one evening he went to a little meeting in Aldersgate Street in London, where someone was reading Luther's "Preface" (actually a sermon) to the Epistle to the Romans. Here is what happened, as Wesley tells it: "About a quarter before nine, while he was describing the change which God works in the heart through faith in Christ, I felt my heart strangely warmed. I felt I did trust in Christ, Christ alone for my salvation. And an assurance was given me that he had taken away *my* sins, even *mine*, and saved *me* from the law of sin and death."[12] Some might argue that Wesley had been saved before this and only came to know it at this point. That may be the case, but Wesley testified that this "warming of the heart" was an important part of what is meant by trusting Christ.

Here is how Calvin put it—after a long section (forty out of fifty pages on "faith") dealing with the element of knowledge or content: "It now remains to pour into the heart itself what the mind has absorbed. For the Word of God is not received by faith if it flits about in the top of the brain, but when it takes root in the depth of the heart that it may be an invincible defense to withstand and drive off all the stratagems of temptation."[13]

The Third Element: Commitment

The third element of faith, which Spurgeon calls "trust" and Lloyd-Jones calls "commitment," is a real yielding of oneself to Christ, which goes beyond having knowledge, however full or accurate, or even being person-

12. John Wesley, *The Works of John Wesley*, vol. 1, *Journal from October 14, 1735, to November 29, 1845* (Grand Rapids: Zondervan, n.d.), p. 103.

13. Calvin, *Institutes of the Christian Religion*, p. 583.

ally moved by the gospel. (Many are moved, even to tears, but are not saved.) It is the point at which we pass over the line from belonging to ourselves (as we think) and become the Lord's disciples. It is what was seen in Thomas when he not only believed in Jesus and his resurrection but fell at his feet in worship, exclaiming, "My Lord and my God!" (John 20:28).

It is at this point that faith joins hands with love, which it closely resembles, and hope is born from that union.

This leads me to the best of all possible illustrations: the way in which a young man and a young woman meet, fall in love, and get married. The first stages of their courtship correspond to the first element in faith; that is, knowledge or content. At this stage each is getting to know the other and trying to determine whether the other is the kind of person whose qualities will contribute to a good and lasting marriage. The second stage is falling in love. It corresponds to the "moving of the heart" element, that is, to the point at which the other person begins to affect the lover in a personal and usually emotional way. The final stage comes when the couple stands in church before the minister and recites the vows by which they pledge themselves to one another.

Jesus pledges himself to us; he has already done it. We pledge ourselves to him through the third element of faith: commitment.

In the wedding service that I use, the vows go: "I, John, take thee, Mary, to be my wedded wife; and I do promise and covenant, before God and these witnesses, to be thy loving and faithful husband: in plenty and in want, in joy and in sorrow, in sickness and in health, as long as we both shall live." The bride says the same words back.

This is how our faith is expressed to Jesus Christ. He died for us, demonstrating the nature of his true love and sterling character. He wooed us, getting us to love him who first loved us. Now he takes the wedding vow, saying, "I, Jesus, take thee, [whoever you may be; put your own name in the space], to be my wedded wife; and I do promise and covenant, before God the Father and these witnesses, to be thy loving and faithful Savior and Bridegroom: in plenty and in want, in joy and in sorrow, in sickness and in health, in this life and for all eternity."

We then look up into his face and repeat the words. "I, [whoever you are; add your own name], take thee, Jesus, to be my loving Savior and Lord; and I do promise and covenant, before God the Father and these witnesses, to be thy loving and faithful wife: in plenty and in want, in joy and in sorrow, in sickness and in health, for this life and for all eternity."

God the Father (not an earthly minister) then pronounces the marriage, and you become the Lord Jesus Christ's forever.

Have you done that? Have you believed on Jesus Christ? Do you love him? Do you know yourself to have been made his forever?

You may say, "Well, I do not know if I have or not."

If you do not know, settle the matter right now. For most wedding services today there are months of preparation during which a church and minister are selected, a guest list is drawn up, clothes are purchased, a license is procured, and many other details are handled. But nothing remains to be done before you are able to make your commitment to Christ. He has done it all. The Father is there. The wedding is prepared. All you must do now is say your vow to him. You must believe and follow Jesus.

Perhaps you say, "But I am unworthy."

Of course you are. How could anybody possibly be worthy of the love of the Lord Jesus Christ? All are unworthy, but it is precisely your awareness of your unworthiness that makes it possible for you to know you need a Savior. Paul reminds us that God has shown "his love for us in this: While we were still sinners, Christ died for us" (Rom. 5:8).

Now you might say, "But my faith is so weak."

Yes, and your love and hope and everything else are weak, too. But it does not take *strong* faith to be saved, just faith. Spurgeon wrote, "The weakness of your faith will not destroy you. A trembling hand may receive a golden gift."[14]

Reach out your hand. Place it in that pierced hand that is stretched out to you. Clasp it to your heart, and love Jesus forever.

14. Spurgeon, *All of Grace*, p. 43.

47

Faith in His Blood

Romans 3:25

God presented him as a sacrifice of atonement, through faith in his blood.

In the last few studies we have explored the multifaceted salvation achieved for us by Jesus Christ, looking at it by such terms as *propitiation, redemption,* and *justification,* and showing its application to us through saving faith. But there is one phrase we have overlooked and to which we must now return: "in his blood." It occurs in Romans 3:25: "God presented him as a sacrifice of atonement, through faith in his blood." This is the key idea and yet one of the most opposed ideas in Romans 3.

Opposition to the words is obvious. A number of years ago I was preaching about the atonement and mentioned the blood of Jesus Christ in my sermon. When I had finished I was accosted by a man who was very antagonistic toward such teaching. "Why are you Fundamentalists always talking about the *blood* of Jesus?" he objected. "Why do you wallow in something so repulsive?" He felt—and his later comments expressed it energetically—that modern Christianity should forget about such ancient concepts and focus instead on things like God's beauty. We should do away with hymns like Robert Lowry's "What can wash away my sin? Nothing but the blood of Jesus." Or William Cowper's "There is a fountain filled with blood Drawn from Immanuel's veins. . . ." According to this man and those who think like him, these hymns are not worthy of "modern" Christianity.

Are they correct in their opinion? I hope to show that not only are they incorrect, but in taking this view they actually miss the very heart of Christianity.

An "Evangelical" Error

Before I do that, however, I need to mention another problem that has arisen with the word *blood*—not from so-called modernists but from people within the evangelical camp. Evangelicals have traditionally believed that the phrase "blood of Christ" is a way of talking about the death of Christ, much like the word *cross*. But the troublesome view I am referring to maintains that Christ's blood stands not for his death but for his life, which was released through his death and thus made available to us.

The idea seems to have originated—of all places—in a work by the great English churchman Brooke Foss Westcott, *The Epistles of St. John*. Westcott wrote:

> The blood is the seat of life in such a sense that it can be spoken of directly as the life itself. . . . By the outpouring of the blood the life which was in it was not destroyed, though it was separated from the organism which it had before quickened. . . . Thus two distinct ideas were included in the sacrifice of a victim, the death of the victim by the shedding of its blood, and the liberation, so to speak, of the principle of life by which it had been animated, so that this life became available for another end.[1]

After Westcott, the idea was picked up by a number of other British Bible scholars, among them Vincent Taylor, C. H. Dodd, and P. T. Forsyth.[2]

What are the grounds for this view? The biblical basis, as Westcott noted in his commentary, is in Leviticus 17:11, "For the life of a creature is in the blood" and Deuteronomy 12:23, "The blood is the life." Unfortunately, these texts do not mean what the proponents of this rather eccentric view suppose.

Beginning with James Denney's *The Death of Christ*, published originally in 1902 but issued many times since,[3] a number of very careful studies of the use of the word *blood* in Scripture have appeared, including: (1) H. E. Guillebaud, "The Meaning of the Blood of Christ" in *Why the Cross?*[4], (2)

1. Brooke Foss Westcott, *The Epistles of St. John* (Grand Rapids: Wm. B. Eerdmans, 1892), pp. 34, 35.

2. See John R. W. Stott, *The Cross of Christ* (Downers Grove, Ill.: InterVarsity Press, 1986), p. 179.

3. James Denney, *The Death of Christ* (Chicago: InterVarsity Press, 1964). For Denney's response to Westcott, see pp. 148–155.

4. H. E. Guillebaud, *Why the Cross?* (Chicago: InterVarsity Christian Fellowship, 1946), pp. 136–140.

Alan M. Stibbs, *The Meaning of the Word "Blood" in Scripture*[5], and (3) Leon Morris, "The Blood" in *The Apostolic Preaching of the Cross.*[6] These studies recognize the scriptural connection between "blood" and "life." But, as Guillebaud says, "Blood is never mentioned except in connection with the shedding of it, or with the use of it after it has been shed. . . . The blood shed is the life poured out, and the poured out life may be used only for atonement."[7]

Morris says about the same thing: "In both the Old and New Testaments the blood signifies essentially the death. . . . [It is] another, clearer expression for the death of Christ in its salvation meaning."[8]

Salvation by Substitution

If you have never heard of the mistaken notion examined above, do not worry about it at all. Dismiss it from your mind. The important thing is to remember that the shedding of Christ's blood has to do with Christ's death, and that the death of Christ in Scripture is always and everywhere set forth as substitutionary. It is by his death that you and I can be saved.

I have referred several times to John R. W. Stott's fine study of *The Cross of Christ.* It is an achievement of this work that, although it thoroughly investigates the biblical images for the meaning of the death of Jesus Christ, it never forgets that the basic idea in every single one of them is substitution—and that by the shedding of Christ's blood.

Let us consider each of the pertinent doctrines once more:

1. *Propitiation.* We have already noted that propitiation has to do with turning aside the wrath of God against sin. But how is that to be accomplished? God's wrath is against sin, and God's justice demands the death of sinners. The soul that sins must die. If the sinner is to escape that fierce wrath of God, the judgment of God upon sin must be poured out upon a substitute. An innocent must die in the guilty person's place. This is what Jesus did for us, and it is why Paul introduces the phrase "in his blood" at this particular place in Romans: "God presented him as a sacrifice of atonement through faith in his blood." Since "sacrifice of atonement" is the New International Version's rendering of "propitiation," the phrase "faith in his blood" in this verse means "faith in his propitiation" or "faith in the atonement."

When we studied "propitiation" I pointed out that the concept is linked to the Mercy Seat of the Ark of the Covenant and that propitiation was

5. Alan M. Stibbs, *The Meaning of the Word "Blood" in Scripture* (London: Tyndale Press, 1948).

6. Leon Morris, *The Apostolic Preaching of the Cross* (Grand Rapids: Wm. B. Eerdmans, 1956). For his study of "The Blood," see pp. 108–124.

7. Guillebaud, *Why the Cross?*, p. 139.

8. Morris, *The Apostolic Preaching of the Cross*, p. 122.

made in Israel when the high priest sprinkled the blood of a slain animal between the symbolic presence of God above the Mercy Seat of the Ark and the law of God within the Ark below it. The blood testified to the substitutionary death of the victim.

It is with this in mind that the author of Hebrews writes, "When Christ came as high priest of the good things that are already here, he went through the greater and more perfect tabernacle that is not man-made, that is to say, not a part of this creation. He did not enter by means of the blood of goats and calves; but he entered the Most Holy Place once for all by his own blood, having obtained eternal redemption. The blood of goats and bulls and the ashes of a heifer sprinkled on those who are ceremonially unclean sanctify them so that they are outwardly clean. How much more, then, will the blood of Christ, who through the eternal Spirit offered himself unblemished to God, cleanse our consciences from acts that lead to death, so that we may serve the living God!" (Heb. 9:11–14).

2. *Redemption.* The idea of blood (and therefore also of death and substitution) is present in references to redemption, too. Redemption has to do with purchasing the sinner from sin's slavery so that he or she does not have to return to sin's marketplace. How is this to be accomplished? Sinners have no resources by which to purchase their redemption. All sinners are bankrupt. Not so the Lord. The Lord is infinitely rich. So he substitutes for us, purchasing our redemption by his own death, or "blood." Here are some pertinent texts (in which I have italicized the key words):

Ephesians 1:7–8: "In him we have redemption *through his blood*, the forgiveness of sins, in accordance with the riches of God's grace that he lavished on us with all wisdom and understanding."

Acts 20:28: "Keep watch over yourselves and all the flock of which the Holy Spirit has made you overseers. Be shepherds of the church of God, which he bought *with his own blood*."

Above all, 1 Peter 1:18–19: "For you know that it was not with perishable things such as silver or gold that you were redeemed from the empty way of life handed down to you from your forefathers, but *with the precious blood of Christ*, a lamb without blemish or defect."

3. *Justification.* Justification, as we have seen, is a legal term, denoting the act by which a judge declares a defendant to be in a right standing before the prevailing law. But here the judge is God. We are the defendants. We want to be declared right before God's holy law. Yet we are not right. We are violators of God's law. How can we be "justified"—declared right? Obviously, only if another makes things right, which is what Jesus has done for us by his death. This is why two chapters further on in Romans we find Paul writing, "We have now been justified by his blood" (Rom. 5:9). It is by Jesus' substitutionary death and the propitiation achieved by it that we are justified.

Here is the way John Stott puts it in his summary, referring to redemption, propitiation, justification, and reconciliation (which we have not yet studied in detail since it is not included in Romans 3:21–31):

All four images plainly teach that God's saving work was achieved through the bloodshedding, that is, the substitutionary sacrifice of Christ. . . . Since Christ's blood is a symbol of his life laid down in violent death, it is also plain in each of the four images that he died in our place as our substitute. The death of Jesus was the atoning sacrifice because of which God averted his wrath from us, the ransom-price by which we have been redeemed, the condemnation of the innocent that the guilty might be justified, and the sinless One being made sin for us.[9]

Where Is the Lamb?

These ideas are so foreign to the thinking of most modern people that it is a difficult matter even to make them comprehensible. But it was not always so. I want you to see in closing that they were actually the steadfast, earnest, and joyful expectation of Old Testament believers, leading up to the coming of Jesus Christ.

To make my point I take you to a question recorded in a passage quite near the beginning of the Bible. Genesis 22 contains the story of Abraham's near-sacrifice of his only son, Isaac, on Mount Moriah, which was a picture of the eventual sacrifice of God's own Son Jesus at that very location several thousand years later. I direct you to it because of the exchange that took place between Abraham and his son while they were making their way up the mountain. Isaac was carrying the wood for the sacrifice. Abraham was carrying the fire and knife. Isaac noticed that there was no animal for the sacrifice.

"Father?" he said.

"Yes, my son," answered Abraham.

"The fire and wood are here," Isaac said. "But where is the lamb for the burnt offering?"

Abraham answered, "God himself will provide the lamb for the burnt offering, my son" (vv. 7–8).

I refer to this exchange because the question asked by Isaac was the most profound question anyone could have asked during the Old Testament period. Indeed, it must have been the chief question of the Old Testament saints. In the same way during this same period, the answer of Abraham was the most profound answer anyone could have given. Think it through with me:

When Adam and Eve sinned in the Garden of Eden, eating from the tree that God had told them not to eat from, God came to them—not to judge them with immediate death as he had said he would, but to show them the way of salvation. He took two animals, probably lambs, killed and skinned

9. Stott, *The Cross of Christ*, p. 202.

them and then clothed our first parents with the fresh skins. Adam, who was probably great in his spiritual understanding, no doubt saw the point immediately. The fact that the animals died showed that sin does indeed bring death. "For the wages of sin is death . . ." (Rom. 6:23). But it also showed that it is possible to have a substitute die in the sinner's place.

Moreover, God promised a deliverer in his judgment on the serpent: "And I will put enmity between you and the woman, and between your offspring and hers; he will crush your head, and you will strike his heel" (Gen. 3:15).

Combining the two revelations, Adam must have reasoned along these lines. "I understand what God is teaching. The principle is substitution, the death of one for another. But I also understand that this can only be a type or symbol of what is coming, since a lamb is not the equivalent of a human being. The death of a lamb does not atone for the sin of a rational man or woman. If a genuine salvation is to be achieved for us, an actual deliverer must come. But when? When will he come?" Adam might well have asked Isaac's question: "Where is the lamb for the burnt offering?"

Abraham was not present on that occasion, of course. But if he had been, he could have answered exactly as he answered Isaac so many years later: "God himself will provide the lamb for the burnt offering." He would have meant, "I do not know when God will do it; but he has promised to do it, and he will certainly send the true lamb at the right time."

I press ahead through the centuries and come to Moses, another great man of God. When God was about to lead the people of Israel out of Egypt into their own land, he passed through Pharaoh's kingdom with one final plague, striking down the firstborn. Only the Jews were spared this fierce judgment, and then only if they had first killed a lamb and had sprinkled its blood upon the doorposts and lintels of their homes. Again, when they had been taken from Egypt and been brought to Mount Sinai, God gave instructions for the Day of Atonement, indicating that on that day other animals were to be killed as sacrifices for the people.

Moses must have understood these symbols, too, just as Adam must have understood the symbols given to him in the garden. If not, there would have been no point in God's having supplied the revelations. But Moses might still have asked Isaac's question. "I understand the principle of substitution," he might have testified. "Animals are being killed in our place. But surely the blood of bulls and goats can never take away sin. The animals point ahead to something finer and more lasting. They point to the true lamb, the great lamb. But where is the lamb for the burnt offering?"

Again, if Abraham had been present, he could have replied, "God himself will provide the lamb for the burnt offering."

David, too, could have asked Isaac's question. He understood the principle of substitution. When he sinned in regard to Bathsheba and later confessed his sin and wrote the great fifty-first Psalm as a pointer to the path to salvation, he put down: "Cleanse me with hyssop, and I will be clean; wash me, and I will be whiter than snow" (v. 7). Hyssop was the plant used by priests to dip into the blood of the sacrifice to sprinkle its blood. So when David wrote, "Cleanse me with hyssop," he was pleading salvation by the blood of the sacrifice. Still, he could have queried its relevance: "I recognize that God has appointed sacrifice as the way of cleansing. But surely a mere lamb does not take away sin. It points to something greater. Where is that greater sacrifice? Where is the lamb for the burnt offering?"

Abraham would have answered, "God himself, in his own time, will provide the lamb for the burnt offering."

Isaiah could have asked Isaac's question, although his prophecy included the greatest statement of the principle of substitutionary sacrifice, or vicarious atonement, in all the Bible: Isaiah 53.

> Surely he took up our infirmities
>   and carried our sorrows,
> yet we considered him stricken by God,
>   smitten by him, and afflicted.
> But he was pierced for our transgressions,
>   he was crushed for our iniquities;
> the punishment that brought us peace was upon him,
>   and by his wounds we are healed.
> We all, like sheep, have gone astray,
>   each of us has turned to his own way;
> and the LORD has laid on him
>   the iniquity of us all.
>
>   (vv. 4–6)

Still, he might have asked— indeed, in one sense that chapter does ask—"Where is the lamb for the burnt offering?"

Abraham would have answered, "God will provide a lamb for the burnt offering."

Jeremiah, Hosea, Habakkuk, Zechariah, Malachi—all the prophets— could have asked this question. And at the time of Jesus there were other faithful people who were asking it, people like Simeon (Luke 2:25–35) and Anna the prophetess, both of whom represented those who were looking for "the redemption of Jerusalem" (Luke 2:38).

"Behold the Lamb"

At last there came a day—the fourth gospel writer tells us about it—when John the Baptist was baptizing by the Jordan River and a relative of his from the north, a man named Jesus, walked by. John, instructed by the Holy Spirit, pointed to Jesus and declared, "Look, the Lamb of God, who takes away the sin of the world!" (John 1:29).

What is that you said, John? Did you say, "Lamb of God"? Are you telling us that the sacrificial lamb we have been looking for and waiting for all these long centuries has come? Has the one who will save us by the shedding of his blood finally arrived on this earth? John answered that this is exactly what he said and that this is indeed the case.

Three short years later, while tens of thousands of lambs were being driven to Jerusalem for Passover, probably in the year A.D. 30, Jesus himself went up to the city on the day we call Palm Sunday. Later that week, at the precise moment when the Passover lambs were being killed, Jesus died in our place, shedding his blood for our salvation.

The world does not like the very idea of the "blood of Jesus," and it is not surprising. His blood represents that for which we have the most extreme aversion: salvation from someone else, the sacrificial death of another in our place. We want to save ourselves, to be our own saviors. But we cannot save ourselves. If we are to be saved at all, it must be by faith in that sacrifice.

"What can wash away my sin?"

It may not be great poetry, but Lowry's hymn answers truthfully and conclusively when it says, "Nothing but the blood of Jesus."

48

No Grounds for Boasting

Romans 3:27–28

Where, then, is boasting? It is excluded. On what principle? On that of observing the law? No, but on that of faith. For we maintain that a man is justified by faith apart from observing the law.

In most modern translations of the Bible, the New International Version included, Romans 3:27 begins a new paragraph—and rightly so. The section it introduces (vv. 27–31) is part of the latter half of the third chapter, in which the way of salvation is fully and brilliantly expounded. But it is also a postscript to verses 21–26. The earlier verses, the first paragraph, tell of the plan God has devised to save men and women. It is by the work of the Lord Jesus Christ, and can be summed up in the words "justification by grace through faith alone." The next five verses, which make up a second paragraph, present three consequences or implications of this plan.

The first is that this way of salvation "by grace through faith" *excludes boasting.*

The second is that it provides one way of salvation *for everybody.*

The third is that, far from allowing a person to indulge in immorality or lawbreaking, as some suppose, it actually *upholds the law.* God's way of salvation provides a level of morality of which mere adherents to law, apart from the grace of God in the gospel, cannot even dream.

These three consequences of the doctrine of justification by grace through faith will occupy us in this and the next two studies, which conclude the section of my commentary I have called "God's Remedy in Christ."

The Greatest of All Sins

It is appropriate that the first implication of the doctrine of justification by faith concerns boasting. For boasting is related to pride—it is an expression of it—and pride is the greatest of all sins, according to biblical Christianity. If pride is the greatest of all sins and God's plan of salvation does not destroy pride—rooting it up, casting it out, and even dusting off the place where it stood—then it is not a good plan. It has failed, and we need a faith other than Christianity.

In the Middle Ages pride was identified by churchmen as the first of the seven deadly sins. This evaluation seems quaint and overstated today. But pride should never be thought of as a harmless flaw, because pride is actually quite deadly.

I do not know of anybody who has written more perceptively about pride in modern times than C. S. Lewis, so let me share a bit of what he had to say on this topic. Lewis begins by calling pride the place where Christian morality differs most sharply from all other moral systems:

> There is one vice of which no man in the world is free; which everyone in the world loathes when he sees it in someone else; and of which hardly any people, except Christians, ever imagine that they are guilty themselves. I have heard people admit that they are bad-tempered, or that they cannot keep their heads about girls or drink, or even that they are cowards. I do not think I have ever heard anyone who was not a Christian accuse himself of this vice. And at the same time I have very seldom met anyone, who was not a Christian, who showed the slightest mercy to it in others. There is no fault which makes a man more unpopular, and no fault which we are more unconscious of in ourselves. And the more we have it ourselves, the more we dislike it in others. The vice I am talking of is Pride.[1]

That is self-evidently true. But it is also a strange thing, isn't it? Why are we so unconscious of this vice in ourselves? And why do we hate in others that of which we are all so guilty?

The answer is in the very nature of pride. Lewis described pride as:

> *essentially* competitive—competitive by its very nature—while the other vices are competitive only, so to speak, by accident. Pride gets no pleasure out of

1. C. S. Lewis, *Mere Christianity* (New York: The Macmillan Company, 1958), p. 94.

having something, only out of having more of it than the next man. We say that people are proud of being rich, or clever, or good-looking, but they are not. They are proud of being richer, or cleverer, or better-looking than others. If everyone else became equally rich, or clever, or good-looking there would be nothing to be proud about. It is the comparison that makes you proud: the pleasure of being above the rest. . . .

The Christians are right: it is Pride which has been the chief cause of misery in every nation and every family since the world began. Other vices may sometimes bring people together: you may find good fellowship and jokes and friendliness among drunken people or unchaste people. But Pride always means enmity—it *is* enmity. And not only enmity between man and man, but enmity to God.[2]

Pride was the very first sin. It was the sin of Satan, who said,

> "I will ascend to heaven;
> I will raise my throne
>   above the stars of God;
> I will sit enthroned on the mount of assembly,
>   on the utmost heights of the sacred mountain.
> I will ascend above the tops of the clouds;
>   I will make myself like the Most High."
> Isaiah 14:13–14

Pride made Satan want to ascend into heaven to the very throne of God, but the Bible says it actually brought him "down to the grave, to the depths of the pit" (v. 15).

Pride was the sin of Eve, who wanted to "be like God, knowing good and evil" (Gen. 3:5). But she did not rise up to become like God. Instead she became like Satan in her perverted and fallen knowledge.

Pride was the sin of Adam, who could not abide even the slightest restriction on his quest for complete autonomy. He could not stand God's law. Adam wanted to be a law unto himself; so he sinned and brought the entire human race into misery.

Pride in Religion

Where in the range of human experience and relationships is pride most evident and at the same time most clearly wrong and inappropriate? Is it in the sphere of daily work? Do we show our pride most in thinking of ourselves as better than other people in what we make or do? Is it in our social relationships? Do we show pride most by thinking that we are more sophisticated or more charming than someone else? Is the person who wants to be the center of attention at the New Year's Eve party the most prideful of the persons we know?

2. Ibid., pp. 95, 96.

No, the sphere of life in which people show the most pride is religion. And there is a good reason for this. Religion—not true Christianity, but religion in the generic sense—is the ultimate setting for the very worst expressions of pride. For it is in religion alone that we are able to claim that God, and not mere human beings, sets his approval on us as superior to other human beings. Moreover, the more demanding or rigorous our "religion" is, the more prideful we become.

Do we need an example? The Lord Jesus Christ provided one when he compared the humility of the tax collector, who was saved by faith in the mercy of God made known in the sacrifices, with the pride of the Pharisee, who boasted of his goodness: "God, I thank you that I am not like other men—robbers, evildoers, adulterers—or even like this tax collector. I fast twice a week and give a tenth of all I get" (Luke 18:11–12). What is the problem here? Was the Pharisee lying? Was he only pretending to give a tenth of all he had to God when actually, like lying Ananias and Sapphira, he was keeping back a part? I do not think so. As mentioned in a previous study, I think he really did fast twice a week. I think he really did give a tenth of all he received to the temple. By outward standards he was significantly superior to the despised tax collector, who even admitted that he was a "sinner" needing mercy.

But that is just it, you see. If the Pharisee had merely been asking a fellow human to appraise his achievements and declare him superior to the tax collector, it would have been unpleasant and perhaps inappropriate. But it could have been done. If we were being asked our opinion, we might have agreed with the Pharisee's assessment—but with a very bad taste in our mouths. We would have acknowledged it but disliked it, without even knowing why.

But the Pharisee was not asking a mere human being for approval. He was *demanding* it of God. And if it is unpleasant and inappropriate to think of submitting one's pride to a human tribunal, it is infinitely more unpleasant and inappropriate—a horror—to think of expecting the holy God to endorse one's own self-inflated judgment. Before God—if he could ever have become truly aware of God—the Pharisee's attainments would have faded away to nothing and he would have seen himself as no different from the tax collector. The fact that he did not see himself as a sinner in need of mercy shows that he did not actually know God at all.

Here is the way Lewis puts it:

> How is it that people who are quite obviously eaten up with Pride can say that they believe in God and appear to themselves very religious? I am afraid it means they are worshiping an imaginary God. They theoretically admit themselves to be nothing in the presence of this phantom God, but are really all the time imagining how he approves of them and thinks them far better than ordinary people: that is, they pay a pennyworth of imaginary humility to him and get out of it a pound's worth of Pride towards their fellow-men. . . .

Whenever we find that our religious life is making us feel that we are good—above all, that we are better than someone else—I think we may be sure that we are being acted on, not by God, but by the devil. The real test of being in the presence of God is that you either forget about yourself altogether or see yourself as a small, dirty object. It is better to forget about yourself altogether.[3]

A Boast-Free Gospel

But how can we possibly forget about ourselves—we who are so filled with pride? It is the very nature of pride to do the opposite. The answer is that in ourselves we cannot. That is what being saved by grace means; it means that we cannot save ourselves. We are no more able to save ourselves or forget about ourselves than are other human beings. But we are enabled to forget about ourselves when God turns our attention to Jesus, who died for us and binds the whole of our hope and life to him through faith.

Which brings us to our Romans 3 text: "Where, then, is boasting? It is excluded. On what principle? On that of observing the law? No, but on that of faith. For we maintain that a man is justified by faith apart from observing the law" (vv. 27–28).

Salvation by grace is the one doctrine that undercuts all boasting.

Think of the possible grounds for boasting that the doctrine of salvation by grace has "excluded."

1. *Morality.* The chief ground on which people suppose they can save themselves is morality, the doing of good things. If they believe that they are saved by this, and others are not similarly saved, they believe that they are approved by God because they are better people. That was the case with the Pharisee, as well as with certain "religious" people today. They look upon religion as the ultimate arena for human achievement. Others—they are very proud here—can achieve in business and gain the acclaim of entrepreneurs and others in high finance. Or they earn accolades in art or literature or an academic field. Ah, but to be acclaimed by God! That is the greatest prize of all. So these people draw up their own little systems of morality, scrupulously adhere to their own sets of laws, and expect God to praise them. They fast and tithe and pray and do "good works" and suppose that by doing those things they become good people—good enough for God to save them—while others, who do not do them, are not good enough and so (quite rightly, they think) perish.

Salvation through the work of Christ undercuts all that. For not even the best of our righteousness can be righteous enough. In fact, it is worse than "not good enough." It is actually evil, for it feeds the pride that lies at the heart of the evil in us all.

3. Ibid., pp. 96, 97.

Over pride in morality, the Bible writes: "'There is no one righteous, not even one. . . . All have turned away, they have together become worthless; There is no one who does good, not even one'" (Rom. 3:10, 12).

2. *Pious feelings.* In past ages people worried about doing good, and for them the danger of trusting in one's morality was very great. People really did think that they could be saved by being better than other people. This has changed somewhat today, along with our declining standards of morality, and it is far more likely now that a person might have pride in his or her feelings. "I have such warm thoughts about God whenever I come to church," such a person might say. "I know I am not a very moral person. But my heart is so tender. I feel so close to God. At times tears even come to my eyes. Surely God must save such a sensitive person as myself."

Must he? If he "must," salvation is not of grace. It is a matter of debt or works. But since, as Romans tells us, salvation is not of good works, it is certain that no one will be saved by pious feelings.

Charles Haddon Spurgeon once wrote on this point:

> Souls, souls, this is work-mongering in its most damnable shape, for it has deluded far more than that bolder sort of work-trusting, which says, "I will rely upon what I do." If you rely upon what you feel, you shall as certainly perish as if you trust to what you do. Repentance is a blessed work of grace, and to be convinced of sin by God the Holy Ghost is a holy privilege, but to think that these in any way win salvation, is to run clean counter to all the teachings of the Word, for salvation is of the free grace of God alone.[4]

Over pride in pious feelings, the Bible writes: "'[There is] . . . no one who seeks God'" (Rom. 3:11).

3. *Knowledge.* Some people think that they are going to be saved by their superior religious knowledge and take pride from that. They are not particularly moral or even especially sensitive people. But they know a great deal of doctrine and have a very sound creed. How could God possibly condemn them when they understand the doctrine of the Trinity so well and when they talk or even teach for hours on such themes as redemption, propitiation, justification, the atonement, election, faith, and perseverance? How can God reject them when they have spent the best years of their lives in Sunday school or memorized "The Westminster Shorter Catechism" or mastered the lists of the kings of Israel?

Ah, but no one will be saved by mere knowledge. Although knowledge is a part of faith, knowledge is not faith itself. The devil understands doctrine far better than we do, yet he is perishing. Besides, if we are not born again,

---

4. Charles Haddon Spurgeon, "Grace Exalted—Boasting Excluded" in *Metropolitan Tabernacle Pulpit* (Pasadena, Tex.: Pilgrim Publications, 1969, 1973), vol. 8, pp. 29, 30.

we do not know God (which is what counts) even if we have such knowledge.

Over pride in our knowledge, the Bible writes: "'There is no one who understands. . . . There is no fear of God before their eyes.'" (Rom. 3:11, 18)

4. *Faith.* The most pernicious ground of all for human boasting is faith. This is a particular danger for the evangelical. For the most part the evangelical knows that he (or she) is not saved by works—he has been taught that since his youth. Usually he does not trust in his feelings, though he thinks rather highly of them. He is even willing to give up on extensive biblical knowledge or sound doctrine as ground for his hope. But it is entirely different with faith. Faith is *the* distinguishing mark of the evangelical. So even though he has been taught there is to be no boasting in heaven, and even though he does not want to boast—and it really pains him to do so—when pressed in his doctrine the evangelical will admit that in the final analysis the reason *he* is going to be in heaven, and another person is not, is that he believed God and trusted Jesus while those who are perishing spurned him.

Sometimes evangelicals express their ideas in the following fashion. They say that God first gave the law to see if anyone could keep it. But since no one did or can, God now comes to us with a slimmed-down or much-facilitated gospel, as if he were saying: "I know you can't keep my law. So let me ask instead for something you *can* do. Just believe in Jesus. If you believe in Jesus, I'll save you."

I am sure that by now you can see clearly what is wrong with that idea. If that is the way God operates, faith becomes a work—something you or I do on the basis of which we are saved—and there *is* ground for boasting. We may not want to boast. But if we are in heaven a million years from now and someone comes up to us and asks why we are there and another person is not, and if we are pressed about it, we will have to admit that we are there because we had faith and the other person had none. Faith is our distinguishing mark. So, although we may not want to boast, honesty will compel us to boast just a little.

But that is not what faith is. Listen to D. Martyn Lloyd-Jones on this subject:

> Faith is nothing but the instrument of our salvation. Nowhere in Scripture will you find that we are justified because of our faith; nowhere in Scripture will you find that we are justified on account of our faith. The Scripture never says that. The Scripture says that we are justified by faith or through faith. Faith is nothing but the instrument or the channel by which this righteousness of God in Christ becomes ours. It is not faith that saves us. What saves us is the Lord Jesus Christ and his perfect work. It is the death of Christ upon Calvary's Cross that saves us. It is his perfect life that saves us. It

is his appearing on our behalf in the presence of God that saves us. It is God putting Christ's righteousness to our account that saves us. This is the righteousness that saves; faith is but the channel and the instrument by which his righteousness becomes mine. The righteousness is entirely Christ's. My faith is not my righteousness and I must never define or think of faith as righteousness. Faith is nothing but that which links us to the Lord Jesus Christ and his righteousness.[5]

So let's have done with boasting in the church of Jesus Christ—"except in the cross of our Lord Jesus Christ" (Gal. 6:14).

Christians are all nothing but sinners saved by grace. If you do not believe that, you are not saved. You are still trusting in your own good works, your feelings, your superior religious knowledge or your faith—not in Jesus.

Jesus saves! That is the message of Christianity. If you believe that, you will forget about yourself and bow low before him.

5. D. M. Lloyd-Jones, *Romans: An Exposition of Chapters 3:20–4:25, Atonement and Justification* (Grand Rapids: Zondervan, 1970), p. 120.

49

One Way for Everybody

Romans 3:29–30

Is God the God of Jews only? Is he not the God of Gentiles too? Yes, of Gentiles too, since there is only one God, who will justify the circumcised by faith and the uncircumcised through that same faith.

When the world seemed larger than it does today and the peoples of the world did not have much contact with one another, the fact that there were many religions hardly troubled anyone. Europeans had their religious doctrines and practices, and it did not bother them that the peoples of Africa or Asia had different ones. Orientals were not troubled by the different faiths of the Europeans. People were not troubled by other people's belief systems, because in most cases they knew very little about them. Today this is different. We know a great deal about the major world religions and often even something about the minor ones. So for many people the question "Which of the world's religions are right and which are wrong?" is very puzzling.

There are three major ways of dealing with this problem.

The first is to suggest that religions are all more or less equal—at least if they are pursued sincerely. Many people in the past anticipated us in thinking along these lines. Edward Gibbon composed a cynical expression of it in *The Decline and Fall of the Roman Empire*, saying that to the common people all religions were "equally true"; to the philosophers they were "equally false"; and to the magistrates they were "equally useful." Today the view is sometimes expressed by the image of a mountain. "God is on the top of the mountain," people say, "and the religions of the world are like roads going up the mountain from the various sides. Some go up one side, some another, but they all get to the same place in the end." This is the characteristic solution of American religious pluralism.

The second way of dealing with this problem is to say that, although the religions of the world all probably have some value (at least to their adherents), some are nevertheless better than others. It follows from this that one of these religions, whatever one it might be, must be the best of all. This view allows everyone to believe that his or her religion is, if not best, at least superior to some others. But it imposes the task of seeking out the "best," which is what many people believe they are doing.

The third view, the Christian one, is that there is only one way to come to God—it is through faith in Jesus Christ—and that the other religions of the world are really only ways of running away from him.

One Way of Salvation

This third solution is so contrary to the accepting or permissive spirit of our times that it is hardly safe to utter it, except behind the strong stone walls of one's church. This is because any such claim to truth, which Christianity certainly makes, is perceived to be narrow, bigoted, hateful, ignorant, wicked, cruel, base, vile, and intolerant—the kind of thinking that has always led to genocide, religious wars, or witch hunts. But it does not lead to any of these things, as we will see.

The teaching that there is only one way to come to God is merely the natural outcome of the basic gospel of grace, which Paul has been expounding in Romans. He has spoken of human failure to live up to God's standards, showing that "'there is no one righteous, not even one. . . . no one who seeks God'" (Rom. 3:10, 11). He has unfolded God's plan of salvation through the redemptive work of Jesus Christ, proving that the salvation provided by God through the work of Christ becomes ours by simple faith. Now, in the second paragraph of Romans 3, he is providing three natural conclusions or inferences from these doctrines, among which is the teaching that in terms of salvation there is but one way of salvation for everybody. These conclusions are:

1. Salvation by grace through faith *excludes boasting* (vv. 27–28),

2. Salvation by grace through faith means that there is *one way of salvation* for everybody, whoever he or she may be or whatever he or she may have done or not done (vv. 29–30), and

3. Salvation by grace through faith *upholds the law of God* rather than subverting it, as some suppose it does (v. 31).

The second point is the one Paul develops in Romans 3:29–30, where he writes, "Is God the God of Jews only? Is he not the God of Gentiles too? Yes, of Gentiles too, since there is only one God, who will justify the circumcised by faith and the uncircumcised through that same faith." These verses teach that the fact that there is only one way of salvation follows from the fact of their being only one God. God is the God of all. So the salvation he provides is but one salvation for all. Far from being narrow or sectarian, this truth actually swings the grand door of salvation wide open for everybody.

The Lord Our God Is One

Each nation has its own set of prejudices, of course. And it is helpful in trying to appreciate this text to realize that Paul was running up against two entirely different sets of prejudices as he composed these verses: those of the Jew, who believed in one God but not in salvation for Gentiles, and those of the Gentile, who believed in salvation for everyone (or at least the possibility of salvation for everyone) but not in one God.

Let us take the Jew first.

The chief theological tenet of Judaism was its monotheism, and it still is today. Judaism is a religion of prayers and sayings, and chief among all the prayers or sayings is the *Shema*, (Hebrew for "Hear"), recited somewhat as a confession of faith prior to the reading of the formal prayers in synagogues each Sabbath: "Hear, O Israel: The LORD our God, the LORD is one" (Deut. 6:6).[1] This is among those great sayings that were to be kept before the people always: "Impress them on your children. Talk about them when you sit at home and when you walk along the road, when you lie down and when you get up. Tie them as symbols on your hands and bind them on your foreheads. Write them on the doorframes of your houses and on your gates" (vv. 7–9).

Nothing so distinguished the Jew from his pagan neighbors as his fierce and uncompromising monotheism. Nothing made his life more difficult, but nothing was so much to his credit. While the nations about worshiped the debased deities described in Romans—"images made to look like mortal man and birds and animals and reptiles" (Rom. 1:23)—the Jew maintained the highest conceptions of the one God and contended for him.

But with this conviction went what one commentator calls "a degenerate theocratic exclusiveness."[2] That is, a scorn of Gentiles to the point of supposing them to be scorned by God also. In the liturgy for morning prayers

1. See George Foot Moore, *Judaism in the First Centuries of the Christian Era: The Age of the Tannaim* (Cambridge: Harvard University Press, 1962), vol. 1, p. 291.

2. Heinrich A. W. Meyer (*Ueber den Brief des Paulus an die Römer*) as quoted by John Murray, *The Epistle to the Romans* (Grand Rapids: Wm. B. Eerdmans, 1968), p. 124.

there was a sentence in which Jewish men thanked God that he had not made them "a Gentile, a slave, or a woman."[3] The Jew said, "God loves Israel alone of all the nations of the earth."[4] A Gentile could be saved, of course, but he had to become a Jew first. Jewish monotheism did not extend so far as to save the Gentile as a Gentile without Judaism.

But the Gentile had overwhelming problems of his own.

Whereas Israel had monotheism with an accompanying exclusiveness, the Gentile had tolerance without monotheism. And what thoughtful person could prefer that? It was said of Athens that there were more gods in the city than people. What is worse, these many and diverse gods permitted and even encouraged the most debased moral practices. Greece was a moral cesspool by the start of the Christian era, and Rome soon became worse. To those who know the characteristics of these times, the portrait of pagan society drawn by Paul in Romans 1:29–33 and Romans 3:13–18 is no exaggeration.

What can be done? If we are firm in our conceptions of one great and moral God, the source of all good, we seem to become narrow, self-righteous, and bigoted. And it is not only the Jew who has been like this.

If we are broad in our doctrines, believing that all are equally right in believing in whatever god or gods suits their fancy, we plunge into polytheism and depravity.

What is the solution? How can anyone find a way out of this dilemma?

The solution is the gospel that Paul has been expounding. It maintains the great high principle of monotheism, for it is the gospel of this one God. It flows from his grace. It has been accomplished by his Son, who died for us. It requires us to be like him. At the same time, the gospel does not promote any kind of exclusiveness, for it is a gospel offered to all alike—apart from their religious advantages or disadvantages, understanding or lack of understanding, good works or very evil deeds.

Here is Charles Hodge's comprehensive statement of this principle:

> We have here the second result of the gospel method of justification: It presents a God as equally a God of the Gentiles as of the Jews. He is such, because "it is one God who justifies the circumcision by faith, and the uncircumcision through faith." He deals with both classes on precisely the same principles; he pursues, with regard to both, the same plan, and offers salvation to both on exactly the same terms. There is, therefore, in this doctrine, the foundation laid for a universal religion, which may be preached to every creature under heaven, which need not, as was the case with the Jewish system, be confined to any one sect or nation. This is the only doctrine which suits the character of God and his relation to all his intelligent creatures

3. William Barclay, *Letters to the Galatians and Ephesians* (Edinburgh: The Saint Andrew Press, 1954), p. 199.

4. William Barclay, *The Letter to the Romans* (Edinburgh: The Saint Andrew Press, 1969), p. 35.

upon earth. God is a universal and not a national God, and this is a method of salvation universally applicable.[5]

No One Cast Out

And that is what I want to do now. I want to apply the gospel developed in Romans 3 as universally as possible. My method is simple. I want to tell you that whoever you are or whatever you may or may not have done, this gospel is for you, because *it is for everybody.* I want you to see that if you will come to God in the way he has appointed for you to come—that is, through faith in his Son, the Lord Jesus Christ, who died for you—he will receive you and will never cast you out.

Let me ask three important questions and then answer them:

1. *Who may come?* The answer is: everybody. All alike are lost in sin, and yet all alike are the objects of Jesus' saving love. The preceding portions of Romans show that the gospel is for the very great sinner as well as for the apparently moral person. It is for the pagan as well as for the one who considers himself or herself to be religious. Even if you are a very great sinner, you may come. Those described in the first chapter of Romans were great sinners, but the way of salvation through faith in the death of Jesus Christ was for them. Even if you are extremely self-righteous, you may come—if you shed your self-righteousness. Those described in Romans 2 were self-righteous, but Paul is expounding the gospel for this type of person also.

What is your sin? Pride? Murder? Stealing? Adultery? It does not matter. If you will come to Jesus, you will be received. It is Jesus who said, "Whoever comes to me I will never drive away" (John 6:37b).

What is your profession? Minister? Gambler? Businessman? Housewife? It does not matter. You may come to God through faith in the atoning work of Jesus Christ.

What is your condition? Are you seeking God? Running away from God? Fighting God? Questioning God? Job was questioning God, but God was never closer to him than when he was.

Are you an indifferent sort of person? Some years ago I met a man who came to Tenth Presbyterian Church occasionally, saying that this was "whenever my friends think I need a dose of religion." That kind of exposure will only inoculate you against true faith in Christ and will give you a false sense of security and well-being. Religion saves no one. It is Jesus Christ who saves. So don't come "to church." Come to Christ. The gospel is for you if you are one of these indifferent people.

2. *How may I come?* You may come as you are. Some years ago there was a fad in the United States known as "come as you are" parties. People would

5. Charles Hodge, *A Commentary on Romans* (Edinburgh and Carlisle, Pa.: The Banner of Truth Trust, 1972), p. 101. (Original edition 1935.)

get an invitation to a party occurring a week or so later, but they were to come to it in exactly the state of dress (or undress) they were in when they got the invitation. Were they dressed to change the oil in the car? They were to come with oil stains. Were they covered with paint from some do-it-yourself household project? They were to come bespeckled. Swimsuits or formal wear! It did not matter. They were to come like that.

In the same way, you are invited to come to Christ in whatever mental or spiritual attire you may find yourself in.

Some come running to Jesus. I have known some. The gospel is preached, and they come like Zacchaeus, who climbed a tree to get a saving view of Jesus Christ. Or they come like Peter, who jumped into the water to swim to Jesus across the Sea of Galilee. Preaching the gospel to people like this is like putting seventy-five cents in a soft-drink machine. The result is immediate. Moreover, they seem to come in full faith and with substantial knowledge. Catholics, many of whom have learned much doctrine but perhaps have not yet quite understood the gospel of grace, often come in this manner. For them the gospel is like the key in the lock that opens the entire treasure house of God at one turning.

Others come limping along with poor, faltering, hesitating steps. But that is all right. They may come, too.

Some years ago members of the staff of Campus Crusade for Christ at the University of Pennsylvania began speaking about Jesus Christ to a young black student. He was not very much interested in spiritual matters. His chief interest was in making the freshman basketball team, and he kept working at this goal all through the fall. They invited him to go to a fall conference at which I had been invited to speak, but he did not want to go. He had no money. They offered him a scholarship. He said he did not have a way of getting there. They provided a ride. When he got to the conference center he was late and had not had any dinner, so he decided to go out for hamburgers instead of going to the first meeting. He came in when the meeting was about half over. I did not notice when he came in, but I was told later that he entered thinking about the tryouts for the team, which were to be held that Monday. I was saying, "God loves you, whoever you are; and he has a special plan for your life." These words struck him as a direct word from God. He sat down and listened. That evening he gave his life to the Lord, and after that he became an extremely effective witness for Christ to the black community.[6]

Some people come kicking and screaming. Paul was reluctant. Saint Augustine resisted until God finally reached him in the garden of a friend's estate near Milan, Italy. C. S. Lewis described himself as "the most dejected and reluctant convert in England."[7]

6. I have told this story in James Montgomery Boice, *The Gospel of John: An Expositional Commentary*, five volumes in one (Grand Rapids: Zondervan, 1985), p. 424. Some of the other material in this section is also borrowed from those pages.

7. C. S. Lewis, *Surprised By Joy* (New York: Harcourt, Brace & World, 1955), p. 228.

3. *When may I come?* You may come at any time. Come as a child. I am delighted when children show an interest in the gospel, which many do, especially if they are being raised in a devout Christian home. Some persons think that children cannot understand the gospel or believe on Jesus meaningfully. But that is not true. Children can understand a great deal if someone will just take the time to explain the things of God to them. Jesus commended the faith of children, saying that we must all come as little children to be saved.

Are you a child? If you are and if you can understand what I am saying now, you can understand three things: (1) you are old enough to sin; (2) you are old enough to die; and (3) you are old enough to come to Jesus. For Jesus himself said, "Let the little children come to me, and do not hinder them, for the kingdom of heaven belongs to such as these" (Matt. 19:14). If you are a child, won't you believe in Jesus and follow him? The way older people are to be saved is for you also.

You may be older. You may be thinking that you probably should have come as a child but that it is too late for you now. "I am getting along in years," you say. "It is hard to change when you are old." True enough! The old do get set in their ways; it is why it is good to come young. But although it is harder to come to Christ when you are older, it is not impossible. And it is never too late. You may not be able to do much for Jesus because of your advanced years, but he can do everything for you. You will not have much time on earth to serve him, but you will have an eternity in heaven to praise him.

Charles Haddon Spurgeon, that great Baptist preacher, wrote:

> Oh, my dear hearers, come to Jesus! Come in the morning when the dew is on your branch, for he will not cast you out. Come in the heat of noon, when the drought of care parches you, and he will not cast you out. Come when the shadows have grown long, and the darkness of the night is gathering about you, for he will not cast you out. The door is not shut; for the gate of mercy closes not so long as the gate of life is open.[8]

Will You Come?

I give this appeal, too: Come to Jesus!

Is God the God of Jews only? Is he not the God of Gentiles, too? Yes, of Gentiles too, since there is only one God, who will justify the circumcised by faith and the uncircumcised through that same faith.

8. Charles Haddon Spurgeon, "High Doctrine and Broad Doctrine" in *Metropolitan Tabernacle Pulpit*, vol. 30 (Pasadena, Tex.: Pilgrim Publications, 1971), pp. 57, 58.

Is God the God of Americans only? Is he not the God of Asians, too? Yes, of Asians, too, since there is only one God, who will justify the Caucasian by faith and the Asian through that same faith.

Is God the God of Catholics only? Is he not the God of Protestants, too? Yes, of Protestants, too, since there is only one God, who will justify the Catholic by faith and the Protestant by that same faith.

Is God the God of upper-middle class people only? Is he not the God of working-class people, too? Yes, of working-class people, too, since there is only one God who will justify the upper-middle class by faith and the working class through that same faith.

Is God the God of elderly people only? Is he not the God of children, too? Yes, of children, too, since there is only one God who will justify the elderly by faith and children through that same faith.

I can only think of one thing that could possibly turn you away from this gracious, embracing, "all are welcome" gospel. And that is that you do not want to go into the Father's house with all those other types of people. But if that is so, do not call Christianity narrow or bigoted or mean or self-righteous or sectarian. It is you who are sectarian, and Christianity is the only thing I know of that can cleanse you of that blight. Only Jesus can give you grace to place your pride aside and step through that wide door of salvation as the rebellious sinner you truly are.

No one else will go through—only sinners who have confessed their sin, turned from it, and believed on Jesus Christ as their Savior.

50

The Law Upheld by Faith

Romans 3:31

Do we, then, nullify the law by this faith? Not at all! Rather, we uphold the law.

Two studies back, I began to explain the final paragraph of Romans 3 (vv. 27–31), pointing out that it contains three conclusions from or implications of the gospel. Let us review them. They may be expressed by saying that the doctrine of justification by grace through faith in Jesus Christ:

1. Excludes boasting (vv. 27–28),
2. Establishes one way of salvation for everybody (vv. 29–30), and
3. Upholds the law of God rather than subverting it, as some seem always to suppose it does (v. 31).

I have called these points "conclusions" from or "implications" of the doctrines of salvation established in verses 21–26. But, strictly speaking, the last of these points is an answer to a false conclusion or erroneous implication that some people, particularly religious people, might draw from the gospel. The apostle has spoken forcefully about salvation by grace apart from law. He has repeated the idea of salvation being apart from law twice, once in verse 21 ("apart from law") and once in verse 28 ("apart from observing the law"). "Well, then," such a person might argue, "if salvation is apart from law, as you say, doesn't the doctrine of salvation by grace set God's law aside and thus show it to be worthless? And if it does that, shouldn't your gospel be rejected as being quite false? Aren't we obliged to reject any doctrine that would nullify the revealed law of God?"

Paul's reply is that the gospel of grace does not nullify God's law. God forbid that it should! If it did that, it *would* be a false gospel, one rightly to be rejected. But it does not nullify the law of God. On the contrary, it establishes the law and is, in fact, the only thing that does or could establish it.

The Law and Sanctification

There are two ways in which this objection to the gospel may be raised, however. One is answered later on in the letter; the other is stated here. The first could be deferred for now, but for the sake of completeness it is worth looking at both of them at one time, although we will consider the first one briefly.

The first (and most obvious) objection concerns the imagined negative impact of the teaching of salvation by grace on the Christian life. In Romans this error is exposed in chapter 6. There Paul imagines a person saying, "Let us go on sinning so that grace may increase" (cf. v. 1). In Galatians, which deals with the problem at even greater length, he imagines a person who says, "Let us use our freedom to indulge the sinful nature" (cf. Gal. 5:13). In both cases the argument is: "If we do not have to keep the law of God in order to be saved, why should any of us want to keep it? If we are saved by grace apart from obeying the law, we must be free to sin. So let's all sin. Let's indulge ourselves by doing any and every sinful thing we want to do—because, after all, we will get to heaven anyway."

It should not be too difficult to see what is wrong with this argument. It is wrong psychologically, if for no other reason. It assumes that the only motivation for right moral conduct is fear of hell or of losing heaven, when actually those are the least significant motivations.

The situation here is similar to what students of corporate management, like Peter F. Drucker, teach about vocational motivation.[1] Many people, perhaps most people, suppose that the best way to motivate an employee is to offer him or her more money. But those who have studied this idea know that such is not the case. Actually, money ranks very low as a work motivator. Feelings of personal worth, being part of something important, respect, pride in the company, or hope for advancement all rank higher. In the same way, it is erroneous to suppose that a person will live a moral life only if by doing so he or she can earn heaven. The highest motivation for godly conduct comes not from fear of hell but from love of God. It is because God has saved us by grace entirely apart from any merit in ourselves that we

---

1. Peter F. Drucker is a management consultant and author of *The Practice of Management, Managing for Results, The Effective Executive,* and other popular volumes.

love and want to please him. Moreover, we recognize the importance of what we have become a part of by God's grace—the kingdom of God on earth—and we want to advance the goals of that kingdom.

The second error is theological. It is the false assumption that when a person is justified by grace through faith in Jesus Christ, he or she is personally unchanged by that process. Or, to put it in other terms, it is to suppose that one can be justified without being regenerated, or born again. Actually, the one effect never occurs without the other. So the one who is justified *always* shows it by striving for righteousness. If a person does not strive to live a moral life according to the law of God, the failure proves that he or she is neither regenerated nor justified.

Here is the way John R. W. Stott puts it. "The justifying work of the Son and the regenerating work of the Spirit cannot be separated. It is for this reason that good works of love follow justification and new birth as their necessary evidence."[2]

The Law and Justification

Yet, as I indicated earlier, this is not the form of the objection that the apostle was thinking of when he composed Romans 3:31. This is because the theme of Romans 3:21–31 is not sanctification (important as that is) but justification, which is achieved for us by the work of Christ. So it is not that the law is upheld by "our faith" in the sense that we inevitably live moral lives if we are living by faith, true as that is, but that the "faith" Paul is describing—that is, the doctrine of justification by grace through faith—upholds the law.

This is so important I need to state it again in different language. The point is not that the law is somehow established by what we do as Christians by the power of the new life of God within. It is rather that the Lord Jesus Christ has established the law in the process of providing salvation for us by his death on the cross.

Or, to put it in still other language, God has established the law by seeing that the demands of the law were met in the way he provided salvation for us.

This needs to be taken in three parts.

1. The doctrine of justification by grace through faith establishes the law by showing that *the law is so high and holy that we who are sinners could never have fulfilled it.*

To see this, let us take a contrary situation. Suppose God had declared the cross of Jesus Christ to be unnecessary. Suppose he had said, "I do not think it will be necessary for me to send my Son, the Lord Jesus Christ, to die for sinners. Rather than saving them in this manner—by grace—I will allow them to be saved in the way they obviously want to be saved, that is, by

2. John R. W. Stott, *The Cross of Christ* (Downers Grove, Ill.: InterVarsity Press, 1986), p. 188.

doing good deeds and by trying to keep the law. They cannot keep the law perfectly, of course, but I will set a certain standard that they will have to attain. We will call it a 'passing grade.' If they reach that, I will save them. If not, they will be lost." Obviously, if God had acted in that fashion, the law would not have been established but rather would have been diminished or nullified—or at least parts of it would have been.

Suppose God set the "passing score" at seventy percent of the law's just requirements. In that case, isn't it evident that he would have nullified the other thirty percent of the law?

If he had put the passing score at fifty, half would have been set aside.

If the passing score were ten percent, ninety percent of the law would have been made worthless.

Of course, the real scenario would actually have been even worse than that. Because, according to the Bible, not one of us keeps even one tiny part of the law of God perfectly, since everything we are and all we do is ruined by our radical and pervasive sin. If the cross were unnecessary and God saved us on the basis of what we could do, since we do not keep even one part of the law perfectly, God would actually be setting aside the entire law, declaring that it is an unimportant standard after all. Instead, the doctrine of justification by faith establishes the law, because it shows that God continues to take each requirement of the law seriously, even though none of us can fulfill it. The law is "holy, . . . righteous and good" (Rom. 7:12). Moreover, it remains the standard and would have condemned everybody, if a way of fulfilling its requirements (by someone other than a mere human being) had not been found.

2. The doctrine of justification by grace through faith establishes the law by showing that *the punishment of sinners by death, as required by the law, has been executed.*

The law had two chief spiritual functions, apart from its more basic role in regulating the civic life of the Jewish nation.

First, it taught that all are sinners. We need to be taught that, of course, because one effect of sin on the mind is to blind us to our true condition. The law was meant to convince us—by its high demands—that there is indeed "no one righteous, not even one . . . no one who understands, no one who seeks God" (Rom. 3:10–11). It teaches us this because, if we are serious about trying to keep its commandments, as Martin Luther was, to give just one example, we soon discover that we cannot.

Second, the law taught that the punishment for sin is death. This teaching goes back as far as the early chapters of Genesis, where God told Adam and Eve, "You must not eat from the tree of the knowledge of good and evil, for when you eat of it, you will surely die" (Gen. 2:17). It is found in Ezekiel 18:4b: "The soul who sins . . . will die." Indeed, in one way or another it is found throughout the Old Testament.

Again, let us imagine a situation contrary to what is actually the case. Let us suppose God to have said, "I know that no one can keep the law. So I will exercise my grace and save people apart from meeting the law's requirements. I will just love sinners into heaven." If God had said that, he would not only have undermined the high and holy standards of the law, suggesting, as we saw above, that thirty percent, half, or even all of the law could be dispensed with. He would also have shown that the punishments for disobeying the law were also arbitrary and that, in the final analysis, they are dispensable. He would have been like a father threatening to spank his child if he or she did not do something he commanded, when he actually had no intention of punishing the child in any way. The law could only have been established by carrying out the penalty of spiritual death—if not on us, then on Jesus Christ as our substitute.

Isn't that obvious? Take a current example. The law of a city specifies that the maximum speed permissible within the bounds of the city is thirty-five miles per hour. A man drives across the city line and continues on into the downtown area, going fifty miles per hour. He is stopped by a policeman. How is the law to be established in the case of the lawbreaker?

By letting him go? Obviously not.

By suggesting that the standard is perhaps too high and that fifty miles per hour actually is close to what probably should be required? No.

By making the offender promise to drive slower the next time? No, that is not a case of establishing the law either.

The only way the law can be established in the case of the speeding motorist is for him to get a ticket and for the necessary fine to be paid. Supposing the motorist had no money? To establish the law in that case, he would have to go to jail, unless someone could be found to pay the fine for him.

It is exactly the same spiritually. When the Lord Jesus Christ died on the cross for us, he showed that God took the law with full seriousness. The law demanded death for infractions. Jesus met that demand by suffering the law's penalty in our place. Therefore, by basing salvation on what was accomplished by Jesus' death rather than on what we could (or, in fact, could not) do, God established the law while at the same time providing a way by which sinners could be saved. Robert Haldane, one of the great commentators on this epistle, asks rhetorically and rightly, "Can there be any greater respect shown to the law, than that when God determines to save men from its curse, he makes his own Son sustain its curse in their stead, and fulfill for them all its demands?"[3]

In this respect, Romans 3:31 is a natural expression of the principle announced in verse 26: "He [that is, God] did it [that is, sent Jesus to be a sacrifice of atonement] to demonstrate his justice at the present time, so as

3. Robert Haldane, *An Exposition of the Epistle to the Romans* (MacDill AFB: MacDonald Publishing, 1958), p. 157.

to be just and the one who justifies those who have faith in Jesus." What is the standard of the justice established by Christ's atonement? Obviously, it is the law. So what Romans 3:26 tells us, to use different language, is that God established the law by having Jesus bear the penalty of the law for those he was saving.

3. The doctrine of justification by grace through faith establishes the law by showing that *it is on the basis of a true righteousness, righteousness that is an exact fulfillment of the law, that we are justified.*

Justification by faith means "justification by faith *in Christ*," and Christ fulfilled the law perfectly. Do you remember the exchange between the Lord Jesus Christ and John the Baptist on the occasion of the Lord's baptism in the Jordan River? John did not want to baptize Jesus, saying that he ought rather to be baptized by Jesus. But Jesus replied, "Let it be so now; it is proper for us to do this to fulfill all righteousness" (Matt. 3:15). The Baptist was right insofar as the meaning of his own baptism was concerned. His was a baptism of repentance, and since Jesus had done nothing sinful there was nothing for him to repent of. John was the sinner. He needed from Jesus a baptism of repentance for his sins.

But Jesus was teaching a greater truth. He was teaching that, having become man, he wanted willingly to submit to the righteous demands of the law of God. He wanted to take these upon himself. Galatians 4:4 describes him as being "born of a woman, born under law, to redeem those under law. . . ." That is, Jesus deliberately placed himself under law as a man, setting out to fulfill the law in each of its particulars.

When God saves us, therefore, it is not just by having the Lord Jesus Christ die in our place, bearing sin's penalty. That is part of it. But the other part, the part I am discussing now, is that God saves us also by imputing to us this actual righteousness of Christ. We do not have it of ourselves. We are sinners. We have fallen short of God's lawful standards. But Jesus has not fallen short. He fulfilled the law perfectly, and his actual righteousness is now, by the grace of God, credited to our account. That is why Paul would later write to the Philippians, ". . . I consider everything a loss compared to the surpassing greatness of knowing Christ Jesus my Lord, for whose sake I have lost all things. I consider them rubbish, that I may gain Christ and be found in him, not having a righteousness of my own that comes from the law, but that which is through faith in Christ—the righteousness that comes from God and is by faith" (Phil. 3:8–9).

This righteousness is not something other than true righteousness. It is that real righteousness possessed and achieved by Jesus Christ. By saving us through this righteousness, and not by any lesser standard, God establishes the law that defines this righteousness.

Haldane asks, "Do we make law void when we conclude that through his faith he [the believer] receives a perfect righteousness, by which, in all its demands and all its sanctions, it is fulfilled?" He answers rightly, "No, it is in this very way we establish it."[4]

The Heart of Scripture

With the exposition of Romans 3:31, which we have now completed, we have come to the end of the most important single passage in the Word of God. As we said at the beginning of our study of verses 21–31, this section of Romans is the very heart of the Bible, the most important and critical passage in all Scripture. We need to end by recalling what it teaches.

There are four great doctrines:

1. *God has provided a righteousness of his own for men and women, a righteousness we do not possess ourselves.* This is the very heart or theme of the Word of God.

2. *This righteousness is by grace.* We do not deserve it. In fact, we are incapable ever of deserving it.

3. *It is the work of the Lord Jesus Christ in dying for his people, redeeming them from their sin, that has made this grace on God's part possible.* Redemption describes the work of Jesus Christ in relation to ourselves; propitiation describes the work of Jesus Christ in relation to the Father; justification describes the act by which God the Father declares us to have met the demands of the law on the basis of Christ's work for us. It is because of Jesus' death that there is a Christian gospel.

4. *This righteousness, which God has graciously provided, becomes ours through simple faith.* Believing and trusting God in regard to the work of Jesus is the only way anyone, whether Jew or Gentile, can be saved. Faith is essential. "And without faith it is impossible to please God . . ." (Heb. 11:6).

These points were stated at the very beginning of the letter, where Paul wrote: "I am not ashamed of the gospel, because it is the power of God for the salvation of everyone who believes: first for the Jew, then for the Gentile. For in the gospel a righteousness from God is revealed, a righteousness that is by faith from first to last, just as it is written: 'The righteous will live by faith'" (Rom. 1:16–17).

The important point is: Have you been saved by what is described in these doctrines? Have you been saved from your sin by Jesus Christ? Do you know that he died in your place to bear the punishment for your sin and offer you, in its place, his own perfect righteousness? Have you believed on the Lord Jesus Christ as your Savior?

We live in a day—perhaps every age has been like this—when people are trying their best to establish other "gospels," other ways of salvation. Some are into good works, some into yoga or reincarnations or crystals or some-

4. Ibid., p. 158.

thing else. But the Bible's gospel is not a human gospel, as those all are. The Bible is God's Word, and this is God's gospel. It is the only true gospel. It is the only way in which a sinful man or woman can be saved. But, praise God, it is the way by which any man or woman may be saved—yourself included.

Believe it. And thank God for it.

PART FIVE

The Gospel Proved from Scripture

51

The Case of Father Abraham

Romans 4:1–5

What then shall we say that Abraham, our forefather, discovered in this matter? If, in fact, Abraham was justified by works, he had something to boast about—but not before God. What does the Scripture say? "Abraham believed God, and it was credited to him as righteousness."

Now when a man works, his wages are not credited to him as a gift, but as an obligation. However, to the man who does not work but trusts God who justifies the wicked, his faith is credited as righteousness.

As Americans living in the twentieth century, we have two things working against us as we begin a study of the fourth chapter of Paul's great letter to the Romans. First, we value what is new more than what is old, and Paul's purpose in this chapter is to prove that the gospel he has explained in Romans 3 is not something new, but is that by which God has been saving people from the dawn of history. Second, we dislike rational proofs, and Romans 4 is an example of classic reasoning.

But it is important that we overcome our cultural liabilities at this point and actually listen to and believe what Paul is saying.

429

No New Doctrine

It might help us to understand what Paul is doing. When Peter preached the first Christian sermon on the day of Pentecost, he had a method that was the exact opposite of the one used by the apostle Paul. Peter's method was to quote an Old Testament text and then explain it, something he does three times in just the one sermon. That is: Scripture first, then explanation. Paul, by contrast, first establishes contact with his readers, analyzing the desperate condition of the human race without God and explaining the gospel as God's answer to that dilemma. Then, after he has analyzed the problem, he proves what he has taught from the Old Testament.

He has done this once already. After describing the dreadful depravity of the race in Romans 1 and 2, using the pagans' own terms for this corruption in 1:29–31, Paul established the same thing by the use of six Old Testament quotations—in 3:10–18.[1] Now, having explained God's way of salvation by the gift of grace through faith in 3:21–31, he proves what he has been teaching by two Old Testament examples: Abraham, the father of the Jewish nation, and King David (4:1–25).

How significant this is! Robert Haldane writes:

> Nothing could be so well calculated to convince both Jewish and Gentile believers, especially the former, how vain is the expectation of those who look for justification by their own works. Abraham was a patriarch, eminently holy, the head of the nation of Israel, the friend of God, the father of all who believe, in whose seed all the nations of the world were to be blessed. David was a man according to God's own heart, the progenitor of the Messiah, his great personal type, and a chosen and anointed king of Israel. If, then, Abraham had not been justified by his works, but by the righteousness of God imputed to him through faith, and David, speaking by the Spirit of God, had declared that the only way in which a man can receive justification is by his sin being covered by the imputation of that righteousness, who could suppose that it was to be attained by any other means? By these two references, the apostle likewise shows that the way of justification was the same from the beginning, both under the old and the new dispensations.[2]

Two times before this, Paul has indicated that salvation through the gift of God's righteousness, apart from law, had been announced beforehand in the Old Testament (Rom. 1:2; 3:21). Now he shows that it is not only something that had been previously announced, but was also the only way anyone either in the Old Testament period or the dawning New Testament era has been saved.

1. The texts are: Psalm 14:1–3 (parallels in Ps. 53:1–3, Eccles. 7:20); Psalm 5:9; Psalm 140:3; Psalm 10:7; Isaiah 59:7–8; and Psalm 36:1.
2. Robert Haldane, *An Exposition of the Epistle to the Romans* (MacDill AFB: MacDonald Publishing, 1958), pp. 159, 160.

Father Abraham

Paul begins with Abraham, and it is clear why he does so. Abraham was the acknowledged father of the Jewish people and, with the exception of Jesus himself, the most important person in the Bible. Abraham is a giant in Scripture.

Think of the other great Old Testament figures. Moses was a very great man. He was the one through whom God broke the power of tyrannous Egypt and led the people forth into a new land. He was the lawgiver, God appearing to him in a special and unique way on Mount Sinai. David was the greatest of Israel's kings. He brought the nation to the pinnacle of its power in the ancient Near East, while expressing its greatest religious feelings and devotion in his psalms. Elijah was great among the prophets. Isaiah was a powerful statesman and a voice of God to Israel in dark days. Daniel was an outstanding statesman as well. But great as these Old Testament figures were, if asked, each would have confessed in an instant that Abraham was his father in the faith.

Early in Genesis we read of God's promise to Abraham that he would become the father of many nations (Gen. 17:5). This promise was fulfilled both physically and spiritually. Physically, Abraham became the father of the Jewish and Arab peoples, through Isaac and Ishmael respectively. Spiritually, Abraham became the father of all true believers, both Jews and Gentiles. He is our father in faith if we have believed on Jesus.

In the New Testament the origins of salvation are always traced to Abraham. Paul does it characteristically, as here in Romans and in the letter to the Galatians (chs. 4, 5). But it is not just Paul who does this. The New Testament begins with such a reference, Matthew's words about "Jesus Christ the son of David, the son of Abraham" (Matt. 1:1). And Luke quotes Mary, Jesus' mother, as exulting: "[God] has helped his servant Israel, remembering to be merciful to Abraham and his descendants forever . . . " (Luke 1:54–55).

Abraham is referred to as God's "friend" three times in the Bible (2 Chron. 20:7; Isa. 41:8; James 2:23). Why is that? The answer, as Paul is about to show, is that Abraham "believed God" and so was credited with righteousness (Rom. 4:3). If Paul can show that Abraham, the father of all the faithful, came into a right relationship with God by faith and not by any amount of human good works, his case is proved. Then the gospel he is expounding is the true gospel; there can be no other. If he cannot prove this, the case is lost and so is Christianity.

No Good in Abraham

Where do we start in considering the case of Father Abraham? The place at which to begin—the same place we ourselves must begin, if we would be saved—is with the acknowledgment that there was nothing in Abraham that could ever have commended him to God.

This point is lost a bit in the New International Version because, for some inexplicable reason, the NIV has translated the Greek words *kata sarka* ("according to the flesh") in Romans 4:1 by the words "in this matter." That is not the idea at all. In the Bible "flesh" refers to human activity apart from God's influence. So the query of verse 1 means, "What did Abraham find to be the case so far as his own human ability was concerned? Did he find that he could be saved by it?"[3] The answer, as Paul shows, is that Abraham was not saved by his own ability or good works but by a gift of God: "Abraham believed God, and it was credited to him as righteousness" (v. 3).

God did not look down from heaven to see whether he could find someone with a little bit of human goodness (even a little bit of human faith), on the basis of which it would be possible to save that person—and then find Abraham. It is not as if God said, "Oh, this is wonderful! In the midst of this corrupt and sinful race, a race which, I have observed, thinks and does 'only evil all the time' [Gen. 6:5], I have discovered at least one individual who wants to serve me. I see Abraham and his goodness. I think I can make something of him." It was not like that at all. How could it be? For, as Paul has just written in Romans 3:10–12 (quoting Ps. 14:1–3 and Ps. 53:1–3):

> "There is no one righteous, not even one;
>   there is no one who understands,
>   no one who seeks God.
> All have turned away,
>   they have together become worthless;
>   there is no one who does good,
>   not even one."

If Abraham had no natural good in him, it is certain that he was not saved by human goodness. How then was he saved? The answer, as we have seen several times already, is by God's gift of righteousness to him, which he received by faith.

3. The words "according to the flesh" can be taken in two ways. (1) They can refer to the fact that Abraham was the Jews' physical progenitor; that is, Abraham was their father according to the flesh. But this is a self-evident truth and hardly needs mentioning. Besides, it subordinates the idea, and in the Greek text the words come last for emphasis. (2) They can refer, as I have taken them to refer, to the sphere of Abraham's experience of which the question is asked: What did Abraham discover as to his natural ability? Was he justified by it? For a fuller discussion see: F. Godet, *Commentary on St. Paul's Epistle to the Romans*, trans. A. Cusin (Edinburgh: T. & T. Clark, n.d.), vol. 1, pp. 283, 284; and D. M. Lloyd-Jones, *Romans: An Exposition of Chapters 3:20–4:25, Atonement and Justification* (Grand Rapids: Zondervan, 1970), pp. 161, 162.

By Proof from the Scriptures

Paul does not merely mention Abraham's example in a general way, however. He refers to a specific Old Testament teaching concerning Abraham, and the text he refers to is Genesis 15:6. The context of the verse is the incident in which God took Abraham out under the night sky and promised him offspring as numerous as the stars of heaven, even though at this time Abraham was eighty-five years old and had no children, and Abraham *believed* God.

From the viewpoint of the doctrine of salvation this is the single most important verse in the entire Bible. This is because in Genesis 15:6 the doctrine of justification by faith is set forth for the first time. It is the first reference in the Bible to (1) faith, (2) righteousness, and (3) justification. Thus, although we know that individuals preceding Abraham were also saved—Adam and Eve, Abel, Enoch, Noah, and others—this is the first time that any specific individual is said to have been justified.

How was this accomplished? Here we have to be extremely careful.

First, we need to dismiss what are clearly two serious misunderstandings of the text. One is the liberal misunderstanding, though it is probably what the great majority of Jews would have thought in Paul's day. It supposes that when the text says "Abraham believed God, and it was credited to him as righteousness," it means that Abraham was just a good or pious man, and that he was justified on that basis. Obviously, if Abraham believed God when God promised him numerous children, Abraham was the kind of person who delighted in believing and obeying God, in doing what God told him to do. And, so this reasoning goes, it was because he was such a good man that God saved him. That is not justification by faith, of course. It is the opposite, justification by works. But it is what many people fervently believe and what liberal scholarship teaches.

D. Martyn Lloyd-Jones, who discusses this error, points out that it is nothing less than the religion of the Pharisee, who went up to the temple to pray, saying, "God, I thank you that I am not like other men—robbers, evildoers, adulterers—or even like this tax collector. I fast twice a week and give a tenth of all I get" (Luke 18:11–12). That is boasting. If that is what Genesis 15:6 means, it is the exact opposite of everything that Paul has been saying thus far in this epistle.

The second misunderstanding is not a liberal but an evangelical one. It goes like this: Since Abraham did not have any righteousness in himself by which he could be justified before God—but since God wanted to save him—God looked for something he could accept in place of righteousness. Since Abraham had faith, at least a little bit, God said, "Even though this little bit of faith is not righteousness, it is something I can work with. I'll treat it as righteousness and so save Abraham."

Even to put it like that shows the absurdity of this interpretation. For God is not a juggler of truth. God does not pretend a thing is something it is not. Consequently, if God counted Abraham as being righteous, it must have been on the basis of a true righteousness—either his or someone else's—and not on the mere fiction of substituting apples for oranges or pretending that the sow's ear of human works is actually the silk purse of salvation.

There are several reasons why we should be warned against this second insidious but very common misunderstanding.

First, when the text says that "it was credited to him as righteousness," what does "it" refer to? What is the antecedent? The evangelical misunderstanding I have been referring to would have to maintain that the antecedent is the fact that Abraham believed God or the fact that he had faith. But this is hard to support grammatically. "It" demands a noun (or at least a verbal noun) as an antecedent, and the text supplies neither. This fact alone suggests that we should look further for what was actually reckoned to Abraham as righteousness.

Second, there is the way faith is referred to in the rest of the Bible, specifically in the writings of Paul. It is never said that people are saved *because* of their faith or even *on the basis of* their faith. They are saved *by* faith. The Greek preposition is *dia* with the genitive, not the dative, and it means "by faith as a channel."

The Greek preposition *dia* can mean either (1) "because of" or (2) "through." If it means "because of" in the phrase *dia pisteos*, faith would indeed be the ground of salvation and a substitute for righteousness. But it does not mean this, because whenever *dia* means "because of" its object is in the accusative case, and this never happens when "faith" is the object. When the Greek word for "faith" occurs with *dia*, it is always in the genitive case, and this is the case the object should be in when *dia* means "by" or "through," indicating that faith is a channel but not the grounds of salvation.

In order to spend a twenty-dollar bill you have to have faith in its purchasing power. But it is not your faith that is the basis of the purchase. It is the value of the money. So also spiritually.

Third, faith cannot be a substitute for righteousness because the important word "credited" does not permit that interpretation. The words (*hasah* in Hebrew, *logizomai* in Greek) are bookkeeping terms. They refer to accounting, a field in which the accountant has to be one hundred percent right. Suppose I am walking around with a dollar in my pocket, and I am aware that this is not very much money. I would like to have more. So I get out my account book and "reckon" one hundred dollars, rather than one dollar, to my account. According to my book I now have one hundred dollars. But this means nothing at all. It is foolishness. If I want to reckon one hundred dollars to my account, I must have one hundred dollars. Reckoning, accounting, or crediting is an acknowledgment or marking down of what is actually the case.

It is the same in justification—which leads to the proper understanding (not a misunderstanding) of this verse. When God saved Abraham he did two things, one negative and one positive:

1. He did what Paul quotes David as saying in verses 7–8 (a quotation of Ps. 32:1–2), namely, *God did not reckon his sin against him.* How so? It is not merely that God simply struck Abraham's transgressions from the ledger book of his life and then forgot about them, as if they could simply be discounted. God does not play imaginary games. True, he did remove the list of Abraham's sins from his ledger, but that was only because he had first transferred it to the ledger book of Jesus Christ. Jesus took the liability of those transgressions on himself and paid their price by dying for them. Abraham's sin was not reckoned to Abraham because it was reckoned to Jesus Christ instead.

2. In a parallel action, God then also *reckoned the righteousness of Christ to Abraham,* which is what Genesis 15:6 teaches. God took Christ's righteousness and wrote it in Abraham's ledger.

That is the only way anybody has ever been saved, and it is precisely what has happened for anybody who has been saved. It is true that there have been different degrees of understanding of what happened. The Old Testament saints understood less (although, as I will show in the next study, Abraham himself probably understood a great deal). New Testament saints understand more. But regardless of the degrees of understanding, the only way we or anybody else is saved is by the imputation of the righteousness of Christ to our account.[4]

Some Practical Points

At the beginning of this study I pointed out two difficulties some of today's readers may have with these teachings. I have tried to address them. But, in closing, I want to balance those with four practical and easy-to-understand applications.

1. *The importance of Scripture.* Paul has been taking three chapters of Romans to explain man's great need and God's perfect remedy for that need in Christ. But here, at the point of proving and clinching his argument, he is ready to base everything he has said on just one Old Testament verse. One verse, followed by just one additional verse to establish the testimony of King David! Then, having stated the biblical teaching, Paul moves on. There is no need to speculate or argue further. For us, in the same way,

---

4. I have borrowed parts of this section with alterations from James Montgomery Boice, *Genesis: An Expositional Commentary,* vol. 2, *Genesis 12:1–36:43* (Grand Rapids: Zondervan, 1985), pp. 99, 100.

any clear statement of the Bible should settle any matter to which the Bible speaks—at once and forever.

2. *The hopelessness of trying to be saved by good works.* Abraham was a good man, even a great man. He is a model of Old Testament piety. Yet Abraham was not saved by his works, nor *could* he be saved by them. If this man could not be saved by good works, it is certain that you and I, who are far less pious and godly than he was, cannot be saved by them.

3. *Confidence in the gospel.* The Lord Jesus Christ testified to Abraham's being a saved man, even speaking on one occasion of "Abraham's bosom" as a synonym for paradise or heaven. Abraham was saved! But if he was saved, not by some ability, godliness, or good works unique to him, but by the same gospel that is being preached today, then we can have a complete and utter trust in that gospel. It saved him. It will save us. It can save anybody.

4. Finally, *all this is proof of Christianity's timelessness and validity.* If Christianity were merely something founded by Jesus Christ some two thousand years ago, it might be interesting but it would have no more ultimate claim upon us than the dogmas of any other human religion. But if—though it was accomplished by Jesus Christ in history some two thousand years ago—it is actually the way of salvation established by God the Father in conjunction with his eternal Son before the world began and through which anyone who has ever been saved was saved, then it is an entirely different matter.

This proves the finality of Christianity as the only true faith. Says Barnhouse, "All other religions are the gropings of man after God. The faith that is in Christ is God's revelation of truth from himself, in the terms and in the manner he wished us to have the truth."[5]

5. Donald Grey Barnhouse, *God's Remedy: Exposition of Bible Doctrines, Taking the Epistle to the Romans as a Point of Departure,* vol. 3, *Romans 3:21–4:25* (Grand Rapids: Wm. B. Eerdmans, 1954), p. 195.

52

Faith Credited as Righteousness

Romans 4:3

What does the Scripture say? "Abraham believed God, and it was credited to him as righteousness."

Anyone who has ever spent time teaching in a religious setting has been asked certain familiar questions often asked of Bible interpreters and thought by the questioners to be either clever or unanswerable, in spite of the fact that they have been answered very well by many people many times:

"Where did Cain get his wife?"

"If God is both good and all-powerful, how come there is evil in the world?"

"What about the innocent pagans who have never had a chance to hear the gospel?"

After hearing such timeworn questions repeatedly, it becomes difficult to take many of them seriously. However, among these questions there is one at least which, whether or not it is asked seriously, is nevertheless important and thoughtful. It is: "How were people saved before the death of Jesus Christ?" The reason it is important is that it assumes some very true things about the gospel. It presupposes (1) the necessity of the death of Christ; (2) the importance of making the good news about his sacrificial death known to lost people; and (3) the need to believe in Jesus. It understands that "without faith it is impossible to please God" (Heb. 11:6). Starting with these presuppositions, the questioner wonders how a person who lived before the time of Christ—and who therefore could not have had an opportunity to hear about or believe on Jesus—could be saved.

How *were* people saved before the birth, life, and death of Christ? The answer is that they were saved in precisely the same way as people who have lived after those events. That is, they were saved by believing on Jesus. The Old Testament saints looked forward to his coming. We look back to it.

What Did Abraham Believe?

This question emerges in our study of Romans 4, for in this chapter Paul is proving, from the Old Testament, the gospel of salvation by grace through the work of Christ. He knows that his Jewish readers would consider the Old Testament and its teaching both true and binding. Therefore, if he can show that Old Testament figures such as Abraham and David were saved by the gospel he has been teaching, he has established his teaching conclusively. If Abraham was saved by faith in Christ, it follows that Christianity is true and there is no other way of salvation.

But how is the apostle to establish this point? He does so by direct appeal to the Old Testament, quoting Genesis 15:6 in reference to Abraham and (as we shall see in the next study) Psalm 32:1–2 in reference to King David.

We have already seen several important things about Genesis 15:6, which is quoted in Romans 4:3 as "Abraham believed God, and it was credited to him as righteousness." We have seen that "it" refers, not to Abraham's faith, but to the righteousness of Christ, which God credited to Abraham. We have seen this as a "bookkeeping" transaction. God took the sin of Abraham from the ledger book of Abraham's life and transferred it to the ledger book of Christ, who died for such sin. And he took the righteousness of Christ from Christ's book and transferred it to Abraham. We also saw that faith is the channel through which this happens.

It is like one's faith in money. You need faith in money's value in order to spend it, but your faith in its purchasing power contributes nothing to the money itself. The value of a twenty-dollar bill is in the bill (or the integrity of the government, which stands behind it), not in the faith of the one using the money. In the same way, the worth of salvation is in the work of Christ, though we must believe on him for that work to be personally effective.

But here comes the question. Genesis 15:6 says, "Abram [Abraham] believed the LORD, and he credited it to him as righteousness." Strictly speaking, the text does not tell us what Abraham believed. We are told of the ultimate object of his faith; that is, the Lord God. But we are left in the dark as to the specific content of God's revelation to Abraham. What did God tell him, and what did Abraham believe as the result of that disclosure?

When we look at the context we see a number of possibilities. Genesis 15:1 records that God told Abraham that he would be Abraham's "shield" and "very great reward." Was that what Abraham believed? God also told Abraham that he would have an "heir" that would come forth from his own body (v. 4). Was that the content of the revelation? Then God speaks of numerous offspring, like the stars of heaven (v. 5). Is that it? Or does the content of Abraham's belief go back even further to the point of God's original call to him to leave Ur of the Chaldeans and go to a new land that God would show him, coupled with a promise of blessing to him and others (Gen. 12:1–7)?

If we had nothing more than Genesis 12 and 15 and Romans 4 to go on, we would have to conclude that Abraham's faith involved all of these—and perhaps things that are not even recorded. That is, we would conclude that Abraham was "credited" with righteousness on the basis of a complete and utterly trusting attitude to God. This is what Martin Luther seems to say in one place, writing, "The expression 'Abraham believed God' is equivalent to saying that he considered God truthful."[1]

We would not be wrong in thinking this; it is part of the story. But there is more to say.

The Problem in Galatia

The interesting thing about Genesis 15:6 is that it is quoted at three places in the New Testament—Romans 4:3 (our text), Galatians 3:6, and James 2:23—and one of these, Galatians 3:6, provides a well-developed answer to our question.

Some background is necessary. Paul had preached to the people of Galatia in southern Asia Minor, which we call Turkey, on his first missionary journey, described in Acts 13 and 14. He had taught them that salvation from sin does not come from keeping the law, or from any other form of good works or character, but from the work of Christ. He had explained that Christ died in our place, bearing the punishment for our sins, and that on the basis of his substitutionary sacrifice God now freely gives his own righteousness to believers. The Galatians understood this, believed it, were baptized, and began to live for Christ. God even worked miracles among them, according to Paul's explicit testimony (Gal. 3:5).

Sometime later—we do not know exactly when—certain Jews came to Galatia from Jerusalem and began to teach the Galatian Christians that it was not enough for them to have believed on Christ. They said it was necessary for them to believe in Moses as well. That is, they had to keep the law.

1. Martin Luther, *Luther's Works*, vol. 25, *Lectures on Romans*, ed. Hilton C. Oswald (St. Louis: Concordia, 1972), p. 255.

Faith was all right, but they also had to be circumcised and begin to keep the ritualistic requirements of the old covenant if they were to be saved. They could be Christians, but they had to become Jews, too.

Paul was aghast when he heard of this, and the letter to the Galatians is his spirited response. It has three parts: a first part, in which he defends his apostleship, no doubt because it had been under attack by these harmful Jewish legalizers; a second part, in which he restates and argues for the gospel; and a third part, in which he shows the inevitable outworking of the gospel of grace in moral living. In the second and chief part he argues that no one, not even Abraham, has been saved in any way but through faith in Jesus.

The Faith of Father Abraham

This is where Paul quotes Genesis 15:6, saying, much as he does in Romans, "Consider Abraham: 'He believed God, and it was credited to him as righteousness'" (Gal. 3:6).

Paul then adds these important words: "The Scripture foresaw that God would justify the Gentiles by faith, and announced the gospel in advance to Abraham: 'All nations will be blessed through you.' So those who have faith are blessed along with Abraham, the man of faith. . . . Christ redeemed us from the curse of the law by becoming a curse for us, for it is written: 'Cursed is everyone who is hung on a tree.' He redeemed us in order that the blessing given to Abraham might come to the Gentiles through Christ Jesus, so that by faith we might receive the promise of the Spirit" (Gal. 3:8–9, 13–14).

Paul's opponents would have argued that Abraham was saved by keeping the law and by being circumcised, but we know from Paul's teaching, both in Galatians and Romans, that he would have answered by reciting the historical sequence of events. The verse that says that Abraham was justified by faith is in Genesis 15. But circumcision is not introduced until years later, as recorded in Genesis 17. And the law was not given until the time of Moses, four hundred years after that. Since Abraham was declared to be a justified man *before* either the law or circumcision, it is certain that he was not justified on the basis of his conformity to either.

"But," Paul's opponents would have countered, "if that is true, then Abraham could not have been justified by faith in Jesus Christ either. For Jesus was not born until an even later date. Abraham did not know of Christ. So how could he have been saved by faith in someone of whom he did not know? Clearly, faith in Christ is not essential for salvation."

At this point we get the real answer to our question. For Paul replies that, on the contrary, Abraham did know of Christ and that he looked forward to his coming and trusted him as his Savior from sin. He makes three points that support this:

1. *Abraham believed the gospel.* This means that Abraham believed God in regard to spiritual matters (Gal. 3:8). The content of the gospel, as Paul explains it in regard to Abraham, was that "'all nations will be blessed through you.'" This quotation is drawn from Genesis 12:3 (repeated in 18:18 and 22:18), from the very beginning of Abraham's pilgrimage. So Paul is saying that from the very beginning, Abraham's faith was not concerned with mere physical things like an earthly heritage or physical posterity, but with spiritual things, like the blessing of salvation to come upon himself, his descendants, and even other nations. It was faith in the gospel, the good news about salvation.

Understand, then, that Abraham's faith was a very high order. He heard the promise of the land and of an earthly seed. He believed those promises. But what really gripped his mind and heart was the spiritual promise of salvation for all nations. It was for the sake of this blessing, not merely a physical land or an earthly posterity (which he could have had in Ur as well as in Canaan), that Abraham left his father's land and people to go to the new land that God was to show him.

This is how the author of the letter to the Hebrews puts it: "He [Abraham] was looking forward to the city with foundations, whose architect and builder is God" (Heb. 11:10).

2. *Abraham's faith concerned redemption.* This is a surprising thing to read, but it is what Paul writes: "Christ redeemed us from the curse of the law. . . . in order that the blessing given to Abraham might come to the Gentiles through Christ Jesus . . ." (Gal. 3:13–14).

"Redemption" is a rich word, as we know from our study of Romans 3:24. It is a commercial term, describing the way in which an object can be ransomed from the marketplace by payment of a price. We know the word chiefly as it is used in the pawn-shop business. If you need money in a hurry, one way of getting it is to take an object of some value to a pawnshop and leave it there, in exchange for a fraction of its worth in cash. Later, when you are better off and want to retrieve the object, you can go back to the pawnbroker and repay the money you were given (plus interest), and you will get it back, assuming the object has not been sold in the meantime.

"Redemption" was also used like this in ancient times, but mostly it was used of the redemption of slaves. Slaves were bought and sold in every marketplace of the ancient world. But a slave could be redeemed from slavery if someone was willing to pay a redemption price for him or her.

This is what Jesus did for us. Jesus delivered us from the bondage of sin at the cost of his own life—because he loved us. And that is what Abraham believed! Did Abraham really foresee and believe that? No doubt Abraham did not know as much as those who have lived after the time of Jesus Christ. Those who live on this side of the incarnation know in detail of Jesus' birth, life, death, resurrection, and ascension. We have four gospels to draw this information from. But we must not be so ready to assume that Abraham knew little. Paul says that God "announced the gospel [to him] in advance" (Gal. 3:8), and Jesus said, "Abraham rejoiced at the thought of seeing my day; he saw it and was glad" (John 8:56). What is more natural than that Abraham looked forward to some work of God in delivering the fallen human race from sin's slavery?

3. *Abraham believed in the coming of Jesus Christ specifically.* This is the final point in Paul's description of Abraham's faith. For having argued that God had announced the gospel to Abraham in advance and that Abraham looked forward to the blessing of God as redemption, Paul says, "The promises were spoken to Abraham and to his seed. The Scripture does not say 'and to seeds,' meaning many people, but 'and to your seed,' meaning one person, who is Christ" (Gal. 3:16).

When we check this out we find that the promise of blessing through a singular descendant of Abraham was given on three occasions: Genesis 12:7; 13:15; and 24:7. Paul is saying that Abraham picked up on this, realizing that this amazing promise was not a promise of blessing through his descendants in some general way but rather a promise of blessing to be achieved by one specific descendant, who was Christ.

Abraham did not know his name, of course. But he was looking forward to the coming of this one individual, and it was through the channel of his faith in Jesus that God declared him to be a justified person.

Faith of the Faithful

We have been studying the faith of Abraham because he is the focus of Paul's attention in this section of Romans. But it is worth saying that the same point can be made about any of the other Old Testament believers. They would all have explained the hope of their salvation in the same terms.

Let's ask a number of them what they "discovered in this matter" (cf. Rom. 4:1).

Here is Adam. Let's start with him. "Adam, you were the first man, and we should assume from this that what you believed in regard to salvation is of value for us. What did you believe in this matter? Did you believe that you could be saved by your works? Or did you have an anticipation of the coming of Jesus Christ and ground your faith in him?"

Adam replies, "You know my sad story, how I sinned by eating of the forbidden fruit and how I carried the human race into sin and death as a result of my transgression. But if you know that, you also know how God appeared to me after my fall and announced the coming of a Savior who would crush the head of Satan, though he would himself be wounded in the process. I did not know who he was at that time, but I believed in him. And I expressed that faith by naming my wife 'Eve,' because she would be the one through whom the gift of spiritual life would come. 'Eve' means 'life giver.' We thought she would give birth to the Messiah. So we named her first son 'Cain,' meaning 'Here he is!' We were wrong in that; it was many thousands of years before our line actually produced Jesus Christ. But we had the right idea, and we were credited with righteousness because of faith in Jesus."

Let's ask Jacob what he "discovered in this matter"—"Jacob, were you saved by your good works or by faith in the deliverer to come?"

Jacob replies, "I wasn't saved by my works—or by my ancestry either, even though I was the grandson of Abraham. I didn't have as much understanding as my grandfather. He was the spiritual giant in our family. But you will recall that as I lay dying I looked forward to the coming of the Savior and said, 'The scepter will not depart from Judah, nor the ruler's staff from between his feet, until he comes to whom it belongs and the obedience of the nations is his' [Gen. 49:10]. I was saved because I believed what God said about that Savior."

Here is Moses. Let's ask him. "Moses, how were you saved?"

Moses replies that even he, the lawgiver, was saved by faith in Jesus Christ and not in any ability he might be supposed to have had to keep God's commandments. "The Lord told me, 'I will raise up for them a prophet like you from among their brothers; I will put my words in his mouth, and he will tell them everything I command him' [Deut. 18:18]. I was saved because I believed that promise."

Our next witness is King David. "Tell us, David, you were called a man after God's own heart, weren't you?"

"Yes," replies David.

"That means you tried to think and act as God does. Does that mean that you were saved by your own good works or obedience?"

David explains that he was an adulterer and murderer. "If I had been trusting my works, I wouldn't have had a chance. No, I was saved because I looked forward in faith to that one who God promised would sit upon my throne forever. I knew that a person who would rule forever was no mere man. He must be the Savior-God. I believed that and was saved by him."

What about Isaiah? Isaiah looked forward to the "man of sorrows" who would take our transgressions on himself: "We all, like sheep, have gone astray, each of us has turned to his own way; and the Lord has laid on him the iniquity of us all" (Isa. 53:6).

Daniel prophesied the coming of "the Anointed One" (Dan. 9:25).

Micah revealed that he would be born in Bethlehem (Mic. 5:2).

At the time of Christ, John the Baptist pointed from himself to Jesus as "the Lamb of God, who takes away the sin of the world!" (John 1:29).[2]

---

2. I have presented much of the material in this chapter in an earlier study, "What Did Abraham Believe?" in James Montgomery Boice, *Genesis: An Expositional Commentary*, vol. 2, *Genesis 12:1–36:43* (Grand Rapids: Zondervan, 1985), pp. 104–109.

God Wants to Be Believed

Now I ask the same question of you. On what basis do you expect to obtain salvation? What do you believe concerning Jesus Christ?

Some years ago Donald Grey Barnhouse, a former pastor of the church I now serve, was talking to a man about the gospel. The conversation had gone on for some time, and the man seemed to be in total darkness. Finally he said, almost in a tone of desperation, "But what does God want? Tell me, what does God want?"

Barnhouse replied in what he believed was the given insight of the moment: "God wants to be believed. More than anything else God wants to be believed."

There was a moment of dawning wonder in the man's face, and then he said, "I think I see. After all, the honor of God is involved." He believed in Jesus Christ at that moment.

Do you believe in Jesus Christ as your Savior? That is what God declares him to be. Abraham believed what God had revealed to him concerning Jesus Christ, and the righteousness of Christ was credited to Abraham as if it were his own. Adam, Jacob, Moses, David, John the Baptist—all believed the same thing. No one has ever been saved in any other way. So I say, if you have not believed in Jesus Christ as your Savior, believe now. Today is always the day of salvation.

53

David's Testimony

Romans 4:6–8

David says the same thing when he speaks of the blessedness of the man to whom God credits righteousness apart from works:

> *"Blessed are they*
> *whose transgressions are forgiven,*
> *whose sins are covered.*
> *Blessed is the man*
> *whose sin the Lord will never count against him."*

It is a principle of Old Testament law, stated clearly in Deuteronomy 19:15, that a legal matter must be established by more than one witness. That verse says, "One witness is not enough to convict a man accused of any crime or offense he may have committed. A matter must be established by the testimony of two or three witnesses."[1]

As a former Pharisee and student of the law, the apostle Paul was undoubtedly well acquainted with that principle. In fact, he seems to be employing it in Romans 4:6–8, where he adds the testimony of King David to that of the patriarch Abraham to support his defense of the gospel of jus-

---

1. The principle is also found in Numbers 35:30 and Deuteronomy 17:6–7.

tification by the grace of God. Paul has already cited the experience of
Abraham, and he will return to him again, for Abraham is referred to
repeatedly throughout the remainder of the chapter. But now he brings in
the witness of David, citing two verses from the magnificent thirty-second
Psalm (vv. 1–2):

> "Blessed are they
>   whose transgressions are forgiven,
>   whose sins are covered.
> Blessed is the man
>   whose sin the Lord will never count against him."

This is a very great testimony.

Greatest of the Kings

When we began our study of Romans 4, taking up the case of Abraham, I
pointed out that, with the exception of Jesus Christ, Abraham is the single
most important person in the Bible—and that all the other biblical figures,
particularly those of the Old Testament, would unquestioningly have
looked to Abraham as their father in the faith. Abraham is a giant.

But this does not mean that David, to whose testimony Paul appeals now,
was insignificant. David was the greatest of Israel's kings as well as the one
who best embodied the nation's devotional spirit and longings, and those to
whom Paul was writing would have had the highest possible regard for
David also. James Hastings wrote in *The Greater Men and Women of the Bible*:

> The David of Israel is not simply the greatest of her kings; he is the man
> great in everything. He monopolizes all her institutions. He is her shepherd
> boy—the representative of her toiling classes. He is her musician—the suc-
> cessor of Jubal and Miriam and Deborah. He is her soldier—the conqueror
> of the Goliaths that would steal her peace. He is her king—numbering her
> armies and regulating her polity. He is her priest—substituting a broken and
> a contrite spirit for the blood of bulls and rams. He is her prophet—presag-
> ing with his last breath the everlastingness of his kingdom. He is her
> poet—most of her psalms are called by his name.[2]

It is hard for us to appreciate the Jews' special regard for King David
unless we think of a person in whom the best qualities and achievements of
George Washington, Thomas Jefferson, and Abraham Lincoln are combined. And perhaps even that would not quite reach this man's stature.

2. James Hastings, *The Greater Men and Women of the Bible*, vol. 3 (Edinburgh: T. & T. Clark,
1914), p. 113.

Importance of the Negative

David is important in the development of Paul's argument in another way also, however, and it is this that makes his testimony particularly telling with us. The words Paul quotes are cast in a negative form, as contrasted with the words about Abraham, which are positive. Abraham was "credited" with righteousness—a positive wording of the justification principle. David speaks of the same principle negatively, even using the same terminology ("credited" means "counted"), saying, "Blessed is the man whose sin the Lord will never count against him."

This negative wording is important for presenting the gospel in our day, as I have indicated, because it speaks to where most people actually are in terms of their spiritual sensitivities.

Let me show what I mean by starting with the positive wording. The positive statement of the justification principle tells us how we can get right with God, which we obviously need to do. But the difficulty is that most people today do not actually feel a need in this area. Martin Luther did; it is what haunted him. He knew he was not right with God, and he anticipated a confrontation with an angry God at the final judgment. God showed him that he could experience a right relationship with God through the work of Jesus Christ. But who feels the intensity of Luther's anguish today? A few people perhaps, but not many. Most people do not think of themselves as being in a wrong relationship to God. On the contrary, they assume that all is well between themselves and God—or at least it ought to be. So they do not feel a need for justification.

This is illustrated by what theologian R. C. Sproul speaks of as "justification by death." Several years ago Sproul tried out the initial question of the Evangelism Explosion program on his son, asking him, "If you should die tomorrow and appear before God at the gates of heaven, and God should ask, 'What right do you have to enter my heaven?' what would you say?"

His son replied, "I'd say, 'Well, I'm dead, aren't I?'"

The point seemed to be that all he needed to do to gain entrance to God's heaven is to die. The righteousness of Christ received by faith did not seem to enter into his son's thinking in the slightest.

Because so many people think or respond this way today, it is necessary to teach the doctrines of justification at length, as I have been trying to do in this exposition of Romans. Yet, when we come to the testimony of King David, just because it is cast in negative form, we come to something that does speak to our contemporaries. It speaks of transgressions. It pictures these as a burden and contrasts them with the blessedness of the person who is freed through God's forgiveness.

This speaks powerfully to our contemporaries, because, as I know from my counseling, nearly everyone carries about the burdens of past sinful actions. Somewhere in the writings of Donald Grey Barnhouse there is a story from early in his ministry—he was about twenty years old at the time—in which a woman came to him for counseling about a terrible crime that had been hanging over her for decades. She was about sixty years old when she came to Barnhouse, and she had killed a man forty years before. He was a boarder in her parents' home, and one day he had abused her sexually. She was so outraged by this that she crept back into his room the next night and turned on the gas jet. The next day, when the police came to investigate the boarder's death, they ruled it an accident, judging that the wind had blown the flame out. Nobody knew what the woman had done, and she had carried the burden of this sin around with her for forty years.

I have never had anyone tell me about a murder he or she has committed, but I have been told enough terrible stories to know that nearly everyone carries around some guilt for past actions.

People have told me of some theft they have committed. Some have harmed other people, lying about them out of jealousy and ruining their chances for promotion, sometimes for marriage.

Others have contributed to the death of another person, not in a direct way (at least so far as what has been told to me), but by their neglect to do what might have saved the person's life or through carelessness—as in a traffic accident, for example.

Men are haunted by dishonesty, even criminal acts, in business.

Women are haunted by the memory of an abortion, sometimes multiple abortions. They have been told that there is nothing to feel guilty about, that all they did was submit to "a surgical procedure." But in their hearts they know they killed their child. I have had women ask, "How can I be forgiven for what I did?"

How would you answer such a question?

Sometimes counselors try to reassure a person by suggesting that the action was all right or at least no more evil than what many other people have done. It is a way of "forgiving" the person, the counselor becoming a priest for the occasion. But many who have gone this route know that human forgiveness, while comforting and nice, is not enough. No mere human being can forgive another's sin, particularly if it is against a third party. The only forgiveness of any true value is God's forgiveness—what David is talking about when he writes, "Blessed are they whose transgressions are forgiven, whose sins are covered. Blessed is the man whose sin the Lord will never count against him."

This is what needs to be said to anyone who is conscious of the guilt of past sins. This is the only thing that works. It is the only thing that matters.

David knew the terrible burden of sin as a result of his transgressions. He had committed adultery with Bathsheba, another man's wife, and then he had arranged for her husband Uriah to be killed in order to cover up his sin. He "covered" it over, true. But the guilt of the act was still there. Why? Because David's cover-up was only a form of self-justification, and no one is able properly to justify himself. It was only when David knew his sin to be "covered" by the blood of Christ (v. 7) that he was freed from guilt and could rightly count himself blessed.[3]

The Bliss of This Thought

Are you suffering from guilt for some past action? Does your mind return again and again to the wrong you have done? Is guilt an ever-present companion? If so, you need to experience what David knew as a result of God's grace in reference to his sin. He says three things about it:

1. *His sin was forgiven.* In the Bible there are a number of Greek words that are translated by our word "forgive" or "forgiveness," all with special meanings. But the word that occurs here is *aphethēsan* (from the irregular verb *aphiēmi*), which means "to send off" or "to send away." It is the word used in Matthew 13:36, where—in the King James Version—Jesus is said to have "sent the multitude away" so he could explain the parables of that chapter privately to his disciples. The idea is that of separation, and the bearing of the word upon the sin question is that it teaches that God is willing to separate the sinner's transgression and guilt from the sinner. We are not able to do that ourselves. When we humans punish a crime it is always by punishing the offender, simply because there is no other way of doing it. But God, for whom all things are possible, does separate the sin from the sinner, placing the sin upon Jesus Christ, where it is punished.

This is what the author of Hebrews was talking about when he said, "Christ was sacrificed once to take away the sins of many people" (Heb. 9:28a).

It is what Peter intended when he wrote, "He himself bore our sins in his own body on the tree, so that we might die to sins and live for righteousness . . ." (1 Peter 2:24).

One of the ways the ancients sometimes punished the crime of murder was to bind the victim's corpse to the murderer so he was forced to carry about the decaying body of his victim until he himself was destroyed. It is a horrible picture, but a true portrait of what it means to bear the burden of one's sin and guilt. It was what Paul was perhaps thinking of when he cried out, later on in Romans, "Who will rescue me from this body of death?" (Rom. 7:24b). Who? Paul gave the answer in the very next verse: God alone through the atonement of Jesus Christ. And what bliss to be delivered! If you can keep the image of the decaying corpse in mind, you may begin to appreciate what it means to be separated from the corrupting influence of the sin you have committed and know the joy of forgiveness.

---

3. David's anticipation of the coming of Christ was noted in the previous study ("Faith Credited as Righteousness"). In Psalm 51:7 David reveals his faith in cleansing by the blood of a sacrifice, for "hyssop," which is mentioned there, was the small shrub used to make the brushes by which the blood of a sacrifice was sprinkled on the altar.

Horatio G. Spafford knew that joy and wrote movingly:

> My sin—O the bliss of this glorious thought!—
>   My sin, not in part, but the whole,
> Is nailed to the cross and I bear it no more;
>   Praise the Lord, praise the Lord, O my soul!

2. *His sin was covered.* This is a different idea from the thought of David's sin being forgiven, or "sent away," but it is not easy at first glance to determine what the term is getting at. The reason is simple. "Covered" (*epekalyph-thēsan*) is one of that special class of words used only once in the New Testament. Obviously, then, the word was not common, and it would probably not even have been used by Paul here except for the fact that it was in the Septuagint version of the Old Testament text he is quoting.

However, the fact that the idea is drawn from the Old Testament gives us an important clue for interpreting it. For as soon as we ask, "Where in the Old Testament do we find the idea of the covering over of sin?" we immediately think of the work the high priest performed on the Day of Atonement. On that day the priest took the blood of a sacrifice, made moments before in the courtyard of the temple, and sprinkled it on the Mercy Seat, the covering of the Ark of the Covenant. The Ark contained the law of Moses, which everyone had broken. Without the sacrifice it is a picture of judgment.[4] But when the broken law was covered by the blood of the sacrifice in this ceremony, God saw that an innocent victim had died in place of those who were guilty, his judgment was turned aside, and his love was released to save sinners.

I think this is what is involved here, and it is why I contrasted David's covering over of his sin with the entirely different "covering" provided by God. David's covering was merely a hiding or denying of his sin. God's covering was a true punishing of sin. It is because sin has actually and truly been punished in Christ that you and I, if we come to Christ, can find release from sin's burden.

If this is what David was thinking of, I find support for this interpretation of "covered" in the thought that the two ideas of sin being "taken away" and "covered" are illustrated by the two parallel acts of the priests of Israel on the Day of Atonement. "Covered" would refer to the covering over of sin by blood sprinkled on the Mercy Seat. "Taken away" would refer to the ceremony performed earlier in the day, in which the sins of the people were confessed over the head of a goat (called the "scapegoat"), which was then driven away into the wilderness. This later rite pictured the removal of the people's sins from them.

---

4. See my previous study in Part Four of this volume, "Propitiation: The Forgotten Doctrine" (Rom. 3:25).

3. *His sin was not counted against him.* The final word David uses of God's handling of his sin is the one we have chiefly been studying here: "counted," "credited," or "reckoned." This is a bookkeeping term, as we have noted, the point being that God would not list the sins of those he was saving in their own ledgers. How would we express this thought? We would probably say, "Happy is the person to whom God has given a clean slate." Or, "How wonderful to be able to start again with no black marks against you."

Perhaps that is too wonderful to be true! Is it? We think so if we think in human terms. But it is not "too wonderful" if we think as God thinks or trust what he says about the striking away of our transgressions.

God says, "I will forgive their wickedness and will remember their sins no more" (Jer. 31:34b). The psalmist declares, "As far as the east is from the west, so far has he removed our transgressions from us" (Ps. 103:12).

Those are great statements, but they are supported by the even greater truth that God has dealt with our sins at the cross of Christ. They have been punished there, and that is why they are removed from us as far as the east is from the west, and why they are remembered by God no more.

Never, Never

There is one more word in Paul's citation of David's testimony that deserves special consideration, because it contrasts so keenly with things human. It is the word *never,* which occurs in the sentence, "Blessed is the man whose sin the Lord will *never* count against him."

Never means never, and it must be taken at full value here, even though the opposite is almost always the case in human relationships. We all know the kind of forgiveness in which a person reluctantly accepts our apology and says that he will forgive us. But we know as he says this that he is not forgetting what happened, that our offense will linger in his mind and will probably be brought out against us in the future. Parents have a way of doing this with their children, never forgetting some foolish action they did years ago and periodically reminding them of it. We adults do it with one another, and it is harmful.

This text tells us that God is not like that. It tells us that once he has forgiven us for our sin through the work of Christ, he will *never, never* bring it up to us again. He will not bring it up in this life, never remind us of something in the past. He will always begin with us precisely where we are in the present. And he will never bring it up at the day of judgment. Why? Because it is truly forgiven. It will *never* be remembered anymore.

That is real "blessedness," which is the terminology David uses. And my concluding question is this: Why trade away that blessedness for the false blessings offered by this world?

The world does offer its blessings, of course. It is how it holds its victims. It offers material things chiefly, but it also offers intangibles such as a good reputation, success, happiness, and such items. Let me remind you that you can have all these things and more and still be miserable—if the burden of your sin is not lifted. David is an example. He was the king of a most favored nation. He had wealth and reputation. But the very psalm from which the verses we have been studying are taken describes what he was like before his sin was forgiven. He wrote that when he kept silent about his sin, trying to hush it up, "my bones wasted away through my groaning all day long. For day and night your hand was heavy upon me; my strength was sapped as in the heat of summer" (Ps. 32:3–4). But because David found forgiveness with God, the burden of his sin rolled away, his strength was restored, and he could write: "Blessed is the man whose sin the Lord will never count against him."

I commend that very great blessing to you.

54

Salvation Without Ceremony

Romans 4:9-12

Is this blessedness only for the circumcised, or also for the uncircumcised? We have been saying that Abraham's faith was credited to him as righteousness. Under what circumstances was it credited? Was it after he was circumcised, or before? It was not after, but before! And he received the sign of circumcision, a seal of the righteousness that he had by faith while he was still uncircumcised. So then, he is the father of all who believe but who have not been circumcised, in order that righteousness might be credited to them. And he is also the father of the circumcised who not only are circumcised but who also walk in the footsteps of the faith that our father Abraham had before he was circumcised.

The human mind is a very subtle thing, and at no point is it more subtle than in trying to make excuses for its conduct. Richard Harris Barham (1788–1845) was an English clergyman who frequently missed morning chapel during his student years at Oxford. Chapel was at 7:00 A.M., but Barham was almost always up too late the night before. When he was reproached for his failure by his tutor, he excused himself by saying, "The fact is, sir, chapel is too late for me. I am a man of regular habits, and I can't sit up until seven in the morning. Unless I get to bed by four or five o'clock at the latest, I'm good for nothing the next day."

My favorite improvised excuse was made by Chico Marx of the famous Marx Brothers. When his wife caught him kissing a chorus girl, Chico explained, "I wasn't kissing her; I was whispering in her mouth."

The Example of Abraham

We remember from our study of the first verses of Romans 4 that in this chapter Paul is attempting to prove the gospel from the Old Testament. His chief example and the basis of the proof is Abraham, patriarch of the Jewish people and the one to whom they looked as their spiritual model. If Paul can show that Father Abraham was saved by the grace of God in Christ, received by the channel of human faith, he has made his point and established the doctrine. Paul shows that Abraham was saved through faith and not by works by quoting Genesis 15:6. That important text says, "Abraham believed God, and it was credited to him as righteousness" (v. 3).

Having proved his point concerning Abraham, Paul then adds a second witness. This witness is David, and the words Paul cites in Romans 4:7–8 are a statement drawn from the thirty-second Psalm: "'Blessed are they whose transgressions are forgiven, whose sins are covered. Blessed is the man whose sin the Lord will never count against him'" (cf. Ps. 32:1–2).

The case should be clear-cut: Abraham was saved by faith apart from human works; we must be saved by faith, too. But here is where the excuse-making subtlety of the unbelieving mind enters in.

"But surely there must be more to it than that," objects the skeptic. "What about circumcision? I know you said earlier that circumcision is an external thing and that God looks not on externals, but on the heart. But, after all, Abraham *was* circumcised, wasn't he? And circumcision *was* given to Abraham by God. It has been practiced by Jews down through the many centuries since Abraham's time. That has to mean something. If it does, then it is not right to say that Abraham was saved by faith alone. He was at least saved by circumcision, too, or perhaps by it rather than by faith. If God gave circumcision, circumcision must be meritorious."

Today, in the same way, people would argue for the redeeming value of baptism or even the Lord's Supper. Jesus Christ gave both to us. Since he did, isn't it right to say that we are saved, at least in part, by the sacraments?

It should not require a degree in logic to see the error of these arguments. They state that if ceremonies are given by God, they must count for something, and if they do, they must be valuable for attaining salvation. But that does not follow. Just because "A" is valuable for "B" does not mean that it is necessarily valuable for "C," unless it can be shown that "B" and "C" are the same thing. If "A" equals "B," and "B" equals "C," then "A" also equals "C." But this is not true if "B" and "C" are different. That is the case here. Circumcision (or any other sacrament) does have value. Paul is going to explain circumcision's value as being a "sign" and a "seal" of the righteousness that is received by faith. But this is not the same thing as saying that it is the ground on which a person receives that righteousness in the first place.

Paul's argument is even stronger than this, however. In these verses Paul asks when it was that Abraham was declared to be righteous by God. That is, when was he saved? Was it after he was circumcised, or before? If it was after, circumcision might be supposed to have entered into his justification in some way. It may have contributed to it. But if it was before, then—whatever circumcision signifies—it obviously does not enter into salvation and is not the basis on which Abraham or anyone else has been justified.

When was it? The answer is clear. As we have already seen in a previous study, Abraham was declared to be justified in Genesis 15:6, but we are not told he was given the sacrament of circumcision until Genesis 17, which describes a period of his life fourteen years later.

Therefore, since Abraham was not saved by circumcision, he can be cited as the father not only of Jews, who are circumcised, but of everyone, even those who are not. He is the father of the justified. Because he was circumcised, he is the spiritual father of those Jewish people who not only are circumcised but who have also believed on Jesus Christ. And because he was declared to be justified *before* he was circumcised, he is also the spiritual father of those who have not been circumcised but who, like believing Jews, have also believed in Jesus.

F. Godet says rightly of this teaching, "The apostle has succeeded in discovering the basis of Christian universalism in the very life of him in whose person theocratic particularism was founded."[1] That is, the Jews had been basing their hopes of being saved as Jews on Abraham. But the example of Abraham actually proves that God saves people through Christ regardless of their origins.

Another writer says, "Paul has turned the Jew's boast upside down. It is not the Gentile that must come to the Jew's circumcision for salvation; it is the Jew who must come to a Gentile faith, such faith as Abraham had long before he was circumcised."[2]

Do you realize the importance of that?

If you are a Jew and are saved, it is not because you are a Jew. It is because of the work of Jesus Christ. If you are a Gentile and are saved, it is not because of anything you are or have done as a Gentile. It is because of the work of Jesus Christ. No one is saved because he or she has been baptized or confirmed or gone to Mass or shared in the communion service. A person is saved through faith in the perfect and completed work of Christ.

---

1. F. Godet, *Commentary on St. Paul's Epistle to the Romans*, trans. A. Cusin (Edinburgh: T. & T. Clark, n.d.), vol. 1, p. 295, 296.

2. Stiftler, quoted by Donald Grey Barnhouse, *God's Remedy*, vol. 3, in an *Exposition of Bible Doctrines, Taking the Epistle to the Romans as a Point of Departure* (Grand Rapids: Wm. B. Eerdmans, 1954), p. 260.

Either you have been saved by him, or you have not been saved at all. It is by faith and not by works that one is justified.

A God-Given Sign

There is a valid question still to be asked at this point, of course, and it is this: If Abraham was saved by faith apart from circumcision, which he must have been if he was declared to be justified fourteen years before circumcision was given to him, why was this rite given? If Abraham was not saved by circumcision, didn't the giving of circumcision just muddy the waters? Or, to put the question in other terms, what is the purpose of the sacraments anyway?

This is a good Bible passage from which to ask these questions, because it contains in one place (in fact, in one verse) the two most important words in the Bible for understanding what the sacraments are about. The words are: (1) "sign" and (2) "seal."

Let's take the word *sign* first. Paul writes that Abraham "received the sign of circumcision" (v. 11). What does that mean? Well, in simple language a sign is a visible object that points to something different from and greater than itself. To review what I noted in a previous study, here are some examples. If you are driving along the New Jersey Turnpike going north and see a sign that says, "New York 125 Miles," you understand that New York City is 125 miles ahead of you. The sign is not New York, but it points to New York. Though it is less than the city—much less—it is not without value.

Here is the other example: You are driving down a certain road and you see a sign over a diner that says, "Joe's Place." This sign does what the sign in my first example does; it points to the diner as "Joe's Place." But in this case, the sign does something more as well. It indicates ownership; it shows that this particular diner is Joe's.

I use that example in addition to the first one because it introduces a second important element into this discussion. On the first level, the sacrament, being a sign, points to something different from and greater than itself. In the case of circumcision, it is a case of pointing to the covenant God established with Abraham based on the work of Christ. In the case of the New Testament sacraments, baptism and the Lord's Supper, it is the same. The Lord's Supper in particular points back to Christ's death: "This is my body given for you . . ." and "This cup is the new covenant in my blood, which is poured out for you" (Luke 22:19–20). But on the second level, these sacraments also indicate ownership. They show that we belong to Christ and that we no longer belong to ourselves.

Baptism especially does this, being an initiatory sacrament. Its whole meaning concerns ownership by or identification with Jesus. This is one reason why, under normal circumstances, baptism is to be a public rather than a private act. It is one important way by which believers are to testify before the world that they are Christ's. On the other hand, baptism is also a testimony to the believers themselves. For if times come into a believer's life, as they seem always to do, when the person begins to doubt whether he or she is actually saved or has been claimed by Christ, the memory of baptism can be an important means of the person's being reassured and strengthened in faith.

This was the case with Martin Luther. It has been reported of Luther that there were times late in his life when he was discouraged and seemed to be confused about everything, no doubt because of the strain and mental fatigue of being in the forefront of the Protestant Reformation in Germany for so many years. Luther questioned the value of the Reformation. He questioned his faith. He even questioned the work of Jesus Christ. But when those times came, we are told, Luther would write in chalk on the table two Latin words: *Baptizatus sum!* ("I have been baptized!"). That reality would strengthen him, and he would remember that he really was Christ's and had been identified with him in his death and resurrection.[3]

A Seal of Christ's Righteousness

The second word Paul uses to discuss the nature of the sacraments, whether circumcision, baptism, or the Lord's Supper, is "seal." He writes that Abraham's circumcision was "a seal of the righteousness that he had by faith while he was still uncircumcised" (v. 11).

What is a seal? We do not use seals very often today, but we have enough examples to illustrate their meaning and importance. Suppose you want to go abroad. You have to secure a passport issued by the government of the United States. You apply for it, submitting two recent pictures of yourself. When it comes you find that one of the photos has been affixed to the passport with a seal: the great seal of the United States. It is stamped into the passport in such a way that it is impossible to remove or alter the photo without damaging and thus invalidating the document. This seal indicates that the authority of the United States government stands behind the passport in affirming that the person whose picture appears there is a true citizen of the United States.

The other use of seals with which we are familiar is the affixing of these to a legal document by a Notary Public. The notary asks us to swear that the representations in the document are true and then affixes his or her seal to validate the transaction.

Sacraments operate in this way. In the case of Abraham, Paul says that circumcision was "a seal of the righteousness that he had by faith while he

3. This is not meant to imply, nor did it imply for Luther, that baptism has some magical property by which a person is joined savingly to Christ. That view was present in the theology of the Roman Catholic Church and has been preserved in some creedal and liturgical statements of Protestantism, but it is unbiblical. The point I am making is that although the sacraments are indeed valuable signs, they are not the reality themselves.

was still uncircumcised." That is, after Abraham had believed God and God had imparted righteousness to him, God gave the seal of circumcision to validate what had happened. In the same way, baptism is a seal that the person being baptized has been identified with Jesus Christ as his disciple, and the elements of the Lord's Supper, when received, indicate that the person has taken Jesus to himself as intimately and as inseparably as eating bread and drinking wine.

Important?

Yes, the sacraments are important as signs and seals of what has happened spiritually and invisibly, *but not as a means of salvation.*

The Father of All

The last portion of our text teaches that because Abraham was saved by faith before he was circumcised, he has become the father of all who are truly saved, both Jew and Gentile. This does not mean that no one had been justified before Abraham. Adam, Abel, Enoch, Noah, and other early believers were also justified by faith. But it does mean that in Abraham's case the way of salvation was made explicit in Scripture for the first time; therefore, all who have been saved trace their spiritual ancestry to him.

What a host of spiritual descendants this man had!

There are Jewish descendants, first of all. Abraham was followed in the faith by Isaac and then by Jacob. They were not the giants Abraham was. But each looked forward to the Messiah who would come, and God referred to himself by using their names, declaring himself many times to be "the God of Abraham, Isaac and Jacob."

David is in that ancestry, as we have already seen. So were all the believing kings. The prophets were in this ancestry, too. Isaiah followed in the steps of Abraham when he trusted, not in his own good works or in his obedience to the sacraments, but in the One who was yet to come. So also did Jeremiah, Ezekiel, Daniel, and all the minor prophets.

At the time of Jesus there were many who took their places in this line of Abraham's descendants, people like Mary and Joseph, Anna, Simeon, and others. And then there at last was John the Baptist, who pointed to Jesus as "the Lamb of God, who takes away the sins of the world!" (John 1:29).

The eleven disciples were among this group of believers: Simon Peter, James, John, Nathanael, Andrew, Philip, Matthew, and the rest. Later, Paul joined their ranks, and Barnabas, and the early deacons of the church. So did John Mark, who wrote the second Gospel.

These were all Jews and were therefore in the great company of those "who not only are circumcised but who also walk in the footsteps of the faith that our father Abraham had before he was circumcised" (v. 12).

What of those other spiritual descendants of Abraham, the Gentiles? At first this was only a trickle, like Israel itself once was. This stream grew slowly, but it contained people like Caleb, who became a member of the tribe of Judah but was originally a Kenizzite or foreigner. There was Rahab of Jericho and Ruth of Moab and Naaman, the Syrian general.

What about the Magi, who are introduced to us at the birth of Jesus? Are we to think that God brought them all the way to Jerusalem from their distant eastern homeland and then allowed them to return unconverted? They were Gentiles and uncircumcised, but they were brought to faith in the Jews' Messiah. These Gentiles saw the Lord Jesus Christ as a child and worshiped him.

During Christ's lifetime we are introduced to such believing Gentiles as the Syro-Phoenician woman and the centurion who approached Jesus on behalf of his paralyzed and suffering servant. Each of these was praised for his or her great faith. There is also, of course, the woman of Samaria.

Later, after the resurrection, Philip preached the gospel to a devout Ethiopian, and the Ethiopian believed. Then Philip went up the coast of Palestine, preaching in Gentile cities where, we may suppose, many more Gentiles believed. Peter took the gospel to the Roman soldier Cornelius, and was used to open the door of the gospel to the Gentiles in an official way.

At Antioch the church grew among Gentiles particularly. Many of its teachers were Gentiles: Simeon called Niger (probably a black man), Lucius of Cyrene, Manaen (who had been brought up with Herod the Tetrarch). When the missionary journeys began, Paul picked up such uncircumcised believers as Luke, who was from Macedonia and who later wrote the third Gospel and Acts, and Titus, who was not circumcised, although pressures were apparently exerted to have him be (cf. Gal. 2:3), and these men worked with him.

In the greetings appended to Paul's letters we discover the names of Gentiles who were added to the church, many through Paul's ministry—people like Apollos, Stephanus, Fortunatus, Philemon, Gaius, and Erastus, and the believing slaves Tertius, Quartus, and Onesimus.

These people were all uncircumcised, but Abraham became their father, too, since "he is the father of all who believe but who have not been circumcised, in order that righteousness might be credited to them" (v. 11).

A Spiritual Ancestor

The great British statesman William Gladstone (1809–1898) once visited an antique shop and was struck by a seventeenth-century oil painting he found there. It portrayed an aristocrat dressed in an old Spanish costume with a ruff, plumed hat, and lace cuffs. Gladstone wanted to buy it, but it was too expensive. Sometime later he visited the home of a rich London merchant and saw the portrait hanging on his wall. His host noticed him looking at the picture and said, "Do you like it? It is a portrait of one of my ancestors, a minister at the court of Queen Elizabeth."

Gladstone, who knew this was untrue, replied, "For three pounds less he would have been my ancestor."

I do not know who your ancestors have been, whether they have been worthy or quite undistinguished, or even whether you know who they are. But I do know this: You can step into the long ranks of the greatest honor roll of ancestors any human being could ever have and it will not cost you even a single cent—though it will cost you your pretensions. It is the ancestral line of Abraham. You need only believe on the Lord Jesus Christ as your Savior, and this great company of the faithful will become your family tree.

55

The Steps of Faith

Romans 4:12

And he is also the father of the circumcised who not only are circumcised but who also walk in the footsteps of the faith that our father Abraham had before he was circumcised.

In Paul's proof of the gospel from the life of Abraham there is a phrase that is worth returning to, even though I have passed by it in the preceding discussion. That phrase is "footsteps of the faith." To walk in another's footsteps means walking in single file so that the ground covered by the leader is covered in turn by each follower.[1] This suggests a journey, and it is for this that I return here to the footsteps idea.

Sometimes we think of the Christian life only in terms of fixed, past decisions like being "born again" or "deciding for Jesus." There are times when decisions must be made, of course, and being born again does indeed happen only once in our lives. But we can go overboard with such an approach, thinking that, if these decisions have been made or these experiences have happened to us once, there is very little to be expected from then on.

---

1. John Murray says, "To 'walk in the footsteps' is to march in file. Abraham is conceived of as the leader of the band and we walk, not abreast, but in file, following in the footprints left by Abraham" (*The Epistle to the Romans* [Grand Rapids: Wm. B. Eerdmans, 1968], p. 139).

461

Actually, those events are only a beginning of the Christian life, and true Christianity is more like a pilgrimage in which every step is to be taken by faith and in the same direction, the direction marked out for us by Abraham.

Abraham was a pilgrim throughout his entire life, and we are to be also. Like him, we are to live "looking forward to the city with foundations, whose builder and maker is God" (Heb. 11:10).

The Obedience of Faith

Abraham's faith is measured by several clearly defined steps, and it is useful to look at each in turn. The first was his calling by God and his response to that call while he was in Ur of the Chaldeans. This is recounted in Genesis 12:1–9 and is referred to in Hebrews 11: "By faith Abraham, when called to go to a place he would later receive as his inheritance, obeyed and went, even though he did not know where he was going" (v. 8).

There are two important things about this initial step in Abraham's faith-pilgrimage. First, it was initiated entirely by God. Abraham did not seek God of himself any more than we do. In fact, Abraham was a worshiper of false gods and at the start had no appreciation of the true God at all (cf. Josh. 24:2). He was in the category of those who have repressed the truth lest the knowledge of the true God spring up to force a change of allegiance in their lives and a reordering of their lifestyles. The fact that Abraham did follow after the true God was due solely to God's initiative.

Nothing could be clearer than this from the verses in Genesis 12 that describe God's call (vv. 1–3, 7). They contain seven great "I will"s.

1. "I will show you [a land]."
2. "I will make you into a great nation."
3. "I will bless you."
4. "I will make your name great."
5. "I will bless those who bless you."
6. "I will curse [those who curse you]" and later, after Abraham had reached Canaan,
7. "I will give [you] this land."

In no case does Abraham do anything to merit the appearance of God to him. Nor does he contribute anything to the promises God utters. It is a matter of election, pure and simple, as in our own salvation.

"But surely Abraham did something?" someone queries. That is true, of course, and it is the second important thing about Abraham's initial step of faith: Abraham obeyed God (Heb. 11:8). But notice, this came after God's commands and was provoked by it. God told Abraham, "Leave your country, your people and your father's household and go to the land I will show you" (v. 1), and Abraham did. The text says, "So Abram [Abraham] left, as the LORD had told him . . ." (v. 4). This is why Hebrews refers to this step as obedience.

We would think about the Christian life more accurately than we do if we would learn to think of our own responses to God in this way. And our presentation of the gospel would be more accurate, too. The way we usually present the gospel suggests that we think of becoming a Christian as a work of ours—"deciding for Jesus" or "letting Jesus into our hearts." But that makes it all man-centered. It would be better if we thought of faith simply as obedience to what God tells us to do.

To Be a Pilgrim

The second stage of Abraham's walk of faith concerns his early years in the Promised Land. In one sense, Abraham had arrived. He was now where God had sent him. But, at the same time, Abraham knew that he was only a pilgrim in this earthly land, since his true goal and inheritance from God was in heaven. The author of Hebrews makes this plain by saying, "By faith he made his home in the promised land like a stranger in a foreign country; he lived in tents, as did Isaac and Jacob, who were heirs with him of the same promise. For he was looking forward to the city with foundations, whose architect and maker is God" (Heb. 11:9–10).

We have a hymn in English that uses the pilgrim image, but in a way that suggests a wrong idea. It states:

> A pilgrim was I, and a wand'ring,
> In the cold night of sin I did roam,
> When Jesus the kind shepherd found me,
> And now I am on my way home.

John W. Peterson, 1958

That is a pretty rhyme, of course, and it is true for the most part. But its use of the word *pilgrim* suggests that this is what we were before Jesus found us and that now we are no longer pilgrims. Actually a pilgrim is what we have become.

To be a pilgrim, two things must have happened to us. First, *we must have left home.* Abraham did that. God told him to leave his country, his people, and his father's household. Similarly, we are called to leave our past to follow Jesus. This is why Jesus told us to deny ourselves and take up our cross daily and follow him (cf. Luke 9:23). It is why he said, "If anyone comes to me and does not hate his father and mother, his wife and children, his brothers and sisters—yes, even his own life—he cannot be my disciple" (Luke 14:26). Of course, the One who taught us to love one another was not teaching us literally to hate members of our family. Rather, he was teaching that all lesser loyalties must be subordinated to our loyalty to him. We must turn our backs on anything that would keep us from one-hundred-percent discipleship.

And that is the second characteristic of a pilgrim: *discipleship,* or *following after Jesus.* A person who has merely left home is not a pilgrim. He is a vagrant, a drifter. To be a pilgrim, a man must have his eyes on the goal to which he is moving.

This does not mean that a Christian cannot have warm human friendships. In fact, Christian friendships will be greater and deeper than those of non-Christians, if only because people will have become more valuable than things to a Christian. And speaking of "things," living the pilgrim life does not mean that Christians cannot also have a reasonable share of earthly riches. Abraham, though a pilgrim, became a rich man. He had flocks and herds and servants. Yet he was a pilgrim still. Why? Donald Grey Barnhouse answers:

> [Because he left] his native land and [began] to walk with God, everything he owned was now held in the reality of its true and eternal value. Nothing was held for any intrinsic worth. Henceforth all that was touched or possessed was looked upon as a gift from God—of value if it enhanced the glory of God and brought the Lord nearer to the heart, and of no value at all if it caused the light of God to grow dim and the memory of the glory to fade.[2]

I am sure that God wants some who are following this study to be more truly pilgrims for God than they have ever been. You may complain that you have too many worldly matters to worry about—a job, a home, a mortgage, and such—and that you are too old to take a rigorous following of Jesus Christ seriously. If that is what you are thinking, consider Abraham. He had many possessions even when he started out from Haran (Gen. 12:5), but they did not stop his pilgrimage. Moreover, Abraham was already seventy-five years old (v. 4). He lived to be one hundred and seventy-five. Even by the life-expectancy standards of his day, he was already what we would call middle-aged when God called him.

How about you? If you are following in the footsteps of Abraham, doesn't God want you to be a true pilgrim?

God of the Impossible

The next stage of Abraham's faith-journey is a great one, but I will not take much time to discuss it now, since it is brought into the story just a few

2. Donald Grey Barnhouse, *God's Remedy: Exposition of Bible Doctrines, Taking the Epistle to the Romans as a Point of Departure,* vol. 3, Romans 3:21–4:25 (Grand Rapids: Wm. B. Eerdmans, 1954), p. 272.

verses further on in Romans (4:18–22). We will consider it in full when we get to that passage, for it is a most important part of the picture.

God had promised Abraham that he would have numerous descendants, as numerous as the stars in heaven (Gen. 15:5). Yet, although Abraham was seventy-five years old when he started out for Canaan, eleven more years passed and he and his wife, Sarah, remained childless. It became a great problem for them—an embarrassment, of course. But more than that, it was a spiritual problem, since God's promise of a deliverer from sin was wrapped up in his promise of a son from Abraham's "own body" (v. 4). Abraham and Sarah's hope was set on this promise, as it should have been. Yet for all those long years no son was born to them.

We know the story. The matter became so unsettling to Sarah that she gave her servant girl, Hagar, to Abraham to see if he could raise up an heir through her. Hagar did conceive. The child was Ishmael. But this was not God's doing, and God later appeared to tell Abraham that he had not forgotten his promise and that the son long anticipated would be born within the year.

At this point Abraham was ninety-nine years old and Sarah was eighty-nine. Earlier, when Ishmael had been conceived, the act of intercourse was by Abraham's own physical strength. Now he was past the age of engendering a child, and Sarah was past the age of childbearing. If there was to be a child at this stage, a miracle was required. But this is precisely what Abraham was enabled to trust God for. That is why the author of Hebrews writes, "By faith Abraham, even though he was past age—and Sarah herself was barren—was enabled to become a father because he considered him faithful who had made the promise. And so from this one man, and he as good as dead, came descendants as numerous as the stars in the sky and as countless as the sand on the seashore" (Heb. 11:11–12).

It is why Paul says in Romans, "Against all hope, Abraham in hope believed and so became the father of many nations, just as it had been said to him, 'So shall your offspring be.' Without weakening in his faith, he faced the fact that his body was as good as dead—since he was about a hundred years old—and that Sarah's womb was also dead. Yet he did not waver through unbelief regarding the promise of God, but was strengthened in his faith and gave glory to God, being fully persuaded that God had power to do what he had promised" (Rom. 4:18–21).

Do you have a faith like that? Faith in the "God of the impossible"?

I admit that this is a very high example of faith, which is why it is so often referred to favorably in the New Testament. But I maintain that in essence this is the same faith we should have—if we are true Christians. The God we worship is the God of Abraham, after all, and God is in the business of bringing forth faith like this in all those who know him. God brings life out of death. Your own conversion is an example! He brings love out of hate, peace out of turmoil, joy out of misery, praise out of cursing, and miracles to those who trust him. Many can testify to these wonders personally if they have been following in the footsteps of Abraham.

In Search of Understanding

The author of Hebrews ends his overview of Abraham's walk of faith with a fourth incident, and, taking my clue from him, I end with this account, too. It concerns Abraham's willingness to sacrifice his son on Mount Moriah. The text says, "By faith Abraham, when God tested him, offered Isaac as a sacrifice. He who had received the promises was about to sacrifice his one and only son, even though God had said to him, 'It is through Isaac that your offspring will be reckoned.' Abraham reasoned that God could raise the dead, and figuratively speaking, he did receive Isaac back from death" (Heb. 11:17–19).

To appreciate this story we must review the previous one, remembering that Isaac had been born to Abraham in his old age and that he had been identified specifically as the son of God's promise. That is, he was the one through whom the Messiah was to come.

Because Isaac had been born so late in Abraham's life, and Abraham had come to love him greatly, the call to sacrifice him was at the very least a test of Abraham's devotion to God. Had Isaac grown too dear to Abraham? Had he begun to take the place of God in the aged patriarch's affections? The Chinese evangelist Watchman Nee thought so and wrote that "Isaac represents many gifts of God's grace. Before God gives them our hands are empty. Afterwards they are full."[3] As a result, when God reaches out his hand to take ours in fellowship, we have no hand to give him and the things that have filled our hands must go. "Isaac can be done without," Nee wrote, "but God is eternal."[4]

Isaac may have begun to take the place of God in Abraham's thinking, though we cannot be sure of that. The Bible does not teach it. But one thing the Bible does teach is that the testing of Abraham was spiritual and that it involved Abraham's perception of who God is and whether or not the aged patriarch would continue to trust him as the only truthful God.

In my more extensive study of this incident in *Genesis: An Expositional Commentary*, I have written:

> The problem was not merely that Abraham loved Isaac. That was true enough. What was even more important was that God had promised that all future blessings, including the blessing of salvation, were to come through Isaac. God had told Abraham that Isaac was to live, marry, and have a family, and that from that family there would come one who would be the deliverer. Now God says that Isaac is to be sacrificed, and for the first time in all

3. Watchman Nee, *Changed Into His Likeness* (Fort Washington, Pa.: Christian Literature Crusade, 1967), p. 62.
4. Ibid.

Abraham's experience with God he is confronted by a conflict between God's command and God's promise. Earlier, Abraham had been tested as to whether he would believe that God could do the seemingly impossible task of giving Abraham and Sarah a son. That was a test, but it was not as hard as this one. This test involved a conflict apparently within the words of God himself. God had *promised* posterity through Isaac. But God had now also *commanded* Abraham to kill him.

How could this problem be resolved? There were only two ways. Abraham could have concluded that God was erratic, wavering from one plan to another because he did not know his own mind. This had not been Abraham's experience of God. The long wait for the son had taught him better than that. Or Abraham could have concluded that, although he—being finite and sinful—was unable to see the resolution of the difficulty, God could nevertheless be trusted to have a resolution, which he would certainly disclose in due time. This was the harder of the two solutions to accept, but Abraham's experience of God led in this direction.

Abraham acted in a manner consistent with his knowledge of God. That is, he trusted him, concluding that whatever God's purposes may or may not have been in this situation, God had at least shown that he could not be his enemy. God was his friend. . . . So Abraham believed God and acted, even though he could not understand the solution to the difficulty.[5]

Did I say "could not understand the solution to the difficulty"? Perhaps in the fullest sense. But the power of the story comes from the fact that Abraham *did* come to understand it somewhat. In other words, it was a case of what Anselm of Canterbury described centuries later by the words "faith in search of understanding."

It must have gone something like this: Abraham must have reasoned, "God is no liar. He told me beyond any question that I would have a son, and I have had one, though in my old age. Isaac stands beside me now. He is a proof of God's faithfulness. But God has also said that Isaac will have children through whom the Messiah will come. Isaac is not married. He has no children. If I put him to death, the promises of God cannot be fulfilled. Here is a contradiction. But there are no contradictions in God. This is a foundational truth. What must I conclude then? Since I am commanded to sacrifice Isaac and since, at the same time, God cannot be unfaithful to himself, the only solution I can imagine is that God is going to do a miracle and bring Isaac back from the dead. There will have to be a resurrection."

But, Abraham, there has *never* been a resurrection in the whole history of the world!

"That does not matter," Abraham replies. "A resurrection is compatible with the nature of God. Since God is the author of life, it would be a small matter for him to bring life back into a dead body. But the one thing God

5. James Montgomery Boice, *Genesis: An Expositional Commentary*, vol. 2, *Genesis 12:1–36:43* (Grand Rapids: Zondervan, 1985), pp. 219, 220.

cannot do is lie. God must tell the truth. He must keep his promises. Therefore, I expect a resurrection."

Apparently, Abraham really did expect a resurrection, for when he got to the base of the mountain he told his servants, "Stay here with the donkey while I and the boy go over there. We will worship and then we [plural!] will come back to you" (Gen. 22:5). In other words, Abraham fully intended to sacrifice his son in obedience to God. But he expected that God would then raise Isaac from the dead so that he and the boy could return home together.

This is true faith. It is faith in search of understanding.

Obedience from First to Last

There is one more thing. At the very end of the account, after Abraham has proceeded to the point of binding Isaac and raising his knife and God has intervened to stay his hand and provide a ram as a substitute, the angel of the Lord speaks to praise Abraham. But what Abraham is praised for—notice this, it is of great importance—is not his perception in figuring out God's plan or even the magnitude of what we might call his "blind faith," but his *obedience*. It is how the story ends. The angel speaks for God again, saying, "Your descendants will take possession of the cities of their enemies, and through your offspring all nations on earth will be blessed, because you have obeyed me" (Gen. 22:18b).

That is where the story began, too—with Abraham's obedience in leaving his own land and setting out for Canaan. Faith begins with obedience. Faith ends with obedience. It is a matter of obedience from the very first to the very last, until we appear before God and see him face to face.

If you are in Abraham's line, if you walk in his footsteps, you must obey God in all things. It is through obedience that faith grows.

56

Salvation Apart from Law

Romans 4:13–17

It was not through law that Abraham and his offspring received the promise that he would be heir of the world, but through the righteousness that comes by faith. For if those who live by law are heirs, faith has no value and the promise is worthless, because law brings wrath. And where there is no law there is no transgression.

Therefore, the promise comes by faith, so that it may be by grace and may be guaranteed to all Abraham's offspring—not only to those who are of the law but also to those who are of the faith of Abraham. He is the father of us all. As it is written: "I have made you a father of many nations." He is our father in the sight of God, in whom he believed—the God who gives life to the dead and calls things that are not as though they were.

During my years of formal education, when I had scores of books to read for classes, I developed a way of looking at the assigned texts that helped me get through them. I regarded the fifteen or twenty books for one course and the dozen or so books for another course as enemy soldiers that had to be shot down before I could win the war. Each time I finished a book I would say, "There's another dead soldier."

I mention this now because there is a sense in which the apostle Paul, too, has been shooting down enemy soldiers. In Romans 4 his war is for the gospel, of course, and the champions that have been sent to do battle against him have been formidable. Thus far there have been two of them. The first was "Works." This is the soldier almost everyone believes in, the people's favorite. But Paul shot him down with an arrow from Genesis 15:6, which proved that Abraham was justified by faith in God's promise, rather than by works. Since Abraham is the Old Testament pattern of a justified and godly man, his experience sets the pattern for those who follow him.

The second soldier was "Circumcision." This champion was peculiar to the Jews and seemed to have the blessing of God behind him, since, after all, God had himself established circumcision. Paul defeats this mighty foe by showing that Abraham was declared to be justified by God years before circumcision was imposed on him and his descendants.

The last of the enemy's heroes is "Law." Paul will shoot this soldier down in the next two paragraphs of his letter (vv. 13–17).

An Additional Argument

It is important to notice his change in strategy, however. When Paul was arguing against circumcision as a way of salvation, he used a temporal or historical argument, as we have seen. He showed that Abraham is said to have been justified when he was about eighty-five years old (cf. Gen. 15:6), but that he was not given the rite of circumcision until he was ninety-nine, about fourteen years later (cf. Gen. 17). Since Abraham was declared to have been justified *before* he was circumcised, the rite of circumcision could not have been the basis of his justification.

That type of argument could also have been used at this later point in the text, in reference to the giving of the law of God to Israel. In fact, in a similar discussion in his letter to the Galatians, this is precisely what Paul does. He says, "The law, introduced 430 years later, does not set aside the covenant previously established by God and thus do away with the promise. For if the inheritance depends on the law, then it no longer depends on a promise; but God in his grace gave it to Abraham through a promise" (Gal. 3:17–18). As an argument from history, the denial of the law's role in salvation is even stronger than the denial of circumcision's role, for the law was given through Moses more than four centuries after Abraham's day, while circumcision was given only fourteen years after the patriarch was said to have been justified.

But Paul does not use this argument in Romans 4. Instead he speaks of the results of trying to live by law, showing that by nature law is contrary to both faith and promise and that the inevitable result for those who choose this bad option is God's wrath.

Why does Paul take this approach? Why does he not argue from a time sequence, as he does in Galatians? It may not be possible to assign a sure reason for this, but we have a clue in the fact that Paul does not use the direct article ("the") before the occurrences of the word *law* in verses

13–15, whereas, by contrast, the article does occur with "law" in Galatians. We remember that the situation in Galatia was one in which Jewish believers were trying to force the Old Testament law on Gentiles, requiring them to be circumcised and take on other specifically Jewish obligations. In that context it was right for Paul to speak of "*the* law," meaning the law of Moses. In Romans it is different. Here Paul is not thinking so much of the specific Jewish law, though nothing he says excludes it, but of law in general. It is the law *principle*, rather than a specific set of laws, that he is thinking about. It is what we commonly call morality.

Is that distinction important? Well, it is for Gentiles, which includes most of us, as well as the bulk of those to whom Paul was specifically writing. The Gentiles of Paul's day generally did not have the advantage of the Old Testament law for moral guidance. But they did have some standards of behavior, just as we do today. And, like us, they wanted to trust in their personal ability to keep that "law," to measure up to those standards, as a way of salvation.

We see that all around us, don't we? And in ourselves, too. People will say that God ought to save them because they have done the best they can, "best" in that statement being defined by their partial attainment of whatever standard they perceive to be a just one. Or because they are good people, "good" being merely the sense that they have done better at living up to some moral code than others.

You will recall from our study of Romans 2:12–15 how C. S. Lewis pointed out that in most arguments we all naturally appeal to some standard, maintaining that the other person has failed to live up to that standard and implying that *we* have. Lewis calls this the Law of Nature, and his point is that there must be a God behind it from whom all such standards of right come.[1] However, this tendency is also evidence of the way we naturally think about salvation. Because we think we have measured up to some moral standard, we believe that God owes us something.

In my opinion, it is because of this universal human error that Paul approaches the third "soldier"—not as if the warrior was clothed in the armor of the law of Moses, but as if he was posing as the moral champion of all mankind.

Because Ideas Have Consequences

Each month I get a newsletter from a think tank in Washington, D.C., which has as its slogan: "Because Ideas Have Consequences." That is true, of course. So, taking my clue from that paper, I ask, as Paul obviously did in writing these verses: What are the consequences if a person tries to achieve

---

1. C. S. Lewis, *Mere Christianity* (New York: The Macmillan Company, 1958), p. 3.

a saved status with God not by faith but by morality or, as Paul says, by the law principle?

Paul says there are three consequences:

1. *Faith has no value* (v. 14). The reason faith has no value if one is living by the law principle is that faith and law are opposites, and if a person is choosing one, he or she is inevitably rejecting the other. It is as impossible to be saved by *both* faith and works as it is to be setting out from Kansas in the direction of California and New York simultaneously.

Here is an example. Quite a few years ago Donald Grey Barnhouse, a former pastor of the church I now serve, produced a gospel film entitled "The Geography of Salvation." It was based on the fact that in the continental United States both the highest point (Mount Whitney) and the lowest point (Death Valley) are in California. Barnhouse compared the state of California to our lost state as sinners and showed that it is impossible to get out of California by going up. A person who starts in Death Valley and travels up to sea level and then on into the mountains may feel that he has made noticeable progress, and he has in terms of elevation. But he is still in California. Similarly, in regard to salvation, what we need is not a higher moral elevation but a change of state. We need to be moved out of our lost state, in which we are under the wrath of God, into a saved state. That is different from going up and by a different means entirely.

To put it another way: Law is man-directed (it points to human abilities), while faith is God-directed (it points to God's accomplishments). So, if you are approaching salvation by trusting man, you cannot be trusting God—and vice versa.

2. *The promise is worthless* (v. 14). The second consequence of living by the law principle is the nullification of God's promise. Why is this so? Well, if the promise of salvation is linked to the law principle, this can only mean that it is necessary for a person to keep the law in order to receive the promise. Of course, God *could* have made this his plan, but it would have meant that the promise was conditional. It would have been as if God had said, "I promise to save you if you will do so and so." But if that were the case, the promise would never have been fulfilled because, as Paul has already proved in the earlier chapters of Romans, there is nobody who has ever done what God's law requires. Not only that, there is nobody who has ever done what *any* law requires. For whenever a person says, "This is my standard," no sooner has he erected that standard than he breaks it. This would exclude him from salvation, *if* salvation were based on that fulfillment. The promise could exist, but it would be worthless in terms of saving anybody.

D. Martyn Lloyd-Jones puts it like this: "Law means failure. Therefore, if the promise had been made through the medium of the Law, what God was giving, as it were, with his right hand, he would have been taking back with his left hand. There would have been no promise at all; it would have had no value whatsoever."[2]

3. *Law brings wrath* (v. 15). The third consequence of trying to achieve a saved status by the law principle is that, instead of achieving salvation, all one actually achieves is wrath. This is an important point, for it goes beyond what has already been established as the first and second consequences. Those consequences tell what a person trying to saved by law *fails* to achieve: he fails to achieve the promise. This point tells us what he actually does achieve: it is wrath.

This is because the law can do nothing but condemn. That is its very essence. The law says, "Do this, and if you do not do it, the punishment is as follows." The law possesses nothing that can enable a person to meet its just demands. Does that mean that the law is evil? Paul asks that question later on in his letter (in Romans 7), answering, "Certainly not! . . . the law is holy, and the commandment is holy, righteous and good" (Rom. 7:7, 12). A mirror is not a defective mirror because it cannot clean your face. That is just not its job. The function of a mirror is to show you that your face is dirty so that, when you know it is dirty, you will get some soap and water and wash it. In the same way, the law is not bad (defective) because it cannot save you. That is not its function. The law was given to show you that you cannot get to heaven by keeping it, so that—having learned that you cannot keep the law and will be condemned if you try—you will turn to Jesus Christ and be saved by him.

If you do not turn from law as a way of salvation and trust the work of God in Jesus Christ, the very standard that you trust condemns you— because you have not kept it and never will.

What does Paul mean when he adds, "Where there is no law there is no transgression" (v. 15)? This could mean the obvious: If there is no law, there can be no transgression of that law. But in the context it probably means: Without the law we do not know we are transgressors. As he says later, ". . . I would not have known what sin was except through the law . . ." (Rom. 7:7).

So, then, there is nothing wrong with law. The problem is in us, and it is the law's sole function to bring that truth to our attention.

A Better Set of Consequences

If you look closely at the New International Version, you will notice that the verses we are studying divide into two paragraphs. This is a proper division. The first paragraph, the one we have been looking at so far, is negative. It deals with the bad consequences of trying to be saved by the law principle: devaluation of faith, nullification of the promise, and wrath. The

---

2. D. M. Lloyd-Jones, *Romans: An Exposition of Chapters 3:20–4:25, Atonement and Justification* (Grand Rapids: Zondervan, 1970), p. 194.

second paragraph, the one we turn to now, is positive. It shows the fortunate consequences of seeking to be justified by God, not on the basis of morality or by the law principle, but by faith—which was the path pursued by Abraham.

Again, as in the case of law (but on the other side of the ledger), there are three consequences.

1. *Faith establishes grace* (v. 16). Why is this so? It is because faith and grace belong together by their very natures, just as works and law belong together. This is very evident in the latter case. Law tells us what we are to do. It points to deeds, action, conduct, and behavior. You cannot think of law without thinking of requirements. In the same way, though by contrast, as soon as you think of faith you inevitably think of grace (if you understand it), and as soon as you think of grace you think of faith. Grace is the unmerited favor of God apart from human works, and it comes to us by simple acceptance, which is faith.

Suppose I agree to work for you for a day for forty dollars. At the end of the day's work I come to collect my wages. Would you claim that you are being gracious in paying me? Not at all. Your payment would not be a matter of grace but of obligation. If I have done the work, you owe me my wages. If, on the other hand, I am sick and out of a job and having financial troubles and you come and offer me forty dollars, that is grace. It has nothing to do with anything I have done or will do. I have only to receive your gift and thank you for it.

Faith establishes grace. Therefore, we must have faith, since it is grace we need.

2. *Faith makes salvation certain* (v. 16). Again, we can see the truth of this by contrast. Suppose salvation were based on our ability to keep some law or live up to some standard of morality. I read in Robert Bellah's study of American mores, *Habits of the Heart*, of a man whose basic moral standard was honesty.[3] Let's take that as a test case. If salvation depends upon our being honest, how honest do we have to be? Here is a very honest man. Let's let him into heaven. Now, here is another man. He is almost as honest as the first, but he has told one more lie than the man we admitted. Should we let him in? If so, how about a man who has told one more lie than that or ten more lies than that? How about a man who is only moderately truthful? Or a man who is quite dishonest? Where do you draw the line? Obviously, in an imperfect and intricately variable world, it is impossible to draw such a line. So anyone who wants to be saved by works can never be certain that he or she has performed well enough—assuming (wrongly) for a moment, that the standard can be less than utter perfection.

3. Robert N. Bellah, *Habits of the Heart* (New York: Harper & Row, 1985). The individual is called Brian Palmer, the first character in the book.

And it is the same for any other moral trait: purity, contentment, charity, or whatever. How pure? How content? How generous do you have to be?

If, by contrast, salvation is not by morality but by the grace of God received through faith, then salvation is certain—because God is faithful and does not waver in his promises. He has done what is necessary through the death of Christ. That work is a perfect and all-sufficient work. Nothing can be added to it. Consequently, the person who rests on that work can be quietly content and confident.

Here is a particularly good way of putting it from the pen of Donald Grey Barnhouse:

> The law is the womb of doubt, and anyone who is attached to the law or its works is going to be besieged by all of the doubts which are born from the law. Any individual who has his eyes upon himself will be miserable. The man who walks by the law walks in the night, and his footsteps echo against the wall of the darkness that goes with the law. These echoes rise to his ears, and each sound from all the troop of doubts gives him fear upon fear. If he pauses, he is in the silence of dread fears, and as he runs from them his footsteps echo all the faster with the increasing tempo of his hysteria of doubt . . . .
>
> But the man who walks by the promise of grace walks in the broad day. His footsteps echo against the light of the promises of God, and he feels himself to be surrounded by the angels of blessing. His eager steps press forward to claim the blessings, and the increasing tempo of his footsteps sets up the echoes of further blessings. If he stops, he finds himself in green pastures and beside still waters. When he walks again he is in the paths of righteousness. He hastens on to the golden city, and the brightness of its prospect takes away any sense of fatigue that might naturally rise from the length of the road. And when the road ends, he finds that he has been supplied with grace at every step and brought on to the triumph of life eternal.[4]

3. *Faith opens the door of salvation to all* (vv. 16–17). The final benefit of faith as the way of salvation is that it opens the door of salvation to everybody, not just to the Jew, who possessed the Old Testament law, or to the few favored Gentiles who had been taught a particularly high standard of morality. It is open to anyone. All may enter. Whoever will may come. This is the point Paul particularly emphasizes in Romans 4, not only in these verses but from verse 9 virtually to the end of the chapter.

I do not know of any human benefit or award or promise of which that can be said, because all human offers have conditions and thereby always exclude some people. There are certain benefits of being an American citizen (or a citizen of some other country), benefits provided by the government. But they are not for those who are not citizens. There are promises

---

4. Donald Grey Barnhouse, *God's Remedy: Exposition of Bible Doctrines, Taking the Epistle to the Romans as a Point of Departure*, vol. 3, Romans 3:21–4:25 (Grand Rapids: Wm. B. Eerdmans, 1954), pp. 296, 297.

that companies make to their employees, but they apply only to those who work for those companies. Labor unions provide securities for their members, but not for other workers or for management. Any human association has built-in limitations.

But this is not true of the way of salvation offered by God through the work of Christ. Because of this, I can say the door is open for you, regardless of who you are or whatever you may have done or not done. If you are a Jew, the gospel is for you. If you are a Gentile, it is for you. It is for those who are good and those who are bad. It is for scholars as well as for the un-educated. It is for religious people and for those who have no religious background whatsoever. None of these things enter into the picture, because we are all reduced to the same level. *Salvation is by the grace of God through faith.*

If you are excluded, it is only because you have refused to walk through that open door. It is because you prefer your own sullied morality to God's grace.

Do not let that be true of you. Instead of refusing grace, accept it and enter into the full joy of God's salvation. That salvation is for you, whoever you may be—if you will have it.

57

The Nature of Abraham's Faith

Romans 4:18–22

Against all hope, Abraham in hope believed and so became the father of many nations, just as it had been said to him, "So shall your offspring be." Without weakening in his faith, he faced the fact that his body was as good as dead—since he was about a hundred years old—and that Sarah's womb was also dead. Yet he did not waver through unbelief regarding the promise of God, but was strengthened in his faith and gave glory to God, being fully persuaded that God had power to do what he had promised. This is why "it was credited to him as righteousness."

Any journey, whether it is geographical or metaphorical, has milestones at which the traveler stops, looks back over the ground already covered, and takes satisfaction in his or her progress before moving on.

We have come to such a milestone in our study. For four chapters the apostle Paul has been laboring up the first great peak of the Himalayan range that is his letter to the Romans. He has analyzed the desperate state of the human race in its rebellion against God and has unveiled the answer to its lost condition in the gospel of Jesus Christ. He has explained the nature of that gospel and has patiently answered all the objections that could possibly be brought against it. He has demonstrated that the gospel of a righteousness from God received by faith is taught in the Old

Testament, proving it from the cases of Abraham and David. He has concluded that "the promise [of salvation] comes by faith, so that it may be by grace and may be guaranteed to all Abraham's offspring . . ." (v. 16). The first four chapters of Romans have been an invigorating climb, and the peak Paul has scaled is a mighty one.

The apostle is now going to discuss the immediate benefits of this God-given salvation and the nature of the resulting Christian life. But, before he moves on to this next great pinnacle, he takes a look back over the ground he has covered and reviews his accomplishment.

He does this in three parts. First, having proved that Abraham was saved by faith (and therefore all other saved people must be), Paul reviews the nature of that faith, using Abraham as an example. (This is the part we will be looking at in the present study.) Second, since the essence of true biblical faith is that it is grounded in God, Paul reviews the character of God, showing that only the true God is an adequate basis for faith. (We will be dealing with that in the next study.) Finally, having explored these matters in regard to Abraham, who has been his chief example of the way of salvation, Paul breaks away from Abraham and speaks about the Christian faith directly, focusing on the death and resurrection of Jesus Christ. (Our study of that faith will conclude the first volume of my commentary on Romans.)

In reviewing the nature of Abraham's faith, Paul highlights five of its most striking characteristics.

Faith in God's Promise

The first important thing about Abraham's faith is that it was faith in God's promise. That is clear in verse 18, where one expression of the promise from Genesis 15 is quoted.[1] But it is also a dominant theme throughout the latter half of Romans 4, in which the noun *promise* appears four times (in vv. 13, 14, 16, 20) and the verb *promised* once (in v. 21). God made a multi-faceted promise to Abraham, involving personal blessing, a land to be given to him and his posterity, blessing on his descendants, and a Redeemer to come. Therefore, the first and most important characteristic of Abraham's faith is that it was faith in this promise.

When we first look at this, the fact that Abraham "believed" God may seem obvious and therefore unimportant. But it is neither obvious nor unimportant.

It is not "obvious," because most of our natural thinking about faith moves in different categories entirely. What do we chiefly think of when we think about faith? We think in subjective terms, don't we? We think of our feelings about something, which really means that we are man-centered in this area rather than God-centered.

---

1. Genesis 15:5. Paul cites the words that immediately precede the proof text regarding Abraham's justification, with which he began this chapter (Gen. 15:6, quoted in v. 3).

Occasionally, when I want to see what others have said about a certain subject, I look in various books of quotations in my library. When I did that in reference to "faith," I found that the quotations made this point dramatically. Here are some that appear in *Roget's International Thesaurus*. The Roman poet Ovid (43 B.C.–A.D. 18) said, "We are slow to believe what hurts when believed." The epic poet Virgil (70–19 B.C.) wrote, "They can because they think they can." The Roman playwright Terence (185–159 B.C.) said, "As many opinions as men." The French writer Montaigne (1533–1592) declared, "Nothing is so firmly believed as that we least know." George Santayana (1863–1952), the Spanish-born American philosopher, spoke of "the brute necessity of believing something so long as life lasts." And then there were popular sayings like: "Believe that you have it, and you have it" and "I believe because it is impossible."[2]

These sayings all have at their root the sense that faith is essentially grounded in man and is a subjective quality. But in the Bible faith is grounded in God and is something that springs from his encounter with the individual.

Again, the fact that biblical faith is faith in God's promise is not "unimportant," because it is along these identical lines that we must believe God today if we, like Abraham, are to be saved. We are not saved because we have a strong subjective faith (that would focus the matter on us), but because we believe the promises of God regarding salvation, promises made known to us in the pages of the Bible. In other words, Christian faith is a Bible faith. Or, to put it in still other words, we are saved not because of our faith but because of God's promises. True faith is receiving these promises and believing them on the basis of God's character.

The Word of God Only

The second characteristic of Abraham's faith is that it was based on what D. Martyn Lloyd-Jones has called "the bare Word of God and on nothing else whatsoever."[3] We go back to Genesis 15 and find that God promised Abraham many offspring (as numerous as the stars in the heavens) at a time when he had no children at all. To be sure, the situation seemed not quite as hopeless as it was later to become. Abraham was then about eighty-five years old, but he was still able to engender a child, as he proved by fathering a child by Sarah's handmaid Hagar. Fourteen years later, at the time of the conception of Isaac, Abraham was not even physically able to father a child. Still, by the time of his life described in Genesis 15, Abraham had lived most of a century without having any children. It seemed that he and Sarah would die childless. Yet here was God promising not only that

2. *Roget's International Thesaurus* (New York: Thomas Y. Crowell, 1953), pp. 323, 324.

3. D. M. Lloyd-Jones, *Romans: An Exposition of Chapters 3:20–4:25, Atonement and Justification* (Grand Rapids: Zondervan, 1970), p. 211.

they would have an heir but that they would eventually have descendants beyond any human possibility of counting.

Where could Abraham find external support to assist him in believing this "wild" promise? There was no such support! From the point of view of human experience, the situation was not promising. He had no prior examples of fecundity in old age that he could rest his belief on. So, if Abraham believed God, as he did, it was only because it was God who had made the promise.

It is the same when we trust God in the matter of salvation today. God says that he has given his Son in death for us so that "whoever believes in him shall not perish but have eternal life" (John 3:16). What else in life can sustain you in believing such a promise except the bare words of God in the Bible. Apart from God's Word, we do not even know anything about eternal life, let alone how to obtain it. The invisible world is hidden from us. No human being can tell us anything. So, if we find salvation, it is by believing God's Word, pure and simple.

Is that too hard to do? In some ways, it is. But why should we not believe God? Human beings can deceive us and often do. But God's word is his bond, and he never changes his mind. Therefore, although we do not have *external* support for believing him, we do not need it. In fact, it would be an insult to the character of God to maintain that we believe God only because of the word or experience of some human being. How can anything human ever support the Eternal? It is rather the other way around.

D. Martyn Lloyd-Jones writes, "There is always this naked element in faith. It does not ask for proofs, it does not seek them; in a sense it does not need them. Faith is content with the bare Word of God, because he is God."[4]

Despite All Contrary Appearances

The vitality of Abraham's faith (and therefore of all true faith) was greater even than this. For, as Paul points out in the closing verses of Romans 4, it was not a case of Abraham's merely believing God in the absence of all external supports; he believed God when the external evidences were actually and sharply to the contrary.

This is the meaning of the sentence "against all hope, Abraham in hope believed" (v. 18). It means that from a human perspective the situation was hopeless. But since God had spoken, Abraham was willing to believe God despite the adverse physical evidence. At this point it is clear that Paul's thought is moving beyond the situation described in Genesis 15 to the utterly "impossible" conditions of Genesis 17. As we have seen, by this time Abraham was ninety-nine years old and there was no longer any hope that the aged couple could have their own child. When they were a bit younger,

4. Ibid.

perhaps. But not at this point, not now. That is why the text says, "Without weakening in his faith, he [Abraham] faced the fact that his body was as good as dead—since he was about a hundred years old—and that Sarah's womb was also dead" (v. 19).

There is an interesting textual variation in this verse which is worth mentioning briefly. In many of the ancient manuscripts there is a negative in the early part of this sentence that would call for the translation "he did *not* consider." If this reading is followed, the sense would be: "Abraham was so strong in faith that he did not consider that his body was as good as dead." Usually, a negative would give an entirely contrary meaning. But in this case, strangely, either of the readings make sense and mean about the same thing. If the negative is omitted, as the New International Version seems to consider correct, the sentence means: "Abraham faced the fact that his body was as good as dead and believed God anyway." If the negative is retained, the course followed by the King James Version, the sentence would be what I suggested earlier. In either case, it means that Abraham was aware of the utter hopelessness of the situation. Yet he believed God in spite of all circumstances.[5]

Moreover, this is what Genesis itself indicates. Although it is not thrown up to Abraham later in the Bible—God seems always to remember the victories and not the failures of his children—Genesis 17:17 tells us that, when the original promise was repeated to Abraham when he was even older, initially he laughed since he knew how preposterous this was: "Abraham fell facedown; he laughed and said to himself, 'Will a son be born to a man a hundred years old? Will Sarah bear a child at the age of ninety?'"

Yet, when the chips were down, Abraham believed God rather than the limitations of his own physical capabilities. And in the following year the promised child was born to Abraham and Sarah.

I do not often cite the testimony of the Swiss theologian Karl Barth in my studies. But Barth had an enviable sense of the greatness of God and, by contrast, the utter weakness and hopelessness of all things human. At this point in his highly esteemed Romans commentary, he quotes with evident approval some strong words about faith by Martin Luther:

> "What could be more irrational and laughable, ridiculous and impossible, than God's words to Abraham? . . . Moreover, all the articles of our Christian belief are, when considered rationally, just as impossible and mendacious and preposterous. Faith, however, is completely abreast of the situation. It grips reason by the throat and strangles the beast. It effects what the whole world

5. For a discussion of the textual problem and its implications see: Bruce M. Metzger, *A Textual Commentary on the Greek New Testament* (London and New York: United Bible Societies, 1971), p. 510; John Murray, *The Epistle to the Romans* (Grand Rapids: Wm. B. Eerdmans, 1968), pp. 149, 150; F. Godet, *Commentary on St. Paul's Epistle to the Romans*, trans. A. Cusin (Edinburgh: T. & T. Clark, n.d.), vol. 1, pp. 306, 307.

and all that is in it is impotent to do. But how can faith do this? By holding on to God's word and by accounting it right and true, however stupid and impossible it may appear. By this means did Abraham imprison his reason. . . . And in the same fashion do all other believers who have entered the dark recesses of faith throttle reason, saying: Listen, Reason, thou blind and stupid fool that understandest not of the things of God. Cease thy tricks and chattering; hold thy tongue and be still! Venture no more to criticize the Word of God. Sit thee down; listen to his words; and believe in him. So do the faithful . . . achieve what the whole world is incompetent to achieve. And thereby they do our Lord God supreme and notable service."[6]

No one should understand this as meaning that faith is "irrational," since nothing is more rational than to believe God even in the face of evidence to the contrary. But it does mean that faith stands always with God and his Word, even when doing so appears foolish from a human perspective.

Full Assurance of Faith

The fourth characteristic of Abraham's faith is assurance. Paul says this in a number of ways: (1) "without weakening in his faith" (v. 19); (2) "he did not waver through unbelief" (v. 20); and (3) he "was strengthened in his faith" (v. 20). But the chief statement is in verse 21: "being fully persuaded that God had power to do what he had promised." Some of the other versions of this verse are worth noting. The Revised Standard Version says that Abraham was "fully convinced." The New English Bible speaks of a "firm conviction." Phillips says that Abraham was "absolutely convinced." The New American Standard Bible speaks of him as "being fully assured."

This is an important point. True faith should always have this assurance.

But how does faith achieve this in a world where flesh is weak and circumstances are usually more powerful than we are? There is only one answer: True faith has assurance because it is directed neither to ourselves nor to circumstances but to God. We are weak, so faith grounded in ourselves is always weak and will weaken further, waver, and slip away, just as Peter's faith wavered when he looked away from Jesus and instead glanced at the churning waves of Galilee over which he was attempting to walk from the disciples' small boat to the Master (Matt. 14:28–31). Faith that is grounded in the being and character of God will go from strength to more strength, since God is faithful.

Faith That Acts

There is one more characteristic of Abraham's faith that we dare not omit and need to remind ourselves of before going on. It is that faith acts.

6. Karl Barth, *The Epistle to the Romans*, trans. Edwyn C. Hoskyns (London, New York and Toronto: Oxford University Press, 1933), pp. 143, 144.

Faith believes God, but it also acts decisively. In fact, I define true biblical faith as "believing God and acting upon it."

Did Abraham believe God? Of course he did. He believed God enough to engender the child of the promise when he was ninety-nine years old. But I have often thought that even greater than that would have been his act of announcing his change of name to those who lived with him—even before Isaac's conception. You know, I am sure, that in its original form Abraham's name was Abram and that Abram meant "father of many" (literally, "father of a people"). That was appropriate in view of God's promise that he and Sarah (originally Sarai) would have many children. But they had had no children for many decades, and the name became an increasing embarrassment for him as the years slipped by.

It must have been a matter of embarrassment for Sarai/Sarah, too. For she was a proud woman and wanted to settle once and for all whether the problem lay in her inability to bear children or in her husband's infertility. What else would cause a woman to send her husband into another woman's arms? But she gave her handmaid Hagar to Abram to see if he could father a child by her, and although Abram should have refused, trusting God to provide the promised heir in his own time, he listened to his wife and so had Ishmael by Hagar. How proud the patriarch was of Ishmael, fathered after years of infertility. Later, when God came to renew the promise of the heir again, Abraham pleaded with God to accept Ishmael (then thirteen years old) instead, saying, "If only Ishmael might live under your blessing!" (Gen. 17:18).

Still there was only one child for a man whose name meant "father of many." The jokes at the patriarch's expense must have been very painful to him.

But when God appeared to Abraham before his hundredth birthday to say that the promise had not been forgotten and that the couple would have a child by the same time next year, God also announced the change in Abram's name. He, in turn, would have announced this to the hundreds of people who were part of his entourage.

What interest there would have been when Abram indicated that he was going to change his name!

"He is going to change his name?"

"I wonder what to."

"He has been Abram, father of many, for so many years. That must have been a difficult thing to live with. Perhaps he is going to change it to Abechad, 'father of one,' since that is all he is, after all."

Then Abraham made his announcement: "God appeared to me last night and told me that I am to change my name from Abram, 'father of many,' to Abraham (which, translated colloquially, means), 'father of a vast, vast multitude' (literally, "father of a nation")."

I suppose the laughter broke out behind the scenes at that point and was only barely suppressed by those who were closest to Abraham. For what could be more ridiculous than such a change of name? Preposterous! Foolish! But it was not foolish, particularly not to Abraham, since he was looking at things from the perspective of God's promise and was willing to act publicly on his convictions regarding God's power, truth, and faithfulness. The next year the son of the promise was born to him.

How about you? Will you act on your faith as Abraham acted? Will you step out in faith, believing the promise of God concerning the gift of salvation through Jesus Christ? You will get little support from the world to help you make such a commitment. On the contrary, the world will hinder you as much as it possibly can and think you are irrational, even foolish. But where is the foolishness found? Is it on the side of those who trust God? Or is it on the side of unbelievers, who trust only themselves and the world, both of which are passing away? I urge you to trust God and act on it.

58

The Ground of Abraham's Faith

Romans 4:18–22

Against all hope, Abraham in hope believed and so became the father of many nations, just as it had been said to him, "So shall your offspring be." Without weakening in his faith, he faced the fact that his body was as good as dead—since he was about a hundred years old—and that Sarah's womb was also dead. Yet he did not waver through unbelief regarding the promise of God, but was strengthened in his faith and gave glory to God, being fully persuaded that God had power to do what he had promised. This is why "it was credited to him as righteousness."

There are times in Bible study when it is necessary to examine every word of a text thoroughly. This is not only a good method; it is also almost always a good place to start. But there are other times when it is helpful to step back from intricate digging and look for the flow of words in a passage and the place of that passage in the chapter or even in the entire book. I want to take the latter approach now in our second and final study of Romans 4:18–22.

What is the flow of these verses?

There is an obvious flow from the thought of Abraham not "weakening in his faith" (v. 19) to being "strengthened in his faith" (v. 20). When we step back from the actual words, that is the first larger picture we see. We can step back even further, and then we see a flow from the idea of hopelessness, with which the section begins ("against all hope," v. 18), to Abraham's being "fully persuaded" of God's promise (v. 21). Nor is this all. If we step back the fullest distance, the embracing flow is from Abraham himself, whose body was "as good as dead" (v. 19) to God, who has "power to do what he had promised" (v. 21). That is another way of expressing what we saw in the preceding study, namely, that Abraham's faith was strong because it was focused on God only.

Read those verses again, this time placing an emphasis on that last idea: "Against all hope, Abraham in hope believed and so became the father of many nations, just as it had been said to him, 'So shall your offspring be.' Without weakening in his faith, he faced the fact that his body was as good as dead—since he was about a hundred years old—and that Sarah's womb was also dead. Yet he did not waver through unbelief regarding the promise of God, but was strengthened in his faith and *gave glory to God*, being fully persuaded that *God had power to do what he had promised*."

Putting this passage in the context of the opening chapters of Romans, we find an interesting contrast. We discover from Romans 1 that the human race rejected God and would not give glory to God (v. 21). But in Romans 4 we find Abraham believing God and making it his utmost concern to glorify him (v. 20).

To God Be the Glory

The overall importance of these points is that they reveal the secret of Abraham's great faith, as we saw in the preceding study. There we looked at the nature of Abraham's faith and saw that it was:

1. Faith in God's promise,
2. Faith based upon the bare words of God and on nothing else whatsoever,
3. Faith despite many strong circumstances to the contrary,
4. Faith that was fully assured, or confident, and
5. Faith that acted in response to God's word.

But as soon as we ask, "How could Abraham's faith achieve such strength and such characteristics when it had no external support and the world was against it?" we see that it was because *Abraham's faith was directed to God*, who alone is the source of all true strength and confidence.

If Abraham's faith had been grounded in himself (or other human beings) or had depended for its nurture upon his own firmness of will or depth of feelings, his faith would have weakened, wavered, and then died. Instead, his faith was strengthened—because it was in Almighty God alone.

This is what the Bible teaches *our* faith is also to be grounded in. I think of Hebrews 12:1–2, for example. These verses, which come immediately after the chapter that lists the great heroes of faith from the Old Testament, teach that we are to look *to God* in faith, as they did. "Therefore, since we are surrounded by such a great cloud of witnesses, let us throw off everything that hinders and the sin that so easily entangles, and let us run with perseverance the race marked out for us. *Let us fix our eyes on Jesus,* the author and perfecter of our faith . . ." (italics mine).

In the preceding chapter of Hebrews we are told that Abraham "was looking forward to the city with foundations" (Heb. 11:10a). But it is even more important to see that Abraham looked to the God who planned and built that city. Abraham looked *forward* to the city, much as we anticipate rewards for faithful service. But, most of all, Abraham looked *to* God and glorified him.

To say that Abraham grounded his faith in God is to say that he fixed his mind on God. This means that he disciplined himself to think about who God is and what he is like. In other words, he contemplated God's attributes. And what is that but giving glory to God? To glorify God is to rehearse his attributes mentally and to praise him for them. What attributes of God did Abraham fill his mind with? The answer, no doubt, is all of them—or at least all the attributes of God he was aware of.

In this study, I want to focus on the attributes of God suggested in our passage.

The God Who Cannot Lie

The first attribute of God that Abraham fixed his mind on was God's truthfulness, the fact that God does not lie. Later, Paul will write this to his friend and co-worker Titus, saying explicitly that our faith is in "God, who does not lie" (Titus 1:2). The truthfulness of God is an underlying assumption in these verses from Romans, and certainly in the life of Abraham as a whole. The truthfulness of God was basic to Abraham's faith in God's promise. If God were not truthful, the promise would have meant nothing to Abraham and would mean nothing to anyone else. It would be only empty words. But because God is truthful, the promise is true and can be trusted implicitly.

Abraham was willing to act on his conviction that God is always truthful. When God told Abraham (Abram) to leave his own land and go to a land that he would show him, Abraham believed God and "set out from Haran" (Gen. 12:4).

When God promised him that he would have descendants as numerous as the stars of heaven, saying "so shall your offspring be," Abraham "believed God and it was credited to him as righteousness" (Gen. 15:5–6; cf. Rom. 4:3).

When God renewed the promise of a son in Abraham's old age, Abraham believed God again and accepted his name change, as well as the rite of circumcision, to show that he believed him (Gen. 17).

Confidence in the truthfulness of God contributed to Abraham's victory in the greatest test of his life: the demand by God that he sacrifice his son on Mount Moriah. Abraham reasoned that since God had promised a numerous posterity through Isaac and since Isaac had not yet married or had children, to keep his word God would have to raise Isaac from the dead (Gen. 22:1–18, esp. v. 5; cf. Heb. 11:17–19). Abraham proceeded on the basis of this faith and was about to perform the sacrifice when God stopped him.

Such complete confidence is vital to any individual's proper relationship to God, since we cannot know, come to, or please God unless we have faith in or believe him (cf. Heb. 11:6).

This is why the Bible, in which God makes his promises to us, has been under such severe attacks by unbelievers in our time. I have participated in many church conferences or consultations in which an ordained minister will say something like this: "I know that the Bible says that, but those words are the product of the limited and erring outlooks of people who lived in that time. We don't have to be bound by them today."

Sometimes they have been more specific: "Paul was wrong when he said that."

Others even say, "Jesus was mistaken," as was implied in a particularly devastating statement made by Dr. Robert G. Bratcher, a translator of the *Good News for Modern Man* Bible. At a three-day national seminar of the Southern Baptist Christian Life Commission, he said: "Quoting what the Bible says in the context of history and culture is not necessarily relevant and helpful—and may be a hindrance in trying to meet and solve the problems we face. . . . Even words spoken by Jesus in Aramaic in the thirties of the first century and preserved in writing in Greek thirty-five to fifty years later do not necessarily wield compelling or authentic authority over us today."[1] That is a powerful expression of unbelief! For Bratcher is not merely saying that the words attributed to Jesus are wrong, being incorrectly reported, but that the very words of Jesus [in Aramaic] may be wrong. And that means that Jesus either was mistaken or lied.

Would Abraham have spoken those words? He would never have done so. He was as far from saying that as the faith of angels is from dogged unbelief.

We are sometimes told that we can believe God without believing the Bible. But it does not require a course in logic to see the absurdity of that statement. If the Bible is not God's Word, to be fully believed because it is God's Word, then where does God tell us anything? Where does God ever show us what needs to be believed? And if there is nowhere that God does

1. From a news report by Dan Martin of the Baptist Press, Nashville, Tennessee.

speak, to say that we can believe him is ridiculous. If God has not spoken to us truthfully in the Bible, then we cannot exercise belief in him—even if we want to.

Look at the possibilities:

1. Either God has spoken to us in the Bible, which is truthful because God is truthful and which we therefore need to believe implicitly, *or*

2. God has not spoken clearly anywhere, and therefore to say that he is truthful and that we believe him is meaningless.

The only possible way to avoid this—a way unfortunately taken by some so-called evangelical scholars of our day—is that God has spoken in the Bible but that the divine and therefore true parts of the Bible are mixed with human error. If that is the case, who is to winnow the divine wheat from the human chaff? The only possible answers are either (1) the individual himself by some subjective process, or (2) the scholar. But in either case, "faith" is not directed to God but to human beings, either ourselves or the scholars, who decide what God has said and what can be trusted. This is not believing God. It is believing in ourselves.

Those who affirm the truthfulness of God always affirm the truthfulness of the biblical revelation.

Great Is Thy Faithfulness

The second attribute of God by which Abraham steadied his faith was God's faithfulness. Nothing in our text says this explicitly, but it is implied by Abraham's steadfast adherence to God's promise. Abraham staked his life on God's promise, and this was based on his conviction not only that God does not lie but also that he does not change his mind.

We know very little of true faithfulness on the part of human beings. In fact, it is far more common to hear of *un*faithfulness today than of faithfulness. People try to wriggle out of contracts. Spouses abandon one another. Individuals promise to do something but then "forget" to do it. God is not like this. Moses said to the Israelites, "God . . . is the faithful God, keeping his covenant of love to a thousand generations of those who love him and keep his commandments" (Deut. 7:9). Paul wrote to Timothy: "If we are faithless, he will remain faithful, for he cannot disown himself" (2 Tim. 2:13). Arthur W. Pink has written: "Everything about God is great, vast, incomparable. He never forgets, never fails, never falters, never forfeits his word. To every declaration of promise or prophecy the Lord has exactly adhered, every engagement or covenant or threatening he will make good, for 'God is not a man, that he should lie; neither the son of man, that he should repent: hath he said, and shall he not do it? or hath he spoken, and shall he not make it good?' (Num. 23:19)."[2]

2. Arthur W. Pink, *The Attributes of God* (Grand Rapids: Baker Book House, 1975), p. 52.

Abraham grounded his faith in God's faithfulness. And so should we, above all whenever we find ourselves to be weak, fearful, or anxious. A. W. Tozer wrote wisely, "The tempted, the anxious, the fearful, the discouraged may all find new hope and good cheer in the knowledge that our Heavenly Father is faithful. . . . The hard-pressed sons of the covenant may be sure that he will never remove his loving-kindness from them nor suffer his faithfulness to fail."[3]

The God Who Is Able

I have been saying that some of the attributes of God to which Abraham directed his mind are not explicit but rather are implied in our passage. But that is not the case with the attribute to which we now come. This attribute is power: "all power," or omnipotence, as we should say. It is stated in several places. In Romans 4:18–22 it occurs in verse 21, which says that Abraham "was fully persuaded that God had power to do what he had promised." In the paragraph before this it is expressed as faith in God "who gives life to the dead and calls things that are not as though they were" (v. 17).

That last phrase—"calls things that are not as though they were"—is particularly interesting because it indicates the frame of thought in which Abraham was moving. What is it speaking of? It is hard to miss that it is a reference to God's power in creation, for it was there above all that God called into being things that were not.

In my studies of creation I have pointed out that there are only four possible explanations of the origin of the universe: (1) that the universe had no origin but rather is eternal; (2) that everything came from a personal something that is good; (3) that everything came from a personal something that is bad; and (4) that there has always been a dualism.[4] These possibilities can be narrowed down to numbers 1 and 2, however, since numbers 3 and 4 do not stand up to careful analysis. This means that the real choice is between an eternity of matter and the Christian view of creation. But the interesting thing is that today non-Christians tend toward another utterly irrational view: that somehow the universe evolved (or brought itself) into being.

It is easy to see how this idea has come about. There has been a rejection of the Christian view of origins on moral grounds, though they are called "scientific." We do not like God, so we dismiss him out of hand. But the idea of an eternity of matter has been destroyed by science itself through what has been called the Big Bang theory.

3. A. W. Tozer, *The Knowledge of the Holy* (New York, Evanston and London: Harper & Row, 1961), p. 87.

4. See James Montgomery Boice, *Foundations of the Christian Faith* (Downers Grove, Ill., and Leicester, England: InterVarsity Press, 1986), pp. 159–162; and *Genesis: An Expositional Commentary*, vol. 1, *Genesis 1:1–11:32* (Grand Rapids: Zondervan, 1982), pp. 31–33. These four points are developed by Francis A. Schaeffer in *Genesis in Space and Time: The Flow of Biblical History* (Downers Grove, Ill.: InterVarsity Press, 1975).

The evidence points to an origin to the universe. But what exactly was that origin? How did the universe come about? If it was not created by God, the only seeming possibility left is that it created itself, which is what unbelievers are coming increasingly to hold. But that is irrational, as I said. For something to create itself, what would be necessary? Obviously, it would have to exist to do the creating, which means that it would have to exist and yet not exist at the same time. Nothing is more manifestly absurd. But that is the way the understanding of our culture has been heading.

Fortunately, Abraham knew better than this and was aware, as believers today are also aware, that God brought all things into being out of nothing—and that because he was able to do that, he was able to keep his promises to Abraham.

"But, Abraham, for God to give you a child in your old age will require a miracle," says a skeptic in the patriarch's time.

"True," Abraham replies, "but not a greater miracle than God's bringing everything in this cosmos into being out of nothing, simply by his own power and the words of his mouth."

Abraham reckoned that what God promised he was able also to perform.

All Christians know this. And that is why believers have been able to believe God in spite of adverse circumstances. Noah believed that God would destroy the earth by a flood. He built the equivalent of an 18,000-ton ship to prepare for it. Gideon believed that God would drive out Israel's enemies, even though he was greatly outnumbered. Obeying God, he routed them with just three hundred soldiers. And what about the Virgin Mary? She believed God's promise that she would give birth to the Messiah, the Savior of the world, even though she had never known a man. Miraculous? Yes. Impossible? Not for the God who has already created all things out of nothing.

Why should it be so impossible for you to trust God? It is highly unlikely that your circumstances even require a miracle. All you need to do is believe God and act upon that faith.

How to Grow Your Faith

A number of years ago the Philadelphia Conference on Reformed Theology held a spring conference on the theme: "How To Grow Your Faith." It was on what theologians call "the means of grace," and it dealt with such subjects as prayer, worship, Bible study, fellowship, and the sacraments. In the course of the weekend it became increasingly evident that the most important, indeed, the *foundational* means of growing faith is Bible study.

Why is that? Because of the very matter we are studying. True biblical faith is not something you and I are capable of working up ourselves, as if we could merely decide to be men and women of faith in the same way we might decide to take up aerobics or pursue degrees in higher education. Faith is only as strong as its object, and it is therefore created in us by God and built up by God through our coming to know him. But how do we do that? The only way we can come to know God is by coming to know his self-revelation in Scripture—and then applying what we learn to our own circumstances.

Here is the way D. Martyn Lloyd-Jones puts it toward the end of his commentary on Romans 3 and 4:

> If you are anxious to know how to have a strong faith, here is the method. It means thorough and deep knowledge of the Bible and of God through it; not suddenly taking up an idea and deciding to "go in" for faith. If you want to have strong faith, read your Bible; go through it from beginning to end. Concentrate on the revelation that God has given of himself and of his character. Keep your eye especially also on prophecy, and then watch his promises being fulfilled. That is the way to develop strong faith—be grounded in all this. Then read the historical portions of the Bible, and the stories of the great heroes. That is why the author of the Epistle to the Hebrews gives that gallery of portraits of these great saints in the eleventh chapter. He says, Look at these men, who were men like yourselves. What was their secret? It was that they knew God, they gave glory to God and relied utterly upon him and his word. Turn that over in your mind, keep on speaking to yourself about it; meditate upon it. . . . Then, finally, you apply all that in practice to particular cases as they arise in your own life and experience. "He staggered not, but gave glory to God." That is the secret of faith. It is our ignorance of God that constitutes our main trouble.[5]

Ours is not an age of great faith—even in evangelical churches. We are weak in faith, and the reason we are weak in faith is that we do not know the Bible's God. Or if we do, we do not put what we do know into practice.

---

5. D. M. Lloyd-Jones, *Romans: An Exposition of Chapters 3:20–4:25, Atonement and Justification* (Grand Rapids: Zondervan, 1970), p. 235.

59

The Christian Faith

Romans 4:23–25

The words "it was credited to him" were written not for him alone, but also for us, to whom God will credit righteousness—for us who believe in him who raised Jesus our Lord from the dead. He was delivered over to death for our sins and was raised to life for our justification.

In several preceding studies we have been working through the apostle Paul's proof from the Old Testament of the doctrine of justification by grace through faith. Paul has given two Old Testament examples, Abraham and King David, but his chief example has been Abraham. Indeed, the fourth chapter of Romans has been almost entirely about him.

But Paul was no mere antiquarian, one who was in love with the past for its own sake. Paul was writing for the present. So, as he comes to the end not only of Romans 4 but of the first major section of the letter, he returns to his first theme, reminding his readers that the things that were written in the Old Testament were written for us and that proof of the doctrine of justification by faith from the case of Abraham is for our present benefit. He concludes, "The words 'it was credited to him' were written not for him alone, *but also for us*, to whom God will credit righteousness—for us who believe in him who raised Jesus our Lord from the dead. He was delivered over to death for our sins and was raised to life for our justification" (vv. 23–25, italics mine).

This passage is a summation of the Christian gospel, and a study of it is an appropriate way to end this first expository volume on the Book of Romans.

The Apostolic Gospel

A number of years ago, a professor from Cambridge University in England named C. H. Dodd wrote a book called *The Apostolic Preaching and Its Developments*. It was a little book—56 pages in all—but it was influential in the field of biblical studies, since it showed in a convincing way that the apostolic preachers all followed a broadly accepted outline of key facts concerning the life and ministry of Jesus Christ when they presented the gospel to unbelievers. Dodd called this list of key facts the *kerygma*, a Greek word that means "proclamation," in order to distinguish it from the ethical and other teachings of Jesus, which were not part of the message proclaimed to unbelievers but which were reserved for the further instruction of converts. Dodd called this additional body of material the *didachē* or "teachings."

One classical statement of the *kerygma* occurs in 1 Corinthians 15:1–7, where it is introduced as something Paul had received from those who were in the faith before him. In that passage it seems to have three parts:

1. "that Christ died for our sins according to the Scriptures" (v. 3),

2. "that he was buried" (v. 4), and

3. "that he was raised on the third day according to the Scriptures" (v. 4).

That brief rehearsal is then followed by a list of those who were witnesses to the resurrection (vv. 5–7).

In the sermons recorded in Acts we see this same pattern, but the list is elaborated to include such items as: the preparatory ministry of John the Baptist, Old Testament prophecies of Christ's coming, evidence of Jesus' divine power by his miraculous works, Jesus' ascension into heaven, and the future role of Jesus in the final judgment. Sometimes the *kerygma* is complete. Sometimes it is abbreviated. In each instance what lies at its heart is a proclamation of the crucifixion and resurrection of the Lord.[1]

These items are important here, because in Romans 4:23–25 we have the basic gospel in its most compact form. Martin Luther wrote, "In these verses the whole of Christianity is comprehended."[2]

Faith in God

The first point in Paul's summary of the gospel in Romans 4 is not strictly part of the *kerygma*, as Dodd defines it. But it is presupposed by the

---

1. C. H. Dodd, *The Apostolic Preaching and Its Developments* (New York: Harper & Brothers, n.d.). The material was first presented in 1935 as a series of three lectures. Examples of the New Testament *kerygma* are: Acts 2:14–39; 3:13–26; 4:10–12; 5:30–32; 10:36–43; 13:17–41; Galatians 1:3–4; and Romans 1:1–4; 8:34; and 10:8–9, but Dodd also sees the *kerygma* even in the basic structure of the four Gospels.

2. Cited by D. M. Lloyd-Jones, *Romans: An Exposition of Chapters 3:20–4:25, Atonement and Justification* (Grand Rapids: Zondervan, 1970), p. 236.

kerygma and is what links the content of this explicitly Christian statement of faith to the case of Abraham. It is belief in God. Paul expresses this by saying, "The words 'it was credited to him' were written not for him alone, but also for us who believe in him who raised Jesus our Lord from the dead."

This sentence involves both continuity with and development beyond Abraham's example. The continuity is important, since the God whom Christians believe in is the same as the God Abraham believed in, and the nature of the faith involved in trusting that God is therefore also the same. This is why we have been able to make practical applications from Abraham's life to our own lives. In discussing Abraham's faith, I pointed out that it was:

1. Faith in God's promise,
2. Faith based on the bare words of God and on nothing else whatever,
3. Faith despite many strong circumstances to the contrary,
4. Faith that was fully assured, and
5. Faith that acts.

That is exactly what our faith is to be and do, and the reason is that it is faith in the God in whom Abraham believed. Moreover, such faith is to grow increasingly strong, because it is grounded not upon itself but upon God. In these ways, Abraham's faith is the same as our own.

But our faith also involves development beyond Abraham's faith, because, as Paul writes, it is faith "in him who raised Jesus our Lord from the dead." True, there are items of continuity even here. Abraham's faith in the promise was an anticipatory faith in Jesus since the promise ultimately was fulfilled in him. Again, the fact that Abraham believed in "God who gives life to the dead" finds a parallel in our belief in Jesus' resurrection. Still, there are also differences due to progressive revelation. Because we live on this side of the incarnation and atonement, we understand that the God in whom we believe is identical with Jesus. He said, "Anyone who has seen me has seen the Father" (John 14:9). Moreover, we recognize that the chief revelation of God is at the cross and in the resurrection.

In other words, Abraham had a promise, but we have a gospel, the Good News. Abraham looked forward to what God had said he would do. We look back to what God has already accomplished.

Delivered to Death for Our Sins

What has God accomplished? This brings us back to the *kerygma* and to the first of its great declarations in our text, namely, that Jesus "was delivered over to death for our sins." According to the Book of Acts, Peter made the identical declaration at Pentecost in these words: "This man was handed over to you by God's set purpose and foreknowledge; and you, with the help of wicked men, put him to death by nailing him to the cross" (Acts 2:23). Later in the same book, when Paul is at Pisidian Antioch, he declares: "The people of Jerusalem and their rulers did not recognize Jesus, yet in condemning him they fulfilled the words of the prophets that are read every Sabbath. Though they found no proper ground for a death sentence, they asked Pilate to have him executed" (Acts 13:27–28).

There are two important points to these classic proclamations of Christ's death.

1. *It was planned by God.* The Revised Standard Version renders part of Romans 4:25 as "Jesus . . . was put to death," but this translation greatly weakens what the apostle is saying. It is not just that Jesus was put to death, that is, "executed," true as that is. It is that Jesus was delivered over to death by God. Sometimes people get into debates over who was responsible for Jesus' crucifixion. Was it the Jews, who hated him and asked Pilate to have him killed? Or was it the Romans, who actually carried out the execution? The passages I have quoted recognize the guilt of both parties, plus that of the masses of Jerusalem. But that is not what they are chiefly concerned about. Their emphasis is upon this being the work of God, who by it was accomplishing salvation for all who would believe on Christ. This is why, in another place, Jesus is referred to as "the Lamb that was slain from the creation of the world" (Rev. 13:8).

It was God the Father who sent the Lord Jesus Christ to the cross. This tells us that the death of Jesus was no accident, but rather the accomplishment of God's plan of redemption, devised even before the universe was created. It is why Jesus came.

2. *It was for others.* The death of Jesus, thus planned by God, was for others, which means that it was substitutionary or vicarious. Paul says that it was "for our sins." Death is God's punishment for sin, its consequence. But Jesus had not sinned and therefore did not deserve death. That he did die was because he was dying in our place as our sin-bearer.

In his great commentary on Bible doctrine, which uses Romans as a "point of departure,"[3] Donald Grey Barnhouse illustrates the substitutionary nature of Christ's death by the story of Barabbas. We know that Barabbas was a robber and murderer who had been arrested by the Romans and was in prison awaiting execution at the time of the trial of Jesus Christ. Pilate had no concern for Barabbas—the world would be better off without him—but he wanted to save Jesus and so hit on the idea of offering the people a choice between the two. It was customary to free a prisoner at the time of the Feast of Passover. "Which of the two do you want me to release to you?" Pilate asked the crowd (Matt. 27:21).

3. Donald Grey Barnhouse, *God's Remedy: Exposition of Bible Doctrines, Taking the Epistle to the Romans as a Point of Departure*, vol. 3, Romans 3:21–4:25 (Grand Rapids: Wm. B. Eerdmans, 1954).

He was astonished when the people replied, "Barabbas!"

Barnhouse pictures Barabbas sitting in the prison, staring at his hands, which were soon to be pierced by nails, and shuddering at any sound of hammering that might remind him with horror of his own impending crucifixion. Suddenly he hears a crowd roaring outside the prison. There are angry voices. "Crucify him! Crucify him!" He thinks he hears his own name. Then a jailer comes to unlock the door of his cell. Barabbas thinks that the time for his execution has come, but instead the jailer tells him that he is being set free. The crowd has called for his release. Jesus of Nazareth is to die instead.

Stunned, Barabbas joins the processional that is making its way to Calvary and watches as Jesus is crucified. He hears the sound of the hammer and knows that the blows that are fastening Jesus to the rough wooden cross were meant for him. He sees the cross lifted high into place and knows that he is the one who should be dying on it.

Jesus cries, "Father, forgive them, for they do not know what they are doing" (Luke 23:34).

The centurion who has commanded the execution party exclaims, "Surely this man was the Son of God!" (Mark 15:39).

Barabbas must have been saying, "That man took my place. I am the one who should have died. I am the condemned murderer. That man did nothing wrong. He is dying for me."

Barnhouse concludes, "Barabbas was the only man in the world who could say that Jesus Christ took his physical place. But [all who are Christians] can say that Jesus Christ took [their] spiritual place." The fact that we are sinners means that we deserve to die. We deserve the eternal punishment of the lake of fire. But Jesus was delivered up for our offenses. He was crucified for our sins. That is why we speak of substitutionary atonement and vicarious suffering, and it is why Jesus' death is so central to the gospel. Nothing that overlooks the death of Christ is the gospel. As Barnhouse says, "Christianity can be expressed in three phrases: I deserved Hell; Jesus took my Hell; there is nothing left for me but his heaven."[4]

Raised for Our Justification

The final part of the gospel in our passage is the resurrection. Paul speaks of it twice: (1) [It was written] "for us who believe in him who raised Jesus our Lord from the dead" (v. 24), and (2) "He . . . was raised to life for our justification" (v. 25).

Why does he say that Jesus was raised "for our justification"? At first glance this seems to be a problem because, according to Paul's own teaching elsewhere, it is the death of Christ (not the resurrection) that is the basis for God's justification of sinners (Rom. 5:9). Even Romans 3 has said

4. Ibid., p. 378.

it: "justified freely by his grace through the redemption that came by Christ Jesus" (v. 24). Redemption has to do with Jesus' death. There is no mention of the resurrection at all in that passage.

There are a number of explanations of the meaning of the phrase "raised to life for our justification," but the one that has commended itself to most expositors is that the resurrection is God's proof, provided for our benefit, that a full payment for sins has been made.

The resurrection proves a great many things. It proves that:

1. There is a God and that the God of the Bible is the true God,
2. Jesus was a teacher sent from God; he was inerrant in his teaching and spoke the very words of God,
3. Jesus is the Son of God,
4. There is a day of judgment coming,
5. Every believer in Christ is justified from all sin,
6. All who are united to Christ by a living faith will live again, and
7. Christians can have victory over sin.[5]

But chiefly the resurrection proves that every believer in Christ is justified from all sin, as Romans 4:25 declares. In other words, it is God's evidence to us that the penalty for our transgressions has been fully paid by Jesus.

When Jesus was on earth, he said that he would die for the sins of others. The time for the crucifixion came, and he did die. But the question remained: Was his death fully acceptable to God for others' sins? Did God accept his atonement? We know that if Jesus had sinned, however slightly, his death could not atone even for his own sin let alone the sin of others. For three days the question remained unanswered. The body of Jesus lay in the cold Judean tomb. But then the hour came. The breath of God swept through the sepulcher, and Jesus rose to appear to his followers and later to ascend to the right hand of the Father. By this means God declared to the entire universe, "I have accepted the atonement Jesus made."

Reuben A. Torrey writes, "When Jesus died, he died as my representative, and I died in him; when he arose, he rose as my representative, and I arose in him. . . . I look at the cross of Christ, and I know that atonement has been made for my sins; I look at the open sepulcher and the risen and ascended Lord, and I know that the atonement has been accepted. There no longer remains a single sin on me, no matter how many or how great my sins may have been. My sins may have been as high as the mountains, but in the light of the resurrection the atonement that covers them is as high as

5. These points are made by R. A. Torrey, *The Bible and Its Christ* (New York: Fleming H. Revell, 1904–1906), pp. 101–111.

heaven. My sins may have been as deep as the ocean, but in the light of the resurrection the atonement that swallows them up is as deep as eternity."[6]

D. Martyn Lloyd-Jones says, "The resurrection is the proclamation of the fact that God is fully and completely satisfied with the work that his Son did upon the Cross."[7]

Point of Decision

We have come to the end of the fourth chapter of Romans and therefore to the end of the first major section of Paul's letter. It has been a long journey.

Paul begins with an analysis of man's lost condition. Far from everything being well with the human race, as the optimists of his day and ours wrongly suppose, the race is actually under the wrath of God for its failure to receive the revelation of himself that God has made in nature, and its refusal to thank God for creation and to seek him out more fully in order to worship him. Instead of following the truth, people have suppressed the truth, and in its place they have created imaginary gods like themselves and even like animals. Having turned from God, who is the source of all good, they have entered on a downhill path marked by sexual and other perversions until they come at last to the point where they are willing to call good evil, and evil good.

No one naturally agrees to this assessment, of course. It is part of what rejecting truth is all about. So Paul next spends time dealing with the arguments of those who would exempt themselves from those conclusions.

One objector is the ethically moral man, who considers Paul's judgments true of others but not of himself. Paul tells him that he stands condemned before God, not only because he has broken God's perfect standard of righteousness, but also because he has not even lived up to his own personal standard, however high or low it may be.

Another objector is the religious person, who thinks that he is exempted because of his religious observances. Paul does not discount the value of religious actions, but he denies that they can change the heart, which is the thing that matters. The end of his argument is that all stand condemned before God: "'There is no one righteous, not even one. . . . no one who understands, no one who seeks God'" (Rom. 3:10–11).

Finally, Paul unfolds the gospel, showing that God has acted to save sinners through the Lord Jesus Christ. We cannot save ourselves. We do not deserve saving. But God is gracious, and because he is, he sent the Lord Jesus Christ to die in our place. By his death, Jesus turned the wrath of God aside and became the grounds upon which God has been able to justify the ungodly. At the end of Romans 4, Paul has returned to this theme after hav-

---

6. Ibid., pp. 107, 108.
7. Lloyd-Jones, *Romans: An Exposition of Chapters 3:20–4:25*, p. 244.

ing shown that this is the same method by which the Old Testament saints, such as Abraham and David, were justified.

But what was written in the Old Testament was not written for these believers alone, Paul says. It was written "also for us," that is, for people living today, so that we might be saved as Abraham was.

Abraham was saved by faith. So the question is: Do you believe in God and trust his promises, as the patriarch did? Although he knew less about the person and work of Jesus than you do, his faith was not different in kind from yours, and for that very reason he remains your example. Remember what we said about his faith? Abraham (1) believed God's promise; (2) believed on the basis of the Word of God only; (3) believed in spite of adverse circumstances; (4) was fully assured that God would do whatever he had promised; and (5) acted on that confidence.

That is what you must do, too. God has promised salvation through the work of Jesus Christ. You must trust his word in this, even though the circumstances of life may seem to rule against it. Abraham looked at himself and considered his body as good as dead. You also are dead to spiritual things. But you must believe what God says, commit yourself to Christ, as he tells you to do, and find that the power of God that was active in quickening Abraham's old body will quicken you.

Abraham "did not waver through unbelief regarding the promise of God, but was strengthened in his faith and gave glory to God" (Rom. 4:20). Neither should your faith falter. Receive the promise, and believe in the God who raised Jesus our Lord from the dead.

Subject Index

Scripture Index